PASSPORT READING

JOURNEYS™ III

TEACHER'S EDITION

PART A

ISBN 978-1-4168-1607-2

Printed in the United States of America 09 10 11 12 13 14 PAD 9 8 7 6 5 4 3 2

Advisers and Consultants

Diane Lapp, Ed.D., Senior Adviser, is the Distinguished Professor of Education in the Department of Teacher Education at San Diego State University. Experienced teacher and researcher, Dr. Lapp's major areas of research and instruction are issues related to struggling readers and writers and their families who live in low socioeconomic areas.

Donald D. Deshler, Ph.D., is a professor in the School of Education and director of the Center for Research on Learning (CRL) at the University of Kansas. Dr. Deshler served as an adviser for *Reading Next: Vision for Action and Research in Middle and High School Literacy*, a recent report from the Carnegie Foundation.

Julia Peyton, Ph.D., is Vice President of Research and Development at Voyager Expanded Learning. Her current research foci include identifying and aligning to best practices for intervention to improve student outcomes, evaluation of program efficacy, assessment development and evaluation, and interpretation of results. She has background experience in reading intervention, teacher training in the area of literacy and intervention, research design, and sustainability of effective innovations.

Janette Klingner, Ph.D., is a professor of Education at the University of Colorado at Boulder. Research foci include reading comprehension strategy instruction for diverse populations, the disproportionate representation of culturally and linguistically diverse students in special education, and special education teacher quality.

Sharon Vaughn, Ph.D., is the H.E. Hartfelder/Southland Corporation Regents Chair at the University of Texas. She is the Co-Principal Investigator at the National Research and Development Center on English Language Learners. Dr. Vaughn is the recipient of the AERA Special Education SIG Award for Research.

Maria Elena Arguelles, Ph.D., is an Education Consultant for Reading First and English Language Learning. Dr. Arguelles is a member of the Governor's Secondary Reading Advisory Panel and a research associate of the Florida Center for Reading Research. She is the coauthor of several publications and a consultant to publishers developing programs for struggling readers and English Language Learners.

Reviewers

ALABAMA
Marsha Savage
Secondary LEA Literacy Coach
Birmingham City Schools
Birmingham, AL

ARIZONA
Jane Przeslica
Teacher of English Language Learners (ELL)
Gilbert School District
Mesa, AZ

Polly Vogt
Secondary Reading Intervention Teacher
Gilbert Public Schools
Gilbert, AZ

Juanita Diggins
Research, Assessment and Evaluation
Sunnyside Unified School District
Tucson, AZ

CALIFORNIA
Deborah McKnight
Special Education Consultant
San Francisco, CA

FLORIDA
Minnie Cardona, Ed.S.
ESOL/World Languages/Foreign Exchange Coordinator
Seminole County Public Schools
Sanford, FL

Patty Adams
Secondary Reading Facilitator
Brevard County School District
Viera, FL

ILLINOIS
Brent Raby
Director of Grants and Learning
McHenry Community High School District 156
McHenry, IL

KENTUCKY
Connie Pohlgeers
Director of School Improvement
Campbell County Schools
Alexandria, KY

LOUISIANA
Rebecca Bordelon
English Language Arts Teacher
Terrebonne Parish School District
Houma, LA

MINNESOTA
Theresa Behnke
Secondary English Language Arts Coach
Saint Paul Public Schools
Saint Paul, MN

OKLAHOMA
Dee Carroll-Cox
Reading Coordinator
Oklahoma City Public Schools
Oklahoma City, OK

PENNSYLVANIA
Barbara S. Heckard, Ed.D.
Assistant Superintendent for Assessment & Accountability
Lebanon School District
Lebanon, PA

SOUTH CAROLINA
Patti Pierce
Coordinator of Special Programs
Georgetown County School District
Georgetown, SC

Susan Shope Thomas, Ph.D.
Director of Programs for Students with Disabilities
Berkeley County School District
Moncks Corner, SC

WASHINGTON
Leah Crudup
Title I/LAP Coordinator
Walla Walla School District 140
Walla Walla, WA

Classroom Trials

FLORIDA
Dawn Roberts
Secondary Reading Intervention Teacher
Brevard School District
Viera, FL

KENTUCKY
Tracey Peavley
Secondary Reading Intervention Teacher
Campbell County Schools
Alexandria, KY

TEXAS
Sara Ramirez
Reading ESL Teacher
Ysleta Independent School District
El Paso, TX

Table of Contents

1

Expedition 1
Who Am I?

Expedition Planner
pages 2 and 3

Expedition Opener
pages 4 and 5

ELL Week 1 Overview
page 6

ELL Week 2 Overview
page 27

Passport Reading Journeys™
Library

Passport Reading Journeys™
Online Technology

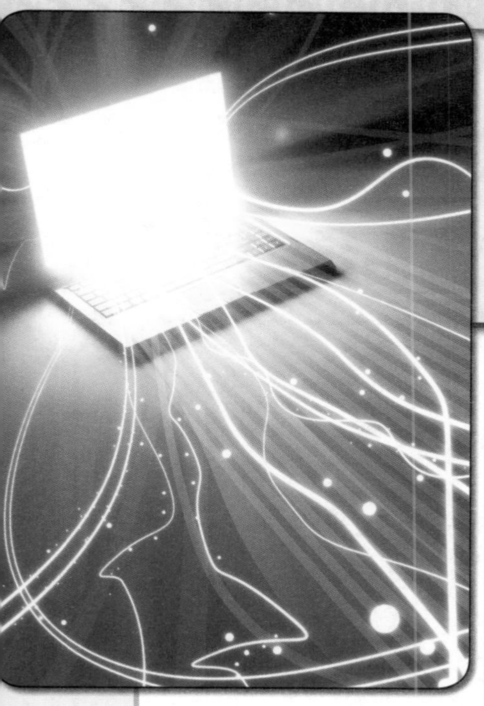

Expedition 2

R U Online?

2

Expedition Planner
pages 48 and 49

Expedition Opener
pages 50 and 51

ELL Week 1 Overview
page 52

ELL Week 2 Overview
page 71

Passport Reading Journeys™
Library

Passport Reading Journeys™
Online Technology

3

Expedition 3
Sounds of Life

Expedition 4

Criminology

Expedition Planner
pages 132 and 133

Expedition Opener
pages 134 and 135

ELL Week 1 Overview
page 136

ELL Week 2 Overview
page 155

Passport Reading Journeys™
Library

Passport Reading Journeys™
Online Technology

5

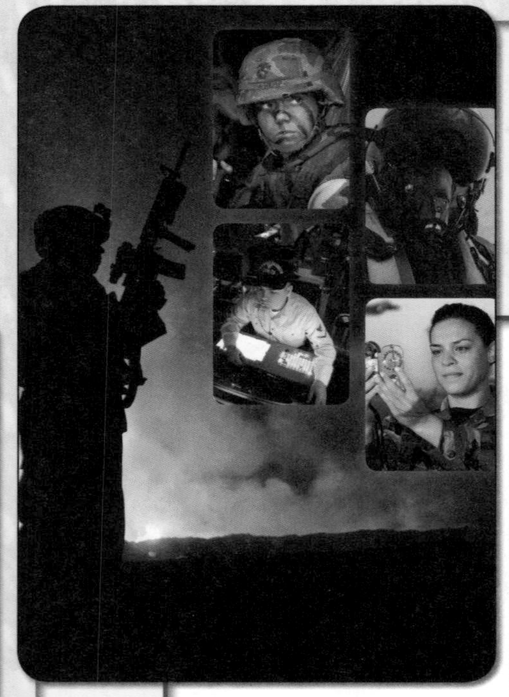

Expedition 5

An Army of Progress

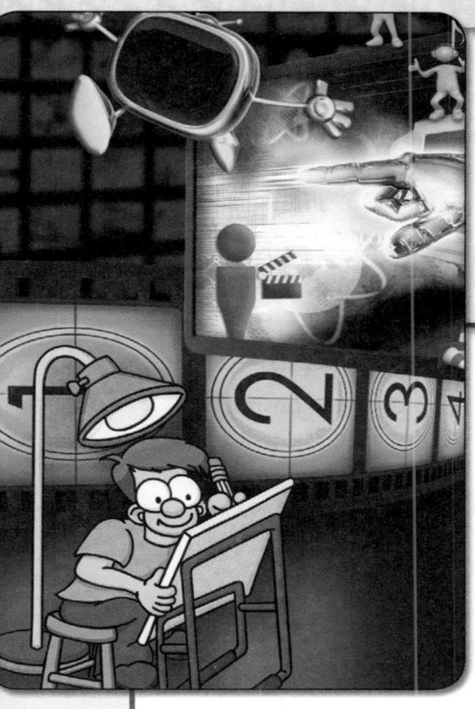

Expedition 6

Now You See It

7

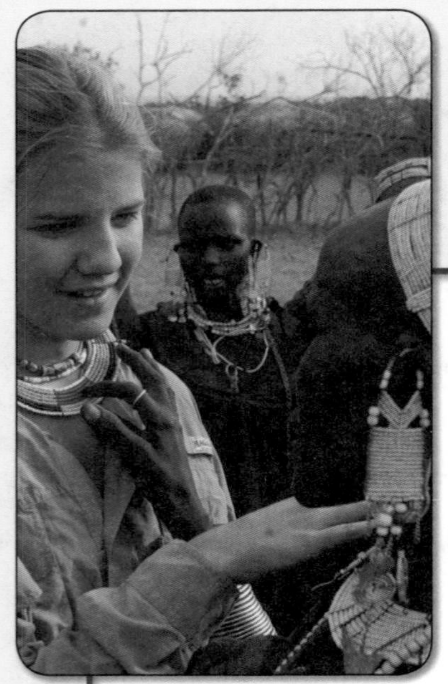

Expedition 7
Across Cultures

Passport Reading Journeys™
Library

Passport Reading Journeys™
Online Technology

Program Components

- **Carefully crafted instruction** in comprehension, academic language, and writing gives high school students the strategies necessary to understand what they read.

- **Effective literacy instruction** embedded in stimulating content promotes the transfer of skills into real-life practice.

- **Self-directed learning** is facilitated through whole-group and small-group instruction combined with collaborative and independent practice using Lexile®-leveled text.

- **Formative and summative assessments and progress monitoring tools** are specifically designed to inform instruction on a regular basis to ensure students maximize reading proficiency.

Teacher's Resource Kit

The comprehensive Teacher's Resource Kit includes all of the necessary guidance and content to effectively teach all facets of *Passport Reading Journeys™ III.*

INSTRUCTIONAL MATERIALS TO SUPPORT DAILY LESSONS

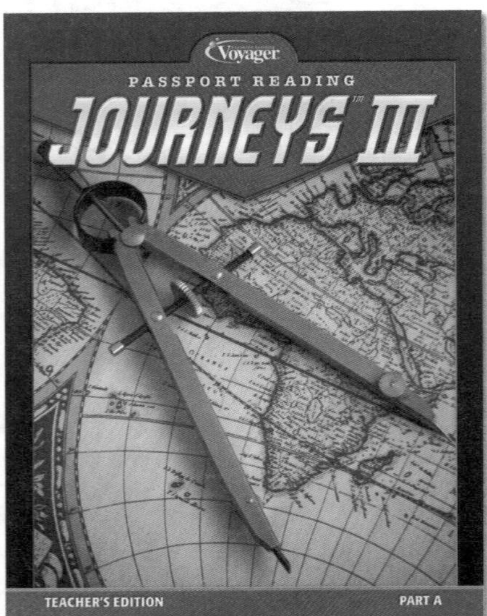

The **Teacher's Edition** features quality instructional guidance for teacher-led instruction that promotes success and student learning. Easy-to-use daily lessons match whole-group with small-group instruction and independent practice and application. Comprehension and vocabulary assessments enable teachers to determine the level of students' ability to apply newly learned strategies to Expedition content.

English Language Learners Blackline Masters combined with strategies and activities listed throughout the lessons provide the extra support needed for English language learners.

DVD videos build and activate background knowledge on real-world and up-to-date topics. High school hosts motivate students to interact with one another about a variety of texts and topics.

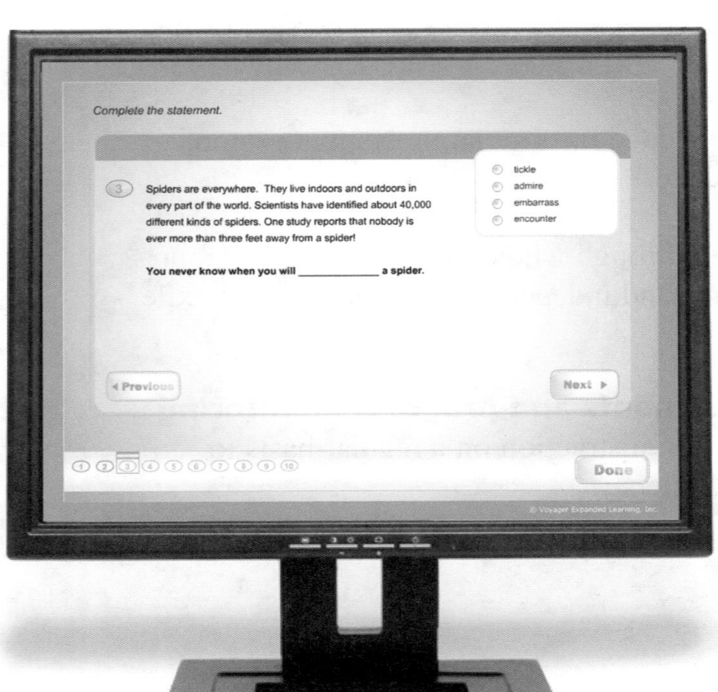

Assessment Management
Reading Benchmark Assessments, the Word Study Screener, and Semester Exams are provided through VPORT® for online or pencil/paper administration. The multiple-stage assessment system within *Passport Reading Journeys III* provides teachers with a complete picture of student progress and achievement.

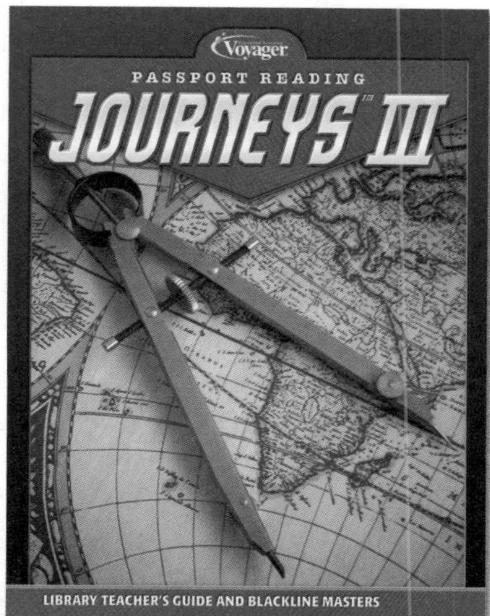

TEACHER SUPPORT FOR SELF-SELECTED READING

The ***Passport Reading Journeys III*** **Library** addresses a wide range of student interest in literature. **The Library Teacher's Guide** provides meaningful instruction on integrating self-selected reading into classroom instruction.

STRATEGIC TUTORING SUPPORTS INDIVIDUAL INSTRUCTION

The ***Word Study Teacher's Guide*** provides short-term, intensive instruction for students who struggle with decoding and fluency. Lesson placement is determined by the Word Study Screener.

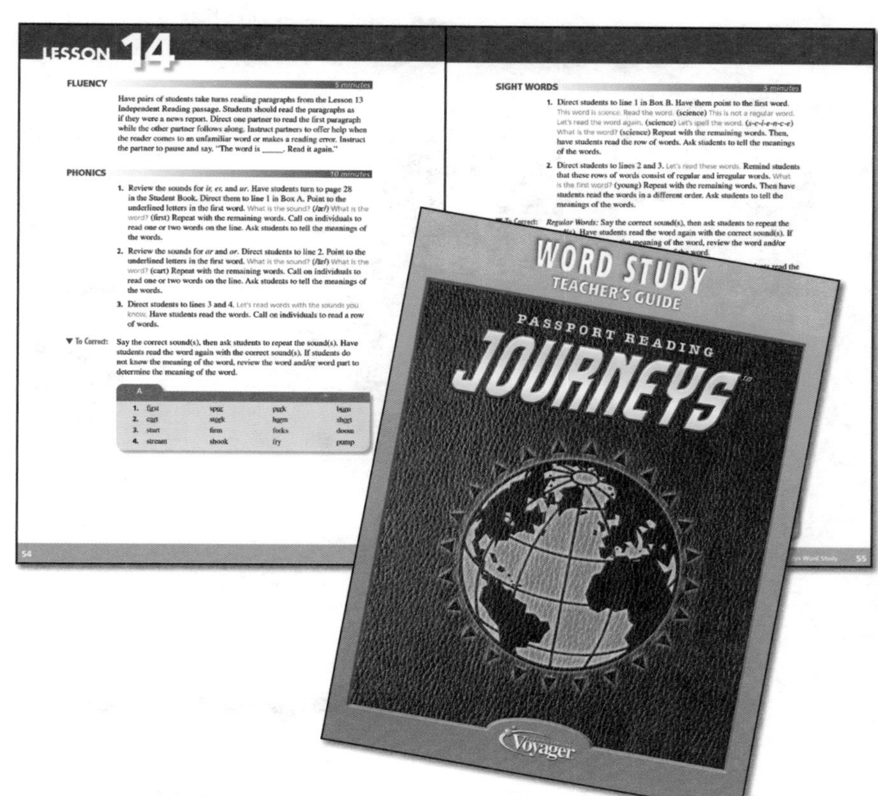

LESSON 14

FLUENCY — 5 minutes

Have pairs of students take turns reading paragraphs from the Lesson 13 Independent Reading passage. Students should read the paragraphs as if they were a news report. Direct one partner to read the first paragraph while the other partner follows along. Instruct partners to offer help when the reader comes to an unfamiliar word or makes a reading error. Instruct the partner to pause and say, "The word is _____. Read it again."

PHONICS — 10 minutes

1. Review the sounds for *ir, er,* and *ur*. Have students turn to page 28 in the Student Book. Direct them to line 1 in Box A. Point to the underlined letters in the first word. What is the sound? (/ər/) What is the word? (first) Repeat with the remaining words. Call on individuals to read one or two words on the line. Ask students to tell the meanings of the words.
2. Review the sounds for *ar* and *or*. Direct students to line 2. Point to the underlined letters in the first word. What is the sound? (/är/) What is the word? (cart) Repeat with the remaining words. Call on individuals to read one or two words on the line. Ask students to tell the meanings of the words.
3. Direct students to lines 3 and 4. Let's read words with the sounds you know. Have students read the words. Call on individuals to read a row of words.

▼ To Correct: Say the correct sound(s), then ask students to repeat the sound(s). Have students read the word again with the correct sound(s). If students do not know the meaning of the word, review the word and/or word part to determine the meaning of the word.

A				
1.	first	spur	perk	burn
2.	cart	stork	harm	short
3.	start	firm	forks	doom
4.	stream	shook	fry	pump

54

SIGHT WORDS — 5 minutes

1. Direct students to line 1 in Box B. Have them point to the first word. This word is science. Read the word. (science) This is not a regular word. Let's read the word again. (science) Let's spell the word. (*s-c-i-e-n-c-e*) What is the word? (science) Repeat with the remaining words. Then, have students read the row of words. Ask students to tell the meanings of the words.
2. Direct students to lines 2 and 3. Let's read these words. Remind students that these rows of words consist of regular and irregular words. What is the first word? (young) Repeat with the remaining words. Then have students read the words in a different order. Ask students to tell the meanings of the words.

▼ To Correct: *Regular Words:* Say the correct sound(s), then ask students to repeat the ... Have students read the word again with the correct sound(s). If ... meaning of the word, review the word and/or ... the word.

55

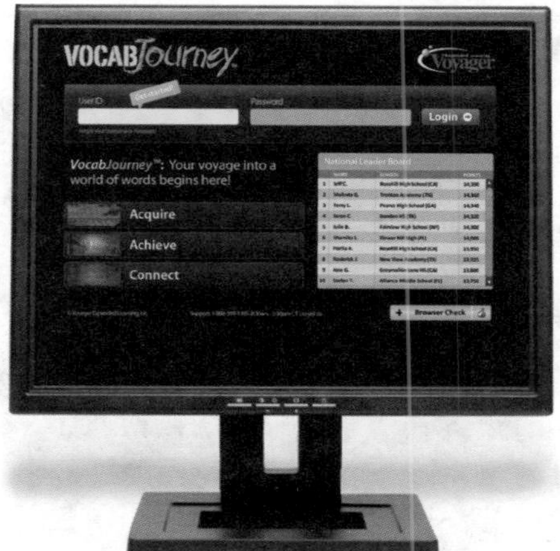

TECHNOLOGY AS A FACILITATOR OF LITERACY

The online technology component combines the strengths of technology-delivered text-based vocabulary lessons. This blended solution optimizes differentiated instruction based on student neds.

Student Resources

Passport Reading Journeys III student materials cultivate higher levels of literacy achievement.

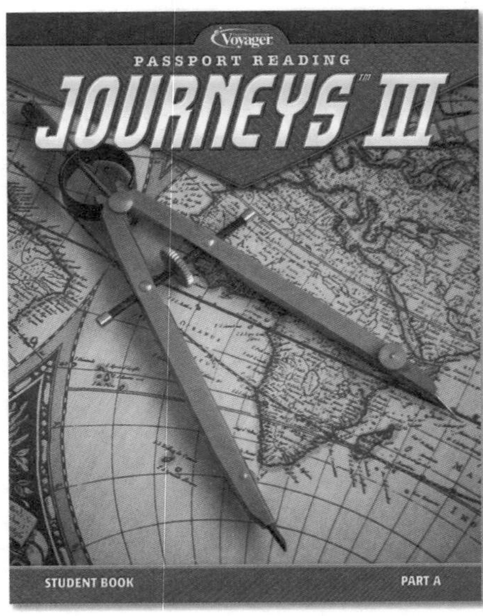

The **Student Book** connects students with meaningful opportunities to practice and apply the comprehension and vocabulary skills being taught throughout the year. Attention to the high-stakes testing formats ensures the Student Book activities are relevant to a students' future success. Assessments include multiple choice, short response, and extended response.

The **Student Anthology** features fiction and nonfiction readings on high-interest science and social studies topics. Transfer of newly learned skills beyond the reading classroom is enhanced by employing academic textbook selections within the exploration of the numerous topics. Career highlights personalize the collaboration around the selections and make them relevant to students' lives.

The **Word Study Student Book** provides strategic tutoring for students who need intensive instruction and practice in fundamental phonics, spelling, and fluency skills.

The **online technology component** offers online instructional reinforcement and individual practice in vocabulary concepts relevant to comprehension. Recognizing the increasing interest adolescents have in technology, the online technology component directs this interest to building academic vocabulary and increasing literacy.

***Passport Reading Journeys III* Library** contains a diverse collection of Lexile-leveled, award-winning and distinctive novels and short stories for independent and partnered reading. The range of topics is of high interest to high school students and connects to their real-world experiences.

- *Stargirl* by Spinelli
- *The Contender* by Lipsyte
- *The Face on the Milk Carton* by Cooney
- *The Floating Island* by Haydon
- *The Green Glass Sea* by Klages
- *The Liberation of Gabriel King* by Going
- *The Lightning Thief* by Riordan
- *The Pigman* by Zindel
- *The True Confessions of Charlotte Doyle* by Avi
- *Walk Two Moons* by Creech
- *Code Orange* by Cooney
- *Drums, Girls & Dangerous Pie* by Sonnenblick
- *Here Lies the Librarian* by Peck
- *Hoops* by Myers
- *Leaving Home* by various authors
- *Loser* by Spinelli
- *Monster* by Myers
- *Nightmare Hour* by Stine
- *The Pinballs* by Byars
- *Scorpions* by Myers

Assessment

Passport Reading Journeys III **provides the highest quality of assessment reporting for placing students and monitoring progress.**

The following diagram demonstrates the four assessment tools used to measure each student's growth in reading, vocabulary, and comprehension.

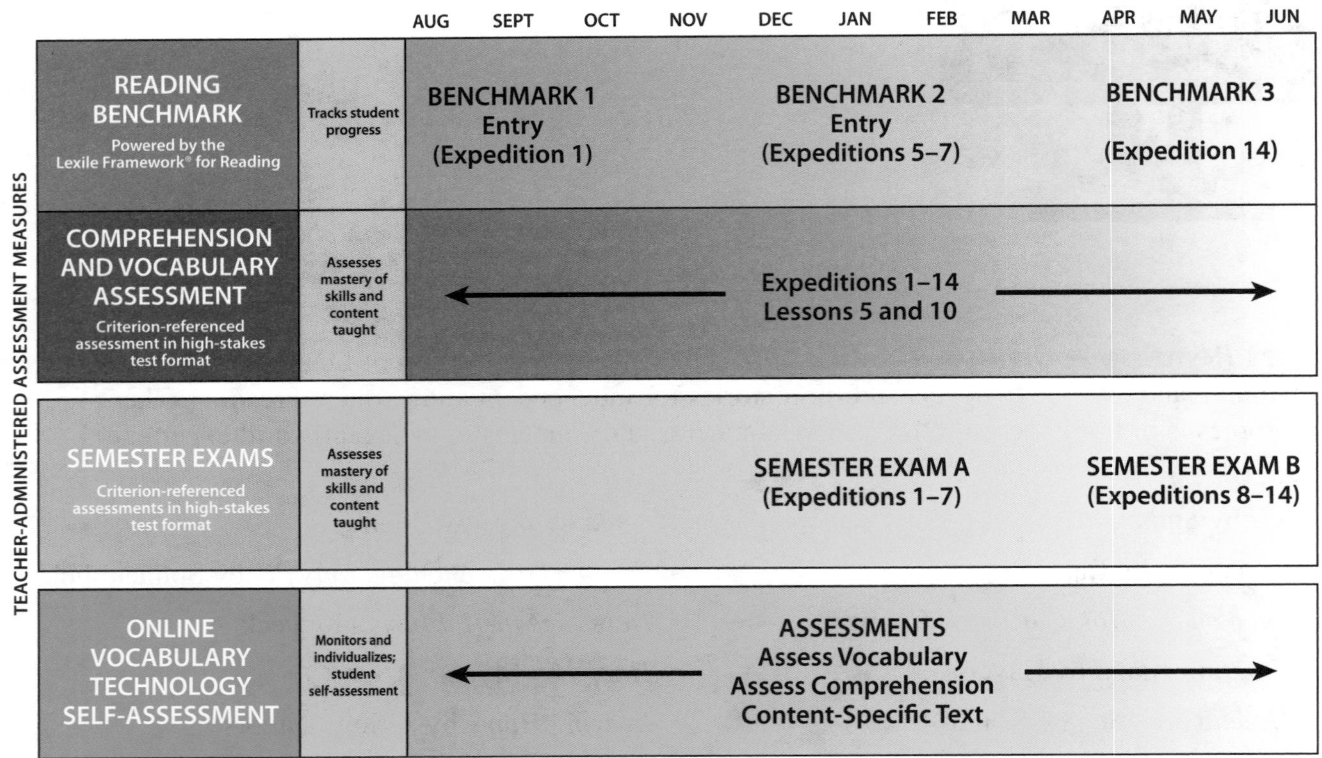

VPORT® Data Management System

Identify Student Instructional Needs

Make informed decisions to determine the specific instructional needs of the students based on VPORT data.

Track Student Progress

Track student progress and measure implementation success with Student and Summary Reports.

Predict Success on High-Stakes Assessments

Collect and use student data to track and predict success on high-stakes assessments.

Get Additional Resources

Access additional implementation ideas, instructional resources, and informational pieces.

Communicate with Coaches and Voyager

Relate implementation concerns and other areas in which you need assistance.

Reading Benchmark Assessments

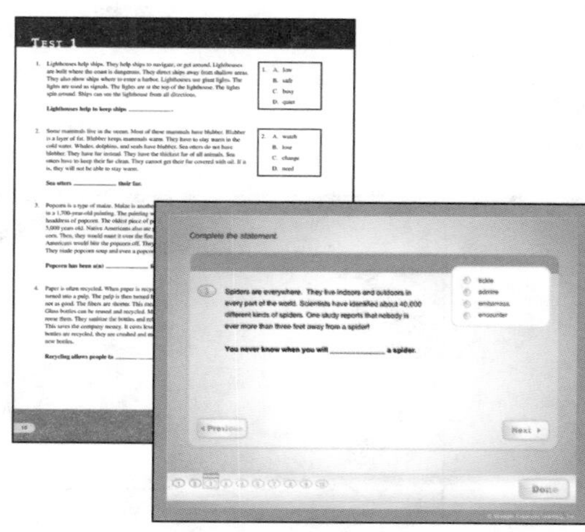

Passport Reading Journeys III uses three standardized Lexile tests to determine the reading level of each student. Appropriate for individual, small-group, and large-group administration, the Reading Benchmark Assessments may be given online or as a paper/pencil administration. The VPORT Data Management System automatically calculates Benchmark Lexile Scores, which are used throughout the year to monitor progress toward reading proficiency.

Semester Exams

Passport Reading Journeys III provides semester exams where students apply the vocabulary and comprehension strategies taught through the Expeditions. The assessments may be given online or as paper/pencil administration.

Comprehension and Vocabulary Assessments

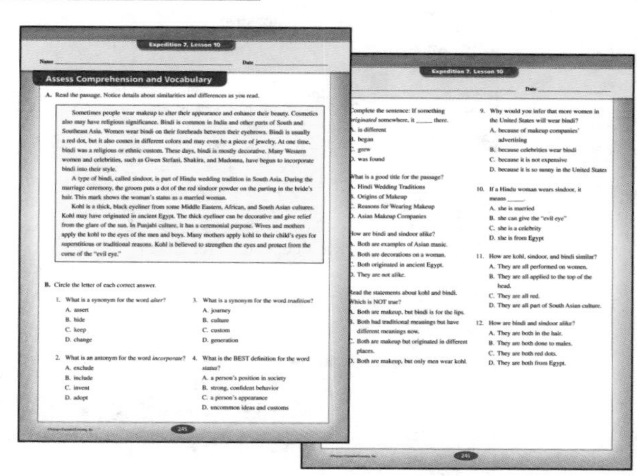

Formative assessments are built into the lessons and are found in the Student Book in Lessons 5 and 10. Each Comprehension and Vocabulary Assessment provides practice in a high-stakes testing format and checks student understanding of the skills focus in the current Expedition.

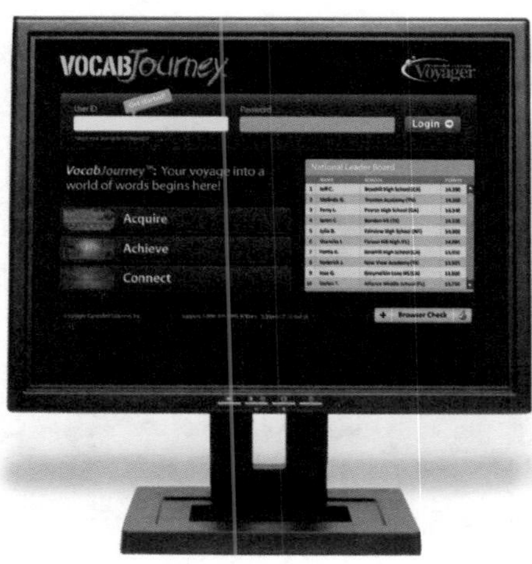

Online Technology Component

In an **online session,** students make choices or select answers as they progress through vocabulary activities. The program monitors student responses and adapts instruction to meet individual needs. The program provides corrective feedback to the student while reporting student progress to VPORT for teachers to monitor and use as a grading opportunity.

Expedition Overview

Each two-week Expedition focuses on a topic related to science or social studies. Students participate in daily lessons to build their vocabulary knowledge and comprehension skills. They also spend time online with an interactive technology component.

Expedition 3

Sounds of Life

"Music with a Message"

Lesson 1	Lesson 2
Introduce the Expedition Discuss probing questions about Sounds of Life. **Before Reading** • Introduce and practice using passage vocabulary. • Apply and practice finding implicit main idea. **During Reading** Read "Music with a Message" and "Follow the Drinking Gourd." **After Reading** Check comprehension. Have students practice vocabulary using the online technology component. Have students select books for independent reading. ELL Extend and practice.	**Prepare to Reread** • Review and practice using passage vocabulary. • Practice using context clues. • Build new words using prefixes. **Reread** • Review and practice finding implicit main idea and details. • Write a paragraph. ELL Extend and practice.

"Evolution of Music"

Lesson 3	Lesson 4
Before Reading • Introduce and practice using passage vocabulary. • Apply the target skill and practice finding implicit main idea and details. • Introduce the passage by previewing and making predictions. **During Reading** Read "Evolution of Music." **After Reading** Check comprehension. Have students practice vocabulary using the online technology component. Have students select books for independent reading. ELL Extend and practice.	**Prepare to Reread** • Review and practice using passage vocabulary. • Practice using context clues. • Build new words using roots. **Reread** • Review and practice finding implicit main idea and details. • Write an interview and a music review. ELL Extend and practice.

Lesson 5—Review, Extend, Assess

Review Vocabulary
Review and practice using passage vocabulary.

Extend Vocabulary
Use base words and affixes to build and understand new words.

Assess Comprehension and Vocabulary
Assess student understanding of vocabulary and finding implicit main idea.

Reteach
Have students complete activity pages for reteaching implicit main idea.

Passport Reading Journeys Library
Have students select books for independent reading.

Technology
Have students practice vocabulary using the online technology component.

Writing Process
Have students use the writing process to write a descriptive essay about a favorite band.

Real-World Reading
Have students read a Web site and complete instructions.

Exploring Careers
Have students read about disc jockeys and complete an activity page.

Teacher's Note
Before beginning the Expedition, ask your librarian to suggest books that will fit with the theme. Books relating to music and sound will be appropriate for this Expedition.

90 Expedition 3

Expedition 3

"Music without Instruments"	
Lesson 6	**Lesson 7**
Before Reading • Introduce and practice using passage vocabulary. • Apply and practice finding implicit main idea and details. • Introduce the passage. **During Reading** Read "Music without Instruments." **After Reading** Check comprehension. Have students practice vocabulary using the online technology component. Have students select books for independent reading. ELL Extend and practice.	**Prepare to Reread** • Review and practice using passage vocabulary. • Practice using context clues. • Build new words using suffixes. **Reread** • Review and practice finding implicit main idea and details. • Write a paragraph. ELL Extend and practice.

"The Science of Sound"	
Lesson 8	**Lesson 9**
Before Reading • Introduce and practice using passage vocabulary. • Apply and practice using text features. • Introduce the passage by previewing and making predictions. **During Reading** Read "The Science of Sound." **After Reading** Check comprehension. Have students practice vocabulary using the online technology component. Have students select books for independent reading. ELL Extend and practice.	**Prepare to Reread** • Review and practice using passage vocabulary. • Practice using context clues. • Build new words using affixes and inflectional endings. **Reread** • Review and practice using text features. • Write a paragraph. ELL Extend and practice.

Lesson 10—Review, Extend, Assess

Review Vocabulary
Review and practice using passage vocabulary.

Extend Vocabulary
Use affixes to build and understand new words.

Assess Comprehension and Vocabulary
Assess student understanding of vocabulary, finding implicit main idea and details, using text features, and other previously taught skills.

Reteach
Have students complete activity pages for reteaching implicit main idea and text features.

Passport Reading Journeys Library
Have students select books for independent reading.

Technology
Have students practice vocabulary using the online technology component.

Expedition Project
Have students conduct an interview and present the findings.

Real-World Reading
Have students read an album review and complete instructions.

Exploring Careers
Have students read about behind-the-scenes music careers and complete an activity page.

Sample Lessons

The **Introduce the Expedition** section introduces teachers and students to the upcoming reading selection. Before students read, they make predictions, build on prior knowledge, generate questions, and review reading strategies.

Opener

Expedition 3

Introduce the Expedition

1. Have students name some of their favorite musicians. **Why are these musicians important to you?** Direct students to think about the Expedition 3 opener photographs on Anthology page 35. **Which of these musicians do you recognize?** (Bono, Björk, Bob Marley) Identify the musicians students do not recognize.
2. Have students discuss possible responses to the following probing questions. Explain that the questions pertain to what they are about to learn.
   - **How has music guided people in the past?**
   - **Where does the music you listen to come from?**
   - **What impact has music had on America's history?**
   - **What is the future of music?**

Build Background DVD 3.1
Have students view a brief DVD that provides background information about music. **As you watch, listen for ideas that connect to the responses you discussed.**

3. Point out the parts of Student Book pages 64 and 65, Expedition Organizer: Sounds of Life. **As you read the passages, you'll record your own ideas about these questions and about the passages.**

   Suggestions for how students can add ideas to the Expedition Organizer appear in this Teacher's Edition at the end of Lessons 2, 4, 7, and 9. If students have responses now, allow them to write on the graphic organizer in Part A.

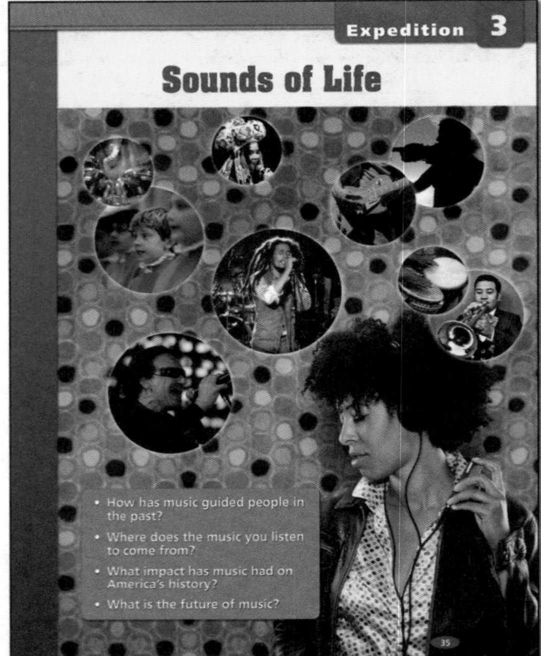
Expedition 3
Sounds of Life
• How has music guided people in the past?
• Where does the music you listen to come from?
• What impact has music had on America's history?
• What is the future of music?
35

Engaging and informative DVD video segments accompany each Expedition to provide background knowledge and capture student interest.

92 Expedition 3

Students refer to **Expedition Organizers** throughout the Expedition as they develop their thoughts about the topics.

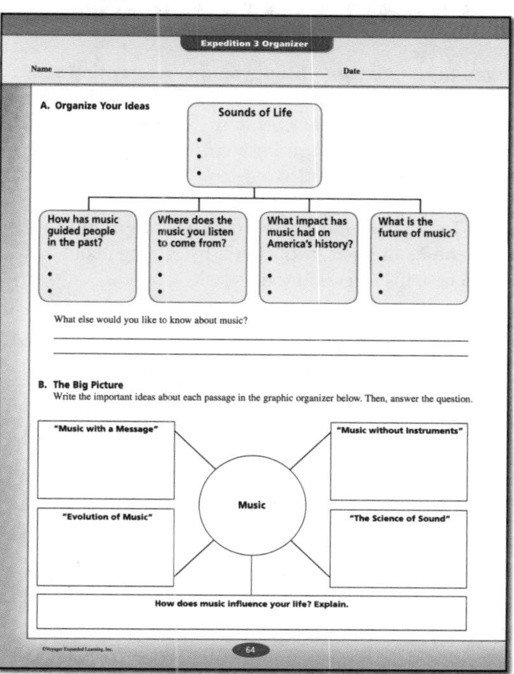

Expedition 3 Organizer

Name ______________________ Date ____________

A. Organize Your Ideas

Sounds of Life

- How has music guided people in the past?
- Where does the music you listen to come from?
- What impact has music had on America's history?
- What is the future of music?

What else would you like to know about music?

B. The Big Picture

Write the important ideas about each passage in the graphic organizer below. Then, answer the question.

"Music with a Message" | "Music without Instruments" | Music | "Evolution of Music" | "The Science of Sound"

How does music influence your life? Explain.

©Voyager Expanded Learning, Inc. 64

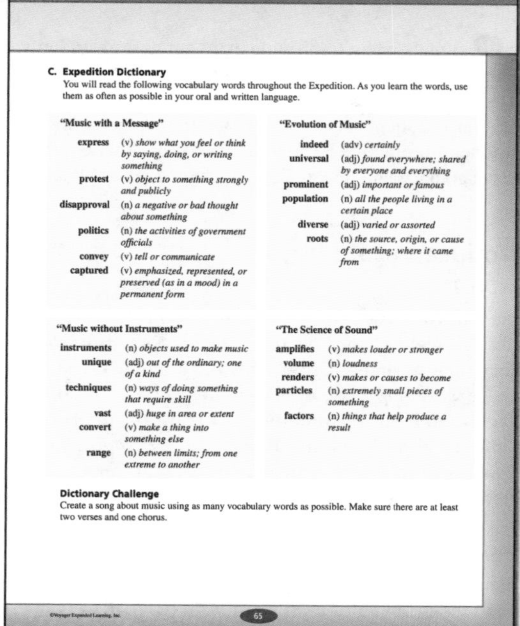

C. Expedition Dictionary

You will read the following vocabulary words throughout the Expedition. As you learn the words, use them as often as possible in your oral and written language.

"Music with a Message"

- **express** (v) *show what you feel or think by saying, doing, or writing something*
- **protest** (v) *object to something strongly and publicly*
- **disapproval** (n) *a negative or bad thought about something*
- **politics** (n) *the activities of government officials*
- **convey** (v) *tell or communicate*
- **captured** (v) *emphasized, represented, or preserved (as in a mood) in a permanent form*

"Evolution of Music"

- **indeed** (adv) *certainly*
- **universal** (adj) *found everywhere; shared by everyone and everything*
- **prominent** (adj) *important or famous*
- **population** (n) *all the people living in a certain place*
- **diverse** (adj) *varied or assorted*
- **roots** (n) *the source, origin, or cause of something; where it came from*

"Music without Instruments"

- **instruments** (n) *objects used to make music*
- **unique** (adj) *out of the ordinary; one of a kind*
- **techniques** (n) *ways of doing something that require skill*
- **vast** (adj) *huge in area or extent*
- **convert** (v) *make a thing into something else*
- **range** (n) *between limits; from one extreme to another*

"The Science of Sound"

- **amplifies** (v) *makes louder or stronger*
- **volume** (n) *loudness*
- **renders** (v) *makes or causes to become*
- **particles** (n) *extremely small pieces of something*
- **factors** (n) *things that help produce a result*

Dictionary Challenge

Create a song about music using as many vocabulary words as possible. Make sure there are at least two verses and one chorus.

©Voyager Expanded Learning, Inc. 65

ELL

Making Connections

Tell students that music is important to people from different cultures and that people identify with different music. Engage students in the music theme by asking them to share different types of music they know and the names for the music in other languages. Have them name prominent artists for each type of music. Discuss who these artists' fans are. Are they popular in certain countries and cultures and with certain age groups? Record their responses in a chart.

Preview the context word *genre* by replacing *type* with *genre* in the chart. Tell students *genre* is another way of saying "type." Ask them to share their favorite genre of music using the sentence frame: *My favorite genre of music is* _________.

If students need support when reading passages that give specific information about different types of music, focus on language support. For example, support them before they read about music with a message by . . .

- asking what they already know about the words *express* and *protest*.
- using everyday or personal examples to explain what *express* and *protest* mean. I *express* friendship by shaking hands. I *express* my opinion when I tell how I feel. The child will *protest* if he disagrees with his mother's rules. The students will *protest* the new law by writing letters to their congressperson.
- connecting to the content by asking how music can be used to *express* feelings or *protest* injustice.

English language learner strategies provide additional vocabulary and comprehension support. They are designed to integrate the five language skills: reading, writing, speaking, viewing, and listening.

Sounds of Life 93

In addition to the integrated strategies, specific ELL activities extend the lessons with additional support, guidance, and modifications for students learning English.

ELL

WEEK 1

English Language Learner Overview

The ELL signals when to provide extra support to students during the lesson. As needed, Blackline Masters for English language learners may provide support. For vocabulary, students also may use the online technology component to practice Expedition words or other content-area vocabulary and designated ELL word sets.

Introduce Vocabulary

Lesson 1

Write the word *disapproval* and tell students that the prefix *dis-* means "not." It can be added to words to change their meaning. Draw a line between the prefix and the base word *approval*. **Approval means "an opinion or feeling in favor of something." I show my approval for a musical performance by clapping. Disapproval means the opposite of approval, or an opinion against something. How would you show disapproval for a musical performance?** (booing; giving the thumbs-down; leaving the performance)

Write the words *agree*, *credit*, and *respect*. Have students explain the meaning of each word. Add the prefix *dis-* to the beginning of each word, and discuss how the meanings change.

Lesson 3

Ask students whether they know a cognate for *universal* in their native language. Read aloud the definition. Ask students what the word for *universal* is in their native language. Have students respond to the following questions.

- **If people all over the world do something, can we say it is universal?** (yes)
- **Is listening to music a universal form of entertainment?** (yes)
- **Is an appreciation for rap music universal?** (no) **Explain.** (Not everyone appreciates rap music.)

Practice Vocabulary

In Lesson 2, provide support for the context words *escalated* and *highlights*. **If something has escalated, it has gotten bigger or stronger. Mr. Rios was running late for work, and his problem escalated when his train was delayed. Did his problem get worse or better?** (It got worse.)

If you highlight something, you draw attention to it. The word highlight reminds me of my highlighter pen, which I use to draw attention to certain words in my reading materials. I can highlight what I say about a topic. For example, if I want to highlight the topic of bicycle safety, I can talk about how I wear a helmet when I ride my bike. How would you highlight the importance of good nutrition? (by talking about the health benefits of good food)

In Lesson 4, provide support for the context word *stressed*. **In the passage, stressed means "emphasized." You can stress beats in music and poetry, and you can stress the syllables in words.** Write the sentence *It's such a perfect day.* on the board. Read the sentence aloud, exaggerating the stressed syllables: **It's SUCH a PERfect DAY.** Touch each syllable as you say it. Have students tell you which syllables are stressed.

Introduce and Apply the Target Skill: Main Idea and Details

Blackline Master page 15 supports students having difficulty identifying main idea and details. Extend practice for Part A, question 2, by having students name other details that support the main idea.

Introduce and Apply the Target Skill: Write a Summary

Support students as they write summaries by providing the following sentence starters. First, have students read the sentence starters and state which words are unfamiliar, such as *concluded*. Use simple definitions when you explain unfamiliar vocabulary.

- *Juan decided to do his research report on music because _________. He found out that ________. He concluded that ________.*

If students have difficulty summarizing, ask the following questions:

- **What did Juan want to find out about music?** (how universal it is)
- **Did Juan find out that music has been the same since the 1950s or that it has changed since the 1950s?** (He found out that it has changed.)
- **Did Juan conclude that music has universal appeal or that only a few people like music?** (Music has universal appeal.)

94 Expedition 3

The Teacher's Edition includes easy-to-use reproductions of the reading passages from the Student Anthology. Highlighted words are taught using context clues.

"Music with a Message"

"Who shot me?
But you punks didn't finish
Now you're 'bout to feel the wrath of a menace . . ."

The lyrics are from the song "Hit 'Em Up" by Tupac Shakur, a West Coast rapper who was shot to death in 1996. The song speaks clearly to his rivals on the East Coast. In the 1990s, a feud, or quarrel, began between East Coast and West Coast rappers. East Coast rapper Tim Dog released a single insulting West Coast rap artists. His song was soon answered. The reply came in the song lyrics of rappers on the West Coast. The feud escalated. During the next few years, as the quarrel grew stronger, rap lyrics were filled with messages and warnings to the rival artists on the opposite coast. Deaths were even associated with the feud.

Messages have always been embedded within musical lyrics. 1 In the 1800s, slaves used songs like "The Drinking Gourd" to reveal hidden messages and **express** their emotions. Rap music is one genre, or style of music, that also frequently contains messages. Rappers have used their music to communicate with one another. They also have used their lyrics to **protest** government injustices and motivate the public to react to current events.

The hip-hop group the Beastie Boys released their single "In a World Gone Mad" in 2003. The song, which protested the Iraq War, expressed the group's **disapproval** of current **politics** in the United States. In the chorus, they sang about how violence and hate prevent people from thinking properly.

Rapper Jadakiss also used his songs to **convey** his political opinions. He **captured** his disdain for President George W. Bush in his single "Why?" In the song, he blamed the president for failing to prevent the destruction of the Twin Towers in New York City on September 11, 2001. Perhaps he hoped his song would encourage others to voice their own disapproval of the president.

Hurricane Katrina devastated the Gulf Coast in 2005. After the storm, many musical artists expressed their feelings in their songs. Many were angered by the government's slow response to those who needed assistance. They used their music to convey this message to the public and to political officials. In his single "Mother Nature," rapper Papoose captures some of the frustration. In the song, he highlights the horrible conditions of life in New Orleans. He asks, "How can I rap about my life and claim honor? When people out in New Orleans don't have water." Many other artists used their songs to draw attention to the problems as well as raise money to help those in need after the storm.

In addition to entertaining their fans, many musicians use their work to express their opinions about current politics and to motivate their listeners to take action. Just as slaves communicated with song, Americans today use music to capture their feelings and speak to one another. 2

Vocabulary

express (v) *show what you feel or think by saying, doing, or writing something*

protest (v) *object to something strongly and publicly*

disapproval (n) *a negative or bad thought about something*

politics (n) *the activities of government officials*

convey (v) *tell or communicate*

captured (v) *emphasized, represented, or preserved (as in a mood) in a permanent form*

1 Understand Words
The prefix *em-* means "in." How does knowing the meaning of the prefix help you understand the word *embedded*?

2 Make Connections
Can you think of other songs that have a message? What do the songs ask you to do or to think about?

36 Expedition 3

Sounds of Life 37

Follow the Drinking Gourd

When the sun comes back,
and the first quail calls,
Follow the drinking gourd.
The old man is a-waiting for to carry you to freedom
If you follow the drinking gourd.

Follow the drinking gourd.
Follow the drinking gourd.
For the old man is a-waiting for to carry you to freedom
If you follow the drinking gourd.

The riverbank will make a mighty good road.
The dead trees show you the way.
Left foot, peg foot, traveling on.
Follow the drinking gourd. 3

Follow the drinking gourd.
Follow the drinking gourd.
For the old man is a-waiting for to carry you to freedom
If you follow the drinking gourd.

The river ends between two hills.
Follow the drinking gourd.
There's another river on the other side.
Follow the drinking gourd.

Follow the drinking gourd.
Follow the drinking gourd.
For the old man is a-waiting for to carry you to freedom
If you follow the drinking gourd.

Where the great big river meets the little river
Follow the drinking gourd.
The old man is a-waiting for to carry you to freedom
If you follow the drinking gourd. End

3 Visualize
i ture the s ene in your mind. What do you see on the ground and in the sky?

3 Expedition 3

Explicit vocabulary instruction focuses on target words that students will encounter in the reading selection.

3 Expedition | Lesson 1

"Music with a Message"

Before Reading

Introduce Vocabulary

1. Have students turn to Part A on Student Book page 66 and scan the boldfaced vocabulary words. **Some of these words may already be familiar to you. Which words do you already know?** Read the instructions aloud, and have students rate their knowledge of each boldfaced word.
2. Have students share which words they know. For each word, tell students to use the word in a sentence.
3. Read aloud the part of speech, definition, and example sentence for each word. **Look back at how you rated each word. Do these definitions match the meanings you knew? Change any ratings you need to.**
4. Have students read the instructions for Part B and complete the activity.

Refer to Blackline Master page 14 to extend vocabulary practice.

Have students use the *Passport Reading Journeys* online technology component to practice and reinforce vocabulary and comprehension skills.

Introduce the Target Skill: Implicit Main Idea and Details

1. The main idea is what the passage is mostly about. **Sometimes the main idea is stated directly, as in this sentence.** Write on the board: *The Displays proved that a garage rock band of 13- and 14-year-olds can amaze people with their talent.* List these details, and have students explain why each detail supports the main idea.
    - *They competed in the Battle of the Bands in Detroit.*
    - *The Displays were judged the best of 10 bands.*
    - *The judges were music professionals.*
2. **Main ideas are not always stated directly.** Direct students to Student Book page 67. **You will find the main idea of a poster by finding the details first.**

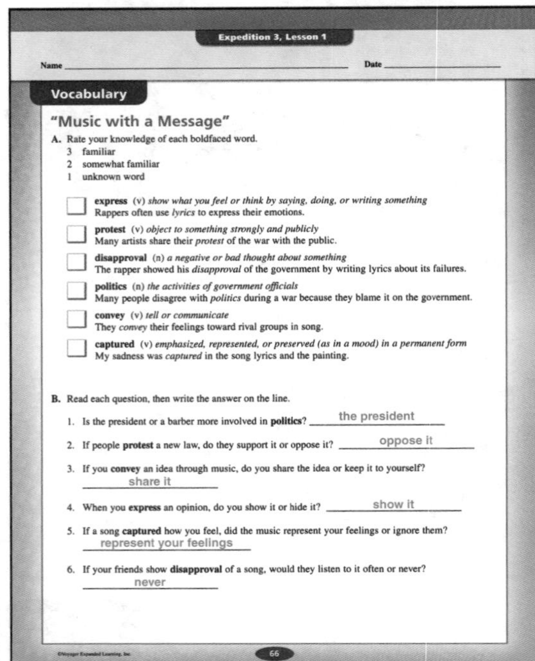

Expedition 3, Lesson 1

Name ____________ Date ____________

Vocabulary

"Music with a Message"

A. Rate your knowledge of each boldfaced word.

3 familiar
2 somewhat familiar
1 unknown word

☐ **express** (v) *show what you feel or think by saying, doing, or writing something*
Rappers often use *lyrics* to express their emotions.

☐ **protest** (v) *object to something strongly and publicly*
Many artists share their *protest* of the war with the public.

☐ **disapproval** (n) *a negative or bad thought about something*
The rapper showed his *disapproval* of the government by writing lyrics about its failures.

☐ **politics** (n) *the activities of government officials*
Many people disagree with *politics* during a war because they blame it on the government.

☐ **convey** (v) *tell or communicate*
They *convey* their feelings toward rival groups in song.

☐ **captured** (v) *emphasized, represented, or preserved (as in a mood) in a permanent form*
My sadness was *captured* in the song lyrics and the painting.

B. Read each question, then write the answer on the line.

1. Is the president or a barber more involved in **politics**? the president
2. If people **protest** a new law, do they support it or oppose it? oppose it
3. If you **convey** an idea through music, do you share the idea or keep it to yourself? share it
4. When you **express** an opinion, do you show it or hide it? show it
5. If a song **captured** how you feel, did the music represent your feelings or ignore them? represent your feelings
6. If your friends show **disapproval** of a song, would they listen to it often or never? never

©Voyager Expanded Learning, Inc. 66

Vocabulary

express	(v) *show what you feel or think by saying, doing, or writing something* Rappers often use lyrics to *express* their emotions.
protest	(v) *object to something strongly and publicly* Many artists share their *protest* of the war with the public.
disapproval	(n) *a negative or bad thought about something* The rapper showed his *disapproval* of the government by writing lyrics about its failures.
politics	(n) *the activities of government officials* Many people disagree with *politics* during a war because they blame it on the government.
convey	(v) *tell or communicate* They *convey* their feelings toward rival groups in song.
captured	(v) *emphasized, represented, or preserved (as in a mood) in a permanent form* My sadness was *captured* in the song lyrics and the painting.

Instruction in carefully selected vocabulary enables students to construct meaning from text.

Comprehension strategies are explicitly taught using teacher modeling, guided practice, and student application of each strategy.

Critical-thinking questions reinforce the comprehension strategies taught in the lesson through review and follow up after reading. The questions help students make connections between what they read and the Expedition content.

3. Have students write the main idea and share their main idea statements.

Introduce the Passage

1. Have students preview "Music with a Message." **What clues tell you what this passage will be about?** (the title and the photos) **What follows the main passage?** (song lyrics)
2. Remind students to pause to read the prompts in the margins. **Think about these prompts as you read the text. Use the vocabulary definitions in the margin when you encounter boldfaced words.**
3. Demonstrate the pronunciation of these terms from the passage:
   - *Tupac* (tū pok)
   - *New Orleans* (nū ȯr lē ənz)
   - *Iraq* (ī rok)
4. Have students predict what they will read about in the main passage. (rappers and how they use music to show their opinions) **How do you think the passage and the lyrics relate to each other?** (Possible response: There is a message in the song.)

   "Follow the Drinking Gourd" began as an American folk song in the 19th century. The song's lyrics gave escaped slaves directions to the north. The "drinking gourd" in the song is the Big Dipper constellation. The constellation looks like a spoon, which is what the squash-like gourds were used for during this time. Many landmarks are mentioned in the song, making it a "map" for the slaves.

During Reading

1. Have students read "Music with a Message" and "Follow the Drinking Gourd." To select reading options that support your students' levels and classroom needs, see Reading Differentiation, page xxxii, if needed.
2. Instruct students to look for the main idea as they read.

After Reading

Check Comprehension

1. **How are the passages related?** (The song was a hidden message, and the passage was about messages in songs.)

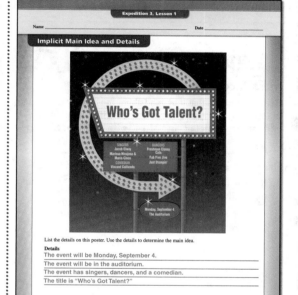

Expedition 3, Lesson 1

Name ____________ Date ____________

Implicit Main Idea and Details

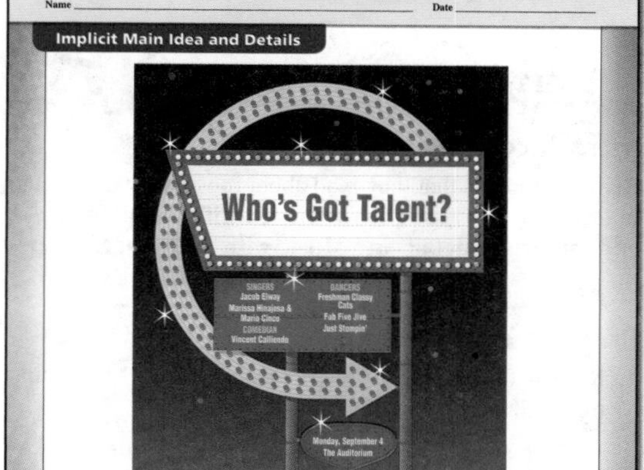

List the details on this poster. Use the details to determine the main idea.

Details

The event will be Monday, September 4.

The event will be in the auditorium.

The event has singers, dancers, and a comedian.

The title is "Who's Got Talent?"

Main Idea

A talent show will be taking place at the school.

67

2. Have students share their responses to the Make Connections margin prompt on Anthology page 37. **What other songs have messages? Are these messages stated directly or not?**
3. **Look at the last paragraph of the first column on page 36. Read the paragraph again. What is the explicit main idea?** (Messages have always been embedded within musical lyrics.) **Sometimes main ideas aren't stated. Let's look at the paragraph before this one. It talks about a feud between two rappers. What is the implicit main idea of this paragraph?** (East and West Coast rappers used song lyrics to speak to one another during a feud in the 1990s.)

ELL For students who have difficulty identifying main idea and details, read paragraphs aloud one at a time. Model using the skill with language such as: *I think the most important point is _________.*

Remind students to choose books from the *Passport Reading Journeys* Library for independent reading.

Suggested **teacher dialogue supports** in-depth teacher modeling opportunities.

Explicit review of the previous lesson's instruction is provided to reinforce content and comprehension.

"Music with a Message"

Prepare to Reread

Introduce the Lesson

Remind students that they read about music with a message in Lesson 1. **In Lesson 2, we will identify the main idea and important details in "Music with a Message."**

Practice Vocabulary

1. Review the vocabulary words from Lesson 1 by asking the following questions.
   - **Who are some artists who have used music to *express* themselves?** (Tupac; Jadakiss)
   - **What issues have artists used their music to *protest*?** (the Iraq War; response to Hurricane Katrina)
   - **The Beastie Boys wrote "In a World Gone Mad" to show their *disapproval* of something. What was it?** (current politics in the United States)
   - **Why did the Beastie Boys criticize current *politics* in the United States?** (They did not like how violence and hate influenced people's thinking.)
   - **What did Jadakiss *convey* in his song "Why?"** (his political opinions)
   - **What are some messages that artists in this passage have *captured* in their music?** (personal messages to rivals; war protests; political criticism; response to Hurricane Katrina)
2. Remind students that they can use context clues to find the meanings of words they don't know. Have students turn to Anthology page 36. **What do you think the word *feud* means?** (a quarrel or fight) **What clue in the text helps you know this?** (The text restates *feud* as a "quarrel.")

   Repeat this process for the following words.
   - **escalated** (v) *increased; grew stronger*, Anthology page 36
   - **embedded** (v) *placed within something else*, Anthology page 36
   - **genre** (n) *style*, Anthology page 36
   - **highlights** (v) *draws attention to something*, Anthology page 37

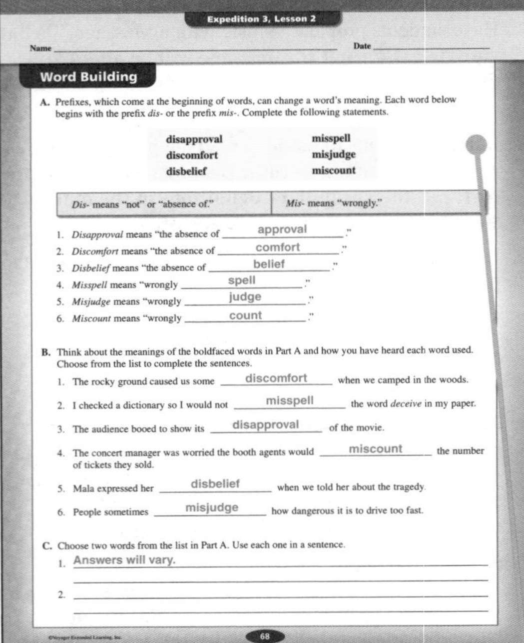

Expedition 3, Lesson 2

Name ____________________ Date ____________

Word Building

A. Prefixes, which come at the beginning of words, can change a word's meaning. Each word below begins with the prefix *dis-* or the prefix *mis-*. Complete the following statements.

disapproval	**misspell**
discomfort	**misjudge**
disbelief	**miscount**

Dis- means "not" or "absence of."	*Mis-* means "wrongly."

1. *Disapproval* means "the absence of approval."
2. *Discomfort* means "the absence of comfort."
3. *Disbelief* means "the absence of belief."
4. *Misspell* means "wrongly spell."
5. *Misjudge* means "wrongly judge."
6. *Miscount* means "wrongly count."

B. Think about the meanings of the boldfaced words in Part A and how you have heard each word used. Choose from the list to complete the sentences.

1. The rocky ground caused us some discomfort when we camped in the woods.
2. I checked a dictionary so I would not misspell the word *deceive* in my paper.
3. The audience booed to show its disapproval of the movie.
4. The concert manager was worried the booth agents would miscount the number of tickets they sold.
5. Mala expressed her disbelief when we told her about the tragedy.
6. People sometimes misjudge how dangerous it is to drive too fast.

C. Choose two words from the list in Part A. Use each one in a sentence.

1. Answers will vary.
2. ____________________

©Voyager Expanded Learning, Inc.

68

ELL Provide examples for the word *genre* by telling students that mysteries and science fiction are different *genres* of books. Have them supply different *genres* of music. List their responses.

3. Have students turn to Student Book page 68. **You learned that the word *disapproval* means "a negative or bad thought about something." This is the opposite of the meaning of *approval*. The prefix *dis-* causes this change in meaning.** Read the instructions for the page aloud. Have students complete the activities, then share their responses.

Guided practice using vocabulary activities allows students to apply newly acquired word knowledge.

Students build confidence and comprehension as they reread the selection from the previous lesson and practice the comprehension skill.

Reread

Apply the Target Skill: Implicit Main Idea and Details

1. Have students turn to Anthology page 36 and reread the first paragraph. **I can find the main idea of this paragraph by identifying details. What are three details in this paragraph?** (An East Coast rapper insulted West Coast rappers in a song; West Coast rappers replied in other song lyrics; rap lyrics became filled with messages.) **What is the main idea?** (Some rappers have put messages to other rappers in their lyrics.)
2. Have students read the instructions on Student Book page 69 and complete the activity.

Refer to Blackline Master page 15 to extend practice with main idea.

ACADEMIC SKILL Remind students that they can use details to figure out a main idea when they read textbooks. They also can use subheadings and other text features.

Write in Response to Reading

1. Prepare students to complete the writing activities on Student Book page 70. **Many artists have expressed their ideas through music. What are some messages they conveyed?** (protesting wars; criticizing current politics; raising money for assistance after Hurricane Katrina) Have students read the instructions and complete Part A.
2. **How are the artists in the passage similar? How are they different?** (They all use music to convey a message, but the messages are different.) Have students read the instructions for Part B and write the paragraph.

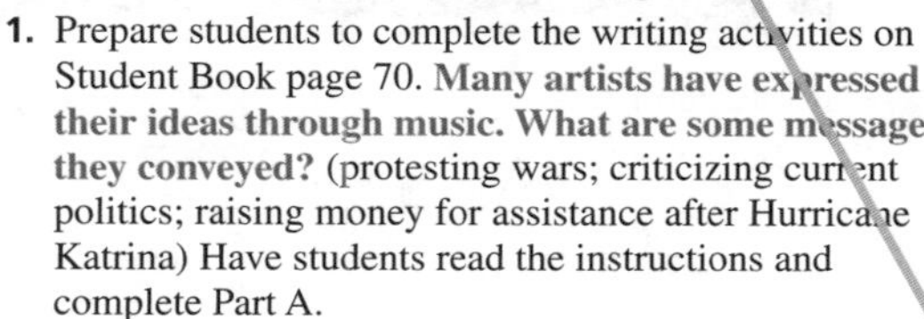

EXPEDITION ORGANIZER **Sounds of Life**

Pause to have students turn to Student Book pages 64 and 65. Have students complete the following:

- Respond to any of the probing questions in Part A. Encourage them to write a question of their own.
- Think about an important idea from "Music with a Message." Tell students to write it in Part B.

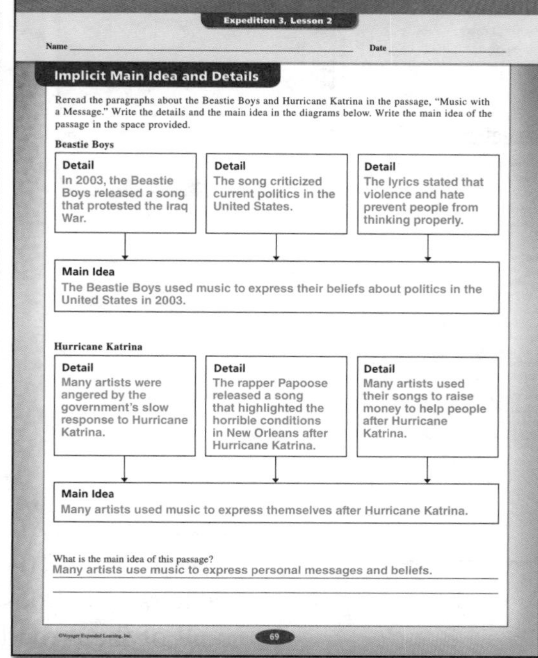

Expedition 3, Lesson 2

Name ______ Date ______

Implicit Main Idea and Details

Reread the paragraphs about the Beastie Boys and Hurricane Katrina in the passage, "Music with a Message." Write the details and the main idea in the diagrams below. Write the main idea of the passage in the space provided.

Beastie Boys

Detail	Detail	Detail
In 2003, the Beastie Boys released a song that protested the Iraq War.	The song criticized current politics in the United States.	The lyrics stated that violence and hate prevent people from thinking properly.

Main Idea
The Beastie Boys used music to express their beliefs about politics in the United States in 2003.

Hurricane Katrina

Detail	Detail	Detail
Many artists were angered by the government's slow response to Hurricane Katrina.	The rapper Papoose released a song that highlighted the horrible conditions in New Orleans after Hurricane Katrina.	Many artists used their songs to raise money to help people after Hurricane Katrina.

Main Idea
Many artists used music to express themselves after Hurricane Katrina.

What is the main idea of this passage?
Many artists use music to express personal messages and beliefs.

69

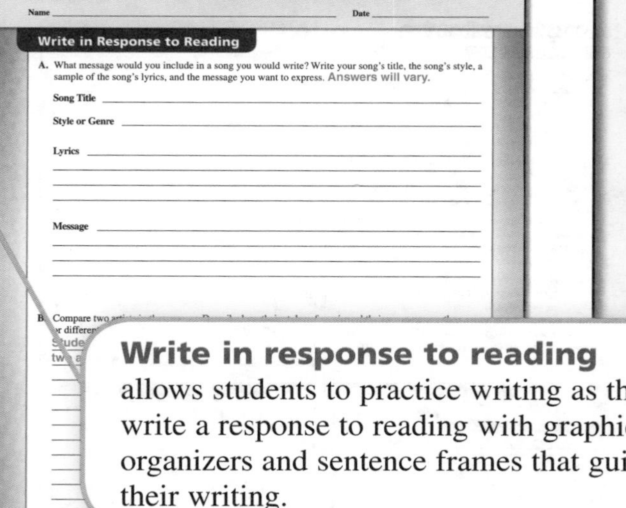

Expedition 3, Lesson 2

Name ______ Date ______

Write in Response to Reading

A. What message would you include in a song you would write? Write your song's title, the song's style, a sample of the song's lyrics, and the message you want to express. Answers will vary.

Song Title ______

Style or Genre ______

Lyrics ______

Message ______

B. Compare two ...

70

Write in response to reading allows students to practice writing as they write a response to reading with graphic organizers and sentence frames that guide their writing.

Review, Extend, Assess

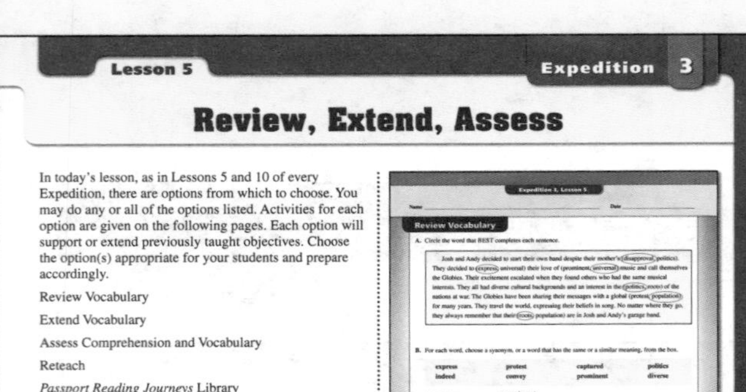

Lesson 5 · Expedition 3

Review, Extend, Assess

In today's lesson, as in Lessons 5 and 10 of every Expedition, there are options from which to choose. You may do any or all of the options listed. Activities for each option are given on the following pages. Each option will support or extend previously taught objectives. Choose the option(s) appropriate for your students and prepare accordingly.

Review Vocabulary
Extend Vocabulary
Assess Comprehension and Vocabulary
Reteach
Passport Reading Journeys Library
Online Technology Component
Writing Process
Real-World Reading
Exploring Careers

Review Vocabulary

Direct students to review the vocabulary for "Music with a Message" and "Evolution of Music" on Student Book page 65.

1. Have students read the words and definitions. Assign partners to quiz each other on the definitions "flash card" style.
2. Have students turn to Student Book page 75. **You encountered most of the vocabulary words in the context of the reading passages. Now you will read the vocabulary in a different context, but the words will have the same meanings. As you complete the review activity, go back and check the definitions in the Anthology to make sure you use the words correctly. Read the instructions aloud, and have** students complete the activities. Have students share their answers for Parts A and B.

CHECKPOINT Have students share their answers for the activities on Student Book page 75. If students have difficulty with a word, reteach the definition by using it in a familiar context, such as one related to school or a popular event.

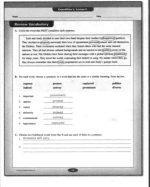

Lesson 5

Extend Vocabulary

1. Direct students to Part A on Student Book page 76. **Knowing the definition of some words can help us understand other words. We can use affixes in the same way.**
2. Write the word *politics* on the board. Ask a student for the definition. Write the word *political* next to *politics* on the board. Ask a student to look up the suffix *-al* in his or her affixionary and read it aloud. Write a class definition of *political* on the board. Instruct students to do the same for the remainder of the words in Part A on Student Book page 76. Review responses when students have finished.
3. Read aloud the instructions for Part B. Tell students they can reread the definitions to help them complete the sentences in Part B. Have students complete the activity, then share their responses.

CHECKPOINT When students share their responses for Part B, be sure that they used the new words in the correct contexts. Pause to explain and correct any errors.

Part A

1. Write the boldfaced words and underline the affix in each of them. Tell students that affixes can change the meaning of a word. Ask them whether they have affixes in their native language.
2. Explore each new word by reading the definition, using the words in a sentence, then asking students to answer a question about the word. **An *expression* is a display of how you feel. When I am happy, my *expression* is a smile. What is your *expression* when you are angry?** Have students answer using the following sentence starter: *When I am angry, my expression is _____.*

Part B

If students have difficulty completing the sentences, turn the sentence frame into a question with the blank as an answer. *Many musicians make _____ statements in their music.* What kind of statements do musicians make? (political)

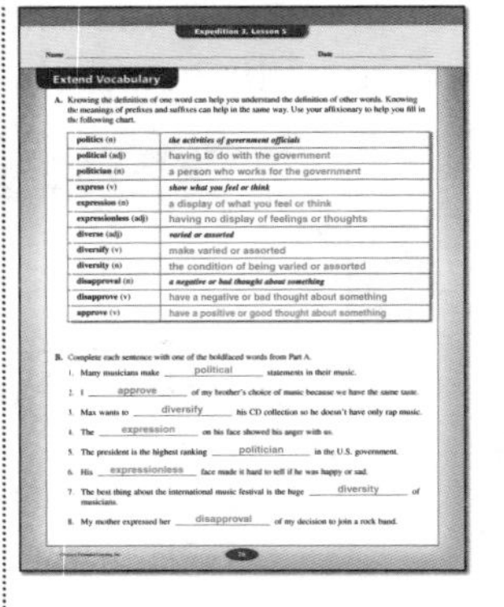

Lessons 5 and 10 offer options from which teachers can choose. Teachers may do any or all of the provided activities.

Lesson 5

Assess Comprehension and Vocabulary

1. Remind students that when they read the passages, they practiced identifying main ideas that were not directly stated. **When you read, you notice details to determine the main idea of a paragraph. You can use the main idea of each paragraph to help you write a summary of the whole passage.**
2. Direct students to Student Book pages 77–79. Preview the pages, showing students that they will read a passage and answer questions about it. Have students complete the pages independently.

   Review student answers. Whenever possible, provide elaborative feedback to student responses. Refer to page xl for examples of elaborative feedback and how to incorporate it in your lessons.

   If students incorrectly answer more than 4 out of 15 Assessment questions, evaluate what kind of reteaching is needed. If students miss vocabulary questions, have them return to the vocabulary activities and work with the words they missed. For main idea errors, use the reteaching suggestions on page 108.

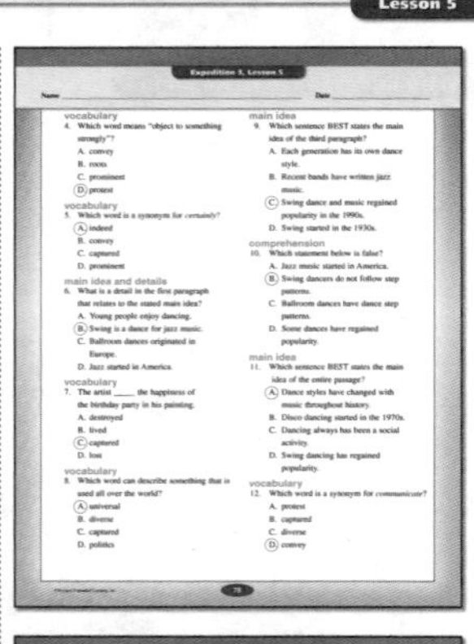

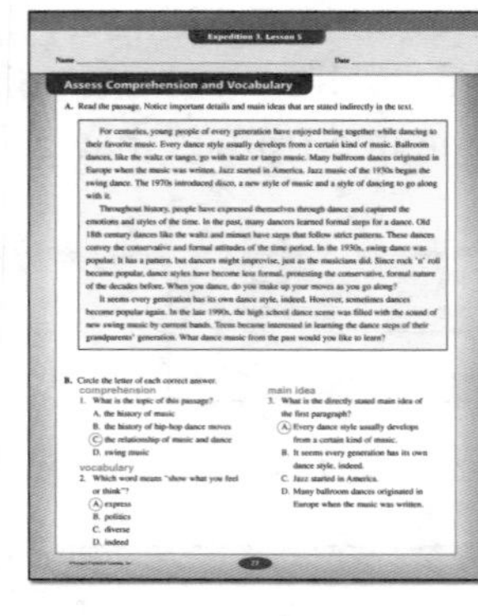

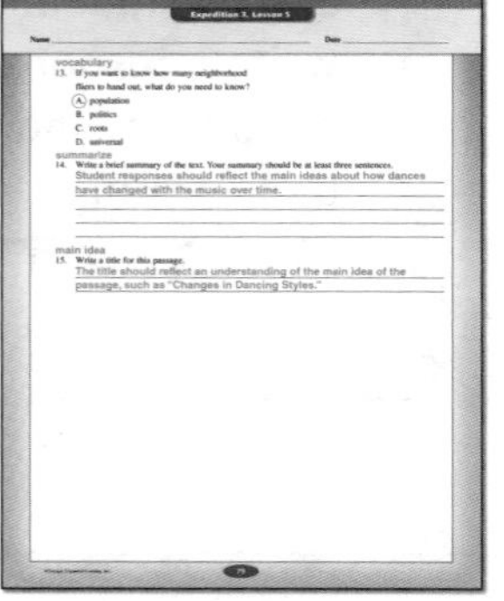

Sounds of Life 107

Lesson 5

Reteach

Main Idea and Details

1. Have students turn to Student Book page 80. Read the passage aloud. **What is the topic of this passage?** (MP3 players) Read aloud the first set of instructions in Part B. **Reread the first sentence and underline it. What has significantly changed?** (how people listen to music) **Each sentence has new information. Underline information that connects to what has changed. The main idea is not directly stated in the second paragraph. Begin with identifying details. Then, put the details together to form the main idea of the paragraph.**
2. Have students complete Parts A and B. If students have difficulty, provide them with two or three words to begin each answer.
3. Have students share their responses to Parts A and B. Write the most common responses on the board. As a class, have students use the details and main ideas to write a summary of the passage. Have a student write the summary on the board.

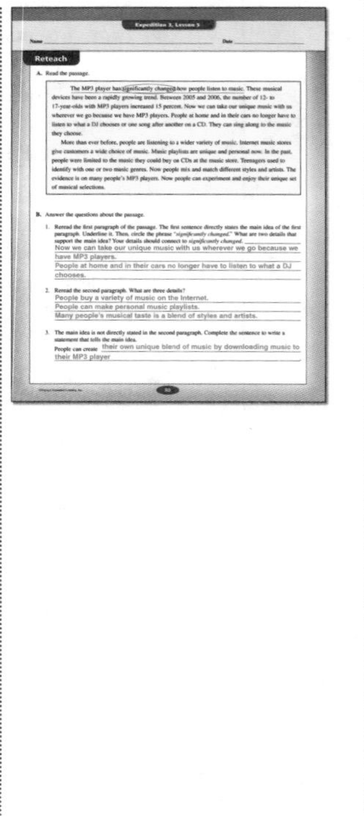

108 Expedition 3

Passport Reading Journeys Library

1. Have students choose reading material from the *Passport Reading Journeys* Library or another approved selection. If students have not finished a previously chosen selection, they may continue reading from that selection. See the *Passport Reading Journeys* Library Teacher's Guide for material on selection guidelines.
2. You also may use this time to allow students to participate in book clubs or book presentations. Use the criteria specified in the *Passport Reading Journeys* Library Teacher's Guide.

Vocabulary Connections

Vocabulary words are listed in the Teacher's Guide for each book. These words are content-related or used frequently in reading material. The selected words can be a basis for independent or small-group discussions and activities.

Student Opportunities

Six copies of each book title are provided in the *Passport Reading Journeys* Library. The number of copies makes it possible for small groups of students to read the same material and share the information they read.

Theme-related titles include *Drums, Girls & Dangerous Pie.*

Technology

1. Depending on your classroom configuration and computer access, you may have all students work through the technology in a lab setting or have individuals or small groups of students work on desktops or laptops while other students participate in other suggested activities, such as the *Passport Reading Journeys* Library.
2. The online technology component provides additional support for students to work with selected vocabulary words. Students will work through a series of activities to strengthen their word knowledge, then apply that knowledge to passage reading. Refer to the online technology component User Guide for more information.

   Theme-related word sets include Physics, U.S. History, English/Language Arts, and Technology.

Writing Process

Descriptive Essay

Distribute copies of Writing Blackline Master page 5. Tell students they will write a three-paragraph essay describing their favorite band or musician. **What kinds of words or phrases will you include in your descriptions?** (adjectives; sensory details) **Adjectives and sensory details create a vivid picture in readers' minds.** Tell students they may include descriptions of these things:

- **Musical genre, sound, instruments, and message of lyrics**
- **Musician's appearance, background, and style**
- **Reasons why you like the musician or band**
- **What the music tells you about the time period in which it was written**

Ask students to look at the assignment and follow along as you explain it. Assign point values and ask students to write them in the rubric. Tell them to make any notes on the page that will help them, but they will turn in the page with the assignment.

Prewrite

Remind students that descriptive writing includes adjectives, or descriptive words that modify nouns. Tell them their essays should use sensory descriptions that appeal to the five senses: sight, smell, hearing, taste, and touch.

If possible, have students listen to the music they will write about. Then they should work independently to write lists of descriptive words and phrases for each sense. Students should focus on sight and hearing, then focus on smell and touch as they apply the context of a concert or musical event. Have groups share their lists with one another. **Use this list of words and phrases as you write your essays.**

Draft

You will use these standards, or criteria, as you write your essays. Write the following on the board, and tell students their descriptive essays must have . . .

- *sensory details that vividly appeal to the senses.*
- *detailed descriptions or explanations about subtopics such as the musicians' backgrounds, music styles, and lyrics.*
- *reasons why they like the musician or band.*
- *what the music tells them about the time period in which it was written.*

Have students work independently to draft their descriptive essays. Tell them they will be able to revise their work.

Revise

Have students reread their drafts, using the revision steps and the following questions. After each step, have students make the revisions and write their final draft. Remind them to do the following steps:

- **Check the explanation.** Did you clearly inform the reader about the band/musician? What parts should you clarify or add more information to?
- **Check your description.** Did you use vivid sensory details and adjectives? Where do you need to add more details or description?
- **Check mechanics.** Do fragments or run-on sentences need to be rewritten? What words might be misspelled? Do all sentences begin with capital letters and end with proper punctuation?

Present

Have students present their essays. If possible, have students play samples of the music their essays describe.

Assess

I will assess your writing and presentation based on the rubric on your page. To assess students' descriptive essays, use the rubric from the Writing Blackline Master.

Real-World Reading

Web Site

1. Direct students to Student Book page 81. Explain that they will read a Web site. Have students preview headings and the menu bar. **What do you think this Web site is for?** (a music event to support American troops)
2. **Follow the instructions to complete the activity.**
3. **Would this Web site entice you to attend the event or donate money to support troops abroad?** Explain. Have students suggest ways that they would improve this Web site.

Expedition 3, Lesson 5

Name ______ Date ______

Real World—Web Site

Look at the Web site. Underline where you would click to find out about the bands performing. Circle the link to e-mail the troops. Draw a box around the link you could click to donate money to the troops.

Exploring Careers

Disc Jockey

1. Have students turn to Anthology page 43. Tell students to preview the title and photos. **What do you already know about a disc jockey's job?** (Possible answer: Disc jockeys work on the radio or at dances. They are familiar with certain styles of music, musicians, and the music industry.) **Pay attention to important details as you read so that you can identify the main idea.**
2. Have students read the passage. **Do you already know how to use equipment such as microphones, speakers, cables, and amplifiers? Do you think your personality would be a good fit for a career as a disc jockey?**
3. Have students turn to Student Book page 82. Have students answer the questions and complete the chart. Tell them they can find the answers by researching the career of disc jockey in books or online. Have students complete the page.

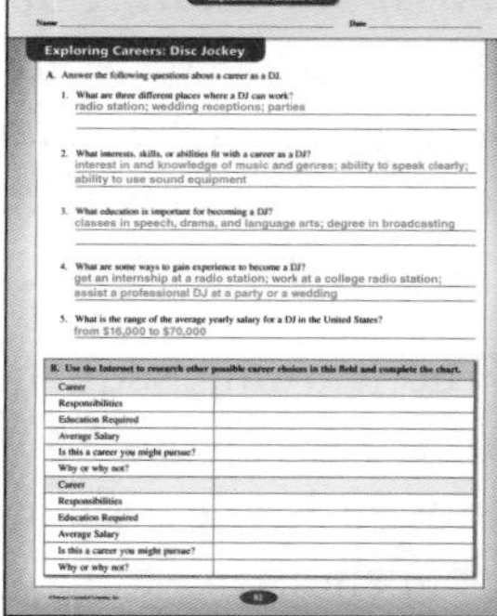
Expedition 3, Lesson 5

Name ______ Date ______

Exploring Careers: Disc Jockey

A. Answer the following questions about a career as a DJ.

1. What are three different places where a DJ can work?
   radio station; wedding receptions; parties
2. What interests, skills, or abilities fit with a career as a DJ?
   interest in and knowledge of music and genres; ability to speak clearly; ability to use sound equipment
3. What education is important for becoming a DJ?
   classes in speech, drama, and language arts; degree in broadcasting
4. What are some ways to gain experience to become a DJ?
   get an internship at a radio station; work at a college radio station; assist a professional DJ at a party or a wedding
5. What is the range of the average yearly salary for a DJ in the United States?
   from $16,000 to $70,000

B. Use the Internet to research other possible career choices in this field and complete the chart.

Career	
Responsibilities	
Education Required	
Average Salary	
Is this a career you might pursue?	
Why or why not?	
Career	
Responsibilities	
Education Required	
Average Salary	
Is this a career you might pursue?	
Why or why not?	

82

Rusty has invitations to every party at school. Everyone knows that without him choosing the music, the party won't be nearly as fun. When he isn't getting his friends out on the dance floor, he spends a lot of time organizing his music on his computer. Sometimes, he evens mixes his own music. He dreams of one day being paid to do this.

Well, he might not be dreaming at all. With a little luck and some work, he just might be able to support himself by doing what he loves. A DJ, or disc jockey, is someone who plays musical recordings. He or she can work in a variety of different places, from parties to wedding receptions to radio stations.

Anyone with a passion for music and the willingness to learn can become a DJ. Most DJs do indeed have an extensive knowledge of music. Some focus on one genre. Others know a lot about a wide range of music. Additionally, they are excellent listeners. Many can easily identify different components of songs just by listening to them.

However, being a DJ involves much more than a passion for music. DJs must be able to express themselves clearly. They announce the artists and titles of the songs they play. Many radio personalities also read the news, interview guests, and do commercials or promotions for their station. They frequently do guest appearances at locations around

Sounds of Life 43

Career

town. They may help celebrate the opening of a new business. Others might entertain guests at a party or a charity auction.

But, having knowledge about music and speaking well are just part of the job. DJs must be able to use a wide range of sound equipment. One key technique to master is the ability to make seamless transitions between songs. Additionally, DJs need to understand how to handle equipment such as microphones, speakers, cables, and amplifiers.

One of the most important qualities for a DJ is connecting with the audience. DJs have to get a feel for what kind of music their listeners crave. That often changes. A DJ has to vary the music to keep people excited and responsive. DJs often are required to multitask. They must watch the clock as songs play and be able to prepare for the next song or commercial. Party and wedding reception DJs also must be able to field requests from guests while playing music.

By nature, most DJs are chatty and have outgoing personalities. Some say that one of the greatest challenges of their jobs is the time spent alone. They often are isolated in a DJ booth. Many radio station DJs have to work overnight or early in the morning when the station is fairly empty. Adjusting to the solitude is just part of the job.

Although higher education is always helpful, you do not need a college degree to become a successful DJ. Many people take speech, drama, and language arts classes in high school to help perfect their speech and delivery. Some choose to pursue broadcasting degrees in college.

On-the-job experience, however, is necessary to become a successful DJ. Internships at radio stations are a great way to learn the ropes. Working at a college radio station is another excellent way to learn the day-to-day tasks and get some on-air experience. A third way to gain hands-on experience is to assist a professional DJ at a party or a wedding.

The pay scale for DJs generally is reflective of where you live, the company you work for, and how much experience you have. The starting annual salary for the average radio DJ is about $25,000. Experienced radio personalities can earn more than $70,000 a year. The average annual salary for a club DJ is about $16,000 a year. However, many club DJs are paid hourly. Their rate also depends on their location and experience. Hourly rates can range from $8 to more than $50.

So, if Rusty is willing to put in some time and learn the ropes, he certainly could become a professional DJ. There are a vast number of opportunities for him to become a success on the air. Soon, he may be able to share his passion for music with listeners everywhere.

44 Expedition 3

VOCABJourney™

VocabJourney™ is a Web-based, interactive program designed to enhance vocabulary and comprehension skills taught in *Passport Reading Journeys III*, teach additional academic vocabulary, and provide vocabulary support for English language learners. The program monitors student responses and adapts instruction to meet individual needs.

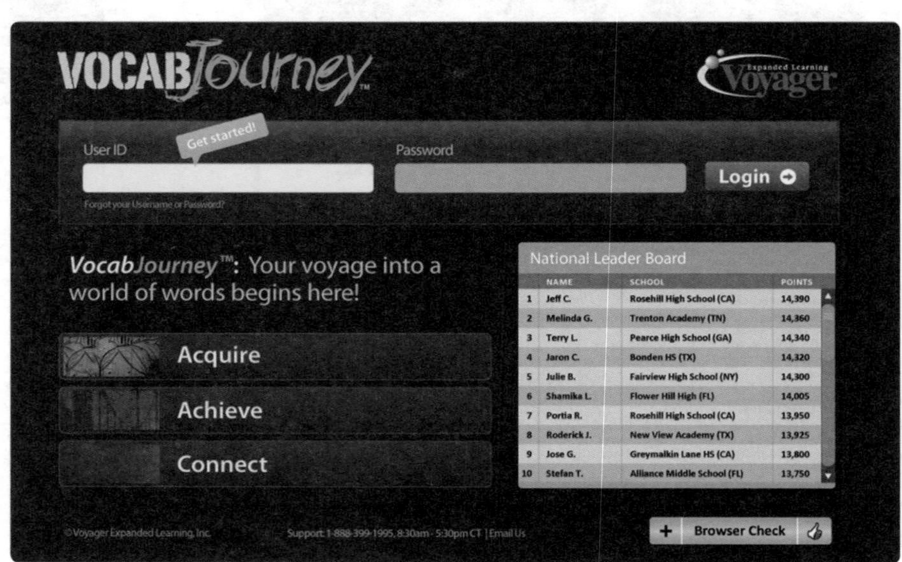

Available 24/7, *VocabJourney* allows students to progress through activities during and outside of class time, extending the classroom instruction and providing teachers with more flexibility to individualize instruction. *VocabJourney* has three major components—**Acquire**, **Achieve**, and **Connect**.

Acquire

In Acquire, students learn new words and practice previously introduced words from each of the *Passport Reading Journeys III* Expeditions. Words are grouped in word sets that students use to build online word cards and engage in interactive tasks that scaffold instruction to help them increase their word knowledge.

The learning sequence includes quick checks of student word knowledge to differentiate each student's experience and provide before-and-after snapshots of student progress.

Students then read the words in the context of high-interest passages and demonstrate their understanding of vocabulary and comprehension in questions that replicate standardized test formats.

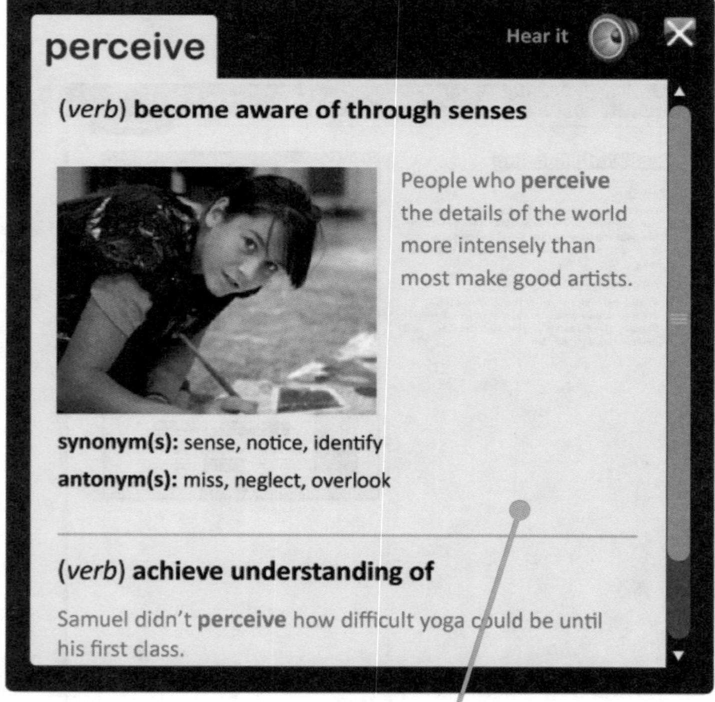

Students build word cards to help them acquire knowledge of a word's definitions, synonyms, antonyms, and context usage. Word cards can be reviewed throughout *VocabJourney*.

Online Technology Component

Achieve

In Achieve, students work to retain what they have learned in Acquire with larger sets of words that they have previously learned. Students play word games and use online flash cards to reinforce their learning and gain additional exposure to multiple meanings of words. Points earned for word activities are displayed on a Leader Board, motivating students to achieve greater word knowledge. Students demonstrate progress toward mastery via regularly scheduled Achieve Tests and Cumulative Tests.

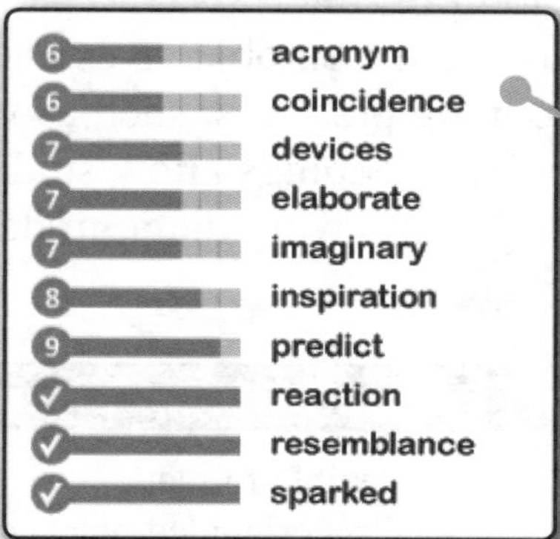

6 acronym
6 coincidence
7 devices
7 elaborate
7 imaginary
8 inspiration
9 predict
reaction
resemblance
sparked

Students can view and monitor their progress on the Achieve dashboard.

Connect

In Connect, students study words organized in categories such as Biology, Chemistry, and World History. Through Connect, students tailor their learning to match their vocabulary needs.

Teacher Center

Log in to www.VocabJourney.com to access the Teacher Center. The Teacher Center facilitates the blending of online and classroom instruction. Teachers can differentiate goals and adapt instruction for the class by creating a pacing calendar for the school year. Teachers also may use the Teacher Center to monitor individual progress and to view grades for assignments that students have completed.

Live Ink®

In *VocabJourney*, students can read all online passages as well as the passages from the Student Anthology using Live Ink®. Live Ink allows students to read more comfortably and effectively in shorter chunks or word groupings.

Live Ink displays text in a cascading format to enhance student ability to read faster, more accurately, and with better recall.

Research shows that readers using the Live Ink format have improved overall reading proficiency and can transfer increased comprehension to traditionally formatted text.* Teachers are encouraged to use the Live Ink format to further differentiate instruction and provide additional support for struggling students.

Robots of Tomorrow

Robots,
both friendly and evil,
have been appearing
in science fiction
for at least a century.

As soon as humans
had invented machines
to do our work,
we began to **predict**
how scientists
might develop those **devices**
in the future.

*Walker, S., Schloss, P., Fletcher, C.R., Vogel, C.A., & Walker, R.C. (2005, May/June). Visual-Syntactic Text Formatting: A new method to enhance online reading. *Reading Online, 8*(6). Available at http://www.readingonline.org/articles/art_index.asp?HREF=r_walker/index.html

Reading Differentiation

Flexible grouping is necessary to provide differentiated instruction. Because each classroom has students with a large range of abilities, interests, and background knowledge, grouping practices need to change to accommodate the lesson objectives and instructional goals. *Passport Reading Journeys III* utilizes several grouping practices, such as whole group, small groups, partners, and individualized instruction. Flexible groupings allow students to maintain high interest and teachers to interact more with students. The following diagram demonstrates some of the grouping practices used in *Passport Reading Journeys III*.

Whole-Group Instruction	Small-Group Instruction	Individual Practice
• Teacher-guided practice, modeling, and think-aloud • Action-packed DVD introduces new Expedition topics and probing questions. • Comprehension strategies • Vocabulary • Writing • Wrap-up DVD review of Expedition content	• Flexible format • Teacher-guided practice, modeling, and think-aloud • Comprehension strategy review • Immediate, corrective feedback • Word Study • Writing in Response to Reading • Writing Process • Expedition Project	• Independent practice and application of skills • Web-based reading practice using *VocabJourney* - Fluency - Vocabulary - Comprehension - Test preparation • *Passport Reading Journeys* Library self-selected readings • Writing in Response to Reading • Writing Process

Depending on the needs of your students, students may listen as you read or read independently, with a partner, or chorally. Use the chart to determine which strategy is appropriate.

Reading Strategy	Definition/Usage	Benefits	When to Use
Read-Aloud	Teacher reads aloud as students follow along, stopping frequently to model comprehension skills.	Students are presented with a model of fluent reading and comprehension strategy usage.	When presenting a new comprehension skill with a difficult text
Choral Reading	Teacher or other skilled reader leads a group reading of the text.	Struggling students are actively engaged in reading while stronger readers model fluency.	When presenting text that may be too difficult for students to read independently but may be able to access with support
Paired Reading	Two students take turns reading aloud a section of the text.	Struggling students can be paired with stronger readers, giving the struggling student a model of fluent reading.	When presenting text at the independent reading level of students
Independent Reading	Individual students read the text silently.	Students practice and apply reading skills and strategies independently.	When presenting text at the students' independent reading level or when asking students to reread a previously introduced text

English Language Learners

Every lesson in *Passport Reading Journeys III* provides opportunities for the English language learner to succeed. The lessons are designed to provide a solid foundation of support as students apply language skills in reading, writing, listening, viewing, and speaking. The following research-supported English language learner practices are integrated into the core instruction in every Expedition.

- **Step-by-step sequencing of instruction** is easy for students to follow and understand.
- **Repeated instructional routines** allow students to be comfortable while new information is presented.
- **Teacher modeling and think-alouds** are embedded throughout each lesson.
- **Teacher-guided practice** allows students to gain confidence and move toward independence.
- **Oral language development** is supported by frequent teacher-student interaction. Students' frequent elaborative responses allow for increased comfort with academic language and questioning.
- **Immediate, corrective feedback** is provided as students respond orally.
- **Graphic organizers** help students link ideas and make connections.
- **Blackline Masters** provide additional instructional support for both vocabulary and comprehension instruction.
- **Additional graphic support** such as illustrations, tables, headings, subheadings, and bold and italicized fonts make the text student friendly.
- **Extensive vocabulary instruction and support activities** allow students to maximize their language-learning potential.
- **Multiple exposures, review, and practice with target vocabulary** enable students to internalize words.
- **Students connect readings to background knowledge** using visuals, videos, photographs, graphic organizers, timelines, and maps.
- **Students work in cooperative groups** to practice language skills.

Students with Special Needs

Passport Reading Journeys III is a scientifically based intervention program that will help to accelerate reading success in students with special needs, as well as those at-risk for referral into special education. The instructional needs of high school students are based on learning large amounts of subject matter material, unlike elementary students who spend a great deal of their instructional day learning strategies for literacy acquisition.

Students with special needs or those at risk of failure need more intensive literacy instruction than content-area classes can provide. To help these students obtain their instructional goals, *Passport Reading Journeys III* provides the instruction and practice necessary to improve their literacy skills.

In addition to providing literacy practice with high-interest passages and activities, students practice applying those skills in other content-area classes. Through practice with text features, taking notes, and summarization, students learn literacy skills that they can use when working with subject-area textbooks. *Passport Reading Journeys III* provides well-designed, explicit, systematic instruction through sequenced skills, immediate feedback, and opportunities for focused review and guided practice.

Because of the high demand on secondary teachers to cover large amounts of in-depth subject matter, there is little time for instruction in basic literacy skills. To this end, *Passport Reading Journeys III* incorporates skills and strategies to enhance students' abilities to access content-area text and subject matter. Through explicit instruction to develop academic vocabulary and emphasis on comprehension skills necessary for understanding expository text, students practice literacy skills while broadening their background knowledge and understanding of subject-area texts. Specific study skill instruction is also provided. Students learn how to evaluate text features, use context clues to define unfamiliar words, and effectively take notes on what they read.

To ensure students understand and transfer what they learn and apply in *Passport Reading Journeys III*, teachers are prompted through the Academic Skill references to make connections to how each comprehension skill taught can be used in subject-area classes.

To further facilitate and differentiate student learning, margin prompts have been placed throughout the Student Anthology. These prompts provide point-of-use vocabulary with definitions and part of speech, as well as strategies for applying active reading skills. As students monitor their own comprehension, they move toward reading independence and practice skills vital to the comprehension of subject-matter text.

Suggestions for Additional Support for Students with Special Needs

Assign Classroom Seating
To maximize benefits from auditory and visual cues, place the student's assigned seat away from the hall and street noise not more than 10 feet from the teacher.

Provide a Quiet Study Area
When a student works with a partner or independently, provide an area free of distractions.

Preteach
Before whole-group instruction, familiarize the student with new vocabulary and content to be covered.

Use Brief Instructions
Paraphrase or restate instructions in a simplified manner to ensure comprehension.

Write Instructions
Provide instructions on a printed sheet of paper. Another student may be assigned as a "buddy" to make sure the student is aware of daily assignments made.

Provide Visual Aids
Write key words or content on the board to provide the student additional visual support.

Monitor Comprehension Closely
Ask the student questions related to the reading or activity, especially during whole-group instruction.

Provide Breaks
Any student with learning or auditory processing difficulties will need frequent breaks. This student will expend more effort in paying attention and discriminating information than other students, and when a student is fatigued, further instruction will likely lead to frustration.

Recommendations from the Advisers

Grouping as a Means to Support Learning for Every Student

Diane Lapp

Ideas for how to group students for instruction are of paramount interest to teachers who wish to accommodate the learning growth of each student. To address this interest, focus on the following two questions: Why should grouping be a part of the instructional plan? What are the characteristics of effective grouping patterns?

Why Should Grouping Be a Part of the Instructional Plan?

For decades, it has been obvious to educators that learning within a group setting that fosters conversation supports growth for all members. This growth includes students who are functioning well above grade level (Navan, 2002) as well as those learning English as a second language and those struggling toward academic proficiency. Success for each student becomes a reality because within these learning clusters, everyone has multiple, secure, and varied opportunities to gain both topical knowledge and language. (Vygotsky, 1978; Lapp, Flood, & Goss, 2000; Langer, 2001; Echevarria, Vogt, & Short, 2004)

What Are the Characteristics of Effective Grouping Patterns?

Effective groups do not just happen by chance. Instead, they are designed by a teacher who realizes that learning becomes possible for every student when he or she is involved in interactive or repetitive, sequential instruction that provides a base of instructional support until independent functioning is reached. This model of instruction often is referred to as the gradual release of explicit instruction (Pearson & Gallagher, 1983) because it initially involves the teacher interactively modeling the new strategy, information, or task for the students. Initial modeling is followed by supportive or guided practice between the teacher and students in a variety of configurations with the teacher offering as much support as warranted by each student's performance. It is during guided practice that students collaborate and practice the information alone or with peers. Finally, when the teacher feels students have learned the information well enough to independently transfer it to novel situations, they are encouraged and supported in doing so. Two major components of this gradual release of explicit instruction are flexible grouping and supportive instructional materials.

Flexible Grouping

A major key to success with instructional grouping is that the groups are flexible, offering students many opportunities to work with their classmates in a variety of contexts and for multiple purposes that include listening, questioning, discussing, and presenting. (Lapp, Fisher, & Wolsey, 2009)

When flexibility is not a component of the grouping plan, students often become members of permanent ability groups commonly referred to as tracking. Within these inflexible groups, students, as well as their teachers, frequently identify the potential for success as limited for those who are seen as struggling to achieve academically. (Slavin & Braddock, 1993; Broussard & Joseph, 1998; Boaler, Wiliam, & Brown, 2000) Repeatedly, struggling learners find themselves designated as such because of their need for additional language or knowledge. Both knowledge and language can be acquired through well-scaffolded instruction occurring through flexible grouping patterns and supported by the appropriate materials.

Flexible grouping plans allow students to work independently or in clusters as a whole class with the teacher as the lead, small groups or individuals receiving guided instruction from the teacher, cooperative and collaborative groups with students working on project tasks with support from the teacher as needed, or partners interacting with teacher support as needed. It is within these contexts that teachers can provide instruction that scaffolds learning from the existing strengths of their students by engaging them in tasks that draw on and extend their knowledge, skills, experiences, and literacy proficiencies.

Supportive Instructional Materials

Within these flexible groups, students often utilize the materials that support independence. The selection of material is important to the total learning process because the learning that occurs from using an instructional material most often occurs during the practice stage of learning and must therefore be considered an extension of the teacher's voice. Effective instructional materials provide students with additional opportunities to practice the newly learned language and information alone or with peers and to then apply these proficiencies to novel tasks. Supportive instructional materials must be aligned closely with the goals the teacher is developing within the gradual release of the instructional model. They must be supportive of flexible grouping opportunities by including differentiated instructional tasks that accommodate the unique differences among students.

Learning becomes a reality for students when they have an effective teacher who designs appropriate learning situations that are supported through flexible grouping and good instructional materials.

To ensure flexible grouping practices in your classroom, observe the following procedures:

- Identify standards, goals, and related instruction.
- Identify learning strengths and needs of students as related to learning goals.
- Identify social strengths of students, such as work habits and behaviors when not supervised by the teacher.
- Determine work time, group compositions, and tasks that support student differences.
- Plan instructional delivery and performance tasks for all groups (whole group, individuals, partners, collaborative groups, and needs-based for students who need teacher-directed instruction on a particular task).
- Determine a rotation plan.
- Demonstrate tasks and create task cards with explicit instruction on how to complete each task for each collaborative group.
- Meet with needs-based groups while collaborative teams work independently.
- Continually assess student performance so that group compositions remain flexible.

Instruction and Discussions that Support Learning the Language of School

Diane Lapp

James A. Winans, a professor of public speaking at Cornell University and later a Cornell University president, wrote: "I confess that I know no better way to improve speaking of all kinds than to encourage and help pupils to acquire something to say worth saying, to think straight, and practice saying it to their fellows." (Winans, 1923) With these words, Winans introduced a model of instruction that helps us realize that language instruction must provide authentic situations where language interchanges with multiple audiences are purposeful and possible—where students have authentic opportunities to use oral language to inquire, discuss, describe, and explain their thinking, and then reflect on how well each purpose was achieved.

Modeling and supporting purposeful language growth occurs as teachers plan instruction, design activities, and select materials that promote their students' oral language proficiencies. The end goal of this instruction is that each student will be independently able to engage in a wide variety of oral interchanges at home and school, in a variety of social situations, and eventually in the workplace. Apply and expand Winans' suggestion in the modern classroom where teachers often attempt to implement an additive model of language development by providing instruction that utilizes each student's existing language base as the foundation upon which to develop content-specific language and also academic language students hear during the school day.

Content and Academic Language

Students primarily encounter content-specific and academic language in textbooks, tests, and the dialogue of the classroom. For example, in science, words such as *transpiration*, which is the process by which plants release water vapor through their leaves, is sometimes a difficult term to understand because it relates to a complex concept. *Longshore drift*, which is the movement of sand along a beach caused by waves coming into shore at an angle, is also important to an understanding of earth science. *Electron*, a foundational term to both physics and chemistry, is typically introduced in upper elementary or middle school, then revisited frequently in high school. These are examples of content-specific words that most students need to be explicitly taught while learning science. These words are related to an understanding of earth science, physics, and chemistry and are referred to as the topical or content vocabulary of these sciences. Words like *evaluation*, *theory*, *hypothesis*, *assumption*, *capacity*, and *validate* are examples of academic English words that teachers use to teach the content of many sciences as well as other content areas. Use of these words implies an academic or formal language style that can be used in multiple contents and contexts. Many students, but not all, have knowledge of academic English terms such as these, if they are members of language communities where they are spoken.

Supporting Students as They Add Academic Dimensions to Their Language

All students come to school with some form of language, and an effective teacher supports their language expansion. All students, including those whose native languages are not English, also need multiple and continuous authentic opportunities to generate language they have neither imitated nor memorized. They need this support until they know the targeted language or language register well enough to independently produce it with accuracy and fluency when needed.

Language instruction that encourages additive language growth includes . . .

- an expert teacher who continually models, guides, and supports authentic language exchanges intended to expand students' understandings of the systems of language. These systems include the phonology, or sound system of the language; the syntax, or rule-governing order, that determines grammatical relationships; the semantics, which is associated with the meanings conveyed by words and combinations of words; and the pragmatics, which highlight the ways in which language is used to communicate ideas.
- teachers providing explicit instructional support across these systems as they strengthen their students' understanding about how these systems work separately and interdependently as they create school talk, which includes targeted topical and academic language.
- time for students to practice in supportive situations, until they know and can independently share their language across situations and audiences.

One's academic and topical language registers are developed in classrooms where an expert teacher designs the curricular activities, selects appropriate materials and programs, then steps aside as students lead conversational dialogic discussions, providing opportunities for students to use these newly acquired dimensions of language. (Adler & Rougle, 2005; Lapp, Fisher, & Wolsey, 2009) These opportunities provide the practice needed by all students, but especially English language learners, to develop oral fluency in academic language. (Cummins, 1994; Rothenberg & Fisher, 2007) Whether thinking, learning, conversing, debating, disagreeing, chatting, or reporting, being linguistically independent means that one has the language needed to take an independent stance and function effectively within the personal, social, and academic situations of life. Diverse voices must be heard to be valued, and it is in classrooms with teachers who are supportive of conversational dialogue that each voice has a chance to grow and to be shared.

To ensure that quality discussion happens in your classroom, observe the following procedures:

- View discussion as conversational time during which students can explore and expand their knowledge and understanding of a topic.
- Work with students to select topics that they find interesting enough to discuss.
- Create with students ground rules for effective listening and conversing.
- Model and encourage, through wondering, how to present and support, with evidence, multiple and diverse perspectives on a topic as a way to enhance knowledge expansion.
- Model and practice with students how to use texts and supporting materials to gain topical knowledge that can be used to expand and support their positions.
- Model with students free-flowing conversational exchanges that do not get stuck in a question-answer-question mode but instead build on presented ideas by listening and speaking to the point.
- Support students as they gain expertise at leading and participating in group conversations.
- Move aside and encourage discussion to happen without you.

Elaborative Feedback

Donald Deshler

For students who have struggled in school, learning a new task can be a difficult process. For learning to take place, there is a need for intensive interaction between the student, the teacher, and the material to be learned. To make new learning sustainable, the process must be active and provide the student with every opportunity for success.

There are many aspects of effective instruction, such as cueing student response, appropriately sequencing instruction, or providing graphic resources to organize information for students. One other aspect of effective instruction is feedback, or the information given in response to a learner's input. Feedback can be as simple as a nod or saying "good job"; however, research has shown that providing elaborative feedback is an effective way to improve student performance toward mastery. (Kline, Schumaker, & Deshler, 1991) Elaborative feedback provides learners with specific information that clearly identifies both the correct and incorrect aspects of a response. Educators employing the strategies of elaborative feedback provide students with one-on-one explicit information about errors and how to correct and avoid similar errors in the future.

Use the following points to guide the elaborative feedback given to students.

- After grading completed student material, analyze the errors, noting the categories of errors made, then return the material to the student for correction.
- Check students' corrections and analyze any remaining errors.
- For students who still have errors, conference with the student to provide specific feedback using the following structure.
  - First, discuss what the student feels he or she understood and did well. Support the student as necessary with a positive statement such as, "You used the correct prefixes for each word," or "You chose the correct vocabulary words to complete three of the sentences."
  - Next, describe one of the categories of errors to the student and point out an example of the error. For example, "The suffixes you added to the words were incorrect."
  - Once the error is identified, provide the student with strategies to correct and avoid the error. For example, for a student confusing affixes, remind him or her to use an affixionary or a dictionary to look up the affix.
  - Model using the strategy, then have the student practice the strategy to correct at least one item with your guidance.
  - Repeat the process for any remaining errors.
  - Finally, summarize the conference by reminding the student of the types of errors and the strategies to avoid the errors in the future.

To expand on this procedure when you close the conference, you may have the student summarize the conference by describing what he or she learned. Also, create a written goal statement to be reviewed by the student before and after attempting the next activity. (Kline, Schumaker, & Deshler, 1991)

References

Adler, M., & Rougle, E. (2005). *Building literacy through classroom discussion: Research-based strategies for developing critical readers and thoughtful writers in middle school.* New York: Scholastic.

Boaler, J., Wiliam, D., & Brown, M. (2000). Students' experiences of ability grouping—disaffection, polarisation and the construction of failure. *British Educational Research Journal, 26*(5), 631–648.

Broussard, C. A., & Joseph, A. L. (1998). Tracking: A form of educational neglect? *Social Work in Education, 20*(2), 110–120.

Cummins, J. (1994). Knowledge, power, and identity in teaching English as a second language. In F. Genesee (Ed.), *Educating second language learners: The whole child, the whole curriculum, the whole community* (pp. 33–58). New York: Cambridge University Press.

Echevarria, J., Vogt, M. E., & Short, D. J. (2004). *Making content comprehensible to English learners: The SIOP model.* Boston: Allyn & Bacon.

Kline, F., Schumaker, J., & Deshler, D. (1991). Development and validation of feedback routines for instructing students with learning disabilities. *Learning Disability Quarterly, 14*(3), 191–207.

Langer, J. A. (2001). Beating the odds: Teaching middle and high school students to read and write well. *American Educational Research Journal, 38*(4), 837–880.

Lapp, D., Fisher, D., & Wolsey, T. D. (2009). *Literacy growth for every child: Differentiated small-group instruction K–6.* New York: The Guilford Press.

Lapp, D., Flood, J., & Goss, K. (2000). Desks don't move—students do: In effective classroom environments. *Reading Teacher, 54*(1), 31–36.

Navan, J. L. (2002). Enhancing the achievement of "all" learners means high ability students too. *Middle School Journal, 34*(2), 45–49.

Pearson, P. D., & Gallagher, M. C. (1983). The instruction of reading comprehension. *Contemporary Educational Psychology, 8*(3), 317–344.

Rothenberg, C., & Fisher, D. (2007). *Teaching English language learners: A differentiated approach.* Upper Saddle River, NJ: Prentice Hall.

Slavin, R. E., & Braddock, J. H. III. (1993). Ability grouping: On the wrong track. *College Board Review*, 168, 11–17.

Vygotsky, L. S. (1978). *Mind in society: The development of higher psychological processes.* (M. Cole, V. John-Steiner, S. Scribner, & E. Souberman (Eds)). Cambridge, MA: Harvard University Press.

Winans, J. A. (1923). Aims and standards in public speaking work. *The English Journal*, *12*, 223–234.

Scope and Sequence

	Expeditions														Additional Components		
	E1	E2	E3	E4	E5	E6	E7	E8	E9	E10	E11	E12	E13	E14	Technology	Word Study	Library
Comprehension Strategies																	
Make Connections	✓	•	•	•	•	•	•	•	•	•	•	•	•	•	•	•	•
Use Prior Knowledge		✓	•	•	•	•	•	•	•	•	•	•	•	•		•	
Preview/Predict	✓	•	•	•	•	•	•	•	•	•	•	•	•	•		•	•
Identify Text Features		✓	•	•	•	•	•	•	•	•	•	•	•	•			•
Identify Main Idea		✓	•	•	•	•	•	•	•	•	•	•	•	•	•	•	•
Make Inferences				✓	•			•		•			•	•	•	•	•
Summarize		✓	•				•	•		•			•	•	•		•
Ask Questions	✓	•	•	•	•	•	•	•	•	•	•	•	•	•	•		•
Identify Author's Purpose						✓				•							
Compare and Contrast							✓				•			•			•
Sequence				✓		•					•		•				•
Identify Cause and Effect					✓				•		•		•	•			•
Take Notes					✓	•	•			•	•						
Visualize	✓	•	•	•	•		•	•	•	•	•	•	•	•			•
Identify Story Elements				✓		•			•		•				•		•
Vocabulary																	
Make Connections Between Words	✓	•	•	•	•	•	•	•	•	•	•	•	•	•	•	•	•
Context Clues	✓	•	•	•	•	•	•	•	•	•	•	•	•	•	•	•	•
Morphology	✓	•	•	•	•	•	•	•	•	•	•	•	•	•		•	•
Dictionary Skills			✓	•	•	•	•	•	•	•	•	•	•	•	•	•	•
High-Frequency Words															•	•	•
Content-Related Words	✓	•	•	•	•	•	•	•	•	•	•	•	•	•	•	•	•
Synonyms and Antonyms	✓	•	•		•	•	•		•		•	•	•	•	•		
Multiple-Meaning Words		✓		•	•	•	•		•						•		
Homophones	✓														•	•	

	Expeditions														Additional Components		
	E1	E2	E3	E4	E5	E6	E7	E8	E9	E10	E11	E12	E13	E14	Technology	Word Study	Library
Fluency																	
Multiple Readings of Passages	✓	•	•	•	•	•	•	•	•	•	•	•	•	•	•	•	•
Prosody	✓	•	•	•	•	•	•	•	•	•	•	•	•	•	•	•	
Word Study																	
Phonemic Awareness																•	
High-Frequency Words															•	•	
Regular Words															•	•	
Irregular Words															•	•	
Word Automaticity	✓	•	•	•	•	•	•	•	•	•	•	•	•	•	•	•	
Phonics	✓	•	•	•	•	•	•	•	•	•	•	•	•	•		•	
Letter Combinations																•	
Rule-Based Words																•	
Prefixes	✓	•	•	•	•	•	•	•	•	•	•	•	•		•	•	
Suffixes			✓	•	•	•	•	•	•	•	•	•	•	•	•	•	
Multisyllabic Words				✓											•	•	
Compound Words		✓														•	
Sight Words																•	
Spelling		✓														•	
Greek/Latin Roots		✓	•	•	•	•	•	•	•	•	•	•	•	•			

	Expeditions														Additional Components		
	E1	E2	E3	E4	E5	E6	E7	E8	E9	E10	E11	E12	E13	E14	Technology	Word Study	Library
Writing																	
Planning to Write	✓	•	•	•	•	•	•	•	•	•	•	•	•	•			
Ideas and Elaboration	✓	•	•	•	•	•	•	•	•	•	•	•	•	•			
Word Choice	✓	•	•	•	•	•	•	•	•	•	•	•	•	•			
Sentence Fluency	✓	•	•	•	•	•	•	•	•	•	•	•	•	•			
Conventions	✓	•	•	•	•	•	•	•	•	•	•	•	•	•			
Organization	✓	•	•	•	•	•	•	•	•	•	•	•	•	•			
Responding to Reading Selections	✓	•	•	•	•	•	•	•	•	•	•	•	•	•	•	•	•
Multiparagraph Writing	✓	•	•	•	•	•	•	•	•	•	•	•	•	•			

Professional Development

The Professional Development Partnership

Voyager's award-winning professional development provides districts and schools with **extensive support across multiple levels,** ensuring a high level of implementation fidelity.

The partnership can include on-site, telephone, and online resources to facilitate . . .

- initial planning.
- teacher training, including ongoing professional development materials.
- consultations with district leadership, principals, and coaches throughout the school year.
- collaboration with teachers and administrators using real-time VPORT data.
- end-of-year assessment analysis and development of next steps.
- access to supplemental support materials.

The Voyager professional development goal is to empower teachers and principals to maximize student potential and improve academic performance.

Implementation Partnership

To ensure success, Voyager offers a professional development partnership that extends throughout the school year and integrates continuous training and support services with detailed reporting for teachers and administrators.

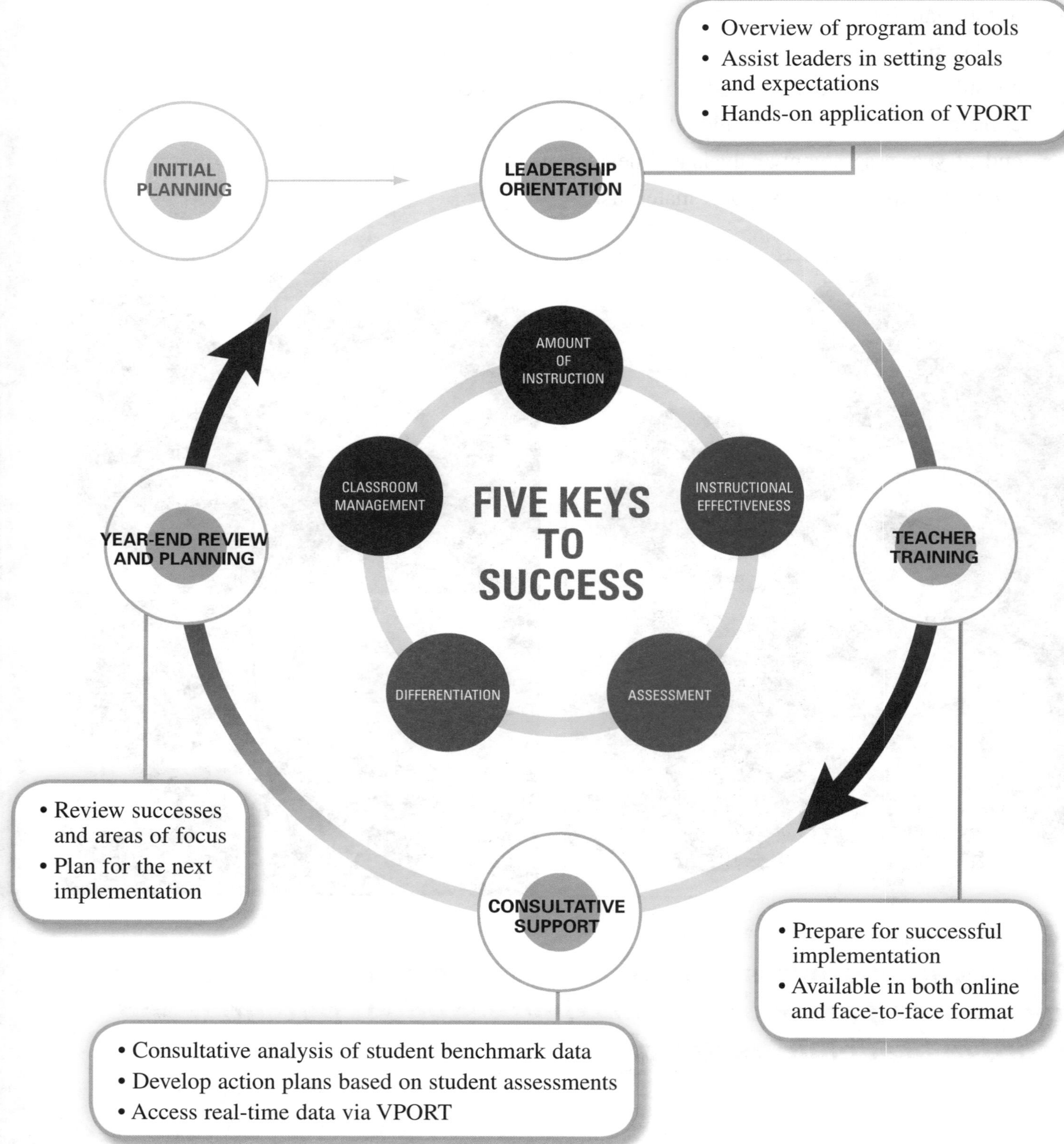

Expeditions

Begin

Who Am I?

Lesson 1 — "You Are What Your Genes Make You—Or *Are* You?"

Introduce the Expedition
- Discuss probing questions about identity.
- Make connections and build background for passages.

Before Reading
- Introduce and practice using passage vocabulary.
- Introduce and practice previewing and making predictions.
- Introduce the passage by previewing and making predictions.

During Reading
Read "You Are What Your Genes Make You—Or *Are* You?"

After Reading
Check comprehension.

Extend and practice.

Lesson 2 — "Nature Versus Nurture—A Story of Genetics"

Before Reading
- Introduce and practice using passage vocabulary.
- Introduce and practice using context clues.
- Introduce the passage by previewing and making predictions.

During Reading
Read "Nature Versus Nurture—A Story of Genetics."

After Reading
Check comprehension.

Extend and practice.

Lesson 3 — "The Truth About Birth Order"

Before Reading
- Introduce and practice using passage vocabulary.
- Introduce and practice asking questions.
- Introduce the passage by previewing and making predictions.

During Reading
Read "The Truth About Birth Order."

After Reading
Check comprehension.

Extend and practice.

Lesson 4 — "The Company You Keep"

Before Reading
- Introduce and practice using passage vocabulary.
- Introduce visualizing.
- Introduce the passage by previewing and making predictions.

During Reading
Read "The Company You Keep."

After Reading
Check comprehension.

Extend and practice.

Lesson 5—Review, Extend, Assess

Review Vocabulary
Review and practice using passage vocabulary.

Extend Vocabulary
Use affixes to build and understand new words.

Assess Comprehension and Vocabulary
Assess student understanding of vocabulary, preview and predict, using context clues, asking questions, and visualizing.

Reteach
Reteach previewing and predicting, using context clues, asking questions, and visualizing using activity pages.

Passport Reading Journeys Library
Have students select books for independent reading.

Technology
Have students practice vocabulary using the online technology component.

Writing Process
Have students use the writing process to write a memoir.

Real-World Reading
Introduce Real-World Reading passages to students.

Exploring Careers
Introduce Exploring Career passages to students.

Teacher's Note
Students will have access to a library of books and an online vocabulary and comprehension component. These will be referenced throughout the remaining Expeditions. Introduce students to these during this Expedition, so you can begin to use them extensively throughout the program.

Lesson 6
"Genes: Assets or Obstacles?"

Before Reading
- Introduce and practice using passage vocabulary.
- Introduce and practice making connections.
- Introduce the passage by previewing and making predictions.

During Reading
Read "Genes: Assets or Obstacles?"

After Reading
Check comprehension.

ELL Extend and practice.

Lesson 7
"When Identical Twins Grow Up Apart, How Identical Are They?"

Before Reading
- Introduce and practice using passage vocabulary.
- Practice using context clues.
- Introduce the passage by previewing and making predictions.

During Reading
- Read "When Identical Twins Grow Up Apart, How Identical Are They?"
- Practice making connections.

After Reading
Check comprehension.

Extend and practice.

Lesson 8
"The Road Not Taken"

Before Reading
- Introduce and practice using passage vocabulary.
- Practice visualizing.
- Introduce the passage by previewing and making predictions.

During Reading
- Read "The Road Not Taken."
- Practice visualizing.

After Reading
Check comprehension.

Extend and practice.

Lesson 9
"You Are What Your Genes Make You—Or *Are* You?" and "Nature Versus Nurture—A Story of Genetics"

Prepare to Reread
- Review and practice using passage vocabulary.
- Practice using context clues.

Reread
- Practice asking questions.
- Practice visualizing.
- Write paragraphs about connections to text.

Extend and practice.

Lesson 10—Review, Extend, Assess

Review Vocabulary
Review and practice using passage vocabulary.

Extend Vocabulary
Use affixes to build and understand new words.

Assess Comprehension and Vocabulary
Assess student understanding of vocabulary, making connections, and other previously taught strategies.

Reteach
Reteach preview and predict, context clues, asking questions, and making connections using activity pages.

Passport Reading Journeys Library
Have students select books for independent reading.

Technology
Have students practice vocabulary using the online technology component.

Expedition Project
Have students research and prepare for an autobiographical presentation.

Real-World Reading
Introduce Real-World Reading passages to students.

Exploring Careers
Introduce Exploring Career passages to students.

Expedition 1

Introduce the Expedition

Teacher's Note
Expedition 1 has a different look and instructional format than the remaining Expeditions. The goal of the Expedition is to teach the five skills that students should use every time they read: preview and predict, use context clues, ask questions, visualize, and make connections. Eight short passages with minimal rereading have been used to accomplish this goal.

1. **The title of Expedition 1 is "Who Am I?"** Direct students to the opening photograph on Anthology page 1. Start a discussion about individual identity by writing *race*, *name*, *interests in and out of school*, and *family* on the board. **What do these words have to do with the theme "Who Am I?" What else could help the students in the picture define who they are?** Encourage students to think about how where a person lives might shape his or her identity. Add student responses to those on the board.

   To make the most of the discussion time, remember to incorporate strategies that encourage and extend student involvement. Refer to page xxxviii for a comprehensive discussion of these strategies.

2. Have students give initial answers to the following probing questions. **You will add to your responses throughout the Expedition.** Record responses on the board.
   - **What makes you who you are?**
   - **Do genetics determine who you are, or do your surroundings?**
   - **What about you is unchangeable?**

Build Background DVD 1.1
Tell students they will view a brief DVD that provides background information about the theme "Who Am I?" As **you watch, listen for ideas that connect to the ideas you discussed.**

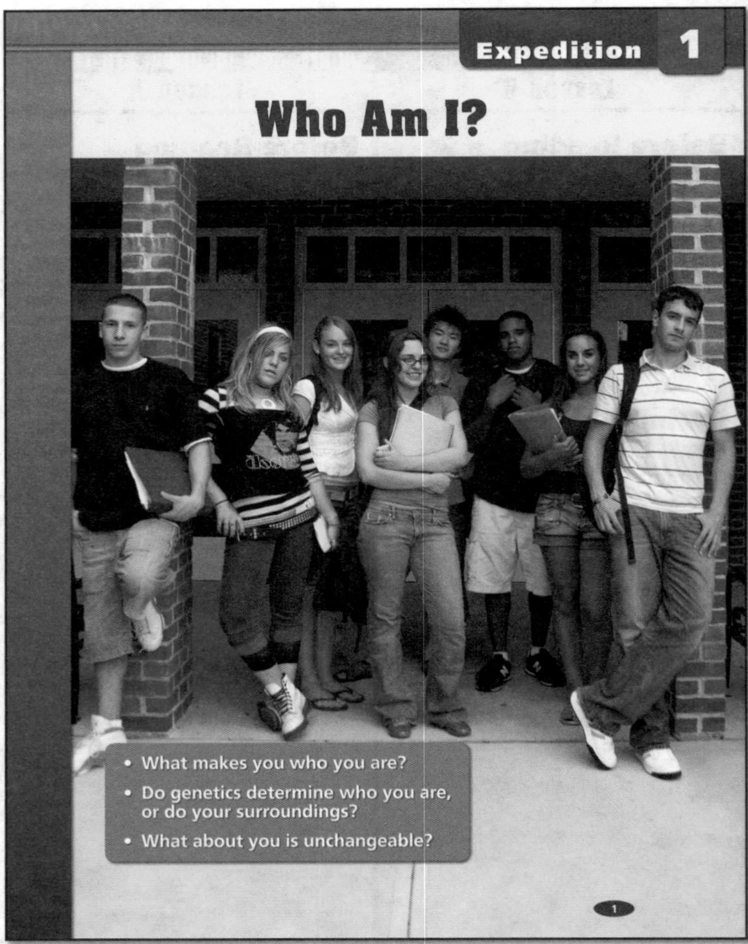
Expedition 1
Who Am I?
• What makes you who you are?
• Do genetics determine who you are, or do your surroundings?
• What about you is unchangeable?
1

3. Have students turn to the Expedition Organizer on Student Book pages 2 and 3. **What ideas or facts from the DVD caught your attention? Do they connect with any of the probing questions?** Have students write any answers to the questions in Part A after watching the DVD.

   Suggestions for how students can add ideas to these pages appear in this Teacher's Edition at the end of Lessons 2, 4, 7, and 9.

   Explain that in Expedition 1, students will learn these strategies: preview and predict, use context clues, ask questions, visualize, and make connections. **We will call these *active reading strategies* because you actively use them when you read for any purpose.** Have students turn to Anthology page 9. **Starting with this passage, you'll see the numbered margin notes. These notes will remind you to practice these strategies as you read.**

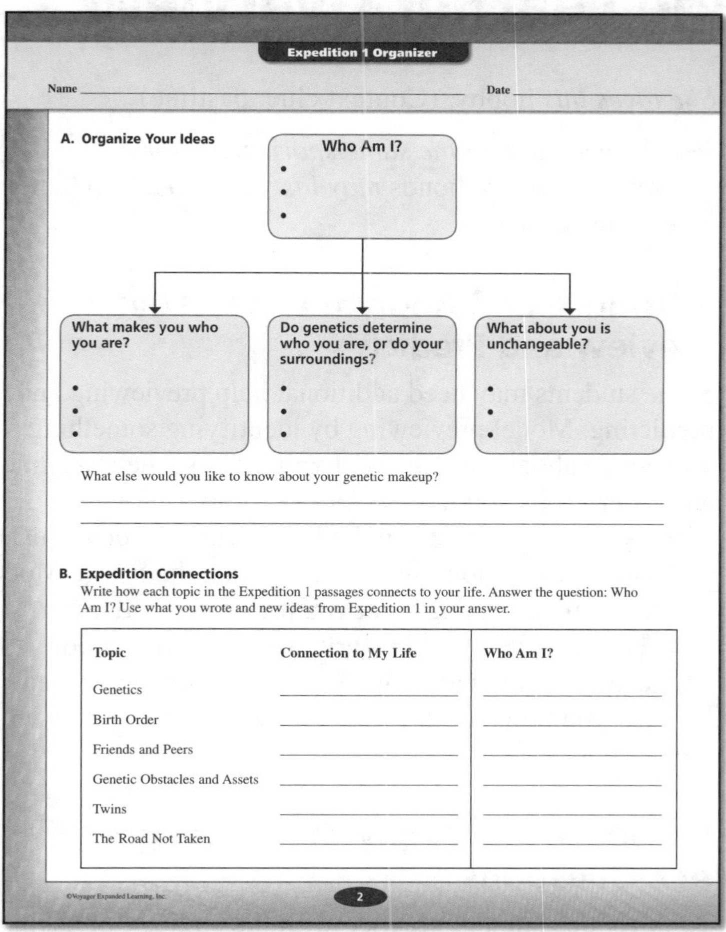

Expedition 1 Organizer

Name ______________________ Date ______________

A. Organize Your Ideas

Who Am I?
-
-
-

What makes you who you are?	Do genetics determine who you are, or do your surroundings?	What about you is unchangeable?
• • •	• • •	• • •

What else would you like to know about your genetic makeup?

____

____

B. Expedition Connections

Write how each topic in the Expedition 1 passages connects to your life. Answer the question: Who Am I? Use what you wrote and new ideas from Expedition 1 in your answer.

Topic	Connection to My Life	Who Am I?
Genetics		
Birth Order		
Friends and Peers		
Genetic Obstacles and Assets		
Twins		
The Road Not Taken		

©Voyager Expanded Learning, Inc. 2

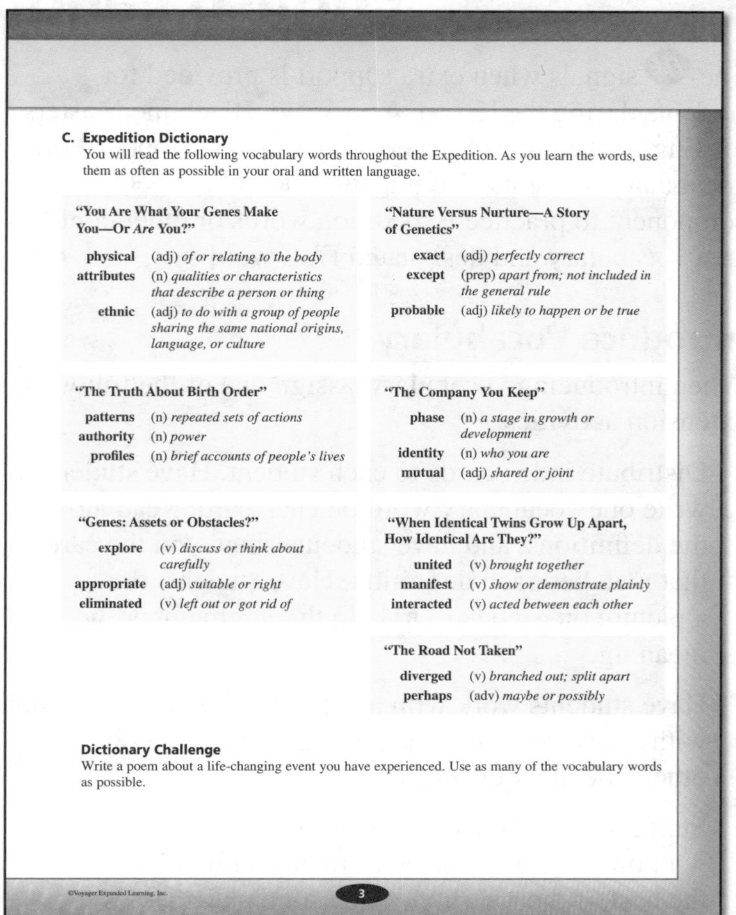

C. Expedition Dictionary

You will read the following vocabulary words throughout the Expedition. As you learn the words, use them as often as possible in your oral and written language.

"You Are What Your Genes Make You—Or *Are* You?"

physical (adj) *of or relating to the body*
attributes (n) *qualities or characteristics that describe a person or thing*
ethnic (adj) *to do with a group of people sharing the same national origins, language, or culture*

"Nature Versus Nurture—A Story of Genetics"

exact (adj) *perfectly correct*
except (prep) *apart from; not included in the general rule*
probable (adj) *likely to happen or be true*

"The Truth About Birth Order"

patterns (n) *repeated sets of actions*
authority (n) *power*
profiles (n) *brief accounts of people's lives*

"The Company You Keep"

phase (n) *a stage in growth or development*
identity (n) *who you are*
mutual (adj) *shared or joint*

"Genes: Assets or Obstacles?"

explore (v) *discuss or think about carefully*
appropriate (adj) *suitable or right*
eliminated (v) *left out or got rid of*

"When Identical Twins Grow Up Apart, How Identical Are They?"

united (v) *brought together*
manifest (v) *show or demonstrate plainly*
interacted (v) *acted between each other*

"The Road Not Taken"

diverged (v) *branched out; split apart*
perhaps (adv) *maybe or possibly*

Dictionary Challenge

Write a poem about a life-changing event you have experienced. Use as many of the vocabulary words as possible.

©Voyager Expanded Learning, Inc. 3

ELL

Making Connections

Expedition 1 offers students opportunities to think about and describe "who they are." They will think, talk, and write about their own personalities, traits, and physical and genetic backgrounds. Some students may not feel comfortable discussing certain personal or family issues in a group.

When students answer questions or write, allow them to reference either their own experiences or experiences of someone they know or have heard of. Students may answer some questions based on their cultural customs or religious beliefs. Allow students to explain the origins of their own viewpoints and invite them to continue studying these.

Help students understand the issues in the Expedition by asking them to think about their personalities, talents, likes, and dislikes. Preview these terms:

genetics *what you are born with that determines your looks and personality and other things that make you who you are*

surroundings *the people, places, and things you encounter during your life*

Have students brainstorm words for *surroundings* in their native language. Tell them that some people believe that surroundings affect people's personalities and choices. Many people also believe that a combination of genetics and surroundings determines "who you are."

If students need support when reading passages that have scientific terms, focus on language support.

Encourage students to keep a personal dictionary of more complex words they learn during the Expedition with definitions and examples as follows:

dominant trait *the stronger trait or one that dominates the weaker recessive traits; brown eyes*

recessive trait *weaker or one that gives way to the other more dominant traits; blue eyes*

English Language Learner Overview

The ELL signals when extra support is provided for students during the lesson. As needed, Blackline Masters for English language learners may provide support. For vocabulary, students also may use the online technology component to practice Expedition words or other content-area vocabulary and designated ELL word sets.

Introduce Vocabulary

When introducing vocabulary, assign one of the following extension activities:

- Distribute index cards to each student. Have students write one vocabulary word on each card. Read aloud the definitions, and have students show you the card that matches each definition. Have students draw a picture on each card to help them remember the meaning.
- Have students work with a partner to create flash cards with the word on one side and the definition on the other side and quiz each other.
- Start a game of charades. Have students draw a card with one of the words on it, then act out the word to the best of their ability. When someone guesses the right term, it is his or her turn to act.

Practice Context Clues

Lesson 3

Provide support for the context words *self-reliant*, *tactful*, and *persistent*. Remind students that context clues can be a restatement of the word you're trying to figure out.

Write the following sentences on the board, and have students identify the context clue in each.

Bindu usually does not ask for help. She tries to be self-reliant. (Context clue: does not ask for help)

Jared does not hurt or offend people. He is very tactful. (Context clue: does not hurt or offend people)

Tina never gives up. She is extremely persistent. (Context clue: never gives up)

Lesson 4

Provide support for the context words *hobby* and *bonds*. Remind students that one type of context clue is a synonym, a word or phrase that means the same thing as the word you're trying to figure out.

Write the following sentences on the board, and have students identify the context clue in each.

Theresa's favorite pastime is building model airplanes. She loves this hobby. (Context clue: pastime)

People who play on the same sports team form connections. These bonds *may last many years.* (Context clue: connections)

Introduce and Apply the Strategy: Preview and Predict

Some students may need additional help previewing and predicting. Model previewing by identifying something you notice about the passage. Explicitly use the academic term *preview* as you model: **As I *preview*, I notice . . . .** Write your observations on the board. Have students make their own observations and write them on the board. Model predicting by rereading what you previewed and using **now I *predict* that . . .**, and write your next prediction on the board. Emphasize that your prediction was based on what you previewed. Have students provide their own predictions.

Introduce and Apply the Strategy: Ask Questions

To introduce student practice with the strategy of asking questions, have them focus on a specific word or phrase and create a question from it. Model the process.

Read aloud the title of Passage 1. **I'm not sure what the word *genes* means. I'll turn it into a question. What are *genes*? Now I'll look back at what I read to find what it means, or I'll keep reading and pay attention to find what it means.** Guide students as they select a part of the passage and formulate their own questions.

Introduce and Apply the Strategy: Visualize

Some students may need further practice visualizing. Have them describe a "mental picture" of a place they know. **You use what you have seen to visualize, and when you read, you can use words to visualize. Write *trains, building, city*.** Have students describe a mental picture using these words. Have students practice the strategy with the short, less complex passages and statements on Blackline Master page 4. Have students answer questions to help them understand how visualizing connects to reading. Partners may share their answers.

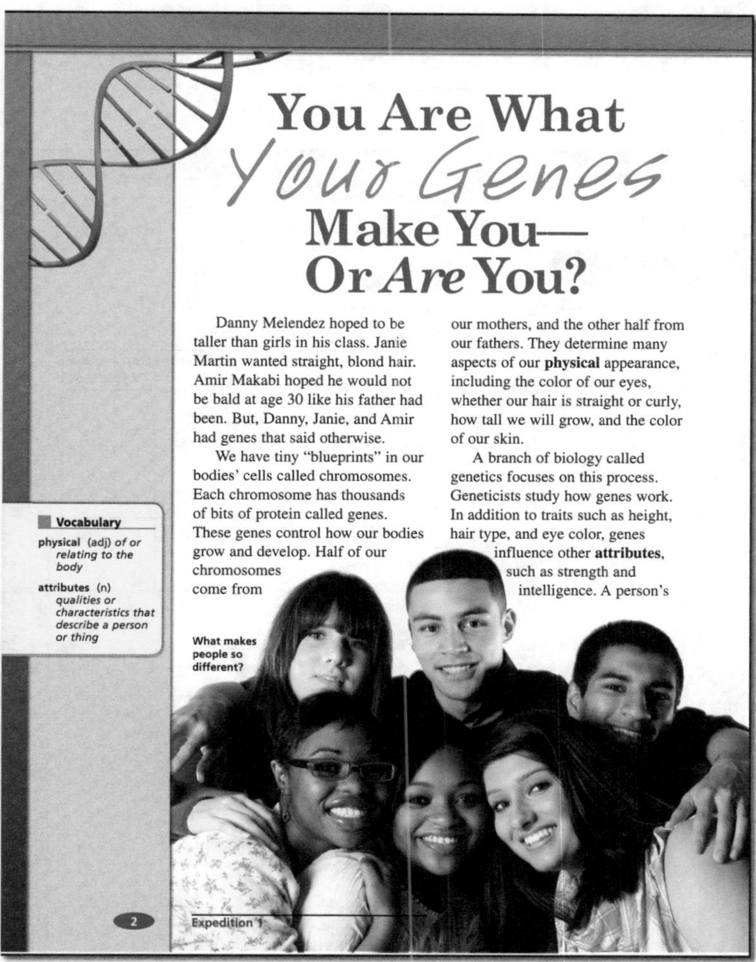

You Are What *Your Genes* Make You—Or *Are* You?

Danny Melendez hoped to be taller than girls in his class. Janie Martin wanted straight, blond hair. Amir Makabi hoped he would not be bald at age 30 like his father had been. But, Danny, Janie, and Amir had genes that said otherwise.

We have tiny "blueprints" in our bodies' cells called chromosomes. Each chromosome has thousands of bits of protein called genes. These genes control how our bodies grow and develop. Half of our chromosomes come from our mothers, and the other half from our fathers. They determine many aspects of our **physical** appearance, including the color of our eyes, whether our hair is straight or curly, how tall we will grow, and the color of our skin.

A branch of biology called genetics focuses on this process. Geneticists study how genes work. In addition to traits such as height, hair type, and eye color, genes influence other **attributes**, such as strength and intelligence. A person's genes can even determine if he or she is particularly susceptible to, or likely to get, a disease.

Vocabulary

physical (adj) *of or relating to the body*

attributes (n) *qualities or characteristics that describe a person or thing*

What makes people so different?

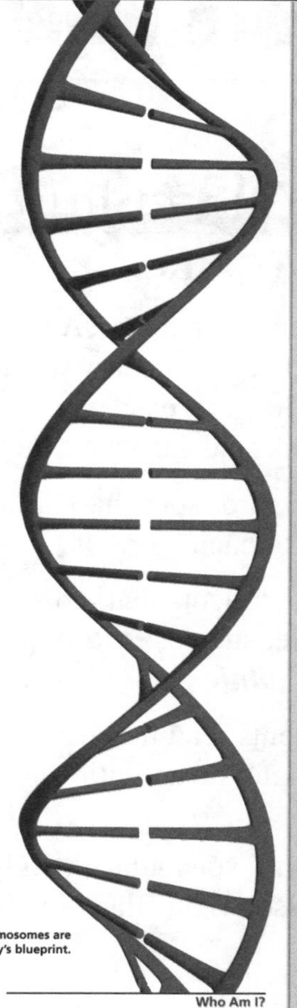

Your **ethnic** heritage, much like your genes, can influence your looks. Each ethnic group has genetic features that influence hair, skin, and eye color. Many families are a blend of different ethnic groups, which may cause offspring to reflect the genetic traits of more than one group.

Genetic research tells us that genes play a role in your physical appearance and what diseases you may be more likely to develop, but things like intelligence, physical strength, and personality are more dependent on how you live and how you use the talents and strengths you have. Your genes can influence your abilities and talents, but your environment and opportunities can enhance your genetic traits. In other words, genetics matters far less than how people choose to live and use their basic talents.

You cannot change some attributes of your genetic makeup. Your height and skin tone are basically unchangeable. However, you can do a lot to affect other parts of your genetic inheritance. You can choose to make the most of the genes that have been passed down to you. With hard work and perseverance, you can continually try to develop your mind and body in ways you desire. End

Vocabulary

ethnic (adj) *to do with a group of people sharing the same national origins, language, or culture*

Your chromosomes are your body's blueprint.

"You Are What Your Genes Make You—Or *Are* You?"

Before Reading

Introduce Vocabulary

1. Have students turn to Part A on Student Book page 4. Read aloud the vocabulary words, and have students rate their knowledge of each word. For words they have seen or know, ask students where they encountered them.
2. Read the part of speech, definition, and example sentence for each word.
3. For words students marked as unknown, give them an example, such as: **Many people who are in the Hispanic *ethnic* group speak Spanish.**
4. Have students read the instructions for Parts B and C and complete the activities.

Lesson 1 vocabulary will be extended at the end of Lesson 2 on Blackline Master page 2.

Introduce and Apply: Preview and Predict

1. **How do you decide what movies you want to see?** (word of mouth; actors; previews) **What is a preview?** (a short clip of the movie) Lead students to tell you that a preview shows who is in the movie, the title of the movie, and some of the scenes. **When you watch or hear a preview, do you predict or guess what the movie will be about? Give me an example of something you might predict from a preview.** (The characters save the world; the couple falls in love; the woman dies; it's funny, scary, or sad.)
2. **It's important to preview and predict so you know what to expect from your reading. When I preview, I don't read all the words in the passage. I look for clues that stand out, then I make predictions.** Model previewing the title, subheadings, and picture in the movie review on Student Book page 5.
3. Read the instructions, and have students complete the activity. Review the answers as a class.

ACADEMIC SKILL Remind students to use previewing and predicting when they read other text types. **When you read a chapter in a science or social studies textbook, it will help you to preview it and make predictions about what you will read.**

Expedition 1, Lesson 1

Name ______ Date ______

Vocabulary

"You Are What Your Genes Make You—Or *Are* You?"

A. Put a check mark in each row to indicate how well you know each boldfaced word.

	Know This Word	Have Seen This Word	Don't Know This Word
physical (adj) *of or relating to the body* The only difference in their *physical* appearance was the color of their eyes.			
attributes (n) *qualities or characteristics that describe a person or thing* Mai has many personal *attributes* that make her different from her friends.			
ethnic (adj) *to do with a group of people sharing the same national origins, language, or culture* Danny and the new student from India share the same *ethnic* background.			

B. Circle the vocabulary word from Part A that BEST completes each sentence.

1. By looking at our (physical, attribute) appearance, you can tell that we are related.
2. We study each country and the (attributes, ethnic) traditions of each.
3. His (physical, attributes) are honesty, loyalty, and friendliness.
4. They had a definite (attributes, physical) type they wanted for the play's role of the mother.
5. My (attributes, ethnic) heritage is a blend of many cultures.
6. My teacher says I have the perfect (ethnic, attributes) to be the class president.

C. Write a sentence using each vocabulary word. Answers will vary.

physical ______

attributes ______

ethnic ______

©Voyager Expanded Learning, Inc. 4

Vocabulary

physical (adj) *of or relating to the body*
The only difference in their *physical* appearance was the color of their eyes.

attributes (n) *qualities or characteristics that describe a person or thing*
Mai has many personal *attributes* that make her different from her friends.

ethnic (adj) *to do with a group of people sharing the same national origins, language, or culture*
Danny and the new student from India share the same *ethnic* background.

Introduce the Passage

1. **You will practice the preview and predict strategy on the passage "You Are What Your Genes Make You—Or *Are* You?" What will you use as clues for previewing?** (title; boldfaced words; photographs; illustrations; captions)
2. **You can use the information from previewing to make a prediction.** Write this sentence starter on the board: *I predict that this passage is* _____. As a class, complete the sentence. (Possible prediction: I predict that this passage is about how genes make people different from one another.) Have students identify the clues they used to make the prediction.
3. Teach these terms from the passage:
   - *chromosomes* (krō' mə sōmz)
   - *Had genes that said otherwise* means "their genes would indicate, or mean, they will not have the trait they hoped for."
   - *Makeup* does not relate to cosmetics but means "what something is made of."

During Reading

1. Have students read "You Are What Your Genes Make You—Or *Are* You?" To select reading options that support your students' levels and classroom needs, see Reading Differentiation, page xxxii, if needed.
2. Remind students to think about their predictions as they read and make changes if needed.

After Reading

Check Comprehension

1. When students finish reading, ask them the following questions.
   - **Where does a person get chromosomes from?** (half from the mother and half from the father)
   - **What do genes control?** (how our bodies grow and develop)
   - **What are some attributes that genes control?** (eye color; hair color and texture; height)
   - **Can you change your genetic makeup? Explain.** (No, genes are in you from birth, and they determine your characteristics.)

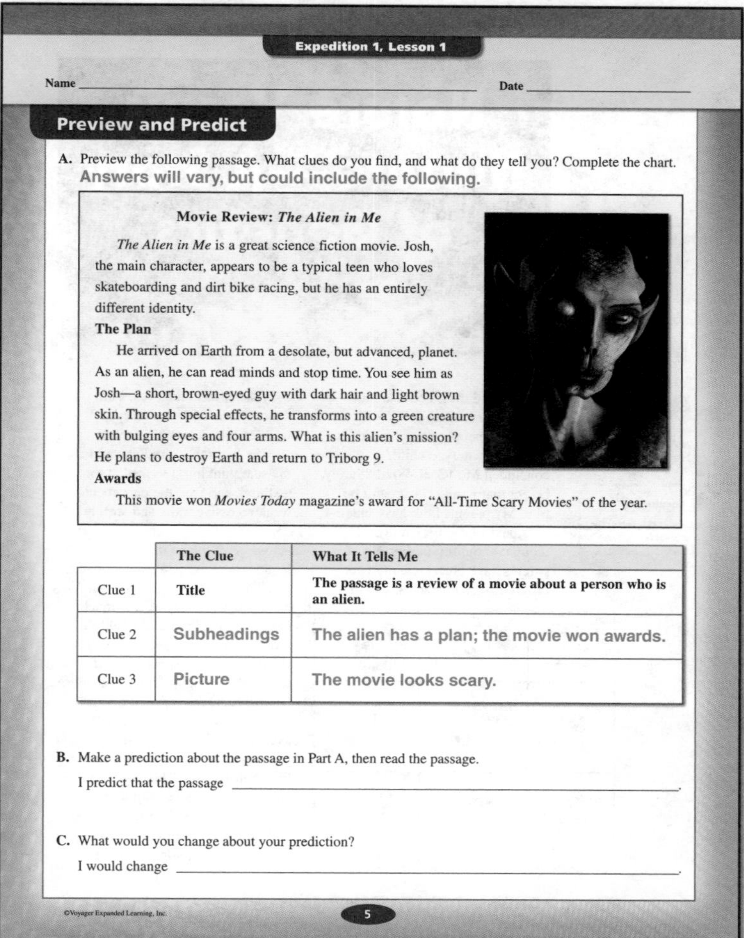

Expedition 1, Lesson 1

Name ______________________ Date ____________

Preview and Predict

A. Preview the following passage. What clues do you find, and what do they tell you? Complete the chart.
Answers will vary, but could include the following.

Movie Review: *The Alien in Me*

The Alien in Me is a great science fiction movie. Josh, the main character, appears to be a typical teen who loves skateboarding and dirt bike racing, but he has an entirely different identity.

The Plan

He arrived on Earth from a desolate, but advanced, planet. As an alien, he can read minds and stop time. You see him as Josh—a short, brown-eyed guy with dark hair and light brown skin. Through special effects, he transforms into a green creature with bulging eyes and four arms. What is this alien's mission? He plans to destroy Earth and return to Triborg 9.

Awards

This movie won *Movies Today* magazine's award for "All-Time Scary Movies" of the year.

	The Clue	What It Tells Me
Clue 1	Title	The passage is a review of a movie about a person who is an alien.
Clue 2	Subheadings	The alien has a plan; the movie won awards.
Clue 3	Picture	The movie looks scary.

B. Make a prediction about the passage in Part A, then read the passage.
I predict that the passage ______________________.

C. What would you change about your prediction?
I would change ______________________.

©Voyager Expanded Learning, Inc.

5

ELL If students have trouble answering these questions, model returning to the text to find the section that will help them answer. Have students read aloud the sentences in the text that answer the questions. Reread the question, and have students answer using what they found in the text.

2. **What did you preview that seemed confusing? What do you understand better now?** (Responses should address the information found in the title, illustrations, captions, or boldfaced words.)
3. Direct students to their prediction statement on the board. **How would you change or add to your prediction? When you read longer passages, pause to check your prediction and change it as you read new information. Changing your prediction is like saying "I get it now" as you read.**

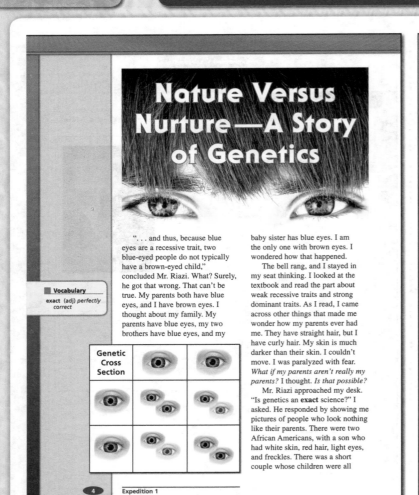

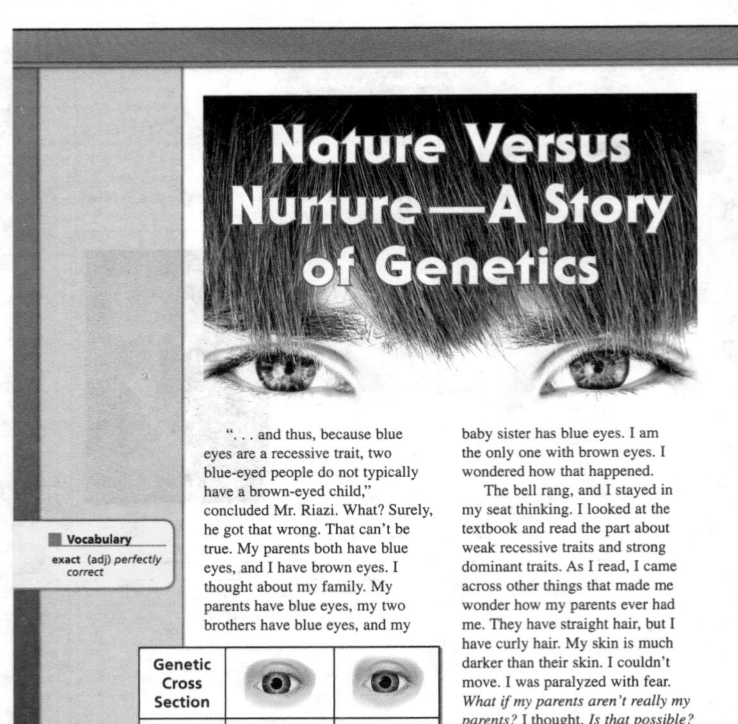

". . . and thus, because blue eyes are a recessive trait, two blue-eyed people do not typically have a brown-eyed child," concluded Mr. Riazi. What? Surely, he got that wrong. That can't be true. My parents both have blue eyes, and I have brown eyes. I thought about my family. My parents have blue eyes, my two brothers have blue eyes, and my baby sister has blue eyes. I am the only one with brown eyes. I wondered how that happened.

Vocabulary
exact (adj) *perfectly correct*

The bell rang, and I stayed in my seat thinking. I looked at the textbook and read the part about weak recessive traits and strong dominant traits. As I read, I came across other things that made me wonder how my parents ever had me. They have straight hair, but I have curly hair. My skin is much darker than their skin. I couldn't move. I was paralyzed with fear. *What if my parents aren't really my parents?* I thought. *Is that possible?*

Genetic Cross Section

Mr. Riazi approached my desk. "Is genetics an **exact** science?" I asked. He responded by showing me pictures of people who look nothing like their parents. There were two African Americans, with a son who had white skin, red hair, light eyes, and freckles. There was a short couple whose children were all short **except** one—who was more than 6 feet tall.

"Nothing in this world is exact," he said.

"I have been listening to your discussion on genetics, and I have read the information in the book. It makes me wonder if my parents are my real parents," I said. "I think it is **probable** that I am adopted."

"It's something you should ask them about. But, do you act like them?"

"Yes."

"Do you like the same things as they do?"

"Yes."

"Do you love them?"

"Yes."

"Then they are your parents—in every way that matters."

"Yes, but you mentioned that sometimes people are susceptible to diseases based on their genetic makeup. Don't I need to know where I came from?"

Mr. Riazi told me he thought it would be a good idea to talk to my parents about my concerns. He said that if I am adopted, it would be good to know my birth parents' health issues and what probabilities I have of contracting a disease.

After basketball practice, I went straight home. I was on a mission. My special task was to find out where I came from. Was I adopted? If so, why did my birth parents put me up for adoption? Why did my parents adopt me when they were able to have kids? Who am I? End

Daughter and mother

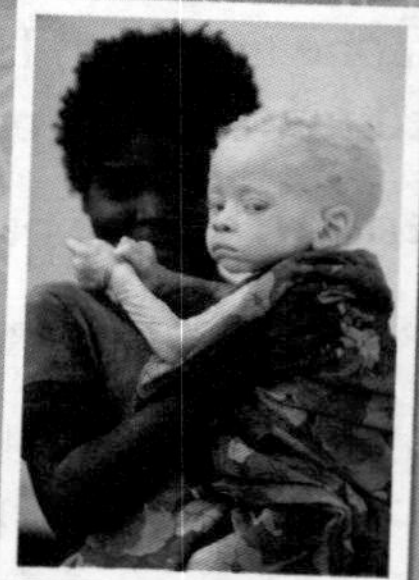
Sister and brother

Vocabulary
except (prep) *apart from; not included in the general rule*
probable (adj) *likely to happen or be true*

"Nature Versus Nurture—A Story of Genetics"

Before Reading

Introduce Vocabulary

1. Have students turn to Part A on Student Book page 6 and scan the boldfaced vocabulary words. **You will see these words as you read "Nature Versus Nurture—A Story of Genetics."** Have students rate their knowledge of each boldfaced word.
2. **Which words do you already know?** Ask students to use the words they know in a sentence. Read aloud the definition and example sentence for each word.
3. Have students read the instructions for Part B and complete the activity.
4. Read the instructions for Part C aloud, and have students complete the section independently. Have partners share their answers.

ELL Refer to Blackline Master page 2 to extend vocabulary practice.

Expedition 1, Lesson 2

Name ______ Date ______

Vocabulary

"Nature Versus Nurture—A Story of Genetics"

A. Rate your knowledge of each boldfaced vocabulary word.
3 familiar
2 somewhat familiar
1 unknown word

☐ **exact** (adj) *perfectly correct*
I am not an *exact* replica of my mom because I have my dad's nose.

☐ **except** (prep) *apart from; not included in the general rule*
We all have the same brown curly hair, *except* my sister, who is blonde.

☐ **probable** (adj) *likely to happen or be true*
Because you share your parents' genes, it is *probable* that you will look like them.

B. Read each sentence, then answer the question.

1. Does an **exact** measurement have mistakes or no mistakes? no mistakes
2. If the weather forecast says that rain is **probable** for your trip, should you pack an umbrella or sunglasses? an umbrella
3. If you order a pizza with everything **except** mushrooms, do you want mushrooms? no mushrooms

C. The words *accept* and *except* sound the same but have different meanings. *Accept* is a verb. One meaning of *accept* is "receive what someone offers." Reread the definition of *except* in Part A. Complete each of the following sentences with *accept* or *except.*

accept (v) *receive what someone offers*
except (prep) *apart from; not included in the general rule*

1. Marta would not accept a gift from the stranger.
2. The thirsty runner was glad to accept a bottle of cold water.
3. Everyone was swimming except one child who played in the sand.

 6

Vocabulary

exact (adj) *perfectly correct*
I am not an *exact* replica of my mom because I have my dad's nose.

except (prep) *apart from; not included in the general rule*
We all have the same brown curly hair, *except* my sister, who is blonde.

probable (adj) *likely to happen or be true*
Because you share your parents' genes, it is *probable* that you will look like them.

Introduce and Apply: Context Clues

1. **When you come across an unfamiliar word, you often can find words and phrases on the same page that help you figure out the meaning of the unfamiliar word. These words and phrases are called context clues.**
2. **Here are some different ways context clues may be used.** Write the following on the board:
   - *A profession is a* <u>*paid occupation*</u>*.*
   - *Many professions,* <u>*including doctors and lawyers,*</u> *require advanced degrees.*
   - *Sia's profession,* <u>*or job*</u>*, is advertising.*
   - *Arun has a* <u>*job*</u> *as a teacher. He has been in this profession for five years.*

   In the last example, the context clue appears in a different sentence. Tell students to look for context clues in the same sentence or in a sentence before or after the unfamiliar word.
3. Explain that a clue might be a definition, a description, an example, a synonym (a word meaning the same thing), or an antonym (a word meaning the opposite).
4. Write the following sentence on the board: *The radio we brought to the beach is portable, or easily carried.* **What does the word *portable* mean?** (easily carried) **What context clues in the sentence helped you find this meaning?** (or easily carried)
5. Have students turn to Student Book page 7. Read the instructions for Parts A and B aloud, and have students complete the activities. Review the answers as a class.

Introduce the Passage

1. **You learned that previewing and predicting can help you understand what a passage is about. Use this strategy before reading this passage.** Have students preview "Nature Versus Nurture—A Story of Genetics." **Look at the title, photos, and chart. What do they tell you about the passage?** (The passage has something to do with genetics.)
2. Have students predict how this passage about genetics might connect to the Expedition 1 theme, "Who Am I?"

During Reading

1. Have students read "Nature Versus Nurture—A Story of Genetics." To select reading options that support your students' levels and classroom needs, see Reading Differentiation, page xxxii, if needed.
2. Remind students to use context clues when they come across unfamiliar words.

ELL Support students as they use context clues to determine the meaning of *dominant*. Write the sentence containing the word, and direct students to contrast the phrases *weak recessive traits* and *strong dominant traits*. Guide them to notice the synonym *strong* to determine the meaning of *dominant*.

After Reading

Check Comprehension

1. When students finish reading, ask them these questions.
   - **What does the narrator discover?** (that he or she might be adopted)
   - **What is the narrator's first clue that she might be adopted?** (He or she has brown eyes, but the parents and siblings have blue eyes.)
2. **How did you predict genetics would connect to the theme "Who Am I?" What other connections did you discover as you read?** (Possible answer: I predicted that the connection would be information about DNA; the passage was actually about genetic traits.)
3. Point out the word *paralyzed* in the passage. **What clue in the text can help you figure out what this word means?** (I couldn't move.)

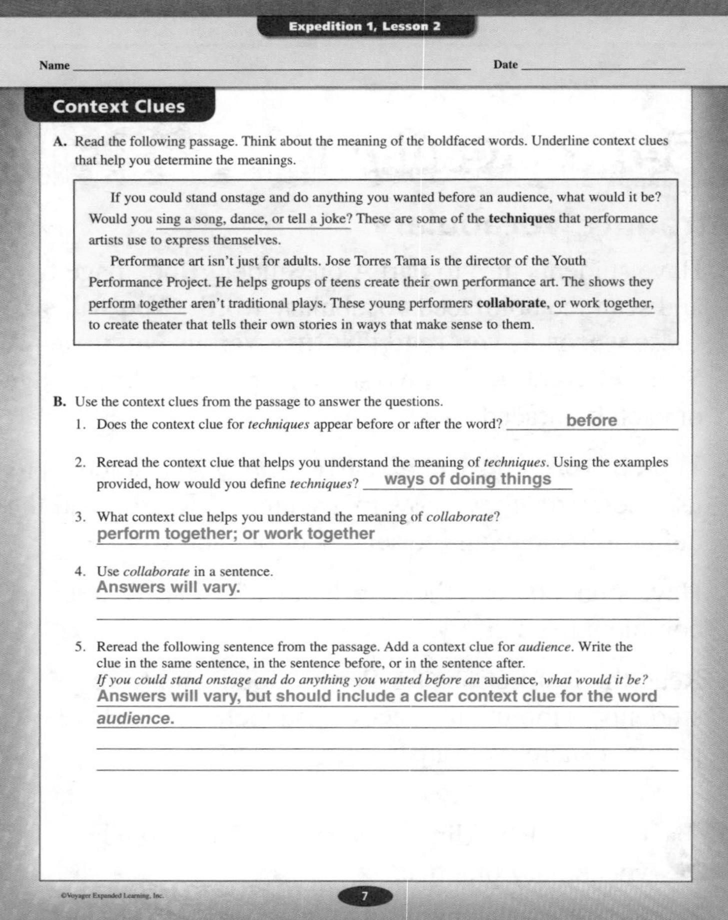

Expedition 1, Lesson 2

Name ______________________ Date ______________

Context Clues

A. Read the following passage. Think about the meaning of the boldfaced words. Underline context clues that help you determine the meanings.

If you could stand onstage and do anything you wanted before an audience, what would it be? Would you sing a song, dance, or tell a joke? These are some of the **techniques** that performance artists use to express themselves.

Performance art isn't just for adults. Jose Torres Tama is the director of the Youth Performance Project. He helps groups of teens create their own performance art. The shows they perform together aren't traditional plays. These young performers **collaborate**, or work together, to create theater that tells their own stories in ways that make sense to them.

B. Use the context clues from the passage to answer the questions.

1. Does the context clue for *techniques* appear before or after the word? before
2. Reread the context clue that helps you understand the meaning of *techniques*. Using the examples provided, how would you define *techniques*? ways of doing things
3. What context clue helps you understand the meaning of *collaborate*? perform together; or work together
4. Use *collaborate* in a sentence. Answers will vary.
5. Reread the following sentence from the passage. Add a context clue for *audience*. Write the clue in the same sentence, in the sentence before, or in the sentence after. *If you could stand onstage and do anything you wanted before an* audience, *what would it be?* Answers will vary, but should include a clear context clue for the word audience.

 7

4. Point out the word *recessive* in the second column of page 4. **What do you think the word *recessive* means?** (weak) **Remember, a clue might come before or after the unfamiliar word. What clues in the text helped you figure out the meaning?** (weak)
5. Point out the words *dominant* and *mission* in the text. Read the following prompts aloud, and wait for a correct response.

   The word *dominant* means "_____." A context clue is _____. (strong; the word *strong*)

   The word *mission* means "_____." A context clue is _____. (a special task; My special task was)

ACADEMIC SKILL Remind students that they can use context clues to help them figure out unfamiliar words or terms in other texts.

EXPEDITION ORGANIZER **Who Am I?**

Pause to have students turn to Student Book pages 2 and 3. Have students complete the following:

- Write answers to one or more of the probing questions in Part A.
- Write how genetics connects to their lives in Part B.

The Truth About Birth Order

President Barack Obama
Oldest Child

News Reporter Barbara Walters
Middle Child

Comedian Whoopi Goldberg
Youngest Child

Vocabulary
patterns (n) *repeated sets of actions*
authority (n) *power*

Are you a bossy person who likes to be the leader, or are you always following others' commands? Do you try to keep the peace and make others happy? Or, are you the clown who makes others laugh hysterically? Your personality may be linked to birth order. Researchers have been looking for **patterns** in people of the same birth order to see how birth order influences personality.

Many observers think an only child gets used to being the center of attention. Only children may get spoiled and overprotected. They tend to lose their temper when they do not get their way. On the other hand, they may feel inept, or foolish, because they see adults do things more easily.

Oldest children with no older siblings as role models are likely to be more self-reliant, or able to do things without help from others. Because they frequently deal with younger siblings, they are natural leaders and often take positions of **authority** and responsibility. More than half of the U.S. presidents were oldest children, and many who weren't the oldest were first-born sons. Twenty-one of the first 25 American astronauts were oldest children. All of the original seven Project Mercury astronauts were first-born children. When blended families add siblings, that changes the birth order. For example, President Obama went from being an only child to an oldest child.

Youngest children are often creative rebels who resist authority. Parents sometimes call them "the babies" of the family—even when they grow up. They may feel like babies because their elders may not take them seriously. They often are described as wonderful storytellers and very persistent, or unwilling to give up. Many youngest children pursue creative careers, like comedy or acting. Eddie Murphy, Jim Carrey, and Whoopi Goldberg are youngest children.

Middle children have to deal with older *and* younger siblings and may feel stuck in the middle. Having been in the middle and often making peace between the siblings, they are likely to grow up to be excellent negotiators. They tend to be very tactful in their speaking, so they rarely offend or hurt people. These are very useful qualities in adult life. Some middle children who have become successful adults include Donald Trump and Barbara Walters.

Do any of these **profiles** sound familiar to you? Does your personality fit the pattern for your birth order? For some people, the personality types are very accurate. Still others have defied the research and become the opposite of what researchers expect them to be.

All theories are likely to have exceptions. Scientists may get it wrong. But, if you want to know whether you fit the profiles, the best way to find out is to ask someone who knows you well. Maybe you would make a great leader, artist, or negotiator, but just don't know it. 

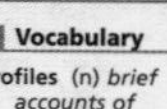
Vocabulary
profiles (n) *brief accounts of people's lives*

"The Truth About Birth Order"

Before Reading

Introduce Vocabulary

1. Have students turn to Part A on Student Book page 8 and scan the boldfaced vocabulary words. **You will see these words as you read "The Truth About Birth Order." Mark how well you know them.** Have students rate their knowledge of each boldfaced word.
2. Have students share which words they know. For each word, have a student use the word in a sentence.
3. Read the words, parts of speech, definitions, and context sentences aloud. **Do you know the word better now? If so, go back and change the rating to show that you understand it better.**
4. Read aloud the instructions for Parts B and C. Have students complete the activity, then compare their responses with a partner.

ELL Lesson 3 vocabulary will be extended at the end of Lesson 4 on Blackline Master page 4.

Introduce and Apply: Ask Questions

1. **Asking questions before, during, or after you read a text is a strategy you can use any time you read.**
2. **Ask questions before you read a text to help you focus on your own reason for reading. For example, if you're reading a passage called "Birthday Traditions Around the World," you can begin by asking a question about the title.** Model by writing on the board: *How are these traditions different from the way I celebrate birthdays?* **Then, focus on the question and read to discover the answer.**
3. **Ask questions while you read too. When you read a confusing part, stop and ask your own question about that part. Reread to find an answer in the text, or keep that question in mind as you keep reading. You might read this sentence in "Birthday Traditions Around the World."** Write on the board: *In Ireland, young men get keys when they turn 21 years old.* **Turn that sentence into a question.** Write student questions on the board. **How will you find the answer?** (Reread or keep reading.)
4. Have students complete page 9 in the Student Book. Review the answers as a class.

Expedition 1, Lesson 3

Name ______________________ Date ______________

Vocabulary

"The Truth About Birth Order"

A. Put a check mark in each row to indicate how well you know each boldfaced word.

	Know This Word	Have Seen This Word	Don't Know This Word
patterns (n) *repeated sets of actions* When children observe *patterns* of bad behavior, they often follow them.			
authority (n) *power* Firstborn children often have *authority* over their younger siblings.			
profiles (n) *brief accounts of people's lives* *Profiles* of astronauts indicate that many of them are firstborn children.			

B. Read the sentences. Circle the word that BEST completes each sentence.

1. The behavior (patterns/authority) of people change as they grow older.
2. Popular sports magazines feature (profiles/patterns) of famous athletes.
3. The teacher told Bernard to pick up the toys because she had (authority/profiles) over him.

C. Some words have more than one meaning. Read the two definitions of the word *profiles*. Write the definition of *profiles* used in each sentence.

A. brief accounts of people's lives
B. outlines of things viewed from the side

1. We drew *profiles* of our faces in art class.
Definition: B. outlines of things viewed from the side

2. The reporter wrote *profiles* of the famous twins.
Definition: A. brief accounts of people's lives

 8

Vocabulary

patterns (n) *repeated sets of actions*
When children observe *patterns* of bad behavior, they often follow them.

authority (n) *power*
Firstborn children often have *authority* over their younger siblings.

profiles (n) *brief accounts of people's lives*
Profiles of astronauts indicate that many of them are firstborn children.

Introduce the Passage

1. **Previewing and predicting help you know what to expect when you read.** Have students preview the title, photos, and captions of "The Truth About Birth Order." **What do you notice about the passage?** (Photos show celebrities; captions tell what order they were in their families.) Have students predict what the passage is about. Write the predictions on the board.
2. Teach this phrase from the passage:

   On the other hand is something that you say when you speak about two different facts or two opposite ways of thinking about a situation.

During Reading

1. Have students prepare to write questions as they read. Begin reading aloud. At the end of the first paragraph, pause to ask a question. **I just read that personality can be connected to birth order. I know that I am someone who always tries to make people laugh. That leaves me with a question. What order of birth are people who make others laugh?** Have students write the question on sheet of paper. Explain that they must read to find the answer.
2. Pause at the end of the second paragraph. Model asking: ***Are only children the only ones who lose their temper easily?* To find the answer, reread or keep the question in mind and keep reading.**
3. Remind students that as they continue reading, they should look for unfamiliar words and use context clues to figure out the meaning. **The word *inept* appears in the second paragraph. The word *foolish* is a context clue that helps you know what *inept* means.**

   Repeat this process for the following words.

   - **self-reliant** (adj) *able to do things without help*, Anthology page 6
   - **persistent** (adj) *unwilling to give up*, Anthology page 7
   - **negotiators** (n) *people who make peace between two sides*, Anthology page 7
   - **tactful** (adj) *without offense*, Anthology page 7
4. **Finish reading "The Truth About Birth Order."** To select reading options that support your students' levels and classroom needs, see Reading Differentiation, page xxxii, if needed.

Expedition 1, Lesson 3

Name ______________________ Date ____________

Ask Questions

Practice asking questions by completing the steps at the right.
Answers will vary, but could include the following.

Birthdays and Brooms

Your birthday can be a special day. Some people celebrate birthdays, while others do not. When you think of birthdays, do you think of traditions like cakes, candles, and gifts? Many people who live outside America celebrate birthdays in other unique and surprising ways.

Germans have a special tradition for men who reach the age of 30 without a wife or girlfriend. On the morning of that man's birthday, he must pick up a broom, march over to city hall, and sweep the front steps clean. He must do this with people watching him. Some of them are the man's friends; they throw dirt on the steps so he has to clean them again!

This tradition is not meant to embarrass the man. It is a way to show any women who pass by city hall that the man has reached the age of 30 and is available. The man's sweeping is supposed to show young women that he will be a good husband who will help her to keep a clean house.

1. Read the title and turn it into a question. Keep your question in mind as you read.
   What do birthdays and brooms have in common?
2. Read the passage. What part is confusing? Turn it into a question.
   Why does he sweep the steps?
3. Write answers to your questions.
   In Germany, unmarried men use a broom to sweep city hall steps on their 30th birthdays. The tradition is a way of getting women to notice these men and to think they will be good husbands.
4. Answer the following critical thinking question.
   What does this custom tell you about the beliefs of the country as a whole?
   Answers will vary.

 9

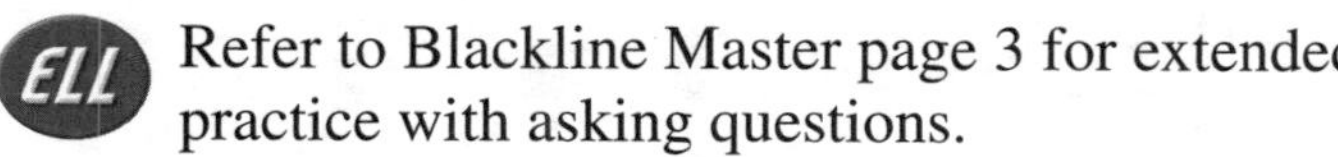

After Reading

Check Comprehension

1. Direct students to read the predictions on the board. **Were the predictions accurate? How would you change them now that you have read the passage?**
2. Have students write answers to the questions they wrote. Allow volunteers to share their questions and answers. **How did the strategy of asking questions help as you read?** (Answers will vary.)
3. **How important do you think birth order is?** As they discuss, have students refer to the passage if needed.

ELL Refer to Blackline Master page 3 for extended practice with asking questions.

ACADEMIC SKILL Remind students that asking questions is a good strategy for any reading. **When you read a textbook in any class, pause to ask your own questions before, during, or after you read a section. This will help ensure you understand what you have read.**

The Company You Keep

Vocabulary

phase (n) *a stage in growth or development*

identity (n) *who you are*

mutual (adj) *shared or joint*

When Clarice Spellings was 12, her favorite activity was going to the mall. She and her friends would shop and talk about movies and music. Clarice's mall hobby lasted until one day in physical education class, when she had to race around the school track. Suddenly, Clarice discovered that she could run quickly, and she began doing something different in her spare time. She started a new **phase** in her life.

"I still do my schoolwork," says Clarice, now 16. "But now, I identify myself as an athlete. I'm on the track team. My specialty event is the 100-meter dash. Although we have meets only in the spring, running is a year-round activity for me. I'm always training and working out. I used to eat tons of junk food, but not anymore. These days, I eat right and get plenty of rest. I think I actually have a good chance of getting a college scholarship—maybe even a free ride. I see a few of my old friends occasionally, but we sort of speak different languages and care about different things now. My close friends are my athlete friends."

Clarice found an **identity** for herself through running, and she developed an exciting awareness of what she could achieve. Her current circle of friends has bonds, or connections, of **mutual** interest. They share a love of competition and self-improvement.

Jeff Castillo, 18, had serious discipline problems a few years ago and did not control his behavior in or out of school. Thinking

8 Expedition 1

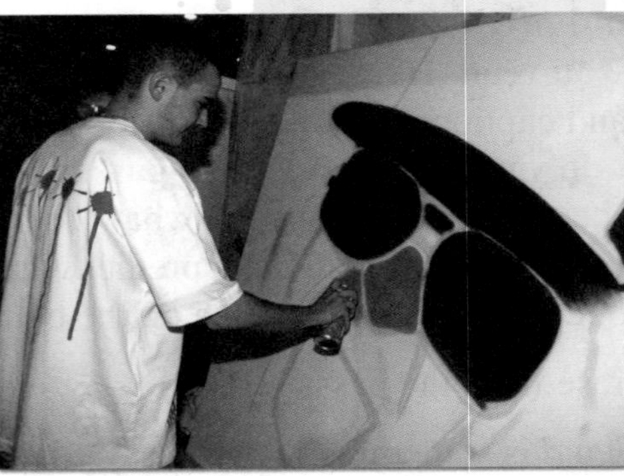

back, he shakes his head. "I am not proud of that phase of my life," he says. "My mom used to say my friends were a bad influence, but I think I was the bad influence. If I hadn't turned things around . . . , who knows what would have happened?"

Jeff had been a "tagger" who spray painted his personal signature on every available wall. One day, a woman caught him tagging the wall of her art gallery.

"Ilene told me I should be doing my stuff on canvas and framing it. She said I was an excellent artist and should be selling my work in her gallery," Jeff says. 1 "She dragged me inside and gave me old canvases and supplies to use. I was never good at studying, but I liked painting. I discovered there were other guys around who liked doing what I did. Just like that, I wasn't a vandal who destroyed people's property anymore. I had a different identity. I was an artist, spending time with other artists who had a mutual understanding and respect for one another's work."

Many people had regarded that part of Jeff's life as destructive. However, his new peers provided him with a different yardstick with which to measure himself.

There are times when all it takes for people to see themselves in a positive light is finding a group that has a similar perspective. That can make all the difference. End

1 Context Clues
Using context clues, what does the word *gallery* mean?

Who Am I? 9

"The Company You Keep"

Before Reading

Introduce Vocabulary

1. Have students turn to Part A on Student Book page 10 and scan the boldfaced vocabulary words. **These words appear in the passage "The Company You Keep." Think about what you already know about each word.** Have students read the instructions, then mark the boxes.
2. Using the words students already know, have them share where they encountered a word. **Use the word in another sentence. Make sure you use the same meaning of the word that you read in the definition.**
3. Read the instructions for Parts B and C. Have students complete the activities independently, then share their answers with a partner.

Refer to Blackline Master page 4 to extend practice with vocabulary.

Introduce and Apply: Visualize

1. **Close your eyes and listen. What do you picture as I read this sentence?** ***Jake's feet crunched on the ice as the wind howled around him.*** Have students identify words that spark an image, such as *crunched*, *ice*, *wind*, and *howled*. **What sense does each word connect to?** (hearing; sight; touch; hearing)
2. **When you picture what you read or hear, you visualize. It is like making a movie in your mind. Start by paying attention to words that appeal to the five senses—sight, taste, touch, smell, and hearing.** Write the following on the board: *The thin boy coughed as he crawled through the smoky tunnel.*

   Have students identify the senses they connect with *thin*, *coughed*, *crawled*, and *smoky*. (Possible responses: sight; hearing; touch; smell) **What do you imagine the tunnel looks like?** Encourage students to describe their own ideas of the tunnel. **Your ideas are different because you added your own experience and knowledge to create the tunnel image. You can add what you know to what you read.**
3. Have students turn to Student Book page 11. Read the instructions for Parts A and B aloud, and have them complete the activity. Have students share their responses.

Expedition 1, Lesson 4

Name ______________________ Date ______________

Vocabulary

"The Company You Keep"

A. Write one or more numbers next to each boldfaced word to show when you have seen, heard, or used this word.

5 I use it in everyday conversation.
4 I heard it on TV or on the radio.
3 I heard or used it in school.
2 I read it in a book, magazine, or online.
1 I have not read, heard, or used this word.

☐ **phase** (n) *a stage in growth or development*
High school seniors expect to have more freedom in the next *phase* of their lives.

☐ **identity** (n) *who you are*
I am much like my friends because they have helped shape my *identity*.

☐ **mutual** (adj) *shared or joint*
We met through a *mutual* friend with whom we both spent time.

B. Read each sentence, then answer the questions.

1. Could a woman describe her **identity** by saying she is someone who loves the outdoors or someone who knows where a rain forest is? who loves the outdoors
2. Is childhood an early or late **phase** of life? early
3. Nicole and Emily had a **mutual** opinion about pepperoni pizza. Did they agree or disagree? agree

C. Write a sentence using each vocabulary word. Answers will vary.

phase ______________________

identity ______________________

mutual ______________________

©Voyager Expanded Learning, Inc. 10

Vocabulary

phase (n) *a stage in growth or development*
High school seniors expect to have more freedom in the next *phase* of their lives.

identity (n) *who you are*
I am much like my friends because they have helped shape my *identity*.

mutual (adj) *shared or joint*
We met through a *mutual* friend with whom we both spent time.

4. Read the instructions for Part C aloud, and have students complete the activity independently. Have partners share their drawings.

Introduce the Passage

1. Have students preview "The Company You Keep." **What is in the photos?** (groups of people; sports teams; taggers) **What do you predict from the title and the photos?** Write predictions on the board.
2. **As you read this passage, pause and ask questions. Create a question based on the title.**
3. Teach these terms from the passage:
   - *Speak different languages* means to talk about things differently.
   - *A free ride* is when your college is paid for through scholarships.

During Reading

1. Have students record what they visualize as they read. Begin reading aloud "The Company You Keep." Pause at the end of the second sentence. **I can visualize the scene. I see three girls walking, talking, and laughing. I can hear giggling and chatter. I can smell the food court.** Read the first two paragraphs.
2. Point out the word *scholarship*. **What do you think the word *scholarship* means?** (money for school) Explain that schools reserve money for some students to attend college. **What clues helped you determine the meaning?** (college; free ride)

   Repeat this process for the following words.
   - **bonds** (n) *connections*, Anthology page 8
   - **gallery** (n) *a place to sell art*, Anthology page 9
   - **vandal** (n) *one who destroys property*, Anthology page 9
3. Have students finish reading the passage while making notes about words or phrases that appeal to the senses. For each note, have them write the sense that the words appeal to. To select reading options that support your students' levels and classroom needs, see Reading Differentiation, page xxxii, if needed.

After Reading

Check Comprehension

1. Have students recall the predictions they made before reading. **Think about what you know after reading the passage. How would you change your prediction?**

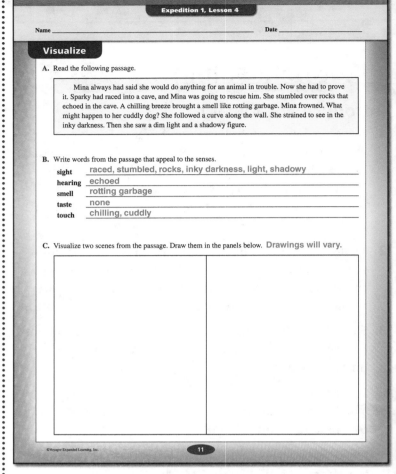

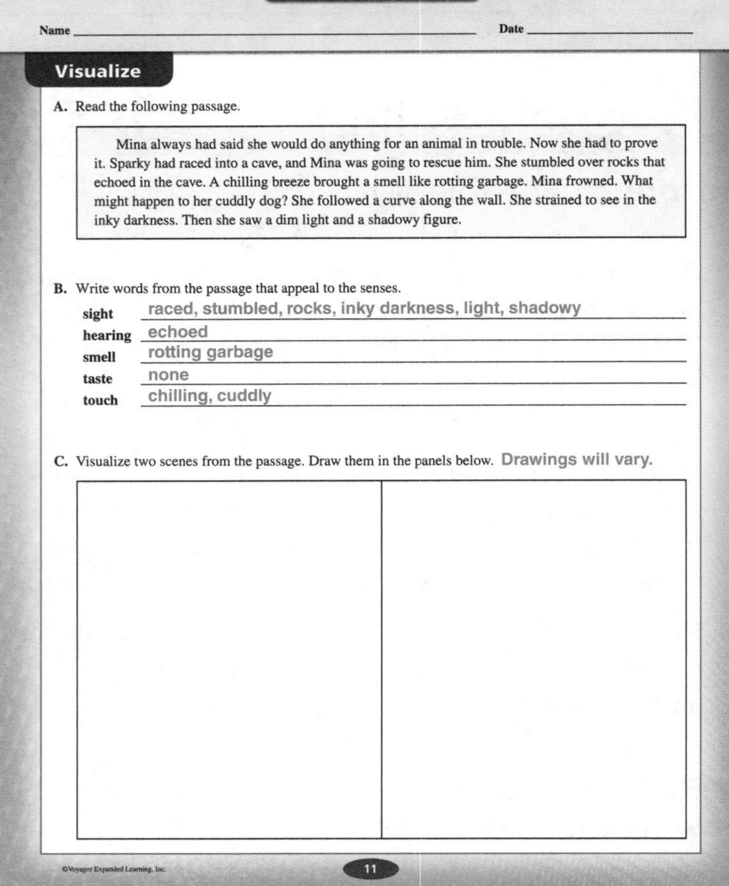

Expedition 1, Lesson 4

Name ______________________ Date ____________

Visualize

A. Read the following passage.

Mina always had said she would do anything for an animal in trouble. Now she had to prove it. Sparky had raced into a cave, and Mina was going to rescue him. She stumbled over rocks that echoed in the cave. A chilling breeze brought a smell like rotting garbage. Mina frowned. What might happen to her cuddly dog? She followed a curve along the wall. She strained to see in the inky darkness. Then she saw a dim light and a shadowy figure.

B. Write words from the passage that appeal to the senses.

sight	raced, stumbled, rocks, inky darkness, light, shadowy
hearing	echoed
smell	rotting garbage
taste	none
touch	chilling, cuddly

C. Visualize two scenes from the passage. Draw them in the panels below. Drawings will vary.

©Voyager Expanded Learning, Inc.

11

2. Have students skim the paragraphs to recall details about Jeff Castillo. **Visualize, then describe what Jeff was like before and after meeting Ilene. Which words helped you visualize the two phases of Jeff's life?** (spray painted; personal signature; on canvas and framing it; old canvases; destructive)
3. **What is one question that you asked yourself while you read?** (Answers will vary.) **Why did you pause to ask that question?** (Answers will vary.)

ACADEMIC SKILL Remind students to visualize while reading textbooks or listening to lectures. This will help them remember the information.

EXPEDITION ORGANIZER **Who Am I?**

Pause to have students turn to Student Book pages 2 and 3. Have students complete the following:

- Write answers to one or more of the probing questions in Part A.
- Write how birth order and peers connect to their lives in Part B.

Review, Extend, Assess

In today's lesson, as in Lessons 5 and 10 of every Expedition, there are options from which to choose. You may do any or all of the options listed. Activities for each option are given on the following pages. Each option will support or extend previously taught objectives. Choose the option(s) appropriate for your students and prepare accordingly.

Review Vocabulary

Extend Vocabulary

Assess Comprehension and Vocabulary

Reteach

Passport Reading Journeys Library

Online Technology Component

Writing Process

Review Vocabulary

Direct students to review the vocabulary for the first four passages on Student Book page 3.

1. Have students read the words and definitions.
2. Have students turn to Student Book page 12. **You have read these vocabulary words in the reading passages. Now you will read these vocabulary words in different contexts. In this activity, you will use these same words and meanings, but the topics will be different.** Read the instructions aloud, and have students complete the activity. As students finish, have them go back and check the definitions to ensure they used the words correctly. Have students share their answers for Parts A and B.
3. In Part A, if students have difficulty identifying antonyms, have them skim the words in the box. You can have students read the sentence twice. For the first time, have them read for the general sentence meaning. For the second time, have students use the phrase *the opposite of* before the underlined word. For Part B, complete three items with students who have difficulty, then have them complete the remaining items independently.

Expedition 1, Lesson 5

Name ______ Date ______

Review Vocabulary

A. Write a boldfaced word from the box that is an antonym, or opposite, for each underlined word.

mutual	**ethnic**	**physical**	**attributes**	**except**	**patterns**
exact	**authority**	**probable**	**profiles**	**identity**	**phase**

1. Aaron used approximate measurements to choose the right frame for his poster. exact
2. My friends and I have separate interests and hobbies. mutual
3. After all his weight lifting, it's unlikely that Will has gotten stronger. probable
4. I downloaded all the songs from the album, plus "Play It Like That." except

B. Write the vocabulary word from Part A defined in context in each sentence.

1. The twins share many similar attributes, like hair color, eye color, and height.
2. The man followed the same patterns every day. His repeated actions included eating breakfast and walking the dog.
3. High school students plan what they will do in the next phase, or stage, of their lives.
4. The referee has been given the authority, or power, to stop the game if there is lightning.
5. Who I am, or my identity, has been influenced by my family and friends.
6. Jet and I are members of the same ethnic group. We speak the same language and are from the same country.
7. We read the presidential profiles, which gave us brief accounts of the presidents' lives.
8. Her physical appearance was very intimidating.

 12

CHECKPOINT Provide additional support for students who had difficulty with context clues in Part B by confirming that students understand the types of context clues: an example, a synonym (a word that means the same), an antonym (a word that means the opposite), or a restatement or appositive (a brief explanation). **In the first sentence, the context clue begins with *like*. What type of context clue includes this word?** (example)

Extend Vocabulary

1. Direct students to Student Book page 13. **A prefix is a word part that is added to the beginning of a word and changes the word's meaning.** Write *un* + *clear* = *unclear* on the board. **The word *clear* is an adjective that means "easily seen through."** Have students provide examples of things that are clear. (water; glass; plastic; air) **The prefix *un-* means "not." *Unclear* describes something that cannot be seen through. What are some examples of things that are *unclear*?** (mud; frosted glass; murky water; smoke; paint) **The prefixes *im-* and *in-* have the same meaning as *un-*. You will work with all three prefixes.**
2. Read the instructions for Parts A and B aloud. Have students complete the activities. Review the answers as a class.

Part A

Explore and practice using the new words. Model using each word in a sentence, and encourage students to provide their own sentence. **When I cook, I make *inexact* measurements, like a pinch. What else is *inexact*?**

Continue the process using the following prompts.

I would never give a baby a video game. It would be *inappropriate*. What is *inappropriate*?

It is *improbable* that it will snow today because the sun is shining. What is it *improbable* that you will do today?

Part B

If students have difficulty writing the paragraph, allow them to write three sentences using the definitions in place of the words. When they finish, have them replace the definitions with the correct words.

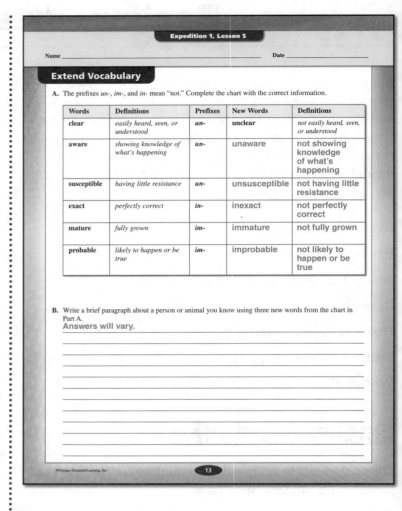

Expedition 1, Lesson 5

Name ______________________ Date ______________

Extend Vocabulary

A. The prefixes *un-*, *im-*, and *in-* mean "not." Complete the chart with the correct information.

Words	Definitions	Prefixes	New Words	Definitions
clear	*easily heard, seen, or understood*	*un-*	unclear	*not easily heard, seen, or understood*
aware	*showing knowledge of what's happening*	*un-*	unaware	not showing knowledge of what's happening
susceptible	*having little resistance*	*un-*	unsusceptible	not having little resistance
exact	*perfectly correct*	*in-*	inexact	not perfectly correct
mature	*fully grown*	*im-*	immature	not fully grown
probable	*likely to happen or be true*	*im-*	improbable	not likely to happen or be true

B. Write a brief paragraph about a person or animal you know using three new words from the chart in Part A.

Answers will vary.

13

Assess Comprehension and Vocabulary

1. **You will use all the active reading strategies you learned as you read the passages. What do you do every time you read?** (preview and predict; use context clues; ask questions; visualize)

2. Direct students to Student Book pages 14–16. Preview the pages, showing students that they will read two passages and answer questions about both. Have students complete the pages independently.

   Review student answers. Whenever possible, provide elaborative feedback to student responses. Refer to page xl for examples of elaborative feedback and how to incorporate it in your lessons.

   If students incorrectly answer more than 4 out of 15 assessment questions, evaluate what kind of reteaching is needed. If students miss vocabulary questions, have them return to the vocabulary activities and work with the words they missed. For active reading strategies errors, use the reteaching suggestions on page 22.

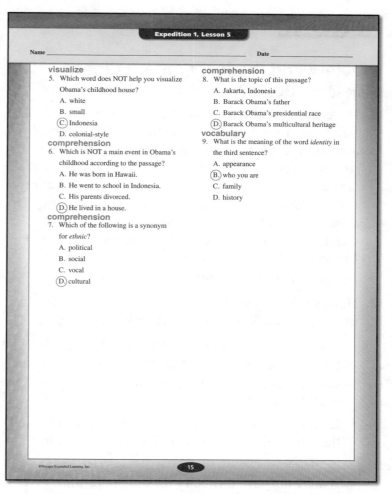

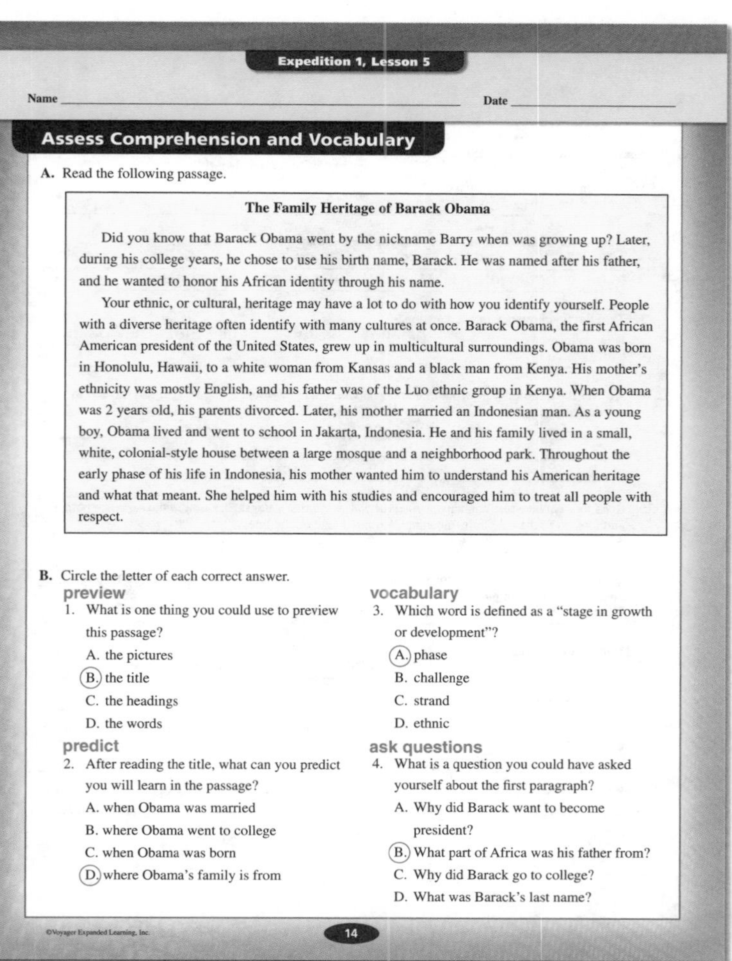

Expedition 1, Lesson 5

Name ______________________ Date ______________

Assess Comprehension and Vocabulary

A. Read the following passage.

The Family Heritage of Barack Obama

Did you know that Barack Obama went by the nickname Barry when was growing up? Later, during his college years, he chose to use his birth name, Barack. He was named after his father, and he wanted to honor his African identity through his name.

Your ethnic, or cultural, heritage may have a lot to do with how you identify yourself. People with a diverse heritage often identify with many cultures at once. Barack Obama, the first African American president of the United States, grew up in multicultural surroundings. Obama was born in Honolulu, Hawaii, to a white woman from Kansas and a black man from Kenya. His mother's ethnicity was mostly English, and his father was of the Luo ethnic group in Kenya. When Obama was 2 years old, his parents divorced. Later, his mother married an Indonesian man. As a young boy, Obama lived and went to school in Jakarta, Indonesia. He and his family lived in a small, white, colonial-style house between a large mosque and a neighborhood park. Throughout the early phase of his life in Indonesia, his mother wanted him to understand his American heritage and what that meant. She helped him with his studies and encouraged him to treat all people with respect.

B. Circle the letter of each correct answer.

preview

1. What is one thing you could use to preview this passage?
   A. the pictures
   (B.) the title
   C. the headings
   D. the words

predict

2. After reading the title, what can you predict you will learn in the passage?
   A. when Obama was married
   B. where Obama went to college
   C. when Obama was born
   (D.) where Obama's family is from

vocabulary

3. Which word is defined as a "stage in growth or development"?
   (A.) phase
   B. challenge
   C. strand
   D. ethnic

ask questions

4. What is a question you could have asked yourself about the first paragraph?
   A. Why did Barack want to become president?
   (B.) What part of Africa was his father from?
   C. Why did Barack go to college?
   D. What was Barack's last name?

 14

Expedition 1, Lesson 5

Name ______________________ Date ______________

visualize

5. Which word does NOT help you visualize Obama's childhood house?
   A. white
   B. small
   (C.) Indonesia
   D. colonial-style

comprehension

6. Which is NOT a main event in Obama's childhood according to the passage?
   A. He was born in Hawaii.
   B. He went to school in Indonesia.
   C. His parents divorced.
   (D.) He lived in a house.

comprehension

7. Which of the following is a synonym for *ethnic*?
   A. political
   B. social
   C. vocal
   (D.) cultural

comprehension

8. What is the topic of this passage?
   A. Jakarta, Indonesia
   B. Barack Obama's father
   C. Barack Obama's presidential race
   (D.) Barack Obama's multicultural heritage

vocabulary

9. What is the meaning of the word *identity* in the third sentence?
   A. appearance
   (B.) who you are
   C. family
   D. history

 15

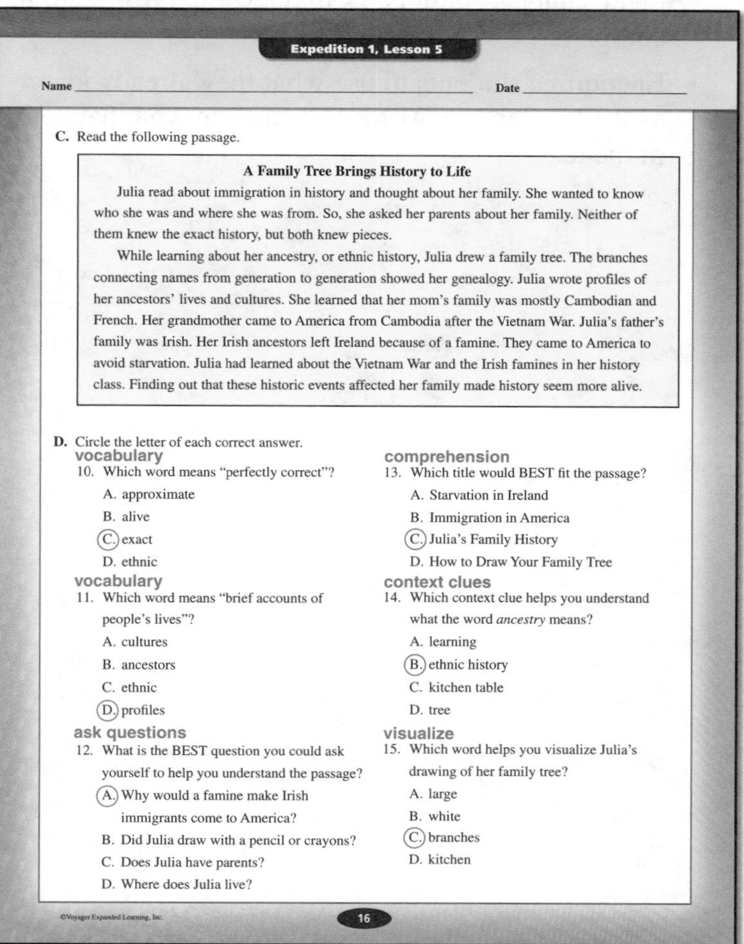

Expedition 1, Lesson 5

Name ______________________ Date ______________

C. Read the following passage.

A Family Tree Brings History to Life

Julia read about immigration in history and thought about her family. She wanted to know who she was and where she was from. So, she asked her parents about her family. Neither of them knew the exact history, but both knew pieces.

While learning about her ancestry, or ethnic history, Julia drew a family tree. The branches connecting names from generation to generation showed her genealogy. Julia wrote profiles of her ancestors' lives and cultures. She learned that her mom's family was mostly Cambodian and French. Her grandmother came to America from Cambodia after the Vietnam War. Julia's father's family was Irish. Her Irish ancestors left Ireland because of a famine. They came to America to avoid starvation. Julia had learned about the Vietnam War and the Irish famines in her history class. Finding out that these historic events affected her family made history seem more alive.

D. Circle the letter of each correct answer.

vocabulary

10. Which word means "perfectly correct"?
    A. approximate
    B. alive
    (C.) exact
    D. ethnic

vocabulary

11. Which word means "brief accounts of people's lives"?
    A. cultures
    B. ancestors
    C. ethnic
    (D.) profiles

ask questions

12. What is the BEST question you could ask yourself to help you understand the passage?
    (A.) Why would a famine make Irish immigrants come to America?
    B. Did Julia draw with a pencil or crayons?
    C. Does Julia have parents?
    D. Where does Julia live?

comprehension

13. Which title would BEST fit the passage?
    A. Starvation in Ireland
    B. Immigration in America
    (C.) Julia's Family History
    D. How to Draw Your Family Tree

context clues

14. Which context clue helps you understand what the word *ancestry* means?
    A. learning
    (B.) ethnic history
    C. kitchen table
    D. tree

visualize

15. Which word helps you visualize Julia's drawing of her family tree?
    A. large
    B. white
    (C.) branches
    D. kitchen

 16

Reteach

Preview and Predict, Context Clues, Ask Questions, Visualize

1. Have students turn to Student Book pages 17 and 18. Read the instructions aloud. Guide students through a preview of the title and subheadings. **When you preview, you don't read details. You look at what stands out on the page. What things usually stand out?** (title; photos; diagrams) **They let you know what to expect when you read.** Discuss possible questions for the first item. **You will ask questions before, during, and after reading.** Have students complete Part A independently.
2. Have students complete Part B. If they have difficulty using the strategies, provide the following support.
   - If student responses include details about the text from previewing, remind them that their prediction can be a guess about the general content to know what to expect.
   - If they don't know where a context clue will be, tell them to look in the same, previous, or following sentence.
   - If students have difficulty forming questions, give them sentence starters, as in question 3, for them to complete.
   - Encourage students to use what they already know as well as sensory words to visualize what happens in the text.

Expedition 1, Lesson 5

Name ______ Date ______

Reteach

A. Read the questions and use them as a guide to reading the passage. Answer the questions.

Clothing that Expresses Identity

Teenagers show their own personalities and identities with their clothing styles. It's a form of self-expression that teens have used for decades. After all, the teen years are an important phase for developing friendships and a sense of identity. Do you know people who are one of a kind? Do people constantly invent new styles? That's why clothing styles can be unique and numerous.

Music Styles and Clothing Styles

Clothing styles can come from different types of music, like goth, punk, or emo. Dark clothing, makeup, and studded denim or leather might be attributes of goth and punk styles. Emo fashion has grown in popularity. Hoodies, tight jeans, and T-shirts with skate shoes characterize this style.

Talents and What You Wear

Sometimes talents or hobbies lead to clothing styles. Athletes might choose jerseys, track pants, or soccer jackets. Artists might create their own designs.

Be Yourself

You'll see new trends at the mall, but feel free to be yourself. Whether you like bright or dark colors, big or small patterns, leather or lace, be confident and let your personality shine through.

Preview and Predict: Read the title and the subheadings. What do you expect to read about in this passage?
how clothes express who you are

Stop after reading the first paragraph. Go back and ask a question about something you're not sure of.
Answers will vary.

What part of the text helped you visualize? Describe your mental picture.
Answers will vary.

 17

Expedition 1, Lesson 5

Name ______ Date ______

B. Answer the questions about the passage.
Answers will vary, but could include the following.

1. How did you preview the passage?
   I read the title and subheadings.
2. How do the title and subheadings help you predict what the passage is about?
   They are clues that the topic is about how a person's clothes can relate to his or her identity, like favorite music, talents, or hobbies.
3. Turn the first sentence into a question.
   How do teens show their own personalities and identities with their clothing styles?
4. Answer the question you wrote in number 3. Use what you wrote in the margin and the text to answer your question. Answers will vary.
5. Read the sentence that contains *self-expression* in the first paragraph. Look in the sentence before and after to find a clue to its meaning. Write the clue on the line.
   show their own personalities and identities
6. Write the context clue that helps you understand the word *unique*. How does the clue help you understand the meaning of *unique*?
   The phrase *one of a kind* explains the word *unique*.
7. What words helped you visualize images while reading?
   dark; studded; tight; hoodies; T-shirts; jeans; skate shoes; track pants
8. Choose one part of the passage that you agree or disagree with. Explain the part and why you agree or disagree with it. Answers will vary.
   I ______ with the part about ______
   because ______ and ______.

 18

Passport Reading Journeys Library

Teacher's Note
The Library and online technology component of *Passport Reading Journeys* will be a part of every Lessons 5 and 10. In the remaining Expeditions, they also will be a part of the daily lessons. Please familiarize yourself with the books in the Library and the online technology component.

1. Have students choose reading material from the *Passport Reading Journeys* Library or another approved selection. If students have not finished a previously chosen selection, they may continue reading from that selection. See the *Passport Reading Journeys* Library Teacher's Guide for material on selection guidelines.
2. You also may use this time to allow students to participate in book clubs or book presentations. Use the criteria specified in the *Passport Reading Journeys* Library Teacher's Guide.

Vocabulary Connections

Vocabulary words are listed in the Teacher's Guide for each book. These words are content-related or used frequently in reading material. The selected words can be a basis for independent or small-group discussions and activities.

Student Opportunities

Six copies of each book title are provided in the *Passport Reading Journeys* Library. The number of copies makes it possible for small groups of students to read the same material and share the information they read.

Theme-related titles include *The Face on the Milk Carton*, *Leaving Home*, and *The Pinballs*.

Technology

1. Depending on your classroom configuration and computer access, you may have all students work through the technology in a lab setting or have individuals or small groups of students work on desktops or laptops while other students participate in other suggested activities, such as the *Passport Reading Journeys* Library.
2. The online technology component provides additional support for students to work with selected vocabulary words. Students will work through a series of activities to strengthen their word knowledge, then apply that knowledge to passage reading. Refer to the online technology component User Guide for more information.

   The theme-related word sets are Biology, Sociology, Psychology, and English/Language Arts.

Writing Process

A Memoir

Distribute Writing Blackline Master page 1. **You will write a memoir.** Explain that a memoir is a story about a memory or experience from the writer's own life. **Your memoir will be a descriptive narrative.** Explain that their memoirs will connect to the Expedition theme "Who Am I?" by retelling a personal experience. **A memoir is autobiographical. The prefix *auto-* means "self." An *autobiography* is a story about oneself.** Ask students if they have seen or read examples of memoirs. **How long or brief was the author's account? Did the memoir span a short or long period in the author's life?** To ensure students understand the characteristics of a memoir, you may have them research memoirs online.

Have students look at the assignment and follow along as you explain. Assign point values and ask students to write them in the rubric. Tell them to make any notes on the page that will help them, but they will turn in the page with the assignment.

Prewrite

A narrative tells a story. Descriptive writing includes adjectives, or descriptive words, that help the reader visualize the story. The word *memoir* comes from the word *memory*. A *memoir* is an autobiographical, true account of a specific experience of one's life as remembered and told by the writer.

Have students think about a personal memory. **You'll tell about the memory from your point of view in your own way. You can brainstorm situations and descriptions with a story web.** Model a story web as a class, using the events of a memorable school activity as the center of the web. Have students expand the web with descriptive words about the event, the setting, and a character. Then, have students select an event and create their own webs.

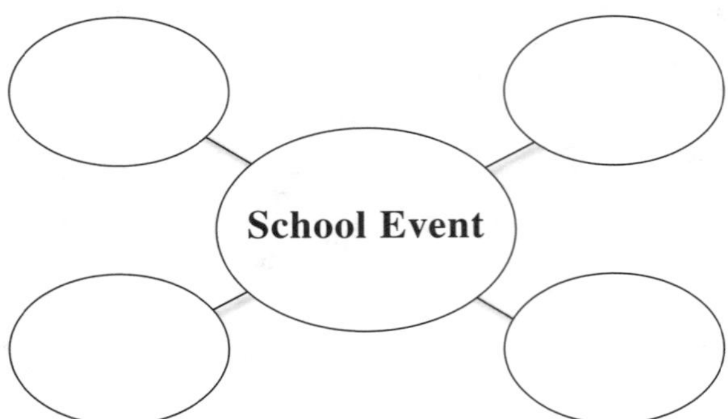

Draft

You will use these standards, or criteria, as you write your memoirs. Write the following criteria on the board:

- *A specific personal memory*
- *A specific setting*
- *A character with traits, actions, feelings, and dialogue*
- *A clear beginning, middle, and end*

Have students independently draft their memoirs. Remind them that they will be able to revise their work.

Revise

Have students reread the drafts, using the following revision steps and questions. After each step, have students make the revisions and write their final draft.

- **Check the organization.** What paragraphs or sentences should you move so that the story flows in the right order?
- **Check your description.** Did you use vivid sensory details and adjectives? Did you use dialogue that sounds like the characters? Where do you need to add more details or description?
- **Check mechanics.** Do fragments or run-on sentences need to be rewritten? What words might be misspelled? Do all sentences begin with capital letters and end with proper punctuation?

Present

Have students present their memoirs. Class members can give feedback to one another. They should tell one another what details and descriptions helped them visualize the story.

Assess

I will assess your writing and presentation based on the rubric on your page. To assess student memoirs, use the rubric on the Writing Blackline Master.

Real-World Reading

1. **Starting with Expedition 2, you will read Real-World Reading passages.** Direct students to the jury summons on Student Book page 118. **How is this like the reading you do in school? How is it different?**
2. **You read for specific purposes outside of school.** Encourage students to suggest other types of real-world reading they see outside of school, such as advertisements and job applications, and to tell the purpose of each type. **Which active reading strategies would you use when you read these?** Encourage students to tell how the strategies they learned would help them read these types of writing. Have students make a poster that illustrates the multiple types of texts they read and write.

Exploring Careers

Career Passages

1. Tell students that starting with Expedition 2, they will read Career passages. **In this Expedition, you have thought about your identity and interests. Career passages will help you think about different careers you might consider.** Have students preview the Career passages on the Anthology Table of Contents, page iii. Have them flip ahead to "Comic Book Writer" on page 103. If students know someone who writes for a living, have them share information about that person and his or her job with the class.
2. **Think about careers you are interested in and would like to read about.** Encourage students to check out books from the library or do Internet searches to learn about careers that interest them. **Which career passage listed in the table of contents interests you? Explain.** Encourage students to tell how the strategies they learned will help them read these types of writings.

English Language Learner Overview

The (ELL) signals when extra support is provided for students during the lesson. As needed, Blackline Masters for English language learners may provide support. For vocabulary, students also may use the online technology component to practice Expedition words or other content-area vocabulary and designated ELL word sets.

Introduce Vocabulary

Lesson 6

Tell students that the word *explore* has a second meaning. Write *travel over new territory for adventure or discovery* on the board. Have students discuss the following questions. **What can you *explore* outdoors? What can you *explore* in a science class? What kind of building would you like to *explore*? What topic would you like to *explore*?** Have students answer using *explore*.

How is *exploring* an idea like *exploring* a place? (You may not know what you will discover.) **How are the two kinds of *exploring* different?** (The first means thinking and talking about a new idea. The second means physically traveling to a new place.)

Lesson 8

The word *diverged* means "split apart." Demonstrate that there can be literal and figurative meanings of the word. **If I say that the small stream *diverged* from the big river, I mean that the stream split apart from the river and moved in a different direction.** Draw a river on the board, then draw a small stream flowing out of the river in another direction. **The river went this way. The stream *diverged* and went another way.**

Tell students *diverged* also can be used to talk about ideas, plans, feelings, and other things that cannot be seen. **If I say that my ideas *diverged* from my parents' ideas, I mean that my ideas were different from my parents'. My ideas went in another direction. If I say that my feelings *diverged* from my friend's feelings, what do I mean about my friend's feelings?** (My friend's feelings were different from mine.)

Practice Context Clues

Provide support for the context words *infancy*, *mannerisms*, *parallel*, and *outgoing*. Remind students that synonyms, restatements, and antonyms can help them figure out the meanings of new words. Write the following sentences on the board and have students identify the context clue in each.

I do not remember my infancy. *Few people remember being babies.* (Context clue: being babies)

He has strange mannerisms. *I've never seen that style of doing things.* (Context clue: style of doing things)

There are parallels *in the way the twins behave. They're a lot alike.* (Context clue: alike)

Charlene is usually outgoing, *but today she is shy.* (Context clue: shy)

Introduce and Apply the Strategy: Make Connections

Some students may need scaffolding to help them make their own connections to the Anthology text. Blackline Master page 5 begins by guiding students to make text-to-world, text-to-text, and text-to-self connections by having them answer specific questions related to different sections of the text. Then, students should be able to make their own connections to another section. Encourage students to use all three types of connections and to reflect on how making connections helps them understand what they read.

Vocabulary

explore (v) *discuss or think about carefully*

appropriate (adj) *suitable or right*

Sally is a scientist. Her mother was a scientist, and her mother's father was a scientist. Was Sally born to be a scientist? Or, did she **explore** other careers and choose this profession on her own? Are we genetically programmed to do certain things well?

Michael Phelps was born to be a swimmer. He is tall with long limbs and large hands and feet. The world record-holding swimmer is an example of having the **appropriate** genes to pursue his dreams. His physical attributes led him toward swimming. His drive and work ethic made him an Olympic gold medal winner. However, not everyone is so lucky.

Many people want to do things they are not genetically programmed to do. Can a 7-foot-tall man become a gymnast? Can a deaf man become a pianist? Can a shy woman become a stand-up comedian? Can a quadriplegic man become a painter? Can a woman of modest means overcome that limitation and become a millionaire? Can a small, nonthreatening man become a menacing defensive lineman for the NFL?

Thirteen-year-old Daniel Torres holding a football while posing in front of fellow uniformed football teammates at Thomas A. Edison Middle School

Vocabulary

eliminated (v) *left out or got rid of*

What if you are born without the appropriate attributes to achieve your goals? What if your body isn't designed to be a swimmer? Many aspects of your heritage are changeable—intelligence, personality, and even your physical makeup. You can make changes or alterations to the color of your hair or the color of your eyes. You may have **eliminated** your need for glasses with surgery or contacts. You can tan your skin, remove body hair, and straighten your teeth. There is much about you that isn't set in stone. But, some things, like your height, cannot be changed. They become either assets, faults, or exceptions.

Spud Webb, a former NBA player, is an example of overcoming not only his genes but also his circumstances. Webb grew up without many advantages. His family was poor, and opportunities for him were minimal. He loved basketball and practiced whenever he had a chance. His vibrant dream of playing in the NBA brightened his days. He thought basketball might be his way to eliminate poverty in his life and explore the world. But, poverty wasn't the only thing holding him back. There was one drastic problem—his height. Most NBA players of the time were more than 6 feet tall, but Webb was only 5 feet 5 inches tall. Webb knew this was a severe limitation, so he worked tirelessly on his skills. He became an offensive and defensive threat on the court. As a senior in high school, he averaged 26 points a game, opening the door to college basketball. By working on his skills and jumping ability, this 5 foot 5 inch player was drafted into the NBA. 1

1 Make Connections
Do you know someone who has worked hard to overcome a genetic trait and eventually accomplished his or her goal?

Michael Phelps used his physical attributes as an asset. Spud Webb made his physical attributes an exception. Neither saw them as a fault or used them as an excuse. They both worked hard and were determined to achieve their goals. Some might say that Phelps had an advantage over Webb. It could be said that Phelps won the genetic lottery, but Webb did not. But, they both had the drive and will to succeed and realize their dreams.

So, what do you think? What are the most important things in determining your future: genes or the will to make things happen for you? What about the people around you? How much do your surroundings influence your future? What is your role in your future? End

"Genes: Assets or Obstacles?"

Before Reading

Introduce Vocabulary

1. Have students turn to Part A on Student Book page 19. Read aloud the three vocabulary words, and have students rate their knowledge of the words in the chart. For words that students rate 3, have them use the words in sentences.
2. Read the part of speech, definition, and example sentence for each word.
3. For words students don't know, have them make sentences using the definitions. **When you use the definition of a word in the sentence, you can substitute the word for the definition and keep the same meaning.** Have students substitute vocabulary words in their sentences and share them with the class.
4. Have students read the instructions for Parts B and C and complete the activities. After they finish, have partners share their responses.

ELL Lesson 6 vocabulary will be extended in Lesson 8 on Blackline Master page 6.

Introduce and Apply: Make Connections

1. Tell students that people make connections with texts in three ways. **You often connect what you read with what you know from your own life or experiences. For example, you might read about someone who is a football coach. You might think of a coach you know. You make a connection to yourself.**
2. Tell students they can make connections between the text and what they know about the world. **In the next passage, you will read about two famous athletes. If this makes you think of other things you have heard or read about them, you make a connection to the world.** Explain that public information is an example of things students know about the world.
3. Tell students that they can make a connection between the text and another text. **When you read the next passage, you may think of something you read in an earlier passage or your science book. Making this text-to-text connection can help you gain a better understanding of identity and genetics.**

Expedition 1, Lesson 6

Name ____________________ Date ____________

Vocabulary

"Genes: Assets or Obstacles?"

A. Rate your knowledge of each boldfaced word.
3 I know what this word means, and I can use it in a sentence.
2 I have an idea of this word's meaning, but I need to know more.
1 I don't know what this word means.

☐ **explore** (v) *discuss or think about carefully*
I need to *explore* my talents before I decide which activity to start.

☐ **appropriate** (adj) *suitable or right*
Swimmers must wear an *appropriate* suit for water.

☐ **eliminated** (v) *left out or got rid of*
They *eliminated* me from the basketball team because I couldn't dribble.

B. Complete each sentence with the correct vocabulary word from Part A.

1. Myra loves to bake desserts, so she wants to explore how to become a pastry chef.
2. Milk products made Keri sick, so she eliminated cheese from her diet.
3. Flowers are an appropriate gift for the hostess of a party.

C. For each underlined word, write an antonym, or a word that has the opposite meaning. Choose your answers from the words in the box.

ignore	improper	included

1. I wanted to explore the ways we could paint the walls to make the room look bigger. ignore
2. Kevin eliminated a lot of the books that used to crowd his bookshelves. included
3. It is appropriate to write thank-you notes to people who give you presents. improper

19

Vocabulary

explore	(v) *discuss or think about carefully*
	I need to *explore* my talents before I decide which activity to start.
appropriate	(adj) *suitable or right*
	Swimmers must wear an *appropriate* suit for water.
eliminated	(v) *left out or got rid of*
	They *eliminated* me from the basketball team because I couldn't dribble.

4. Have students turn to Student Book page 20. Read the instructions aloud, and have them complete the activities.

ACADEMIC SKILL Remind students that making connections will help them when they read other texts. **Making connections helps you better understand the deeper meanings of a text.**

Introduce the Passage

1. Have students preview the passage. **What do you think the title "Genes: Assets or Obstacles?" means?** (whether your genetic makeup helps or hinders you) **What clues about the passage are in the photos and captions?** (The image of the athletes indicates that the passage may talk about how genes affect athletes.) Have students make predictions and check them as they read.
2. **Before reading, you can ask questions about the text. What questions can you make from the title?** (When could genes be an asset? When could genes be an obstacle?) **Ask questions after reading a confusing part.**
3. Teach this phrase from the passage:

   Won the genetic lottery means to have the physical or mental traits needed for a specific purpose.

During Reading

1. Have students prepare to note any connections to the text. Begin reading the passage aloud.
2. Pause after the first paragraph. **I can make a connection with this paragraph. My dad is a coach, so everyone thinks I should be good in sports.** Continue reading to the end of the second paragraph. **I have heard about Michael Phelps. I remember when he won the gold medals.**
3. **As you read, stop when you reach an unfamiliar word.** Point out the word *alterations* in the first paragraph on Anthology page 11. **This is an unfamiliar word. What context is around it?** (change) ***Alterations* must be changes.** Remind students to use context with unfamiliar words.

   Repeat this process for the following words.

   - **modest** (adj) *small*, Anthology page 10
   - **menacing** (adj) *big; scary*, Anthology page 10
   - **vibrant** (adj) *bright*, Anthology page 11
   - **drastic** (adj) *extreme*, Anthology page 11
4. **Read the rest of "Genes: Assets or Obstacles?"** To select reading options that support your students' levels and classroom needs, see Reading Differentiation, page xxxii, if needed.

Expedition 1, Lesson 6

Name ______________________ Date ____________

Make Connections

Read the passage. Complete the activities in the right margin.
Answers will vary.

"Seeing" Past a Genetic Flaw

Su Kim was born blind. She had difficulty learning to walk because she could not see others walk. She had difficulty learning to eat with a spoon because she could not see others eat. Su had difficulty doing many things, but one thing came naturally to her—playing the piano.

Su first played the piano when she was 4 years old. Her mother had sung a lullaby to her since she was born. One night, she sat at the family piano and played along with her mother. She couldn't see the keys or read any music, but she didn't need to. Su could play the song because she had heard it before.

Over the next several years of her life, Su played for audiences around the world. She would listen to a song and play it. Often, the audience tried to stump her with an original song that she had never heard before. But, Su never failed. She was amazing.

Su was born with a genetic flaw. Because of this flaw, she used other assets to her benefit. She wasn't able to see, so she focused on her ability to hear. After awhile, she was able to hear things so clearly that it was committed to her memory. She took her flaw and made it an asset.

1. Mark 1 by a part of the text you connect with your own experience or what you already know. Tell what the connection is.
2. Mark 2 by a part of the text you connect with what you know about the world. Tell what the connection is.
3. Mark 3 by a part of the text you connect with something you read in an earlier passage. Tell what the connection is.

©Voyager Expanded Learning, Inc. 20

After Reading

Check Comprehension

1. When students finish reading, ask these questions:
   - **What do Michael Phelps and Spud Webb have in common?** (Both men have been successful in their sport.)
   - **What genetic assets does Michael Phelps have?** (He has long limbs and large hands and feet.)
   - **How did Spud Webb overcome the obstacles in his way?** (He worked hard to achieve his goals.)
2. Have students look back at the predictions they made before reading. **How would you change your prediction now that you have read the passage?**
3. Have students refer to the connections they made to the text. Have volunteers share a connection and what type it was. **How have you overcome obstacles you have faced? How did the connections you made help you?**

Refer to Blackline Master page 5 for extra practice making connections.

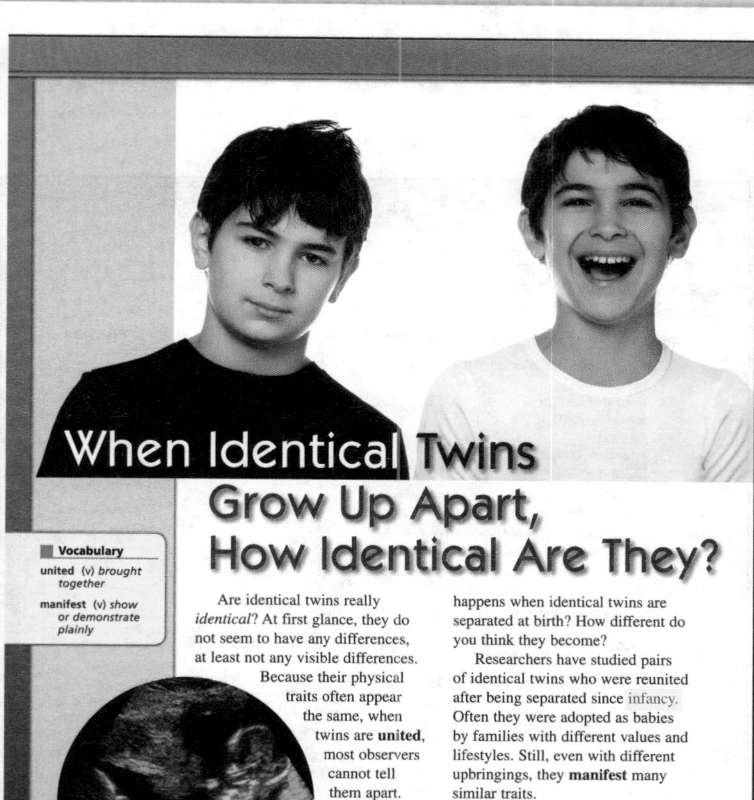

When Identical Twins Grow Up Apart, How Identical Are They?

Vocabulary

united (v) *brought together*

manifest (v) *show or demonstrate plainly*

Are identical twins really *identical*? At first glance, they do not seem to have any differences, at least not any visible differences. Because their physical traits often appear the same, when twins are **united**, most observers cannot tell them apart. But, what happens when identical twins are separated at birth? How different do you think they become?

Ultrasound scan of twins at 4 months

Researchers have studied pairs of identical twins who were reunited after being separated since infancy. Often they were adopted as babies by families with different values and lifestyles. Still, even with different upbringings, they **manifest** many similar traits.

For example, a set of identical British twins had no connection for 40 years before being reunited. Both women had dyed their hair auburn, preferred cold coffee, and would push up their noses with their palms, a practice they each called "squidging." For their meeting, they chose to wear the same color of clothes. Each had two sons and a daughter. There was only a one-point difference in their IQs, and they both had the same health problems. The manifestation of these similarities was probably not a coincidence. They were most likely products of shared genes.

Vocabulary

interacted (v) *acted between each other*

Other sets of identical twins follow the same pattern. When they first met as adults, a pair of male twins found they used the same type of shaving lotion, toothpaste, and hair product. They went back home after their time together and sent each other birthday presents. Each sent the other the exact same gift.

After long separations, many reunited pairs of twins demonstrate similar attitudes and mannerisms, or ways of doing things. Though they have not **interacted** as young children, they feel close ties. Two brothers had opened fitness clubs and cared a great deal about good physical health. A set of sisters had edited their high school newspapers and gone to film school. This kind of similarity, or parallel, happens in case after case.

However, there are always distinctions. One twin may be outgoing and social, while the other is quiet and shy. They may not share all the same likes and dislikes. This, of course, might be because of nurture, or how one is raised, rather than nature. Even after years apart, it seems likely, though, that identical twins will have many striking similarities to each other.

On the other hand, even when identical twins grow up interacting with each other, there are differences. Their personalities can be quite distinct. And, in case you were wondering, no, they do *not* have the same fingerprints. 1 In other words, no two people are ever exactly alike. End

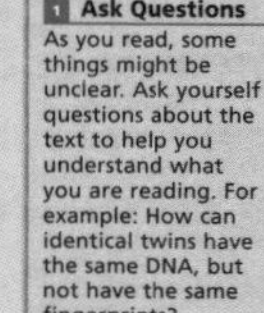

1 Ask Questions

As you read, some things might be unclear. Ask yourself questions about the text to help you understand what you are reading. For example: How can identical twins have the same DNA, but not have the same fingerprints?

"When Identical Twins Grow Up Apart, How Identical Are They?"

Before Reading

Introduce Vocabulary

1. Have students turn to Part A on Student Book page 21 and read aloud the three vocabulary words. **You will see these words in the passage.** Have students rate their knowledge of the words in the chart.
2. Read the part of speech, definition, and example sentence for each word.
3. Have students note the words they marked with a 2. **Use word parts to help you remember a word's meaning. For example, for the word *interacted*, *inter-* means "between." Combine that with the rest of the word, and you have most of the meaning—*acted between*.**
4. Have students read the instructions for Parts B and C and complete the activities independently. After they finish, have partners share their responses.

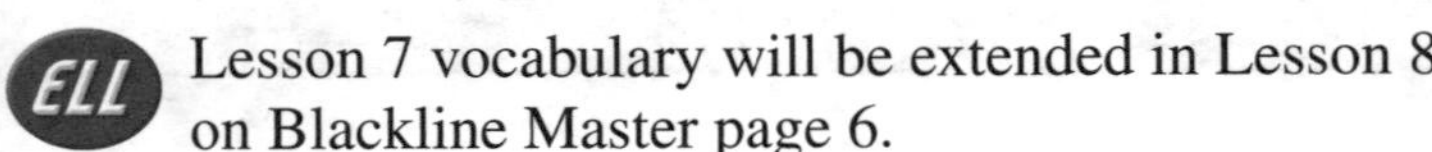

ELL Lesson 7 vocabulary will be extended in Lesson 8 on Blackline Master page 6.

Apply the Strategy: Make Connections

1. **Remember that as you read, it helps to make text connections.**
2. **What kind of connections can you make?** (text-to-self; text-to-world; text-to-text)
3. **I will read aloud a topic, and you give me a connection.**
   - **Lunch**
   - **Music**
   - **School**
   - **Wealth**
   - **Difficulty**
   - **Pride**

Introduce the Passage

1. Have students turn to Anthology page 12 and preview the photos that appear with the passage. **What do you see in the photos?** (twins; an ultrasound of twins) **Now read the title. What do you think the passage is about?** (The passage compares identical twins who grow up apart from each other.) Have students write their predictions on a sheet of paper.

Expedition 1, Lesson 7

Name ________________ Date ________

Vocabulary

"When Identical Twins Grow Up Apart, How Identical Are They?"

A. Rate your knowledge of each boldfaced word.
3 familiar
2 somewhat familiar
1 unknown word

☐ **united** (v) *brought together*
I was *united* with my sister for the first time at age 10.

☐ **manifest** (v) *show or demonstrate plainly*
Twins often *manifest* the same habits and tastes.

☐ **interacted** (v) *acted between each other*
The twins *interacted* so well with other people.

B. Complete each sentence with the correct vocabulary word from Part A.

1. Zelda will ___manifest___ her problem-solving ability when she shows her new invention.
2. Bella and her father ___united___ the two dogs from different shelters.
3. When Karen and her sister ___interacted___ with adults, they were polite and friendly.

C. Some word endings, or inflections, can change the meaning of a word. The ending *-ed* changes a word from present tense to past tense. Notice how the underlined parts of the definitions change.

Present Tense Verbs		Past Tense Verbs
interact *act between each other*	+ *-ed*	**interacted** *acted between each other*
manifest *show or demonstrate plainly*		**manifested** *showed or demonstrated plainly*

Choose a present or past tense verb from the lists to complete each sentence.

1. When you meet new people, how do you ___interact___ with them?
2. William ___manifested___ his bravery by rescuing a drowning child.

©Voyager Expanded Learning, Inc. 21

Vocabulary

united	(v) *brought together* I was *united* with my sister for the first time at age 10.
manifest	(v) *show or demonstrate plainly* Twins often *manifest* the same habits and tastes.
interacted	(v) *acted between each other* The twins *interacted* so well with other people.

2. Read aloud the title. **This title is in the form of a question, so you already have one question you can ask about this passage. What is another question?** (Why would twins grow up apart?) Remind students to pause and ask questions if they are confused while reading the passage.
3. Teach this term from the passage:

   IQ is an intelligence quotient, or one way to measure how smart you are.

During Reading

1. **Read "When Identical Twins Grow Up Apart, How Identical Are They?"** To select reading options that support your students' levels and classroom needs, see Reading Differentiation, page xxxii, if needed.
2. Have students note any connections they make to the text as they read. Remind them to write where they found the connection in the text and what type of connection it is.
3. Remind students to use context clues for unfamiliar words. Point out the word *mannerisms* on page 13 in the second full paragraph. **What does this word mean?** (ways of doing things) **What context clue helps you understand this meaning?** (or ways of doing things)

   Repeat this process for the following words.

   - **infancy** (n) *time as babies*, Anthology page 12
   - **parallel** (n) *similarity*, Anthology page 13
   - **outgoing** (adj) *social*, Anthology page 13

After Reading

Check Comprehension

1. When students finish reading, ask them these questions:
   - **Why do some identical twins grow up apart from each other?** (They are adopted by different families.)
   - **What similarities did the British twins have?** (They dyed their hair the same color; they both liked cold coffee; they both did "squidging.")
   - **What may be the cause of the similarities in twins who do not grow up together?** (They share the same genes.)

ELL Read each question aloud, and identify key words to look for in the text. Read aloud the paragraph from the text with the answer. Have students provide the answer. Rephrase as a yes/no question if needed.

2. Have partners compare the predictions they made. **Explain to your partner the prediction you made and why you made that prediction. Explain either how you changed your prediction after reading or why you think your prediction is accurate.**
3. **Let's look at the list of connections you made to the text.** Generate a discussion with the following questions.
   - **What connections did you make to other texts?** If needed, provide an example: **This passage connects with the passage we read earlier that dealt with nature versus nurture.**
   - **What connections did you make to the world?** If needed, provide an example: **I saw a talk show with separated twins who dressed the same.**
   - **What connections did you make to yourself?** (Answers will vary.)

   To make the most of the discussion time, remember to incorporate strategies that encourage and extend student involvement. Refer to page xxxviii for a comprehensive discussion of these strategies.
4. **Imagine you have a twin who grew up in a very different family. Draw a picture of you and your twin. Next to the drawing, list similarities and differences between you and your twin.** Have individuals share their drawings with the class.

ACADEMIC SKILL Tell students that finding context clues is especially important in their science classes. **You may come across unfamiliar terms. Use context clues to help you understand what these terms mean.**

EXPEDITION ORGANIZER **Who Am I?**

Pause to have students turn to Student Book pages 2 and 3. Have students complete the following:

- Write answers to one or more of the probing questions in Part A.
- Write how overcoming or using genetic traits connects to their lives in Part B.

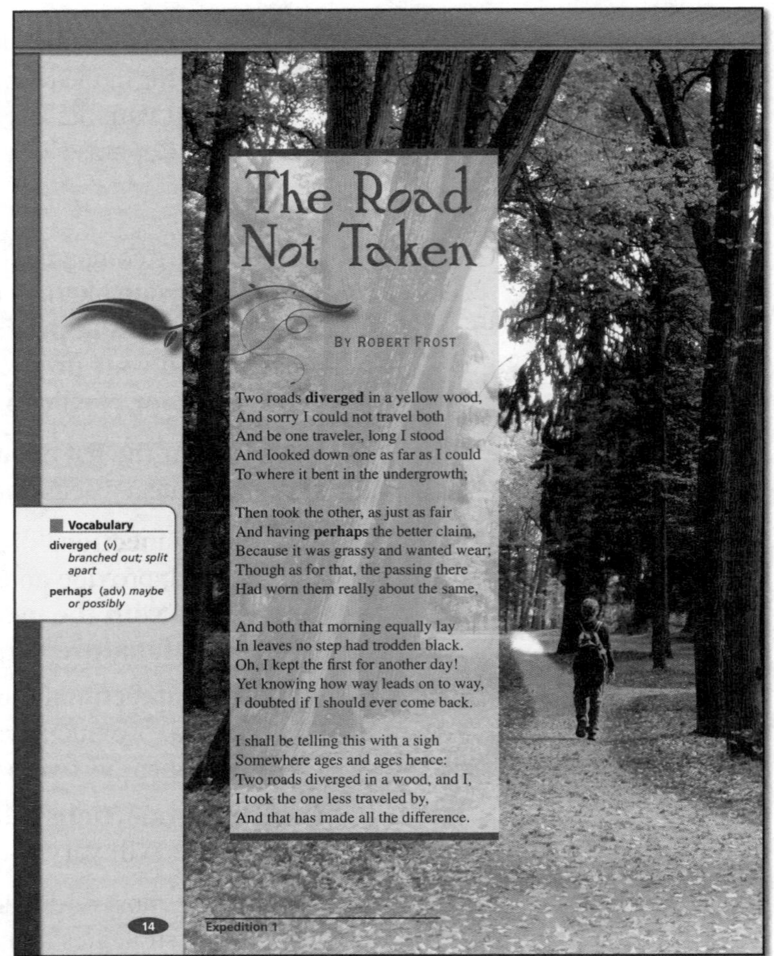
The Road Not Taken
By Robert Frost
Two roads **diverged** in a yellow wood,
And sorry I could not travel both
And be one traveler, long I stood
And looked down one as far as I could
To where it bent in the undergrowth;

Then took the other, as just as fair
And having **perhaps** the better claim,
Because it was grassy and wanted wear;
Though as for that, the passing there
Had worn them really about the same,

And both that morning equally lay
In leaves no step had trodden black.
Oh, I kept the first for another day!
Yet knowing how way leads on to way,
I doubted if I should ever come back.

I shall be telling this with a sigh
Somewhere ages and ages hence:
Two roads diverged in a wood, and I,
I took the one less traveled by,
And that has made all the difference.
Vocabulary
diverged (v) branched out; split apart
perhaps (adv) maybe or possibly
14
Expedition 1

"The Road Not Taken"

Before Reading

Introduce Vocabulary

1. Have students turn to Part A on Student Book page 22 and read aloud the two boldfaced vocabulary words. **You will see these words as you read "The Road Not Taken."** Have students rate their knowledge of these words.
2. Read the parts of speech, definitions, and example sentences for the words.
3. For words that students did not know, have them write an example sentence using the meaning they just learned. Have students share their sentences.
4. Read the instructions for Parts B and C aloud. Have students complete the activities independently. After they finish, have partners share responses.

ELL Refer to Blackline Master page 6 to extend vocabulary practice.

Apply the Strategy: Visualize

1. **What do you imagine when you hear the word *beach*? Close your eyes and think about what you know and have experienced about beaches.** Have students list details they associate with beaches, such as sand, water, shells, wind, and waves. Then, have students identify the senses that each term or detail appeals to.
2. **When you read, you visualize by noticing details that appeal to your senses. Use those details to create a kind of movie in your mind of what is happening in the text.** Write on the board: *Larissa felt the wind whip her long red hair as she walked along the beach.*

   Which details appeal to your senses? Some details can appeal to more than one sense.

   - sight (long red hair; ocean)
   - hearing (wind; whip)
   - taste (salty)
   - smell (ocean)
   - touch (ocean; hair; whip; wind)

Expedition 1, Lesson 8

Name ______________________ Date ______________

Vocabulary

"The Road Not Taken"

A. Write one or more numbers next to each boldfaced word to show when you have seen, heard, or used this word.

5 I use it in everyday conversation.
4 I heard it on TV or on the radio.
3 I heard or used it in school.
2 I read it in a book, magazine, or online.
1 I have not read, heard, or used this word.

☐ **diverged** (v) *branched out; split apart*
One road *diverged* into two roads.

☐ **perhaps** (adv) *maybe or possibly*
Perhaps I might like to visit the forest.

B. Read each sentence, then answer each question.

1. If your plan **diverged** from your friend's plan, did you agree or disagree with your friend? disagree
2. If your friend states, "**perhaps** I will go to the party," is he sure or unsure that he will attend? unsure

C. The word *diverged* contains the Latin root *verge. Verge* can mean "to lean toward or to incline." Another word that contains *verge* is the verb *converged.* Complete each sentence with either *diverged* or *converged.*

diverged	*branched out; split apart*
converged	*met at a point; came together*

1. The two sides of the triangle started out wide apart, but converged at the corner.
2. The huge rushing river diverged into two smaller, gentler streams.
3. Even though one plane took off from New York and the other took off from Los Angeles, they both converged at the same airport in Cleveland, Ohio.

 22

Vocabulary

diverged (v) *branched out; split apart*
One road *diverged* into two roads.

perhaps (adv) *maybe or possibly*
Perhaps I might like to visit the forest.

Introduce the Poem

1. Explain to students that the genre is poetry, not a passage or story. **When you read a poem, notice the sounds and rhythms of the words as much as the words themselves.**
2. Focus student attention on the title of the poem. **Do you think the author is actually talking about a road?** (no) **What could *road* actually mean?** (a path; decision) **Think about times when you could have gone one way but did not, or times when you made a decision to do one thing but not another. Did it change your life? What do you think the poem is about?** Remind them that they will return to these predictions later.
3. **Read the title. What is one question that you can make from it?** (What will happen because he doesn't take that road?) **Keep this question in mind as you read and try to find the answer in the text.**
4. Teach these terms from the passage:
   - *Undergrowth* is low-growing plants in a forest.
   - *Trodden* means "trampled; walked on."
   - *Hence* means "from this time."

During Reading

1. Give each student sticky notes. If sticky notes are unavailable, have students use their own paper to mark parts of the passage where they can visualize. On the sticky notes, have them identify descriptive words in the text and the senses they are using.
2. Explain that visualizing is an important strategy to use when reading poetry. **Let's try it. Follow along as I read.** Begin reading the poem aloud. Stop after reading the line: *In leaves no step had trodden black.* ***Trodden* means "trampled or walked on." What do you picture in your mind when you read *trodden black*?** (wet leaves mashed until they are black) **Now think of the words and your mental picture. What do you "see"?** (a road that people don't walk on often) **How do the phrase and your visualization make you feel about that road?** (inviting with colorful leaves; a nice day) Accept more than one interpretation if students can support their thinking.
3. Finish reading the poem aloud.
4. Have students reread "The Road Not Taken." Remind them to visualize while reading. To select reading options that support your students' levels and classroom needs, see Reading Differentiation, page xxxii, if needed.

After Reading

Check Comprehension

1. When students finish reading, ask these questions:
   - **What did the roads look like?** (They looked very similar. The first one was more worn, and the second one was grassier/leafier.)
   - **Why was the second road not as worn down?** (Fewer people walked down that road.)
   - **Which road did the traveler take, and how did he feel about it?** (He took the road less traveled by, and it was a very important decision in his life.)
   - **Which senses did this poem touch? What did you visualize?**
2. Have partners share their predictions. **Would you change your prediction now that you have read the whole poem?**
3. **The traveler took the road less traveled. What does that mean? Can you connect to this? Have you or someone you know ever made a decision to do something that was the opposite of what your peers were doing?** Have students make text-to-self and text-to-world connections about the traveler's choice. **Have you heard about people who make decisions like the traveler made? Explain whether you think they made the right decision.** Ask individuals to explain other connections they made. Finally, have them make a text-to-text connection with a passage they read previously or in another book. If students have difficulty, have them think about a recently read novel where the characters had to make a tough choice that affected their life. You might say, "This reminded me of *Twilight* by S. Meyer. I'm wondering how Bella's life would have differed if she hadn't fallen for Edward—if she had chosen another road."

ACADEMIC SKILL Remind students that they can visualize when they read texts for other classes. Visualizing can help students better understand unfamiliar people and places.

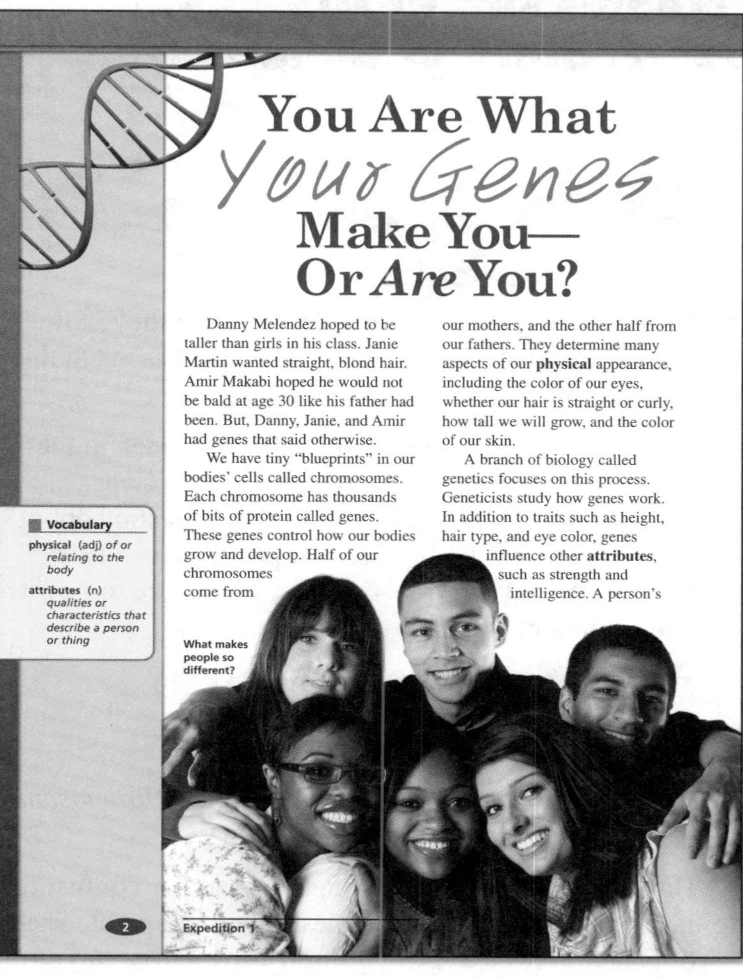

You Are What *Your Genes* Make You— Or *Are* You?

Danny Melendez hoped to be taller than girls in his class. Janie Martin wanted straight, blond hair. Amir Makabi hoped he would not be bald at age 30 like his father had been. But, Danny, Janie, and Amir had genes that said otherwise.

We have tiny "blueprints" in our bodies' cells called chromosomes. Each chromosome has thousands of bits of protein called genes. These genes control how our bodies grow and develop. Half of our chromosomes come from our mothers, and the other half from our fathers. They determine many aspects of our **physical** appearance, including the color of our eyes, whether our hair is straight or curly, how tall we will grow, and the color of our skin.

A branch of biology called genetics focuses on this process. Geneticists study how genes work. In addition to traits such as height, hair type, and eye color, genes influence other **attributes**, such as strength and intelligence. A person's genes can even determine if he or she is particularly susceptible to, or likely to get, a disease.

Vocabulary
physical (adj) *of or relating to the body*
attributes (n) *qualities or characteristics that describe a person or thing*

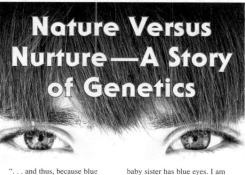

What makes people so different?

Your **ethnic** heritage, much like your genes, can influence your looks. Each ethnic group has genetic features that influence hair, skin, and eye color. Many families are a blend of different ethnic groups, which may cause offspring to reflect the genetic traits of more than one group.

Genetic research tells us that genes play a role in your physical appearance and what diseases you may be more likely to develop, but things like intelligence, physical strength, and personality are more dependent on how you live and how you use the talents and strengths you have. Your genes can influence your abilities and talents, but your environment and opportunities can enhance your genetic traits. In other words, genetics matters far less than how people choose to live and use their basic talents.

You cannot change some attributes of your genetic makeup. Your height and skin tone are basically unchangeable. However, you can do a lot to affect other parts of your genetic inheritance. You can choose to make the most of the genes that have been passed down to you. With hard work and perseverance, you can continually try to develop your mind and body in ways you desire. End

Vocabulary
ethnic (adj) *to do with a group of people sharing the same national origins, language, or culture*

Your chromosomes are your body's blueprint.

Nature Versus Nurture—A Story of Genetics

". . . and thus, because blue eyes are a recessive trait, two blue-eyed people do not typically have a brown-eyed child," concluded Mr. Riazi. What? Surely, he got that wrong. That can't be true. My parents both have blue eyes, and I have brown eyes. I thought about my family. My parents have blue eyes, my two brothers have blue eyes, and my baby sister has blue eyes. I am the only one with brown eyes. I wondered how that happened.

The bell rang, and I stayed in my seat thinking. I looked at the textbook and read the part about weak recessive traits and strong dominant traits. As I read, I came across other things that made me wonder how my parents ever had me. They have straight hair, but I have curly hair. My skin is much darker than their skin. I couldn't move. I was paralyzed with fear. *What if my parents aren't really my parents?* I thought. *Is that possible?*

Mr. Riazi approached my desk. "Is genetics an **exact** science?" I asked. He responded by showing me pictures of people who look nothing like their parents. There were two African Americans, with a son who had white skin, red hair, light eyes, and freckles. There was a short couple whose children were all short **except** one—who was more than 6 feet tall.

Vocabulary
exact (adj) *perfectly correct*

Genetic Cross Section

"Nothing in this world is exact," he said.

"I have been listening to your discussion on genetics, and I have read the information in the book. It makes me wonder if my parents are my real parents," I said. "I think it is **probable** that I am adopted."

"It's something you should ask them about. But, do you act like them?"

"Yes."

"Do you like the same things as they do?"

"Yes."

"Do you love them?"

"Yes."

"Then they are your parents—in every way that matters."

"Yes, but you mentioned that sometimes people are susceptible to diseases based on their genetic makeup. Don't I need to know where I came from?"

Mr. Riazi told me he thought it would be a good idea to talk to my parents about my concerns. He said that if I am adopted, it would be good to know my birth parents' health issues and what probabilities I have of contracting a disease.

After basketball practice, I went straight home. I was on a mission. My special task was to find out where I came from. Was I adopted? If so, why did my birth parents put me up for adoption? Why did my parents adopt me when they were able to have kids? Who am I? End

Vocabulary
except (prep) *apart from; not included in the general rule*
probable (adj) *likely to happen or be true*

Daughter and mother

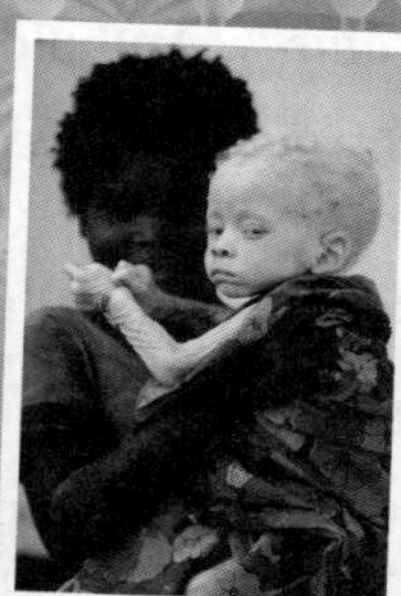

Sister and brother

"You Are What Your Genes Make You—Or *Are* You?" and "Nature Versus Nurture—A Story of Genetics"

Prepare to Reread

Remind students that they read about how genes help determine who a person is in "You Are What Your Genes Make You—Or *Are* You?" and "Nature Versus Nurture—A Story of Genetics." **Now you'll revisit those passages to use the strategies you learned.**

Practice Vocabulary

1. Have students think about how vocabulary words from Lessons 1 and 2 were used in the passages.
   - **Does your *ethnic* heritage influence your genetic makeup?** (yes)
   - **What part of a person's *physical* appearance may be influenced by his or her genetics?** (height; eye and hair color)
   - **Without any tools, can you find the *exact* distance in centimeters from your finger to your thumb.** (no)
   - **None of the planets are inhabitable, *except* which one?** (Earth)
   - **What are the *attributes* of your favorite actor?** (Answers will vary.)
   - **Is it *probable* for people to want to change something about themselves?** (yes)
2. **Remember, you can use context clues to find the meaning of unfamiliar words.** Have students turn to Anthology pages 2 and 3. Reread the third paragraph. **What do you think the word *susceptible* means?** (likely to have)
3. Repeat this process for the following words.
   - **traits** (n) *features*, Anthology page 3
   - **inheritance** (n) *genes passed down from parents*, Anthology page 3
   - **perseverance** (n) *continually trying*, Anthology page 3

ELL Support students using context clues to determine the meaning of *perseverance*. Write the sentence containing the word, and guide students to notice the phrases *hard work* and *continually try*. For further practice, refer to Blackline Master page 7.

Reread

Apply the Strategies

1. Explain to students that in today's lesson they will review the strategies taught in previous lessons in this Expedition.
2. Have students find a confusing phrase or idea in the second paragraph of "You Are What Your Genes Make You—Or *Are* You?" and write a question about it. **What is a confusing idea or phrase from this paragraph? What question can you make out of it?** Guide students to . . .
   - locate a sentence, such as "We have tiny 'blueprints' in our bodies' cells called chromosomes."
   - formulate a question, such as *What do chromosomes have to do with genes?*

   Have students scan the passage for another confusing idea or phrase and write a question on a separate sheet of paper. **Where might you find the answer to your question?** (reread to find the meanings of what they read; continue reading, keeping the question in mind)
3. Have students turn to "Nature Versus Nurture—A Story of Genetics" on Anthology page 4. **In fiction text, visualizing can help you know what a character looks like and how a character feels.** Direct student attention to the second paragraph. **Use sensory details to help you visualize. What sensory words can you use to create a picture in your mind?** (straight hair; curly hair; darker skin) **What do these details show you about the narrator and her family?** (She looks a lot different from her family.)
4. **You also can visualize by adding details from your own experiences.** Read aloud the following text from the first paragraph: **That can't be true. My parents both have blue eyes, and I have brown eyes. I thought about my family.** Have students draw what the narrator looks like on a separate sheet of paper. Use these prompts: **How might the narrator feel at that moment? What is her expression?** Have partners compare and contrast their drawings.

ELL Extend practice visualizing by prompting students to visualize other aspects of the passage, such as the setting. Allow students to pause and create their own mental pictures of where the scene takes place and what objects they might see in that room. Have students describe their mental pictures. (a classroom; books; desks; science posters on the wall) Write student responses on the board. Ask how visualizing helped them understand what they read.

Write in Response to Reading

1. Direct students to Student Book page 23. Remind students that when they make a text-to-world connection, something in the passage sparks an idea, and they remember something they read about, heard about on TV, or learned in school. Clarify that a text-to-world connection is not about their personal experience. Have students complete Part A.
2. For Part B, point out that student connections will be different, but they must show a connection to the text.
3. Allow students to extend their Part C responses creatively by writing a paragraph, a poem, or a rap. They also may create a diagram showing different influences that make them who they are. Provide examples if needed.

   My brother isn't quite like me because he's a he, and I am a she. He likes to sail and can tell a good tale. I like to run and also to have fun. Our eyes are brown, and we both like to clown. Too bad we don't live in the same town.

EXPEDITION ORGANIZER **Who Am I?**

Pause to have students turn to Student Book pages 2 and 3. Have students complete the following:

- Answer the probing questions in Part A. Answer the question that they wrote.
- Write how twins and Robert Frost's poem connect to their lives in Part B.
- Complete the dictionary challenge in Part C.

Expedition 1, Lesson 9

Name ____________ Date ____________

Write in Response to Reading

A. What connections did you make between the passages and the world around you? Write them in the chart. Answers will vary.

Passage	Connection to Something I Know About
"You Are What Your Genes Make You—Or *Are* You?"	
"Nature Versus Nurture—A Story of Genetics"	

B. What do you think makes you who you are? Is it your genes, your life experiences, or something else?
Student responses should reflect an understanding of how genetics and life experience are separate forces that work together to create who people are.

C. Write a paragraph, poem, rap, or song about the things that make you who you are.
Answers will vary.

 23

Build Background DVD 1.2

Briefly discuss the Expedition passages. Then, watch the DVD together. After watching, review student responses to the probing questions using the Expedition Organizer.

Review, Extend, Assess

In today's lesson, as in Lessons 5 and 10 of every Expedition, there are options from which to choose. You may do any or all of the options listed. Activities for each option are given on the following pages. Each option will support or extend previously taught objectives. Choose the option(s) appropriate for your students and prepare accordingly.

Review Vocabulary

Extend Vocabulary

Assess Comprehension and Vocabulary

Reteach

Passport Reading Journeys Library

Online Technology Component

Expedition Project

Review Vocabulary

Direct students to review the vocabulary for the last three passages on Student Book page 3.

1. Have students read the words and definitions.
2. Have students turn to Student Book page 24. **You have read these vocabulary words in the reading passages. Now you will read these vocabulary words again in a new context. The words will have the same meanings. As you finish, go back and check the definitions to ensure you used the words correctly.** Read the instructions aloud, and have students complete the activity. Have them share their answers for Parts A and B.

CHECKPOINT Provide support for students who had difficulty choosing synonyms in Part A. Explain that synonyms are words that have the same or similar meanings. **The sentence meaning will be the same with both the underlined word and the synonym. Test the word by reading the sentence to see if it makes sense. What is the synonym for *split*?** (diverged) **Does *diverged* make sense in the sentence?** (yes) Continue asking students to test the synonyms in the sentence context.

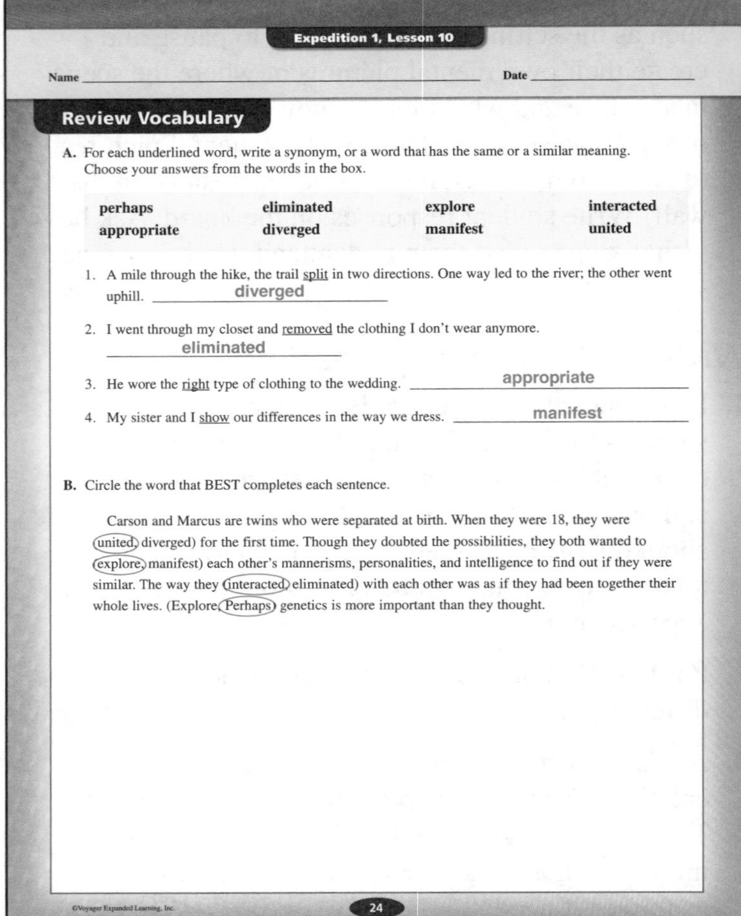

Expedition 1, Lesson 10

Name ______ Date ______

Review Vocabulary

A. For each underlined word, write a synonym, or a word that has the same or a similar meaning. Choose your answers from the words in the box.

perhaps	eliminated	explore	interacted
appropriate	diverged	manifest	united

1. A mile through the hike, the trail split in two directions. One way led to the river; the other went uphill. diverged
2. I went through my closet and removed the clothing I don't wear anymore. eliminated
3. He wore the right type of clothing to the wedding. appropriate
4. My sister and I show our differences in the way we dress. manifest

B. Circle the word that BEST completes each sentence.

Carson and Marcus are twins who were separated at birth. When they were 18, they were (united, diverged) for the first time. Though they doubted the possibilities, they both wanted to (explore, manifest) each other's mannerisms, personalities, and intelligence to find out if they were similar. The way they (interacted, eliminated) with each other was as if they had been together their whole lives. (Explore, Perhaps) genetics is more important than they thought.

 24

Extend Vocabulary

1. Direct students to Student Book page 25. **A prefix is a word part at the beginning of a word. It adds meaning to the word.** Write *inter-* = *in the middle of; between; among* on the board. **The word *interacted* means "acted between each other."** Write *interacted* and the definition on the board. Underline the word *between* in the definition.
2. Write *interrupt* = *break or stop in the middle of an activity* on the board. **How does the prefix *inter-* relate to the definition?** (The definition has the word *middle* in it.) Underline the word *middle* on the board.
3. Read aloud the instructions for Parts B and C. Complete the first item of Part B along with the students. When students complete Part B, have them share their answers.

CHECKPOINT When students share their answers for Part B, make sure they notice the context clues in the sentences that will help them fill in the correct words.

Part A

1. Distribute five index cards to each student. Have students write one word from Part A on each card.
2. Read aloud the definition of *interacted*. Provide a sample sentence, such as *Teachers and students interacted at the school picnic.* Have students complete a sentence starter, such as *Friends and families interacted at* ________. (a holiday celebration)
3. Have students draw a clue on the back of each card. Model thinking aloud about what would make a good clue then drawing your clue to help you remember.

Part B

1. Read aloud the sentence frames. Have students show you the card that best completes each sentence.
2. Ask students which clue they drew on the back to help them remember each word. Encourage students to share other ways they remember words.

Part C

For added support, allow partners to work together while writing sentences.

Expedition 1, Lesson 10

Name ______________________ Date __________

Extend Vocabulary

A. When you read, you learn what words mean and how they are used. Each of the following words begins with *inter-*. This prefix often means "in the middle of; between; among." Read the words and their meanings.

interacted (v)	*acted between each other*
interrupt (v)	*stop in the middle of an activity*
interstate (n)	*system of highways existing between states*
intermission (n)	*a break between parts of a play, movie, or concert*
interview (n)	*a face-to-face meeting between people*

B. Complete each sentence with a word from Part A.

1. In a magazine, I read an __interview__ with my favorite actress.
2. Last summer, my family and I traveled on the __interstate__ through four states.
3. Please don't __interrupt__ me when I'm talking. Wait until I've finished telling my story.
4. The play was so long that there was an __intermission__ in the middle of it.
5. The cats __interacted__ playfully with each other.

C. Choose three words from the list in Part A and use each in a sentence.

1. Answers will vary.
2. ______________________
3. ______________________

 25

Assess Comprehension and Vocabulary

1. **You will use the active reading strategies as you read the passages. When you read, what do you make connections with?** (what you know about the world; your life; other texts) **What else do you do every time you read?** (ask questions; preview and predict; use context clues; visualize)

2. Direct students to Student Book pages 26–28. Preview the pages, showing students that they will read two passages and answer questions. Have students complete the pages independently.

   Review student answers. Whenever possible, provide elaborative feedback to student responses. Refer to page xl for examples of elaborative feedback and how to incorporate it in your lessons.

   If students incorrectly answer more than 4 out of 15 assessment questions, evaluate what kind of reteaching is needed. If students miss vocabulary questions, have them return to the vocabulary activities and work with the words they missed. For active reading strategies errors, use the reteaching suggestions on page 43.

Expedition 1, Lesson 10

Name ______________________ Date ____________

Assess Comprehension and Vocabulary

A. Read the following passage.

Different People, Different Personalities

Look around you. People look different, and they have different personalities as well. Some people follow the same patterns of behavior. How can you recognize these patterns? Perhaps you can take a personality test to better understand yourself and others. These tests give you a general sense of your identity. They are not an exact measurement of who you are. You will learn that a variety of attributes make up a person's personality.

Some people are extroverts. They are outgoing, or sociable, and gain energy by being around people. Introverts might be more quiet or reflective. They feel most comfortable doing things alone instead of interacting with a group. A test might ask you how you react to an event, such as seeing a hot air balloon rise up into the sky. You might think about what causes the balloon to rise and about other facts. Someone else will think about how it looks and how it makes him or her feel. A test might ask you how you make decisions. You might use reason, logic, and facts. Someone else might think more about how other people will be affected. It can be interesting to explore your personality.

B. Circle the letter of each correct answer.

vocabulary
1. Which word is a synonym for *possibly*?
   A. absolutely
   B. somehow
   C. appropriate
   (D) perhaps

vocabulary
2. Which word is defined as "think about carefully"?
   A. plunge
   B. diverge
   C. interact
   (D) explore

context clues
3. The examples *outgoing* and *quiet* are context clues that help you define ________.
   (A) attributes
   B. person
   C. variety
   D. measurement

context clues
4. Which word is a context clue that helps you define *outgoing*?
   A. quiet
   (B) sociable
   C. reflective
   D. logical

Expedition 1, Lesson 10

Name ______________________ Date ____________

preview
5. What did you use to help you preview this passage?
   A. pictures and a graph
   B. paragraph count
   (C) title
   D. word count

context clues
6. Which of the following is NOT a context clue that helps you understand the meaning of the word *extroverts*?
   A. outgoing
   B. sociable
   (C) people
   D. energy

context clues
7. Which of the following is a context clue that helps you understand the meaning of the word *introverts*?
   (A) quiet
   B. people
   C. things
   D. comfortable

make connections
8. Which of the following is a possible connection that could be made to this text?
   (A) My uncle is an extrovert who needs to be around people all the time.
   B. My dog likes to roll in the dirt.
   C. What is an extrovert?
   D. Do people need to take tests to figure out who they are?

ask questions
9. Which of the following is a question you might ask yourself while reading to help you better understand the passage?
   A. Why do I need to read this?
   (B) Why would someone take a personality test?
   C. What do dogs and cats have in common?
   D. What is my locker combination?

make connections
10. Think about someone you know who is an extrovert. How does the person's personality compare with yours?
    Answers will vary.

make connections
11. What connection can be made to "They feel most comfortable doing things alone instead of interacting with a group"?
    A. My brother is annoying.
    B. My mom is very helpful.
    (C) My sister spends much of her time alone in her room.
    D. My dad works a lot.

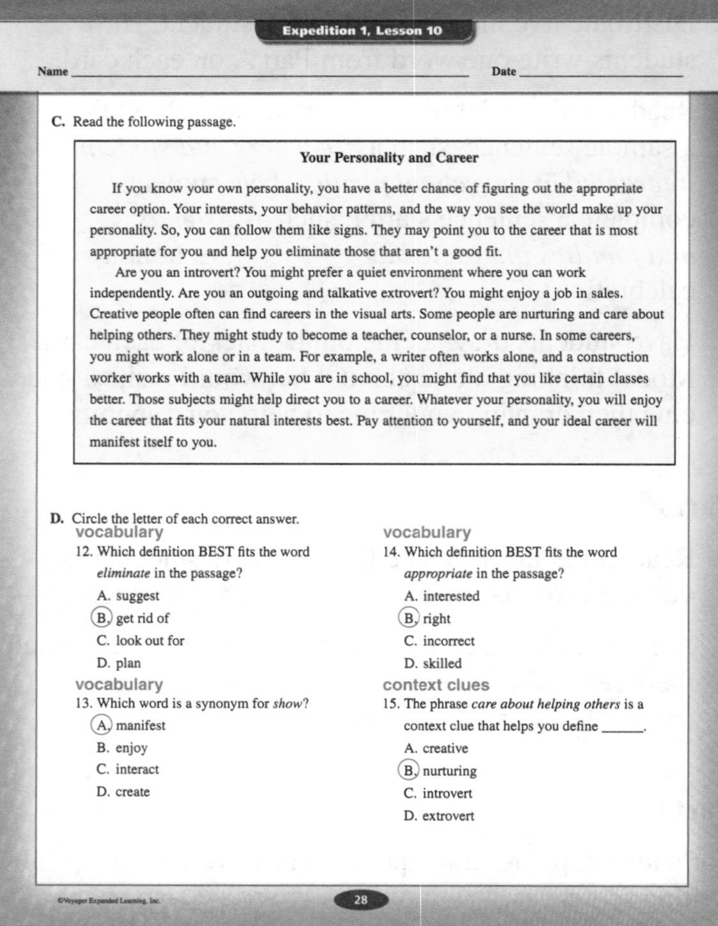
Expedition 1, Lesson 10

Name ______________________ Date ____________

C. Read the following passage.

Your Personality and Career

If you know your own personality, you have a better chance of figuring out the appropriate career option. Your interests, your behavior patterns, and the way you see the world make up your personality. So, you can follow them like signs. They may point you to the career that is most appropriate for you and help you eliminate those that aren't a good fit.

Are you an introvert? You might prefer a quiet environment where you can work independently. Are you an outgoing and talkative extrovert? You might enjoy a job in sales. Creative people often can find careers in the visual arts. Some people are nurturing and care about helping others. They might study to become a teacher, counselor, or a nurse. In some careers, you might work alone or in a team. For example, a writer often works alone, and a construction worker works with a team. While you are in school, you might find that you like certain classes better. Those subjects might help direct you to a career. Whatever your personality, you will enjoy the career that fits your natural interests best. Pay attention to yourself, and your ideal career will manifest itself to you.

D. Circle the letter of each correct answer.

vocabulary
12. Which definition BEST fits the word *eliminate* in the passage?
    A. suggest
    (B) get rid of
    C. look out for
    D. plan

vocabulary
13. Which word is a synonym for *show*?
    (A) manifest
    B. enjoy
    C. interact
    D. create

vocabulary
14. Which definition BEST fits the word *appropriate* in the passage?
    A. interested
    (B) right
    C. incorrect
    D. skilled

context clues
15. The phrase *care about helping others* is a context clue that helps you define ______.
    A. creative
    (B) nurturing
    C. introvert
    D. extrovert

Reteach

Preview and Predict, Context Clues, Ask Questions, Make Connections, Visualize

1. Have students turn to Student Book page 29. Read the instructions aloud. **What do you predict the passage is about based on the title?** Read the instructions and passage with students.
2. Preview the chart with students. Explain that they should read the tips to help them practice the strategy. Offer these suggestions, as needed:
   - For preview and predict, remind students that when they preview, they don't read the passage's main words. They look for clues in the title, subheadings, and illustrations. Then they can make predictions.
   - For context clues, have students check the meaning of a clue by substituting it in the sentence to see if it makes sense.
   - To ask questions, remind students that they may have to reread or read further to find details in the text that answer their question.
   - To make connections, have students recall events, situations, and emotions they have experienced that can help them connect to the passage.

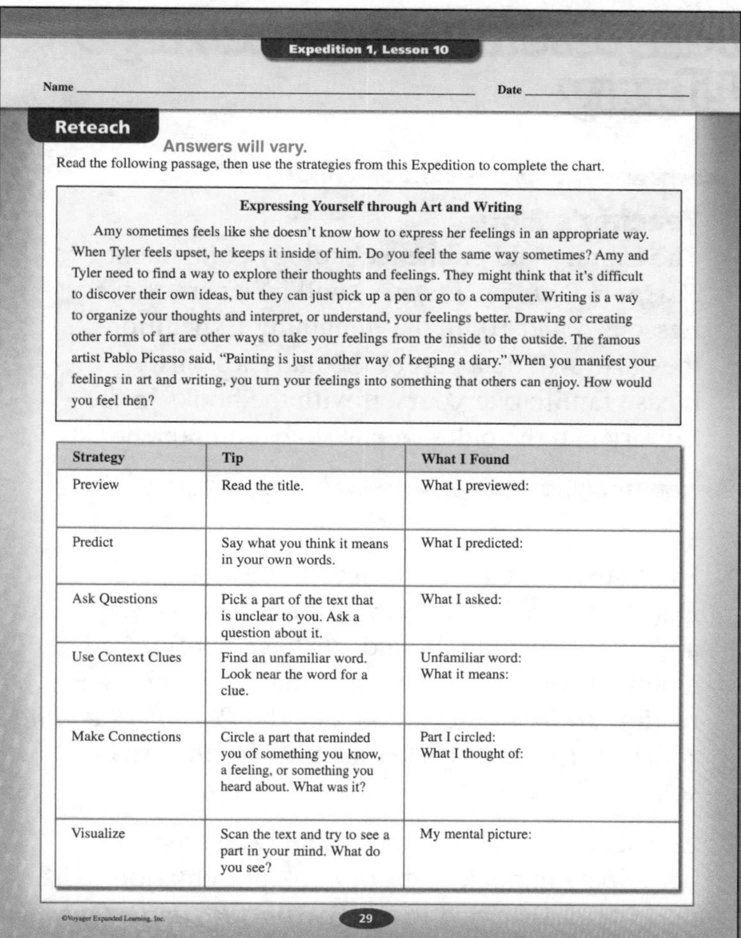

Expedition 1, Lesson 10

Name ______ Date ______

Reteach

Answers will vary.

Read the following passage, then use the strategies from this Expedition to complete the chart.

Expressing Yourself through Art and Writing

Amy sometimes feels like she doesn't know how to express her feelings in an appropriate way. When Tyler feels upset, he keeps it inside of him. Do you feel the same way sometimes? Amy and Tyler need to find a way to explore their thoughts and feelings. They might think that it's difficult to discover their own ideas, but they can just pick up a pen or go to a computer. Writing is a way to organize your thoughts and interpret, or understand, your feelings better. Drawing or creating other forms of art are other ways to take your feelings from the inside to the outside. The famous artist Pablo Picasso said, "Painting is just another way of keeping a diary." When you manifest your feelings in art and writing, you turn your feelings into something that others can enjoy. How would you feel then?

Strategy	Tip	What I Found
Preview	Read the title.	What I previewed:
Predict	Say what you think it means in your own words.	What I predicted:
Ask Questions	Pick a part of the text that is unclear to you. Ask a question about it.	What I asked:
Use Context Clues	Find an unfamiliar word. Look near the word for a clue.	Unfamiliar word: What it means:
Make Connections	Circle a part that reminded you of something you know, a feeling, or something you heard about. What was it?	Part I circled: What I thought of:
Visualize	Scan the text and try to see a part in your mind. What do you see?	My mental picture:

29

Passport Reading Journeys Library

Teacher's Note
The Library and online technology component of *Passport Reading Journeys* will be a part of every Lessons 5 and 10. In the remaining Expeditions, they also will be a part of the daily lessons. Please familiarize yourself with the books in the Library and the online technology component.

1. Have students choose reading material from the *Passport Reading Journeys* Library or another approved selection. If students have not finished a previously chosen selection, they may continue reading from that selection. See the *Passport Reading Journeys* Library Teacher's Guide for material on selection guidelines.
2. You also may use this time to allow students to participate in book clubs or book presentations. Use the criteria specified in the *Passport Reading Journeys* Library Teacher's Guide.

Vocabulary Connections

Vocabulary words are listed in the Teacher's Guide for each book. These words are content-related or used frequently in reading material. The selected words can be a basis for independent or small-group discussions and activities.

Student Opportunities

Six copies of each book title are provided in the *Passport Reading Journeys* Library. The number of copies makes it possible for small groups of students to read the same material and share the information they read.

Theme-related titles include *The Face on the Milk Carton*, *Leaving Home*, and *The Pinballs*.

Technology

1. Depending on your classroom configuration and computer access, you may have all students work through the technology in a lab setting or have individuals or small groups of students work on desktops or laptops while other students participate in other suggested activities, such as the *Passport Reading Journeys* Library.
2. The online technology component provides additional support for students to work with selected vocabulary words. Students will work through a series of activities to strengthen their word knowledge, then apply that knowledge to passage reading. Refer to the online technology component User Guide for more information.

   The theme-related word sets are Biology, Sociology, Psychology, and English/Language Arts.

Expedition Project

Biographical Presentation

Distribute copies of Project Blackline Master page 2. Have students think about their own hobbies, interests, families, cultural backgrounds, and personalities. **What things make you who you are? What do you want to find out about new friends when you are getting to know them?**

Have students look at the assignment and follow along as you explain. Assign point values and ask students to write them in the rubric. Tell them to make any notes on the page that will help them, but they will turn in the page with the assignment.

Have students choose partners and follow these steps:

1. **Introduce yourself to your partner.** Have students share a few brief things about themselves, such as hobbies, interests, families, and cultural backgrounds.
2. Students should use what their partner shared about himself or herself as brainstorming material for the biographical presentations. Partners will present each other to the class.
3. Have students ask questions about their partner and their families.
4. **Your presentations should fit the following criteria:**
   - **Thorough explanation of personal attributes**
   - **Detailed visuals that connect to the presentation**
   - **Organized delivery and personal connection to topics of the Anthology passages**
5. Have students gather or create visuals. Visuals might be posters, photographs, favorite possessions, cultural objects, or items used for their hobbies.
6. Have students rehearse presentations. Partners should give feedback for improvement. Make sure the presentation has each of the criteria listed.
7. Have students present biographical presentations during class.
8. **I will assess your presentation based on the rubric on your page.** To assess student presentations, use the rubric from the Project Blackline Master.

Real-World Reading

1. **Starting with Expedition 2, you will read Real-World Reading passages.** Direct students to the FaceStart Wall-to-Wall on Student Book pages 193 and 194. **How is this like the reading you do in school? How is it different?**
2. **You read for specific purposes outside of school.** Encourage students to suggest other types of real-world reading they see outside of school, such as advertisements and job applications, and to tell the purpose of each type. **Which active reading strategies would you use when you read these?** Encourage students to tell how the strategies they learned would help them read these types of writing. Have students make a poster that illustrates the multiple types of texts they read and write.

Exploring Careers

Career Passages

1. Tell students that starting with Expedition 2, they will read Career passages. **In this Expedition, you have thought about your identity and interests. Career passages will help you think about different careers you might consider.** Have students preview the Career passages on the Anthology Table of Contents, page iii. Have them flip ahead to "Courtroom Professionals" on page 63. If students know someone who works in a courtroom, have them share information about that person and his or her job with the class.
2. **Think about careers you are interested in and would like to read about.** Encourage students to check out books from the library or do Internet searches to learn about careers that interest them. **Which career passage listed in the table of contents interests you? Explain.** Encourage students to tell how the strategies they learned will help them read these types of writings.

R U Online?

"Friends or Foes?"		"DotComGuy: A Life Alone on the Internet"	
Lesson 1	**Lesson 2**	**Lesson 3**	**Lesson 4**
Introduce the Expedition Discuss probing questions about the Internet. **Before Reading** • Introduce and practice using passage vocabulary. • Introduce and practice identifying main idea and details. **During Reading** Read "Friends or Foes?" **After Reading** Check comprehension. Have students practice vocabulary using the online technology component. Have students select books for independent reading. ELL Extend and practice.	**Prepare to Reread** • Review and practice using passage vocabulary. • Practice using context clues. • Practice using multiple-meaning words. **Reread** • Review and practice identifying main idea and details. • Write advice. ELL Extend and practice.	**Before Reading** • Introduce and practice using passage vocabulary. • Apply the target skill and practice identifying main idea and details. • Introduce the passage by previewing and making predictions. **During Reading** Read "DotComGuy: A Life Alone on the Internet." **After Reading** Check comprehension. Have students practice vocabulary using the online technology component. Have students select books for independent reading. ELL Extend and practice.	**Prepare to Reread** • Review and practice using passage vocabulary. • Practice using context clues. • Build new words using the Latin root *term*. **Reread** • Practice identifying main idea and details. • Write an interview and To Do list. ELL Extend and practice.

Lesson 5—Review, Extend, Assess

Review Vocabulary
Review and practice using passage vocabulary.

Extend Vocabulary
Use prefixes *en-* and *ex-* to build and understand new words.

Assess Comprehension and Vocabulary
Assess student understanding of identifying main idea and details and other previously taught skills.

Reteach
Reteach main idea and details using student activity pages.

Passport Reading Journeys Library
Have students select books for independent reading.

Technology
Have students practice vocabulary using the online technology component.

Writing Process
Have students use the writing process to write a review.

Real-World Reading
Have students read a blog.

Exploring Careers
Have students read about a Web designer and complete an activity page.

Teacher's Note
Before beginning the Expedition, ask your librarian to suggest books that will fit the theme. Books relating to the Internet will be appropriate for this Expedition.

"Truth, Lies, and the Internet"		"Online Shopping Versus Brick-and-Mortar Stores"	
Lesson 6	**Lesson 7**	**Lesson 8**	**Lesson 9**
Before Reading • Introduce and practice using passage vocabulary. • Apply the target skill and practice identifying main idea and details. • Introduce the passage by previewing and making predictions. **During Reading** Read "Truth, Lies, and the Internet." **After Reading** Check comprehension. Have students practice vocabulary using the online technology component. Have students select books for independent reading. ELL Extend and practice.	**Prepare to Reread** • Review and practice using passage vocabulary. • Practice using context clues. • Build and use compound words. **Reread** • Review and practice identifying main idea and details. • Write a blog. ELL Extend and practice.	**Before Reading** • Introduce and practice using passage vocabulary. • Introduce the target skill and practice using text features. • Introduce the passage by previewing and making predictions. **During Reading** Read "Online Shopping Versus Brick-and-Mortar Stores." **After Reading** Check comprehension. Have students practice vocabulary using the online technology component. Have students select books for independent reading. ELL Extend and practice.	**Prepare to Reread** • Review and practice using passage vocabulary. • Practice using context clues. • Build new words using affixes. **Reread** • Use text features and identify main idea. • Write descriptions. ELL Extend and practice.

Lesson 10—Review, Extend, Assess

Review Vocabulary
Review passage vocabulary.

Extend Vocabulary
Use suffixes to build and understand new words.

Assess Comprehension and Vocabulary
Assess student understanding of main idea and details and text features.

Reteach
Reteach main idea and details and text features using student activity pages.

Passport Reading Journeys Library
Have students select books for independent reading.

Technology
Have students practice vocabulary using the online technology component.

Expedition Project
Design a Web site.

Real-World Reading
Read an online news article and answer questions.

Exploring Careers
Read about careers in information technology and complete student activity page.

Expedition 2

Introduce the Expedition

1. Discuss with students how you use the Internet. For example, *I use the Internet to check local movie times, catch up on daily news, and find information.* Have students share different ways they use the Internet and look at the Expedition 2 opening photo on Anthology page 15.
2. Have students generate questions they most often hear people ask about using the Internet. Write their questions on the board. Have students follow along as you read the probing questions.
   - **What are some benefits of the Internet?**
   - **What are some of the problems with using the Internet as a way of communicating with people around the world?**
   - **How has the Internet changed the way people interact with one another?**

   Have partners discuss their initial responses to these questions. To make the most of the discussion time, remember to incorporate strategies that encourage and extend student involvement. Refer to page xxxviii for a comprehensive discussion of these strategies.

Build Background DVD 2.1
Tell students they will view a brief DVD that provides background information about the Internet. **As you watch, listen for ideas that connect to the responses you discussed.**

Expedition 2
R U Online?
• What are some benefits of the Internet?
• What are some of the problems with using the Internet as a way of communicating with people around the world?
• How has the Internet changed the way people interact with one another?
15

3. Point out the Expedition 2 Organizer on Student Book pages 30 and 31. **As you read the passages, you'll pause to record your own ideas about these questions and about the passages.**

   Suggestions for how students can add ideas to these pages appear in this Teacher's Edition at the end of Lessons 2, 4, 7, and 9. Allow students to write initial responses in the probing questions graphic organizer in Part A.

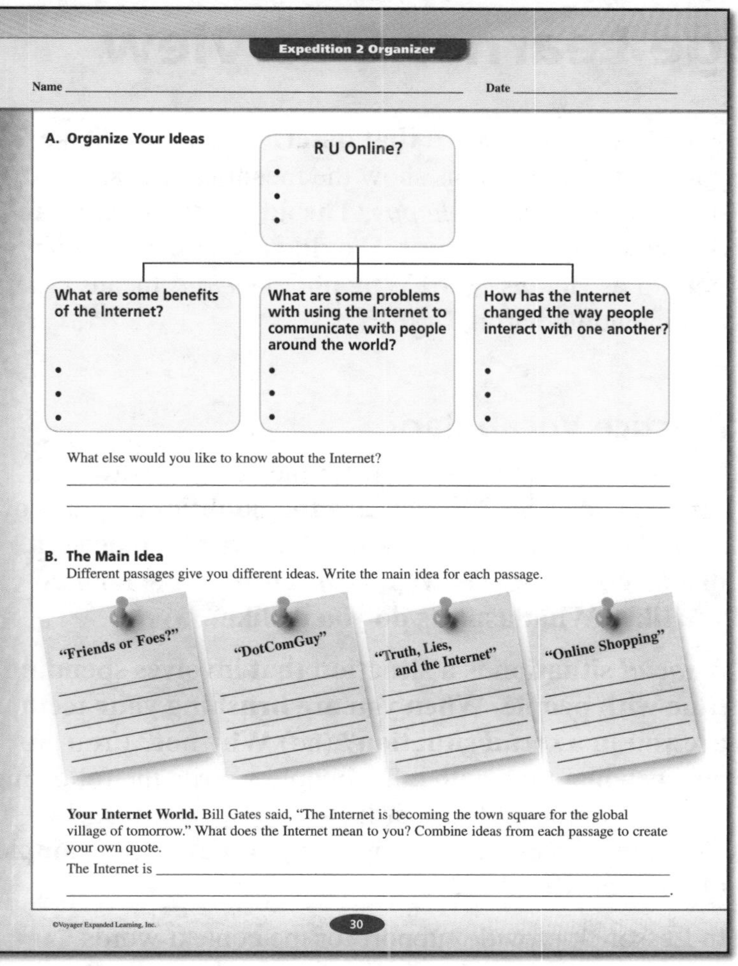
Expedition 2 Organizer

Name ______________________ Date ____________

A. Organize Your Ideas

R U Online?
-
-
-

What are some benefits of the Internet?	What are some problems with using the Internet to communicate with people around the world?	How has the Internet changed the way people interact with one another?
• • •	• • •	• • •

What else would you like to know about the Internet?

____

B. The Main Idea
Different passages give you different ideas. Write the main idea for each passage.

"Friends or Foes?"
"DotComGuy"
"Truth, Lies, and the Internet"
"Online Shopping"

Your Internet World. Bill Gates said, "The Internet is becoming the town square for the global village of tomorrow." What does the Internet mean to you? Combine ideas from each passage to create your own quote.

The Internet is ______________________.

©Voyager Expanded Learning, Inc. 30

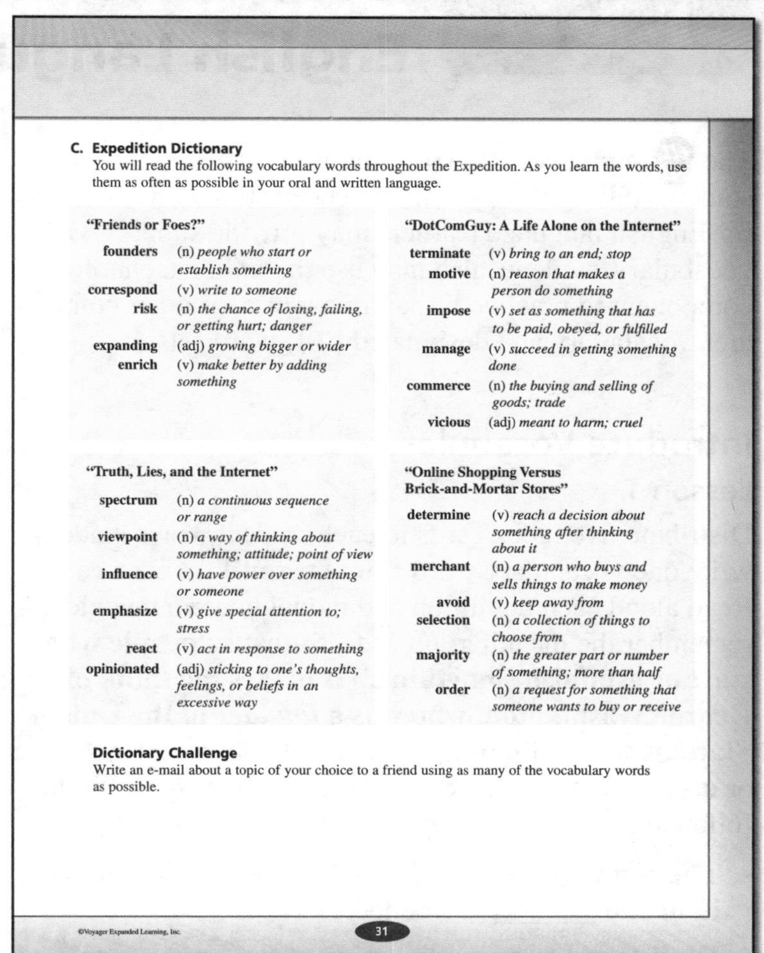
C. Expedition Dictionary
You will read the following vocabulary words throughout the Expedition. As you learn the words, use them as often as possible in your oral and written language.

"Friends or Foes?"

founders (n) *people who start or establish something*
correspond (v) *write to someone*
risk (n) *the chance of losing, failing, or getting hurt; danger*
expanding (adj) *growing bigger or wider*
enrich (v) *make better by adding something*

"DotComGuy: A Life Alone on the Internet"

terminate (v) *bring to an end; stop*
motive (n) *reason that makes a person do something*
impose (v) *set as something that has to be paid, obeyed, or fulfilled*
manage (v) *succeed in getting something done*
commerce (n) *the buying and selling of goods; trade*
vicious (adj) *meant to harm; cruel*

"Truth, Lies, and the Internet"

spectrum (n) *a continuous sequence or range*
viewpoint (n) *a way of thinking about something; attitude; point of view*
influence (v) *have power over something or someone*
emphasize (v) *give special attention to; stress*
react (v) *act in response to something*
opinionated (adj) *sticking to one's thoughts, feelings, or beliefs in an excessive way*

"Online Shopping Versus Brick-and-Mortar Stores"

determine (v) *reach a decision about something after thinking about it*
merchant (n) *a person who buys and sells things to make money*
avoid (v) *keep away from*
selection (n) *a collection of things to choose from*
majority (n) *the greater part or number of something; more than half*
order (n) *a request for something that someone wants to buy or receive*

Dictionary Challenge
Write an e-mail about a topic of your choice to a friend using as many of the vocabulary words as possible.

©Voyager Expanded Learning, Inc. 31

ELL

Making Connections

Encourage students to show how they cross cultures through technology and discuss different ways they use the Internet to connect with their home culture or how they use their home language on the Internet. Have them name online newspapers and magazines and the types of information they read in their home languages. Ask them to share how the Internet connects them to other parts of the world. Write student examples on the board. Encourage them to tell whether they use the Internet to visit social networking sites, send e-mail, shop online, or find information.

Students may need additional information about common problems associated with using the Internet. Use the following background material as needed to help students prepare to read the Expedition.

Internet Security

Using the Internet for personal communications and shopping can be convenient. However, people want to know that information they share through the Internet is secure and cannot be seen or used by anyone else. Internet companies spend a lot of time and money ensuring no one can break into their sites and access confidential information. Many computer experts know how to hack into Web sites or guess passwords and use other methods to view private information. These hackers can steal and use personal information, such as credit card numbers.

Reliable Information

The Internet provides a lot of information, but not all the information is correct. People can publish information online without anyone's approval. For this reason, information found on personal Web sites, blogs, and even some encyclopedias may be incorrect or outdated. Web sites of credible institutions, such as universities and government organizations, and established newspapers and magazines usually contain reliable information. Remember that many Web sites are commercial, or used to sell things, and may contain biased information that tries to persuade people to buy a certain product.

English Language Learner Overview

The (ELL) signals when extra support is provided for students during the lesson. As needed, Blackline Masters for English language learners may provide support. For vocabulary, students also may use the online technology component to practice Expedition words or other content-area vocabulary and designated ELL word sets.

Introduce Vocabulary

Lesson 1

Distribute five index cards to each student. Have students write one vocabulary word from Lesson 1 on each card. Read aloud each definition and model how you would remember the meaning. ***Founders*** **means "people who start or establish something." It makes me think of George Washington, who was a *founder* of the United States. I will write that on the card.** Have students write or draw a clue on each card. Have students complete the following sentences using words from the cards.

- **The company is named after the people who started it, or the ________.** (founders)
- **We listened to an audio guide at the museum to ________ our experience.** (enrich)
- **I use only Internet sites I know to avoid the ________ of incorrect information.** (risk)
- **Helena moved to a new city, so she and her friends ________ by e-mail.** (correspond)
- **Because I read the newspaper, my knowledge of current events is ________.** (expanding)

Lesson 3

Have students tell the part of speech of each vocabulary word. Write the heads *Nouns, Verbs,* and *Adjectives* on the board. List words under the correct headings. **A noun is a person, place, thing, or idea.** Show items around the classroom as you give examples of nouns, such as *table*. ***Motive*** **is a noun. Is a *motive* a person, place, thing, or idea?** (idea) Repeat the process with the noun *commerce*.

A verb is an action word. Act out or have volunteers act out examples of verbs, such as walk. ***Terminate*** **is a verb. If you *terminate* something, do you start it or stop it?** (stop it) Repeat the process with the verbs *impose* and *manage*.

An adjective is a word that describes a noun. Make your facial expressions show the meaning of examples of adjectives, such as *happy*. **The adjective *vicious* can describe different nouns. Would you describe a nice person as *vicious*?** (no) **Why not?** (*Vicious* means cruel and intending harm.)

Practice Vocabulary

In Lesson 2, provide support for the context words *aspects* and *social*. ***Aspects*** **are the qualities or parts of something. You may like some *aspects* of a place but dislike other aspects. What *aspects* of our school do you like? What aspects do you dislike?**

A *social* situation is a situation that involves spending time with people. When you are brushing your teeth, are you in a *social* situation? (no) **Why not?** (You are not spending time with other people.) Write the following sentence frame on the board: ________ *is a social situation.* (a party; a sporting event) **What is an example of a *social* situation?**

In Lesson 4, provide support for the context words *restrictions* and *merits*. ***Restrictions*** **are usually the things you are not allowed to do. What *restrictions* do we have in our school?** (no offensive language on clothing; no cell phones in class)

If a person *merits* a reward, that person deserves a reward. If someone worked very hard for a goal, would that person *merit* success? (yes)

Apply the Target Skill: Main Idea and Details/Summarize

In Lesson 4, some students may need additional practice identifying main idea and details. Blackline Master page 10 has an article about the Internet and submarines. Students are asked questions about the main idea of the article and the details that support it. Part B asks them to use the main idea and details to write a summary. Have students respond orally to the instructions in Part B before they write their summaries.

Friends or Foes?

Vocabulary

founders (n) *people who start or establish something*

correspond (v) *write to someone*

risk (n) *the chance of losing, failing, or getting hurt; danger*

Michelle recently joined a networking site. When she logged on, she found that a lot of her friends and classmates were already a part of this virtual community. They could use this seemingly real community to instantly catch up with one another during the weekend instead of waiting until Monday morning at school. **1** Through this online social network, people can "get together," communicate with others, share photographs, and meet new people. When Michelle got her hair cut one day after school, her friends didn't have to wait to see it at school the next day. They got to see it right away because she posted a photo of her new haircut as soon as she got home.

1 Context Clues
What does the word *virtual* mean? What clues help you discover the meaning?

2 Make Connections
How do you and your friends use networking sites?

The **founders** of one online networking site that connects people from all over the world said they wanted to make it easy for friends to catch up and hang out with each other online. Michelle was able to do this and meet new people on the site. Soon, she had friends all across the country. She said she likes to meet new people and **correspond** with them online. **2**

However, Michelle found there was a downside to this new form of communication. A guest speaker came to her school to talk about the **risk** of online networking. As she listened to him, she never imagined she would soon learn firsthand that the dangers are very real.

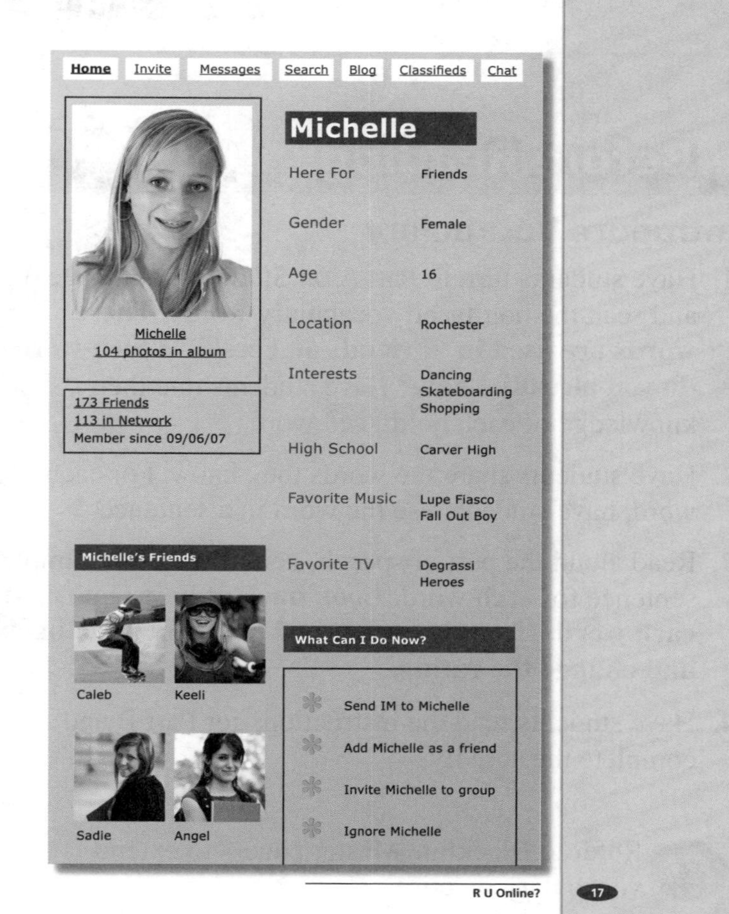

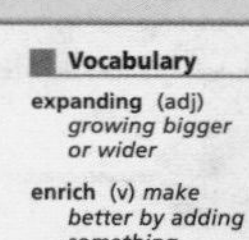

Vocabulary

expanding (adj) *growing bigger or wider*

enrich (v) *make better by adding something*

Before the end of the week, Michelle learned that some of the new friends in her **expanding** social network were not who they said they were. Michelle began corresponding with a young woman her age who had the same favorite band and liked horror films. One day Michelle's new friend said she wanted to buy something online but didn't have a credit card. So, she asked Michelle for her credit card number and promised to mail her a check to pay her back. Fortunately, Michelle had heard about this Internet scam from the guest speaker and knew she couldn't trust her new "friend." Michelle spent a few days chatting with a young man who said he was her age and loved the same music she did. A few days later, she tried to find him in an online yearbook search and learned he was much older. He wasn't a student at all; he was an adult with his own house and business. She told her parents in case they needed to alert the police and make them aware of the older man.

"I was lucky to figure this out before we became any closer," Michelle recalled. "There are a lot of creepy people out there. There is a risk they can turn into stalkers, or worse."

Michelle realized there were rewarding aspects, or features, of virtual communities. However, she learned to keep herself safe from people who might be lying about who they are. She also learned she should never give out personal information or take the risk of meeting her new friends in person. However, if she ever did decide to meet an online friend in person, she should tell her parents, bring along several trusted friends, and meet in a public place. **3**

3 Make Connections
What safe practices do you follow while using networking sites?

"Online networking is cool. It can really **enrich** your relationships and expand your circle of friends," she said. "You need to be really careful though. Enriching your life isn't as important as your personal safety." End

"Friends or Foes?"

Before Reading

Introduce Vocabulary

1. Have students turn to Part A on Student Book page 32 and scan the boldfaced vocabulary words. **These words are used in "Friends or Foes?" Which words do you already know?** Have students rate their knowledge of each boldfaced word.
2. Have students share the words they know. For each word, have students use the word in a sentence.
3. Read aloud the part of speech, definition, and example sentence for each word. **Look back at how you rated each word. If you know a word better now, go back and change the rating.**
4. Have students read the instructions for Part B and complete the activity.

Refer to Blackline Master page 8 to extend vocabulary practice.

Have students use the *Passport Reading Journeys* online technology component to practice and reinforce vocabulary and comprehension skills.

Introduce the Target Skill: Main Idea and Details

1. Tell students that the main idea is what the passage is mostly about, or the central point, and that important details support this main idea.
2. **People pay attention to main ideas and details all the time. For example, your history teacher announces an upcoming test. He or she may tell what it will cover and when it will be. The main idea is that there is a test soon. The details are when it will be and what it will cover.**
3. **There are two types of main ideas: explicit and implicit.** Explain that explicit main ideas are stated directly and implicit main ideas are implied, or indirectly stated. **You will learn to identify explicit main ideas first.**

Expedition 2, Lesson 1

Name ______________________ Date ____________

Vocabulary

"Friends or Foes?"

A. Put a check mark in each row to indicate how well you know each boldfaced word.

	Know This Word	Have Seen This Word	Don't Know This Word
founders (n) *people who start or establish something* Tom Anderson was one of the original *founders* of MySpace.			
correspond (v) *write to someone* We used to *correspond* by e-mail, but now we post messages on MySpace as a way of writing to each other.			
risk (n) *the chance of losing, failing, or getting hurt; danger* People who do not share personal information online want to avoid the *risk* of strangers knowing about them.			
expanding (adj) *growing bigger or wider* Tom Anderson now has an *expanding* circle of friends because of MySpace.			
enrich (v) *make better by adding something* Tom probably thinks joining MySpace will *enrich* your life because you can meet people from all over the world.			

B. Read each statement. Circle true or false.

1. The **founders** of a company are the people who started it. (true) false
2. If you **enrich** something, you remove something from it. true (false)
3. If something is a **risk**, it is safe. true (false)
4. One way to **correspond** with someone is to send an e-mail. (true) false
5. If something is **expanding**, it is shrinking. true (false)

©Voyager Expanded Learning, Inc. 32

Vocabulary

founders (n) *people who start or establish something*
Tom Anderson was one of the original *founders* of MySpace.

correspond (v) *write to someone*
We used to *correspond* by e-mail, but now we post messages on MySpace to each other as a way of writing.

risk (n) *the chance of losing, failing, or getting hurt; danger*
People who do not share personal information online want to avoid the *risk* of strangers knowing about them.

expanding (adj) *growing bigger or wider*
Tom Anderson now has an *expanding* circle of friends because of MySpace.

enrich (v) *make better by adding something*
Tom probably thinks joining MySpace will *enrich* your life because you can meet people from all over the world.

4. Have students turn to Anthology page 3 and read the first paragraph. **The explicit main idea, the central point that is directly stated in this paragraph, is "Your ethnic heritage can influence your looks."**

5. **How do the next sentences support the main idea?** (They tell how ethnic heritage influences looks.)

Introduce the Passage

1. Have students preview "Friends or Foes?" on Anthology page 16. Remind students that the Expedition is about the Internet. **Look at the title and the photos. What do you think this passage is about?** (online sites and some of the dangers of using the Internet)
2. Remind students to read the margin prompts. **These prompts will guide your thinking about the passage as you read. The vocabulary notes will remind you of the meanings of the new words you learned.**
3. Have students predict some of the information in the passage by saying: **You know this passage will be about the Internet. Who do you think could be friends online? Who could be foes?** Allow students to discuss their predictions.

During Reading

1. To select reading options that support your students' levels and classroom needs, see Reading Differentiation, page xxxii, if needed.
2. **As you read "Friends or Foes?" think about the main idea and the details that support it.**

After Reading

Check Comprehension

1. **Did your prediction match what you read in the passage?** Have students discuss their predictions and why they did or did not match what they read.
2. Reread the Context Clues margin prompt on Anthology page 16. Have students share responses. **What part of the text helped you figure out the meaning of the word *virtual*?** (seemingly real)
3. Have students share their responses to the Make Connections margin prompt on Anthology page 16. **How is your experience with sites like this one similar to or different from Michelle's experiences?** Allow students to discuss their experiences.
4. Review student responses to the Make Connections margin prompt on Anthology page 18.

   To make the most of the discussion time, remember to incorporate strategies that encourage and extend student involvement. Refer to page xxxviii for a comprehensive discussion of these strategies.
5. Have students look back at Anthology page 16. **The main idea is stated in each paragraph. Which sentence in the first paragraph states the main idea?** (Through this online social network, people can "get together," communicate with others, share photographs, and meet new people.)
6. **Find a detail that supports this main idea.** (Many of Michelle's friends and classmates are part of her online community.) **What are two other supporting details?** (Friends can share photographs. Classmates can catch up over the weekend.) Explain that students will find the main idea and details for the remaining paragraphs in the next lesson.

ACADEMIC SKILL Remind students that paying attention to main ideas and details will help them when they read textbooks. **The main idea of a section of a text will be supported by details.**

Remind students to choose books from the *Passport Reading Journeys* Library for independent reading.

"Friends or Foes?"

Prepare to Reread

Introduce the Lesson

Remind students they read about virtual communities in Lesson 1. **In this lesson, we'll revisit "Friends or Foes?" and identify main ideas and important details.**

Practice Vocabulary

1. Remind students of the vocabulary words from Lesson 1 and how they were used in the passage by asking the following questions.
    - **This passage mentions the *founders* of an online networking site. What else could have *founders*?** (a school; a club)
    - **Michelle can *correspond* with people online. Can people *correspond* another way?** (letters)
    - **In this passage, Michelle learns there is *risk* in online networking. What is one *risk* she discovers?** (identity theft)
    - **Michelle's social network is *expanding*. What is happening to her social network to make it *expand*?** (adding more friends)
    - **In this passage, Michelle says an online community can *enrich* your life. What is one way online communities *enrich* Michelle's life?** (make it easier to communicate with new friends)
2. Remind students they used context clues to find the meaning of the word *virtual*. Have students turn to Anthology page 18. **What do you think the word *aspects* means?** (features) **What clues in the text help you?** (The word *features* comes right after *aspects*.)

    Repeat this process for the following words.
    - **networking** (adj) *pertaining to a supportive system of sharing information among individuals*, Anthology page 16
    - **social** (adj) *characterized by friendly companionship or relations*, Anthology page 16
    - **scam** (n) *fraudulent scheme, especially for making a quick profit*, Anthology page 18
    - **alert** (v) *make aware*, Anthology page 18

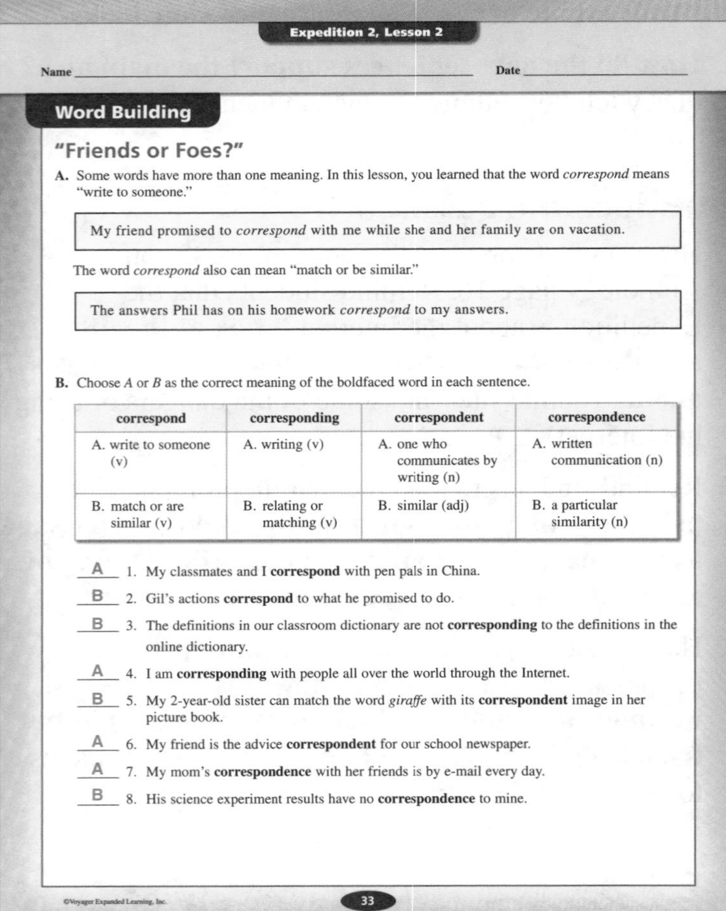

Expedition 2, Lesson 2

Name ______________________ Date ______________

Word Building

"Friends or Foes?"

A. Some words have more than one meaning. In this lesson, you learned that the word *correspond* means "write to someone."

My friend promised to *correspond* with me while she and her family are on vacation.

The word *correspond* also can mean "match or be similar."

The answers Phil has on his homework *correspond* to my answers.

B. Choose *A* or *B* as the correct meaning of the boldfaced word in each sentence.

correspond	corresponding	correspondent	correspondence
A. write to someone (v)	A. writing (v)	A. one who communicates by writing (n)	A. written communication (n)
B. match or are similar (v)	B. relating or matching (v)	B. similar (adj)	B. a particular similarity (n)

A 1. My classmates and I **correspond** with pen pals in China.
B 2. Gil's actions **correspond** to what he promised to do.
B 3. The definitions in our classroom dictionary are not **corresponding** to the definitions in the online dictionary.
A 4. I am **corresponding** with people all over the world through the Internet.
B 5. My 2-year-old sister can match the word *giraffe* with its **correspondent** image in her picture book.
A 6. My friend is the advice **correspondent** for our school newspaper.
A 7. My mom's **correspondence** with her friends is by e-mail every day.
B 8. His science experiment results have no **correspondence** to mine.

©Voyager Expanded Learning, Inc. 33

3. Have students turn to Student Book page 33. Read Part A aloud. Have students read the instructions for Part B and complete the page independently. Have partners compare their responses.

ELL Explain the definitions of the words used in context. Allow students to find clues in the text that support the definitions. Refer to English Language Learner Overview page 52 for more activities supporting these words.

Reread

Apply the Target Skill: Main Idea and Details

1. Remind students they practiced identifying the main idea and important details as they read in Lesson 1.

2. Students will identify the main idea and important details for each paragraph in the rest of the passage on Student Book page 34. Complete the diagram for paragraph 2 together.
3. Have students turn to Anthology page 16. **The main idea is stated in each paragraph. Which sentence in the second paragraph states the main idea?** (Social networking sites make it easy to catch up and hang out online.)
4. **Find a detail that supports this main idea.** (These sites connect people all over the world.) **What are two other supporting details?** (Michelle met new people on the site. She made friends from all over the country.)

ELL For students who have difficulty identifying main idea and details, read paragraphs aloud one at a time. Model finding the main idea with language, such as *I think the most important point is* _________.

Write in Response to Reading

1. Have students turn to Student Book page 35. **What risks in online networking does Michelle discover?** (Internet scams; people lying about their identities) Students will write advice to Michelle about how to avoid risks of online networking. Have students complete the activity independently.
2. When students finish writing, have partners share their advice.

EXPEDITION ORGANIZER **R U Online?**

Pause to have students turn to Student Book pages 30 and 31. Have students complete the following:

- Write answers or notes below one or more of the probing questions in Part A. Encourage students to write a question of their own.
- Think about the most important idea from "Friends or Foes?" and write it in the appropriate note in Part B.

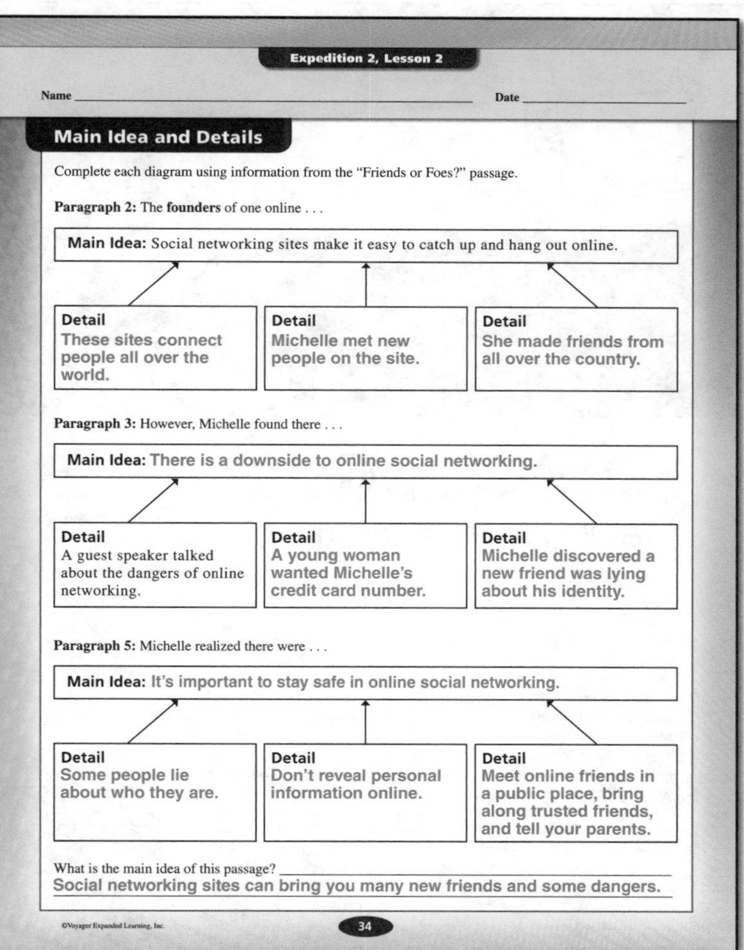

Expedition 2, Lesson 2

Name ______________________ Date __________

Main Idea and Details

Complete each diagram using information from the "Friends or Foes?" passage.

Paragraph 2: The **founders** of one online . . .

Main Idea: Social networking sites make it easy to catch up and hang out online.

Detail	Detail	Detail
These sites connect people all over the world.	Michelle met new people on the site.	She made friends from all over the country.

Paragraph 3: However, Michelle found there . . .

Main Idea: There is a downside to online social networking.

Detail	Detail	Detail
A guest speaker talked about the dangers of online networking.	A young woman wanted Michelle's credit card number.	Michelle discovered a new friend was lying about his identity.

Paragraph 5: Michelle realized there were . . .

Main Idea: It's important to stay safe in online social networking.

Detail	Detail	Detail
Some people lie about who they are.	Don't reveal personal information online.	Meet online friends in a public place, bring along trusted friends, and tell your parents.

What is the main idea of this passage? Social networking sites can bring you many new friends and some dangers.

©Voyager Expanded Learning, Inc. 34

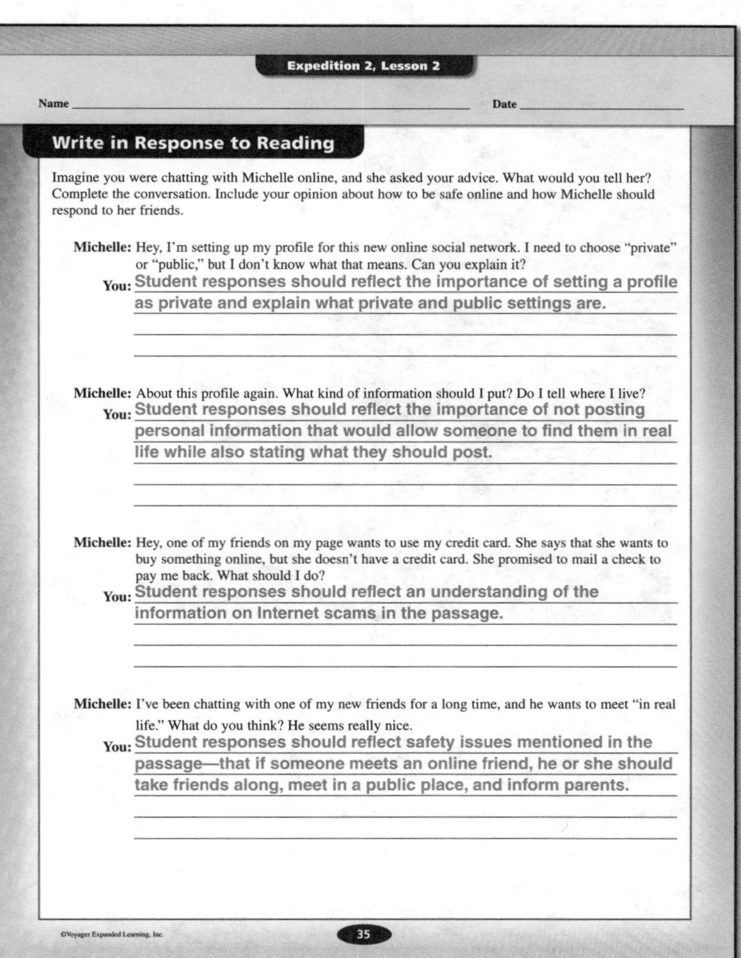

Expedition 2, Lesson 2

Name ______________________ Date __________

Write in Response to Reading

Imagine you were chatting with Michelle online, and she asked your advice. What would you tell her? Complete the conversation. Include your opinion about how to be safe online and how Michelle should respond to her friends.

Michelle: Hey, I'm setting up my profile for this new online social network. I need to choose "private" or "public," but I don't know what that means. Can you explain it?

You: Student responses should reflect the importance of setting a profile as private and explain what private and public settings are.

Michelle: About this profile again. What kind of information should I put? Do I tell where I live?

You: Student responses should reflect the importance of not posting personal information that would allow someone to find them in real life while also stating what they should post.

Michelle: Hey, one of my friends on my page wants to use my credit card. She says that she wants to buy something online, but she doesn't have a credit card. She promised to mail a check to pay me back. What should I do?

You: Student responses should reflect an understanding of the information on Internet scams in the passage.

Michelle: I've been chatting with one of my new friends for a long time, and he wants to meet "in real life." What do you think? He seems really nice.

You: Student responses should reflect safety issues mentioned in the passage—that if someone meets an online friend, he or she should take friends along, meet in a public place, and inform parents.

©Voyager Expanded Learning, Inc. 35

DotComGuy:
A Life Alone on the Internet

His name was Mitch Maddox, but he legally changed his name to DotComGuy. He decided not to leave his house for a full year. To begin his experiment, he moved into an empty house in Dallas, Texas. He brought nothing with him. UPS delivered his computer less than an hour after he walked into the empty house.

Why did he **terminate** his face-to-face interactions with the outside world? What was his **motive**? It was the year 2000, and Mitch was a 26-year-old systems manager. He wanted to **impose** this confinement upon himself to prove something. He would prove that he could **manage** with only a computer to access the outside world. He said he was motivated to show the world how all-embracing electronic **commerce**, or e-commerce, had become.

In January 2000, DotComGuy began his project by setting up his home with his laptop. For an entire year, he imposed the following rule upon himself: He would use only his computer to get everything he needed. He ordered absolutely everything he needed online. He purchased furniture and dishes for his home, books to read, and even all his groceries online. 1 He communicated with people who

Vocabulary

terminate (v) *bring to an end; stop*

motive (n) *reason that makes a person do something*

impose (v) *set as something that has to be paid, obeyed, or fulfilled*

manage (v) *succeed in getting something done*

commerce (n) *the buying and selling of goods; trade*

1 Visualize
Imagine your house without anything in it. What would you need to buy online so you could live in it for one year?

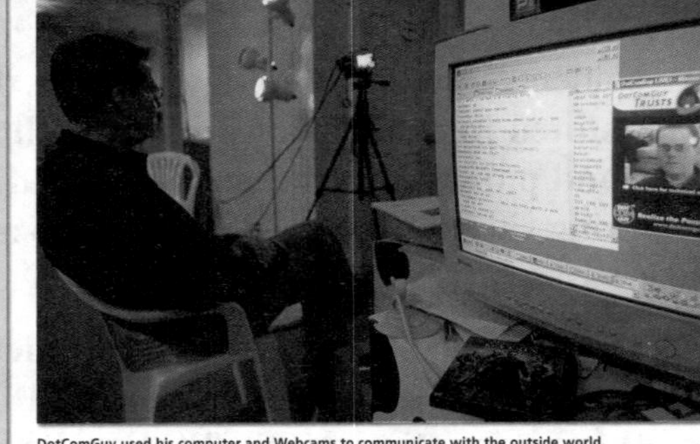
DotComGuy used his computer and Webcams to communicate with the outside world.

wrote to him on his Web site. People everywhere could watch him on their computers because he installed cameras all over his house. He turned them off only when he went to sleep or to the bathroom. Friends and family would stop by, and he gave interviews for the media. He even had a personal trainer who visited regularly, but DotComGuy never left his house.

Why did he choose to impose these restrictions on himself? DotComGuy said he did it "to show people the extreme possibilities of the Internet." He said he also wanted people "to go watch my experiences, learn from them, and also discuss e-commerce." 2

After the year ended, he returned to the outside world, not much the worse for wear. He posted a farewell message on his Web site that read, "It's been a great year everyone. Now it is time for DotComGuy to re-enter society." When he reflected back on the year, he admitted he'd been bored now and then. But, he claimed he never felt desperate or unhappy or trapped. On the other hand, after he terminated his project, he returned to his old life, took his original name back, and has not repeated the experiment.

As Mitch proved, you certainly can manage to live without going to the store. E-commerce has made that possible. But, is it a good idea? The Internet allows people to make new friends around the world and keep in touch with distant family members. However, for many users,

2 Make Connections
If you performed DotComGuy's experiment, what would you miss the most?

DotComGuy even installed cameras in his bathroom.

DotComGuy ordered everything for living in his home on the computer and had it delivered to his house.

it may be replacing important day-to-day human interactions.

Today, computers are an important part of everyday life. Many people spend time each day in front of their monitors. They e-mail, shop, play games, listen to music, and chat with friends. But, they do it alone. Instead of face-to-face contact, people are isolating themselves from the world by spending their time with their computers. 3 Terminating face-to-face contact with others may become a huge problem.

Mental health professionals and observers have noted this growing trend with alarm. Computer addicts distance themselves from their families, their friends, and the world at large. Because computer addicts all behave in similar ways, some

3 Context Clues
What clues in this sentence help you determine the meaning of *isolating*?

Vocabulary

vicious (adj) *meant to harm; cruel*

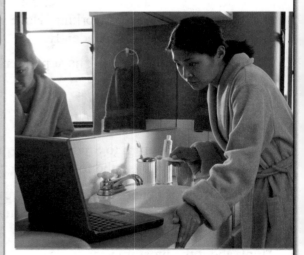

psychologists think that computer addiction should be a recognized syndrome, and many studies have been written about it. Computer addicts are less and less motivated to spend time with family and friends. Their computers become their most important companions.

Computer addiction can be a **vicious** cycle; the less contact computer addicts have with flesh-and-blood human beings, the more difficult such contact becomes for them. Their social skills weaken, and any fears they have concerning the outside world get bigger and less manageable. Experts claim that excessive Internet use can lead to depression, isolation, and failure at work or school.

The key to solving this growing problem is finding the right balance and learning how to manage your time. However, there are a growing number of computer addicts that represent the dark side of the constantly changing computer world. Many feel this dark side merits serious examination and is worthy of concern. Human beings are by nature social animals. Just because it's possible to exist without regular human contact does not mean it's a good idea. 4 End

4 Ask Questions
After reading this passage, what questions would you like to ask DotComGuy?

"DotComGuy: A Life Alone on the Internet"

Before Reading

Introduce Vocabulary

1. Have students turn to Student Book page 36 and scan the boldfaced vocabulary words. **You will read these words in "DotComGuy: A Life Alone on the Internet." How familiar is each of these words?** Have students rate their knowledge of each word.
2. Have students share which words they know. For each word, have students use the word in a sentence.
3. Read aloud the part of speech, definition, and example sentence for each word.
4. Have students read the instructions for Part B and complete the activity.

Refer to Blackline Master page 9 to extend vocabulary practice.

Have students use the *Passport Reading Journeys* online technology component to practice and reinforce vocabulary and comprehension skills.

Expedition 2, Lesson 3

Name ______ Date ______

Vocabulary

"DotComGuy: A Life Alone on the Internet"

A. Rate your knowledge of each boldfaced vocabulary word.
3 familiar
2 somewhat familiar
1 unknown word

- **terminate** (v) *bring to an end; stop*
  He decided to *terminate* all personal contact with stores and only shop online.
- **motive** (n) *reason that makes a person do something*
  What was your *motive* for talking to your friends only by computer?
- **impose** (v) *set as something that has to be paid, obeyed, or fulfilled*
  It was good for DotComGuy to *impose* his strange experiment on himself and not on me.
- **manage** (v) *succeed in getting something done*
  I tried not to laugh at my brother's haircut, but I couldn't *manage* it.
- **commerce** (n) *the buying and selling of goods; trade*
  The Internet has active *commerce* every day, and some businesses make a lot of money from it.
- **vicious** (adj) *meant to harm; cruel*
  Limiting contact with people might create a *vicious* cycle that causes you to lose contact with friends.

B. Complete each sentence with the correct vocabulary word from Part A.

1. The new principal will impose strict rules about Internet use in school.
2. The convenience of shopping online has contributed to an increase in Internet commerce.
3. The business partners decided to terminate their agreement and close the business.
4. There was a vicious rumor posted on an Internet site about my favorite singer, but it was not true.
5. My motive for writing a blog while I am on vacation is that I want to let my friends know what I am doing.
6. Even when I am busy, I manage to keep in touch with my friends through online networking.

 36

Introduce the Target Skill: Main Idea and Details/Summarize

1. Remind students that the main idea is the central point and important details support the main idea.
2. **Finding the main idea and details can help you summarize the text. When you summarize, you briefly restate in your own words what the text was about. An example of giving a summary from the main idea and details is when you tell a friend about a TV show or movie you watched.**
3. **When you summarize, it is important to tell the most important information and not every detail.** Have partners take 2 minutes to tell each other about a TV show they have seen recently. Ask students whether they could tell what the show was about based on their partner's summary.

Vocabulary

terminate (v) *bring to an end; stop*
He decided to *terminate* all personal contact with stores and only shop online.

motive (n) *reason that makes a person do something*
What was your *motive* for talking to your friends only by computer?

impose (v) *set as something that has to be paid, obeyed, or fulfilled*
It was good for DotComGuy to *impose* his strange experiment on himself and not on me.

manage (v) *succeed in getting something done*
I tried not to laugh at my brother's haircut, but I couldn't *manage* it.

commerce (n) *the buying and selling of goods; trade*
The Internet has active *commerce* every day, and some businesses make a lot of money from it.

vicious (adj) *meant to harm; cruel*
Limiting contact with people might create a *vicious* cycle that causes you to lose contact with friends.

Introduce the Passage

1. Have students preview "DotComGuy: A Life Alone on the Internet." **Read the title and look at the photos.** Explain that this passage is about a person who chose to live "alone on the Internet" without leaving his house. **Why do you think this person chose to live "alone on the Internet"? How long do you think he did this?** Have students discuss their predictions.
2. Remind students to pause to read the margin prompts. **Think about these prompts as you read the passage.**
3. Teach this term from the passage:
    - *Not much the worse for wear* means "not harmed in any way."

During Reading

1. To select reading options that support your students' levels and classroom needs, see Reading Differentiation, page xxxii, if needed.
2. Have students read the passage, paying attention to main ideas and details of the paragraphs.

After Reading

Check Comprehension

1. **What was DotComGuy's reason for living "alone on the Internet"? Does this match your prediction?** (He wanted to demonstrate that commerce over the Internet is quite powerful.)
2. **According to the passage, what are some dangers of relying on the Internet too much?** (distance from family and friends; depression; isolation) Write student responses on the board.
3. Have students share their responses to the Visualize margin prompt on Anthology page 19. **What did you picture when you imagined your home without anything in it? What is one thing you would want to buy right away?** Allow students to brainstorm their ideas.
4. Reread the Ask Questions margin prompt on Anthology page 22. **What questions would you like to ask? What part of the text sparked those questions?**

Whenever possible, provide elaborative feedback to student responses. Refer to page xl for examples of elaborative feedback and how to incorporate it in your lessons.

ELL If students have trouble thinking of questions to ask DotComGuy, write *who, what, where, when, why,* and *how* on the board. Model asking a question, such as *What did you miss the most?*

5. Have students turn to Anthology page 19. Work with students to find the main idea and supporting details of paragraph 2. Record student responses on the board. (Main idea: He said he was motivated to show the world how all-embracing electronic commerce, or e-commerce, had become. Supporting details: He terminated his face-to-face interactions. He wanted to prove he could manage with only a computer.)
6. Have students summarize the paragraph. To help them keep their summaries brief, have students imagine that each word used in the summary costs a dollar. Challenge students to see who can write the most effective, but least expensive summary. (Possible summary: DotComGuy wanted to prove how all-embracing e-commerce is by terminating face-to-face contact and using only a computer.)

ACADEMIC SKILL Remind students that paying attention to main ideas and details will help them summarize when they read textbooks. **Summarizing can be helpful when you are studying or trying to learn something new.**

Remind students to choose books from the *Passport Reading Journeys* Library for independent reading.

"DotComGuy: A Life Alone on the Internet"

Prepare to Reread

Introduce the Lesson

Remind students that they read about DotComGuy in Lesson 3. **In this lesson, we'll revisit the passage to look at important details and the main idea.**

Practice Vocabulary

1. Ask the following questions to remind students of the vocabulary words from Lesson 3. Encourage students to use the vocabulary words in their responses.
   - **What did DotComGuy *impose* on himself?** (He imposed his confinement.)
   - **What did DotComGuy *terminate*?** (He terminated face-to-face interactions with the outside world.)
   - **DotComGuy used electronic *commerce* for a year. What does that mean?** (He only bought things online.)
   - **What was DotComGuy's *motive* for this experiment?** (His motive was to show how powerful e-commerce had become.)
   - **What did DotComGuy prove he could *manage*?** (He could manage to live with only a computer for commerce and communication for a year.)
   - **According to this passage, who could be caught in a *vicious* cycle?** (computer addicts)
2. Remind students they can use context clues to find the meanings of new words. Have students turn to Anthology page 19. Reread the second paragraph. **What do you think the word *confinement* means?** (being held or restricted to a limited space or area) **What clues in the text help you?** (Sentences earlier in the passage describe his situation.)

   Repeat this process for the following words.
   - **restrictions** (n) *rules*, Anthology page 20
   - **syndrome** (n) *a group of symptoms that together are characteristics of a specific disorder*, Anthology page 22
   - **companions** (n) *one that keeps company with another*, Anthology page 22
   - **merits** (v) *deserves; needs*, Anthology page 22

Expedition 2, Lesson 4

Name ______ Date ______

Word Building

"DotComGuy: A Life Alone on the Internet"

A. Many words have Greek or Latin roots. You've learned that the word *terminate* means "bring to an end." The Latin root *term* means "boundary, limit, or end." Read other words that use the root *term*. Knowing which part of speech each word is will help you use it correctly in a sentence.

terminate (v) *bring to an end*
The teacher might *terminate* your Internet access rights if she finds you playing online games.

term (n) *a limited or definite extent of time*
Our science class will go outside to launch the rockets we made during the spring *term*.

terminal (adj) *leading to death; fatal*
Luckily, the doctors do not think his cancer is *terminal* and will start treatment immediately.

termination (n) *an end or conclusion*
We were disappointed at the *termination* of our favorite television show.

terminology (n) *technical or special words that are limited to a particular subject*
That novel contains a lot of science *terminology* that is difficult for me to understand.

B. Complete each sentence with one of the words from Part A. Consider which part of speech is needed for the missing word.

1. I will take a computer class next term at school.
2. Julio decided to terminate his membership to that online community.
3. Computer terminology is hard for me to understand because some words sound odd.
4. After the termination of his subscription to *All Star Soccer* magazine, Mark would read soccer articles online.
5. Shantelle reassured her worried little brother that chicken pox was not a terminal disease.

C. Choose the correct usage of the multiple-meaning words in the sentences.

term	**terminal**
A. a limited or definite extent of time	A. leading to death; fatal
B. word or phrase	B. a main station for trains, airplanes, or buses

B 1. I'll meet you at the bus **terminal**.
A 2. That actor played the part of a man with a **terminal** disease.
B 3. I told my mother I was updating my blog, but she didn't understand the **term** *blog*.
A 4. Does the spring **term** end in May or June?

 37

ELL Provide extra support for students by telling them the definition of the words used in context. Allow them to find the context clues in the text that support the definition.

3. Have students turn to Student Book page 37. **Many words have Greek or Latin roots. The word *terminate* uses the Latin root *term*.** Read Part A and the instructions for Parts B and C aloud. Have students complete the page, then compare their answers with a partner.

CHECKPOINT After students complete Part B, have them identify one item that was difficult. Have students explain how they used the meaning of *term* or another clue in the sentence to determine the correct answer.

Reread

Apply the Target Skill: Main Idea and Details/Summarize

1. Remind students they practiced identifying the main idea and important details of paragraphs and using those to create a summary. **Readers can use these main ideas to create a summary of an entire text.**
2. Have students turn to Anthology page 19. **Each paragraph of this passage has a main idea that is stated directly.**
3. Have students turn to Student Book page 38 and read the Part A instructions. Have students complete the activity.
4. If students have difficulty, ask: **What is the paragraph mostly about? Which sentence contains that main idea?**
5. Read aloud the instructions for Part B. Have students complete the activity.

Refer to Blackline Master page 10 to extend practice writing summaries.

Write in Response to Reading

1. Have students turn to Student Book page 39. Read aloud the Part A instructions. Have partners write an interview with DotComGuy. Have students share their responses.
2. **How do you think DotComGuy prepared for his year in an empty house? How would you prepare for an experiment like this?** Have students complete Part B and share their lists with a partner.

EXPEDITION ORGANIZER **R U Online?**

Pause to have students turn to Student Book pages 30 and 31. Have students complete the following:

- Write answers or notes below one or more of the probing questions. If they have not yet added a question of their own, encourage them to add one.
- Think about the main idea from "DotComGuy: A Life Alone on the Internet" and write it in the appropriate note.

Expedition 2, Lesson 4

Name ______ Date ______

Main Idea and Details

A. Write the directly stated main idea of each paragraph in the box. The first one is done for you.

Main Idea Paragraph 2: He said he was motivated to show the world how all-embracing electronic commerce, or e-commerce, had become.

Main Idea Paragraph 3: He would use only his computer to get everything he needed.

Main Idea Paragraph 4: DotComGuy said he did it "to show people the extreme possibilities of the Internet."

Main Idea Paragraph 5: After he terminated his project, he returned to his old life, took his original name back, and has not repeated the experiment.

Main Idea Paragraph 6: For many users, it [the Internet] may be replacing important day-to-day human interactions.

Main Idea Paragraph 7: Instead of face-to-face contact, people are isolating themselves from the world by spending their time with their computers.

Main Idea Paragraph 8: Computer addiction should be a recognized syndrome.

Main Idea Paragraph 9: Computer addiction can be a vicious cycle.

Main Idea Paragraph 10: The key to solving this growing problem is finding the right balance and learning how to manage your time.

B. Use the statements in Part A to write a three- to five-sentence summary of "DotComGuy: A Life Alone on the Internet."

Student responses should include three main points: DotComGuy isolated himself with the Internet to show the power of e-commerce and the possibilities of the Internet; computer addiction can be a serious problem; and it's important to find a balance between computer usage and human interaction.

 38

Expedition 2, Lesson 4

Name ______ Date ______

Write in Response to Reading

A. If you could interview DotComGuy, what would you ask him? How do you think he would respond? Write an interview between a reporter and DotComGuy.

Reporter: Student responses should reflect an engagement with the passage.

DotComGuy: ______

Reporter: ______

DotComGuy: ______

Reporter: ______

DotComGuy: ______

Reporter: ______

DotComGuy: ______

Reporter: ______

DotComGuy: ______

B. Imagine you had to live for a year with only your computer. How would you prepare? What would you do? Make a To Do list.

Before the Year Begins	During the Year	When the Year Ends
Student responses should reflect an understanding of DotComGuy's experiment, especially the fact that he relied on the Internet completely.		

 39

Review, Extend, Assess

In today's lesson, as in Lessons 5 and 10 of every Expedition, there are options from which to choose. You may do any or all of the options listed. Activities for each option are given on the following pages. Each option will support or extend previously taught objectives. Choose the option(s) appropriate for your students and prepare accordingly.

Review Vocabulary

Extend Vocabulary

Assess Comprehension and Vocabulary

Reteach

Passport Reading Journeys Library

Online Technology Component

Writing Process

Real-World Reading

Exploring Careers

Review Vocabulary

Direct students to review the vocabulary for "Friends or Foes?" and "DotComGuy: A Life Alone on the Internet" on Student Book page 31.

1. Have students turn to Student Book page 40. Read the instructions aloud for Parts A and B.
2. **As you complete the review activity, go back and check the definitions to ensure you used the words correctly.** Remind students the definitions are on Student Book page 31. Have students complete the activity. When all students finish, have them share their answers.

CHECKPOINT Have students share their responses for Part B. If student responses vary, have them explain reasons for their choices.

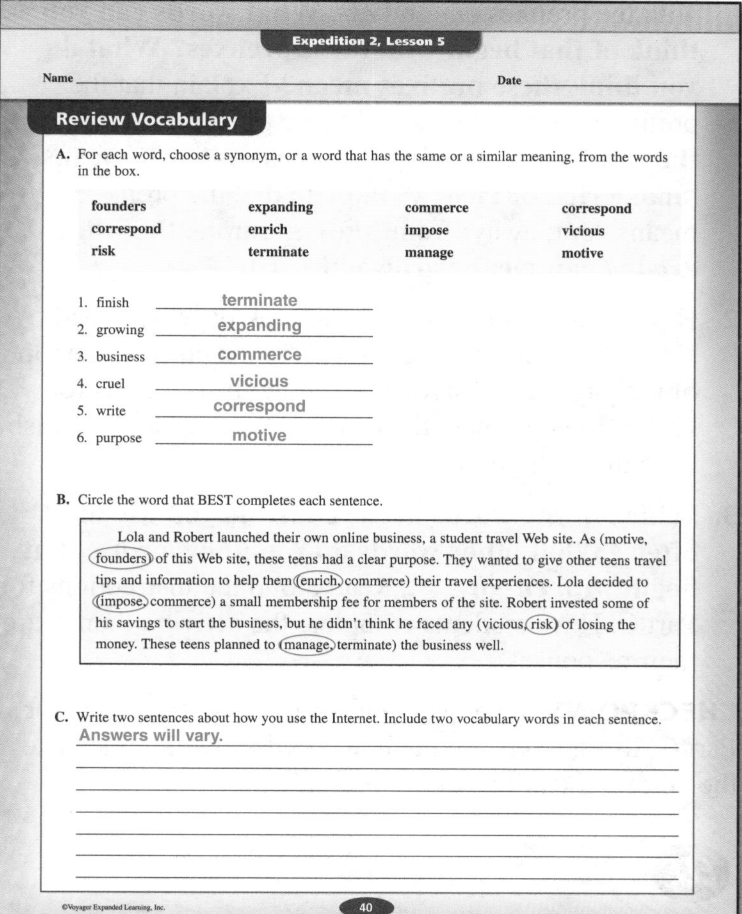

Expedition 2, Lesson 5

Name ______________________ Date ______________

Review Vocabulary

A. For each word, choose a synonym, or a word that has the same or a similar meaning, from the words in the box.

founders	expanding	commerce	correspond
correspond	enrich	impose	vicious
risk	terminate	manage	motive

1. finish terminate
2. growing expanding
3. business commerce
4. cruel vicious
5. write correspond
6. purpose motive

B. Circle the word that BEST completes each sentence.

Lola and Robert launched their own online business, a student travel Web site. As (motive, founders) of this Web site, these teens had a clear purpose. They wanted to give other teens travel tips and information to help them (enrich, commerce) their travel experiences. Lola decided to (impose, commerce) a small membership fee for members of the site. Robert invested some of his savings to start the business, but he didn't think he faced any (vicious, risk) of losing the money. These teens planned to (manage, terminate) the business well.

C. Write two sentences about how you use the Internet. Include two vocabulary words in each sentence.
Answers will vary.

©Voyager Expanded Learning, Inc. 40

Extend Vocabulary

1. Tell students they will work with words that begin with the prefixes *en-* and *ex-*. **What words can you think of that begin with these prefixes? What do you think these prefixes mean?** Explain that the prefix *en-* means "make or cause to." **For example, the word *enrich* begins with this prefix. It means "make rich or richer."** Explain that the prefix *ex-* means "out; away; from." **For example, the word *expand* can mean "grow outward."**
2. Have students turn to Student Book page 41. Read aloud the words and definitions in the chart at the top of the page. Have students read the instructions for Part B and complete the activity. When students finish, have them share their answers.
3. **Which of the words in the chart do you use most often? What other words do you know or use that begin with *en-* or *ex-*?** Read aloud the instructions for Part C. Have students complete the activity, then share their responses.

CHECKPOINT When students share their responses for Part C, listen to ensure the new words they included use the correct meanings of the prefixes.

Part A

1. Distribute eight index cards to each student and have them write one word from the chart on each.
2. Have students write or draw a clue for each word on the cards. Model writing clues. ***Enforce* means "cause to be obeyed." I know that police officers *enforce* the law. I'll write that sentence on the card: Police officers *enforce* the law.**

Part B

Read the instructions for Part B. Then read the sentences. Have students show the card that best completes each sentence. If students have trouble providing the correct card, give them two choices. Read the sentence using both the correct choice and the incorrect choice and ask them which makes sense.

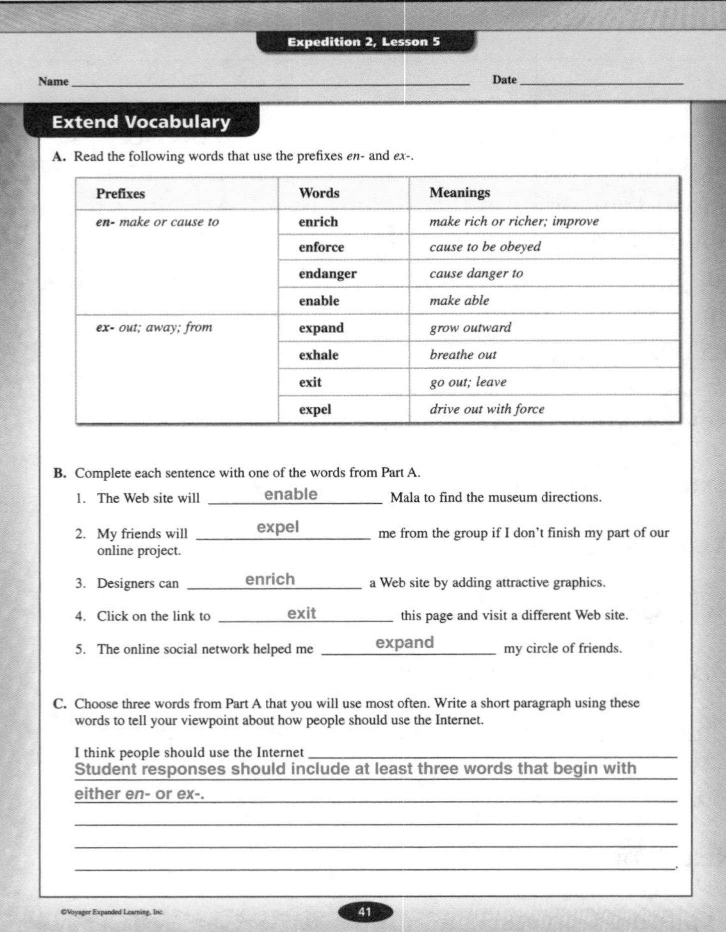

Expedition 2, Lesson 5

Name ______________________ Date ____________

Extend Vocabulary

A. Read the following words that use the prefixes *en-* and *ex-*.

Prefixes	Words	Meanings
en- *make or cause to*	**enrich**	*make rich or richer; improve*
	enforce	*cause to be obeyed*
	endanger	*cause danger to*
	enable	*make able*
ex- *out; away; from*	**expand**	*grow outward*
	exhale	*breathe out*
	exit	*go out; leave*
	expel	*drive out with force*

B. Complete each sentence with one of the words from Part A.

1. The Web site will ___enable___ Mala to find the museum directions.
2. My friends will ___expel___ me from the group if I don't finish my part of our online project.
3. Designers can ___enrich___ a Web site by adding attractive graphics.
4. Click on the link to ___exit___ this page and visit a different Web site.
5. The online social network helped me ___expand___ my circle of friends.

C. Choose three words from Part A that you will use most often. Write a short paragraph using these words to tell your viewpoint about how people should use the Internet.

I think people should use the Internet ___
Student responses should include at least three words that begin with either *en-* or *ex-*.

©Voyager Expanded Learning, Inc. 41

Part C

1. Before students choose their words, have them rate each word from 1 to 3. Words that receive a 1 are words the student has never seen before. Words that receive a 2 are words the student has heard but is not sure about. Words that receive a 3 are words the student uses in conversation or in school.
2. Have students choose words that received a 2 or 3 for the activity. If students do not have enough words rated 2 or 3, have them look at the clues they wrote on the index cards and choose words with the most helpful clues.

Assess Comprehension and Vocabulary

1. Remind students they have practiced identifying main ideas that were directly stated and supporting details. **It is important to notice details that support the main idea of a paragraph to understand what you read. Paying attention to the main idea of each paragraph can help you write a summary of the entire text.**
2. Have students turn to Student Book pages 42–44. Read aloud the instructions. Have students complete the assessment.

   Review student answers. Whenever possible, provide elaborative feedback to student responses. Refer to page xl for examples of elaborative feedback and how to incorporate it in your lessons.

   If students incorrectly answer more than 4 out of 15 assessment questions, evaluate what kind of reteaching is needed. If students miss vocabulary questions, have them return to the vocabulary activities and work with the words they missed. If students have trouble with main idea and details, use the reteaching suggestions on page 66.

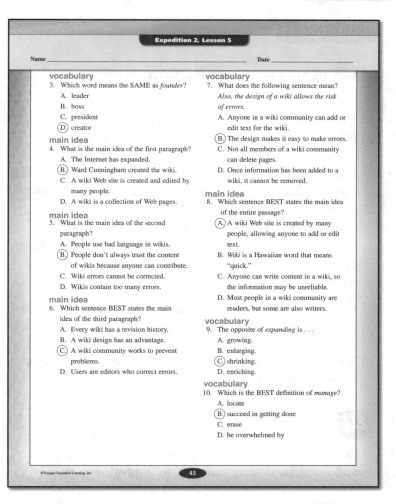

Expedition 2, Lesson 5

Name ______________________ Date ____________

vocabulary

3. Which word means the SAME as *founder*?
   A. leader
   B. boss
   C. president
   (D.) creator

main idea

4. What is the main idea of the first paragraph?
   A. The Internet has expanded.
   (B.) Ward Cunningham created the wiki.
   C. A wiki Web site is created and edited by many people.
   D. A wiki is a collection of Web pages.

main idea

5. What is the main idea of the second paragraph?
   A. People use bad language in wikis.
   (B.) People don't always trust the content of wikis because anyone can contribute.
   C. Wiki errors cannot be corrected.
   D. Wikis contain too many errors.

main idea

6. Which sentence BEST states the main idea of the third paragraph?
   A. Every wiki has a revision history.
   B. A wiki design has an advantage.
   (C.) A wiki community works to prevent problems.
   D. Users are editors who correct errors.

vocabulary

7. What does the following sentence mean?
   Also, the design of a wiki allows the risk of errors.
   A. Anyone in a wiki community can add or edit text for the wiki.
   (B.) The design makes it easy to make errors.
   C. Not all members of a wiki community can delete pages.
   D. Once information has been added to a wiki, it cannot be removed.

main idea

8. Which sentence BEST states the main idea of the entire passage?
   (A.) A wiki Web site is created by many people, allowing anyone to add or edit text.
   B. *Wiki* is a Hawaiian word that means "quick."
   C. Anyone can write content in a wiki, so the information may be unreliable.
   D. Most people in a wiki community are readers, but some are also writers.

vocabulary

9. The opposite of *expanding* is . . .
   A. growing.
   B. enlarging.
   (C.) shrinking.
   D. enriching.

vocabulary

10. Which is the BEST definition of *manage*?
    A. locate
    (B.) succeed in getting done
    C. erase
    D. be overwhelmed by

©Voyager Expanded Learning, Inc. 43

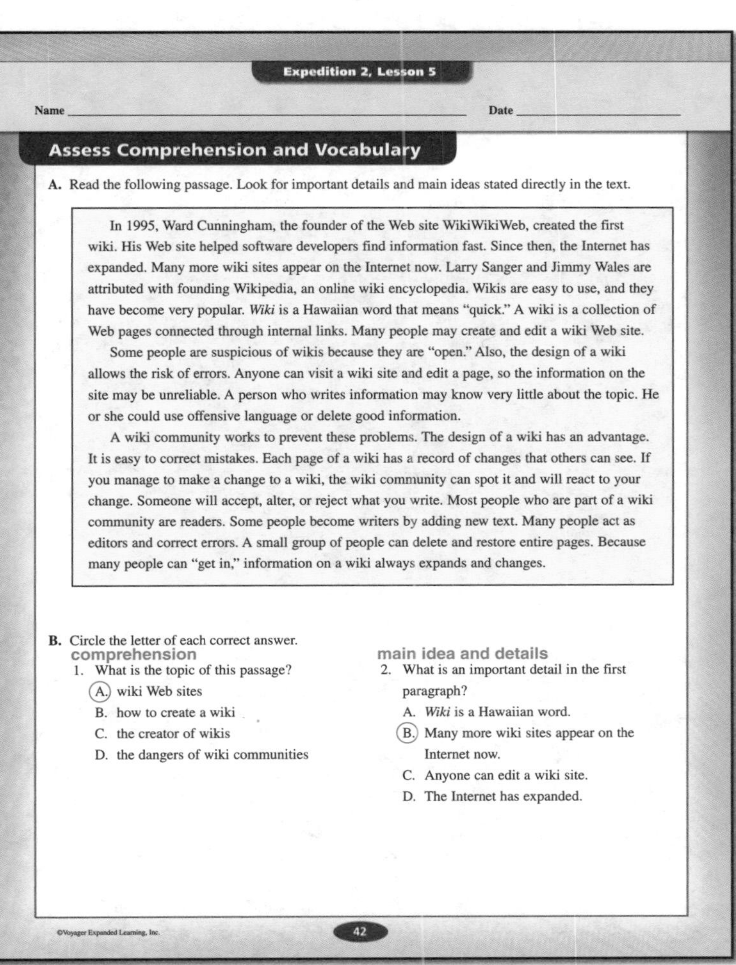
Expedition 2, Lesson 5

Name ______________________ Date ____________

Assess Comprehension and Vocabulary

A. Read the following passage. Look for important details and main ideas stated directly in the text.

In 1995, Ward Cunningham, the founder of the Web site WikiWikiWeb, created the first wiki. His Web site helped software developers find information fast. Since then, the Internet has expanded. Many more wiki sites appear on the Internet now. Larry Sanger and Jimmy Wales are attributed with founding Wikipedia, an online wiki encyclopedia. Wikis are easy to use, and they have become very popular. *Wiki* is a Hawaiian word that means "quick." A wiki is a collection of Web pages connected through internal links. Many people may create and edit a wiki Web site.

Some people are suspicious of wikis because they are "open." Also, the design of a wiki allows the risk of errors. Anyone can visit a wiki site and edit a page, so the information on the site may be unreliable. A person who writes information may know very little about the topic. He or she could use offensive language or delete good information.

A wiki community works to prevent these problems. The design of a wiki has an advantage. It is easy to correct mistakes. Each page of a wiki has a record of changes that others can see. If you manage to make a change to a wiki, the wiki community can spot it and will react to your change. Someone will accept, alter, or reject what you write. Most people who are part of a wiki community are readers. Some people become writers by adding new text. Many people act as editors and correct errors. A small group of people can delete and restore entire pages. Because many people can "get in," information on a wiki always expands and changes.

B. Circle the letter of each correct answer.

comprehension

1. What is the topic of this passage?
   (A.) wiki Web sites
   B. how to create a wiki
   C. the creator of wikis
   D. the dangers of wiki communities

main idea and details

2. What is an important detail in the first paragraph?
   A. *Wiki* is a Hawaiian word.
   (B.) Many more wiki sites appear on the Internet now.
   C. Anyone can edit a wiki site.
   D. The Internet has expanded.

©Voyager Expanded Learning, Inc. 42

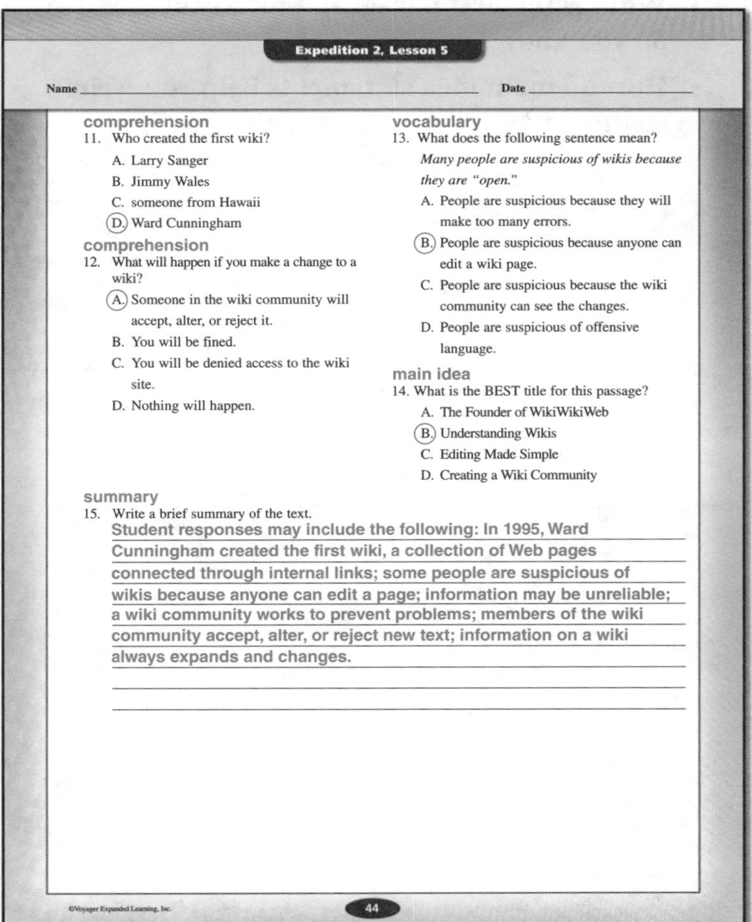
Expedition 2, Lesson 5

Name ______________________ Date ____________

comprehension

11. Who created the first wiki?
    A. Larry Sanger
    B. Jimmy Wales
    C. someone from Hawaii
    (D.) Ward Cunningham

comprehension

12. What will happen if you make a change to a wiki?
    (A.) Someone in the wiki community will accept, alter, or reject it.
    B. You will be fined.
    C. You will be denied access to the wiki site.
    D. Nothing will happen.

vocabulary

13. What does the following sentence mean?
    Many people are suspicious of wikis because they are "open."
    A. People are suspicious because they will make too many errors.
    (B.) People are suspicious because anyone can edit a wiki page.
    C. People are suspicious because the wiki community can see the changes.
    D. People are suspicious of offensive language.

main idea

14. What is the BEST title for this passage?
    A. The Founder of WikiWikiWeb
    (B.) Understanding Wikis
    C. Editing Made Simple
    D. Creating a Wiki Community

summary

15. Write a brief summary of the text.
    Student responses may include the following: In 1995, Ward Cunningham created the first wiki, a collection of Web pages connected through internal links; some people are suspicious of wikis because anyone can edit a page; information may be unreliable; a wiki community works to prevent problems; members of the wiki community accept, alter, or reject new text; information on a wiki always expands and changes.

©Voyager Expanded Learning, Inc. 44

Reteach

Main Idea and Details/Summarize

1. Have students turn to Student Book page 45. Read the passage aloud. **What is the topic of this passage?** (an organization called Teens for Technology) **Look back at the first paragraph. Each sentence has information. What information do you think is the most important? What main idea do these details support? Underline the sentence in the text that states the main idea.** Have students complete the activity. If students have difficulty, provide them with two or three words to begin each answer.
2. Have students share their responses. Write the most common responses on the board. **Use these details and main ideas to write a summary of the passage. Your summary should be three to five sentences long.** Have partners share their summaries.

ELL Focus on finding main idea statements in the text to reteach main idea and details for students who had difficulty with the skill. Read the article aloud and confirm student answers to the following:

- **What is the first paragraph mostly about? How do you know?**
- **How do main idea statements help you write a summary?**

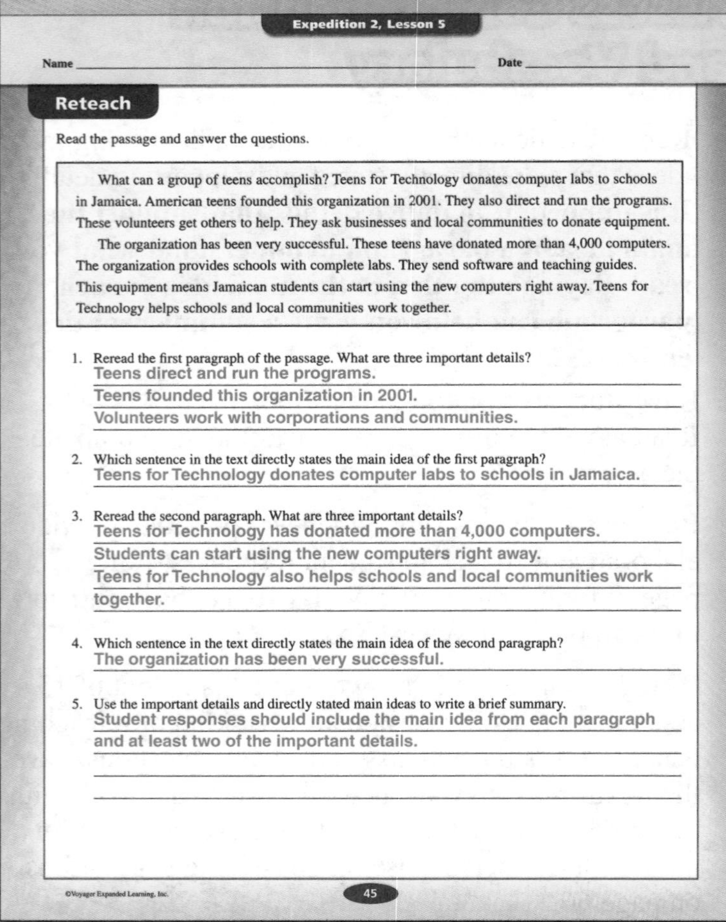

Expedition 2, Lesson 5

Name ____________ Date ____________

Reteach

Read the passage and answer the questions.

What can a group of teens accomplish? Teens for Technology donates computer labs to schools in Jamaica. American teens founded this organization in 2001. They also direct and run the programs. These volunteers get others to help. They ask businesses and local communities to donate equipment.

The organization has been very successful. These teens have donated more than 4,000 computers. The organization provides schools with complete labs. They send software and teaching guides. This equipment means Jamaican students can start using the new computers right away. Teens for Technology helps schools and local communities work together.

1. Reread the first paragraph of the passage. What are three important details?
   Teens direct and run the programs.
   Teens founded this organization in 2001.
   Volunteers work with corporations and communities.
2. Which sentence in the text directly states the main idea of the first paragraph?
   Teens for Technology donates computer labs to schools in Jamaica.
3. Reread the second paragraph. What are three important details?
   Teens for Technology has donated more than 4,000 computers.
   Students can start using the new computers right away.
   Teens for Technology also helps schools and local communities work together.
4. Which sentence in the text directly states the main idea of the second paragraph?
   The organization has been very successful.
5. Use the important details and directly stated main ideas to write a brief summary.
   Student responses should include the main idea from each paragraph and at least two of the important details.

45

Passport Reading Journeys Library

1. Have students choose reading material from the *Passport Reading Journeys* Library or another approved selection. If students have not finished a previously chosen selection, they may continue reading from that selection. See the *Passport Reading Journeys* Library Teacher's Guide for material on selection guidelines.
2. You also may use this time to have students participate in book clubs or book presentations. Use the criteria specified in the *Passport Reading Journeys* Library Teacher's Guide.

Vocabulary Connections

Vocabulary words for each book are listed in the Teacher's Guide. These words are content related or used frequently in reading material. The selected words can be a basis for independent or small-group discussions and activities.

Student Opportunities

Six copies of each book title are provided in the *Passport Reading Journeys* Library. The number of copies makes it possible for small groups of students to read the same material and share the information they read.

Theme-related titles include *Code Orange.*

Technology

1. Depending on your classroom configuration and computer access, you may have students work through the technology in a lab setting or have individuals or small groups of students work on desktops or laptops while other students participate in other suggested activities, such as the *Passport Reading Journeys* Library.
2. The online technology component provides additional support for students to work with selected vocabulary words. Students will work through a series of activities to strengthen their word knowledge, then apply that knowledge to passage reading. Refer to the online technology component User Guide for more information.

   Theme-related word sets include Math and Technology.

Writing Process

Write a Review

For this activity, students will evaluate a Web site. If computer access is available, choose a few popular online stores you consider safe for students to access. List the URL addresses of the sites on the board. Distribute copies of Writing Blackline Master page 3. Refer to the screen shot on this Blackline Master throughout the lesson when referring to a Web site. If students do not have access to the Internet, have them evaluate the screenshot on the Writing Blackline Master.

You will write a review of a Web site. Where have you seen reviews? (newspapers; magazines; online) **People write reviews when they have opinions about products or events. Many people who aren't professional critics post reviews online.** Explain that people often write reviews because they are experts or have experience about a topic and want to share their evaluations, or judgments, about a product, movie, or something else. Tell students these reviewers want to convince other people their evaluations are correct.

Prewrite

Think about your favorite Web site. Why do you like it? What makes it good? Explain that to convince other people something is good, students must include clear reasons and specific evidence.

Have students work in small groups to brainstorm what qualities make a Web site good or successful.

For students to have a meaningful experience completing tasks as a group, certain strategies need to be employed. Group dynamics and interactions can be improved with strategic planning for group work. Refer to page xxxvi for information on effective grouping strategies.

Have groups share their ideas. Write student responses on the board. (Possible responses might address usability, content, design, or organization.) **Use these ideas to create a list of four to five standards you think make a good Web site.** Instruct students to choose and access one of the Web sites from your list. **Now look at your Web site. How does it meet these standards?** Have students write their ideas on a separate sheet of paper.

Draft

You will use these standards, or criteria, as you write your reviews. Assign point values to the rubric as you tell students their reviews must have . . .

- a description of the Web site, including what features it has.
- four or five standards a Web site must meet to be considered good.
- specific ways your Web site meets these standards.

Have students work independently to draft their reviews. Remind students that they will be able to revise their work.

Revise

Have students reread their drafts, using the following revision steps and questions. After each step, have students make the revisions and write their final draft.

- **Check the explanation.** Did you clearly explain each of the reasons you presented? Where do you need to add more details?
- **Check your purpose.** Did you present enough evidence to convince the reader the Web site is good? What other features of the Web site could you describe?
- **Check mechanics.** Do fragments or run-on sentences need to be rewritten? What words might be misspelled? Do all sentences begin with capital letters and end with proper punctuation?

Present

Have students present their reviews to one another in small groups. Each group should share the most convincing review with the whole class.

Assess

To assess students' written Web site reviews, use the Writing Rubric at the bottom of the Writing Blackline Master.

Real-World Reading

Blog

1. Have students turn to Student Book page 46. Explain they will read a blog. **A *blog* is a Web log.** Write *Web log* on the board and circle the letters *b log*. **It's a Web site people create to write about topics of interest. What blogs do you know about? How often do you read blogs? What do you think the person who writes this blog is like?** (Possible answer: I think this person is a male high school student.)
2. **Look at the blog. Underline the parts of the page that show you when Joe wrote each piece of text.** (the dates) **How often does Joe add to this blog?** (every few weeks) **What do you call each piece of text on this page?** (a post or entry) **Blogs are organized last-to-first chronologically, so the newest post is always at the top of the page. Begin reading this blog with the post at the bottom and work your way up.** Have students read the blog posts.
3. **What is this blog about?** (Joe has started an organization to help his friend pay for rehab.) **How is reading this blog different from reading an article about the topic?** (You hear someone's personal experience.) **What are advantages to writing a blog like this?** (You have a chance to help other people; you connect with people experiencing similar things.) **What are disadvantages to writing a blog like this?** (You lose some privacy.)
4. **If you wanted to find out more about this topic, what keywords would you use in your research? Highlight them in the text of the blog.** (rehab; depression; fund-raising)
5. **Post a short response to Joe's blog in the lines provided.** Have partners share their responses.

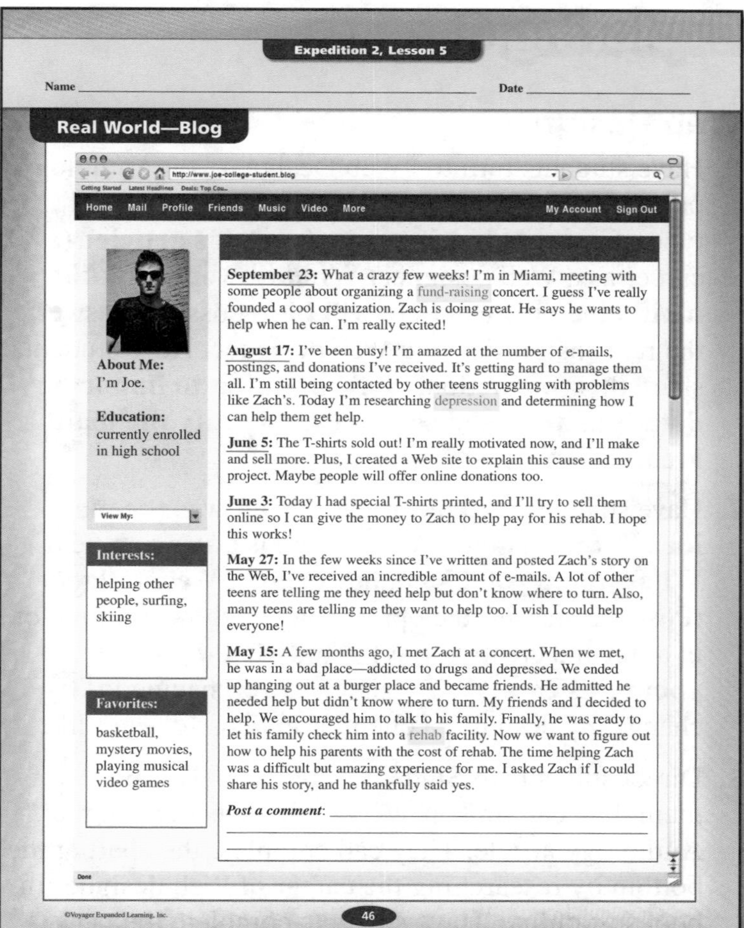

Expedition 2, Lesson 5

Name ______ Date ______

Real World—Blog

About Me:
I'm Joe.

Education:
currently enrolled in high school

Interests:
helping other people, surfing, skiing

Favorites:
basketball, mystery movies, playing musical video games

September 23: What a crazy few weeks! I'm in Miami, meeting with some people about organizing a fund-raising concert. I guess I've really founded a cool organization. Zach is doing great. He says he wants to help when he can. I'm really excited!

August 17: I've been busy! I'm amazed at the number of e-mails, postings, and donations I've received. It's getting hard to manage them all. I'm still being contacted by other teens struggling with problems like Zach's. Today I'm researching depression and determining how I can help them get help.

June 5: The T-shirts sold out! I'm really motivated now, and I'll make and sell more. Plus, I created a Web site to explain this cause and my project. Maybe people will offer online donations too.

June 3: Today I had special T-shirts printed, and I'll try to sell them online so I can give the money to Zach to help pay for his rehab. I hope this works!

May 27: In the few weeks since I've written and posted Zach's story on the Web, I've received an incredible amount of e-mails. A lot of other teens are telling me they need help but don't know where to turn. Also, many teens are telling me they want to help too. I wish I could help everyone!

May 15: A few months ago, I met Zach at a concert. When we met, he was in a bad place—addicted to drugs and depressed. We ended up hanging out at a burger place and became friends. He admitted he needed help but didn't know where to turn. My friends and I decided to help. We encouraged him to talk to his family. Finally, he was ready to let his family check him into a rehab facility. Now we want to figure out how to help his parents with the cost of rehab. The time helping Zach was a difficult but amazing experience for me. I asked Zach if I could share his story, and he thankfully said yes.

***Post a comment*:** ______

©Voyager Expanded Learning, Inc.

46

Exploring Careers

Web Designer

1. Have students turn to "Web Designer" on Anthology page 23. Have them preview the title, photo, and type of page. **What is the topic of this article?** (a career as a Web designer) **What do you think the main idea of the article will be?** (Possible answer: the responsibilities of a Web designer) Have students share their predictions. **Pay attention to important details as you read so you can identify the main idea.**

2. Have students read the article. **What was the main idea of this article?** (Web design is a growing field.) **What would you like about being a Web designer?** (Possible answer: the opportunity to show information in a fun and creative way) **What would you dislike about this career?** (Possible answer: having to change my design if a client or my boss doesn't like it)

3. Direct students to Student Book page 47. Tell them they can find answers to the questions in the Anthology article. They can complete the chart at the bottom by researching the career of Web designer in books or online. Have students complete the page.

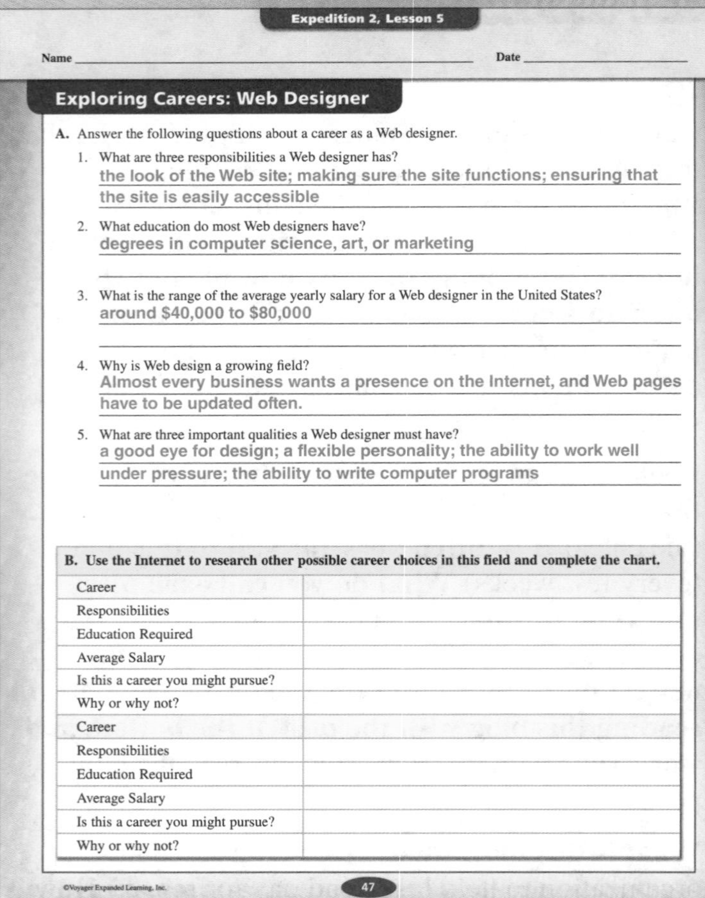

Expedition 2, Lesson 5

Name ______________________ Date ______________

Exploring Careers: Web Designer

A. Answer the following questions about a career as a Web designer.

1. What are three responsibilities a Web designer has?
the look of the Web site; making sure the site functions; ensuring that the site is easily accessible

2. What education do most Web designers have?
degrees in computer science, art, or marketing

3. What is the range of the average yearly salary for a Web designer in the United States?
around $40,000 to $80,000

4. Why is Web design a growing field?
Almost every business wants a presence on the Internet, and Web pages have to be updated often.

5. What are three important qualities a Web designer must have?
a good eye for design; a flexible personality; the ability to work well under pressure; the ability to write computer programs

B. Use the Internet to research other possible career choices in this field and complete the chart.

Career	
Responsibilities	
Education Required	
Average Salary	
Is this a career you might pursue?	
Why or why not?	
Career	
Responsibilities	
Education Required	
Average Salary	
Is this a career you might pursue?	
Why or why not?	

©Voyager Expanded Learning, Inc. 47

Career

Web Designer

Everyone at school is talking about Melissa Tait's Web page. She has great photos, music, and links—but everyone has those. Her page really stands out because of the design. She put together a mixture of colors, fonts, photos, and boxes to create an amazing look. Now many of her friends are asking for help. They want their pages to look as enticing too.

After designing a few more pages, Melissa began to think. She enjoyed doing the design, and she often had original page design ideas that worked well. Melissa decided to see whether she could turn this hobby into a career. She began to research the possibility of becoming a Web designer.

Web designers are responsible for a wide range of tasks. They create and arrange a Web site. They are usually responsible for the layout of the pages. Web designers have to be able to combine fonts, type size, color, images, and sometimes even sound to create their final product. Sometimes Web designers write computer programs to make the Web

R U Online? 23

Career

page more interesting. They also work to make sure the Web site functions properly. Finally, they are responsible for making sure the pages work on a variety of browsers.

Melissa learned that most designers have college degrees in computer science, art, or marketing. However, others are self-taught. Some people start off like Melissa, playing around at home with a personal Web page, and find they have a passion for this type of work. Many designers then explore their skills further by doing volunteer work for nonprofit organizations. With some hands-on experience, they are then able to turn their talent into a well-paid career. Estimated average salaries for Web designers in 2008 ranged from $40,000 to $80,000 a year.

However, Web designers need to have much more than a good design eye. They need to have a flexible personality to be able to work with many different kinds of clients. They also need to be able to take constructive criticism in stride and not allow their feelings to be hurt. During a project, they frequently receive client requests for changes and alterations. These requests need to be accepted and implemented quickly. Another key element to becoming a successful designer is the ability to meet deadlines and work well under pressure. Finally, most Web designers learn to write computer programs.

There is a need for Web designers in most every industry. Since almost all businesses have a Web site, they all use designers. This allows designers to pursue many different passions. For example, a Web designer who loves cars may be able to combine the best of both worlds and design Web pages for a car company.

Today, Web design is a growing field. There are many opportunities for growth and advancement. Employment for talented designers is expected to grow at a steady rate for the next 10 years. As demand continues to grow, more jobs will be created. Almost every business Web site needs to be constantly updated. These changes keep information current and make sure people return to visit the site.

Melissa thinks this may be the perfect job. She now dreams of heading off to work each morning to design Web pages. Melissa is sure she would enjoy this career path.

"It would be a great way to earn a paycheck," she said. "I would love to see my ideas come to life online and to work with other designers to create Web pages. Maybe I could even influence other Web designers!"

24 Expedition 2

English Language Learner Overview

The ELL signals when extra support is provided for students during the lesson. As needed, Blackline Masters for English language learners may provide support. For vocabulary, students also may use the online technology component to practice Expedition words or other content-area vocabulary and designated ELL word sets.

Introduce Vocabulary

Lesson 6

Distribute six index cards to each student. Have students write one vocabulary word on each card. Read aloud the following clues, and have students show you the word card that matches each clue. Then have students write or draw their own clue on each card to help them remember the meaning.

- **Having strong feelings** (opinionated)
- **A range of possibilities** (spectrum)
- **Affect people's behavior or decisions** (influence)
- **Way you think or feel about something** (viewpoint)
- **Respond** (react)
- **Show that something is important** (emphasize)

Lesson 8

Have students read aloud the definition of each vocabulary word. Then ask the following questions.

- **Can you *determine* whether you will buy something without knowing the price?** (no)
- **Is a bookseller an example of a *merchant*?** (yes)
- **Do you *avoid* things you like doing?** (no)
- **If a store has a large *selection*, does it sell just one thing?** (no)
- **Do the *majority* of shoppers like to save money?** (yes)
- **If you place an *order* for something, do you expect to receive it?** (yes)

Practice Vocabulary

In Lesson 7, provide support for the context words *interpretations* and *subjective*. ***Interpretations* are different ways of understanding or explaining something. My friend and I had different *interpretations* of the movie we saw last night.**

Write the following sentence frame on the board and have students complete the sentence aloud: *If two people have different interpretations of a movie, they think ________ about the movie.* (different things)

When something is *subjective*, it is based on personal opinions and feelings. Am I being *subjective* when I say the sky is usually blue? (no) **Why not?** (It is a fact that the sky is usually blue.) **Am I being *subjective* when I say the sky is beautiful?** (yes) **Why?** (It is an opinion to say the sky is beautiful.)

In Lesson 9, provide support for the context words *entice* and *guarantee*. **If you try to *entice* someone, you try to get the person to do something. I tried to *entice* my dog to go outside by throwing its toy.**

When you *guarantee* something, you promise it will happen. I can *guarantee* that I will be at school on Monday. Can I guarantee that it is going to rain tomorrow? (no) **Why not?** (No one can control the weather.) **What are some things you can guarantee?** Make a list of student responses.

Apply the Target Skill: Main Idea and Details

Support student understanding of the relationship between the main idea and the details in a paragraph. Model asking yourself questions aloud to identify the main idea, such as *What is this paragraph mostly about?* or *What important idea does the author want me to understand when I read this paragraph?* Then read aloud sentences that provide details and model connecting those details to the main idea with language: *This detail about articles on Martin Luther King supports the main idea. The main idea is that many articles on the Internet reflect subjective viewpoints.*

Apply the Target Skill: Text Features

In Lesson 9, some students may need additional practice identifying text features. Blackline Master page 13 begins with a brief activity that asks students to write a title and subheadings from the passages in Expedition 2. Then, students write to explain whether or not a picture helped them understand the text. Support students in this activity by having them first discuss why or why not the pictures were helpful. Write useful phrases used in the discussion on the board.

Truth, Lies, and the Internet

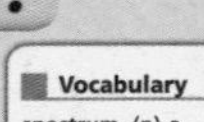

Vocabulary

spectrum (n) *a continuous sequence or range*

Michael recently heard some kids talking during class about the arrest of one of his favorite musicians. Michael logged onto his computer to find out what had happened. A quick online search supplied him with the following results:

1. Hip-Hop Star the Subject of Drug Probe
2. Self-Indulgent Lifestyle Finally Catches Up to Hip-Hop Star
3. Scandal Sheets Smear Hip-Hop Star with Lies!

Michael was confused by the headlines. How could there be so many interpretations of the same event? How could he figure out which stories to trust? **1**

Thanks to the Internet, there is a broad **spectrum** of information at your fingertips. But, what you read is not always true. Anyone can write and publish a blog or a Web page.

1 Context Clues
What does the word *interpretations* mean? Which clues from the text helped you determine the meaning?

Vocabulary

viewpoint (n) *a way of thinking about something; attitude; point of view*

influence (v) *have power over something or someone*

emphasize (v) *give special attention to; put stress upon*

react (v) *act in response to something*

opinionated (adj) *sticking to one's thoughts, feelings, or beliefs in an excessive way*

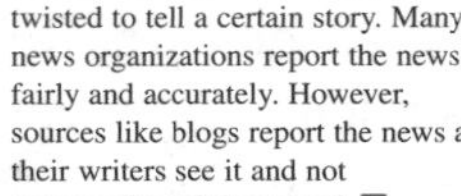

Because of this, facts may get twisted to tell a certain story. Many news organizations report the news fairly and accurately. However, sources like blogs report the news as their writers see it and not necessarily as it happened. **2**

A newspaper cites sources to show where the information came from, but a blog frequently reflects a subjective **viewpoint**. Being subjective means that you base your opinion on your own feelings and thoughts rather than facts. A writer's feelings can **influence** which facts he or she chooses to **emphasize**. Feelings also influence which facts the writer decides to omit or downplay in the article.

So, how can you get a sense of the spectrum of viewpoints that lie behind the news you read before you **react** to it? Probably the best way to begin is to identify the viewpoint of the writer or the Web site. Most people who publish information want to influence readers to adopt their viewpoint. As a result, they will often pick and choose facts and data to make their case.

For example, try a search of Dr. Martin Luther King, Jr. It will bring up more than nine million results. The results reflect a wide spectrum of information. There are many sites with accurate, historical information, but there are also quite a few articles written by **opinionated** authors. Some of these

2 Ask Questions
A good question you might ask right now is: "How can you know if the information is correct or true?" Keep reading to see if this question is answered.

sites admire King's work for equal rights. These sites emphasize his nonviolent, positive leadership that helped change people's lives for the better. Others choose to show King in a negative light. They emphasize his relationships with communists, people who hold political ideas that the government should control all social and economic activities of a country. They even accuse him of plagiarism. Plagiarism is copying someone's written work and saying that you wrote it yourself.

Another popular example of sometimes unreliable information is Wikipedia. The online encyclopedia has become a popular reference source. This site is often a great place to start a research project. However, it may supply information that is not accurate. Wikipedia articles can be written by anyone, even you. Other readers can edit your article and add to the collection online. Wikipedia does post a warning at the top of some pages to alert readers that an article may be missing citations, making it hard to determine where the facts were obtained. **3** However, Wikipedia authors don't need to have any qualifications to write or post an article. Some people or groups use this site to emphasize their own opinions and influence readers.

3 Context Clues
What are *citations*? Which words in the sentences help you determine the meaning?

Before you react to the information as the truth, you might want to check another source. Find another article on the same topic that is based on factual information. The facts may offer a different viewpoint.

Another clue to the position of the writer may be in the Web address of the site. Web sites that end in .edu are used by educational institutions, like colleges and universities. Those that end in .gov are maintained by the U.S. government. Both of these sources are generally reliable. Others, like those that end in .com or .net, are often commercial and are not restricted. Therefore, the information may or may not be accurate. Finally, .org Web sites are linked to a specific organization, which may be lobbying for a certain goal. Knowing the position of the writer before reading the article may help you decide whether the reporting is opinionated or factual.

Armed with all of this information, Michael looked back through his search results. He read each headline again. He guessed that the first story was probably the most objective. The second appeared to be a story written by someone who has a poor opinion of the celebrity. The third headline seemed to be written by someone who is a fan of this star. Michael decided to read all three because he is a big fan. Because he knew that some of the search results were biased, he was able to filter the information as he read and then react to the story. **4** **End**

4 Ask Questions
Think about what you read. Ask yourself if you could describe to a friend how to recognize whether something is fact or opinion.

"Truth, Lies, and the Internet"

Before Reading

Introduce Vocabulary

1. Have students turn to Student Book page 48 and scan the boldfaced vocabulary words. **You will read these words in "Truth, Lies, and the Internet."** Read aloud the instructions, then have students complete Part A.
2. Have students share which words they know. For each word, have students use the word in a sentence.
3. Read aloud the words, parts of speech, definitions, and example sentences. As you read each word, have students repeat the pronunciation. Clarify any confusion students may have about word meanings.
4. Read aloud the instructions for Part B. Have students complete the activity individually, then compare answers with a partner.

ELL Refer to Blackline Master page 11 to extend vocabulary practice.

Have students use the *Passport Reading Journeys* online technology component to practice and reinforce vocabulary and comprehension skills.

Expedition 2, Lesson 6

Name ____________ Date ____________

Vocabulary

"Truth, Lies, and the Internet"

A. Put a check mark in each row to indicate how well you know each boldfaced word.

	Know This Word	Have Seen This Word	Don't Know This Word
spectrum (n) *a continuous sequence or range* A whole *spectrum* of Web sites will give good information about your research topic.			
viewpoint (n) *a way of thinking about something; attitude; point of view* The *viewpoint* of that blog obviously favors banning soda machines from schools.			
influence (v) *have power over something or someone* That negative article will not *influence* my opinion of that actor; I still like him.			
emphasize (v) *give special attention to; put stress upon* I love our superintendent's blog because she tries to *emphasize* positive things happening in our schools.			
react (v) *act in response to something* What made Jose *react* like he was mad?			
opinionated (adj) *sticking to one's thoughts, feelings, or beliefs in an excessive way* Yolanda is so *opinionated* about her favorite author that no one can say anything negative about him.			

B. Complete each sentence with the correct vocabulary word from Part A.

1. The Internet has a ___spectrum___ of sites for researching a variety of topics.
2. Tanisha posts her reactions on blogs to ___influence___ other readers.
3. Many bloggers are ___opinionated___, so readers need to check the facts.
4. To understand global warming, Cade visited Web sites with different ___viewpoints___.
5. If you received an e-mail message in all capital letters, how would you ___react___?
6. Two health articles I read online ___emphasize___ the importance of exercise.

 48

Vocabulary

spectrum (n) *a continuous sequence or range*
A whole *spectrum* of Web sites will give good information about your research topic.

viewpoint (n) *a way of thinking about something; attitude; point of view*
The *viewpoint* of that blog obviously favors banning soda machines from schools.

influence (v) *have power over something or someone*
That negative article will not *influence* my opinion of that actor; I still like him.

emphasize (v) *give special attention to; put stress upon*
I love our superintendent's blog because she tries to *emphasize* positive things happening in our schools.

react (v) *act in response to something*
What made Jose *react* like he was mad?

opinionated (adj) *sticking to one's thoughts, feelings, or beliefs in an excessive way*
Yolanda is so *opinionated* about her favorite author that no one can say anything negative about him.

Apply the Target Skill: Main Idea and Details

1. Remind students that details are statements about the main idea, or what the passage is mostly about. **When I read, I look for examples and other details to support the main idea. After I read, I think about what was most important about the paragraph or the text.**

2. Read aloud the following paragraph. Have students identify the main idea and supporting details. **The Internet is a great resource. Students can use the Internet to complete research on a topic. Many reliable sites have good information about almost any imaginable topic. Many people think it is also much less time consuming to do an Internet search than it is to do library research.**

Main idea: The Internet is a great resource.

Detail: Students can use the Internet to complete research on a topic.

Detail: It is also much less time consuming to do an Internet search than it is to do library research.

Introduce the Passage

1. Have students preview "Truth, Lies, and the Internet." Remind students that the Expedition is about the Internet. **Read the title and the three numbered search results in the first paragraph. What do you think this passage is about?** (misleading and conflicting facts or opinions on the Internet)

ELL Write the three search results on the board and have students read them aloud. Ask students what *star* means in the first title. (a famous person) Repeat this process for the terms *subject* and *probe*.

2. Remind students to pause to read the margin prompts. **Think about the prompts as you read the passage. The vocabulary notes in the margin will remind you of the meanings of the new words.**
3. **We already know this passage is about the Internet. How can a person decide what is the truth and what are lies on the Internet?** Have students discuss their responses.

   To make the most of discussion time, remember to incorporate strategies that encourage and extend student involvement. Refer to page xxxviii for a comprehensive discussion of these strategies.

During Reading

1. To select reading options that support your students' levels and classroom needs, see Reading Differentiation, page xxxii, if needed.
2. Have students read "Truth, Lies, and the Internet," looking for main ideas and supporting details.

After Reading

Check Comprehension

1. **Before you read this passage, you predicted what it would be about. Did your prediction match what you read?** Allow students to discuss their predictions and the passage.
2. **What is the main idea of the first paragraph?** (Michael logged onto his computer to find out what had happened.)
3. Remind students that Michael learned how to figure out which stories to trust. **The passage gives three main ways a reader can determine which stories to trust. What are they?** Have students scan the passage to find the answers. (identify the viewpoint; find another source; identify the type of Web address) Write student responses on the board.

Remind students to choose books from the *Passport Reading Journeys* Library for independent reading.

"Truth, Lies, and the Internet"

Prepare to Reread

Introduce the Lesson

Remind students that they read about finding trustworthy Internet sources. **In this lesson, we'll revisit "Truth, Lies, and the Internet" and identify main ideas and details.**

Practice Vocabulary

1. Ask the following questions to help students practice the vocabulary words from Lesson 6 and recall how they were used in the passage.
   - **Does a *spectrum* of information mean a range in variety or a limited scope?** (a range in variety)
   - **What were two *viewpoints* of the articles Michael found?** (a poor opinion and a fan of the musician)
   - **If a group tries to *influence* you, what are its members doing?** (trying to get you to agree with their viewpoint)
   - **What do some writers *emphasize* to make their point?** (facts that are favorable to their opinions)
   - **How did Michael *react* to the headlines?** (He was confused.)
   - **Which story was the least *opinionated*?** (the first story) **Which details from the text supports your thinking?** (Answers will vary.)
2. Remind students that they can use context clues to find the meanings of unknown words. Have students turn to Anthology page 25. **What do you think the word *interpretations* means?** (ways something is explained or what it means) **Which clues in the text helped you figure out the meaning?** (The headlines above the text are different ways of telling the same story.)

   Repeat this process for the following words.
   - **cites** (v) *shows where information was obtained*, Anthology page 26
   - **subjective** (adj) *affected by your own opinions, feelings, and thoughts rather than facts*, Anthology page 26
   - **communists** (n) *people who hold political ideas that the government should control all social and economic activities of a country*, Anthology page 27
   - **plagiarism** (n) *copying someone's written work and claiming it as yours*, Anthology page 27

Expedition 2, Lesson 7

Name ____________ Date ____________

Word Building

"Truth, Lies, and the Internet"

A. Divide each compound word into two separate words. Then write the definitions. The first one is done for you.

viewpoint	view	+	point	point of view
workplace	work	+	place	place of work
seaside	sea	+	side	side of the sea
snowbound	snow	+	bound	bound by snow
snowflake	snow	+	flake	flake of snow
hilltop	hill	+	top	top of a hill
moonlight	moon	+	light	light of the moon

B. Use the compound words from Part A to complete the paragraph.

It was a cold winter evening in New Hampshire. David left his workplace ready for a relaxing weekend. He headed to his home on a hilltop overlooking the seaside. It was dark, but he could see the road ahead in the moonlight. David's car radio reported that a winter storm was coming. Then a snowflake landed on the windshield. The flurries increased as he arrived home. David knew he'd be snowbound all weekend, but he didn't mind. His viewpoint was that storms were a great excuse to stay inside and play online skiing and other games.

C. Read the following definitions. Think of a compound word for each definition.

playground — the grounds at a school or a park where children play
daylight — the light of day
crosswalk — a marked area of a road for walking across the street
campfire — a fire in a camp used for cooking
underground — under the surface of the ground

 49

3. Have students turn to Student Book page 49. **You have learned the word *viewpoint*, which is a compound word.** Remind them that *viewpoint* means "a way of thinking about something; attitude; point of view" and that it is made by combining two words, *view* and *point*. **If an unfamiliar word is a compound word, you can think about the separate words to understand it better.** Read aloud Part A, then have students complete the page independently.

CHECKPOINT After students complete the activity, have them identify anything they could not answer. Have students identify clues in the sentences that helped them determine which compound words to choose.

Reread

Apply the Target Skill: Main Idea and Details

1. Remind students that it is helpful for readers to notice the main ideas and supporting details of paragraphs. **When I read, I notice the main idea and details in each paragraph, and I think about how they relate to the main idea of the whole passage.**
2. Have students turn to Student Book page 50. Read the instructions.
3. Have students reread the passage and complete the outline with main ideas and details.
4. Have partners share their responses.

ACADEMIC SKILL Remind students that they can write main ideas and details when they read other types of texts, such as science textbooks.

Write in Response to Reading

1. Have students turn to Student Book page 51. **Think about how the writer of the passage tried to influence the readers. How do writers do this?** (They choose facts that emphasize their opinions.) Read aloud the instructions for Part A, then have students complete the exercise.
2. **In the reading passage, you read that people who write blogs often are opinionated and subjective. Choose a topic and write your own blog entry. How will you emphasize your opinion?** Read aloud the instructions for Part B and tell students they can choose other topics, such as their favorite music, movie, or book. Have students complete the exercise. If students seem unsure, have partners first discuss what they plan to include.

EXPEDITION ORGANIZER **R U Online?**

Pause to have students turn to Student Book pages 30 and 31. Have students complete the following:

- Write answers or notes below one or more of the probing questions. If they have not yet added a question of their own, encourage them to add one.
- Think about the main idea from "Truth, Lies, and the Internet" and write it in the appropriate place in Part B.

Expedition 2, Lesson 7

Name ______ Date ______

Main Idea and Details

Briefly complete the outline notes with paragraph main ideas and details from "Truth, Lies, and the Internet." Then write the main idea of the passage.

Answers will vary, but could include the following.

I. Main Idea Paragraph 2: Michael was confused by the headlines.
Detail: Different sources have different interpretations.

II. Main Idea Paragraph 3: There is a broad spectrum of information available on the Internet.
A. Detail: Anyone can publish a blog/Web page.
B. Detail: Many news organizations are fair and accurate.

III. Main Idea Paragraph 4: A blog frequently reflects a subjective viewpoint.
A. Detail: Newspapers cite sources.
B. Detail: Feelings affect writer's emphasis.

IV. Main Idea Paragraphs 5 and 6: Identify the viewpoint of the writer.
Detail: Writers pick facts/data to defend opinions and influence readers.

V. Main Idea Paragraph 7: A popular example of unreliable information is Wikipedia.
A. Detail: Writers don't have to have qualifications.
B. Detail: Articles could be opinionated.

VI. Main Idea Paragraph 9: Another clue to the position of the writer may be in the Web address.
Detail: Reliable: .edu, .gov; may/may not be accurate: .com, .net; might be biased: .org

VII. Main Idea Paragraph 10: Because he knew that some Web sites were biased, he was able to filter information.
Detail: Writer positions: objective; poor opinion; fan

Main Idea of the Passage: Learn to figure out writer bias/accuracy of the source to filter information.

 50

Expedition 2, Lesson 7

Name ______ Date ______

Write in Response to Reading

A. The following three school newspaper headlines tell about the news story from different viewpoints. Write a brief article for each headline that supports the viewpoint. Answers will vary.

News Story: On Monday, the school cafeteria added two vegetarian meals to the usual menu.

Meat-eaters have no choices at school

My first vegetarian meal eaten at school

Vegetarians succeed at last!

B. Write a blog entry about a topic on which you are opinionated. Your topic could be an event or issue related to your school, neighborhood, or town. Emphasize your own opinions. Try to influence what your readers think.

Date: ______

Opinion: ______

 51

Online Shopping

Versus Brick-and-Mortar Stores

For a long time, people have bought items without going to the store. Mail-order catalogs like Sears Roebuck have been around for more than 100 years. Catalog shopping is still common today. However, the rise in popularity of the personal computer has changed the shopping world. Today, more and more people are doing their shopping online. But, has Internet shopping improved the experience for shoppers? How has this affected the business done in so-called "brick-and-mortar" stores?

Benefits of Online Shopping

Today, many people love to shop with online retailers, or sellers. One of the main benefits is convenience. Shoppers can "visit" many different stores quickly. This allows them to compare styles and brands instantly. Online shoppers can also quickly **determine** which stores have the best prices. An Internet **merchant** is often able to offer better prices than traditional stores. Internet merchants can **avoid** some of the costs of traditional stores, like paying a sales staff. Online operations like Amazon.com carry a wide **selection** of products. They also offer price and shipping discounts. As a result, a **majority** of shoppers often find them to be convenient one-stop shops.

Shopping at home is also appealing to some. It is great for people who like to avoid crowded parking lots and stores, especially during the holiday season. Online stores never close. People can log on, shop, and place their **order**

Vocabulary

determine (v) *reach a decision about something after thinking about it*

merchant (n) *a person who buys and sells things to make money*

avoid (v) *keep away from*

selection (n) *a collection of things to choose from*

majority (n) *the greater part or number of something; more than half*

order (n) *a request for something that someone wants to buy or receive*

Some people prefer the quiet solitude of shopping online to the chaos of shopping at a store.

anytime they like. Additionally, the rising price of gasoline can also entice people to shop at home. This allows them to save money on fuel. Others report online shopping is ideal when buying gifts that need to be shipped. By ordering online, gifts are purchased and mailed in one step. This saves the buyer a trip to the post office.

These benefits have lured some shoppers away from traditional stores. Unfortunately, the volume of business done by online sites has happened at the expense of brick-and-mortar stores. That is, it takes away from their business. 1

1 Ask Questions
Review what you read by asking yourself, "What are the benefits mentioned of online shopping?"

Traditional Shopping Has Benefits

Not everyone is ready to make the switch to online merchants. A

majority of people prefer shopping in traditional brick-and-mortar stores. Shoppers like to touch and try on some types of products, like clothing and shoes. That is how they determine which ones they like. Shopping online for these types of items can be difficult. There may be no guarantee, or promise, the product will look like the image on the screen. Some people report that returning or exchanging items purchased online is a lot of trouble.

Another downside to online shopping is inaccurate information. Many Web sites offer a wide selection of items. However, some sites don't include enough information about a product. Without clear pictures, a size chart, or accurate measurements, shoppers are often frustrated. Other Web sites are slow to update their sites to reflect product availability or shipping times.

Many people simply prefer the experience of shopping in a traditional store. Some view a shopping trip as a social event. It is a great way to catch up with family and friends. For others, online shopping can feel like work. They spend all day at work and do not want to shop in front of their computers. For some products, like books, many shoppers like to browse and read different parts of a book before they purchase the item. Therefore, they prefer the in-store experience. 2

2 Ask Questions
Review what you read by asking yourself, "What are the benefits mentioned of traditional shopping?"

Best of Both Worlds

As their popularity grows, online retailers are taking business away from brick-and-mortar stores. In order to keep up, many traditional merchants are creating and updating their Web sites. Studies have

Increased online shopping could take away business from brick-and-mortar stores.

Online stores ship orders from large warehouses like this one.

shown that many people use their computer to do research. For major purchases, like a car, they look online. They determine what they want online. Finally, they make the purchase at a traditional store.

Additionally, many brick-and-mortar stores are working harder to improve their stores. They are improving lighting, store layouts, and customer service. Some stores are working to provide online shopping along with their brick-and-mortar stores. They are carrying a limited assortment of products in their stores and offering a wider selection online. Others are offering in-store pickup for orders placed online. Larger stores and chains have developed their own e-shopping sites to combat the exclusively online operations.

Both online and traditional stores continue to refine their operations. They are always trying to find new ways to lure shoppers.

It's unlikely that the rise of e-shopping will mean the end of the brick-and-mortar store. The two forms of commerce will find ways to coexist. 3 Perhaps they will even boost each other's business. End

3 Context Clues
What does the word *coexist* mean? Use what you know about the root word *exist* and context clues to determine the meaning.

"Online Shopping Versus Brick-and-Mortar Stores"

Before Reading

Introduce Vocabulary

1. Have students turn to Part A on Student Book page 52. Read the instructions aloud. Have students scan the boldfaced vocabulary words and rate their knowledge of each word.
2. Have students find words marked with a 3 rating and use them in sentences.
3. Read aloud the vocabulary words, parts of speech, definitions, and context sentences. For each word, ask: **Does the word seem more or less familiar in this context? What other context do you know for that word?** (Answers will vary.)
4. Have students read the instructions for Part B, complete the activity, and share their responses with a partner.

ELL Refer to Blackline Master page 12 to extend vocabulary practice.

Have students use the *Passport Reading Journeys* online technology component to practice and reinforce vocabulary and comprehension skills.

Introduce the Target Skill: Text Features

1. **To better undertand a chapter or article, it is helpful to preview the text.** Provide examples of textbooks from a content area, such as social studies or science. **When you preview a chapter or article in a textbook, notice the features that surround the text or stand out from the regular text. Text features include photographs, headings, lists, charts, diagrams, maps, sidebars, graphs, and boldfaced words. Readers preview text features to know what to expect from the reading.**
2. Write the following rating scale on the board.

   1. I read or view each text feature carefully.

   2. I read certain text features and ignore others.

   3. I ignore the text features.

Expedition 2, Lesson 8

Name ____________ Date ____________

Vocabulary

"Online Shopping Versus Brick-and-Mortar Stores"

A. Write one or more numbers next to each boldfaced word to show when you have seen, heard, or used this word.

5 I heard or used it in school.
4 I heard it on TV or radio.
3 I use it in everyday conversation.
2 I read it in a book, magazine, or online.
1 I have not read, heard, or used this word.

☐ **determine** (v) *reach a decision about something after thinking about it*
I can *determine* which music I want to buy after I listen to it.

☐ **merchant** (n) *a person who buys and sells things to make money*
Kelton will check prices with an Internet *merchant* before driving to the store.

☐ **avoid** (v) *keep away from*
My neighbor will shop online just so she can *avoid* a crowded shopping center.

☐ **selection** (n) *a collection of things to choose from*
This store has only a small *selection* of T-shirts.

☐ **majority** (n) *the greater part or number of something; more than half*
The *majority* of people still shop at stores because they get their purchase immediately.

☐ **order** (n) *a request for something that someone wants to buy or receive*
I placed an *order* on the Web site for a CD, and I should receive it by Friday.

B. Complete each sentence with the correct vocabulary word from Part A.

1. You can choose from a wide ___selection___ of luggage in the new mall store.
2. I use the Internet daily, just like the ___majority___ of students I know.
3. When I meet people on the Internet, I ___avoid___ becoming friends with anyone who asks for my credit card number.
4. The online shoe store could not fill my ___order___ for size 15 hiking boots.
5. I buy my hats from an online company owned by a teen ___merchant___.
6. Before I believe what I read on a Web site, I ___determine___ where the site gets its information.

 52

Vocabulary

determine (v) *reach a decision about something after thinking about it*
I can *determine* which music I want to buy after I listen to it.

merchant (n) *a person who buys and sells things to make money*
Kelton will check prices with an Internet *merchant* before driving to the store.

avoid (v) *keep away from*
My neighbor will shop online just so she can *avoid* a crowded shopping center.

selection (n) *a collection of things to choose from*
This store has only a small *selection* of T-shirts.

majority (n) *the greater part or number of something; more than half*
The *majority* of people still shop at stores because they get their purchase immediately.

order (n) *a request for something that someone wants to buy or receive*
I placed an *order* on the Web site for a CD, and I should receive it by Friday.

Have students read the list and rate how they usually use text features in their reading. Have them tell which text features they find most useful.

3. **It is important to view or read text features with as much attention as the regular text because these features contain important information that supports understanding. The information in text features helps explain more about the text or extends the information found in the text.** Remind students that reading text features that appear in tests also can help them answer questions correctly.

Introduce the Passage

1. Have students turn to "Online Shopping Versus Brick-and-Mortar Stores." **Preview the text features in this passage.** Have students name these text features:
   - Main heading and subheadings
   - Photos
   - Examples of print ads
2. Direct student attention to the margin prompts. **What reading strategy do these notes suggest?** (Ask questions and identify context clues as you read.)
3. Tell students they will read the expression *brick-and-mortar store*. Have them tell what they think this is and what would be its opposite. (a store you must travel to; a traditional store; its opposite would be a catalog or online store) Write the word part *e-* on the board. **What words use this word part? What does it mean?** (*e-mail; e-commerce; e-shopping*; it means "electronic")
4. Have students think about what they previewed. **Where would you find this type of passage? What do you think the purpose of the passage is? Why do you think this?** (The passage is a textbook article. Its purpose is to contrast online shopping and brick-and-mortar stores. The headings and images are clues to the purpose.) Remind students to use the text features they previewed as they make predictions.

ELL Support the term *brick-and-mortar store*. Draw several bricks on the board as part of a wall. Then explain that *mortar* holds the bricks together. Tell students that the term *brick-and-mortar store* means a store in a building of some kind.

During Reading

1. To select reading options that support your students' levels and classroom needs, see Reading Differentiation, page xxxii.
2. Have students read "Online Shopping Versus Brick-and-Mortar Stores," and use the text features to identify important information about the text.

After Reading

Check Comprehension

1. When students finish reading, ask the following questions and encourage them to look in the text to find answers.
   - **Why do some people prefer online shopping?** (convenience; wide variety of products; ease of comparing products and prices; no travel)
   - **What are benefits of going to a store to shop?** (Seeing and trying on the product can be fun.)
   - **When do people use both online and brick-and-mortar stores?** (when they research products online, then buy the product in a brick-and-mortar store)
   - **How have brick-and-mortar stores changed to compete with online stores?** (including their Web sites in ads; improving the appearance of the store and offering special services)
2. **Were your predictions correct? Explain.** (Answers will vary.)
3. **Name two text features you think add information to help you understand the text better. Give reasons for your answer.** (Students should identify text features and explain how the text features added more information to what was written in the text.)

ACADEMIC SKILL Remind students that paying attention to text features will help them when they read other types of texts, such as science textbooks.

Remind students to choose books from the *Passport Reading Journeys* Library for independent reading.

"Online Shopping Versus Brick-and-Mortar Stores"

Prepare to Reread

Introduce the Lesson

Have students think about recent shopping experiences. **Connecting your experiences with what you read in "Online Shopping Versus Brick-and-Mortar Stores" might help you better understand the passage. In this lesson, we'll use text features to find the main idea.**

Practice Vocabulary

1. Write *determine*, *merchant*, *avoid*, *selection*, *majority*, and *order* on the board. **You can use these words to talk about shopping, but you also can use them to talk about other topics.** Have students answer the following questions in complete sentences. (Answers will vary.)
   - **A traveler searching online could *determine* the best way to get somewhere. What can an online shopper *determine*?**
   - **A *merchant* can sell items on the Internet. What is your favorite *merchant*?**
   - **Internet merchants *avoid* some costs. What conditions should drivers *avoid*?**
   - **Online merchants carry a wide *selection* of products. What kind of *selection* of songs does your favorite radio station play?**
   - **The *majority* of shoppers think online shopping is convenient. What do the *majority* of your friends do in their free time?**
   - **People can place an *order* online at any time. How else can a person place an *order*?**
2. **When we find unfamiliar words, we can look for text clues.** Have students find the word *retailers* on Anthology page 29 and its meaning. (sellers) **What clues in the text help you?** (the word *sellers* in text)

   Repeat this process for the following words.
   - **convenience** (n) *anything that saves work*, Anthology page 29
   - **entice** (v) *lure or attract*, Anthology page 30
   - **guarantee** (n) *promise or assurance*, Anthology page 31
   - **browse** (v) *inspect something in a casual way*, Anthology page 31

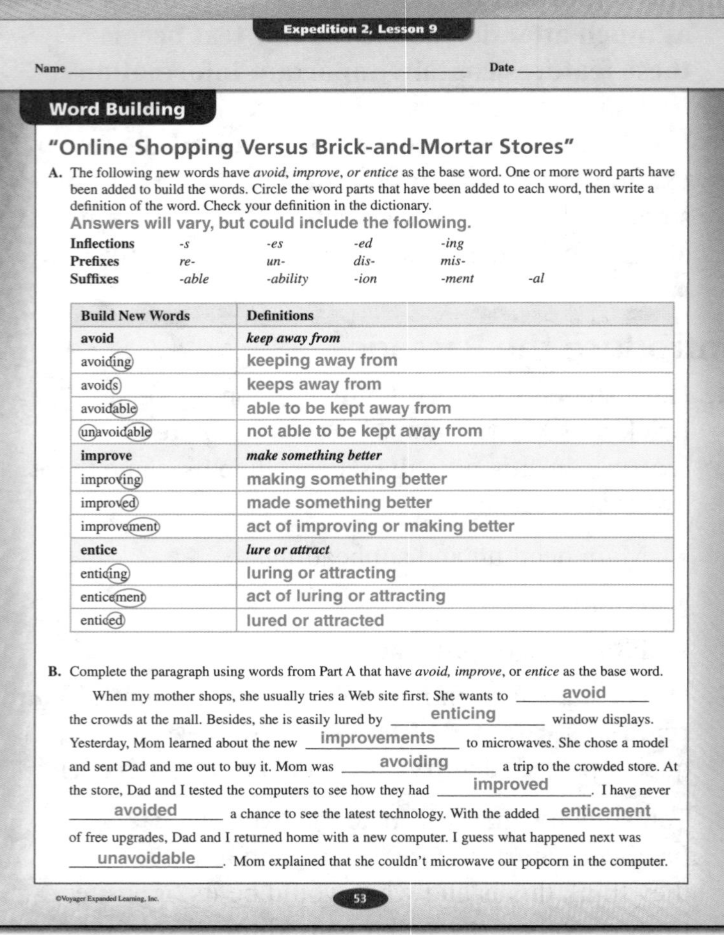

Expedition 2, Lesson 9

Name ______________________ Date ______________

Word Building

"Online Shopping Versus Brick-and-Mortar Stores"

A. The following new words have *avoid, improve, or entice* as the base word. One or more word parts have been added to build the words. Circle the word parts that have been added to each word, then write a definition of the word. Check your definition in the dictionary.

Answers will vary, but could include the following.

Inflections	*-s*	*-es*	*-ed*	*-ing*	
Prefixes	*re-*	*un-*	*dis-*	*mis-*	
Suffixes	*-able*	*-ability*	*-ion*	*-ment*	*-al*

Build New Words	Definitions
avoid	***keep away from***
avoid(ing)	keeping away from
avoid(s)	keeps away from
avoid(able)	able to be kept away from
(un)avoid(able)	not able to be kept away from
improve	***make something better***
improv(ing)	making something better
improv(ed)	made something better
improve(ment)	act of improving or making better
entice	***lure or attract***
entic(ing)	luring or attracting
entice(ment)	act of luring or attracting
entic(ed)	lured or attracted

B. Complete the paragraph using words from Part A that have *avoid, improve*, or *entice* as the base word.

When my mother shops, she usually tries a Web site first. She wants to ___avoid___ the crowds at the mall. Besides, she is easily lured by ___enticing___ window displays. Yesterday, Mom learned about the new ___improvements___ to microwaves. She chose a model and sent Dad and me out to buy it. Mom was ___avoiding___ a trip to the crowded store. At the store, Dad and I tested the computers to see how they had ___improved___. I have never ___avoided___ a chance to see the latest technology. With the added ___enticement___ of free upgrades, Dad and I returned home with a new computer. I guess what happened next was ___unavoidable___. Mom explained that she couldn't microwave our popcorn in the computer.

53

ELL Provide extra support for students by telling them the definitions of the words used in context. Then allow them to find the context clues in the text that support the definitions.

3. Have students turn to Student Book page 53. Explain that by learning the meaning of one word and understanding word parts, students can learn other words in the same word family. Read aloud the instructions for Part A and have students complete the section. Have partners compare their responses. Then have students complete Part B independently.

CHECKPOINT If students have difficulty with Part B, suggest they look back at the list of word parts to make new words that will fit the answer.

Reread

Apply the Target Skill: Text Features

1. **Why should readers pay attention to text features?** (to know what to expect from the reading)
2. Direct students to Student Book page 54. Read aloud the instructions for Parts A and B. Make sure students recognize that the headings state the main topic of the sections. Have students complete the activity independently.
3. When students finish, have them share their answers.

Refer to Blackline Master page 13 to extend practice using text features.

Write in Response to Reading

1. **Think about your own opinions and whether you like or dislike online shopping. Your opinions are based on your experiences or the experiences of someone you know.**
2. **You will describe your shopping experiences and opinions about the passage's main ideas. Turn to Student Book page 55.** Read the instructions aloud.
3. After students complete their writing, have them share their opinions.

EXPEDITION ORGANIZER **R U Online?**

Pause to have students turn to Student Book pages 30 and 31. Have students complete the following:

- Think about the main idea from "Online Shopping Versus Brick-and-Mortar Stores" and write it in the appropriate space.
- Have students read "Your Internet World." Explain that *town square* as used here refers to an open area of a town where the community would gather and visit. *Global village* refers to the world being one village when everyone is connected by the Internet. For students who need additional support, explain that Bill Gates is the founder of Microsoft.

Build Background DVD 2.2

Briefly discuss the Expedition passages. Then, watch the DVD together. After watching, review student responses to the probing questions using the Expedition Organizer.

Expedition 2, Lesson 9

Name ______________________ Date ____________

Text Features

A. Look at the following images in your Anthology. Tell how they helped you understand more about the text. Answers will vary, but could include the following.

Photo of catalog, page 29 helped understand about mail-order catalogs

Photo and caption, page 30 helped visualize the difference between online shopping and shopping at a store

Photo and caption, page 31 helped realize the impact that online shopping has on brick-and-mortar stores

Photo and caption, page 32 helped understand how online warehouses work

B. List the headings from "Online Shopping" in the boxes provided. The headings state the main topic of each section. Reread the section and list details that support the main topic.

Benefits of Online Shopping

convenience; visit many stores quickly; compare styles and brands instantly; determine who has best price; prices might be better or offer discounts; wide selection; stores never close; no crowds or parking problems; saves gas; gifts can be shipped

Traditional Shopping Has Benefits

can touch and try on; can see what you're getting; can return or exchange easily; online product information can be inaccurate; social event to shop; chance to get away from home or work; can read any part of a book before purchasing

Best of Both Worlds

research product online; buy at the store; brick-and-mortar stores working with online stores to be better

 54

Expedition 2, Lesson 9

Name ______________________ Date ____________

Write in Response to Reading

In the following boxes, write a description of when you or someone you know shopped in a brick-and-mortar store and online. Include descriptive details in first person, such as what it was like to shop and place your order or make your purchase, what you bought, and what happened afterward. Finally, tell your opinions about both ways of shopping. Give reasons for your opinions. Answers will vary.

I remember the time when I went to the store and bought . . .

Another time, I decided to go online to buy . . .

After these two experiences, I think . . .
Student descriptions should include several of the descriptive elements suggested in the instructions, and the opinions should be accompanied by reasons.

 55

Review, Extend, Assess

In today's lesson, as in Lessons 5 and 10 of every Expedition, there are options from which to choose. You may do any or all of the options listed. Activities for each option are given on the following pages. Each option will support or extend previously taught objectives. Choose the option(s) appropriate for your students and prepare accordingly.

Review Vocabulary

Extend Vocabulary

Assess Comprehension and Vocabulary

Reteach

Passport Reading Journeys Library

Online Technology Component

Expedition Project

Real-World Reading

Exploring Careers

Review Vocabulary

Direct students to review the vocabulary for "Truth, Lies, and the Internet" and "Online Shopping Versus Brick-and-Mortar Stores" on Student Book page 30.

1. Have students turn to Student Book page 56. Tell them to focus on the meanings of the words they learned. **As you complete the review activity, go back and check the definitions to make sure you use the words correctly.**
2. Read the instructions for Part A aloud, and have students read through the blog comments before they choose answers. For Part B, tell them all the words are vocabulary words that have definitions in the Student Book.

CHECKPOINT Have students share their answers for Student Book page 56. If students have difficulty with a word, reteach the definition by using it in a familiar context, such as one related to school.

Expedition 2, Lesson 10

Name ______ Date ______

Review Vocabulary

A. Read the following blog comments. Remember to begin reading from the bottom. Circle the word that BEST completes each sentence.

April 14: Do people even know about the ban? The state has to publicize the laws and (emphasize, guarantee) that they will keep our roads safer for everyone. Posted by Amit 3:44 p.m.

April 12: It's a fact that teens are the biggest risk-takers of any age group! The ban helps teens (browse, avoid) unnecessary risks. So, I think cell phone laws should be enforced. Posted by Porfirio 7:20 a.m.

April 11: Are you going to ban just teens or the whole (spectrum, majority) of drivers from using cell phones? The habits of adults (influence, emphasize) how teens act, even if most teens don't admit it. Posted by Jake 10:01 p.m.

April 10: I support laws that ban using cell phones while driving. Teen drivers who talk on cell phones (react, determine) poorly to problems while they drive. This is not just my (selection, viewpoint)! Research proves this. Posted by Kerri 12:39 a.m.

B. Read the interview. Write a word from your Expedition Dictionary that BEST completes each sentence. Use the words in parentheses as clues.

This chat site was founded by Della Dorett, a high school student with a passion for publishing many viewpoints in her online magazine. Here's a "say it" session.

Della: Do the majority (greater than half) of your friends like to shop online?

Barry: Yes, most of them do because they can place an order (request to buy something) quickly. Some have a favorite online shop.

Della: What about you? Do you like a certain online merchant (person who buys and sells things)?

Barry: I totally avoid (keep away from) sellers who treat their employees badly. If a company has unfair labor rules, nothing can entice (lure) me to shop there.

Della: You are certainly opinionated (strongly sticking to your opinion)! How do you know which shops treat workers well?

Barry: I joined an organization that fights for worker rights. Its researchers show statistics that help me determine (reach a decision about) which shops are OK.

 56

Extend Vocabulary

1. Have students turn to Student Book page 57. **You can make new words with suffixes, or word parts you add to the end of a word.** Read the instructions for Part A. **Are the majority of the students in this class girls or boys?** After students answer, tell them you could also say that *the major group in this class is boys/girls.* **Because you know the meaning of the base word *major*, you can understand the meaning of the word *majority*.**
2. If needed, complete the second row with students before they work independently. Have students tell which words they have used before. For the words they have not used before, provide an example sentence.
3. Have students complete Part B independently.

CHECKPOINT Check that students correctly spelled the new words. Have them compare the spellings in Part A and Part B and make any corrections.

Part A

Explore and practice the base words. Ask students if they know the meanings. If not, provide a simple definition, then model using each word in a sentence. ***Major* means "larger or more important." A *major* point of the article was that we should be careful about what Internet sources we use. What is a *major* reason the Internet is useful?** Write the following sentence starter on the board to help students respond: *One* major *reason the Internet is useful is* _________.

Continue the process using the following prompts.

- **When you *interpret* something, you figure out what it means. I *interpret* your smile to mean that you are happy. How would you *interpret* a frown?** *I* interpret *a frown to mean* ________.
- **If you *avoid* something, you stay away from it. I *avoid* going out in the rain. What kinds of movies do you *avoid*?** *I* avoid *movies that* ________.
- **When something is *personal*, it is specific to you. My *personal* information includes my name, address, and telephone number. When would you need your *personal* information?** *I need my* personal *information when* _________.

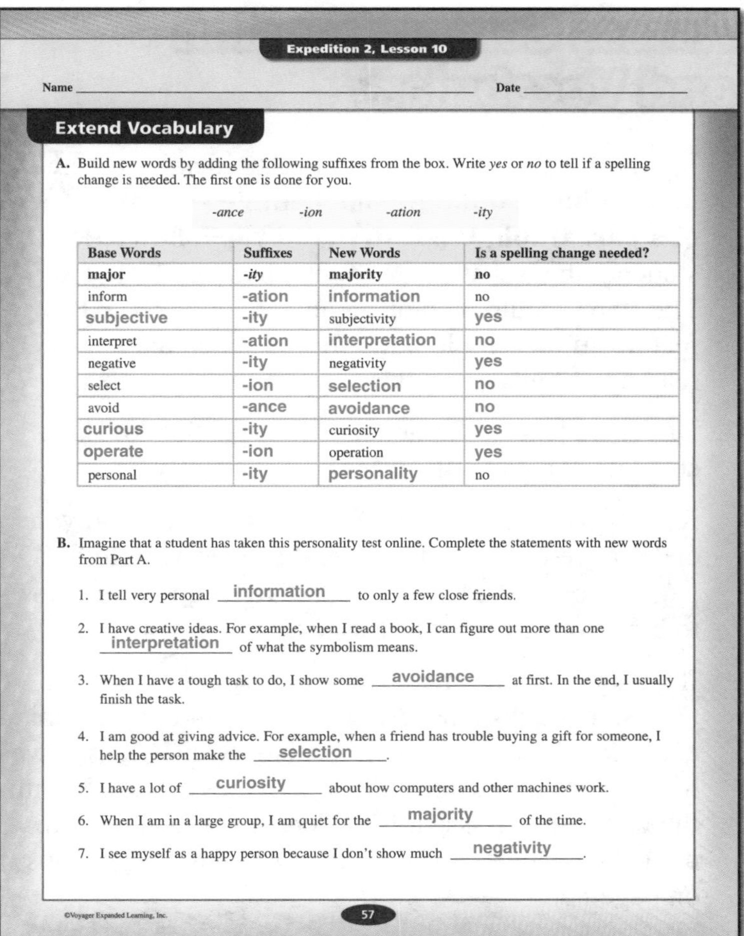

Expedition 2, Lesson 10

Name ______________________ Date ______________

Extend Vocabulary

A. Build new words by adding the following suffixes from the box. Write *yes* or *no* to tell if a spelling change is needed. The first one is done for you.

-ance *-ion* *-ation* *-ity*

Base Words	Suffixes	New Words	Is a spelling change needed?
major	***-ity***	**majority**	**no**
inform	-ation	information	no
subjective	-ity	subjectivity	yes
interpret	-ation	interpretation	no
negative	-ity	negativity	yes
select	-ion	selection	no
avoid	-ance	avoidance	no
curious	-ity	curiosity	yes
operate	-ion	operation	yes
personal	-ity	personality	no

B. Imagine that a student has taken this personality test online. Complete the statements with new words from Part A.

1. I tell very personal ___information___ to only a few close friends.
2. I have creative ideas. For example, when I read a book, I can figure out more than one ___interpretation___ of what the symbolism means.
3. When I have a tough task to do, I show some ___avoidance___ at first. In the end, I usually finish the task.
4. I am good at giving advice. For example, when a friend has trouble buying a gift for someone, I help the person make the ___selection___.
5. I have a lot of ___curiosity___ about how computers and other machines work.
6. When I am in a large group, I am quiet for the ___majority___ of the time.
7. I see myself as a happy person because I don't show much ___negativity___.

57

Part B

Explore the meanings of the new words students build by using the process above. If students have trouble completing Part B, read aloud the sentence frames. Then rephrase them as questions. For example, rephrase *I tell very* personal ________ *to only a few close friends.* as *What would you only tell to close friends?*

Assess Comprehension and Vocabulary

1. Review the process students used to identify the main idea. **Think about how you identified the main idea of a paragraph. What steps did you follow?** Have students suggest steps and write them on the board. The steps should include paying attention to text features if present, looking for the stated main idea, reading to find details that support the main idea.

2. Direct students to Student Book pages 58–60. Have students complete the pages independently.

   Review student answers. Whenever possible, provide elaborative feedback to student responses. Refer to page xl for examples of elaborative feedback and how to incorporate it in your lessons.

   If students incorrectly answer more than 4 out of 15 assessment questions, evaluate what kind of reteaching is needed. If students miss vocabulary questions, have them return to the vocabulary activities and work with the words they missed. If students have trouble with main idea and details, use the reteaching suggestions on page 85.

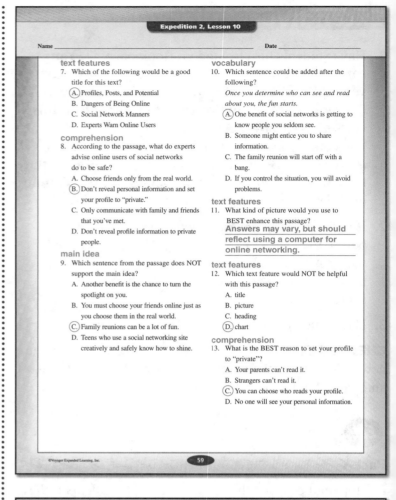

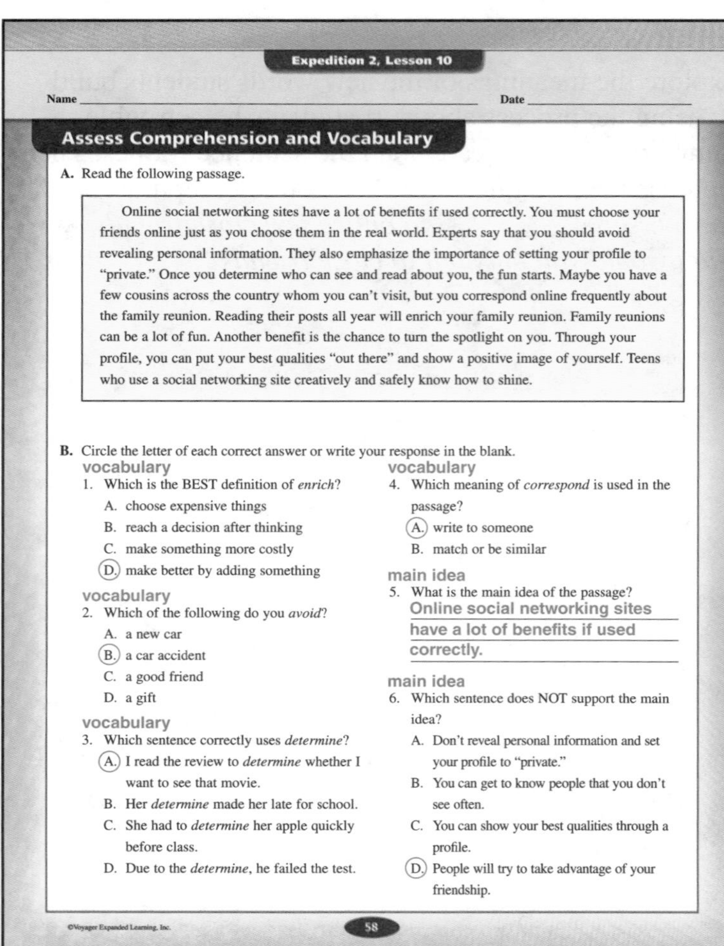

Expedition 2, Lesson 10

Name ______ Date ______

Assess Comprehension and Vocabulary

A. Read the following passage.

Online social networking sites have a lot of benefits if used correctly. You must choose your friends online just as you choose them in the real world. Experts say that you should avoid revealing personal information. They also emphasize the importance of setting your profile to "private." Once you determine who can see and read about you, the fun starts. Maybe you have a few cousins across the country whom you can't visit, but you correspond online frequently about the family reunion. Reading their posts all year will enrich your family reunion. Family reunions can be a lot of fun. Another benefit is the chance to turn the spotlight on you. Through your profile, you can put your best qualities "out there" and show a positive image of yourself. Teens who use a social networking site creatively and safely know how to shine.

B. Circle the letter of each correct answer or write your response in the blank.

vocabulary
1. Which is the BEST definition of *enrich*?
   - A. choose expensive things
   - B. reach a decision after thinking
   - C. make something more costly
   - (D.) make better by adding something

vocabulary
2. Which of the following do you *avoid*?
   - A. a new car
   - (B.) a car accident
   - C. a good friend
   - D. a gift

vocabulary
3. Which sentence correctly uses *determine*?
   - (A.) I read the review to *determine* whether I want to see that movie.
   - B. Her *determine* made her late for school.
   - C. She had to *determine* her apple quickly before class.
   - D. Due to the *determine*, he failed the test.

vocabulary
4. Which meaning of *correspond* is used in the passage?
   - (A.) write to someone
   - B. match or be similar

main idea
5. What is the main idea of the passage?
   Online social networking sites have a lot of benefits if used correctly.

main idea
6. Which sentence does NOT support the main idea?
   - A. Don't reveal personal information and set your profile to "private."
   - B. You can get to know people that you don't see often.
   - C. You can show your best qualities through a profile.
   - (D.) People will try to take advantage of your friendship.

©Voyager Expanded Learning, Inc. 58

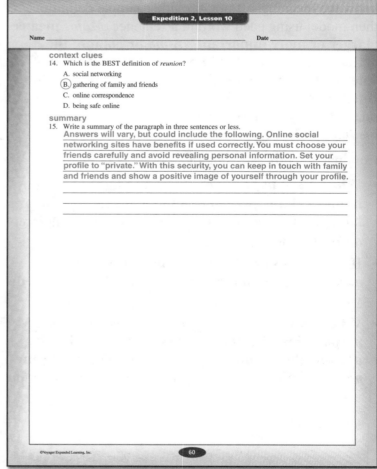

Expedition 2, Lesson 10

Name ______ Date ______

text features
7. Which of the following would be a good title for this text?
   - (A.) Profiles, Posts, and Potential
   - B. Dangers of Being Online
   - C. Social Network Manners
   - D. Experts Warn Online Users

comprehension
8. According to the passage, what do experts advise online users of social networks do to be safe?
   - A. Choose friends only from the real world.
   - (B.) Don't reveal personal information and set your profile to "private."
   - C. Only communicate with family and friends that you've met.
   - D. Don't reveal profile information to private people.

main idea
9. Which sentence from the passage does NOT support the main idea?
   - A. Another benefit is the chance to turn the spotlight on you.
   - B. You must choose your friends online just as you choose them in the real world.
   - (C.) Family reunions can be a lot of fun.
   - D. Teens who use a social networking site creatively and safely know how to shine.

vocabulary
10. Which sentence could be added after the following?
    Once you determine who can see and read about you, the fun starts.
    - (A.) One benefit of social networks is getting to know people you seldom see.
    - B. Someone might entice you to share information.
    - C. The family reunion will start off with a bang.
    - D. If you control the situation, you will avoid problems.

text features
11. What kind of picture would you use to BEST enhance this passage?
    Answers may vary, but should reflect using a computer for online networking.

text features
12. Which text feature would NOT be helpful with this passage?
    - A. title
    - B. picture
    - C. heading
    - (D.) chart

comprehension
13. What is the BEST reason to set your profile to "private"?
    - A. Your parents can't read it.
    - B. Strangers can't read it.
    - (C.) You can choose who reads your profile.
    - D. No one will see your personal information.

 59

Expedition 2, Lesson 10

Name ______ Date ______

context clues
14. Which is the BEST definition of *reunion*?
    - A. social networking
    - (B.) gathering of family and friends
    - C. online correspondence
    - D. being safe online

summary
15. Write a summary of the paragraph in three sentences or less.
    Answers will vary, but could include the following. Online social networking sites have benefits if used correctly. You must choose your friends carefully and avoid revealing personal information. Set your profile to "private." With this security, you can keep in touch with family and friends and show a positive image of yourself through your profile.

 60

Reteach

Main Idea and Details/Text Features

1. Have students turn to Student Book page 61. Read the passage aloud. **Sometimes a main idea is stated directly in the paragraph or passage.** For Part A, have students scan the passage and draw two lines under the main idea. Have students share what they underlined and confirm their answers. Then have them write the answer to the first item. **You can check whether you know what the main idea is by finding details that support it.** Have students identify the details, discuss their choices, and complete the activity.
2. For Part B, read aloud each item in the list of text features. Have students scan textbooks or magazines to find examples of text features. **If you spot a text feature that is not listed in the Student Book, add it to the appropriate category.** Discuss new text features students find. Then complete the first question, calling attention to the clues in it, such as the comparison of products, prices, and models. **If we do not see clues in the question, we should think about the title and use our own knowledge of the topic to decide what belongs in the article.**

ELL For students who had difficulty with the main idea and details, reteach by having them underline specific parts of the assessment passage. **Reread the first two sentences. Underline the main idea.** (Online social networking sites have a lot of benefits if used correctly.) Have students continue underlining words and phrases in the remaining sentences that support the main idea.

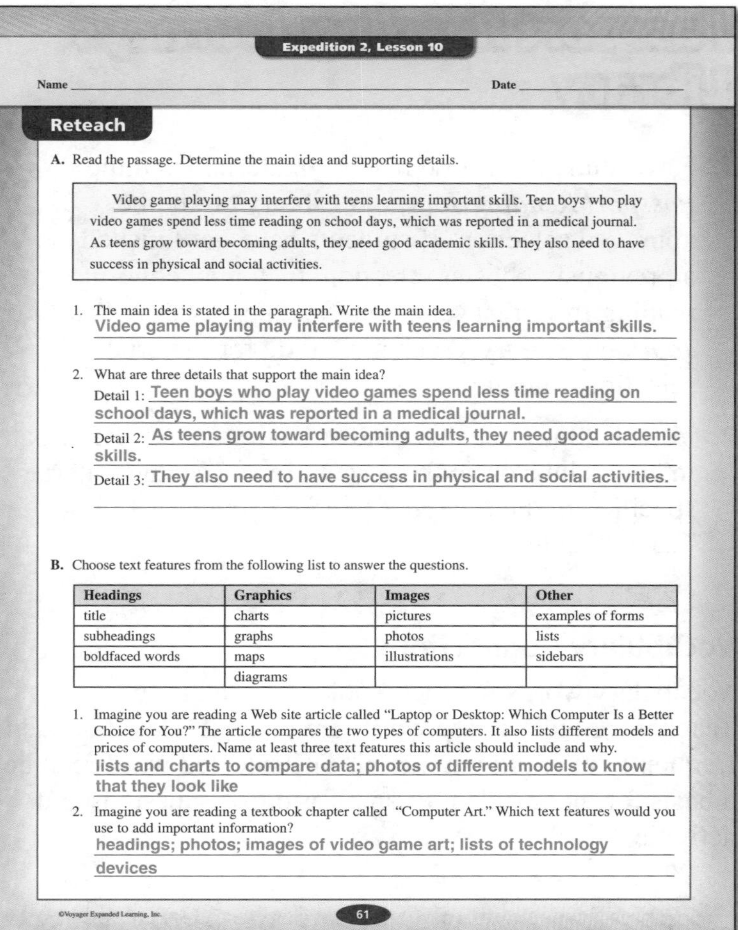

Expedition 2, Lesson 10

Name ______ Date ______

Reteach

A. Read the passage. Determine the main idea and supporting details.

Video game playing may interfere with teens learning important skills. Teen boys who play video games spend less time reading on school days, which was reported in a medical journal. As teens grow toward becoming adults, they need good academic skills. They also need to have success in physical and social activities.

1. The main idea is stated in the paragraph. Write the main idea.
Video game playing may interfere with teens learning important skills.

2. What are three details that support the main idea?
Detail 1: Teen boys who play video games spend less time reading on school days, which was reported in a medical journal.
Detail 2: As teens grow toward becoming adults, they need good academic skills.
Detail 3: They also need to have success in physical and social activities.

B. Choose text features from the following list to answer the questions.

Headings	Graphics	Images	Other
title	charts	pictures	examples of forms
subheadings	graphs	photos	lists
boldfaced words	maps	illustrations	sidebars
	diagrams		

1. Imagine you are reading a Web site article called "Laptop or Desktop: Which Computer Is a Better Choice for You?" The article compares the two types of computers. It also lists different models and prices of computers. Name at least three text features this article should include and why.
lists and charts to compare data; photos of different models to know that they look like

2. Imagine you are reading a textbook chapter called "Computer Art." Which text features would you use to add important information?
headings; photos; images of video game art; lists of technology devices

61

Passport Reading Journeys Library

1. Have students choose reading material from the *Passport Reading Journeys* Library or another approved selection. If students have not finished a previously chosen selection, they may continue reading from that selection. See the *Passport Reading Journeys* Library Teacher's Guide for material on selection guidelines.
2. You also may use this time to have students participate in book clubs or book presentations. Use the criteria specified in the *Passport Reading Journeys* Library Teacher's Guide.

Vocabulary Connections

Vocabulary words for each book are listed in the Teacher's Guide. These words are content related or used frequently in reading material. The selected words can be a basis for independent or small-group discussions and activities.

Student Opportunities

Six copies of each book title are provided in the *Passport Reading Journeys* Library. The number of copies makes it possible for small groups of students to read the same material and share the information they read.

Theme-related titles include *Code Orange.*

Technology

1. Depending on your classroom configuration and computer access, you may have students work through the technology in a lab setting or have individuals or small groups of students work on desktops or laptops while other students participate in other suggested activities, such as the *Passport Reading Journeys* Library.
2. The online technology component provides additional support for students to work with selected vocabulary words. Students will work through a series of activities to strengthen their word knowledge, then apply that knowledge to passage reading. Refer to the online technology component User Guide for more information.

   Theme-related word sets include Math and Technology.

Expedition Project

Web Site

Distribute copies of Project Blackline Master page 4. Have students look at the page and follow along as you explain the assignment. Assign point values, and have students write them in the rubric. Tell them to make any notes on the page that will help them, but they will turn in the page with the assignment. Have students think about "cool graphics" and other elements that attract them to a Web site. Have students also think about the standards they listed in Lesson 5. **What makes a Web site a good one? You will design a Web site that sells a product and demonstrates these elements.** Have students form small groups and direct them to follow these steps:

1. Students may refer to the Web sites used in Lesson 5 Writing Process (or to the screen shot of the Web site on Writing Blackline Master page 3 if students do not have access to the Internet) as needed for ideas.
2. Have students follow these steps to create their Web site:
   - Decide what your Web site will sell.
   - Design three screens to be accessed on your site.
     - a home page with a link to a catalog
     - a catalog screen that shows the product with a link to the checkout
     - a checkout screen that shows how to order the product
   - Assign one screen to one (or two) group members to design. Sketch your ideas on paper.
3. When everything is mapped out, have students create posters showing the three screens for their Web site. They should use labels to show the different features. Instruct students to use colored pencils or markers and magazine cutouts or drawings.
4. Have students use at least three vocabulary words from the Expedition in the Web site posters and three more words in the oral presentations.
5. Students will present their Web site plan to the class. Allow time to rehearse the presentations. Each group member should talk about his or her particular screen, explaining all the features.
6. Have students present their Web sites during class.
7. To assess student presentations, use the rubric provided at the bottom of the Project Blackline Master.

Real-World Reading

Online News Article

1. Direct students to Student Book page 62. Explain that all readers should use reading strategies when they read real-world materials, such as news stories and blogs online. Have students preview the headings and other text features. **What do you know about the text already?** (These are two online newspaper articles from the *Los Angeles Post* and Celeb Blog!) **What do you predict the author's purpose is for writing "Drug Charges Dropped"? Why?** (The purpose is to state news. The dateline is Los Angeles. It shows it is news from a certain place. The headline indicates the article has facts, not opinions.) **What do you predict the author's purpose is for writing "Will Staci Face the Music"? Why?** (The purpose is to give an opinion. The author is writing a blog, which is a way to share opinions about facts from other sources.)
2. Write the following instructions on the board. Tell students to mark the text as they read.
   - *Underline with two lines the sources the authors cite.*
   - *Underline with one line the key facts in both articles.*
   - *Circle clues that show opinions of the author.*
3. Have students read and place a check mark by the following words. Then have them tell the meanings. Clarify their understanding as needed:
   - *Issue* (passage 1) means "send out."
   - *Circulating* (passage 2) means "distributing in a wide area."
4. **Do you think the author of *Celeb Blog!* is convincing? Explain.** Have students use the information they marked in the passages and their own ideas to answer.

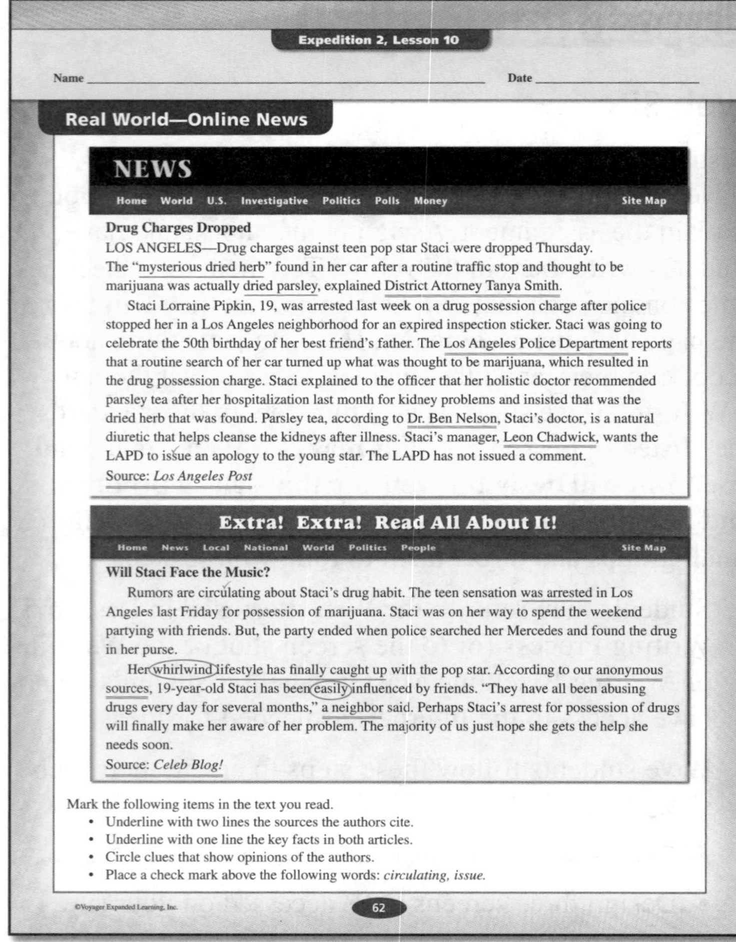

Expedition 2, Lesson 10

Name ____________ Date ____________

Real World—Online News

NEWS

Home World U.S. Investigative Politics Polls Money Site Map

Drug Charges Dropped

LOS ANGELES—Drug charges against teen pop star Staci were dropped Thursday. The "mysterious dried herb" found in her car after a routine traffic stop and thought to be marijuana was actually dried parsley, explained District Attorney Tanya Smith.

Staci Lorraine Pipkin, 19, was arrested last week on a drug possession charge after police stopped her in a Los Angeles neighborhood for an expired inspection sticker. Staci was going to celebrate the 50th birthday of her best friend's father. The Los Angeles Police Department reports that a routine search of her car turned up what was thought to be marijuana, which resulted in the drug possession charge. Staci explained to the officer that her holistic doctor recommended parsley tea after her hospitalization last month for kidney problems and insisted that was the dried herb that was found. Parsley tea, according to Dr. Ben Nelson, Staci's doctor, is a natural diuretic that helps cleanse the kidneys after illness. Staci's manager, Leon Chadwick, wants the LAPD to issue an apology to the young star. The LAPD has not issued a comment.

Source: *Los Angeles Post*

Extra! Extra! Read All About It!

Home News Local National World Politics People Site Map

Will Staci Face the Music?

Rumors are circulating about Staci's drug habit. The teen sensation was arrested in Los Angeles last Friday for possession of marijuana. Staci was on her way to spend the weekend partying with friends. But, the party ended when police searched her Mercedes and found the drug in her purse.

Her whirlwind lifestyle has finally caught up with the pop star. According to our anonymous sources, 19-year-old Staci has been easily influenced by friends. "They have all been abusing drugs every day for several months," a neighbor said. Perhaps Staci's arrest for possession of drugs will finally make her aware of her problem. The majority of us just hope she gets the help she needs soon.

Source: *Celeb Blog!*

Mark the following items in the text you read.
- Underline with two lines the sources the authors cite.
- Underline with one line the key facts in both articles.
- Circle clues that show opinions of the authors.
- Place a check mark above the following words: *circulating, issue.*

62

Exploring Careers

Careers in Information Technology (IT) and Computers

1. Direct students to "Information Technology" on Anthology page 33. Have students preview the photo and title and type of page. **What do you think this article will be about?** (careers in computers) **Turn the title into a question.** Have students share their responses. (Possible response: Which information technology careers interest me?) **Focus on answering your question as you read.**
2. Have students read the article. When all students finish reading, have them share one answer they found to their question.
3. Direct students to Student Book page 63. Have them answer the questions using information they read in the Anthology article. Then they can complete the chart at the bottom by researching a career in IT in books or online.

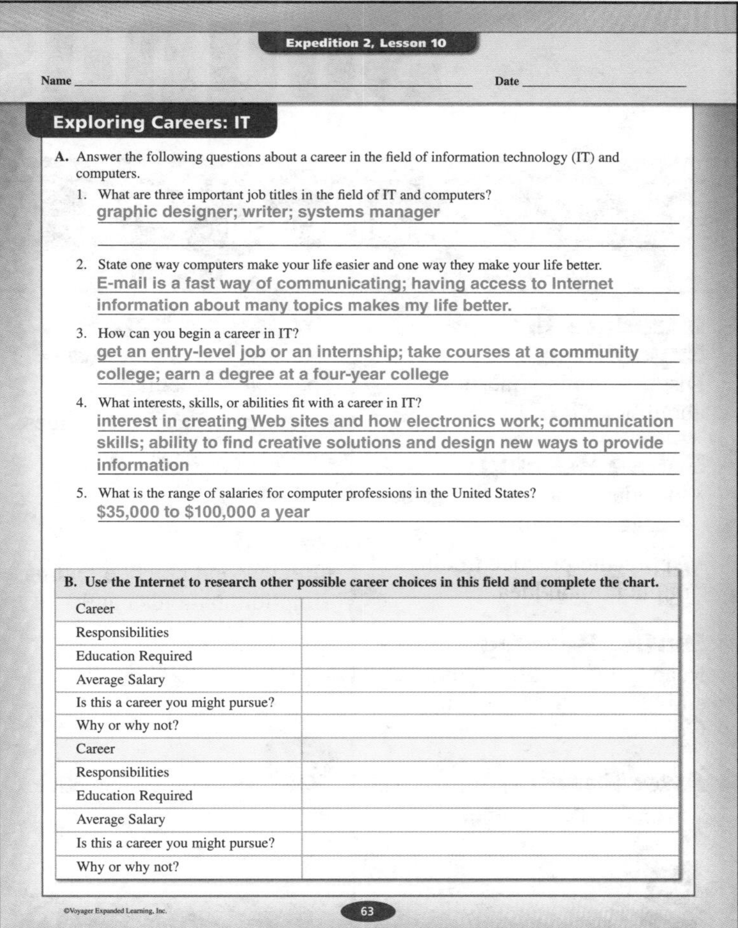

Expedition 2, Lesson 10

Name ______________________ Date ____________

Exploring Careers: IT

A. Answer the following questions about a career in the field of information technology (IT) and computers.

1. What are three important job titles in the field of IT and computers?
graphic designer; writer; systems manager
2. State one way computers make your life easier and one way they make your life better.
E-mail is a fast way of communicating; having access to Internet information about many topics makes my life better.
3. How can you begin a career in IT?
get an entry-level job or an internship; take courses at a community college; earn a degree at a four-year college
4. What interests, skills, or abilities fit with a career in IT?
interest in creating Web sites and how electronics work; communication skills; ability to find creative solutions and design new ways to provide information
5. What is the range of salaries for computer professions in the United States?
$35,000 to $100,000 a year

B. Use the Internet to research other possible career choices in this field and complete the chart.

Career	
Responsibilities	
Education Required	
Average Salary	
Is this a career you might pursue?	
Why or why not?	
Career	
Responsibilities	
Education Required	
Average Salary	
Is this a career you might pursue?	
Why or why not?	

©Voyager Expanded Learning, Inc. 63

Webmaster. Graphic designer. Writer. Systems manager. Technical support specialist. Advertising agent. Product manager. Each of these job titles represents a career available to those wishing to work in the Information Technology (IT) field.

Information Technology is defined as the development, installation, and implementation of computer systems, hardware, and software. In other words, it includes any job related to computers. A majority of businesses depend on computers to manage their staff, communicate internally, and compute their payroll. They also rely on technology to keep in touch with their clients and the rest of the outside world. As a result, IT professionals are often responsible for keeping their companies running.

You may think you want no part of this field, that only computer geeks could be happy in an IT job. But, you probably use and enjoy more benefits of IT than you realize. From sending e-mail and text messages to playing video games, technology touches our lives in many ways. There is a wide selection of jobs to consider. Some people are involved with building the hardware. Others develop the programs that make businesses operate properly. Some IT career options involve designing Web sites, setting up computer networks, or managing software systems, to name just a few. Information Technology is an all-encompassing field.

There are many different ways in which to enter this field. Many people attend college and pursue degrees in computer science or computer engineering. Others decide to get

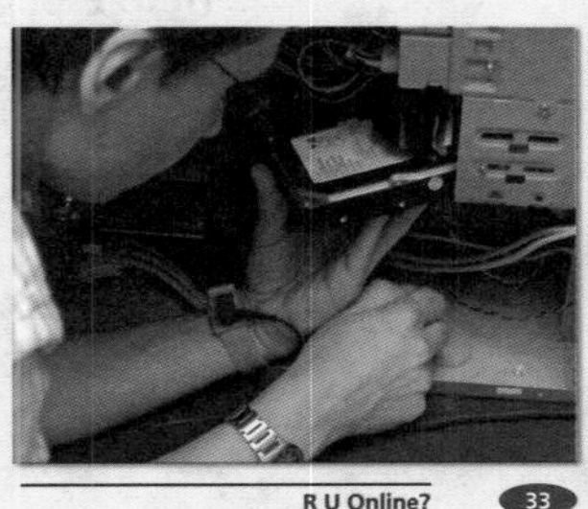

R U Online? 33

Career

vocational training at a technical college. Finally, some people just learn by doing. Others start by creating their own Web site or by developing a program for others to use. Or, some people begin with an entry-level position and work to gain knowledge and experience on the job.

One attractive element of IT is the wide variety of jobs available. There are positions at all levels, from data entry positions to the chief information officer of a large corporation. If you think you might like to explore an IT career, an entry-level job or internship may be the best way to get a taste of the industry. By working alongside professionals, you can easily learn the day-to-day details of life in the IT world. It is no surprise that IT offers people the chance to work in almost any industry, from accounting to television production. Everyone needs computers and wants them running efficiently.

Technology is advancing and changing. With the rise in popularity of the Internet, more and more jobs are being created. As a result, IT jobs are also thriving. There is a strong demand for qualified IT people. Many IT positions are expected to grow at a faster-than-average pace during the next 10 years. There are good benefits in the IT world. Salaries for these types of jobs can range from $35,000 to more than $100,000 a year.

Today, more and more people turn to Digg, YouTube, and Google to get their news and entertainment. The Internet has been a strong influence on businesses. As a result, the IT industry continues to grow. People with a passion for computers can become Webmasters, systems managers, computer programmers, or any number of other occupations in the IT field.

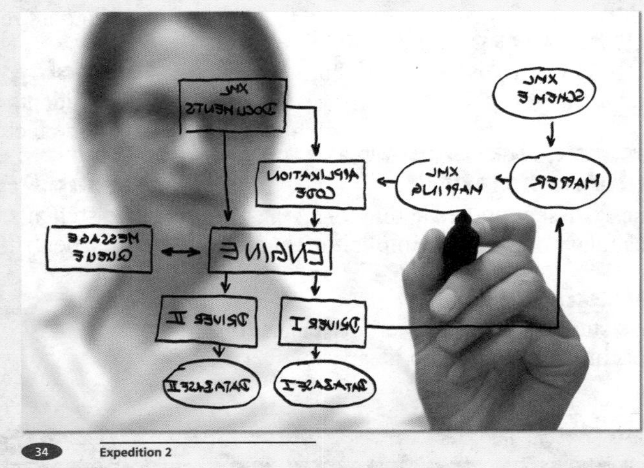

34 Expedition 2

Sounds of Life

"Music with a Message"		"Evolution of Music"	
Lesson 1	**Lesson 2**	**Lesson 3**	**Lesson 4**
Introduce the Expedition Discuss probing questions about Sounds of Life. **Before Reading** • Introduce and practice using passage vocabulary. • Apply and practice finding implicit main idea. **During Reading** Read "Music with a Message" and "Follow the Drinking Gourd." **After Reading** Check comprehension. Have students practice vocabulary using the online technology component. Have students select books for independent reading. ELL Extend and practice.	**Prepare to Reread** • Review and practice using passage vocabulary. • Practice using context clues. • Build new words using prefixes. **Reread** • Review and practice finding implicit main idea and details. • Write a paragraph. ELL Extend and practice.	**Before Reading** • Introduce and practice using passage vocabulary. • Apply the target skill and practice finding implicit main idea and details. • Introduce the passage by previewing and making predictions. **During Reading** Read "Evolution of Music." **After Reading** Check comprehension. Have students practice vocabulary using the online technology component. Have students select books for independent reading. ELL Extend and practice.	**Prepare to Reread** • Review and practice using passage vocabulary. • Practice using context clues. • Build new words using roots. **Reread** • Review and practice finding implicit main idea and details. • Write an interview and a music review. ELL Extend and practice.

Lesson 5—Review, Extend, Assess		
Review Vocabulary Review and practice using passage vocabulary. **Extend Vocabulary** Use base words and affixes to build and understand new words. **Assess Comprehension and Vocabulary** Assess student understanding of vocabulary and finding implicit main idea. **Reteach** Have students complete activity pages for reteaching implicit main idea.	**Passport Reading Journeys Library** Have students select books for independent reading. **Technology** Have students practice vocabulary using the online technology component. **Writing Process** Have students use the writing process to write a descriptive essay about a favorite band.	**Real-World Reading** Have students read a Web site and complete instructions. **Exploring Careers** Have students read about disc jockeys and complete an activity page. **Teacher's Note** Before beginning the Expedition, ask your librarian to suggest books that will fit with the theme. Books relating to music and sound will be appropriate for this Expedition.

"Music without Instruments"		"The Science of Sound"	
Lesson 6	**Lesson 7**	**Lesson 8**	**Lesson 9**
Before Reading • Introduce and practice using passage vocabulary. • Apply and practice finding implicit main idea and details. • Introduce the passage. **During Reading** Read "Music without Instruments." **After Reading** Check comprehension. Have students practice vocabulary using the online technology component. Have students select books for independent reading. ELL Extend and practice.	**Prepare to Reread** • Review and practice using passage vocabulary. • Practice using context clues. • Build new words using suffixes. **Reread** • Review and practice finding implicit main idea and details. • Write a paragraph. ELL Extend and practice.	**Before Reading** • Introduce and practice using passage vocabulary. • Apply and practice using text features. • Introduce the passage by previewing and making predictions. **During Reading** Read "The Science of Sound." **After Reading** Check comprehension. Have students practice vocabulary using the online technology component. Have students select books for independent reading. ELL Extend and practice.	**Prepare to Reread** • Review and practice using passage vocabulary. • Practice using context clues. • Build new words using affixes and inflectional endings. **Reread** • Review and practice using text features. • Write a paragraph. ELL Extend and practice.

Lesson 10—Review, Extend, Assess

Review Vocabulary
Review and practice using passage vocabulary.

Extend Vocabulary
Use affixes to build and understand new words.

Assess Comprehension and Vocabulary
Assess student understanding of vocabulary, finding implicit main idea and details, using text features, and other previously taught skills.

Reteach
Have students complete activity pages for reteaching implicit main idea and text features.

Passport Reading Journeys Library
Have students select books for independent reading.

Technology
Have students practice vocabulary using the online technology component.

Expedition Project
Have students conduct an interview and present the findings.

Real-World Reading
Have students read an album review and complete instructions.

Exploring Careers
Have students read about behind-the-scenes music careers and complete an activity page.

Expedition 3

Introduce the Expedition

1. Have students name some of their favorite musicians. **Why are these musicians important to you?** Direct students to think about the Expedition 3 opener photographs on Anthology page 35. **Which of these musicians do you recognize?** (Bono, Björk, Bob Marley) Identify the musicians students do not recognize.
2. Have students discuss possible responses to the following probing questions. Explain that the questions pertain to what they are about to learn.
   - **How has music guided people in the past?**
   - **Where does the music you listen to come from?**
   - **What impact has music had on America's history?**
   - **What is the future of music?**

Build Background DVD 3.1
Have students view a brief DVD that provides background information about music. **As you watch, listen for ideas that connect to the responses you discussed.**

3. Point out the parts of Student Book pages 64 and 65, Expedition Organizer: Sounds of Life. **As you read the passages, you'll record your own ideas about these questions and about the passages.**

   Suggestions for how students can add ideas to the Expedition Organizer appear in this Teacher's Edition at the end of Lessons 2, 4, 7, and 9. If students have responses now, allow them to write on the graphic organizer in Part A.

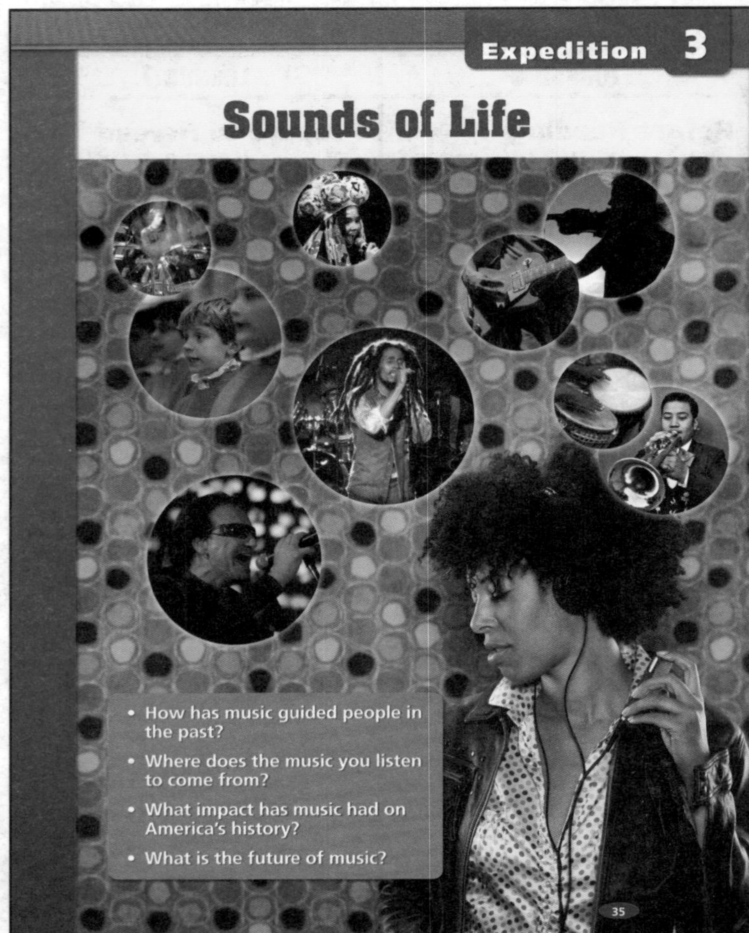
Expedition 3
Sounds of Life
• How has music guided people in the past?
• Where does the music you listen to come from?
• What impact has music had on America's history?
• What is the future of music?
35

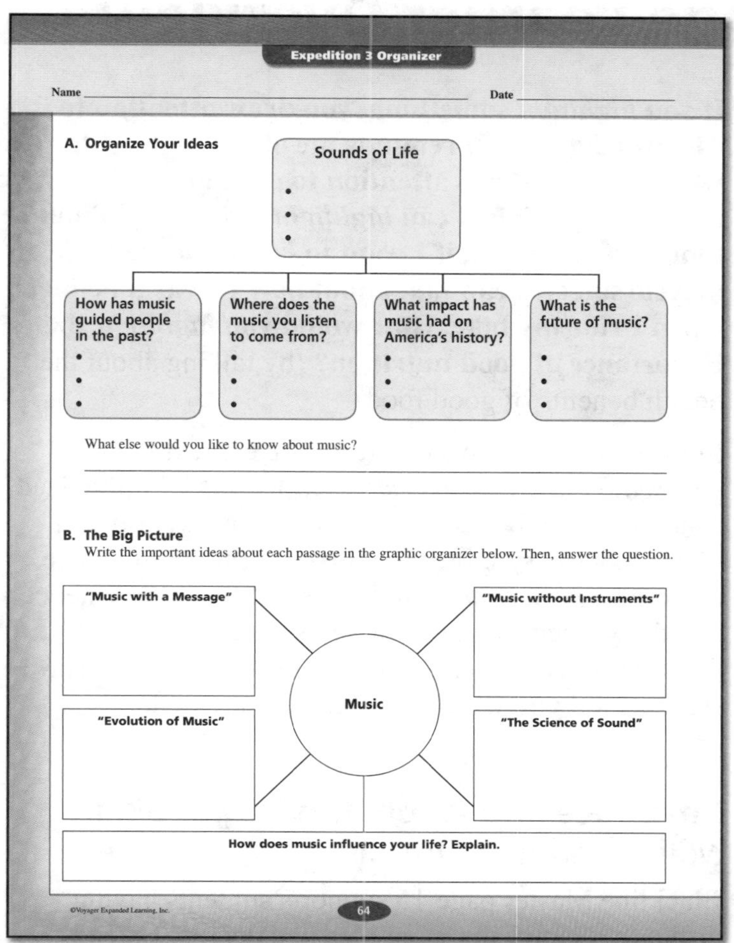

Expedition 3 Organizer

Name ______________________ Date ____________

A. Organize Your Ideas

Sounds of Life
•
•
•

How has music guided people in the past?	Where does the music you listen to come from?	What impact has music had on America's history?	What is the future of music?
• • •	• • •	• • •	• • •

What else would you like to know about music?

B. The Big Picture

Write the important ideas about each passage in the graphic organizer below. Then, answer the question.

"Music with a Message"

"Music without Instruments"

Music

"Evolution of Music"

"The Science of Sound"

How does music influence your life? Explain.

©Voyager Expanded Learning, Inc. 64

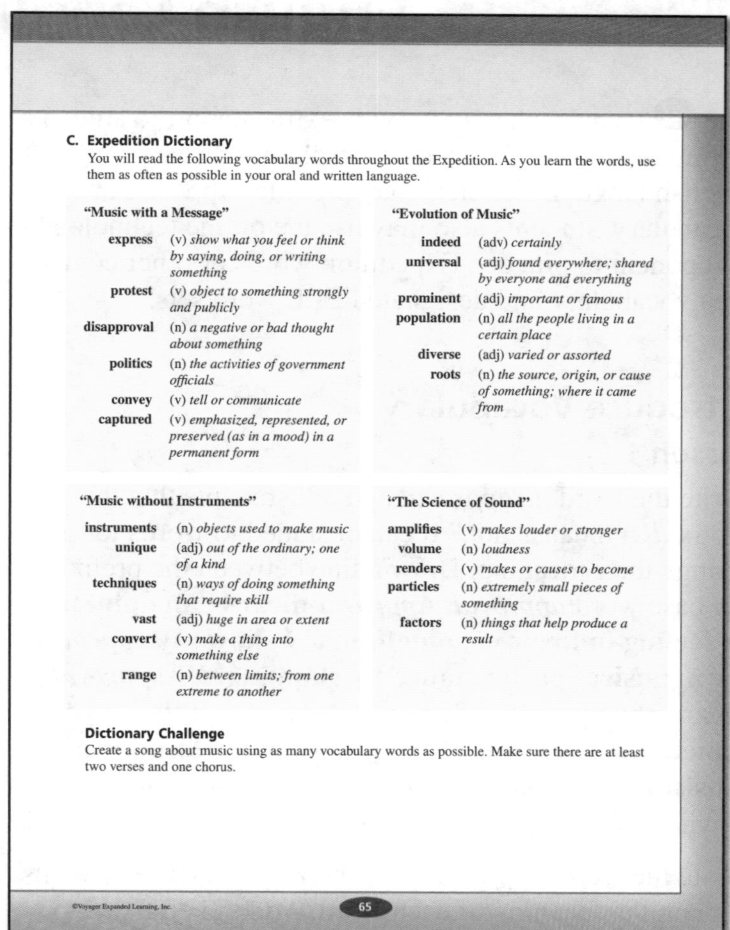

C. Expedition Dictionary

You will read the following vocabulary words throughout the Expedition. As you learn the words, use them as often as possible in your oral and written language.

"Music with a Message"

express (v) *show what you feel or think by saying, doing, or writing something*
protest (v) *object to something strongly and publicly*
disapproval (n) *a negative or bad thought about something*
politics (n) *the activities of government officials*
convey (v) *tell or communicate*
captured (v) *emphasized, represented, or preserved (as in a mood) in a permanent form*

"Evolution of Music"

indeed (adv) *certainly*
universal (adj) *found everywhere; shared by everyone and everything*
prominent (adj) *important or famous*
population (n) *all the people living in a certain place*
diverse (adj) *varied or assorted*
roots (n) *the source, origin, or cause of something; where it came from*

"Music without Instruments"

instruments (n) *objects used to make music*
unique (adj) *out of the ordinary; one of a kind*
techniques (n) *ways of doing something that require skill*
vast (adj) *huge in area or extent*
convert (v) *make a thing into something else*
range (n) *between limits; from one extreme to another*

"The Science of Sound"

amplifies (v) *makes louder or stronger*
volume (n) *loudness*
renders (v) *makes or causes to become*
particles (n) *extremely small pieces of something*
factors (n) *things that help produce a result*

Dictionary Challenge

Create a song about music using as many vocabulary words as possible. Make sure there are at least two verses and one chorus.

©Voyager Expanded Learning, Inc. 65

ELL

Making Connections

Tell students that music is important to people from different cultures and that people identify with different music. Engage students in the music theme by asking them to share different types of music they know and the names for the music in other languages. Have them name prominent artists for each type of music. Discuss who these artists' fans are. Are they popular in certain countries and cultures and with certain age groups? Record their responses in a chart.

Type of Music	Words in Other Languages	Artists	How or Why They Are Popular

Preview the context word *genre* by replacing *type* with *genre* in the chart. Tell students *genre* is another way of saying "type." Ask them to share their favorite genre of music using the sentence frame: *My favorite genre of music is* ________.

If students need support when reading passages that give specific information about different types of music, focus on language support. For example, support them before they read about music with a message by . . .

- asking what they already know about the words *express* and *protest*.
- using everyday or personal examples to explain what *express* and *protest* mean. I *express* friendship by shaking hands. I *express* my opinion when I tell how I feel. The child will *protest* if he disagrees with his mother's rules. The students will *protest* the new law by writing letters to their congressperson.
- connecting to the content by asking how music can be used to *express* feelings or *protest* injustice.

English Language Learner Overview

The ELL signals when to provide extra support to students during the lesson. As needed, Blackline Masters for English language learners may provide support. For vocabulary, students also may use the online technology component to practice Expedition words or other content-area vocabulary and designated ELL word sets.

Introduce Vocabulary

Lesson 1

Write the word *disapproval* and tell students that the prefix *dis-* means "not." It can be added to words to change their meaning. Draw a line between the prefix and the base word *approval*. ***Approval* means "an opinion or feeling in favor of something." I show my *approval* for a musical performance by clapping. *Disapproval* means the opposite of approval, or an opinion against something. How would you show *disapproval* for a musical performance?** (booing; giving the thumbs-down; leaving the performance)

Write the words *agree*, *credit*, and *respect*. Have students explain the meaning of each word. Add the prefix *dis-* to the beginning of each word, and discuss how the meanings change.

Lesson 3

Ask students whether they know a cognate for *universal* in their native language. Read aloud the definition. Ask students what the word for *universal* is in their native language. Have students respond to the following questions.

- **If people all over the world do something, can we say it is universal?** (yes)
- **Is listening to music a universal form of entertainment?** (yes)
- **Is an appreciation for rap music universal?** (no) **Explain.** (Not everyone appreciates rap music.)

Practice Vocabulary

In Lesson 2, provide support for the context words *escalated* and *highlights*. **If something has *escalated*, it has gotten bigger or stronger. Mr. Rios was running late for work, and his problem *escalated* when his train was delayed. Did his problem get worse or better?** (It got worse.) **If you *highlight* something, you draw attention to it. The word *highlight* reminds me of my highlighter pen, which I use to draw attention to certain words in my reading materials. I can *highlight* what I say about a topic. For example, if I want to *highlight* the topic of bicycle safety, I can talk about how I wear a helmet when I ride my bike. How would you *highlight* the importance of good nutrition?** (by talking about the health benefits of good food)

In Lesson 4, provide support for the context word *stressed*. **In the passage, *stressed* means "emphasized." You can *stress* beats in music and poetry, and you can *stress* the syllables in words.** Write the sentence *It's such a perfect day.* on the board. Read the sentence aloud, exaggerating the stressed syllables: **It's SUCH a PERfect DAY.** Touch each syllable as you say it. Have students tell you which syllables are stressed.

Introduce and Apply the Target Skill: Main Idea and Details

Blackline Master page 15 supports students having difficulty identifying main idea and details. Extend practice for Part A, question 2, by having students name other details that support the main idea.

Introduce and Apply the Target Skill: Write a Summary

Support students as they write summaries by providing the following sentence starters. First, have students read the sentence starters and state which words are unfamiliar, such as *concluded*. Use simple definitions when you explain unfamiliar vocabulary.

- *Juan decided to do his research report on music because _________. He found out that ________. He concluded that ________.*

If students have difficulty summarizing, ask the following questions:

- **What did Juan want to find out about music?** (how universal it is)
- **Did Juan find out that music has been the same since the 1950s or that it has changed since the 1950s?** (He found out that it has changed.)
- **Did Juan conclude that music has universal appeal or that only a few people like music?** (Music has universal appeal.)

"Who shot me?
But you punks didn't finish
Now you're 'bout to feel the wrath of a menace . . . "

The lyrics are from the song "Hit 'Em Up" by Tupac Shakur, a West Coast rapper who was shot to death in 1996. The song speaks clearly to his rivals on the East Coast. In the 1990s, a feud, or quarrel, began between East Coast and West Coast rappers. East Coast rapper Tim Dog released a single insulting West Coast rap artists. His song was soon answered. The reply came in the song lyrics of rappers on the West Coast. The feud escalated. During the next few years, as the quarrel grew stronger, rap lyrics were filled with messages and warnings to the rival artists on the opposite coast. Deaths were even associated with the feud.

Messages have always been embedded within musical lyrics. 1 In the 1800s, slaves used songs like "The Drinking Gourd" to reveal hidden messages and **express** their emotions. Rap music is one genre, or style of music, that also frequently contains messages. Rappers have used their music to communicate with one another. They also have used their lyrics to **protest** government injustices and motivate the public to react to current events.

The hip-hop group the Beastie Boys released their single "In a World Gone Mad" in 2003. The song, which protested the Iraq War, expressed the group's **disapproval** of current **politics** in the United States. In the chorus, they sang about how violence and hate prevent people from thinking properly.

Rapper Jadakiss also used his songs to **convey** his political opinions. He **captured** his disdain for President George W. Bush in his single "Why?" In the song, he blamed the president for failing to prevent the destruction of the Twin Towers in New York City on September 11, 2001. Perhaps he hoped his song would encourage others to voice their own disapproval of the president.

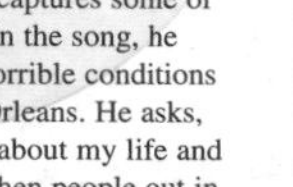

Hurricane Katrina devastated the Gulf Coast in 2005. After the storm, many musical artists expressed their feelings in their songs. Many were angered by the government's slow response to those who needed assistance. They used their music to convey this message to the public and to political officials. In his single "Mother Nature," rapper Papoose captures some of the frustration. In the song, he highlights the horrible conditions of life in New Orleans. He asks, "How can I rap about my life and claim honor? When people out in New Orleans don't have water." Many other artists used their songs to draw attention to the problems as well as raise money to help those in need after the storm.

In addition to entertaining their fans, many musicians use their work to express their opinions about current politics and to motivate their listeners to take action. Just as slaves communicated with song, Americans today use music to capture their feelings and speak to one another. 2

Vocabulary

express (v) *show what you feel or think by saying, doing, or writing something*

protest (v) *object to something strongly and publicly*

1 Understand Words
The prefix *em-* means "in." How does knowing the meaning of the prefix help you understand the word *embedded*?

Vocabulary

disapproval (n) *a negative or bad thought about something*

politics (n) *the activities of government officials*

convey (v) *tell or communicate*

captured (v) *emphasized, represented, or preserved (as in a mood) in a permanent form*

2 Make Connections
Can you think of other songs that have a message? What do the songs ask you to do or to think about?

36 Expedition 3

Sounds of Life 37

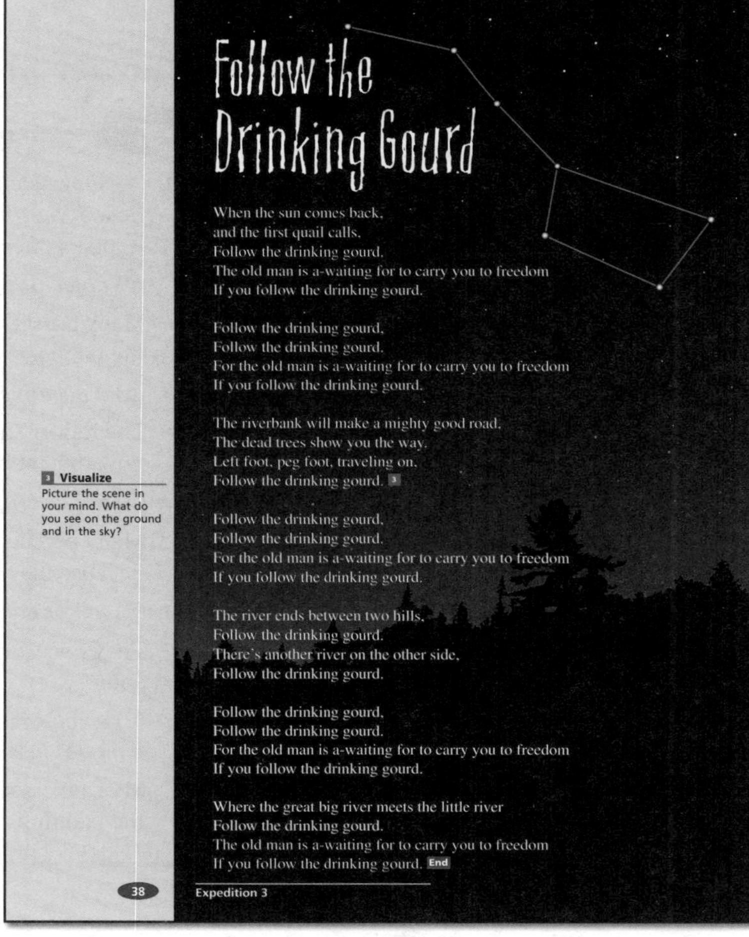

Follow the Drinking Gourd

When the sun comes back,
and the first quail calls,
Follow the drinking gourd.
The old man is a-waiting for to carry you to freedom
If you follow the drinking gourd.

Follow the drinking gourd,
Follow the drinking gourd,
For the old man is a-waiting for to carry you to freedom
If you follow the drinking gourd.

The riverbank will make a mighty good road,
The dead trees show you the way,
Left foot, peg foot, traveling on,
Follow the drinking gourd. 3

Follow the drinking gourd,
Follow the drinking gourd,
For the old man is a-waiting for to carry you to freedom
If you follow the drinking gourd.

The river ends between two hills,
Follow the drinking gourd.
There's another river on the other side,
Follow the drinking gourd.

Follow the drinking gourd,
Follow the drinking gourd,
For the old man is a-waiting for to carry you to freedom
If you follow the drinking gourd.

Where the great big river meets the little river
Follow the drinking gourd.
The old man is a-waiting for to carry you to freedom
If you follow the drinking gourd. End

3 Visualize
Picture the scene in your mind. What do you see on the ground and in the sky?

38 Expedition 3

"Music with a Message"

Before Reading

Introduce Vocabulary

1. Have students turn to Part A on Student Book page 66 and scan the boldfaced vocabulary words. **Some of these words may already be familiar to you. Which words do you already know?** Read the instructions aloud, and have students rate their knowledge of each boldfaced word.
2. Have students share which words they know. For each word, tell students to use the word in a sentence.
3. Read aloud the part of speech, definition, and example sentence for each word. **Look back at how you rated each word. Do these definitions match the meanings you knew? Change any ratings you need to.**
4. Have students read the instructions for Part B and complete the activity.

Refer to Blackline Master page 14 to extend vocabulary practice.

Have students use the *Passport Reading Journeys* online technology component to practice and reinforce vocabulary and comprehension skills.

Introduce the Target Skill: Implicit Main Idea and Details

1. The main idea is what the passage is mostly about. **Sometimes the main idea is stated directly, as in this sentence.** Write on the board: *The Displays proved that a garage rock band of 13- and 14-year-olds can amaze people with their talent.* List these details, and have students explain why each detail supports the main idea.
   - *They competed in the Battle of the Bands in Detroit.*
   - *The Displays were judged the best of 10 bands.*
   - *The judges were music professionals.*
2. **Main ideas are not always stated directly.** Direct students to Student Book page 67. **You will find the main idea of a poster by finding the details first.** List the details as a class.

Expedition 3, Lesson 1

Name ____________________ Date ____________

Vocabulary

"Music with a Message"

A. Rate your knowledge of each boldfaced word.
3 familiar
2 somewhat familiar
1 unknown word

☐ **express** (v) *show what you feel or think by saying, doing, or writing something*
Rappers often use *lyrics* to express their emotions.

☐ **protest** (v) *object to something strongly and publicly*
Many artists share their *protest* of the war with the public.

☐ **disapproval** (n) *a negative or bad thought about something*
The rapper showed his *disapproval* of the government by writing lyrics about its failures.

☐ **politics** (n) *the activities of government officials*
Many people disagree with *politics* during a war because they blame it on the government.

☐ **convey** (v) *tell or communicate*
They *convey* their feelings toward rival groups in song.

☐ **captured** (v) *emphasized, represented, or preserved (as in a mood) in a permanent form*
My sadness was *captured* in the song lyrics and the painting.

B. Read each question, then write the answer on the line.

1. Is the president or a barber more involved in **politics**? the president
2. If people **protest** a new law, do they support it or oppose it? oppose it
3. If you **convey** an idea through music, do you share the idea or keep it to yourself? share it
4. When you **express** an opinion, do you show it or hide it? show it
5. If a song **captured** how you feel, did the music represent your feelings or ignore them? represent your feelings
6. If your friends show **disapproval** of a song, would they listen to it often or never? never

66

Vocabulary

express (v) *show what you feel or think by saying, doing, or writing something*
Rappers often use lyrics to *express* their emotions.

protest (v) *object to something strongly and publicly*
Many artists share their *protest* of the war with the public.

disapproval (n) *a negative or bad thought about something*
The rapper showed his *disapproval* of the government by writing lyrics about its failures.

politics (n) *the activities of government officials*
Many people disagree with *politics* during a war because they blame it on the government.

convey (v) *tell or communicate*
They *convey* their feelings toward rival groups in song.

captured (v) *emphasized, represented, or preserved (as in a mood) in a permanent form*
My sadness was *captured* in the song lyrics and the painting.

3. Have students write the main idea and share their main idea statements.

Introduce the Passage

1. Have students preview "Music with a Message." **What clues tell you what this passage will be about?** (the title and the photos) **What follows the main passage?** (song lyrics)
2. Remind students to pause to read the prompts in the margins. **Think about these prompts as you read the text. Use the vocabulary definitions in the margin when you encounter boldfaced words.**
3. Demonstrate the pronunciation of these terms from the passage:
   - *Tupac* (tū pok)
   - *New Orleans* (nū ȯr lē ənz)
   - *Iraq* (ī rok)
4. Have students predict what they will read about in the main passage. (rappers and how they use music to show their opinions) **How do you think the passage and the lyrics relate to each other?** (Possible response: There is a message in the song.)

   "Follow the Drinking Gourd" began as an American folk song in the 19th century. The song's lyrics gave escaped slaves directions to the north. The "drinking gourd" in the song is the Big Dipper constellation. The constellation looks like a spoon, which is what the squash-like gourds were used for during this time. Many landmarks are mentioned in the song, making it a "map" for the slaves.

During Reading

1. Have students read "Music with a Message" and "Follow the Drinking Gourd." To select reading options that support your students' levels and classroom needs, see Reading Differentiation, page xxxii, if needed.
2. Instruct students to look for the main idea as they read.

After Reading

Check Comprehension

1. **How are the passages related?** (The song was a hidden message, and the passage was about messages in songs.)

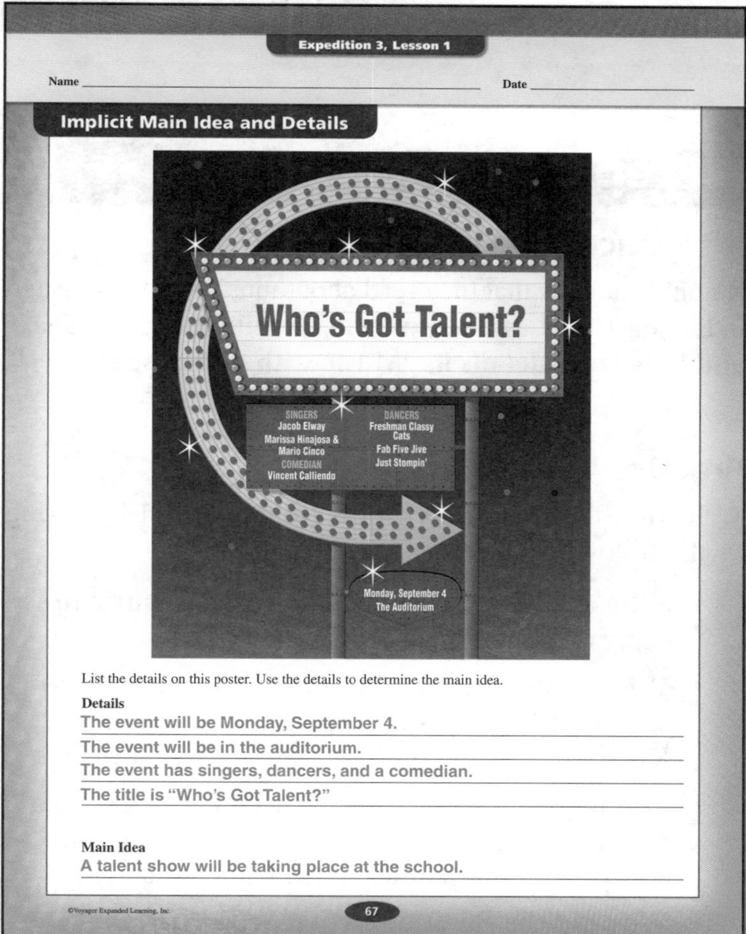

Expedition 3, Lesson 1

Name ______________________ Date ____________

Implicit Main Idea and Details

List the details on this poster. Use the details to determine the main idea.

Details
The event will be Monday, September 4.
The event will be in the auditorium.
The event has singers, dancers, and a comedian.
The title is "Who's Got Talent?"

Main Idea
A talent show will be taking place at the school.

©Voyager Expanded Learning, Inc. 67

2. Have students share their responses to the Make Connections margin prompt on Anthology page 37. **What other songs have messages? Are these messages stated directly or not?**
3. **Look at the last paragraph of the first column on page 36. Read the paragraph again. What is the explicit main idea?** (Messages have always been embedded within musical lyrics.) **Sometimes main ideas aren't stated. Let's look at the paragraph before this one. It talks about a feud between two rappers. What is the implicit main idea of this paragraph?** (East and West Coast rappers used song lyrics to speak to one another during a feud in the 1990s.)

ELL For students who have difficulty identifying main idea and details, read paragraphs aloud one at a time. Model using the skill with language such as: *I think the most important point is* __________.

Remind students to choose books from the *Passport Reading Journeys* Library for independent reading.

"Music with a Message"

Prepare to Reread

Introduce the Lesson

Remind students that they read about music with a message in Lesson 1. **In Lesson 2, we will identify the main idea and important details in "Music with a Message."**

Practice Vocabulary

1. Review the vocabulary words from Lesson 1 by asking the following questions.
   - **Who are some artists who have used music to *express* themselves?** (Tupac; Jadakiss)
   - **What issues have artists used their music to *protest*?** (the Iraq War; response to Hurricane Katrina)
   - **The Beastie Boys wrote "In a World Gone Mad" to show their *disapproval* of something. What was it?** (current politics in the United States)
   - **Why did the Beastie Boys criticize current *politics* in the United States?** (They did not like how violence and hate influenced people's thinking.)
   - **What did Jadakiss *convey* in his song "Why?"** (his political opinions)
   - **What are some messages that artists in this passage have *captured* in their music?** (personal messages to rivals; war protests; political criticism; response to Hurricane Katrina)
2. Remind students that they can use context clues to find the meanings of words they don't know. Have students turn to Anthology page 36. **What do you think the word *feud* means?** (a quarrel or fight) **What clue in the text helps you know this?** (The text restates *feud* as a "quarrel.")

   Repeat this process for the following words.
   - **escalated** (v) *increased; grew stronger*, Anthology page 36
   - **embedded** (v) *placed within something else*, Anthology page 36
   - **genre** (n) *style*, Anthology page 36
   - **highlights** (v) *draws attention to something*, Anthology page 37

Expedition 3, Lesson 2

Name ______________________ Date ____________

Word Building

A. Prefixes, which come at the beginning of words, can change a word's meaning. Each word below begins with the prefix *dis-* or the prefix *mis-*. Complete the following statements.

disapproval	**misspell**
discomfort	**misjudge**
disbelief	**miscount**

Dis- means "not" or "absence of."	*Mis-* means "wrongly."

1. *Disapproval* means "the absence of approval."
2. *Discomfort* means "the absence of comfort."
3. *Disbelief* means "the absence of belief."
4. *Misspell* means "wrongly spell."
5. *Misjudge* means "wrongly judge."
6. *Miscount* means "wrongly count."

B. Think about the meanings of the boldfaced words in Part A and how you have heard each word used. Choose from the list to complete the sentences.

1. The rocky ground caused us some discomfort when we camped in the woods.
2. I checked a dictionary so I would not misspell the word *deceive* in my paper.
3. The audience booed to show its disapproval of the movie.
4. The concert manager was worried the booth agents would miscount the number of tickets they sold.
5. Mala expressed her disbelief when we told her about the tragedy.
6. People sometimes misjudge how dangerous it is to drive too fast.

C. Choose two words from the list in Part A. Use each one in a sentence.

1. Answers will vary.
2. ______________________

©Voyager Expanded Learning, Inc. 68

ELL Provide examples for the word *genre* by telling students that mysteries and science fiction are different *genres* of books. Have them supply different *genres* of music. List their responses.

3. Have students turn to Student Book page 68. **You learned that the word *disapproval* means "a negative or bad thought about something." This is the opposite of the meaning of *approval*. The prefix *dis-* causes this change in meaning.** Read the instructions for the page aloud. Have students complete the activities, then share their responses.

Reread

Apply the Target Skill: Implicit Main Idea and Details

1. Have students turn to Anthology page 36 and reread the first paragraph. **I can find the main idea of this paragraph by identifying details. What are three details in this paragraph?** (An East Coast rapper insulted West Coast rappers in a song; West Coast rappers replied in other song lyrics; rap lyrics became filled with messages.) **What is the main idea?** (Some rappers have put messages to other rappers in their lyrics.)
2. Have students read the instructions on Student Book page 69 and complete the activity.

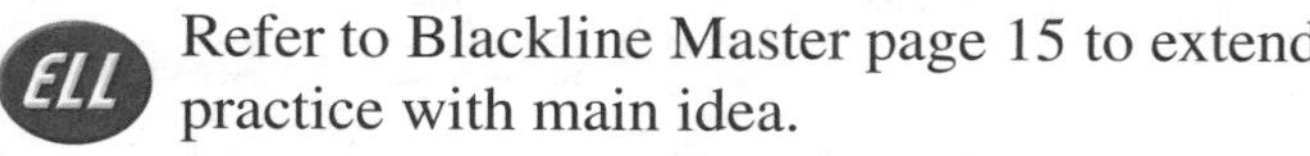

ELL Refer to Blackline Master page 15 to extend practice with main idea.

ACADEMIC SKILL Remind students that they can use details to figure out a main idea when they read textbooks. They also can use subheadings and other text features.

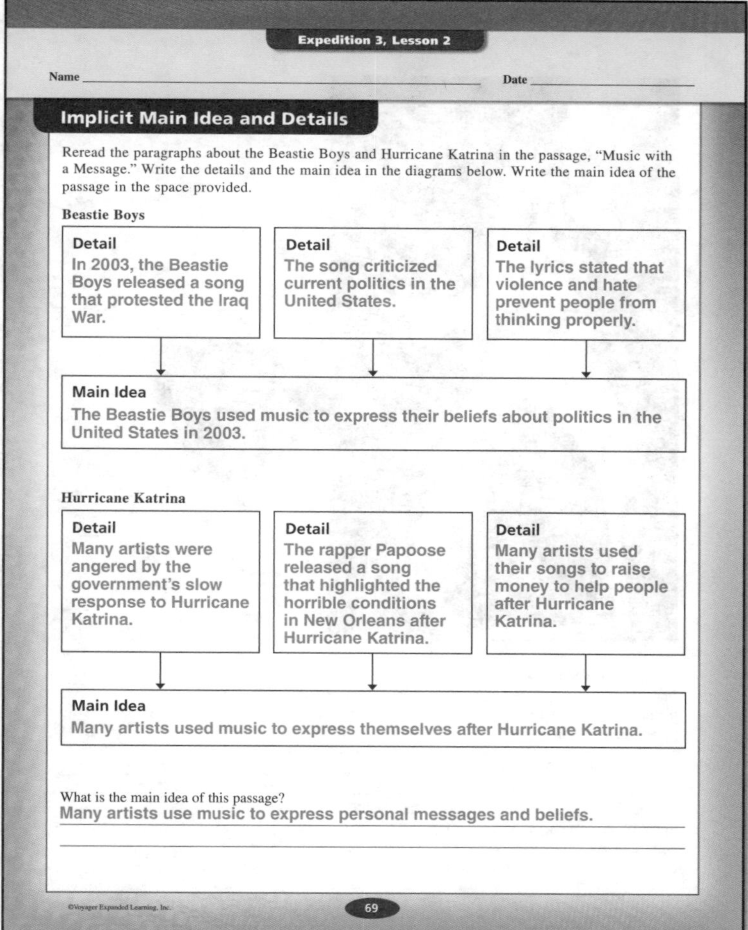

Expedition 3, Lesson 2

Name ______________________ Date ____________

Implicit Main Idea and Details

Reread the paragraphs about the Beastie Boys and Hurricane Katrina in the passage, "Music with a Message." Write the details and the main idea in the diagrams below. Write the main idea of the passage in the space provided.

Beastie Boys

Detail	Detail	Detail
In 2003, the Beastie Boys released a song that protested the Iraq War.	The song criticized current politics in the United States.	The lyrics stated that violence and hate prevent people from thinking properly.

Main Idea: The Beastie Boys used music to express their beliefs about politics in the United States in 2003.

Hurricane Katrina

Detail	Detail	Detail
Many artists were angered by the government's slow response to Hurricane Katrina.	The rapper Papoose released a song that highlighted the horrible conditions in New Orleans after Hurricane Katrina.	Many artists used their songs to raise money to help people after Hurricane Katrina.

Main Idea: Many artists used music to express themselves after Hurricane Katrina.

What is the main idea of this passage?
Many artists use music to express personal messages and beliefs.

©Voyager Expanded Learning, Inc. 69

Write in Response to Reading

1. Prepare students to complete the writing activities on Student Book page 70. **Many artists have expressed their ideas through music. What are some messages they conveyed?** (protesting wars; criticizing current politics; raising money for assistance after Hurricane Katrina) Have students read the instructions and complete Part A.
2. **How are the artists in the passage similar? How are they different?** (They all use music to convey a message, but the messages are different.) Have students read the instructions for Part B and write the paragraph.

Expedition 3, Lesson 2

Name ______________________ Date ____________

Write in Response to Reading

A. What message would you include in a song you would write? Write your song's title, the song's style, a sample of the song's lyrics, and the message you want to express. Answers will vary.

Song Title ______________________

Style or Genre ______________________

Lyrics ______________________

Message ______________________

B. Compare two artists in the passage. Describe how their styles of music and their messages are the same or different. Then, tell why you agree or disagree with these artists' messages.
Student responses should reflect an understanding of the messages in two artists' songs and how they are similar and different.

©Voyager Expanded Learning, Inc. 70

EXPEDITION ORGANIZER **Sounds of Life**

Pause to have students turn to Student Book pages 64 and 65. Have students complete the following:

- Respond to any of the probing questions in Part A. Encourage them to write a question of their own.
- Think about an important idea from "Music with a Message." Tell students to write it in Part B.

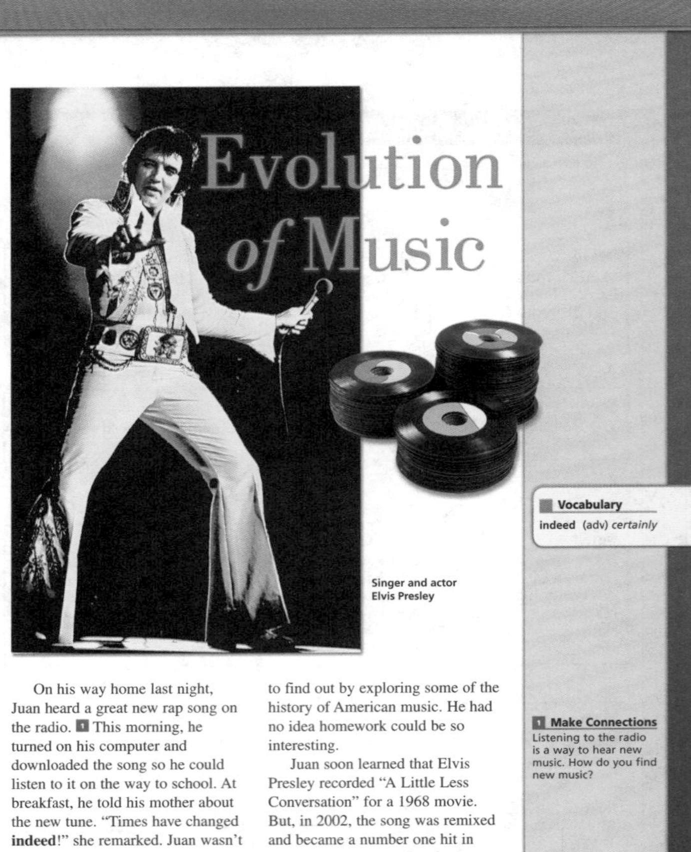

Evolution of Music

Singer and actor Elvis Presley

> **Vocabulary**
> **indeed** (adv) *certainly*

On his way home last night, Juan heard a great new rap song on the radio. **1** This morning, he turned on his computer and downloaded the song so he could listen to it on the way to school. At breakfast, he told his mother about the new tune. "Times have changed **indeed**!" she remarked. Juan wasn't quite sure what she meant. With a research paper due soon, he decided to find out by exploring some of the history of American music. He had no idea homework could be so interesting.

Juan soon learned that Elvis Presley recorded "A Little Less Conversation" for a 1968 movie. But, in 2002, the song was remixed and became a number one hit in 20 countries. The remix of this popular Elvis tune was also used in

> **1 Make Connections**
> Listening to the radio is a way to hear new music. How do you find new music?

> **Vocabulary**
> **universal** (adj) *found everywhere; shared by everyone and everything*
> **prominent** (adj) *important or famous*
> **population** (n) *all the people living in a certain place*
> **diverse** (adj) *varied or assorted*
> **roots** (n) *the source, origin, or cause of something; where it came from*

Little Richard rocks and rolls on his piano.

movies, advertisements, television shows, and presidential campaigns. It was even the theme song of the 2007 NBA All-Star Game. Juan began to see how **universal** rock 'n' roll is and wanted to learn more. This is what he found out.

The Birth of Rock 'n' Roll

Rock 'n' roll began in the United States in the 1950s. Since then, American music has never been the same. Rock 'n' roll grew from the blending of rhythm and blues with country and western music. Loud instruments and heavily stressed, or emphasized, beats defined the music and gave it universal appeal. The sounds of rock 'n' roll quickly swept the nation. Two **prominent** artists in the early years of rock 'n' roll were Little Richard and Elvis Presley.

The first weekly *Billboard* chart was released in 1955. This chart is based on the sales of songs and albums. *Billboard* magazine creates the chart to estimate, or make a rough guess of, the popularity of an artist or group and assign a position from 1 to 100. Soon, the American **population** watched these charts to see where their favorite songs ranked. Today, there are about 20 different charts. Some categories include jazz, dance, hip-hop, and Top 40.

The Music of the 1960s and 1970s

American music represents the country's **diverse** population. Regional music continued to develop distinct sounds. Many of its genres reflected the ethnicity of the artists. The music also reflected American culture and lifestyle. Motown emerged in Detroit in 1959. This style of music has its **roots** in gospel music. This distinct style of singing was combined with rhythm and blues instrumentation. Motown was also one of the first genres of pop music that featured female groups.

By 1977, disco was the new

craze. Enthusiastic Americans were dancing to songs such as "Stayin' Alive" and "The Hustle." **2** While people danced under disco strobe lights, another new sound was emerging. The hip-hop sound was developed by DJs in New York City. It quickly became popular with African American and Hispanic listeners. Rap, with its strong rhythmic beats and spoken lyrics, also became a prominent sound in the music world. Indeed, these two genres quickly developed a large following.

More Changes in the Music World

In the early 1980s, music videos made their way into American homes with the introduction of MTV. Soon, videos became almost as important as lyrics and music in determining the popularity of a song. **3**

Popular music in the 1990s came

> **2 Context Clues**
> What clues from the second sentence help you understand the meaning of *craze*?

> **3 Make Connections**
> Do you watch music videos? Do they affect your attitude toward songs?

Actor John Travolta dances with Karen Lynn Gorney in a disco scene from the 1977 movie *Saturday Night Fever* directed by John Badham.

The Rock and Roll Hall of Fame and Museum in Cleveland, Ohio, is the preeminent home for the celebration and study of rock 'n' roll music.

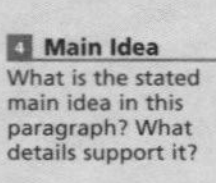

> **4 Main Idea**
> What is the stated main idea in this paragraph? What details support it?

from a variety of different types of musicians. In the 90s, grunge entered the popular music scene. With its roots in 1970s hard rock, grunge put Seattle's music scene on the map. Alternative punk, metal/hardcore, and techno music also became popular during this decade.

In 1995, the Rock and Roll Hall of Fame and Museum opened in Cleveland, Ohio. The museum features a huge collection of artifacts from prominent musicians of the past. The exhibits showcase the roots of rock and new sounds on the music charts.

Today, music from all eras of history is available. Many popular clubs feature music from only one decade, such as the 1970s. Others play a single genre, such as hip-hop. The next popular sound is just around the corner, as garage bands and vocalists work out their latest arrangements. Many people turn to the Internet to explore new sounds, and they download their favorite music. **4**

As Juan finished his research, he thought about his mother's comment. The popularity of different types of music has come and gone over the years, but one thing remains the same: The American population loves to listen and dance to music. Music has a universal appeal. While it helps some people express their individuality, it unites others. It entertains and inspires. Above all, it does indeed reflect the diversity of the American people. **End**

"Evolution of Music"

Before Reading

Introduce Vocabulary

1. Have students turn to Part A on Student Book page 71 and scan the boldfaced vocabulary words. **You'll read these vocabulary words in the passage "Evolution of Music." Think about what you already know about each word.** Have students rate their understanding of each vocabulary word.
2. Have students identify words they rated as a 3. Tell them to use their own words to share a definition they know with a partner and use it in a sentence or phrase.
3. Read aloud the words, parts of speech, definitions, and example sentences. **Check the definitions of the words you assigned a 3 rating. Were your definitions correct? Reread the definitions and sentences of the words you rated a 2 or 1.**
4. Read aloud the instructions for Part B. Have students complete the word association activity independently, then compare answers with a partner.

Refer to Blackline Master page 16 to extend vocabulary practice.

Have students use the *Passport Reading Journeys* online technology component to practice and reinforce vocabulary and comprehension skills.

Apply the Target Skill: Implicit Main Idea and Details

1. Remind students that the main idea is the most important idea, or what the text is mostly about, and that details support the main idea.

Expedition 3, Lesson 3

Name ______________________ Date ____________

Vocabulary

"Evolution of Music"

A. Rate your knowledge of each boldfaced word.
3 I know what this word means, and I can use it in a sentence.
2 I have an idea of this word's meaning, but I need to know more.
1 I don't know what this word means.

☐ **indeed** (adv) *certainly*
Music has *indeed* affected American society.

☐ **universal** (adj) *found everywhere; shared by everyone and everything*
Hip-hop has spread around the world and become a *universal* form of music.

☐ **prominent** (adj) *important or famous*
Jimi Hendrix was a *prominent* musician in the 1960s who influenced the way people play guitar.

☐ **population** (n) *all the people living in a certain place*
Rock 'n' roll has had a big impact on the *population* of the United States.

☐ **diverse** (adj) *varied or assorted*
Because he likes many different types of music, Juan has a quite *diverse* CD collection.

☐ **roots** (n) *the source, origin, or cause of something; where it came from*
Rock 'n' roll has some of its *roots* in country and western music.

B. Answer each question with a boldfaced word from Part A.

1. Which word goes with "the origins of a country song"? roots
2. Which word goes with "a positive reaction from audiences around the world"? universal
3. Which word would you use to describe the number of people who live in your town? population
4. Which word would you use to indicate that your grandma certainly doesn't like rap music. indeed
5. Which word goes with a rock band that has millions of fans? prominent
6. Which word goes with the types of music CDs you can buy online? diverse

©Voyager Expanded Learning, Inc. 71

Vocabulary

indeed (adv) *certainly*
Music has *indeed* affected American society.

universal (adj) *found everywhere; shared by everyone and everything*
Hip-hop has spread around the world and become a *universal* form of music.

prominent (adj) *important or famous*
Jimi Hendrix was a *prominent* musician in the 1960s who influenced the way people play guitar.

population (n) *all the people living in a certain place*
Rock 'n' roll has had a big impact on the *population* of the United States.

diverse (adj) *varied or assorted*
Because he likes many different types of music, Juan has a quite *diverse* CD collection.

roots (n) *the source, origin, or cause of something; where it came from*
Rock 'n' roll has some of its *roots* in country and western music.

2. **Sometimes the main idea of a paragraph is not directly stated. You might figure out the main idea by first paying attention to the details.** Read aloud the following paragraph:

   What makes the alternative rock band Coldplay different? They make their fans aware of issues, such as torture and poverty, because the band supports Amnesty International and Oxfam. Coldplay gives 15 percent of its profits to charity because the band wants to help others. What does this information make you think of Coldplay?

3. **What are the details?** (The band supports Amnesty International and Oxfam. The band gives 15 percent of its profits to charity. Fans become aware of torture and poverty.)

4. **What is the main idea?** (Coldplay is a band that helps people and makes them aware of issues.)

Introduce the Passage

1. Have students preview "Evolution of Music." Remind students that the Expedition is about music. **What clues do you notice that help you predict what this passage is about?** (The title and the photos are clues that the passage will be about the history of American music.)
2. Direct student attention to the margin prompts. **As you read this passage, pause to respond to the prompts. The vocabulary notes in the margin will remind you of the meanings of the new words you learned.**
3. Teach these terms from the passage:
   - *Strobe lights* are lights that produce regular flashes of light to make things appear to be in slow motion.
   - *Swept the nation* means "became popular."
4. **You know this passage is about the history of American music. What kinds of American musical periods and styles do you already know about? What do you expect to learn?** Have partners discuss their prior knowledge.

During Reading

1. Have students think of the main idea as they read "Evolution of Music." To select reading options that support your students' levels and classroom needs, see Reading Differentiation, page xxxii, if needed.
2. When students finish reading the passage, have partners create a timeline of the music periods, styles, musicians, and trends in the passage. **When did rock 'n' roll begin? Who was a famous rock 'n' roll artist of that time? What do the words of the songs tell you about the artists' thoughts about society at the time?** Tell students to think about these questions as they create their timelines.

   ELL Add to the timeline by drawing marks labeled 1970, 1980, 1990, and 2000. Have students scan the text for years. Have students read sentences that contain years. Add this information to the timeline.

3. To extend the activity, students may further research music online and add details and photos to their timelines.

After Reading

Check Comprehension

1. Have students think about the predictions they made about this passage. **What information was in the passage that you expected? What didn't you expect to read? Discuss your predictions with a partner.**
2. **Now that you have read the passage and determined if your predictions are correct, what is the passage mostly about?** (American music is diverse and comes from many different styles of the past.)
3. Have students share their responses to the Make Connections margin prompt on Anthology page 41. **How do music videos affect your attitude toward songs?** (Possible answer: Sometimes music videos affect how I interpret what the song is about.)

   To make the most of the discussion time, remember to incorporate strategies that encourage and extend student involvement. Refer to page xxxviii for a comprehensive discussion of these strategies.

Remind students to choose books from the *Passport Reading Journeys* Library for independent reading.

"Evolution of Music"

Prepare to Reread

Introduce the Lesson

In Lesson 4, you will revisit the "Evolution of Music," practice vocabulary, and identify main ideas.

Practice Vocabulary

1. Remind students of the vocabulary words from Lesson 3 and how they were used in the passage.
   - **If your teacher says, "You have done well *indeed*," what does *indeed* mean?** (surely)
   - **Rock 'n' roll is *universal* because people everywhere like it. What is a musical activity that is *universal*?** (dancing; playing instruments)
   - **Would a *prominent* person probably be remembered or forgotten?** (remembered)
   - **If you were interested in a certain *population*, what would you study?** (a group of people)
   - **Would you find more *diverse* animals at a zoo or at an animal shelter?** (zoo)
   - **If you discovered the *roots* of a tradition, what did you discover?** (how the tradition started)
2. Remind students that they can use context clues to find the meanings of unknown words. Have students turn to Anthology page 40. **What do you think the word *stressed* means?** (emphasized; made important) **What clues in the text helped you figure out the meaning?** (The word *stressed* is restated as "emphasized.")

   Repeat this process for the following words.
   - **estimate** (v) *make a guess*, Anthology page 40
   - **ranked** (v) *assigned a position to something*, Anthology page 40
   - **craze** (n) *excessive enthusiasm or excitement*, Anthology page 41
   - **artifacts** (n) *man-made objects from the past*, Anthology page 42
3. Have students turn to Student Book page 72. **You have learned the word *population*. It comes from the root word *populus*, which means "people." You can build on *population* to learn new words.** Have students read the instructions and complete the page independently.

Expedition 3, Lesson 4

Name ______ Date ______

Word Building

A. Each word below comes from the Latin root word *populus*, which means "people." Read the words and their meanings below. Notice how all the word meanings connect to the word *people*.

population (n)	*all the people living in a certain place*
popular (adj)	*liked by many people*
populate (v)	*inhabit; form the group of people living in a region*
populous (adj)	*full of people; densely populated*
popularize (v)	*cause to become known or enjoyed by many people*

B. Think about the meanings of the boldfaced words in Part A and how you have heard each word used. Choose from the list to complete the sentences.

1. When a movie star wears a certain style of clothes, the style often becomes very popular.
2. The streets are crowded in the most populous cities of India.
3. The city's parks attract the local population during the summer.
4. People often move from the cities to populate land that used to be farmland.
5. Radio stations often popularize songs from new albums.

C. Choose two boldfaced words from the list in Part A. Use each one in a sentence.

1. Answers will vary.
2. ______

 72

CHECKPOINT After students complete Part B, have them identify clues that helped them determine the word.

Reread

Apply the Target Skill: Implicit Main Idea; Summarize

1. Have students turn to Anthology page 39 and reread the first paragraph. **Each paragraph of this passage has a main idea. Sometimes the main idea is not stated directly. What details do you notice?** (Juan downloaded a song; his mom said times have changed; he decided to explore the history of American music; it was interesting.) **What is the main idea? Begin with "Juan found out that . . ."** (. . . exploring the history of American music is interesting.)

2. Have students turn to Student Book page 73. Read the instructions for Part A, and have partners complete the activity.

ELL Remind students that a summary contains only the most important ideas. If a friend asked what the passage was mostly about, he or she would give a summary, rather than explaining every detail.

3. **Reread the main idea statements you chose from the passage.** Read aloud the instructions for Part B. **Use these statements to write three to five sentences to explain what the whole passage is about.**

ACADEMIC SKILL Remind students to look for indirectly stated main ideas when they read textbooks, then use those main idea statements to create a summary. Explain that the subheadings in textbooks can help with this process.

Write in Response to Reading

1. Prepare students to complete the writing activities on Student Book page 74. Have students brainstorm interview questions and conduct their interviews. Direct them to ask *who*, *what*, *where*, *when*, *why*, and *how* questions.
2. **Music reviews often make judgments or state opinions about a musician or music style. You will be a reviewer writing for a popular magazine.** Have students read the instructions and write their reviews. Remind them to state an opinion.

EXPEDITION ORGANIZER **Sounds of Life**

Pause to have students turn to Student Book pages 64 and 65. Have students complete the following:

- Write answers to one or more of the probing questions in Part A. Have students write their own question in the space provided.
- Think about the big idea from "Evolution of Music." Add this to Part B.

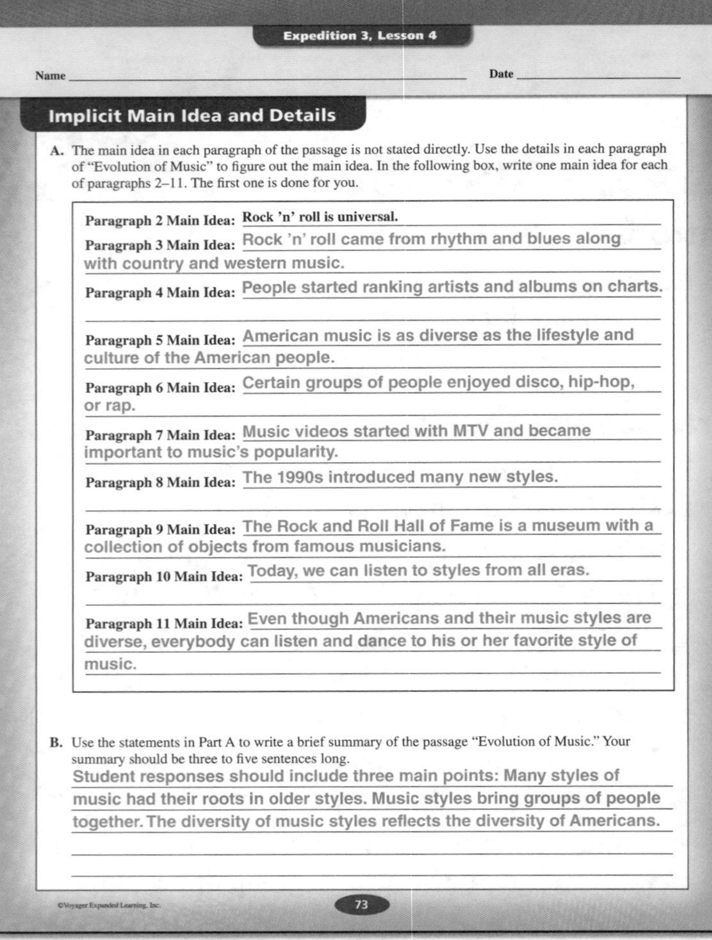

Expedition 3, Lesson 4

Name ______ Date ______

Implicit Main Idea and Details

A. The main idea in each paragraph of the passage is not stated directly. Use the details in each paragraph of "Evolution of Music" to figure out the main idea. In the following box, write one main idea for each of paragraphs 2–11. The first one is done for you.

Paragraph 2 Main Idea: Rock 'n' roll is universal.

Paragraph 3 Main Idea: Rock 'n' roll came from rhythm and blues along with country and western music.

Paragraph 4 Main Idea: People started ranking artists and albums on charts.

Paragraph 5 Main Idea: American music is as diverse as the lifestyle and culture of the American people.

Paragraph 6 Main Idea: Certain groups of people enjoyed disco, hip-hop, or rap.

Paragraph 7 Main Idea: Music videos started with MTV and became important to music's popularity.

Paragraph 8 Main Idea: The 1990s introduced many new styles.

Paragraph 9 Main Idea: The Rock and Roll Hall of Fame is a museum with a collection of objects from famous musicians.

Paragraph 10 Main Idea: Today, we can listen to styles from all eras.

Paragraph 11 Main Idea: Even though Americans and their music styles are diverse, everybody can listen and dance to his or her favorite style of music.

B. Use the statements in Part A to write a brief summary of the passage "Evolution of Music." Your summary should be three to five sentences long.

Student responses should include three main points: Many styles of music had their roots in older styles. Music styles bring groups of people together. The diversity of music styles reflects the diversity of Americans.

 73

Expedition 3, Lesson 4

Name ______ Date ______

Write in Response to Reading

A. Interview a classmate about his or her favorite musician or musical style. Ask what dance or clothing trends represent the type of music and other questions that address *who, what, where, when, why,* and *how*. Write your interview below.

You: Interviews should include questions and answers that closely relate to the student's favorite musician or music style and

Classmate: include questions with *who, what, where, when, why*, and *how* and related answers.

You:

Classmate:

You:

Classmate:

You:

Classmate:

You:

Classmate:

B. You are a music reviewer during one of the periods in "Evolution of Music." Write a review of a musician, an album, a song, or style of music. Explain your opinion about the music or musician, and explain what you have learned about the world through the eyes of the musician and the lyrics.

Reviews should include an opinion of the musician or song and reasons for the opinion.

 74

Review, Extend, Assess

In today's lesson, as in Lessons 5 and 10 of every Expedition, there are options from which to choose. You may do any or all of the options listed. Activities for each option are given on the following pages. Each option will support or extend previously taught objectives. Choose the option(s) appropriate for your students and prepare accordingly.

Review Vocabulary

Extend Vocabulary

Assess Comprehension and Vocabulary

Reteach

Passport Reading Journeys Library

Online Technology Component

Writing Process

Real-World Reading

Exploring Careers

Review Vocabulary

Direct students to review the vocabulary for "Music with a Message" and "Evolution of Music" on Student Book page 65.

1. Have students read the words and definitions. Assign partners to quiz each other on the definitions "flash card" style.
2. Have students turn to Student Book page 75. **You encountered most of the vocabulary words in the context of the reading passages. Now you will read the vocabulary in a different context, but the words will have the same meanings. As you complete the review activity, go back and check the definitions in the Anthology to make sure you use the words correctly.** Read the instructions aloud, and have students complete the activities. Have students share their answers for Parts A and B.

CHECKPOINT Have students share their answers for the activities on Student Book page 75. If students have difficulty with a word, reteach the definition by using it in a familiar context, such as one related to school or a popular event.

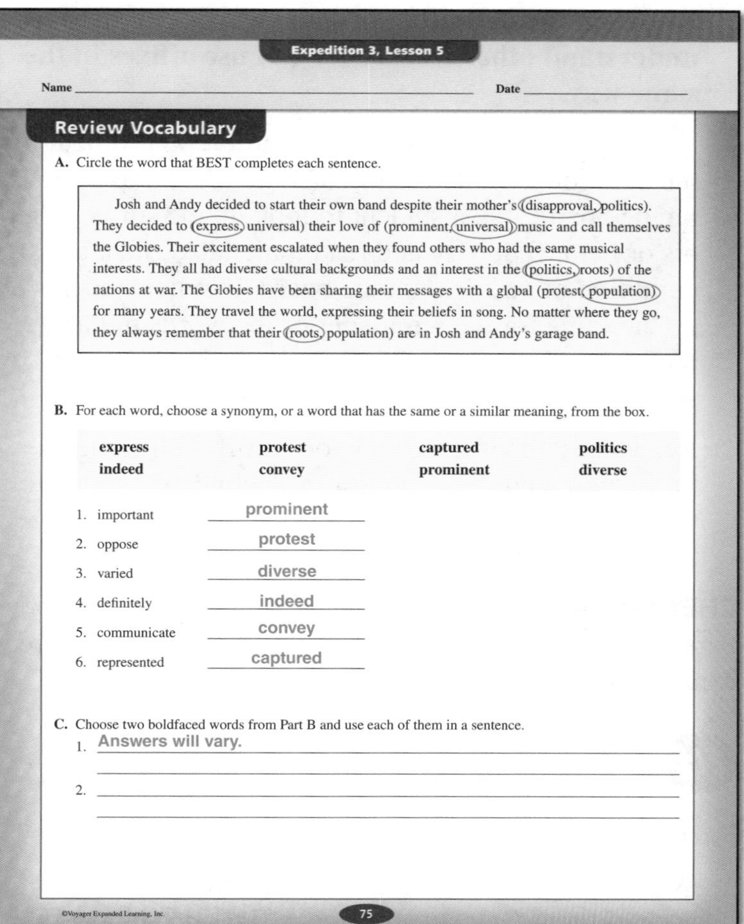

Expedition 3, Lesson 5

Name ______ Date ______

Review Vocabulary

A. Circle the word that BEST completes each sentence.

Josh and Andy decided to start their own band despite their mother's (disapproval, politics). They decided to (express, universal) their love of (prominent, universal) music and call themselves the Globies. Their excitement escalated when they found others who had the same musical interests. They all had diverse cultural backgrounds and an interest in the (politics, roots) of the nations at war. The Globies have been sharing their messages with a global (protest, population) for many years. They travel the world, expressing their beliefs in song. No matter where they go, they always remember that their (roots, population) are in Josh and Andy's garage band.

B. For each word, choose a synonym, or a word that has the same or a similar meaning, from the box.

express	**protest**	**captured**	**politics**
indeed	**convey**	**prominent**	**diverse**

1. important prominent
2. oppose protest
3. varied diverse
4. definitely indeed
5. communicate convey
6. represented captured

C. Choose two boldfaced words from Part B and use each of them in a sentence.

1. Answers will vary.
2. ______

75

Extend Vocabulary

1. Direct students to Part A on Student Book page 76. **Knowing the definition of some words can help us understand other words. We can use affixes in the same way.**
2. Write the word *politics* on the board. Ask a student for the definition. Write the word *political* next to *politics* on the board. Ask a student to look up the suffix *-al* in his or her affixionary and read it aloud. Write a class definition of *political* on the board. Instruct students to do the same for the remainder of the words in Part A on Student Book page 76. Review responses when students have finished.
3. Read aloud the instructions for Part B. Tell students they can reread the definitions to help them complete the sentences in Part B. Have students complete the activity, then share their responses.

CHECKPOINT When students share their responses for Part B, be sure that they used the new words in the correct contexts. Pause to explain and correct any errors.

Part A

1. Write the boldfaced words and underline the affix in each of them. Tell students that affixes can change the meaning of a word. Ask them whether they have affixes in their native language.
2. Explore each new word by reading the definition, using the words in a sentence, then asking students to answer a question about the word. **An *expression* is a display of how you feel. When I am happy, my *expression* is a smile. What is your *expression* when you are angry?** Have students answer using the following sentence starter: *When I am angry, my expression is _____.*

Part B

If students have difficulty completing the sentences, turn the sentence frame into a question with the blank as an answer. *Many musicians make _____ statements in their music.* **What kind of statements do musicians make?** (political)

Expedition 3, Lesson 5

Name ____________ Date ____________

Extend Vocabulary

A. Knowing the definition of one word can help you understand the definition of other words. Knowing the meanings of prefixes and suffixes can help in the same way. Use your affixionary to help you fill in the following chart.

politics (n)	***the activities of government officials***
political (adj)	having to do with the government
politician (n)	a person who works for the government
express (v)	***show what you feel or think***
expression (n)	a display of what you feel or think
expressionless (adj)	having no display of feelings or thoughts
diverse (adj)	***varied or assorted***
diversify (v)	make varied or assorted
diversity (n)	the condition of being varied or assorted
disapproval (n)	***a negative or bad thought about something***
disapprove (v)	have a negative or bad thought about something
approve (v)	have a positive or good thought about something

B. Complete each sentence with one of the boldfaced words from Part A.

1. Many musicians make ___political___ statements in their music.
2. I ___approve___ of my brother's choice of music because we have the same taste.
3. Max wants to ___diversify___ his CD collection so he doesn't have only rap music.
4. The ___expression___ on his face showed his anger with us.
5. The president is the highest ranking ___politician___ in the U.S. government.
6. His ___expressionless___ face made it hard to tell if he was happy or sad.
7. The best thing about the international music festival is the huge ___diversity___ of musicians.
8. My mother expressed her ___disapproval___ of my decision to join a rock band.

76

Assess Comprehension and Vocabulary

1. Remind students that when they read the passages, they practiced identifying main ideas that were not directly stated. **When you read, you notice details to determine the main idea of a paragraph. You can use the main idea of each paragraph to help you write a summary of the whole passage.**

2. Direct students to Student Book pages 77–79. Preview the pages, showing students that they will read a passage and answer questions about it. Have students complete the pages independently.

   Review student answers. Whenever possible, provide elaborative feedback to student responses. Refer to page xl for examples of elaborative feedback and how to incorporate it in your lessons.

   If students incorrectly answer more than 4 out of 15 Assessment questions, evaluate what kind of reteaching is needed. If students miss vocabulary questions, have them return to the vocabulary activities and work with the words they missed. For main idea errors, use the reteaching suggestions on page 108.

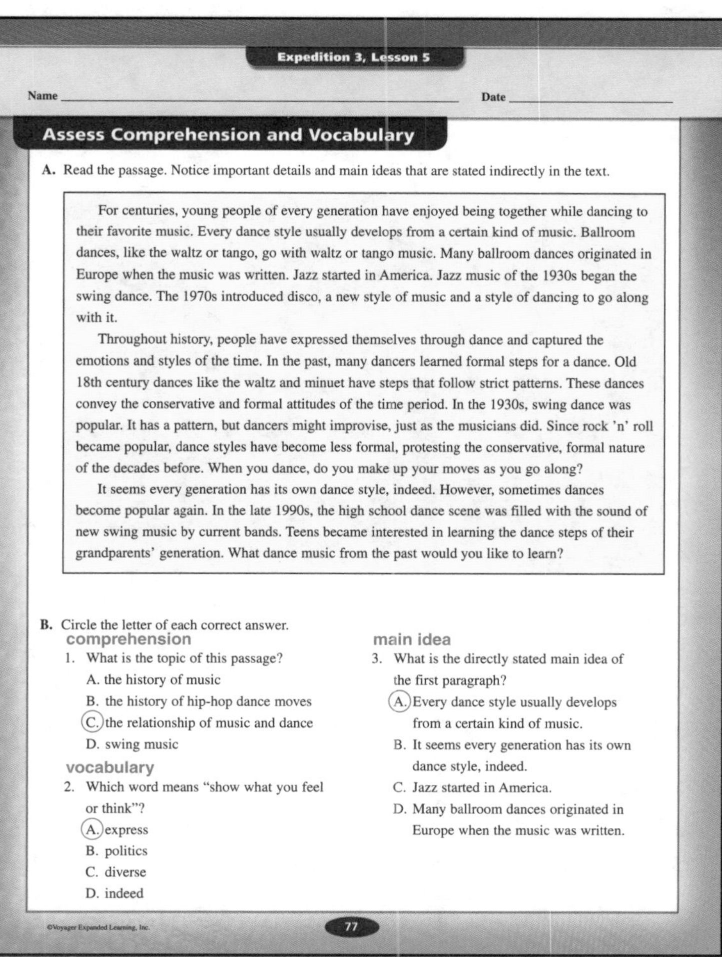

Expedition 3, Lesson 5

Name ______ Date ______

Assess Comprehension and Vocabulary

A. Read the passage. Notice important details and main ideas that are stated indirectly in the text.

For centuries, young people of every generation have enjoyed being together while dancing to their favorite music. Every dance style usually develops from a certain kind of music. Ballroom dances, like the waltz or tango, go with waltz or tango music. Many ballroom dances originated in Europe when the music was written. Jazz started in America. Jazz music of the 1930s began the swing dance. The 1970s introduced disco, a new style of music and a style of dancing to go along with it.

Throughout history, people have expressed themselves through dance and captured the emotions and styles of the time. In the past, many dancers learned formal steps for a dance. Old 18th century dances like the waltz and minuet have steps that follow strict patterns. These dances convey the conservative and formal attitudes of the time period. In the 1930s, swing dance was popular. It has a pattern, but dancers might improvise, just as the musicians did. Since rock 'n' roll became popular, dance styles have become less formal, protesting the conservative, formal nature of the decades before. When you dance, do you make up your moves as you go along?

It seems every generation has its own dance style, indeed. However, sometimes dances become popular again. In the late 1990s, the high school dance scene was filled with the sound of new swing music by current bands. Teens became interested in learning the dance steps of their grandparents' generation. What dance music from the past would you like to learn?

B. Circle the letter of each correct answer.

comprehension
1. What is the topic of this passage?
   A. the history of music
   B. the history of hip-hop dance moves
   (C.) the relationship of music and dance
   D. swing music

vocabulary
2. Which word means "show what you feel or think"?
   (A.) express
   B. politics
   C. diverse
   D. indeed

main idea
3. What is the directly stated main idea of the first paragraph?
   (A.) Every dance style usually develops from a certain kind of music.
   B. It seems every generation has its own dance style, indeed.
   C. Jazz started in America.
   D. Many ballroom dances originated in Europe when the music was written.

©Voyager Expanded Learning, Inc. 77

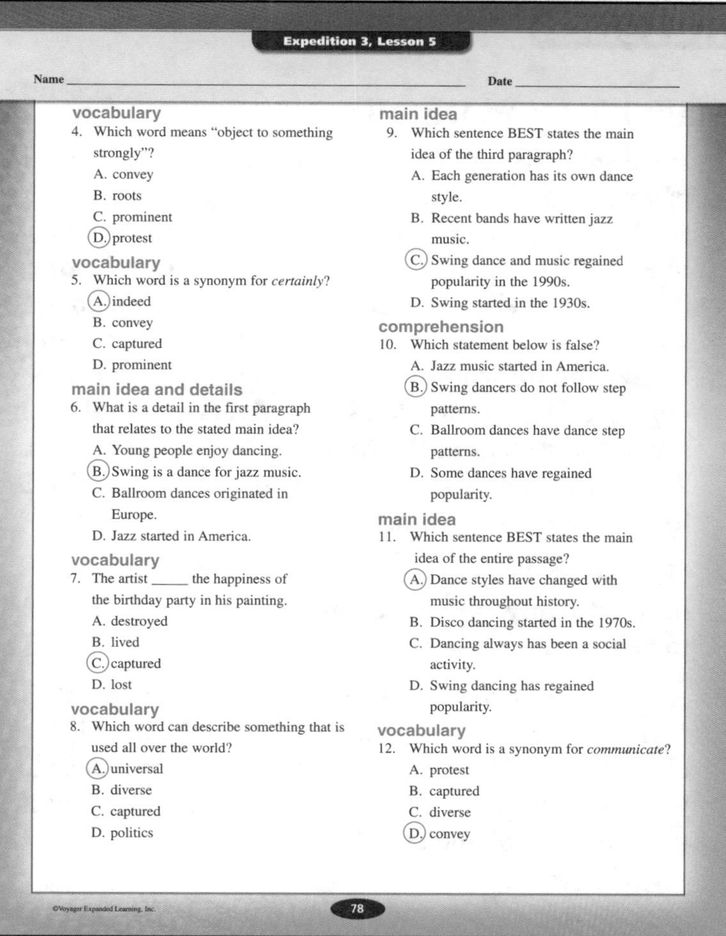

Expedition 3, Lesson 5

Name ______ Date ______

vocabulary
4. Which word means "object to something strongly"?
   A. convey
   B. roots
   C. prominent
   (D.) protest

vocabulary
5. Which word is a synonym for *certainly*?
   (A.) indeed
   B. convey
   C. captured
   D. prominent

main idea and details
6. What is a detail in the first paragraph that relates to the stated main idea?
   A. Young people enjoy dancing.
   (B.) Swing is a dance for jazz music.
   C. Ballroom dances originated in Europe.
   D. Jazz started in America.

vocabulary
7. The artist _____ the happiness of the birthday party in his painting.
   A. destroyed
   B. lived
   (C.) captured
   D. lost

vocabulary
8. Which word can describe something that is used all over the world?
   (A.) universal
   B. diverse
   C. captured
   D. politics

main idea
9. Which sentence BEST states the main idea of the third paragraph?
   A. Each generation has its own dance style.
   B. Recent bands have written jazz music.
   (C.) Swing dance and music regained popularity in the 1990s.
   D. Swing started in the 1930s.

comprehension
10. Which statement below is false?
   A. Jazz music started in America.
   (B.) Swing dancers do not follow step patterns.
   C. Ballroom dances have dance step patterns.
   D. Some dances have regained popularity.

main idea
11. Which sentence BEST states the main idea of the entire passage?
   (A.) Dance styles have changed with music throughout history.
   B. Disco dancing started in the 1970s.
   C. Dancing always has been a social activity.
   D. Swing dancing has regained popularity.

vocabulary
12. Which word is a synonym for *communicate*?
   A. protest
   B. captured
   C. diverse
   (D.) convey

©Voyager Expanded Learning, Inc. 78

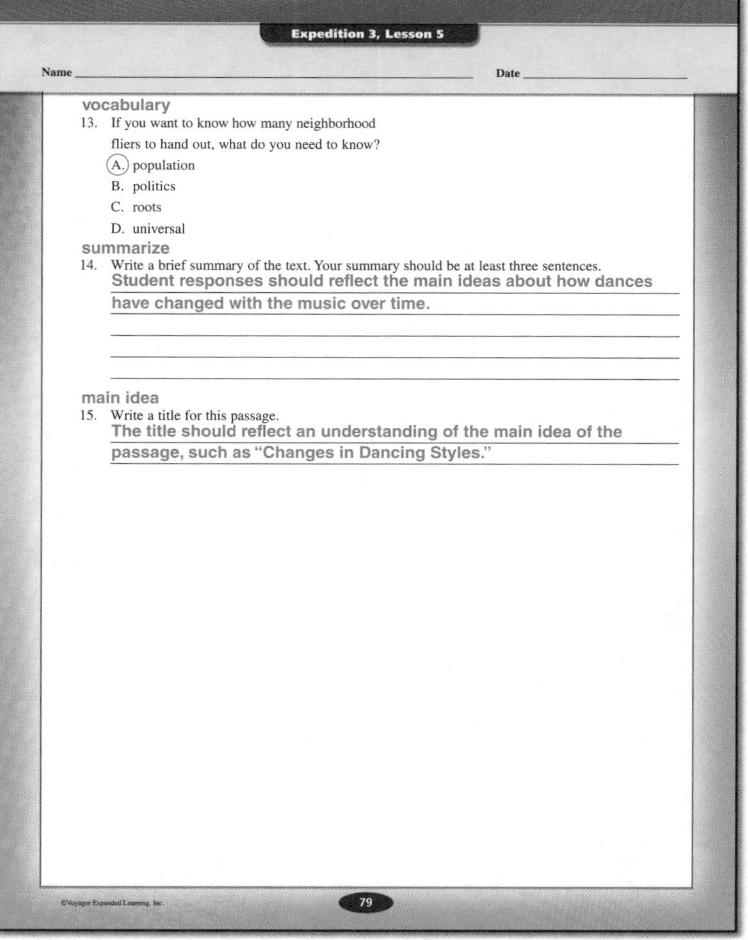

Expedition 3, Lesson 5

Name ______ Date ______

vocabulary
13. If you want to know how many neighborhood fliers to hand out, what do you need to know?
   (A.) population
   B. politics
   C. roots
   D. universal

summarize
14. Write a brief summary of the text. Your summary should be at least three sentences.
   Student responses should reflect the main ideas about how dances have changed with the music over time.

main idea
15. Write a title for this passage.
   The title should reflect an understanding of the main idea of the passage, such as "Changes in Dancing Styles."

©Voyager Expanded Learning, Inc. 79

Reteach

Main Idea and Details

1. Have students turn to Student Book page 80. Read the passage aloud. **What is the topic of this passage?** (MP3 players) Read aloud the first set of instructions in Part B. **Reread the first sentence and underline it. What has significantly changed?** (how people listen to music) **Each sentence has new information. Underline information that connects to what has changed. The main idea is not directly stated in the second paragraph. Begin with identifying details. Then, put the details together to form the main idea of the paragraph.**
2. Have students complete Parts A and B. If students have difficulty, provide them with two or three words to begin each answer.
3. Have students share their responses to Parts A and B. Write the most common responses on the board. As a class, have students use the details and main ideas to write a summary of the passage. Have a student write the summary on the board.

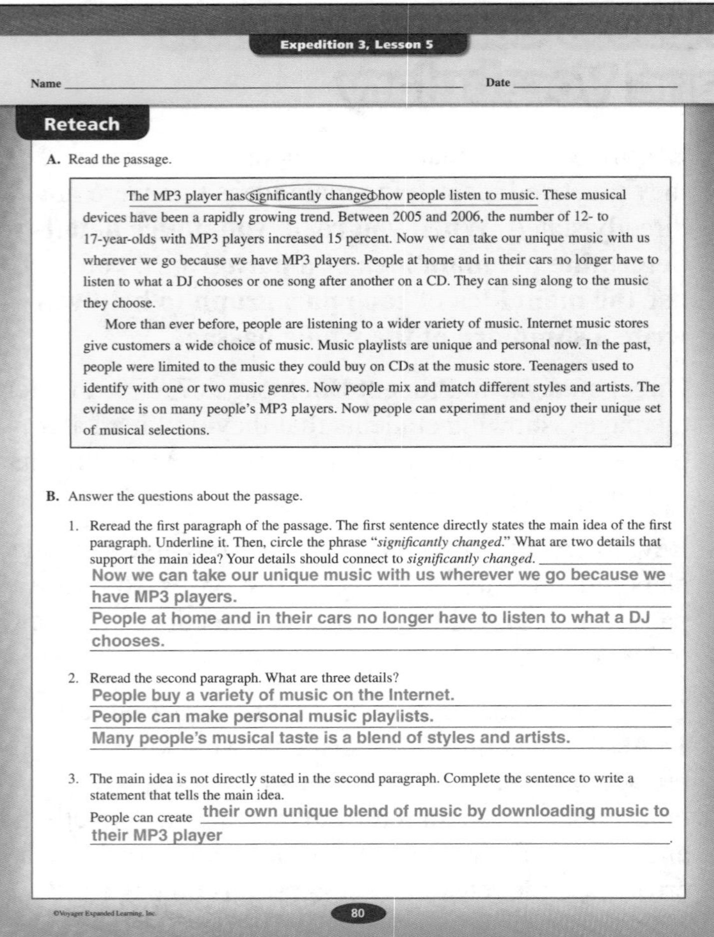

Expedition 3, Lesson 5

Name ______ Date ______

Reteach

A. Read the passage.

The MP3 player has significantly changed how people listen to music. These musical devices have been a rapidly growing trend. Between 2005 and 2006, the number of 12- to 17-year-olds with MP3 players increased 15 percent. Now we can take our unique music with us wherever we go because we have MP3 players. People at home and in their cars no longer have to listen to what a DJ chooses or one song after another on a CD. They can sing along to the music they choose.

More than ever before, people are listening to a wider variety of music. Internet music stores give customers a wide choice of music. Music playlists are unique and personal now. In the past, people were limited to the music they could buy on CDs at the music store. Teenagers used to identify with one or two music genres. Now people mix and match different styles and artists. The evidence is on many people's MP3 players. Now people can experiment and enjoy their unique set of musical selections.

B. Answer the questions about the passage.

1. Reread the first paragraph of the passage. The first sentence directly states the main idea of the first paragraph. Underline it. Then, circle the phrase "*significantly changed.*" What are two details that support the main idea? Your details should connect to *significantly changed.*
   Now we can take our unique music with us wherever we go because we have MP3 players.
   People at home and in their cars no longer have to listen to what a DJ chooses.
2. Reread the second paragraph. What are three details?
   People buy a variety of music on the Internet.
   People can make personal music playlists.
   Many people's musical taste is a blend of styles and artists.
3. The main idea is not directly stated in the second paragraph. Complete the sentence to write a statement that tells the main idea.
   People can create their own unique blend of music by downloading music to their MP3 player.

80

Passport Reading Journeys Library

1. Have students choose reading material from the *Passport Reading Journeys* Library or another approved selection. If students have not finished a previously chosen selection, they may continue reading from that selection. See the *Passport Reading Journeys* Library Teacher's Guide for material on selection guidelines.
2. You also may use this time to allow students to participate in book clubs or book presentations. Use the criteria specified in the *Passport Reading Journeys* Library Teacher's Guide.

Vocabulary Connections

Vocabulary words are listed in the Teacher's Guide for each book. These words are content-related or used frequently in reading material. The selected words can be a basis for independent or small-group discussions and activities.

Student Opportunities

Six copies of each book title are provided in the *Passport Reading Journeys* Library. The number of copies makes it possible for small groups of students to read the same material and share the information they read.

Theme-related titles include *Drums, Girls & Dangerous Pie.*

Technology

1. Depending on your classroom configuration and computer access, you may have all students work through the technology in a lab setting or have individuals or small groups of students work on desktops or laptops while other students participate in other suggested activities, such as the *Passport Reading Journeys* Library.
2. The online technology component provides additional support for students to work with selected vocabulary words. Students will work through a series of activities to strengthen their word knowledge, then apply that knowledge to passage reading. Refer to the online technology component User Guide for more information.

   Theme-related word sets include Physics, U.S. History, English/Language Arts, and Technology.

Writing Process

Descriptive Essay

Distribute copies of Writing Blackline Master page 5. Tell students they will write a three-paragraph essay describing their favorite band or musician. **What kinds of words or phrases will you include in your descriptions?** (adjectives; sensory details) **Adjectives and sensory details create a vivid picture in readers' minds.** Tell students they may include descriptions of these things:

- **Musical genre, sound, instruments, and message of lyrics**
- **Musician's appearance, background, and style**
- **Reasons why you like the musician or band**
- **What the music tells you about the time period in which it was written**

Ask students to look at the assignment and follow along as you explain it. Assign point values and ask students to write them in the rubric. Tell them to make any notes on the page that will help them, but they will turn in the page with the assignment.

Prewrite

Remind students that descriptive writing includes adjectives, or descriptive words that modify nouns. Tell them their essays should use sensory descriptions that appeal to the five senses: sight, smell, hearing, taste, and touch.

If possible, have students listen to the music they will write about. Then they should work independently to write lists of descriptive words and phrases for each sense. Students should focus on sight and hearing, then focus on smell and touch as they apply the context of a concert or musical event. Have groups share their lists with one another. **Use this list of words and phrases as you write your essays.**

Draft

You will use these standards, or criteria, as you write your essays. Write the following on the board, and tell students their descriptive essays must have . . .

- *sensory details that vividly appeal to the senses.*
- *detailed descriptions or explanations about subtopics such as the musicians' backgrounds, music styles, and lyrics.*
- *reasons why they like the musician or band.*
- *what the music tells them about the time period in which it was written.*

Have students work independently to draft their descriptive essays. Tell them they will be able to revise their work.

Revise

Have students reread their drafts, using the revision steps and the following questions. After each step, have students make the revisions and write their final draft. Remind them to do the following steps:

- **Check the explanation.** Did you clearly inform the reader about the band/musician? What parts should you clarify or add more information to?
- **Check your description.** Did you use vivid sensory details and adjectives? Where do you need to add more details or description?
- **Check mechanics.** Do fragments or run-on sentences need to be rewritten? What words might be misspelled? Do all sentences begin with capital letters and end with proper punctuation?

Present

Have students present their essays. If possible, have students play samples of the music their essays describe.

Assess

I will assess your writing and presentation based on the rubric on your page. To assess students' descriptive essays, use the rubric from the Writing Blackline Master.

Real-World Reading

Web Site

1. Direct students to Student Book page 81. Explain that they will read a Web site. Have students preview headings and the menu bar. **What do you think this Web site is for?** (a music event to support American troops)
2. **Follow the instructions to complete the activity.**
3. **Would this Web site entice you to attend the event or donate money to support troops abroad? Explain.** Have students suggest ways that they would improve this Web site.

Expedition 3, Lesson 5

Name ______ Date ______

Real World—Web Site

Look at the Web site. Underline where you would click to find out about the bands performing. Circle the link to e-mail the troops. Draw a box around the link you could click to donate money to the troops.

Rock for the Troops

SATURDAY, OCTOBER 14 | 8:00 PM
DOWNTOWN ARENA | CHICAGO, IL

HOME
MUSICAL ACTS
VENUE
INFORMATION
TICKETS
STORE
DONATE NOW
CONTACT US

Join us for a historic event as musicians from all over America join together in song. This groundbreaking event will feature a wide variety of artists who are coming together to support our troops serving overseas. Together, we will send a message of support to the men and women in the armed forces. All proceeds from the event will be used to send supplies and care packages to service men and women stationed abroad.

TICKETS ON SALE SATURDAY, AUGUST 22
CALL: 800-555-1234 | www.ticketsonline.com

BEHIND THE SCENES
Go behind the scenes as we plan this event. Read blogs, see photos, and more.

PHOTO GALLERY

E-MAIL THE TROOPS
Use these quick links to send a note to members of the armed forces serving overseas.

©Voyager Expanded Learning, Inc.

81

Exploring Careers

Disc Jockey

1. Have students turn to Anthology page 43. Tell students to preview the title and photos. **What do you already know about a disc jockey's job?** (Possible answer: Disc jockeys work on the radio or at dances. They are familiar with certain styles of music, musicians, and the music industry.) **Pay attention to important details as you read so that you can identify the main idea.**
2. Have students read the passage. **Do you already know how to use equipment such as microphones, speakers, cables, and amplifiers? Do you think your personality would be a good fit for a career as a disc jockey?**
3. Have students turn to Student Book page 82. Have students answer the questions and complete the chart. Tell them they can find the answers by researching the career of disc jockey in books or online. Have students complete the page.

Expedition 3, Lesson 5

Name ______________________ Date ____________

Exploring Careers: Disc Jockey

A. Answer the following questions about a career as a DJ.

1. What are three different places where a DJ can work?
   radio station; wedding receptions; parties
2. What interests, skills, or abilities fit with a career as a DJ?
   interest in and knowledge of music and genres; ability to speak clearly; ability to use sound equipment
3. What education is important for becoming a DJ?
   classes in speech, drama, and language arts; degree in broadcasting
4. What are some ways to gain experience to become a DJ?
   get an internship at a radio station; work at a college radio station; assist a professional DJ at a party or a wedding
5. What is the range of the average yearly salary for a DJ in the United States?
   from $16,000 to $70,000

B. Use the Internet to research other possible career choices in this field and complete the chart.	
Career	
Responsibilities	
Education Required	
Average Salary	
Is this a career you might pursue?	
Why or why not?	
Career	
Responsibilities	
Education Required	
Average Salary	
Is this a career you might pursue?	
Why or why not?	

 82

Career

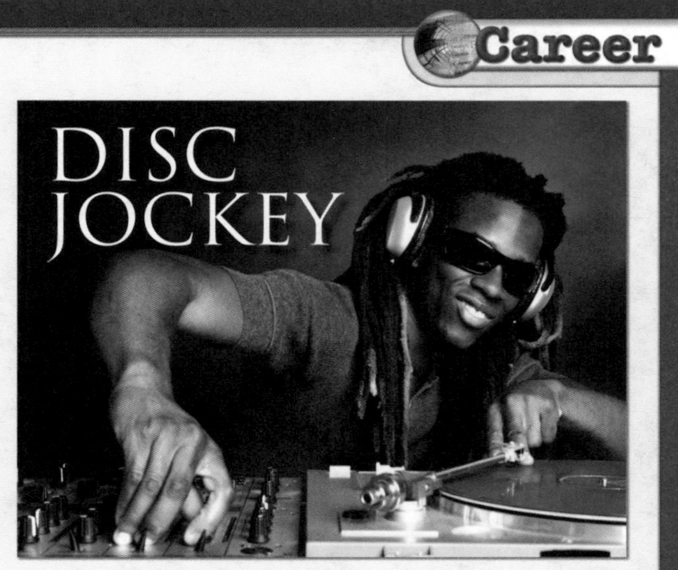

Rusty has invitations to every party at school. Everyone knows that without him choosing the music, the party won't be nearly as fun. When he isn't getting his friends out on the dance floor, he spends a lot of time organizing his music on his computer. Sometimes, he evens mixes his own music. He dreams of one day being paid to do this.

Well, he might not be dreaming at all. With a little luck and some work, he just might be able to support himself by doing what he loves. A DJ, or disc jockey, is someone who plays musical recordings. He or she can work in a variety of different places, from parties to wedding receptions to radio stations.

Anyone with a passion for music and the willingness to learn can become a DJ. Most DJs do indeed have an extensive knowledge of music. Some focus on one genre. Others know a lot about a wide range of music. Additionally, they are excellent listeners. Many can easily identify different components of songs just by listening to them.

However, being a DJ involves much more than a passion for music. DJs must be able to express themselves clearly. They announce the artists and titles of the songs they play. Many radio personalities also read the news, interview guests, and do commercials or promotions for their station. They frequently do guest appearances at locations around

Sounds of Life  43

Career

town. They may help celebrate the opening of a new business. Others might entertain guests at a party or a charity auction.

But, having knowledge about music and speaking well are just part of the job. DJs must be able to use a wide range of sound equipment. One key technique to master is the ability to make seamless transitions between songs. Additionally, DJs need to

understand how to handle equipment such as microphones, speakers, cables, and amplifiers.

One of the most important qualities for a DJ is connecting with the audience. DJs have to get a feel for what kind of music their listeners crave. That often changes. A DJ has to vary the music to keep people excited and responsive. DJs often are required to multitask. They must watch the clock as songs play and be able to prepare for the next song or commercial. Party and wedding reception DJs also must be able to field requests from guests while playing music.

By nature, most DJs are chatty and have outgoing personalities. Some say that one of the greatest challenges of their jobs is the time spent alone. They often are isolated in a DJ booth. Many radio station DJs have to work overnight or early in the morning when the station is fairly empty. Adjusting to the solitude is just part of the job.

Although higher education is always helpful, you do not need a college degree to become a successful DJ. Many people take speech, drama, and language arts classes in high school to help perfect their speech and delivery. Some choose to pursue broadcasting degrees in college.

On-the-job experience, however, is necessary to become a successful DJ. Internships at radio stations are a great way to learn the ropes. Working at a college radio station is another excellent way to learn the day-to-day tasks and get some on-air experience. A third way to gain hands-on experience is to assist a professional DJ at a party or a wedding.

The pay scale for DJs generally is reflective of where you live, the company you work for, and how much experience you have. The starting annual salary for the average radio DJ is about $25,000. Experienced radio personalities can earn more than $70,000 a year. The average annual salary for a club DJ is about $16,000 a year. However, many club DJs are paid hourly. Their rate also depends on their location and experience. Hourly rates can range from $8 to more than $50.

So, if Rusty is willing to put in some time and learn the ropes, he certainly could become a professional DJ. There are a vast number of opportunities for him to become a success on the air. Soon, he may be able to share his passion for music with listeners everywhere.

44 Expedition 3

English Language Learner Overview

The ELL signals when to provide extra support to students during the lesson. As needed, Blackline Masters for English language learners may provide support. For vocabulary, students also may use the online technology component to practice Expedition words or other content-area vocabulary and designated ELL word sets.

Introduce Vocabulary

Lesson 6

Distribute six index cards to each student. Have students write one vocabulary word on each card. Read aloud the following clues, and have students show the card that matches each clue. Then, have students write an example or draw their own clue on each card to help them remember the meaning.

- **Nothing else is like it.** (unique)
- **All shades of gray between black and white** (range)
- **Huge** (vast)
- **Guitar and piano** (instruments)
- **Change into something else** (convert)
- **Ways of doing things** (techniques)

Lesson 8

Have students read aloud the definition of each vocabulary word. Ask the following questions.

- **When you *amplify* something, do you make it smaller?** (no)
- **Is practice one of the *factors* that help people become good musicians?** (yes)
- **If you cannot hear music, do you need to make the *volume* softer?** (no)
- **Do you think a drum *renders* the same sound as a trumpet?** (no)
- **Are *particles* of dust hard to see?** (yes)

Practice Vocabulary

In Lesson 7, provide support for the context words *aspiring* and *integrating*. **When you are *aspiring* to do something, you are hoping and trying. *Aspiring* actors take acting lessons and audition for parts. What do *aspiring* musicians do?** Write the following sentence starter on the board: *Aspiring musicians* ________. (take music lessons; practice their instruments; play in bands)

***Integrating* something means "blending it with something else." Mashup artists record songs, *integrating* sounds from different sources. Do they put these different sounds together, or do they keep them separate?** (put them together)

In Lesson 9, provide support for the context words *counsel* and *navigate*. **When you give someone *counsel*, you tell the person what you think they should do. I went to my parents for *counsel* when I was trying to decide on a career. What kind of person would you ask for *counsel*?** (someone you trust) Write the following sentence starter on the board: *I trust the counsel I receive from* _________. (my parents; my teachers; my friends)

When you *navigate* a place, you find your way through it. It took me about a year to learn to *navigate* this city. How do you *navigate* a new city? (maps; asking directions) **What do you call a person whose job it is to *navigate* through water?** (a ship captain; a sailor) **Who *navigates* through air?** (an airplane or helicopter pilot)

Apply the Target Skill: Main Idea and Details

Support academic language by exploring the word *main* in *main idea*. Write *main* on the board and ask students what it means. (Students may have an answer because they have worked with main idea already.) Write a simple definition, such as "most important." Have students give examples of other contexts where they have heard *main*, both in academic uses or everyday language, such as *main goal*, *main character*, or *main road into town*.

Apply the Target Skill: Text Features

Some students may need additional practice identifying text features. Blackline Master page 19 begins with a sample passage and asks students to explain the function of different text features. To extend this activity, return to Passages 3 and 4 and ask similar questions about text features, such as *Which text feature helps you locate facts about the causes of different sounds?*

Glenn Weyant uses a cello bow and a cardboard tube to play a section of the wall in Arizona that separates the United States from Mexico.

Vocabulary

instruments (n) *objects used to make music*

unique (adj) *out of the ordinary; one of a kind*

techniques (n) *ways of doing something that require skill*

Glenn Weyant has always been a musician at heart. Like many aspiring artists, he achieved his goal and recorded a song. But, his **instruments** were anything but ordinary. In a project called The Anta Project, Weyant played a three-mile-long section of a steel wall that separates the United States from Mexico. Using chopsticks, egg beaters, and a cello bow to make music, Weyant recorded his song. He even used the sound of the wind vibrating the fence and the noise from the U.S. Department of Homeland Security helicopters to add depth to his music. 1

Weyant's project and his **unique techniques** have received a lot of media attention. "All of us has [*sic*] an inner artist, an inner musician," he said. "Playing found objects allows us to bypass obstacles to expressing that musicianship. It gets

1 Ask Questions
Be sure you understand what you read by asking questions. For example, what objects did Weyant use to make music?

Vocabulary

vast (adj) *huge in area or extent*

convert (v) *make a thing into something else*

range (n) *between limits; from one extreme to another*

to the core of the connections that exist between people and music."

Today, many people take a **vast** array of ordinary objects and combine sounds to make music. This new format is becoming quite popular. The Portland Bike Ensemble performs live music by playing actual bicycles. The Oregon-based group turns the vehicles upside down and attaches microphones to them that **convert** the bikes into an orchestra. They then pluck the spokes like a harp and turn cranks to keep the beat. They even touch their microphones to spinning wheels to create new sounds. This technique creates a unique sound that delights audiences.

Matmos is another group that uses a vast **range** of everyday sounds in their music. They recorded the sounds of liposuction and other forms of surgery. By converting the sounds into beats and melodies, they created an entire album from this recording. The duo is featured on a Björk album. A solo on one of the tracks is made from a deck of cards being shuffled. Björk said, "All their noises are recorded around the home." These everyday sounds really add depth to the music.

Recording artists are also exploring new techniques that can be used to make music. For example, mashups have become very popular. A mashup is a song that combines the vocals from one song with the music from another. On Girl Talk's 2008 album *Feed the Animals*, there are 14 tracks of mashups from more than 300 artists. This album is made up almost entirely of samples from music by other artists. Listeners can hear everything from Pachelbel, a 17th century German composer and organist, to Vampire Weekend, an indie rock band. These songs are then mashed with a wide range of hip-hop hooks.

"United State of Pop" by DJ Earworm is another example of this style. This song is a conversion of the top 25 billboard hits of 2007 into one hit song—the ultimate mashup. 2

Other musical artists are bringing everyday sounds into their albums in different ways. The sounds from Nintendo games play a prominent role in many tracks on Beck's *Guero* album. Critics say the Nintendo sounds lend a techno feel to the songs.

STOMP is a Broadway musical that also captured this trend. In the show, the performers use anything

2 Summarize
What are some examples of mashups?

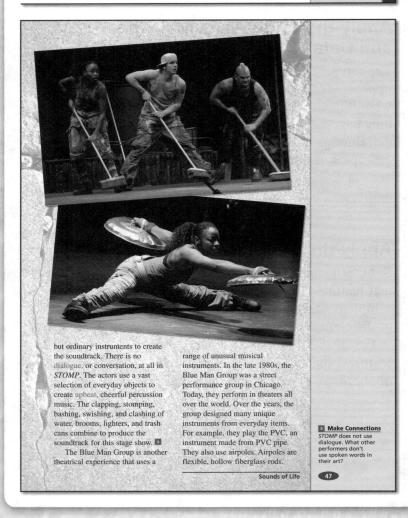

but ordinary instruments to create the soundtrack. There is no dialogue, or conversation, at all in *STOMP*. The actors use a vast selection of everyday objects to create upbeat, cheerful percussion music. The clapping, stomping, bashing, swishing, and clashing of water, brooms, lighters, and trash cans combine to produce the soundtrack for this stage show. 3

The Blue Man Group is another theatrical experience that uses a range of unusual musical instruments. In the late 1980s, the Blue Man Group was a street performance group in Chicago. Today, they perform in theaters all over the world. Over the years, the group designed many unique instruments from everyday items. For example, they play the PVC, an instrument made from PVC pipe. They also use airpoles. Airpoles are flexible, hollow fiberglass rods.

3 Make Connections
STOMP does not use dialogue. What other performers don't use spoken words in their art?

When moved through the air they make a "swoosh" sound. Finally, they even "play" a group member's dog. They call this instrument the "dogulum." The dog is stroked until he is content. The group records the noises he makes once satisfied, and uses them in their songs. 4

Countless other famous and not-so-famous musical acts are integrating, or blending, everyday noises and objects into their performances. So, the next time you hear water dripping in the sink or trains passing each other on the tracks, listen closely. You may just have front row seats at the best concert in town. End

4 Visualize
Look over what you have read. Picture in your mind what a *STOMP* or Blue Man Group performance might look like.

"Music without Instruments"

Before Reading

Introduce Vocabulary

1. Have students turn to Part A on Student Book page 83 and scan the boldfaced vocabulary words. **You will see these new words in "Music without Instruments." Remember that what you already know will help you learn new vocabulary.** Have students rate their knowledge of each boldfaced word.
2. Have students find words they assigned a 3 rating, share the meaning they know, and use the word in a sentence or phrase.
3. Read the part of speech, definition, and example sentence for each word. **Check that words you marked with a 3 have the meaning that you know. Pay special attention to the words you assigned a 1 rating. Has that rating changed?**
4. Have students read the instructions for Part B and complete the activity.

Refer to Blackline Master page 17 to extend vocabulary practice.

Have students use the *Passport Reading Journeys* online technology component to practice and reinforce vocabulary and comprehension skills.

Apply the Target Skill: Implicit Main Idea and Details

1. Tell students that when people read or listen to information, they try to understand the most important, or main, idea. **Why do people focus on the main idea of a text?** (Understanding the main idea helps you understand the rest of the information in the text.)

Expedition 3, Lesson 6

Name ______________________ Date ______________

Vocabulary

"Music without Instruments"

A. Write one or more numbers next to each boldfaced word to show when you have seen, heard, or used this word.

5 I use it in everyday conversation.
4 I heard it on TV or on the radio.
3 I heard or used it in school.
2 I read it in a book, magazine, or online.
1 I have not read, heard, or used this word.

☐ **instruments** (n) *objects used to make music*
There are many kinds of *instruments* in the band.

☐ **unique** (adj) *out of the ordinary; one of a kind*
No one else had ever played the *unique* instrument.

☐ **techniques** (n) *ways of doing something that require skill*
He uses strange *techniques* to play the guitar, but they work.

☐ **vast** (adj) *huge in area or extent*
There is a *vast* number of songs on the concert playlist.

☐ **convert** (v) *make a thing into something else*
It is easy to *convert* a strange sound into pleasing music.

☐ **range** (n) *between limits; from one extreme to another*
A marching band uses a wide *range* of instruments from the flute to the bass drum.

B. Read each statement. Circle true or false.

1. Basketball players usually bring **instruments** to practice. true (false)
2. If something is **unique**, many things are just like it. true (false)
3. Different artists may use different **techniques** to create art. (true) false
4. Walking across a **vast** field could take a long time. (true) false
5. When you **convert** something, you make sure it stays the same. true (false)
6. Restaurants that sell only hot dogs sell a wide **range** of foods. true (false)

 83

Vocabulary

instruments (n) *objects used to make music*
There are many kinds of *instruments* in the band.

unique (adj) *out of the ordinary; one of a kind*
No one else had ever played the *unique* instrument.

techniques (n) *ways of doing something that require skill*
He uses strange *techniques* to play the guitar, but they work.

vast (adj) *huge in area or extent*
There is a *vast* number of songs on the concert playlist.

convert (v) *make a thing into something else*
It is easy to *convert* a strange sound into pleasing music.

range (n) *between limits; from one extreme to another*
A marching band uses a wide *range* of instruments from the flute to the bass drum.

2. **When I want to figure out the main idea, I read and make a statement about it.** Read aloud the first paragraph of the passage. **For example, I can say that the main idea of this paragraph is *Weyant uses unusual things as musical instruments.* Then I find details that directly support that main idea. One detail is *Weyant used chopsticks to make music.*** Have students identify other details. **Name one detail that does not directly support the main idea.** (Weyant has always been a musician at heart.) Explain that students have correctly identified the main idea when they can find several details that support it.

Introduce the Passage

1. Have students preview "Music without Instruments." Remind students that the Expedition is about music. **What clues in the title and photos tell you what the passage is about?** (The title and photos suggest the passage is about ways to make music without traditional instruments.) **How might people make music without instruments?** (Clues like the photographs suggest that people might use bicycles or other ordinary objects to make music.)
2. Have students notice the margin prompts. **As you read the passage, pause to read these prompts. Respond to them based on what you read. The vocabulary notes in the margin will remind you of the meanings of the boldfaced words.**
3. Teach these terms from the passage:
   - *Liposuction* is a plastic surgery procedure for removing fat.
   - *Björk* (byȯrk)
   - *ensemble* (on som' buhl)
   - *Pachelbel* (po' ku bel)
   - *PVC pipe* is white plastic piping used in plumbing.
   - [*sic*] is used when a quote in the text has something misspelled or grammatically incorrect.
4. **When have you seen or heard people make music without instruments? How was that music different from music made with traditional instruments?** Have students discuss their experiences, including the effect that hearing the music had on them.

   To make the most of the discussion time, remember to incorporate strategies that encourage and extend student involvement. Refer to page xxxviii for a comprehensive discussion of these strategies.

ELL Provide sentence frames to help students share their experiences. *I saw people using _______ to make music.* If students do not have experiences to share, have them suggest possibilities. *People could use _______ to make music.*

During Reading

1. Have students look for details as they read the passage. To select reading options that support your students' levels and classroom needs, see Reading Differentiation on page xxxii, if needed.
2. When students finish reading, have them return to the text to identify the main idea of the third paragraph and find one detail that directly supports the main idea and one detail that does not support it directly. (Main idea: Many people take a vast array of objects and combine sounds to make music. Direct supporting detail: The Portland Bike Ensemble uses bicycles as instruments. Detail that does not support it directly: The new format is becoming popular.)

After Reading

Check Comprehension

1. **Before you read the passage, you predicted ways people might make music without instruments. Which of your predictions were mentioned in the passage? Which techniques were new to you?**
2. Have students share their responses to the Summarize margin prompt on Anthology page 46. **What are some examples of mashups?** (Girl Talk's 2008 album, which uses samples of classical and modern music; DJ Earworm's "The United States of Pop" combines 25 top songs into one.)
3. Reread the Visualize margin prompt on Anthology page 48. Have students share what they visualized. **How can visualizing help you during reading?** (It helps connect the text to the real-life situation it describes.)

Remind students to choose books from the *Passport Reading Journeys* Library for independent reading.

"Music without Instruments"

Prepare to Reread

Introduce the Lesson

In Lesson 7, we'll revisit "Music without Instruments" and practice identifying the main idea and details.

Practice Vocabulary

1. Have students think about how vocabulary words from Lesson 6 were used in the passage.
   - **What kind of *instruments* does Glenn Weyant use?** (a steel wall; chopsticks; egg beaters; a cello bow)
   - **In what way is Weyant's music *unique*?** (No one else uses these objects as musical instruments.)
   - **What *techniques* do the Portland Bike Ensemble use to make music?** (They play the spokes of bicycle wheels and turn cranks.)
   - **These musicians say they have a *vast* number of ways to make music. Why would they say this?** (They make music with ordinary objects, so it is limitless.)
   - **Give an example of an ordinary object you can *convert* into a musical instrument.** (a bicycle)
   - **Does the Blue Man Group use a wide or narrow *range* of "instruments"? How do you know?** (wide; they play anything from a dog to PVC pipes.)
2. Remind students that they can use context clues to find the meaning of unfamiliar words. Have students turn to Anthology page 45. Reread the first three sentences. **What do you think the word *aspiring* means?** (hoping to do something) **What clues in the text help you figure out the meaning?** (He achieved his goal.)

   Repeat this process for the following words.
   - **dialogue** (n) *conversation*, Anthology page 47
   - **upbeat** (adj) *cheerful*, Anthology page 47
   - **content** (adj) *satisfied*, Anthology page 48
   - **integrating** (v) *blending*, Anthology page 48
3. Have students turn to Student Book page 84. Read the instructions, and have them complete the activities.

Expedition 3, Lesson 7

Name ______________________ Date ______________

Word Building

A. Suffixes, which come at the end of words, can change a word's meaning. Each word in the box ends with the suffix *-ly*. Complete the statements below.

technically	**vastly**	**safely**
uniquely	**perfectly**	**correctly**

-ly means "in a ______ way."

1. *Technically* means "in a technical way."
2. *Uniquely* means "in a unique way."
3. *Vastly* means "in a vast way."
4. *Perfectly* means "in a perfect way."
5. *Safely* means "in a safe way."
6. *Correctly* means "in a correct way."

What vocabulary word is similar to *technical*? techniques

Using the definition of the vocabulary word, define *technical*. done with skill

B. Use the boldfaced words in Part A to fill in the blanks.

1. The roads were icy and dangerous, but she arrived home safely.
2. After many months of practicing the skills, Juan gave a technically sound performance.
3. The man from Hawaii was vastly more comfortable in the ocean than the man from Kansas.
4. She correctly completed the math problem.
5. The odd piece of pottery was uniquely created by my friend, Mai.
6. She perfectly rounded the pot to make it flawless and smooth.

C. Use two of the boldfaced words from Part A in a descriptive sentence about yourself.

1. Answers will vary.
2. ______________________

84

ELL Support the adjectives *content* and *upbeat* by directly explaining the definitions. Have students answer questions using facial expressions and gestures. *How do you look when you are content? How would you act upbeat?*

Reread

Apply the Target Skill: Implicit Main Idea and Details

1. **I want to know the main idea of this passage. So, I scan each paragraph for the important ideas. Then, I put them together to figure out the main idea of the whole passage.**

2. Write the main idea on the board: *People can make music by using everyday objects as instruments.* **Now I can scan the first paragraph to find details that support this main idea.** Provide this example: **Glenn Weyant uses unusual instruments, such as chopsticks, egg beaters, and a steel wall. How does the example directly support the main idea?** (Chopsticks, egg beaters, and a steel wall are everyday objects that are not designed to be musical instruments.) Tell students they also can write details first, then figure out the main idea from the details.
3. Have students turn to Student Book page 85. Direct them to reread the text and locate details supporting the main idea. **Check that each detail directly supports the main idea.** For Part B, have students write a summary of the passage. **You can use the information in the diagram to write the summary.**

ELL Support academic language by exploring the word *detail*. Write a simple definition, such as *a small part of a whole thing*. Ask students to describe *details* they like on vehicles.

ACADEMIC SKILL Remind students that they can determine the main idea and details when they read texts for other classes, such as science. Science textbooks often have stated main ideas or subheadings that can help them comprehend the main idea.

Write in Response to Reading

1. **Think about famous musicians who use interesting sounds and techniques to make their music stand out from other performers' music.** Have students turn to Student Book page 86. Read the instructions for Part A aloud, and have students complete the activity.
2. Have students describe a mashup in their own words. Tell students they will imagine and describe a mashup of two of their favorite songs. Read the instructions for Part B aloud.

EXPEDITION ORGANIZER **Sounds of Life**

Pause to have students turn to Student Book pages 64 and 65. Have students complete the following:

- Write answers to one or more of the probing questions in Part A. Encourage them to add a question.
- Write an important idea about "Music without Instruments" in Part B.

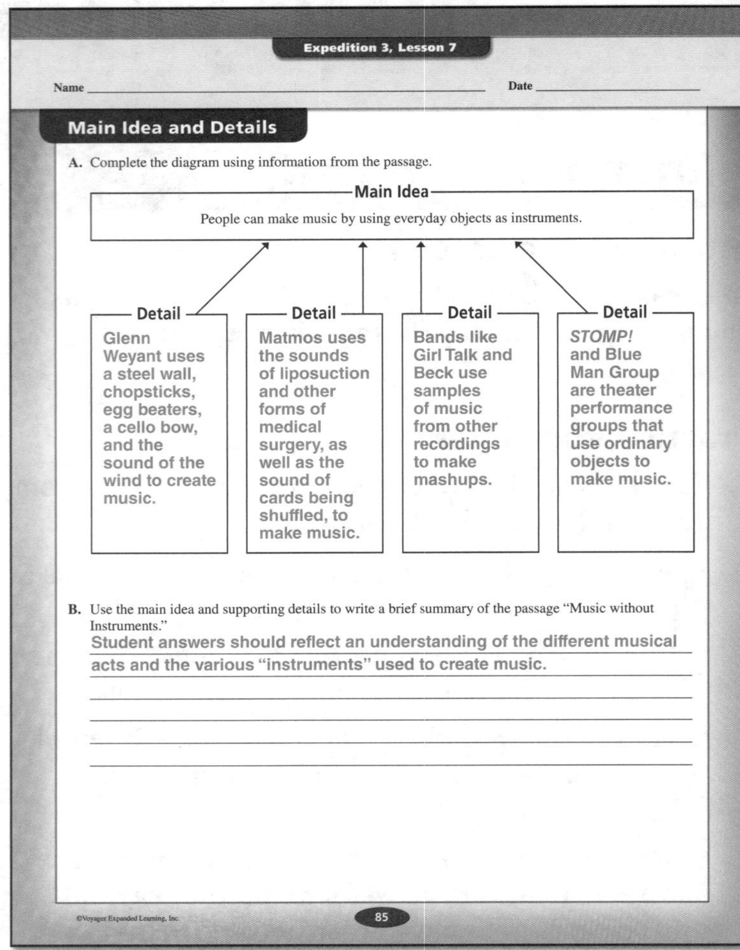

Expedition 3, Lesson 7

Name ______________________ Date __________

Main Idea and Details

A. Complete the diagram using information from the passage.

Main Idea

People can make music by using everyday objects as instruments.

Detail	Detail	Detail	Detail
Glenn Weyant uses a steel wall, chopsticks, egg beaters, a cello bow, and the sound of the wind to create music.	Matmos uses the sounds of liposuction and other forms of medical surgery, as well as the sound of cards being shuffled, to make music.	Bands like Girl Talk and Beck use samples of music from other recordings to make mashups.	*STOMP!* and Blue Man Group are theater performance groups that use ordinary objects to make music.

B. Use the main idea and supporting details to write a brief summary of the passage "Music without Instruments."

Student answers should reflect an understanding of the different musical acts and the various "instruments" used to create music.

©Voyager Expanded Learning, Inc. 85

Expedition 3, Lesson 7

Name ______________________ Date __________

Write in Response to Reading

A. What kind of music do you listen to? What kinds of sounds do you hear in each performer's music? Complete the chart with information about three of your favorite musical performers. Include each performer's name, genre (the kind of music), and some unique sounds that you hear in the songs.

Answers will vary.

Performer's Name	Genre	Unique Sounds

B. In the passage, you read about mashups that combine parts of two different songs to make a new song. What would a mashup of two of your favorite songs sound like? Imagine the sound of the new song and describe it on the following lines. Include how each performer contributes to the new, unique sound.

Student answers should reflect an understanding of mashups and how they combine elements of two songs to make a new work of musical art.

©Voyager Expanded Learning, Inc. 86

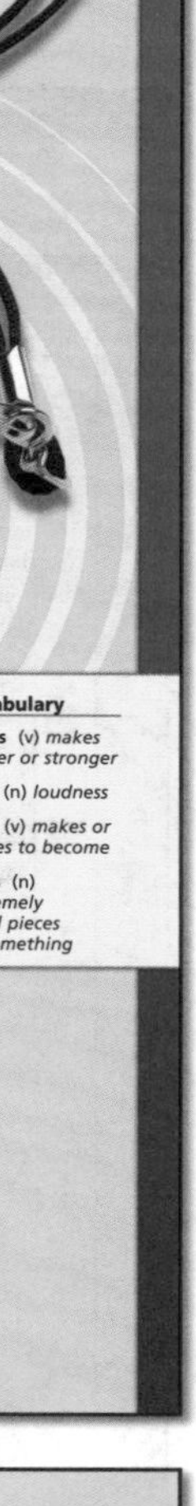

THE SCIENCE of SOUND

The crowd screams as the home team scores a basket. Thump. Thump. Thump. The basketball echoes as it is dribbled up the court. The loudspeaker system **amplifies** the announcer's voice as he relays the score. In the next row, a couple talks about their plans after the game. A vendor selling programs walks through the section and calls, "Programs!" The guy in row L gets caught up in the excitement of the last quarter and shares his counsel, or advice, with the coach.

At the basketball game, there are many different types of sounds—some loud and some soft. All of these sounds interact with one another. So, depending on your location, the sounds may be different from the ones a friend across the arena hears. The pitch and **volume** of the sound varies based on your location.

What Is Sound?

Guitar strings vibrate, or move quickly back and forth, to produce music. In the same way, when we speak, our vocal cords vibrate, creating the sound of our voices. Sound is a vibration that travels through matter. The matter can be a solid, liquid, or gas. When an object vibrates, it **renders** movement in the air **particles**. As the particles

Vocabulary

amplifies (v) *makes louder or stronger*

volume (n) *loudness*

renders (v) *makes or causes to become*

particles (n) *extremely small pieces of something*

Vocabulary

factors (n) *things that help produce a result*

bump into one another, they create sound waves. If you are within range, your ears will pick up these vibrations. You hear them as sounds. The closer you are to the root of the sound, the louder the volume will be. 1

Sound cannot travel through a vacuum, or airless space, because there is nothing to vibrate—it is empty. Outer space is a vacuum. Because there are no particles to vibrate in outer space, sounds cannot be transferred from the source of the sound. If there were an explosion in outer space, you would only be able to see it. You would not hear it. The next time you see a movie with a battle that takes place in outer space, you'll know the sounds were added for dramatic effect.

What Causes Different Sounds?

Why are there so many different sounds? The frequency, amplitude, and wavelength of the sound waves are **factors** that combine to determine which sound you hear. Sound waves travel 340 meters, or about three football fields, per second through air. In water, sound travels more than four times as quickly, at a rate of 1,500 meters per second.

The frequency is the number of waves that pass a given point per second. Another way to describe the frequency is to describe how quickly the particles vibrate. The faster the waves move, the higher the pitch of the sound. The pitch is how the note or noise sounds compared to other notes or noises. A foghorn renders a low-pitched sound. A dog whistle renders a high-pitched sound.

1 Summarize
What is sound?

An explosion in space can be seen, but not heard. Why?

Wavelength is another factor that affects the pitch. The wavelength is the distance from the top of one wave to the top of the next. Another way to describe it is the distance between matching points on a wave. The slower the frequency, the longer the wavelength will be. Therefore, the longer the wavelength, the lower pitched the sound. 2

Another factor that determines the sound you hear is the amplitude. The amplitude is the amount of energy in a sound wave. The volume of a sound is determined by the amplitude. The height of the wave is used to measure this. The taller the wave, the louder the

2 Text Features
Look at the diagram below. It says that the waveforms have the same frequency. Which waveform has the lower pitched sound?

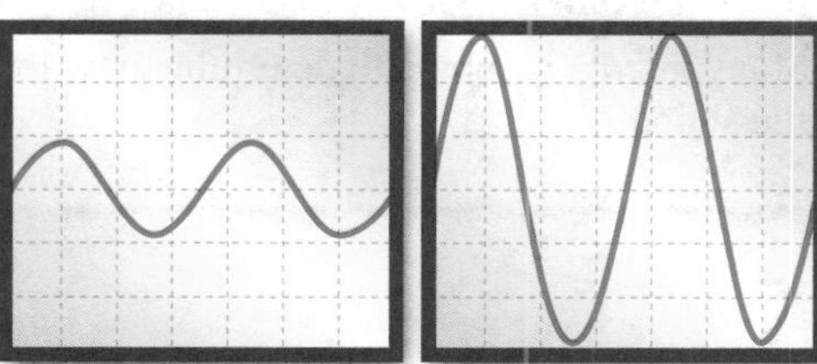

The waveform on the left has a smaller amplitude, but the same number of peaks in a given time (frequency). The only difference between the sounds is that the first one is quieter because it has less energy.

sound. An amplifier is a device specifically designed to make a sound louder. It does so by increasing the amplitude of a signal. Many electronics products, from computers to televisions, have devices in them that amplify the sound. 3

Communicating with Sound Waves

Although they don't have vocal cords or words, dolphins have communicated with one another for centuries using sound waves. A mother dolphin often whistles to her baby for several days after giving birth. This allows the calf to identify his mother simply by the pitch of her whistle. Dolphins also use sound waves to navigate their way through the dark waters, as well as hunt and communicate.

Recent studies show that teenagers can hear higher pitches of notes than adults. Some businesses have installed devices that emit a high-pitched sound to keep teens from loitering. The inventor says most people who are older than 30 cannot hear this sound. Some teens have figured out how to benefit from this ability. They have created a new ringtone, the mosquito. Now, they can receive text message notifications on their cell phones without adults knowing. 4

Sounds are everywhere. They allow us to communicate with each other and take in our surroundings. Sounds also provide us with entertainment and help us learn. So, the next time you hear a soothing sound that brings a smile to your face—or a horrible screech that makes you crazy, stop and think about how the sound was created. End

3 Ask Questions
What questions would you ask yourself about frequency, wavelength, and amplitude before you describe the science of sound to a friend?

4 Make Connections
Do you know anyone who uses the mosquito ringtone?

"The Science of Sound"

Before Reading

Introduce Vocabulary

1. Have students turn to Part A on Student Book page 87 and scan the boldfaced vocabulary words. **As you read "The Science of Sound," you will encounter these words.** Have students rate their knowledge of each boldfaced word.
2. Have students share the meanings of words they know with the class and give an example sentence or phrase using each word.
3. Read the definition, part of speech, and example sentence for each word. **Which meanings surprise you? Are you more familiar with any word meaning than you thought?** Have students change ratings if needed.
4. Have students read the instructions for Part B. Have them complete the activity, then compare their answers with partners. Prompt them to provide reasons for their answers.

Refer to Blackline Master page 18 to extend vocabulary practice.

Have students use the *Passport Reading Journeys* online technology component to practice and reinforce vocabulary and comprehension skills.

Apply the Target Skill: Content Area Text Features

1. Remind students that it is important to preview a text before they read. Provide real-world examples of texts like newspapers, magazines, and Internet articles. **In these kinds of readings, you expect to see features like headings, charts and graphs, and pictures with captions. What features do you usually find in a newspaper?** (headings; pictures with captions) Ask students to share other kinds of text features they have seen in texts they have read.
2. **Think about textbooks you used this week. What features helped you understand the text better?**

Expedition 3, Lesson 8

Name ______________________ Date ______________

Vocabulary

"The Science of Sound"

A. Put a check mark in each row to show how well you know each boldfaced word.

	Know This Word	Have Seen This Word	Don't Know This Word
amplifies (v) *makes louder or stronger* A microphone *amplifies* her singing voice so she can be heard by everyone.			
volume (n) *loudness* The *volume* of the radio forced me to speak very loudly.			
renders (v) *makes or causes to become* A guitar string *renders* a different sound when pressed.			
particles (n) *extremely small pieces of something* *Particles* we can't see are in the air at all times.			
factors (n) *things that help produce a result* Many *factors* combine to determine how loud the sound is.			

B. Choose the word from Part A that BEST completes each sentence.

1. David increased the ___volume___ on the radio because he couldn't hear the music.
2. In order to see the ___particles___ of dust, Cordelia had to use a magnifying glass.
3. Drivers should be careful after an ice storm because it ___renders___ the streets slippery and dangerous.
4. Many ___factors___, like a broken traffic light and a slick road, combined to cause the car accident.
5. Becca ___amplifies___ her voice when she screams as loud as she can.

87

Vocabulary

amplifies (v) *makes louder or stronger*
A microphone *amplifies* her singing voice so she can be heard by everyone.

volume (n) *loudness*
The *volume* of the radio forced me to speak very loudly.

renders (v) *makes or causes to become*
A guitar string *renders* a different sound when pressed.

particles (n) *extremely small pieces of something*
Particles we can't see are in the air at all times.

factors (n) *things that help produce a result*
Many *factors* combine to determine how loud the sound is.

Introduce the Passage

1. Have students turn to "The Science of Sound." Preview the text features in this passage. Have students locate and identify these text features:
   - Main heading and subheadings
   - Diagrams
   - Photos
2. Direct student attention to the margin prompts. **As you read the passage, pause to read the margin prompts. Think about what you already know and the information you read in the text to respond to these prompts.**
3. Teach these terms to prepare students for the passage:
   - *Within range* means "close enough to something to be affected by it or to experience it."
   - *For dramatic effect* describes something done to cause an emotional reaction in people.
4. Have students preview the text and think of the text features as clues to what the passage is about. Then, have students use those clues to make a prediction. **What do you think the passage is about?** (how sound works from a scientific point of view) **How did the text features help you predict?** (The title, headings, and the diagram of sound waves give clues to what the passage is about.)

During Reading

1. Instruct students to pay attention to the text features as they read "The Science of Sound." To select reading options that support your students' levels and classroom needs, see Reading Differentiation on page xxxii, if needed.
2. Ask students the following questions, and encourage them to return to the text to check for answers.
   - **Think about the relationship between matter and sound. Why is matter necessary for sound?** (Particles of matter must vibrate to create sound.)

ELL Support the first bulleted question by directing students to the third paragraph. Write *Sound is a vibration that travels through matter.* Explain that air is one kind of matter, so sound can travel through air.

   - **The passage states that there are low-pitched sounds and high-pitched sounds. What is an example of a low-pitched sound?** (a foghorn) **How would you describe the frequency of this sound?** (The waves pass a certain point slower than many other sounds.)
   - **How does sound travel?** (Sound travels in waves through matter.)
   - **What is the main reason that people use sound?** (to communicate with one another)

After Reading

Check Comprehension

1. **What did you predict the passage was about? How does your prediction compare with what you know now about the passage?** (Answers will vary.) Ask students to point out the text features they used to think of their predictions.
2. **Reread the Summarize margin prompt on Anthology page 50. How did you answer this?** (Sound starts with a vibration. As the vibration moves through the air, it moves particles. Particles bumping into one another create sound waves.) If students have difficulty summarizing, have them scan the section for the most important facts about sound.
3. **Reread the Text Features margin prompt on Anthology page 51. What was tricky about this question?** (The answer is neither.) **Sometimes you are asked questions that don't have a correct answer. It is not a good idea to assume there has to be a correct answer. Go with your first instinct, once you have carefully thought it through.**

Remind students to choose books from the *Passport Reading Journeys* Library for independent reading.

"The Science of Sound"

Prepare to Reread

Introduce the Lesson

In Lesson 9, we'll look more closely at text features in "The Science of Sound."

Practice Vocabulary

1. Have students answer the following questions in complete sentences.
   - **A loudspeaker system *amplifies* sounds you hear. What *amplifies* your ability to see things?** (A pair of glasses *amplifies* my ability to see things.)
   - **The *volume* of a sound affects how well you can hear that sound. What level of *volume* do you use when you whisper?** (When you whisper, you speak at a low *volume*.)
   - **When particles in the air bump into each other, they *render* sound waves. What are some ways that you could *render* a picture of something?** (You could use a camera to *render* a picture.)
   - **Many *particles* in the air are so small that you cannot see them. What kinds of *particles* can you see?** (You can see dust *particles* and crumbs on the floor.)
   - **Three *factors* that determine sound are frequency, wavelength, and amplitude. What are some *factors* that affect how a plant grows?** (Water, sunlight, and fertile soil are some *factors* that affect plant growth.)
2. Remind students that context clues can help readers understand unfamiliar words. Have students find the word *vendor* on Anthology page 49 and tell its meaning. (one who sells goods) **Which word or words help you know what this word means?** (selling programs)

   Repeat this process for the following words.
   - **counsel** (n) *advice*, Anthology page 49
   - **vibrate** (v) *move quickly back and forth*, Anthology page 49
   - **vacuum** (n) *a completely empty space*, Anthology page 50
   - **navigate** (v) *make your way through something*, Anthology page 52

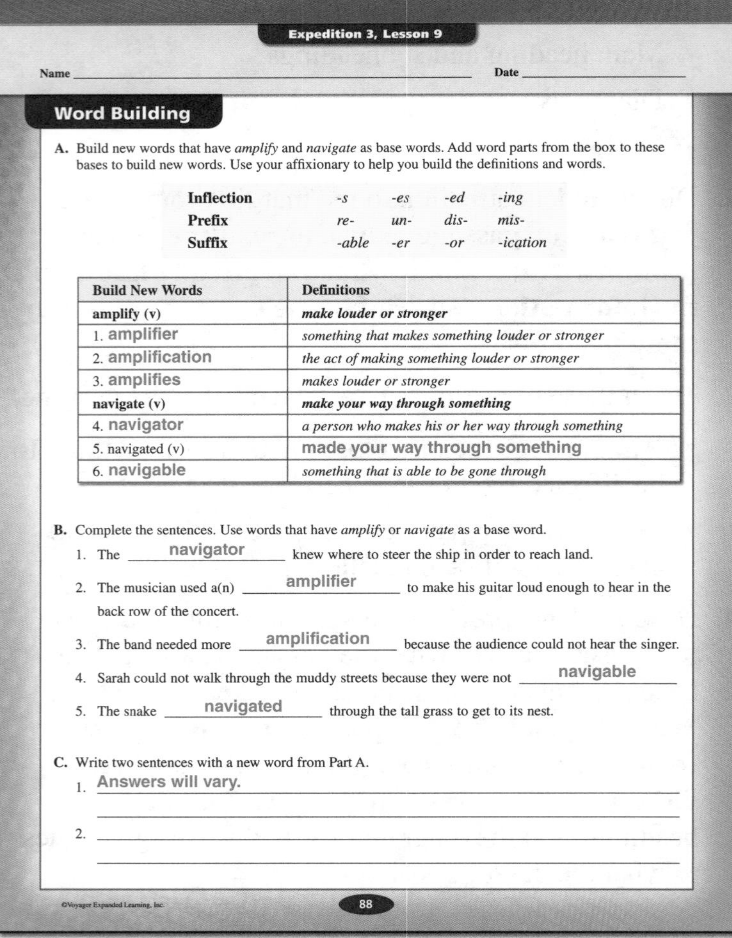

Expedition 3, Lesson 9

Name ______________________ Date ____________

Word Building

A. Build new words that have *amplify* and *navigate* as base words. Add word parts from the box to these bases to build new words. Use your affixionary to help you build the definitions and words.

Inflection	*-s*	*-es*	*-ed*	*-ing*
Prefix	*re-*	*un-*	*dis-*	*mis-*
Suffix	*-able*	*-er*	*-or*	*-ication*

Build New Words	Definitions
amplify (v)	***make louder or stronger***
1. amplifier	*something that makes something louder or stronger*
2. amplification	*the act of making something louder or stronger*
3. amplifies	*makes louder or stronger*
navigate (v)	***make your way through something***
4. navigator	*a person who makes his or her way through something*
5. navigated (v)	made your way through something
6. navigable	*something that is able to be gone through*

B. Complete the sentences. Use words that have *amplify* or *navigate* as a base word.

1. The navigator knew where to steer the ship in order to reach land.
2. The musician used a(n) amplifier to make his guitar loud enough to hear in the back row of the concert.
3. The band needed more amplification because the audience could not hear the singer.
4. Sarah could not walk through the muddy streets because they were not navigable
5. The snake navigated through the tall grass to get to its nest.

C. Write two sentences with a new word from Part A.

1. Answers will vary.
2. ______________________

©Voyager Expanded Learning, Inc. 88

Directly explain the definition of *vendor* and have students give examples.

3. Have students turn to Student Book page 88. Read the word parts at the top of the page. Explain that the vocabulary word *amplifies* contains the word *amplify*. ***Amplify* is a base word. You can create new words by adding prefixes, suffixes, and inflectional endings to base words. Words that share the same base word are in the same word family.** Read aloud the instructions for Part A, and have students complete the activity. Have partners share their answers. Have them complete Parts B and C independently.

CHECKPOINT If students have difficulty with Part B or C, suggest they check the meanings of the words in a dictionary.

Reread

Apply the Target Skill: Content Area Text Features

1. **Reread "The Science of Sound." The text you read is an informational passage. Why is it a good idea to include text features with a passage like this?** (to help readers understand a complicated topic)
2. Direct students to Student Book page 89. Read aloud the instructions, and have students complete the page.

ELL Refer to Blackline Master page 19 to extend practice using text features.

Write in Response to Reading

1. Prepare students to complete the writing activities on Student Book page 90. Point out that people use technology to appeal to all five senses. **Think about how you encounter sound every day and how you use sound. Could you use another sense to do the same thing?** Read aloud the instructions, and have students complete the activity.
2. **Sounds can create emotional responses in all of us.** Have students think of a sound they enjoy or dislike. Read the instructions for Part B aloud, and have students complete the activity.

EXPEDITION ORGANIZER **Sounds of Life**

Pause to have students turn to Student Book pages 64 and 65. Have students complete the following:

- Write answers or notes below one or more of the probing questions in Part A.
- Think about the big idea from "The Science of Sound." Tell students to write it in the graphic organizer in Part B. Complete the remainder of the graphic organizer.
- Complete the Dictionary Challenge in Part C.

Build Background DVD 3.2

Briefly discuss the Expedition passages, then watch the DVD together. After watching, review student responses to the probing questions using the Expedition Organizer.

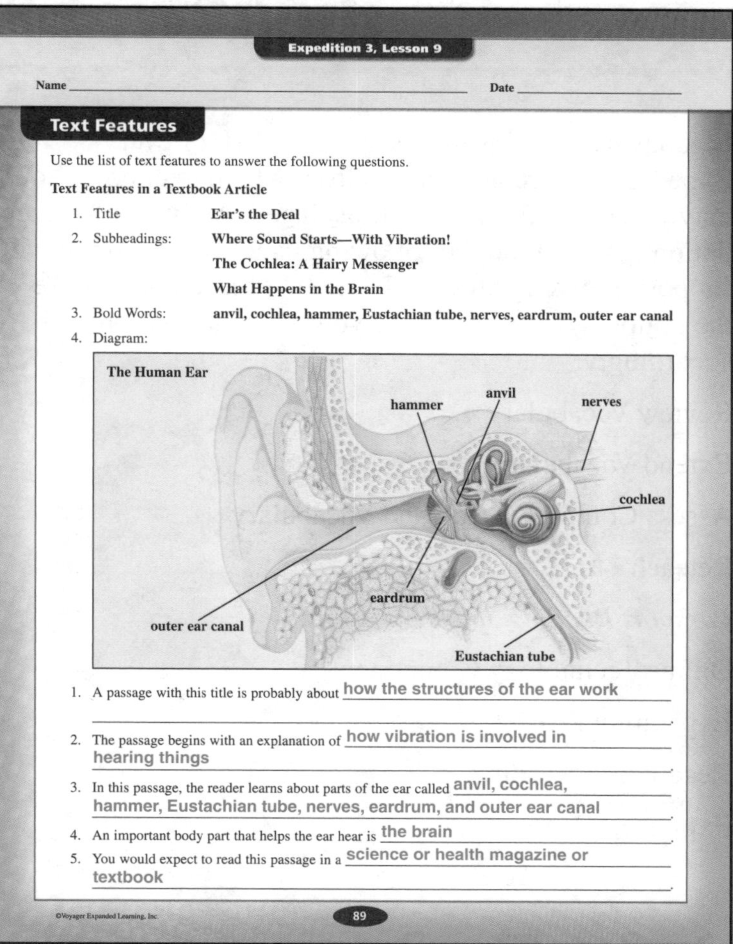

Expedition 3, Lesson 9

Name ______ Date ______

Text Features

Use the list of text features to answer the following questions.

Text Features in a Textbook Article

1. Title **Ear's the Deal**
2. Subheadings: **Where Sound Starts—With Vibration!** **The Cochlea: A Hairy Messenger** **What Happens in the Brain**
3. Bold Words: **anvil, cochlea, hammer, Eustachian tube, nerves, eardrum, outer ear canal**
4. Diagram:

1. A passage with this title is probably about how the structures of the ear work.
2. The passage begins with an explanation of how vibration is involved in hearing things.
3. In this passage, the reader learns about parts of the ear called anvil, cochlea, hammer, Eustachian tube, nerves, eardrum, and outer ear canal.
4. An important body part that helps the ear hear is the brain.
5. You would expect to read this passage in a science or health magazine or textbook.

 89

Expedition 3, Lesson 9

Name ______ Date ______

Write in Response to Reading

A. How would life be different without sound? Use the chart to invent ways to replace sounds you depend on. In the left column, list sounds you hear and use every day. In the middle column, write how you use each sound. In the right column, write how you could replace the sound. The first item is done for you.
Answers will vary.

Sound	How the Sound Is Used	How to Replace the Sound
school bell	tells when classes begin and end	A screen in the room flashes when classes begin and end.

B. Describe two sounds that produce a feeling in you. Tell where you hear the sounds, what makes them, and how you feel when you hear them.
Student descriptions should include two sounds, the settings where they hear them, what produces the sounds, and the emotions that the sounds evoke.

 90

Review, Extend, Assess

In today's lesson, as in Lessons 5 and 10 of every Expedition, there are options from which to choose. You may do any or all of the options listed. Activities for each option are given on the following pages. Each option will support or extend previously taught objectives. Choose the option(s) appropriate for your students and prepare accordingly.

Review Vocabulary

Extend Vocabulary

Assess Comprehension and Vocabulary

Reteach

Passport Reading Journeys Library

Online Technology Component

Expedition Project

Real-World Reading

Exploring Careers

Review Vocabulary

Direct students to review the vocabulary for "Music without Instruments" and "The Science of Sound" on Student Book page 65.

1. Have students read the words and definitions. **Do you think you will be able to understand these words when you read them in context? Which words can you use correctly when speaking?**
2. Have students turn to Student Book page 91. Tell them to focus on the meanings of the words they learned. **As you complete the activity, go back and check the definitions to make sure you use the words correctly.**
3. Read the instructions for Parts A and B aloud. Tell them to briefly check the meanings in the Expedition Dictionary on Student Book page 65.

Expedition 3, Lesson 10

Name ______ Date ______

Review Vocabulary

A. Complete each sentence by writing a context clue that supports the meaning of the boldfaced word. A context clue can be an example, a synonym, an antonym, or a brief explanation. The first one is done for you. Possible responses are given.

1. His drumming **techniques**, or __methods__, were extremely impressive.
2. A violin **renders**, or __creates__, sound when the strings vibrate.
3. This band likes to **convert**, or __change__, regular objects into percussion instruments.
4. A microphone **amplifies** a singer's voice; it doesn't __mute or silence__ the voice.
5. Many **instruments**, such as the __flute__ and the __drums__ are played in a marching band.
6. The **volume**, or __loudness__, of a trumpet depends on how hard you blow into it.
7. I swallowed the **particles** in my drink because I couldn't see the __small pieces__.

B. Read the interview. Write a vocabulary word from "Music without Instruments" or "The Science of Sound" that BEST completes each sentence. Use the words in parentheses as clues.

James: Thank you for having this dialogue with me. Tell me, what __factors__ (things that help produce a result) make these concerts so appealing to you?

Angel: Two factors are that the concerts are free and easy to get to. I feel good when I listen to the upbeat music at the Latin Music Festival. My friends and I just love being there and are never bored listening to so many __unique__ (not ordinary) musical groups.

Anna: I never miss watching Irish dancers at the Celtic Music Festival. I am an aspiring dancer myself.

Angel: Another factor is the __vast__ (huge in extent) variety of concerts. You're sure to find at least one you want to attend.

James: How do you navigate the crowds and get to the performances you want to see?

Anna: Each festival has its own informational Web site. I like to browse the __range__ (from one extreme to another) of musicians. Then I plan my schedule.

 91

Extend Vocabulary

1. Direct students to Student Book page 92, and read the instructions. **A suffix is a word part at the end of a word that changes the meaning.** Write the suffixes *-ate* and *-ion* on the board along with their meanings.
2. Point out that words ending in *-ion* become nouns. Complete the first two items in Part A with the whole group. Then, have students work independently. Tell students to watch for changes in spelling as they build words.
3. Have students read the instructions and complete Part B. Tell them to check their answers by looking in Part A to find the definitions. Have partners share their answers after completing both parts.

CHECKPOINT When students share their answers, make sure they use the correct parts of speech in the sentence syntax and that the new words are spelled correctly. Pause to explain and correct any errors.

Part A

Explore and practice the words in the first column. Ask students whether they know the meanings. If not, give a simple definition and model using each word in a sentence. **We saw the word *vibrate* in Passage 4. It means "move quickly back and forth." My cell phone *vibrates* when someone calls me. What does the *vibration* create?** Write the following sentence starter on the board to help students respond: *The vibration creates* ________.

Part B

If students have difficulty completing Part B, read aloud the sentence frames. Then, support the items with a think-aloud. For item 1: **The band writes music for an blank of acoustic and electric instruments. I know that acoustic and electric are two styles of instruments. What word can mean something that brings two different types together?** (integration) **Let's see if that word makes sense in the sentence.** Read the sentence with *integration* in the blank. Ask students whether that answer makes sense.

Continue the process for the remaining items.

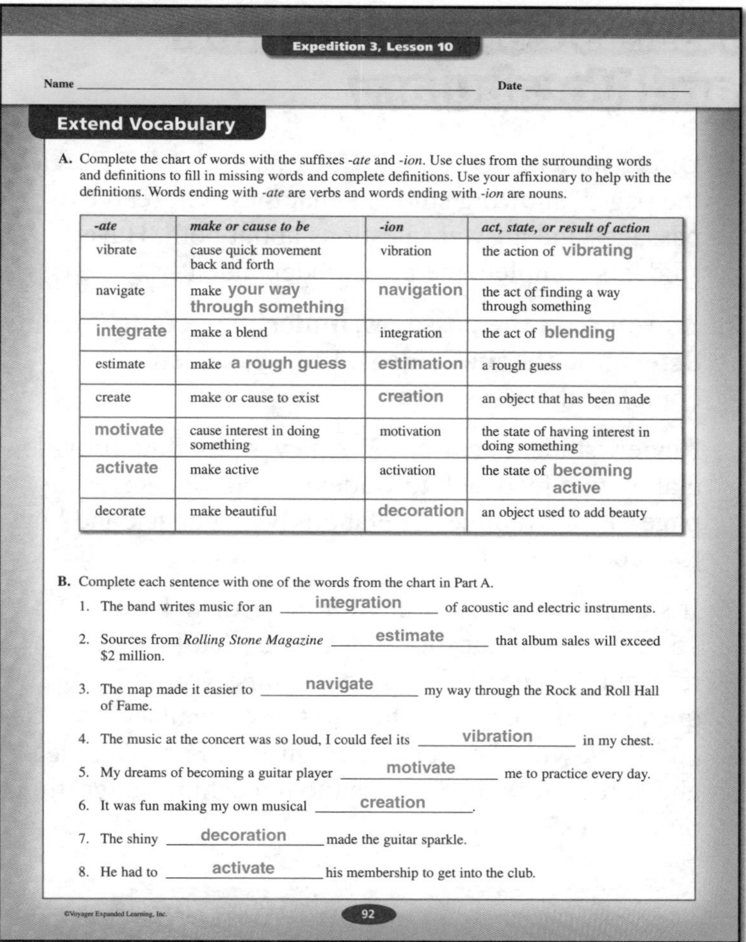

Expedition 3, Lesson 10

Name ________ Date ________

Extend Vocabulary

A. Complete the chart of words with the suffixes *-ate* and *-ion*. Use clues from the surrounding words and definitions to fill in missing words and complete definitions. Use your affixionary to help with the definitions. Words ending with *-ate* are verbs and words ending with *-ion* are nouns.

-ate	*make or cause to be*	*-ion*	*act, state, or result of action*
vibrate	cause quick movement back and forth	vibration	the action of vibrating
navigate	make your way through something	navigation	the act of finding a way through something
integrate	make a blend	integration	the act of blending
estimate	make a rough guess	estimation	a rough guess
create	make or cause to exist	creation	an object that has been made
motivate	cause interest in doing something	motivation	the state of having interest in doing something
activate	make active	activation	the state of becoming active
decorate	make beautiful	decoration	an object used to add beauty

B. Complete each sentence with one of the words from the chart in Part A.

1. The band writes music for an integration of acoustic and electric instruments.
2. Sources from *Rolling Stone Magazine* estimate that album sales will exceed $2 million.
3. The map made it easier to navigate my way through the Rock and Roll Hall of Fame.
4. The music at the concert was so loud, I could feel its vibration in my chest.
5. My dreams of becoming a guitar player motivate me to practice every day.
6. It was fun making my own musical creation.
7. The shiny decoration made the guitar sparkle.
8. He had to activate his membership to get into the club.

 92

Assess Comprehension and Vocabulary

1. Direct students to Student Book pages 93–95. Preview the pages, showing students that they will read two passages and answer questions about both. Have students complete the pages independently.
2. **As you read the passages, underline details. Then, determine the main ideas.** Instruct students to complete the assessment.

   Review student answers. Whenever possible, provide elaborative feedback to student responses. Refer to page xl for examples of elaborative feedback and how to incorporate it in your lessons.

   If students incorrectly answer more than 4 out of 15 Assessment questions, evaluate what kind of reteaching is needed. If students miss vocabulary questions, have them return to the vocabulary activities and work with the words they missed. For main idea and text features errors, use the reteaching suggestions on page 127.

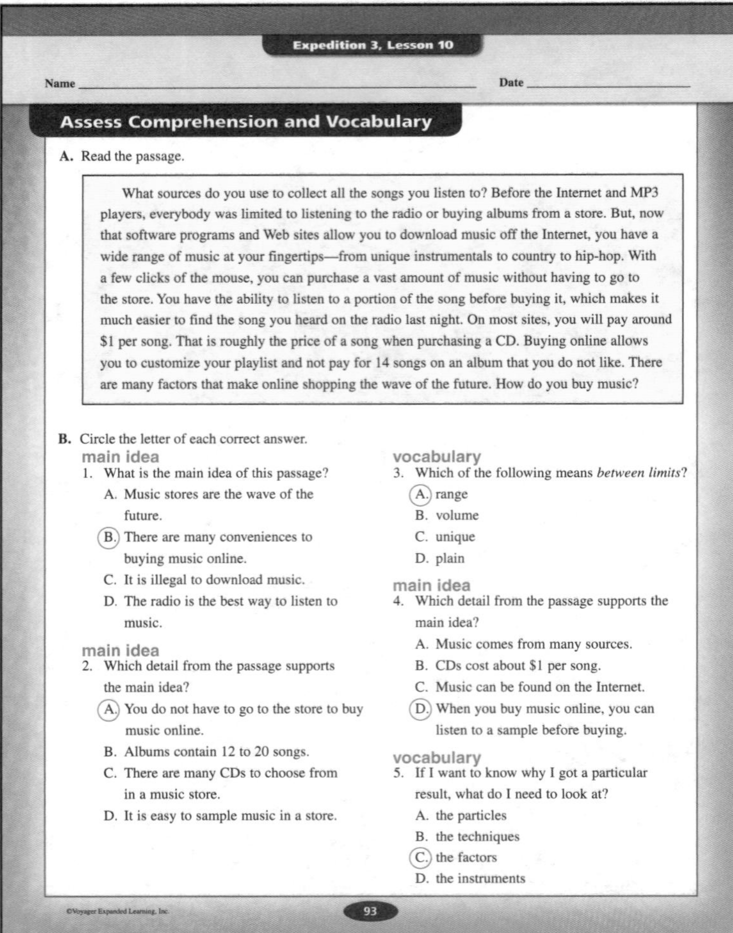

Expedition 3, Lesson 10

Name ______________________ Date ____________

Assess Comprehension and Vocabulary

A. Read the passage.

What sources do you use to collect all the songs you listen to? Before the Internet and MP3 players, everybody was limited to listening to the radio or buying albums from a store. But, now that software programs and Web sites allow you to download music off the Internet, you have a wide range of music at your fingertips—from unique instrumentals to country to hip-hop. With a few clicks of the mouse, you can purchase a vast amount of music without having to go to the store. You have the ability to listen to a portion of the song before buying it, which makes it much easier to find the song you heard on the radio last night. On most sites, you will pay around $1 per song. That is roughly the price of a song when purchasing a CD. Buying online allows you to customize your playlist and not pay for 14 songs on an album that you do not like. There are many factors that make online shopping the wave of the future. How do you buy music?

B. Circle the letter of each correct answer.

main idea
1. What is the main idea of this passage?
   A. Music stores are the wave of the future.
   (B.) There are many conveniences to buying music online.
   C. It is illegal to download music.
   D. The radio is the best way to listen to music.

main idea
2. Which detail from the passage supports the main idea?
   (A.) You do not have to go to the store to buy music online.
   B. Albums contain 12 to 20 songs.
   C. There are many CDs to choose from in a music store.
   D. It is easy to sample music in a store.

vocabulary
3. Which of the following means *between limits*?
   (A.) range
   B. volume
   C. unique
   D. plain

main idea
4. Which detail from the passage supports the main idea?
   A. Music comes from many sources.
   B. CDs cost about $1 per song.
   C. Music can be found on the Internet.
   (D.) When you buy music online, you can listen to a sample before buying.

vocabulary
5. If I want to know why I got a particular result, what do I need to look at?
   A. the particles
   B. the techniques
   (C.) the factors
   D. the instruments

©Voyager Expanded Learning, Inc. 93

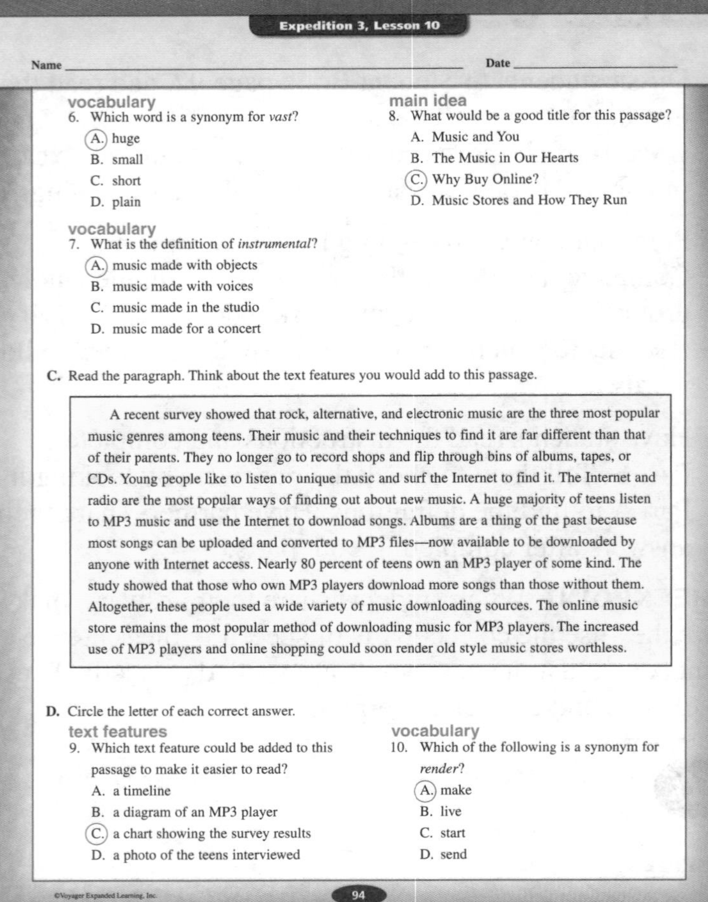

Expedition 3, Lesson 10

Name ______________________ Date ____________

vocabulary
6. Which word is a synonym for *vast*?
   (A.) huge
   B. small
   C. short
   D. plain

vocabulary
7. What is the definition of *instrumental*?
   (A.) music made with objects
   B. music made with voices
   C. music made in the studio
   D. music made for a concert

main idea
8. What would be a good title for this passage?
   A. Music and You
   B. The Music in Our Hearts
   (C.) Why Buy Online?
   D. Music Stores and How They Run

C. Read the paragraph. Think about the text features you would add to this passage.

A recent survey showed that rock, alternative, and electronic music are the three most popular music genres among teens. Their music and their techniques to find it are far different than that of their parents. They no longer go to record shops and flip through bins of albums, tapes, or CDs. Young people like to listen to unique music and surf the Internet to find it. The Internet and radio are the most popular ways of finding out about new music. A huge majority of teens listen to MP3 music and use the Internet to download songs. Albums are a thing of the past because most songs can be uploaded and converted to MP3 files—now available to be downloaded by anyone with Internet access. Nearly 80 percent of teens own an MP3 player of some kind. The study showed that those who own MP3 players download more songs than those without them. Altogether, these people used a wide variety of music downloading sources. The online music store remains the most popular method of downloading music for MP3 players. The increased use of MP3 players and online shopping could soon render old style music stores worthless.

D. Circle the letter of each correct answer.

text features
9. Which text feature could be added to this passage to make it easier to read?
   A. a timeline
   B. a diagram of an MP3 player
   (C.) a chart showing the survey results
   D. a photo of the teens interviewed

vocabulary
10. Which of the following is a synonym for *render*?
   (A.) make
   B. live
   C. start
   D. send

©Voyager Expanded Learning, Inc. 94

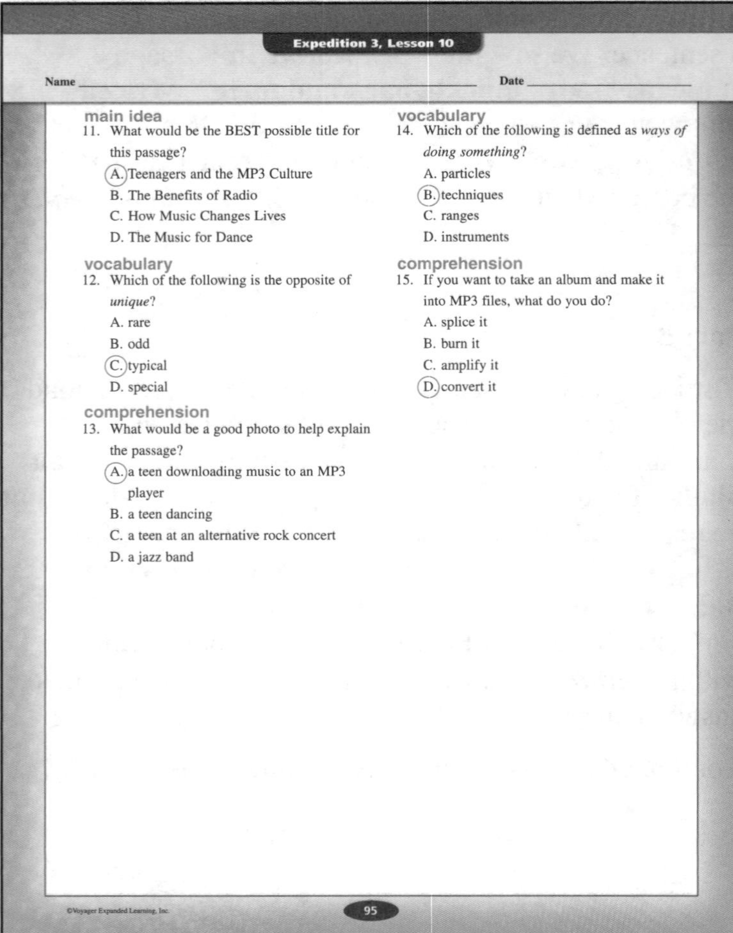

Expedition 3, Lesson 10

Name ______________________ Date ____________

main idea
11. What would be the BEST possible title for this passage?
   (A.) Teenagers and the MP3 Culture
   B. The Benefits of Radio
   C. How Music Changes Lives
   D. The Music for Dance

vocabulary
12. Which of the following is the opposite of *unique*?
   A. rare
   B. odd
   (C.) typical
   D. special

comprehension
13. What would be a good photo to help explain the passage?
   (A.) a teen downloading music to an MP3 player
   B. a teen dancing
   C. a teen at an alternative rock concert
   D. a jazz band

vocabulary
14. Which of the following is defined as *ways of doing something*?
   A. particles
   (B.) techniques
   C. ranges
   D. instruments

comprehension
15. If you want to take an album and make it into MP3 files, what do you do?
   A. splice it
   B. burn it
   C. amplify it
   (D.) convert it

©Voyager Expanded Learning, Inc. 95

Reteach

Main Idea and Details; Text Features

1. Direct students to Student Book pages 96 and 97 and read the instructions aloud. **Sometimes a main idea is not stated directly in the paragraph or passage. The main idea in this passage is an opinion.** Read the passage aloud. **What is the opinion?** Have students complete the sentence starter in the first item. **You can check if you know what the main idea is by finding details that support it.** Have students find the details, discuss their choices, and complete the activity.

2. For Part C, read aloud each item in the list of text features. Provide students with textbooks, magazines, and sticky notes. Allow them to work in pairs as they use sticky notes to label each text feature and write how each adds to the message of the passage. Have students share their responses.

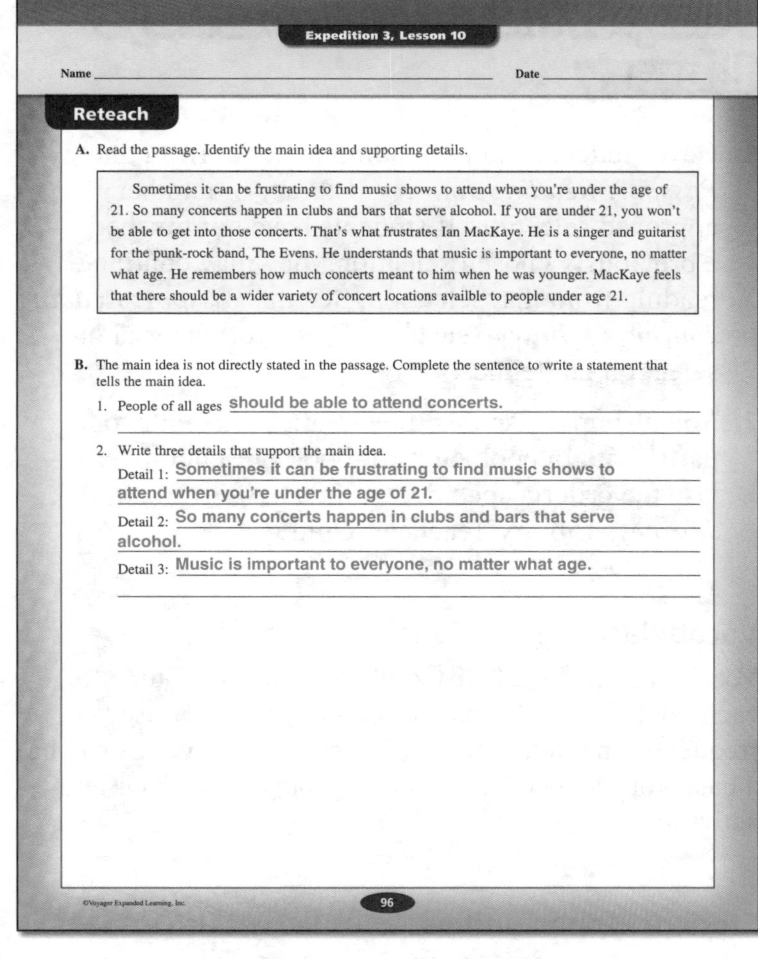

Expedition 3, Lesson 10

Name ______ Date ______

Reteach

A. Read the passage. Identify the main idea and supporting details.

Sometimes it can be frustrating to find music shows to attend when you're under the age of 21. So many concerts happen in clubs and bars that serve alcohol. If you are under 21, you won't be able to get into those concerts. That's what frustrates Ian MacKaye. He is a singer and guitarist for the punk-rock band, The Evens. He understands that music is important to everyone, no matter what age. He remembers how much concerts meant to him when he was younger. MacKaye feels that there should be a wider variety of concert locations availble to people under age 21.

B. The main idea is not directly stated in the passage. Complete the sentence to write a statement that tells the main idea.

1. People of all ages should be able to attend concerts.

2. Write three details that support the main idea.

Detail 1: Sometimes it can be frustrating to find music shows to attend when you're under the age of 21.

Detail 2: So many concerts happen in clubs and bars that serve alcohol.

Detail 3: Music is important to everyone, no matter what age.

96

Expedition 3, Lesson 10

Name ______ Date ______

C. Choose text features from the following lists to answer the questions.

Headings	Diagrams	Images	Other
title subheadings bold words	charts graphs maps	pictures photos illustrations drawings with labels	forms lists sidebars

1. List three or more text features that you think would add useful information to the passage.
Possible answers: title; photos of MacKaye, his band, and students being turned away from a club; a list of places that would be considered free

2. Find one example of each type of text feature in a textbook, newspaper, or magazine. Explain how the text features would help you understand the message of the passage.
Answers will vary.

97

Passport Reading Journeys Library

1. Have students choose reading material from the *Passport Reading Journeys* Library or another approved selection. If students have not finished a previously chosen selection, they may continue reading from that selection. See the *Passport Reading Journeys Library* Teacher's Guide for material on selection guidelines.
2. You also may use this time to allow students to participate in book clubs or book presentations. Use the criteria specified in the *Passport Reading Journeys* Library Teacher's Guide.

Vocabulary Connections

Vocabulary words are listed in the Teacher's Guide for each book. These words are content-related or used frequently in reading material. The selected words can be a basis for independent or small-group discussions and activities.

Student Opportunities

Six copies of each book title are provided in the *Passport Reading Journeys* Library. The number of copies makes it possible for small groups of students to read the same material and share the information they read.

Theme-related titles include *Drums, Girls & Dangerous Pie*.

Technology

1. Depending on your classroom configuration and computer access, you may have all students work through the technology in a lab setting or have individuals or small groups of students work on desktops or laptops while other students participate in other suggested activities, such as the *Passport Reading Journeys* Library.
2. The online technology component provides additional support for students to work with selected vocabulary words. Students will work through a series of activities to strengthen their word knowledge, then apply that knowledge to passage reading. Refer to the online technology component User Guide for more information.

   Theme-related word sets include Physics, U.S. History, English/Language Arts, and Technology.

Expedition Project

Interview

Distribute copies of Project Blackline Master page 6. Remind students that they have read about different music groups and styles in their Anthology passages. **In Lesson 5, you described your favorite band or musician. Now you will interview an adult you know about a favorite band or musical style from when he or she was your age.** Have students form small groups and direct them to follow the steps.

For students to have a meaningful experience completing tasks as a group, certain strategies need to be employed. Group dynamics and interactions can be improved with strategic planning for group work. Refer to page xxxvi for information on effective grouping strategies.

Ask students to look at the assignment and follow along as you explain the assignment. Assign point values as you see fit, and ask students to write them in the rubric. Tell them to make any notes on the page that will help them, but they will turn in the page with the assignment.

1. Have students write seven specific questions to ask their subject. Tell them to be sure to ask *who*, *what*, *where*, *when*, *why*, and *how* questions. **Ask your subject about dance or clothing trends that were associated with the type of music or about details, such as concerts, instruments, or lyrical messages. Try to determine if everyone in their age group liked the same kinds of music. If not, why are periods of music mostly associated with one segment of the whole society? What does this tell you about society as a whole?**
2. Assign the role of recorder/note taker to one group member. Instruct this person to take notes during the interview.
3. **Prepare a presentation that includes the interview and background related to the subject's favorite band or musician.** Have students do research if necessary.

   Presentations should have the following elements:

   - **Vivid, accurate descriptions and background of the musical genre or musicians**
   - **Quotations and other detailed information from the interview based on specific questions**
   - **Connection to musical origins, culture, history, politics, or topical connections to the Anthology passages**
4. **Gather or create visuals, such as posters, band memorabilia, album covers, and T-shirts.** Have students plan how to use samples of actual recordings of the music discussed in the interview during the presentation.
5. Have students rehearse the presentation. Each group member should take one role, such as presenting the trends related to the musical genre or connections to politics. Students should revise the information. **Make sure the presentation has each of the features listed in the previous steps.**
6. **Present the interview and other findings to the class.**
7. **I will assess your presentation based on the rubric on your page.** To assess students' presentations, use the rubric from the Project Blackline Master.

Real-World Reading

Album Review

1. Direct students to Student Book page 98. Have them preview the article and predict what it is about. (an album review) **Where have you seen album reviews before, and why do people write them?** (newspapers; magazines; online; critics write album reviews to state their opinions about a musician's new album and convince readers of their opinions.)
2. Have students read the review and complete the activity.
3. **What does the author of the review think about Sketchbook? Explain whether the author is convincing.** Have students share their reviews.

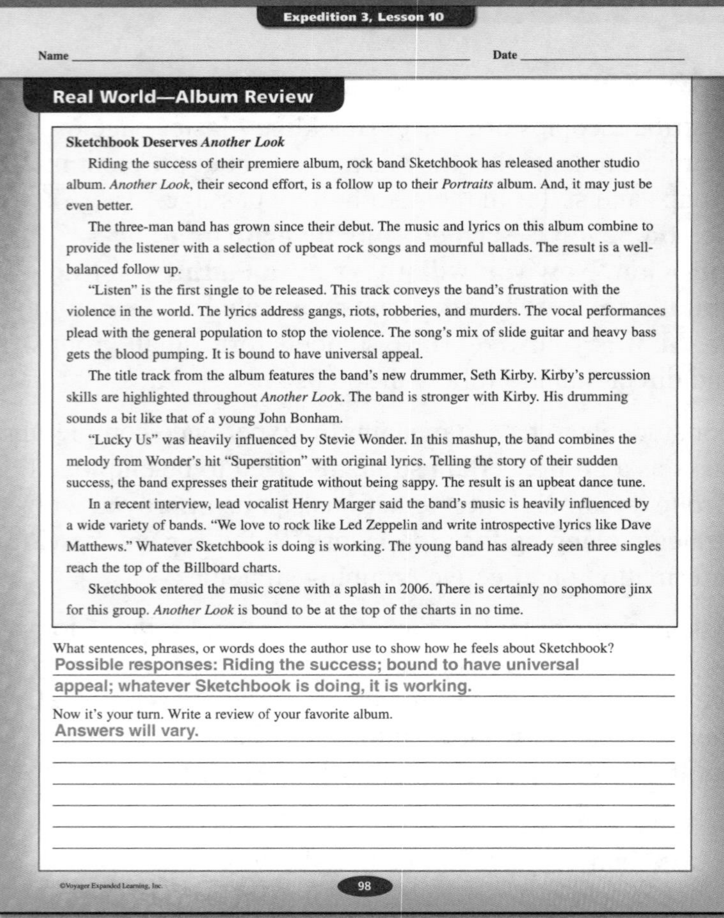

Expedition 3, Lesson 10

Name ______________________ Date ____________

Real World—Album Review

Sketchbook Deserves *Another Look*

Riding the success of their premiere album, rock band Sketchbook has released another studio album. *Another Look*, their second effort, is a follow up to their *Portraits* album. And, it may just be even better.

The three-man band has grown since their debut. The music and lyrics on this album combine to provide the listener with a selection of upbeat rock songs and mournful ballads. The result is a well-balanced follow up.

"Listen" is the first single to be released. This track conveys the band's frustration with the violence in the world. The lyrics address gangs, riots, robberies, and murders. The vocal performances plead with the general population to stop the violence. The song's mix of slide guitar and heavy bass gets the blood pumping. It is bound to have universal appeal.

The title track from the album features the band's new drummer, Seth Kirby. Kirby's percussion skills are highlighted throughout *Another Look*. The band is stronger with Kirby. His drumming sounds a bit like that of a young John Bonham.

"Lucky Us" was heavily influenced by Stevie Wonder. In this mashup, the band combines the melody from Wonder's hit "Superstition" with original lyrics. Telling the story of their sudden success, the band expresses their gratitude without being sappy. The result is an upbeat dance tune.

In a recent interview, lead vocalist Henry Marger said the band's music is heavily influenced by a wide variety of bands. "We love to rock like Led Zeppelin and write introspective lyrics like Dave Matthews." Whatever Sketchbook is doing is working. The young band has already seen three singles reach the top of the Billboard charts.

Sketchbook entered the music scene with a splash in 2006. There is certainly no sophomore jinx for this group. *Another Look* is bound to be at the top of the charts in no time.

What sentences, phrases, or words does the author use to show how he feels about Sketchbook?
Possible responses: Riding the success; bound to have universal appeal; whatever Sketchbook is doing, it is working.

Now it's your turn. Write a review of your favorite album.
Answers will vary.

 98

Exploring Careers

Behind-the-Scenes Music Careers

1. Have students turn to Anthology page 53. Tell students to preview the title and photos. **Pay attention to important details as you read so you can identify the main idea of each paragraph.**
2. Have students read the passage. **As you read, think about jobs that appeal to you.**
3. Have students turn to Student Book page 99 and answer the questions and complete the chart. Tell them they can find the answers by researching careers in the music industry in books or online. Have students complete the page.

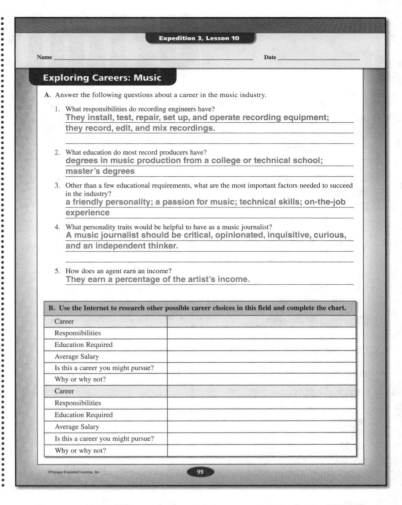

Expedition 3, Lesson 10

Name ______________________ Date ____________

Exploring Careers: Music

A. Answer the following questions about a career in the music industry.

1. What responsibilities do recording engineers have?
They install, test, repair, set up, and operate recording equipment; they record, edit, and mix recordings.
2. What education do most record producers have?
degrees in music production from a college or technical school; master's degrees
3. Other than a few educational requirements, what are the most important factors needed to succeed in the industry?
a friendly personality; a passion for music; technical skills; on-the-job experience
4. What personality traits would be helpful to have as a music journalist?
A music journalist should be critical, opinionated, inquisitive, curious, and an independent thinker.
5. How does an agent earn an income?
They earn a percentage of the artist's income.

B. Use the Internet to research other possible career choices in this field and complete the chart.	
Career	
Responsibilities	
Education Required	
Average Salary	
Is this a career you might pursue?	
Why or why not?	
Career	
Responsibilities	
Education Required	
Average Salary	
Is this a career you might pursue?	
Why or why not?	

Career

Behind-the-Scenes Music Careers

Everyone knows what it takes to become a singer or musician. But, what if your passion for music doesn't come with a talent for singing or playing an instrument? Can you still earn a living in the music industry? Absolutely! There are a wide variety of job opportunities for those wanting to work behind the scenes in the music world. Here is a look at a few of them.

Recording Engineers

Recording engineers install, test, repair, set up, and operate the electronic equipment used to record songs. They must be able to use a wide range of equipment. They also must have the necessary skills to record, edit, and mix musical recordings. There are no specific educational requirements for becoming a recording engineer. However, most recording engineers have some formal education from a technical school or four-year college. Technical skills and on-the-job experience are the two most critical needs for engineers. Many engineers gain valuable hands-on experience as interns at recording studios. The average engineer earns about $36,000 a year.

Record Producers

Record producers work with the talent, session musicians, and the recording engineer to produce the recordings. They make sure projects are done on time and within budget. The producer's job includes planning every detail of a recording project. He or she supervises the recording session and helps

Career

the artists achieve a certain sound. Most producers start as sound engineers or music editors. After gaining experience in the recording studio, they move up to become producers. Many producers have degrees in music production from a college or technical school. Some earn a master's degree. The salary range for producers is wide. Starting salaries can be around $20,000 a year. Successful producers can earn more than $1 million annually. Additionally, some artists pay their producers royalties if their song or album becomes a commercial success.

Music Journalists

For those who like to write as well as listen to music, being a music journalist or critic might be the perfect job. Music critics listen to new music and review it for the public. They also write about performers and music trends. Some review concerts. Many music journalists also interview musicians. They write for newspapers, magazines, Web sites, and even television. In addition to writing well, critics must give fair and honest reviews of the music. They must be able to express themselves clearly. Journalists must be able to work independently and meet critical deadlines. To get started, most critics earn a bachelor's degree in English or journalism. Many critics begin as freelance writers. They take small jobs or submit their reviews to local papers or Web sites. Average starting salaries for this position range from $25,000 to $36,000 a year. Experienced critics can earn more than $60,000 annually.

Radio Plugger

A radio plugger promotes music to radio stations. Hired by record labels, pluggers get music of the artists they work for played on the air. They work to get songs put on radio stations' playlists. Pluggers may also set up on-air interviews or concerts for the artists. Radio pluggers generally work job to job. Frequently they negotiate a fee for working a particular album or tour. They generally do not have a regular salary. But, experienced pluggers can be well paid. To get started, many people will work for free or for a reduced rate. By doing so, they gain valuable experience. They also begin to establish contacts at radio stations.

Artist Manager

An artist manager, or agent, supervises the business side of the band or singer. An agent books gigs and finds work for the artist. Additionally, the job includes promotion and negotiating contracts. Excellent communication and people skills are two of the most important qualities of an agent. Most managers are paid a percentage of an artist's income. Generally, they earn between 20 percent and 30 percent of an artist's salary. Many people begin as interns at a management or entertainment company. Others meet and quickly bond with an artist. They then decide to work together and enter the entertainment world as a team.

So, even if you do not have the vocal talent to become America's next pop star, you can still earn a living in the music industry. You can channel your interest and passion for music into one of these exciting behind-the-scenes music careers.

Criminology

"Ax Murderer or Beloved Daughter?"

Lesson 1

Introduce the Expedition
Discuss probing questions about criminology.

Before Reading
- Introduce and practice using passage vocabulary.
- Introduce and practice making inferences.

During Reading
Read "Ax Murderer or Beloved Daughter?"

After Reading
Check comprehension.

Have students practice vocabulary using the online technology component.

Have students select books for independent reading.

Extend and practice.

Lesson 2

Prepare to Reread
- Review and practice using passage vocabulary.
- Practice using context clues.
- Build new words using the prefixes *trans-* and *sub-*.

Reread
- Review and practice making inferences.
- Write a dialogue.

Extend and practice.

"CSI at the Lizzie Borden Crime Scene"

Lesson 3

Before Reading
- Introduce and practice using passage vocabulary.
- Introduce the target skill and practice asking questions.
- Introduce the passage by previewing and making predictions.

During Reading
Read "CSI at the Lizzie Borden Crime Scene."

After Reading
Check comprehension.

Have students practice vocabulary using the online technology component.

Have students select books for independent reading.

Extend and practice.

Lesson 4

Prepare to Reread
- Review and practice using passage vocabulary.
- Practice using context clues.
- Build new words using the suffix *-ment*.

Reread
- Practice asking questions to check comprehension.
- Write answers to interview questions and complete an evidence log.

Extend and practice.

Lesson 5—Review, Extend, Assess

Review Vocabulary
Review and practice using passage vocabulary.

Extend Vocabulary
Use Latin root words to build and understand new words.

Assess Comprehension and Vocabulary
Assess student understanding of making inferences, asking questions, and other previously taught skills.

Reteach
Reteach target skills with student activity pages.

Passport Reading Journeys Library
Have students select books for independent reading.

Technology
Have students practice vocabulary using the online technology component.

Writing Process
Have students use the writing process to write closing arguments in the Lizzie Borden case.

Real-World Reading
Have students read a jury summons and complete instructions.

Exploring Careers
Have students read about bailiffs and court reporters and complete an activity page.

Teacher's Note

Before beginning the Expedition, ask your librarian to suggest books that will fit with the theme. Books relating to criminology, Sherlock Holmes, Lizzie Borden, or mysteries will be appropriate for this Expedition.

"The Red-Headed League," Part 1

Lesson 6

Before Reading
- Introduce and practice using passage vocabulary.
- Introduce the target skill and practice identifying story elements.

During Reading
Read "The Red-Headed League," Part 1.

After Reading
Check comprehension.

Have students practice vocabulary using the online technology component.

Have students select books for independent reading.

ELL Extend and practice.

Lesson 7

Prepare to Reread
- Review and practice using passage vocabulary.
- Practice using context clues.
- Use word parts to change a word's part of speech.

Reread
- Review and practice identifying story elements.
- Write a job ad and resignation letter.

ELL Extend and practice.

"The Red-Headed League," Part 2

Lesson 8

Before Reading
- Introduce and practice using passage vocabulary.
- Introduce the target skill and practice identifying story elements and making inferences.

During Reading
Read "The Red-Headed League," Part 2.

After Reading
Check comprehension.

Have students practice vocabulary using the online technology component.

Have students select books for independent reading.

ELL Extend and practice.

Lesson 9

Prepare to Reread
- Review and practice using passage vocabulary.
- Practice using context clues.
- Build new words using the suffix *-ly*.

Reread
- Practice identifying story elements and making inferences.
- Write an alternate ending, and draw a map.

ELL Extend and practice.

Lesson 10—Review, Extend, Assess

Review Vocabulary
Review passage vocabulary.

Extend Vocabulary
Use base words to build and understand new words.

Assess Comprehension and Vocabulary
Assess student understanding of making inferences, asking questions, and identifying story elements.

Reteach
Reteach target skills with student activity pages.

Passport Reading Journeys Library
Have students select books for independent reading.

Technology
Have students practice vocabulary using the online technology component.

Writing Process
Have students research and prepare for a debate dialogue.

Real-World Reading
Have students read movie reviews and complete student activity page.

Exploring Careers
Have students read about a career as a graphic artist and complete an activity page.

Expedition 4

Introduce the Expedition

1. Have students name television shows about crime and forensics, such as *CSI*. Have partners talk about the characteristics of shows that deal with crime and forensics. Prompt them with the following questions: **What do these shows have in common? What do the characters on these shows do?** (forensic science; investigate crime scenes) **The stories in shows like these are based on the study of crime and the impact crime has on society. The scientific study of crime is known as criminology.** Have students think about the Expedition 4 opening photograph on Anthology page 55. **What words and images come to mind when you look at the title and picture? Think about your own lives, TV, and what you've read that will help you determine what kinds of information and stories you might read in this Expedition.** Write students' ideas on the board.
2. Have partners discuss possible responses to the following probing questions. Explain that the questions will guide what they are about to learn.
   - **How have advances in science made it more difficult to get away with a crime?**
   - **Has criminology reduced the number of crimes that are committed? Why or why not?**
   - **Why do some crimes still go unsolved?**

   To make the most of this discussion time, remember to incorporate strategies that encourage and extend student involvement. Refer to page xxxviii for a comprehensive discussion of these strategies.

Build Background DVD 4.1
Tell students they will view a brief DVD that provides background information about criminology. **As you watch the DVD, think about questions you would like to have answered.**

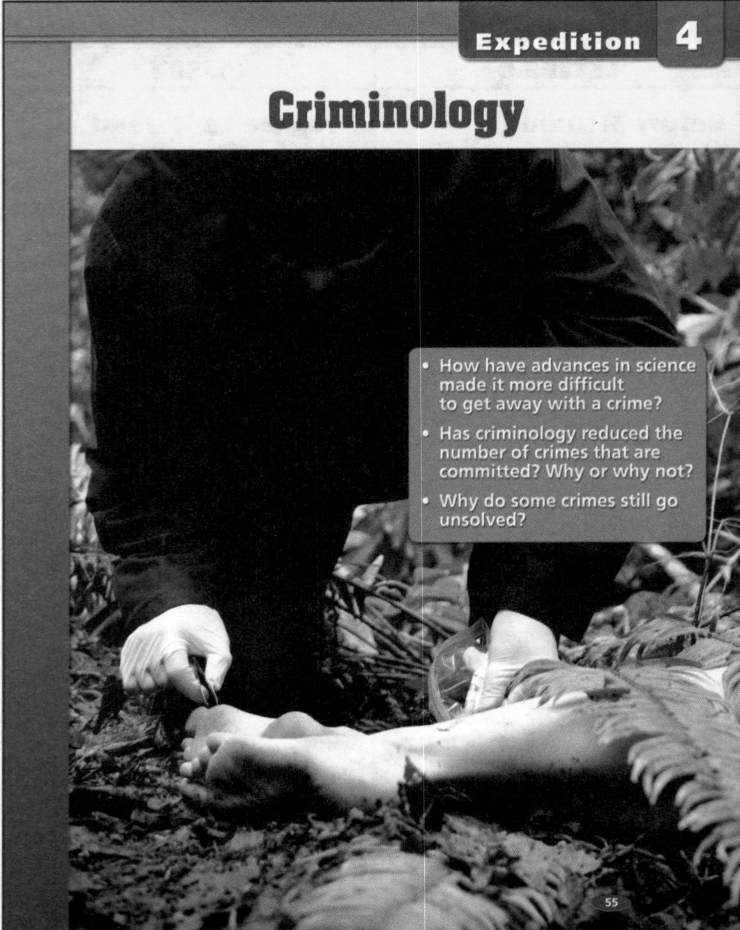

3. Have students turn to the Expedition Organizer on Student Book pages 100 and 101. **Now, think about what you viewed on the DVD. If you have answers or thoughts about the probing questions, write them under the questions. Then, think of questions you have about solving crimes and write them on this page. We'll revisit these questions at the end of the Expedition.**

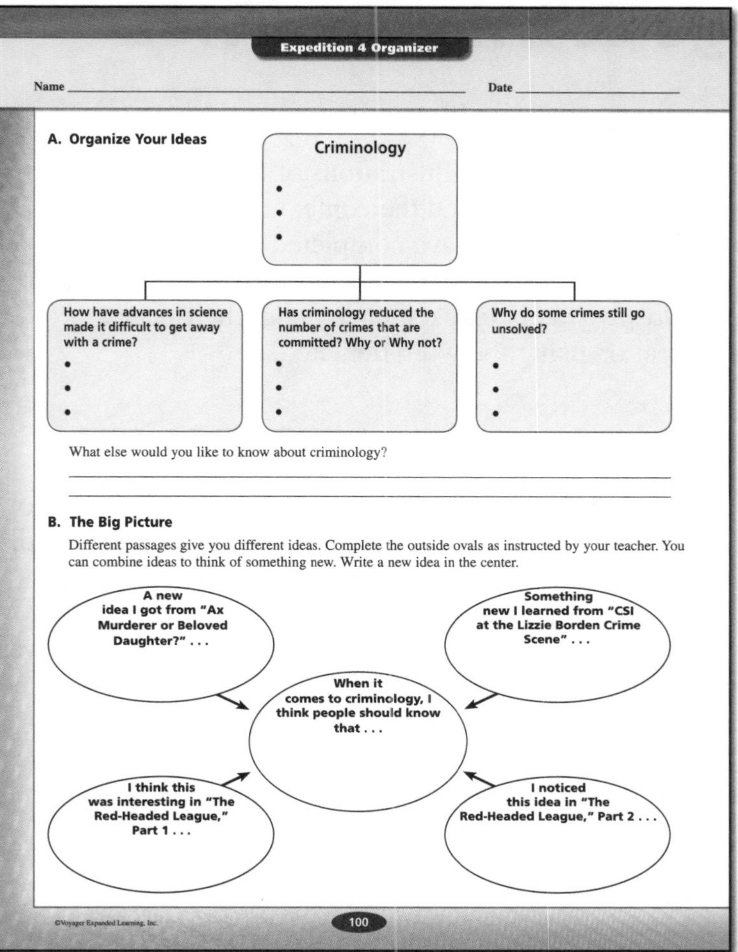

Expedition 4 Organizer

Name ______________________ Date ______________

A. Organize Your Ideas

Criminology
-
-
-

How have advances in science made it difficult to get away with a crime?
-
-
-

Has criminology reduced the number of crimes that are committed? Why or Why not?
-
-
-

Why do some crimes still go unsolved?
-
-
-

What else would you like to know about criminology?

B. The Big Picture

Different passages give you different ideas. Complete the outside ovals as instructed by your teacher. You can combine ideas to think of something new. Write a new idea in the center.

A new idea I got from "Ax Murderer or Beloved Daughter?" . . .

Something new I learned from "CSI at the Lizzie Borden Crime Scene" . . .

When it comes to criminology, I think people should know that . . .

I think this was interesting in "The Red-Headed League," Part 1 . . .

I noticed this idea in "The Red-Headed League," Part 2 . . .

©Voyager Expanded Learning, Inc.

100

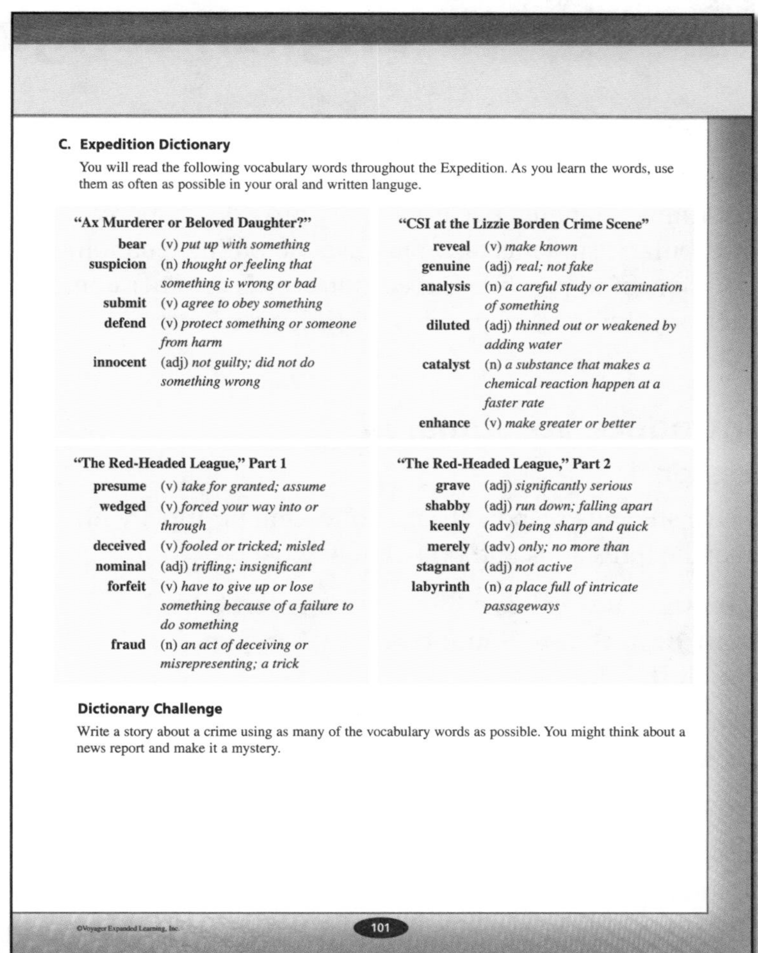

C. Expedition Dictionary

You will read the following vocabulary words throughout the Expedition. As you learn the words, use them as often as possible in your oral and written languge.

"Ax Murderer or Beloved Daughter?"
- **bear** (v) *put up with something*
- **suspicion** (n) *thought or feeling that something is wrong or bad*
- **submit** (v) *agree to obey something*
- **defend** (v) *protect something or someone from harm*
- **innocent** (adj) *not guilty; did not do something wrong*

"CSI at the Lizzie Borden Crime Scene"
- **reveal** (v) *make known*
- **genuine** (adj) *real; not fake*
- **analysis** (n) *a careful study or examination of something*
- **diluted** (adj) *thinned out or weakened by adding water*
- **catalyst** (n) *a substance that makes a chemical reaction happen at a faster rate*
- **enhance** (v) *make greater or better*

"The Red-Headed League," Part 1
- **presume** (v) *take for granted; assume*
- **wedged** (v) *forced your way into or through*
- **deceived** (v) *fooled or tricked; misled*
- **nominal** (adj) *trifling; insignificant*
- **forfeit** (v) *have to give up or lose something because of a failure to do something*
- **fraud** (n) *an act of deceiving or misrepresenting; a trick*

"The Red-Headed League," Part 2
- **grave** (adj) *significantly serious*
- **shabby** (adj) *run down; falling apart*
- **keenly** (adv) *being sharp and quick*
- **merely** (adv) *only; no more than*
- **stagnant** (adj) *not active*
- **labyrinth** (n) *a place full of intricate passageways*

Dictionary Challenge

Write a story about a crime using as many of the vocabulary words as possible. You might think about a news report and make it a mystery.

©Voyager Expanded Learning, Inc.

101

ELL

Making Connections

1. Some students may be unfamiliar with popular movies or TV shows about criminology. Make connections to their prior knowledge by describing the roles of police officers and detectives responsible for solving crimes through investigating the crime scene, interviewing witnesses, and following other leads. Explain that there are people with specialized jobs within a police department who are responsible for looking for evidence when a crime is committed. The people who investigate crimes often have specialized skills and college degrees relating to the study of crime scenes. Further explain that the average police officer that students see directing traffic is not the police officer responsible for investigating crimes. However, some police departments do require investigators to work some of these regular "beats" periodically.
2. Students may need more information about Lizzie Borden and Sherlock Holmes. Use the following background information as needed to help students connect to the Expedition.

Lizzie Borden

Lizzie Borden was the central figure in the hatchet murders of her father and stepmother on Aug. 4, 1892, in Fall River, Massachusetts. The slayings, trial, and media attention made Lizzie Borden and the crime infamous. Although Lizzie Borden was acquitted, she was widely believed to be guilty; no one else was ever arrested or tried, and she has remained notorious in American folklore. Dispute over the identity of the killer or killers continues to this day.

Sherlock Holmes

Sherlock Holmes, a London detective, is a fictional character of the late 19th and early 20th centuries. He is the creation of author and physician Sir Arthur Conan Doyle. Holmes is famous for his skillful use of deductive reasoning and astute observation to solve cases. Holmes was first introduced to the world in 1887 in short stories published in a magazine. The character of Sherlock Holmes was said to be based on a real person, Dr. Joseph Bell. Doyle had worked as Bell's clerk at the Edinburgh Royal Infirmary. Like Sherlock Holmes, Bell was noted for drawing large conclusions from the smallest observations. Bell also assisted the police in solving crimes.

English Language Learner Overview

The ELL signals when extra support is provided for students during the lesson. As needed, Blackline Masters for English language learners may provide support. For vocabulary, students also may use the online technology component to practice Expedition words or other content-area vocabulary and designated ELL word sets.

Introduce Vocabulary

Lesson 1

Have students respond to the following prompts with facial expressions and body language.

You have a *suspicion* that someone left a trick book in your desk that will make noise when you touch it.

Your friend is being teased. You try to *defend* him or her.

You can't *bear* to listen to the same song one more time.

You are accused of cheating on a test, but you are *innocent*.

***Transport* your pen to the desk beside you.**

You must *submit* to being questioned.

Lesson 3

Distribute six index cards to each student. Have students write one vocabulary word from Lesson 3 on each card. Read aloud each definition, and have students show you the card with the word matching the definition. Next, read the following sentences aloud. Have students show you the card with the word that best completes each sentence.

I decided to _______ my room by painting it. (enhance)

After careful _______, they decided the fire was an accident. (analysis)

The _______ that caused the reaction had to be added slowly. (catalyst)

The orange juice was so _______ it barely looked orange. (diluted)

I didn't believe the necklace had a _______ diamond in it. (genuine)

They told me I couldn't _______ the name of the winner until after dinner. (reveal)

Practice Vocabulary

Have students create illustrations of the context words, depicting the words and the context in which they are used. After students have completed their illustrations, have them share their work with a partner. Each partner should write a context sentence under their partner's illustration using the word depicted.

Apply the Target Skill: Inference

Further practice making inferences may be necessary for some students. Students may need to practice the skill of making inferences with a shorter, less complex passage with which they can interact. Blackline Master page 21 begins with a short passage. Students are asked to answer questions about what they already know. These questions lead to making an inference. This will allow students to have concrete practice identifying text evidence and adding what they already know to make an inference.

Introduce the Target Skill: Ask Questions

To increase students' practice with the skill of asking questions, have students work with a partner to share their questions and responses. Help students monitor whether their questions and answers are helpful to understanding the passage.

Vocabulary
bear (v) *put up with something*
suspicion (n) *thought or feeling that something is wrong or bad*

Lizzie Borden took an ax
And gave her mother forty whacks.
When she saw what she had done,
She gave her father forty-one.

1 Make Connections
Have you ever been so bothered by something you saw or heard that you couldn't think straight?

All that most people know about me is that awful rhyme. But, there is more to my story. I was the one who found my father's body lying in a pool of blood. The slashed face, sliced and bleeding, looked up at me like a stranger in my father's clothing. It was more than I could **bear**. I screamed in horror at the sight. Bridget, our maid, was the first to come to my aid. I didn't even think to look for anyone else. 1

They found Mrs. Borden, my stepmother, dead too. She and my father had been brutally, violently murdered with an ax. The police at first thought Bridget might have done it. I was shocked when their **suspicion** shifted from her to me. How could I, a 32-year-old Sunday school teacher and respected church member, have possibly done something so vicious, so cruel?

The police thought my motive was money. My father was wealthy. Mrs. Borden was a gold digger who wanted his money. The police believed that I killed them so his money would go to me—not her. Father was good to me. Why would I kill him?

No one was home the day of the murders except Bridget and me. So that left only us as witnesses. We had to **submit** to endless hours of questioning until I couldn't bear to hear another question. Bridget tried to **defend** herself by saying she was

Vocabulary
submit (v) *agree to obey something*
defend (v) *protect something or someone from harm*

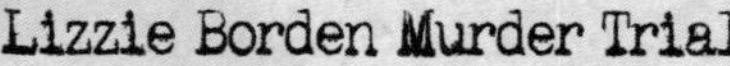
Lizzie Borden Murder Trial

Lizzie Borden
murder suspect

Andrew Borden
Lizzie's father

Abby Borden
Lizzie's stepmother

Emma Borden
Lizzie's sister

Bridget Sullivan
maid

Borden home

Abby Borden's body
in bedroom

Andrew Borden's body
in living room

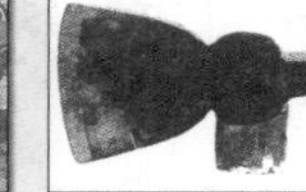
Ax
murder weapon

Vocabulary
transport (v) *move from one place to another*
innocent (adj) *not guilty; did not do something wrong*

2 Ask Questions
Asking yourself questions about the case will help your understanding. Why would the clerk lie and say Lizzie tried to buy poison?

3 Summarize
Tell all the reasons police thought Lizzie was guilty.

napping during the murders, so the police let her go. I told police I was in the barn when my father was killed. Investigators said there were no footprints in the dust on the barn floor, so I must be lying.

A drugstore clerk falsely reported that I came in looking for poison a few days earlier. 2 Police used this to determine that I poisoned my parents like helpless rats, then chopped them up like lumber. There was no poison found in either of their stomachs. Still, I was officially accused of double homicide. Did the police think I was somehow able to **transport** myself from the barn to the house, up the stairs to kill my stepmother, down the stairs to kill my father, to the bathroom to wash up, to the basement to dispose of the weapon, and back again without being seen or heard by neighbors?

There was no blood on my clothes, my face, or my hands. They found a half-burnt hatchet handle with no blood on it in the fireplace that they claimed was the weapon I tried to burn. A few days after the murder, a neighbor saw me burning a dress that had paint on it. She thought it was suspicious and told police. They used that against me in court, claiming I must have been burning my bloodstained clothing. 3

Thankfully, the jury understood. They found me, Lizzie Borden, **innocent**. My sister and I inherited everything, receiving all of Father's money. I lived the rest of my life quietly in a mansion. End

"Ax Murderer or Beloved Daughter?"

Before Reading

Introduce Vocabulary

1. Have students turn to Part A on Student Book page 102 and scan the boldfaced vocabulary words. **You will see these new words in "Ax Murderer or Beloved Daughter?"** Have students rate their knowledge of each boldfaced word.
2. Have students share words they assigned a 3 rating, share the meaning they know, and use the word in a sentence or phrase.
3. Read the part of speech, definition, and example sentence for each word. **Check that words you assigned a 3 have the meanings that you know.**
4. Have students read the instructions for Part B and complete the activity.

Refer to Blackline Master page 20 to extend vocabulary practice.

Have students use the *Passport Reading Journeys* online technology component to practice and reinforce vocabulary and comprehension skills.

Introduce the Target Skill: Inference

1. Tell students when people want to figure out why or how something happened, they use what they know and what they see, read, or hear. **For example, if you came home from school and saw no one was home, what would you think?** (My parents are still at work.)
2. **Figuring out why or how something happened by using what you see, hear, or read and what you already know is called making an inference.** Write on the board:

   Read or Observe + Already Know = Inference

   For example, a visitor comes to this school and sees the halls are mostly empty. The visitor already knows it is a regular school day. What could the visitor infer? (The visitor has come during a class period, and students are in class.)
3. Have students turn to Student Book page 103.

Expedition 4, Lesson 1

Name ______________________ Date ______________

Vocabulary

"Ax Murderer or Beloved Daughter?"

A. Rate your knowledge of each boldfaced word.
3 I know what this word means, and I can use it in a sentence.
2 I have an idea of this word's meaning, but I need to know more.
1 I don't know what this word means.

☐ **bear** (v) *put up with something*
I could not *bear* to be accused of something I didn't do.

☐ **suspicion** (n) *thought or feeling that something is wrong or bad*
The *suspicion* shifted to Lizzie, but no one thought she could commit the crime.

☐ **submit** (v) *agree to obey something*
Lizzie had to *submit* to endless questions without an attorney.

☐ **defend** (v) *protect something or someone from harm*
How could Lizzie *defend* herself if everyone thought she did it?

☐ **transport** (v) *move from one place to another*
Lizzie could *transport* the murder weapon to another part of the house.

☐ **innocent** (adj) *not guilty; did not do something wrong*
Many people do not think Lizzie Borden is *innocent*.

B. Complete each sentence with the correct vocabulary word.

1. A police car will ___transport___ the prisoners to jail.
2. Mr. Farley cannot ___bear___ to be accused of wrongdoing.
3. We blamed the broken window on our neighbor but found out he was ___innocent___.
4. When Hank saw the open door, he had a ___suspicion___ that a stranger was in the house.
5. The police fought to ___defend___ the city.
6. To be cleared of the crime, we will ___submit___ to the DNA testing.

102

Vocabulary

bear (v) *put up with something*
I could not *bear* to be accused of something I didn't do.

suspicion (n) *thought or feeling that something is wrong or bad*
The *suspicion* shifted to Lizzie, but no one thought she could commit the crime.

submit (v) *agree to obey something*
Lizzie had to *submit* to endless questions without an attorney.

defend (v) *protect something or someone from harm*
How could Lizzie *defend* herself if everyone thought she did it?

transport (v) *move from one place to another*
Lizzie could *transport* the murder weapon to another part of the house.

innocent (adj) *not guilty; did not do something wrong*
Many people do not think Lizzie Borden is *innocent*.

Read aloud the instructions on the top of the page. **What do you understand about this picture that is not directly shown? What are the clues? What can you infer?** Have students complete the page.

4. Have students share inferences and clues. **Which inferences make sense? Why?** Have students explain how the clues lead to the inferences.

Introduce the Passage

1. Have students turn to Anthology page 56 to preview "Ax Murderer or Beloved Daughter?" **What clues in the title and photos tell you what the passage is about? What clues tell you when these events take place?** (The passage is about a murder; I can tell from the pictures the events happened in the past; it is not certain who the murderer is.)

   Tell students the passage is fictional, but Lizzie Borden was a real person. **This passage is what Lizzie might have said about the murders of her father and stepmother.**

2. Direct students' attention to the margin prompts. As you read the passage, pause to read these prompts. Use the text to answer them.
3. Teach this term from the passage:

   Gold digger means "someone who uses charm to get money or gifts from others."

During Reading

1. To select reading options that support your students' levels and classroom needs, see Reading Differentiation, page xxxii, if needed.
2. **Lizzie is narrating the events surrounding the murder. As you read, make inferences about her claim to be innocent.**

After Reading

Check Comprehension

1. **What are five important details Lizzie tells us to prove her innocence? Make inferences about why these details prove her innocence.** (Possible answers: She was a church member; she was in the barn; there was no blood on her clothes; neighbors did not hear anything; she didn't need the money.)

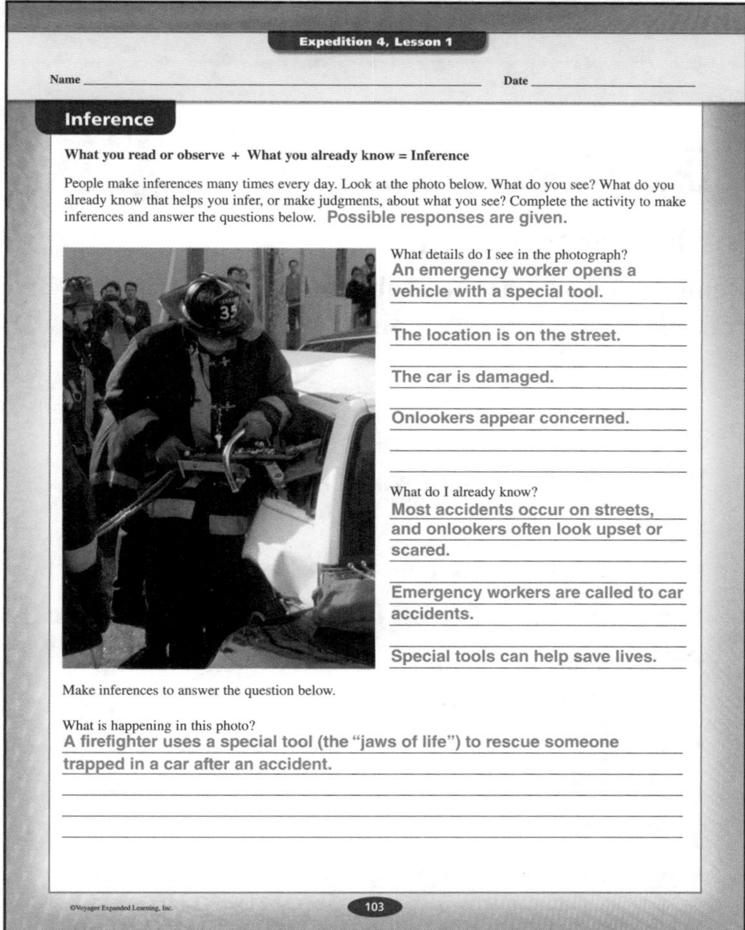

Expedition 4, Lesson 1

Name ______________________ Date ______________

Inference

What you read or observe + What you already know = Inference

People make inferences many times every day. Look at the photo below. What do you see? What do you already know that helps you infer, or make judgments, about what you see? Complete the activity to make inferences and answer the questions below. Possible responses are given.

What details do I see in the photograph?
An emergency worker opens a vehicle with a special tool.
The location is on the street.
The car is damaged.
Onlookers appear concerned.

What do I already know?
Most accidents occur on streets, and onlookers often look upset or scared.
Emergency workers are called to car accidents.
Special tools can help save lives.

Make inferences to answer the question below.

What is happening in this photo?
A firefighter uses a special tool (the "jaws of life") to rescue someone trapped in a car after an accident.

©Voyager Expanded Learning, Inc. 103

2. **What is your own opinion about the outcome of the trial? Did you base your opinion on what you read, prior experience, or a combination of both?**
3. Have students share their responses to the Make Connections margin prompt on Anthology page 56. **How did this connection affect how you felt about Lizzie?**
4. Reread the Summarize margin prompt on Anthology page 58. Have students share their summaries. **How can summarizing help you during reading?** (Summarizing helps confirm that you understand what you read.)

ELL Model how to make inferences using text evidence by telling whether you believe Lizzie Borden was guilty or not and showing what information in the text led to your inference.

Remind students to choose books from the *Passport Reading Journeys* Library for independent reading.

"Ax Murderer or Beloved Daughter?"

Prepare to Reread

Introduce the Lesson

Remind students they read about Lizzie Borden. **We will reread the story and practice making inferences.**

Practice Vocabulary

1. Review the vocabulary words by asking the following questions.
   - **What could Lizzie not *bear*?** (seeing her father)
   - **Who had a *suspicion* in the passage?** (the police)
   - **Who had to *submit* to hours of questioning?** (Lizzie and Bridget)
   - **Whom did Bridget try to *defend*?** (herself)
   - **What did Lizzie say she couldn't *transport*?** (herself)
   - **Whom did the jury declare *innocent*?** (Lizzie)
2. Write *bear*, *suspicion*, *submit*, *defend*, *transport*, and *innocent* on the board. **Zach thinks someone took his umbrella. Which vocabulary word would you connect with this sentence? Why?** (suspicion; he thinks someone has done something wrong.) Follow this process for the remaining vocabulary words.
   - **Rosa moves the table into the kitchen.** (transport)
   - **We realized the dog had not eaten the steak.** (innocent)
   - **Vanessa protects her cat from the storm.** (defend)
   - **We agree to let our bags be searched.** (submit)

Ask students to use each word in a sentence that mirrors the context in which it is used.

3. Remind students they can use context clues to find the meaning of unknown words. Have students turn to Anthology page 56. Reread the first paragraph. **What do you think the word *slashed* means?** (cut with rough, sweeping strokes) **Find clues in the text that help you figure out the meaning.** (The sentence with *body* and *pool of blood* is a clue that the face is badly cut. The words *sliced and bleeding* with *slashed* also offer a clue.)

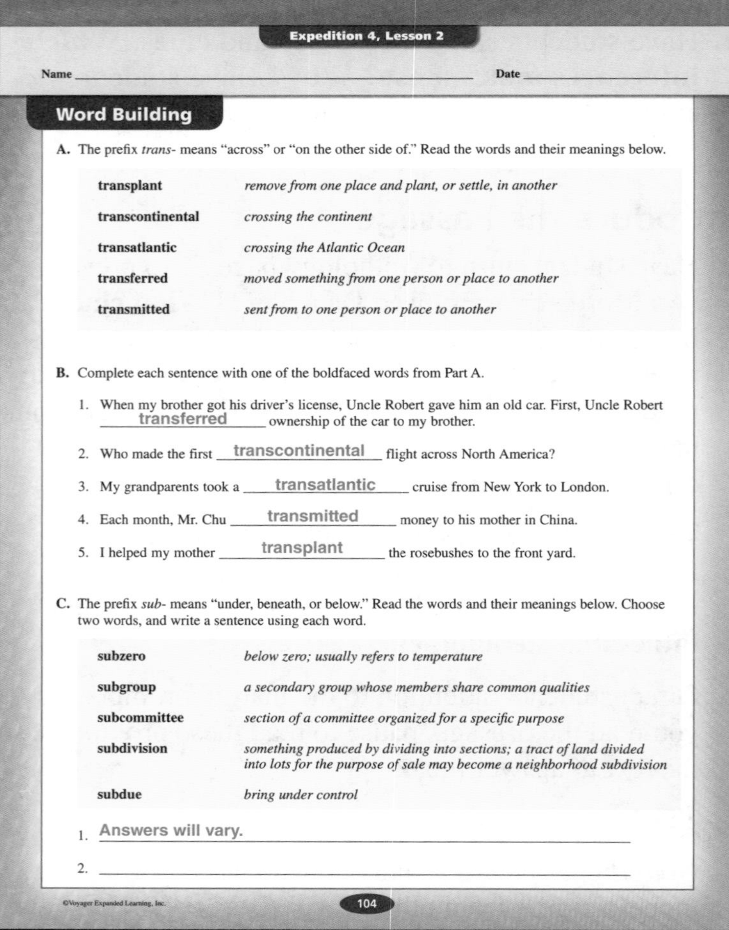

Expedition 4, Lesson 2

Name ______________________ Date ______________

Word Building

A. The prefix *trans-* means "across" or "on the other side of." Read the words and their meanings below.

transplant	*remove from one place and plant, or settle, in another*
transcontinental	*crossing the continent*
transatlantic	*crossing the Atlantic Ocean*
transferred	*moved something from one person or place to another*
transmitted	*sent from to one person or place to another*

B. Complete each sentence with one of the boldfaced words from Part A.

1. When my brother got his driver's license, Uncle Robert gave him an old car. First, Uncle Robert __transferred__ ownership of the car to my brother.
2. Who made the first __transcontinental__ flight across North America?
3. My grandparents took a __transatlantic__ cruise from New York to London.
4. Each month, Mr. Chu __transmitted__ money to his mother in China.
5. I helped my mother __transplant__ the rosebushes to the front yard.

C. The prefix *sub-* means "under, beneath, or below." Read the words and their meanings below. Choose two words, and write a sentence using each word.

subzero	*below zero; usually refers to temperature*
subgroup	*a secondary group whose members share common qualities*
subcommittee	*section of a committee organized for a specific purpose*
subdivision	*something produced by dividing into sections; a tract of land divided into lots for the purpose of sale may become a neighborhood subdivision*
subdue	*bring under control*

1. Answers will vary.
2. ______________________

©Voyager Expanded Learning, Inc. 104

Repeat this process for the following words.

- **brutally** (adj) *very cruelly or done without feeling,* Anthology page 56
- **homicide** (n) *the killing of one human by another,* Anthology page 58
- **dispose** (v) *get rid of,* Anthology page 58
- **inherited** (v) *received something from a person who has died,* Anthology page 58

4. Have students turn to Student Book page 104. **You learned the word *transport*, which begins with the prefix *trans-*. You can build on what you know about *transport* to learn other words that begin with *trans-*.** Read aloud the instructions for each part of the page, and have students complete the page.

Reread 

Apply the Target Skill: Inference

1. Write the definition of inference on the board:

   Read or Observe + *Already Know* = *Inference*

2. Have students turn to Student Book page 105 and read aloud the instructions. **You read that Lizzie called her stepmother "Mrs. Borden." Many children call their stepmothers "Mom" or use their first names. What inference can you make?** Have students write their responses on their page.

3. Have students complete the second inference chart. Direct them to reread the text and locate details that lead to their inferences. When all students finish, have them share their responses.

Refer to Blackline Master page 21 for students who are having difficulty making inferences.

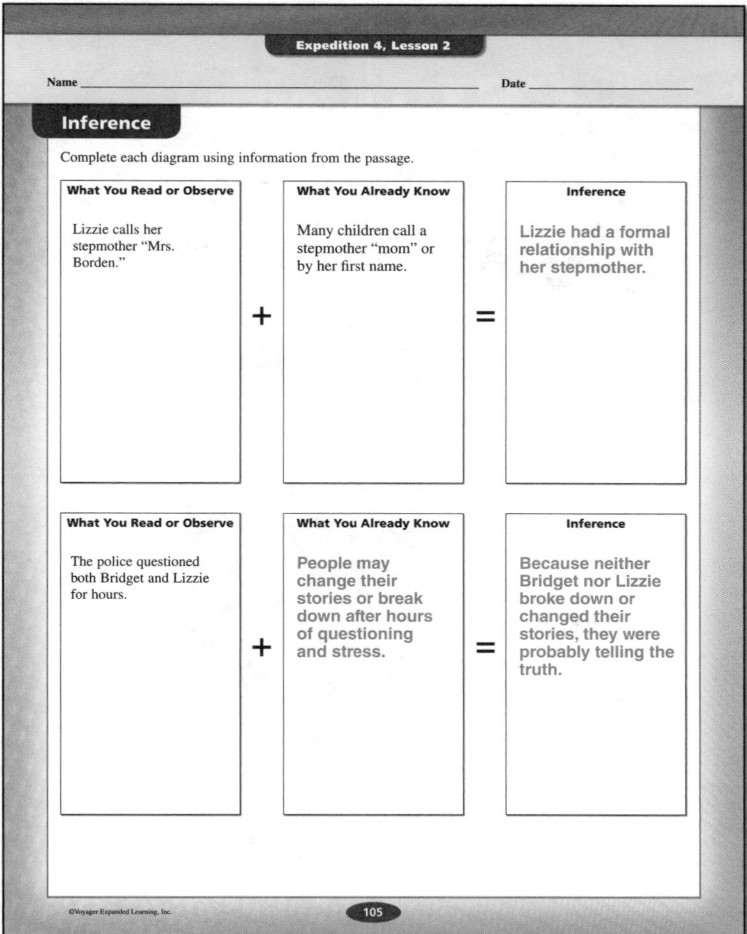

Expedition 4, Lesson 2

Name ______________________ Date ____________

Inference

Complete each diagram using information from the passage.

What You Read or Observe		What You Already Know		Inference
Lizzie calls her stepmother "Mrs. Borden."	+	Many children call a stepmother "mom" or by her first name.	=	Lizzie had a formal relationship with her stepmother.

What You Read or Observe		What You Already Know		Inference
The police questioned both Bridget and Lizzie for hours.	+	People may change their stories or break down after hours of questioning and stress.	=	Because neither Bridget nor Lizzie broke down or changed their stories, they were probably telling the truth.

©Voyager Expanded Learning, Inc. 105

Write in Response to Reading

1. Have students turn to Student Book page 106. **Do you believe Lizzie is telling the truth about Bridget?**

2. Read aloud the instructions for Parts A and B. **News articles are often organized around the questions *who*, *what*, *when*, *where*, *why*, and *how*. When you finish, check that you have included all the information.** Have students complete the page, then share their responses with a partner.

Allow students to extend oral language by acting out the scene between Lizzie and Bridget.

Expedition 4, Lesson 2

Name ______________________ Date ____________

Write in Response to Reading

A. Lizzie said Bridget, the maid, was the only person at home with her when her father and stepmother were murdered. Imagine the scene. Write a dialogue below that might have taken place between Bridget and Lizzie at that moment. Then, create a comic strip showing the scene complete with dialogue.

Scene Bridget finds Lizzie screaming at the sight of the dead bodies.

Bridget: Answers will vary.

Lizzie: ____________________

Bridget: ____________________

Lizzie: ____________________

Bridget: ____________________

B. You are a reporter at the trial of Lizzie Borden. The jury just announced they have found Lizzie innocent of the crime of murder. Write a news article that tells how the trialed ended. Include the reaction of people in the courtroom, such as Lizzie, the lawyers, and spectators.

Answers will vary.

©Voyager Expanded Learning, Inc. 106

EXPEDITION ORGANIZER **Criminology**

Pause to have students turn to Student Book pages 100 and 101. Have students complete the following:

- Write answers or notes below one or more of the probing questions. Encourage them to write a question of their own.
- Think about their own idea from "Ax Murderer or Beloved Daughter?" and write it in the oval in Part B.

CSI at the Lizzie Borden Crime Scene

Crime scene investigation (CSI) and the science of forensics have made it possible to solve crimes that 100 years ago would have gone unsolved, like the case of Lizzie Borden. If a CSI team from today could be transported through time and space and arrive on the scene at the same time those turn-of-the-century investigators did, the case of Lizzie Borden might not be so mysterious. 1

Andrew Borden's skull   Murder weapon

Investigators secure the scene so they can make a careful analysis of the crime.

Vocabulary
reveal (v) *make known*

1 Make Connections
Think about what you read in the last passage about Lizzie Borden as you read what the CSI might do at the site.

Steps of the CSI

The first thing CSI team members would have done is to secure the scene so they could take fingerprints. This would **reveal** for certain whether someone besides Lizzie, Bridget, and Mr. and Mrs. Borden had been in the house.

Modern-day investigators would not determine the time of death by relying on touch to measure the temperature of a body as they did in the Borden case. Instead, they would use an internal thermometer and take

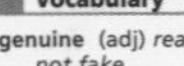

Vocabulary
genuine (adj) *real; not fake*
analysis (n) *a careful study or examination of something*
diluted (adj) *thinned out or weakened by adding water*

An investigator analyzes items found at a crime scene.

temperatures over a period of time. Even so, they could determine the time of death only within a few hours of the murder.

There was much debate about the dress that Lizzie wore that day. Was it indeed the light blue dress she later burned, or was it a dark blue dress? CSI would have recorded the scene by taking photographs and videos of everyone there, including Lizzie in her dress. The video also would have shown how Lizzie reacted to the scene. Were her emotions **genuine**, or was she a clever actress? 2

Today, a CSI team would use blood spatter **analysis** to reveal many clues to the mystery. The CSI team would collect bloodstain data at the scene, and a blood spatter expert would interpret the blood patterns. The results would reveal the positions of the victims, of objects in the room at the time of death, and of the assailant, or attacker. The analysis would also help the investigators establish the type of weapon used and the number of blows. The trajectory, or path, of blood spatter would help estimate the height of the assailant and the movements of the victim and assailant after blood was shed. 3

Finally, the modern-day crime scene investigators would use high-intensity light to search for blood at the crime scene. **Diluted** blood leaves a brownish stain where someone has tried to clean it. The team would use modern techniques to detect blood that seeped into cracks in the floorboards or behind baseboards. If the investigators discovered what looked like blood on the floor that someone attempted to clean up, the floorboards would be removed and taken to the crime lab for further testing. 4

2 Ask Questions
Think about what you just read. Ask yourself, "Why are photographs and video of a crime scene helpful?"

3 Visualize
Think about how the trajectory would help estimate the height of the assailant. Draw a picture, if necessary.

4 Summarize
What are the steps a CSI team might take to investigate a crime scene?

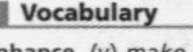

Vocabulary
catalyst (n) *a substance that makes a chemical reaction happen at a faster rate*

POLICE LINE DO NOT CROSS

Chemical Reactions

Many techniques used today in criminal investigations involve a chemical test of the evidence found at a crime scene. Tests performed by the investigators often result in a chemical reaction from one chemical mixing with another. During a chemical reaction, tiny invisible particles or molecules of one substance react with molecules from another substance. The molecules of each substance undergo a change. This change is a chemical reaction that produces totally different chemicals. Chemical reactions are common and occur around you and inside your body each day. Digesting the food you eat is a common type of chemical reaction. So is iron changing to rust and gasoline burning in a car engine.

Luminol

Today, crime investigators use a chemical reaction to detect blood at a crime scene. In this chemical reaction, investigators use a special chemical called luminol to identify blood particles that may be invisible to the naked eye. Before luminol will work, it has to undergo a chemical reaction with blood. When luminol reacts chemically with blood, it changes and produces a substance that has a greenish blue glow. Locating a trail of blood using luminol could help reveal the escape route of a murderer who is either bleeding or carrying a bloody weapon. Luminol could even reveal the presence of blood on a suspected murder weapon. 5

How Luminol Works

Luminol is a powder made up of nitrogen, hydrogen, oxygen, and carbon molecules. Criminalists will mix luminol powder with hydrogen peroxide, distilled water, and washing soda to form a liquid that is poured into a spray bottle. The liquid is then sprayed on a surface thought to contain traces of blood. If blood is present, it will react with the luminol and start to glow in the dark.

Before the luminol can glow, a chemical reaction must take place. To make a chemical reaction, the liquid luminol needs a **catalyst**, or something to cause the molecules from the luminol to start reacting

5 Summarize
Name some ways luminol is helpful with crime scene investigation.

Vocabulary
enhance (v) *make greater or better*

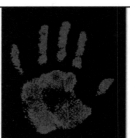

A bloody handprint glows in the dark after luminol is sprayed on it.

with the molecules in the blood. The catalyst needed is iron. Hemoglobin, an oxygen-carrying protein in blood, contains iron. Molecules of luminol react with the iron contained in hemoglobin. When criminalists spray the luminol mixture on the surface of an object where there is blood, they will see a green glow from the chemical reaction.

The chemical reaction that takes place is called an oxidation reaction. In the oxidation reaction, the luminol loses nitrogen and hydrogen atoms and gains oxygen atoms. (See the diagram.) The result is a completely new compound called *3-aminophthalate*. 6 This new compound glows in the dark because it releases extra energy in the form of light particles called photons. It is this same chemical reaction that causes fireflies and light sticks to glow in the dark. In a dark room, luminol will make a bloody footprint or fingerprint glow.

Drawbacks of Luminol

Luminol, however, is not the CSI's first choice for detecting blood. If a bloodstain is so diluted that it can only be made visible with luminol, the chemical also will destroy the sample so no further testing can be done with the blood. For example, DNA tests could not be performed to confirm whose blood it is because the luminol would destroy the DNA. Also, luminol can react with other iron molecules, copper molecules, and even urine, giving a false positive reaction. But, as a final step, when used with a high-intensity light, luminol is ideal to **enhance** bloody fingerprints and shoeprints. End

6 Word Reading
Sometimes it may not be necessary to pronounce a word correctly to understand the text. Do the best you can quickly, then keep reading.

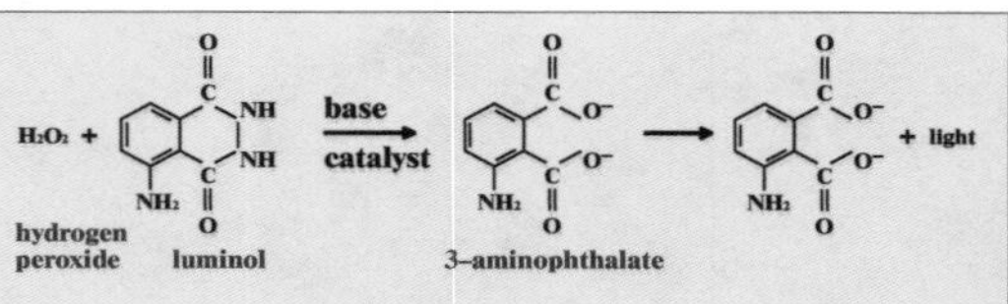

This diagram shows how molecules are exchanged during the oxidation reaction that happens when hydrogen peroxide and luminol react with a base catalyst (iron found in hemoglobin).

"CSI at the Lizzie Borden Crime Scene"

Before Reading

Introduce Vocabulary

1. Have students turn to Part A on Student Book page 107 and scan the boldfaced vocabulary words. **You will see these words in "CSI at the Lizzie Borden Crime Scene."** Read aloud the instructions, and have students complete Part A.
2. Have students share the words they already know. **Which words have you seen or heard before? Where?** Read aloud the words, parts of speech, definitions, and example sentences. Discuss with students any confusion they have about the word meanings or pronunciations.
3. Read aloud the instructions for Part B. Have students complete the activity independently, then compare answers with a partner.

Refer to Blackline Master page 22 to extend vocabulary practice.

Have students use the *Passport Reading Journeys* online technology component to practice and reinforce vocabulary and comprehension skills.

Introduce the Target Skill: Ask Questions

1. Remind students when they come across a word or idea they don't know, they should figure out a question to ask about the part they don't understand, then look for answers in the text. **When do you ask questions? Before reading? During? After?** (before, during, and after) Remind students they should ask questions as they read all kinds of texts.
2. **One way to ask questions is to preview the title and subheadings in a passage.** Have students turn to Anthology page 59. **For example, before reading this passage, I could look at the title and ask, "What does *CSI* mean?" or "Was there really a CSI team at the Lizzie Borden crime scene?" Then I would read on to find the answer.**

Expedition 4, Lesson 3

Name ______ Date ______

Vocabulary

"CSI at the Lizzie Borden Crime Scene"

A. Put a check mark in each row to indicate how well you know each word.

	Know This Word	Have Seen This Word	Don't Know This Word
reveal (v) *make known* Many things investigators do at a crime scene can *reveal* who committed the crime.			
genuine (adj) *real; not fake* The police did not believe Lizzie's tears were *genuine* because she didn't even like her stepmother.			
analysis (n) *a careful study or examination of something* An *analysis* of the data will show what caused the problem.			
diluted (adj) *thinned out or weakened by adding water* The *diluted* blood left a different color of stain.			
catalyst (n) *a substance that makes a chemical reaction happen at a faster rate* When added to vinegar, baking soda acts as a *catalyst* that causes a quick reaction.			
enhance (v) *make greater or better* The CSI team uses tools to *enhance* blurry photographs.			

B. Match the beginning of each sentence with its ending. Write the correct sentence ending for each line.

an analysis of the data — **had been diluted** — **enhance their presentations** — **started the chemical reaction** — **were genuine** — **the secret formula**

1. The baking soda was the catalyst that started the chemical reaction.
2. The scientists would not reveal how they made the secret formula.
3. The police said the fingerprints were genuine.
4. They could not use the bloodstains as evidence because they had been diluted.
5. Speakers use visual aids to enhance their presentations.
6. The researchers took the results and performed an analysis of the data.

©Voyager Expanded Learning, Inc. 107

Vocabulary

reveal (v) *make known*
Many things investigators do at a crime scene can *reveal* who committed the crime.

genuine (adj) *real; not fake*
The police did not believe Lizzie's tears were *genuine* because she didn't even like her stepmother.

analysis (n) *a careful study or examination of something*
An *analysis* of the data will show what caused the problem.

diluted (adj) *thinned out or weakened by adding water*
The *diluted* blood left a different color of stain.

catalyst (n) *a substance that makes a chemical reaction happen at a faster rate*
When added to vinegar, baking soda acts as a *catalyst* that causes a quick reaction.

enhance (v) *make greater or better*
The CSI team uses tools to *enhance* blurry photographs.

3. Have students preview the remaining headings. **Use these headings to ask questions. What questions could you ask about Steps of the CSI?** Have students form their own questions using the other headings in the passage. Write students' questions on the board. **Keep these questions in mind as you read "CSI at the Lizzie Borden Crime Scene."** Remind students to pause for the margin prompts as they read.

Introduce the Passage

1. Have students look at the other features in the passage. **What kinds of images do you see?** (photographs, a diagram, fingerprints, footprints) **What genre, or type of text, do you think this passage is? Why?** (nonfiction; it has a diagram like a textbook; it has realistic photos and factual captions.)

ELL Explain that this passage is similar to what students might see in their science class. Explain how to use captions, headings, photographs, and diagrams to enhance understanding of the text.

2. Tell students they will encounter scientific and technical terms in the passage. Have students turn to Anthology page 62. **The margin prompt on this page says sometimes it may not be necessary to pronounce a word correctly to understand the text, and you can just keep reading. Why do you think it is good to do this?** (It helps the reader focus on what the main idea is and learn more as he or she keeps reading.)
3. Have students use the headings and pictures to make a prediction about the passage. **What modern techniques do you think this article will focus on?** Have students write their responses on a sheet of paper, then share them with a partner.

During Reading

1. To select reading options that support your students' levels and classroom needs, see Reading Differentiation, page xxxii, if needed.
2. Have students use the Ask Questions strategy by pausing at difficult parts in their reading and forming questions about those parts. **To find the answer, you can reread the part that comes before or read on.**

After Reading

Check Comprehension

1. Have students refer to the predictions they made about this passage. **What information was in the passage that you didn't expect?**
2. Reread the Make Connections margin prompt on Anthology page 59. Have students share the connections they made between "Ax Murderer or Beloved Daughter?" and this passage. (Students' answers should reflect that the investigation of the Borden murders had little technology and the outcome of the trial may have been different if modern investigation techniques were used.)
3. Have students look back at the headings. **What steps does a CSI team take?** (A CSI team takes fingerprints, determines time of death, takes photographs and videos, searches for blood, and uses blood splatter analysis.) **What special chemical does a CSI team use?** (luminol to find blood) **How does luminol work?** (It reacts with the iron in hemoglobin.) **What are the drawbacks of luminol?** (It can destroy the sample, and it can give a false-positive result.)

ACADEMIC SKILL Remind students they can turn text headings into questions when they read text in science, social studies, and other classes.

Remind students to choose books from the *Passport Reading Journeys* Library for independent reading.

"CSI at the Lizzie Borden Crime Scene"

Prepare to Reread

Introduce the Lesson

Ask students what a CSI team would have discovered at the Borden crime scene. **We'll revisit "CSI at the Lizzie Borden Crime Scene" and practice making inferences.**

Practice Vocabulary

1. Review the vocabulary words by asking the following questions.
   - **When you *reveal* something, do you show it or hide it?** (show it)
   - **Is something that is *genuine* real or fake?** (real)
   - **Is it best to do an *analysis* before or after reaching a conclusion? Why?** (before; The analysis helps you reach the conclusion.)
   - **When something is *diluted*, is it stronger or weaker?** (weaker)
   - **Does a *catalyst* help things stay the same, or does it change them?** (changes them)
   - **When you *enhance* something, do you make it better or worse?** (better)
2. Remind students they can use context clues to find the meanings of unknown words. Have students turn to Anthology page 60. **What do you think the word *assailant* means?** (attacker) **How do you know?** (The word *assailant* is restated as "attacker.")

   Repeat this process for the following words.
   - **trajectory** (n) *path*, Anthology page 60
   - **molecules** (n) *tiny, invisible particles*, Anthology page 61
   - **hemoglobin** (n) *the oxygen-carrying protein in blood*, Anthology page 62
3. Have students turn to Student Book page 108. **You learned the word *enhance*. You can add the suffix *-ment* to the verb *enhance* and some other verbs to create noun forms of the words.** Read Part A aloud as students follow along. Read aloud the instructions for Parts B and C. Have students complete the page independently. When students finish, have partners compare their responses.

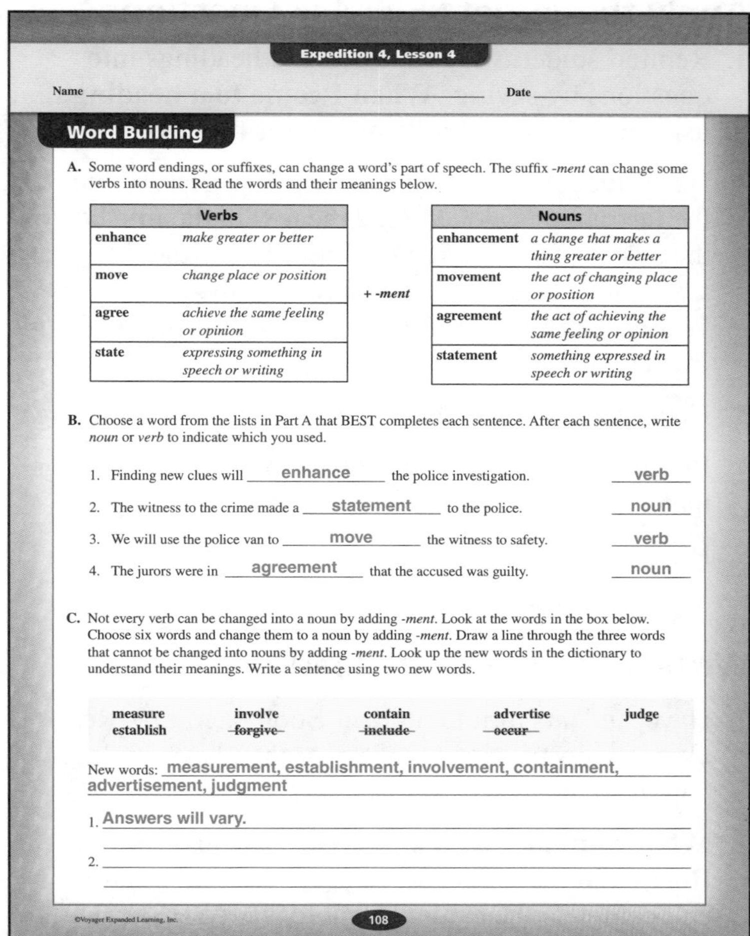

Expedition 4, Lesson 4

Name ______ Date ______

Word Building

A. Some word endings, or suffixes, can change a word's part of speech. The suffix *-ment* can change some verbs into nouns. Read the words and their meanings below.

Verbs			Nouns	
enhance	*make greater or better*	+ *-ment*	enhancement	*a change that makes a thing greater or better*
move	*change place or position*		movement	*the act of changing place or position*
agree	*achieve the same feeling or opinion*		agreement	*the act of achieving the same feeling or opinion*
state	*expressing something in speech or writing*		statement	*something expressed in speech or writing*

B. Choose a word from the lists in Part A that BEST completes each sentence. After each sentence, write *noun* or *verb* to indicate which you used.

1. Finding new clues will __enhance__ the police investigation. __verb__
2. The witness to the crime made a __statement__ to the police. __noun__
3. We will use the police van to __move__ the witness to safety. __verb__
4. The jurors were in __agreement__ that the accused was guilty. __noun__

C. Not every verb can be changed into a noun by adding *-ment*. Look at the words in the box below. Choose six words and change them to a noun by adding *-ment*. Draw a line through the three words that cannot be changed into nouns by adding *-ment*. Look up the new words in the dictionary to understand their meanings. Write a sentence using two new words.

measure	involve	contain	advertise	judge
establish	~~forgive~~	~~include~~	~~occur~~	

New words: measurement, establishment, involvement, containment, advertisement, judgment

1. Answers will vary.

2. ______

©Voyager Expanded Learning, Inc. 108

CHECKPOINT If students have difficulty creating sentences for Part C, have them make sure they are using the new word as a noun.

ELL Allow students to work with partners to complete Parts B and C of Student Book page 108 or complete it orally with small groups.

Reread

Apply the Target Skill: Ask Questions

1. Remind students to turn titles and headings into questions by saying: **When I come to a heading, I ask myself what it tells me about the text.**
2. Have students turn to Student Book page 109, and read the instructions aloud. Read the text in the first box on the sidebar aloud, and model how to use the title to ask a question. **I can turn this title into the questions, *What is criminal justice?* or *How is it different in the United States?***
3. Have students read the passage and complete the page.
4. Remind students to underline the parts of the passage that answer their questions.
5. Have partners share their questions.

Write in Response to Reading

1. Have students turn to Student Book page 110. Read aloud the instructions for Part A, then have students complete the interview questions.
2. **What would a CSI team have discovered at the Borden home?** Have students read the instructions and complete the evidence log for Part B.

EXPEDITION ORGANIZER **Criminology**

Pause to have students turn to Student Book pages 100 and 101. Have students complete the following:

- Write answers or notes below one or more of the probing questions. Encourage them to write a question of their own.
- Think about their own idea from "CSI at the Lizzie Borden Crime Scene." Tell students to write it in the appropriate oval in Part B.

Expedition 4, Lesson 4

Name ____________________ Date __________

Ask Questions

Asking questions is a good strategy to ensure you're actively reading. Before, during, and after reading the passage below, ask yourself questions to check your understanding. Underline the parts of the text that answer your questions.

Criminal Justice in the United States

Criminal justice is the system of practices and organizations used by national and local governments to control crime and prosecute those who violate laws with criminal penalties. The criminal justice system consists of three main parts: (1) law enforcement or police, (2) courts, and (3) corrections or jails and prisons.

Law Enforcement

Police or law enforcement agencies and officers use force and legal means to control the public and social order. The term is most commonly associated with police departments of a state or city. Law enforcement agencies maintain public order and are responsible for arresting people accused of committing a crime. Law enforcement is not responsible for prosecuting or arguing that the accused is truly guilty of a crime.

Courts

The courts are where disputes are settled and justice is administered. In the United States, guilt or innocence is decided through the adversarial system. In this system, two parties will offer their version of events and argue their case in front of a judge or jury.

Read the title and the subheadings. Ask a question about what you expect to read in this passage.
What is criminal justice in the United States?

Stop after reading the second paragraph. What question do you have about the next paragraph?
Who is responsible for making sure a criminal is held accountable?

What other question do you have about this paragraph?
Answers will vary.

 109

Expedition 4, Lesson 4

Name ____________________ Date __________

Write in Response to Reading

A. Imagine you will interview for a job as an investigator for a CSI team. What would you tell the interviewer about yourself? Complete the statements explaining why you would be a good investigator.

CSI Team Position Available

I am very good at Student responses should reflect that CSI investigators need to have a strong background in science and an interest in solving problems or puzzles.

I am interested in ____________________.

I have experience ____________________.

B. If a modern CSI team was transported back in time to the Lizzie Borden crime scene, what do you think team members would find, and how would they investigate? What would this evidence mean? Complete the evidence log with your ideas.

Evidence Log for Borden Crime Scene

Found in living room: Student responses should be reasonable given the
How CSI investigated: facts of the Borden case, the techniques and tools a
Conclusion: CSI team uses, and what a CSI team investigates.

Found in basement: ____________________
How CSI investigated: ____________________
Conclusion: ____________________

Found in barn: ____________________
How CSI investigated: ____________________
Conclusion: ____________________

 110

Review, Extend, Assess

In today's lesson, as in Lessons 5 and 10 of every Expedition, there are options from which to choose. You may do any or all of the options listed. Activities for each option are given on the following pages. Each option will support or extend previously taught objectives. Choose the option(s) appropriate for your students and prepare accordingly.

Review Vocabulary

Extend Vocabulary

Assess Comprehension and Vocabulary

Reteach

Passport Reading Journeys Library

Technology

Writing Process

Real-World Reading

Exploring Careers

Review Vocabulary

Direct students to review the vocabulary for "Ax Murderer or Beloved Daughter?" and "CSI at the Lizzie Borden Crime Scene" on Student Book page 101.

1. Have students reread the meanings of those words.
2. Have students turn to Student Book page 111. **As you complete the review activity, go back and check the definitions to make sure you used words correctly.** Read the instructions aloud and have students complete the activity. Have students share their answers.

CHECKPOINT Provide support for students who had difficulty creating context clues by confirming that students understand the types of context clues: an example, a synonym (a word that means the same), an antonym (a word that means the opposite), or a brief explanation (restatement or appositive). **In sentence 1, the context clue begins with *which are.* What type of context clue would you need to add?** (brief explanation) Continue having students identify the type of context clue they need to write to prompt their answers.

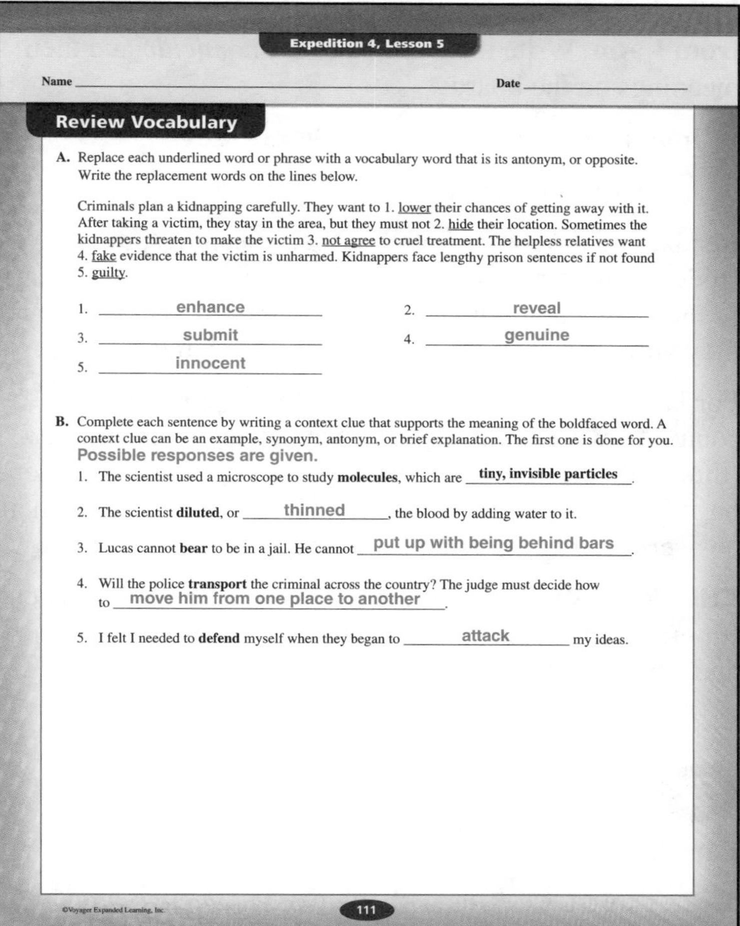

Expedition 4, Lesson 5

Name ____________ Date ____________

Review Vocabulary

A. Replace each underlined word or phrase with a vocabulary word that is its antonym, or opposite. Write the replacement words on the lines below.

Criminals plan a kidnapping carefully. They want to 1. lower their chances of getting away with it. After taking a victim, they stay in the area, but they must not 2. hide their location. Sometimes the kidnappers threaten to make the victim 3. not agree to cruel treatment. The helpless relatives want 4. fake evidence that the victim is unharmed. Kidnappers face lengthy prison sentences if not found 5. guilty.

1. enhance
2. reveal
3. submit
4. genuine
5. innocent

B. Complete each sentence by writing a context clue that supports the meaning of the boldfaced word. A context clue can be an example, synonym, antonym, or brief explanation. The first one is done for you. Possible responses are given.

1. The scientist used a microscope to study **molecules**, which are tiny, invisible particles.
2. The scientist **diluted**, or thinned, the blood by adding water to it.
3. Lucas cannot **bear** to be in a jail. He cannot put up with being behind bars.
4. Will the police **transport** the criminal across the country? The judge must decide how to move him from one place to another.
5. I felt I needed to **defend** myself when they began to attack my ideas.

Extend Vocabulary

Direct students to Part A on Student Book page 112. **Many words in English, such as *homicide*, come from Latin.** Write the word parts for *homicide* and their meanings on the board:

homo + cide = homicide

human + killing of

Read aloud the Latin roots and their meanings, then have students answer the questions. Remind them the spelling of the Latin ending may be *i* or *o* in the English word, and they will need to use a dictionary to check the spelling.

For Part B, have students practice by tapping out the sounds of words like *dispose* (two syllables) and *diluted* (three syllables) to allow them to hear the syllables. Then, have them complete the activity. Have students share their answers after completing both parts.

CHECKPOINT When students share their answers, listen for errors common to several students. Pause to explain and correct the answers.

Part A

1. Prepare index cards with the words *regicide, fungicide, insecticide, matricide, genocide, infanticide,* and *herbicide* for student pairs.
2. Orally review the Latin word parts and English meanings with students.
3. Next, read the questions in Part A aloud and have student pairs show the card with the correct response for each question.

Part B

1. Read the words aloud, emphasizing the syllable breaks.
2. After students have listed the words, have them work with a partner to draw a line at the syllable breaks.

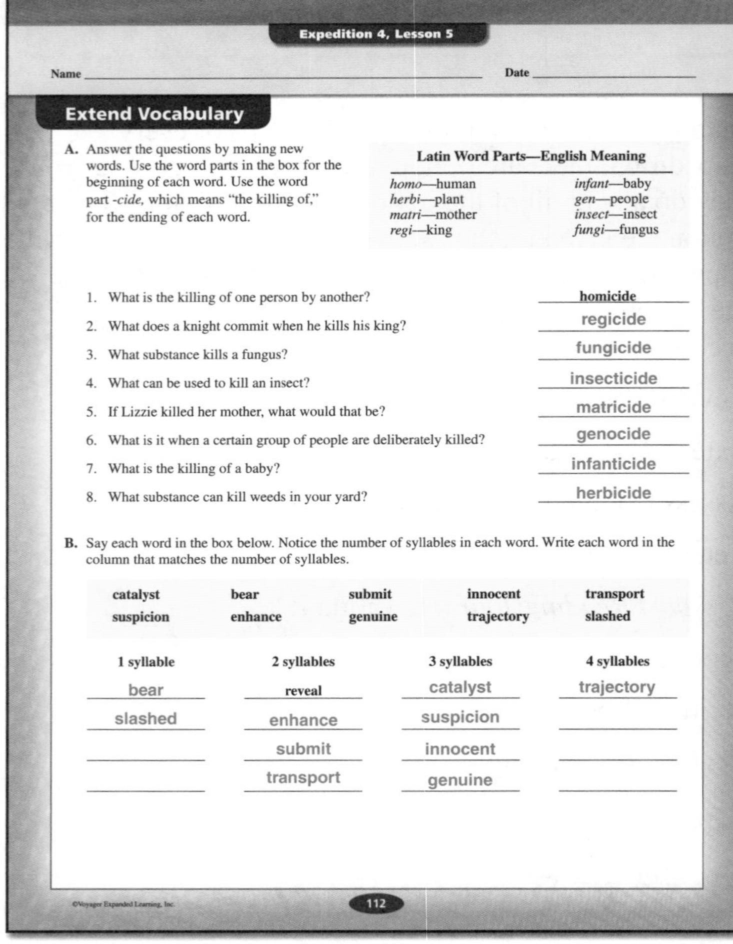

Expedition 4, Lesson 5

Name ______ Date ______

Extend Vocabulary

A. Answer the questions by making new words. Use the word parts in the box for the beginning of each word. Use the word part *-cide,* which means "the killing of," for the ending of each word.

Latin Word Parts—English Meaning	
homo—human	*infant*—baby
herbi—plant	*gen*—people
matri—mother	*insect*—insect
regi—king	*fungi*—fungus

1. What is the killing of one person by another? **homicide**
2. What does a knight commit when he kills his king? regicide
3. What substance kills a fungus? fungicide
4. What can be used to kill an insect? insecticide
5. If Lizzie killed her mother, what would that be? matricide
6. What is it when a certain group of people are deliberately killed? genocide
7. What is the killing of a baby? infanticide
8. What substance can kill weeds in your yard? herbicide

B. Say each word in the box below. Notice the number of syllables in each word. Write each word in the column that matches the number of syllables.

catalyst	**bear**	**submit**	**innocent**	**transport**
suspicion	**enhance**	**genuine**	**trajectory**	**slashed**

1 syllable	2 syllables	3 syllables	4 syllables
bear	**reveal**	catalyst	trajectory
slashed	enhance	suspicion	
	submit	innocent	
	transport	genuine	

112

Assess Comprehension and Vocabulary

1. Remind students that they learned how to make inferences.
   - **If I see police dogs, *I would infer*** (a police officer might be in the neighborhood.)
   - **If I see a police photographer, *I would infer*** (she or he is photographing evidence.)
   - **If I see the ambulance leaving empty, *I would infer*** (no one was hurt badly.)
2. Direct students to Student Book pages 113–115. Have students complete the pages independently.

   Review student answers. Whenever possible, provide elaborative feedback to student responses. Refer to page xl for examples of elaborative feedback and how to incorporate it in your lessons.

   If students incorrectly answer more than 4 out of 15 assessment questions, evaluate what kind of reteaching is needed. If students miss vocabulary questions, have them return to the vocabulary activities and work with the words they missed. For errors with making inferences or asking questions, use the reteaching suggestions on page 150.

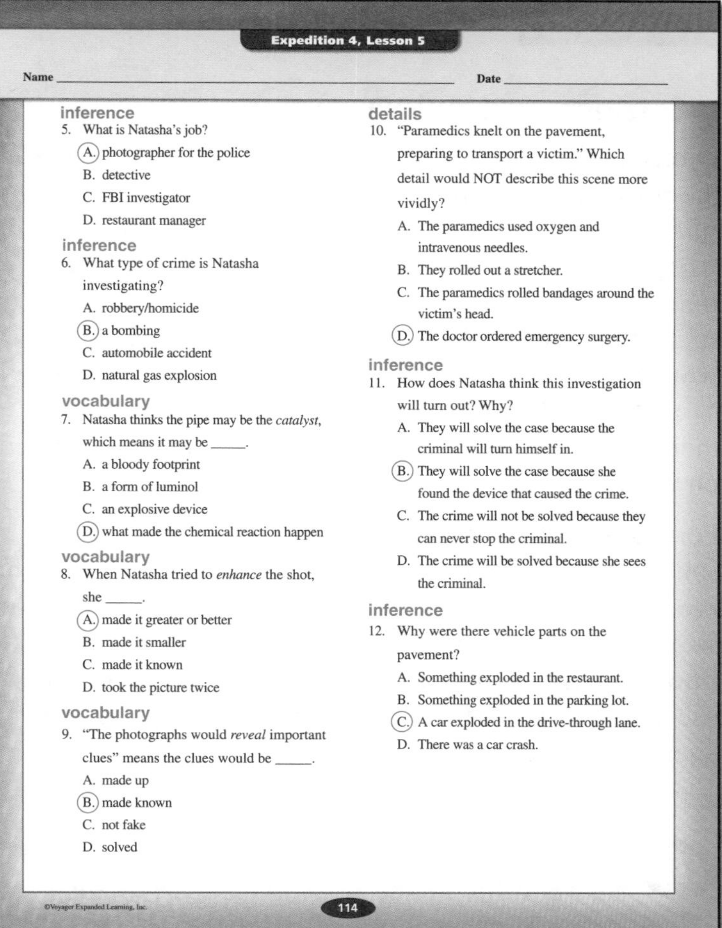

Expedition 4, Lesson 5

Name ______ Date ______

inference
5. What is Natasha's job?
   (A) photographer for the police
   B. detective
   C. FBI investigator
   D. restaurant manager

inference
6. What type of crime is Natasha investigating?
   A. robbery/homicide
   (B) a bombing
   C. automobile accident
   D. natural gas explosion

vocabulary
7. Natasha thinks the pipe may be the *catalyst*, which means it may be ______.
   A. a bloody footprint
   B. a form of luminol
   C. an explosive device
   (D) what made the chemical reaction happen

vocabulary
8. When Natasha tried to *enhance* the shot, she ______.
   (A) made it greater or better
   B. made it smaller
   C. made it known
   D. took the picture twice

vocabulary
9. "The photographs would *reveal* important clues" means the clues would be ______.
   A. made up
   (B) made known
   C. not fake
   D. solved

details
10. "Paramedics knelt on the pavement, preparing to transport a victim." Which detail would NOT describe this scene more vividly?
   A. The paramedics used oxygen and intravenous needles.
   B. They rolled out a stretcher.
   C. The paramedics rolled bandages around the victim's head.
   (D) The doctor ordered emergency surgery.

inference
11. How does Natasha think this investigation will turn out? Why?
   A. They will solve the case because the criminal will turn himself in.
   (B) They will solve the case because she found the device that caused the crime.
   C. The crime will not be solved because they can never stop the criminal.
   D. The crime will be solved because she sees the criminal.

inference
12. Why were there vehicle parts on the pavement?
   A. Something exploded in the restaurant.
   B. Something exploded in the parking lot.
   (C) A car exploded in the drive-through lane.
   D. There was a car crash.

©Voyager Expanded Learning, Inc. 114

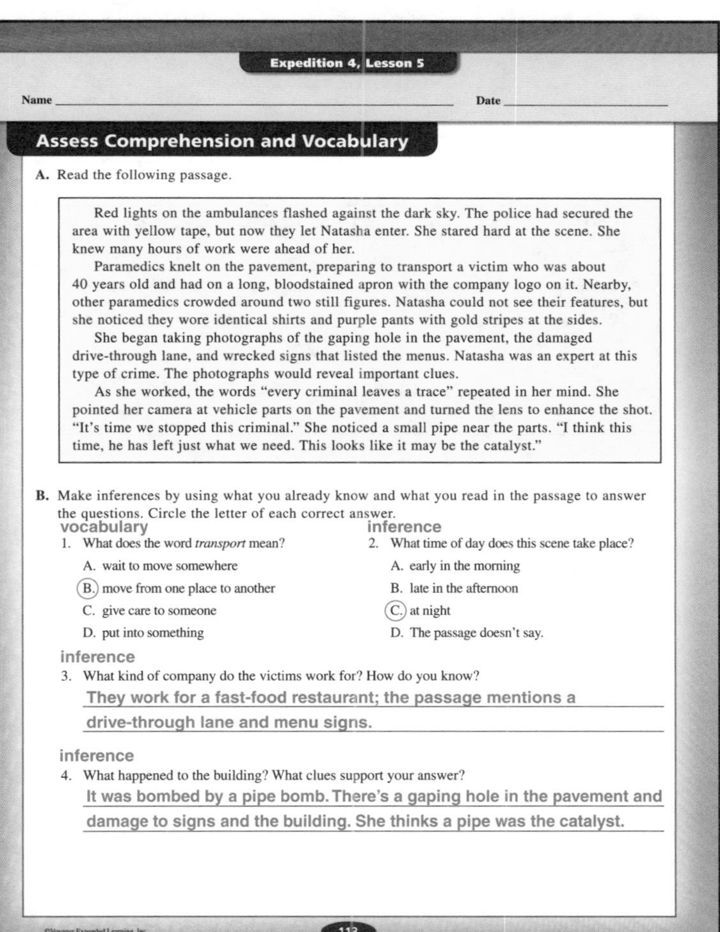

Expedition 4, Lesson 5

Name ______ Date ______

Assess Comprehension and Vocabulary

A. Read the following passage.

Red lights on the ambulances flashed against the dark sky. The police had secured the area with yellow tape, but now they let Natasha enter. She stared hard at the scene. She knew many hours of work were ahead of her.

Paramedics knelt on the pavement, preparing to transport a victim who was about 40 years old and had on a long, bloodstained apron with the company logo on it. Nearby, other paramedics crowded around two still figures. Natasha could not see their features, but she noticed they wore identical shirts and purple pants with gold stripes at the sides.

She began taking photographs of the gaping hole in the pavement, the damaged drive-through lane, and wrecked signs that listed the menus. Natasha was an expert at this type of crime. The photographs would reveal important clues.

As she worked, the words "every criminal leaves a trace" repeated in her mind. She pointed her camera at vehicle parts on the pavement and turned the lens to enhance the shot. "It's time we stopped this criminal." She noticed a small pipe near the parts. "I think this time, he has left just what we need. This looks like it may be the catalyst."

B. Make inferences by using what you already know and what you read in the passage to answer the questions. Circle the letter of each correct answer.

vocabulary
1. What does the word *transport* mean?
   A. wait to move somewhere
   (B) move from one place to another
   C. give care to someone
   D. put into something

inference
2. What time of day does this scene take place?
   A. early in the morning
   B. late in the afternoon
   (C) at night
   D. The passage doesn't say.

inference
3. What kind of company do the victims work for? How do you know?
   They work for a fast-food restaurant; the passage mentions a drive-through lane and menu signs.

inference
4. What happened to the building? What clues support your answer?
   It was bombed by a pipe bomb. There's a gaping hole in the pavement and damage to signs and the building. She thinks a pipe was the catalyst.

©Voyager Expanded Learning, Inc. 113

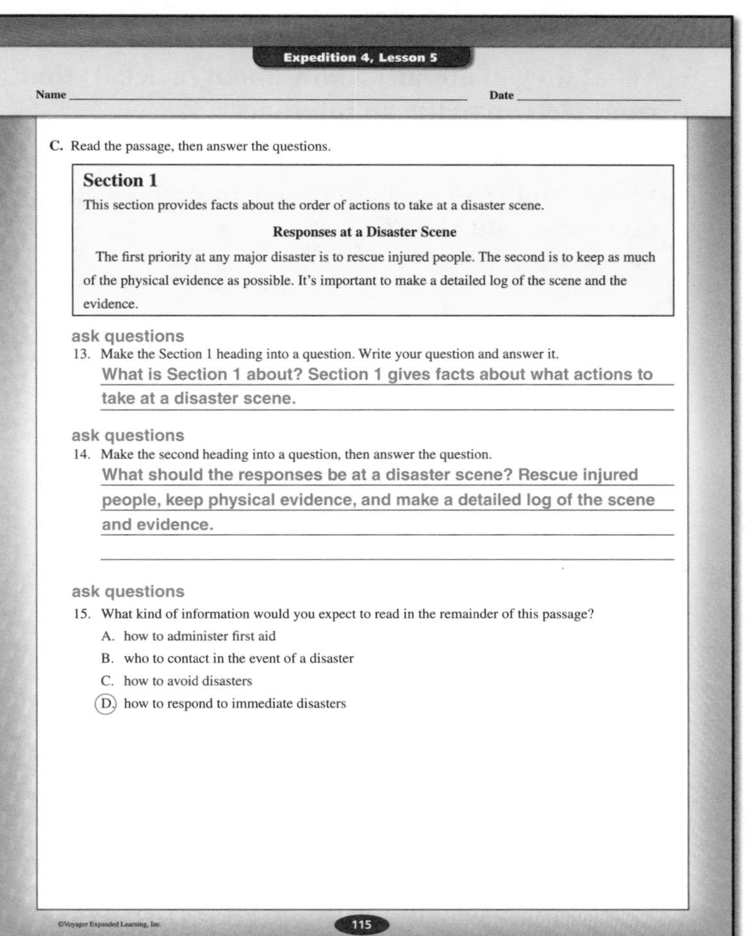

Expedition 4, Lesson 5

Name ______ Date ______

C. Read the passage, then answer the questions.

Section 1

This section provides facts about the order of actions to take at a disaster scene.

Responses at a Disaster Scene

The first priority at any major disaster is to rescue injured people. The second is to keep as much of the physical evidence as possible. It's important to make a detailed log of the scene and the evidence.

ask questions
13. Make the Section 1 heading into a question. Write your question and answer it.
   What is Section 1 about? Section 1 gives facts about what actions to take at a disaster scene.

ask questions
14. Make the second heading into a question, then answer the question.
   What should the responses be at a disaster scene? Rescue injured people, keep physical evidence, and make a detailed log of the scene and evidence.

ask questions
15. What kind of information would you expect to read in the remainder of this passage?
   A. how to administer first aid
   B. who to contact in the event of a disaster
   C. how to avoid disasters
   (D) how to respond to immediate disasters

©Voyager Expanded Learning, Inc. 115

Reteach

Inference and Ask Questions

Direct students to Student Book pages 116 and 117. Read the passage aloud. **You can make inferences about the underlined sentence by thinking about the details and what you already know.** Have students complete the first box independently. For the second box, use prompts such as: **What would a Navajo detective be like? How would he or she be different from a detective in New York City?** Have students complete Part A and share their inferences. Encourage students to add details based on what they know.

For Parts B and C, explain that students should stop to ask their own questions and continue reading. **When you read and ask questions, it is like having a conversation with the author or the text. Sometimes you read on to find the answer to your questions.** Prompt students to use unfamiliar words from the headings or text in their questions. Have students compare their questions.

Use these prompts to help students go back and answer difficult questions in the assessment.

- **What details in the passage relate to the question? Use them to help you make an inference.**
- **What do you already know about** [a detail] **that can help you make an inference?**
- **Why will asking a question about a heading before you read make it easier to understand the text when you read?**

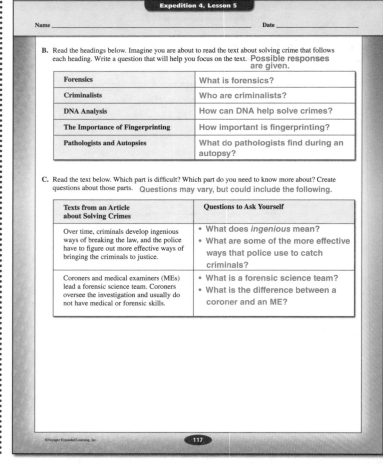

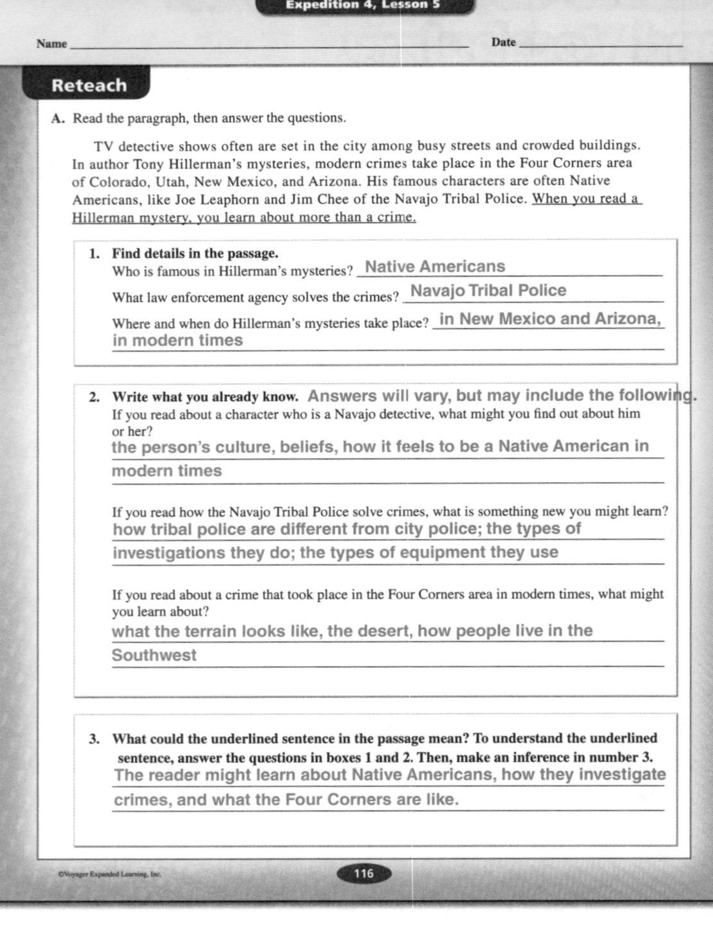

Expedition 4, Lesson 5

Name ______________________ Date ____________

Reteach

A. Read the paragraph, then answer the questions.

TV detective shows often are set in the city among busy streets and crowded buildings. In author Tony Hillerman's mysteries, modern crimes take place in the Four Corners area of Colorado, Utah, New Mexico, and Arizona. His famous characters are often Native Americans, like Joe Leaphorn and Jim Chee of the Navajo Tribal Police. When you read a Hillerman mystery, you learn about more than a crime.

1. **Find details in the passage.**
   Who is famous in Hillerman's mysteries? Native Americans
   What law enforcement agency solves the crimes? Navajo Tribal Police
   Where and when do Hillerman's mysteries take place? in New Mexico and Arizona, in modern times

2. **Write what you already know.** Answers will vary, but may include the following.
   If you read about a character who is a Navajo detective, what might you find out about him or her?
   the person's culture, beliefs, how it feels to be a Native American in modern times
   If you read how the Navajo Tribal Police solve crimes, what is something new you might learn?
   how tribal police are different from city police; the types of investigations they do; the types of equipment they use
   If you read about a crime that took place in the Four Corners area in modern times, what might you learn about?
   what the terrain looks like, the desert, how people live in the Southwest

3. **What could the underlined sentence in the passage mean? To understand the underlined sentence, answer the questions in boxes 1 and 2. Then, make an inference in number 3.**
   The reader might learn about Native Americans, how they investigate crimes, and what the Four Corners are like.

©Voyager Expanded Learning, Inc. 116

Expedition 4, Lesson 5

Name ______________________ Date ____________

B. Read the headings below. Imagine you are about to read the text about solving crime that follows each heading. Write a question that will help you focus on the text. Possible responses are given.

Forensics	What is forensics?
Criminalists	Who are criminalists?
DNA Analysis	How can DNA help solve crimes?
The Importance of Fingerprinting	How important is fingerprinting?
Pathologists and Autopsies	What do pathologists find during an autopsy?

C. Read the text below. Which part is difficult? Which part do you need to know more about? Create questions about those parts. Questions may vary, but could include the following.

Texts from an Article about Solving Crimes	Questions to Ask Yourself
Over time, criminals develop ingenious ways of breaking the law, and the police have to figure out more effective ways of bringing the criminals to justice.	• What does *ingenious* mean? • What are some of the more effective ways that police use to catch criminals?
Coroners and medical examiners (MEs) lead a forensic science team. Coroners oversee the investigation and usually do not have medical or forensic skills.	• What is a forensic science team? • What is the difference between a coroner and an ME?

©Voyager Expanded Learning, Inc. 117

Passport Reading Journeys Library

1. Have students choose reading material from the *Passport Reading Journeys* Library or another approved selection. If students have not finished a previously chosen selection, they may continue reading from that selection. See the *Passport Reading Journeys* Library Teacher's Guide for material on selection guidelines.
2. You also may use this time to allow students to participate in book clubs or book presentations. Use the criteria specified in the *Passport Reading Journeys* Library Teacher's Guide.

Vocabulary Connections

Vocabulary words are listed in the Teacher's Guide for each book. These words are content-related or used frequently in reading material. The selected words can be a basis for independent or small-group discussions and activities.

Student Opportunities

Six copies of each book title are provided in the *Passport Reading Journeys* Library. The number of copies makes it possible for small groups of students to read the same material and share the information they read.

Theme-related titles include *Monster* and *Scorpions*.

Technology

1. Depending on your classroom configuration and computer access, you may have all students work through the technology in a lab setting or have individuals or small groups of students work on desktops or laptops while other students participate in other suggested activities, such as the *Passport Reading Journeys* Library.
2. The online technology component provides additional support for students to work with selected vocabulary words. Students will work through a series of activities to strengthen their word knowledge, then apply that knowledge to passage reading. Refer to the online technology component User Guide for more information.

   Theme-related word sets include U.S. History, Literature, and Chemistry.

Writing Process

Write a Closing Argument

1. Tell students that police, detectives, and CSI teams find evidence, but lawyers, a judge, and often a jury evaluate the evidence and decide who is guilty or innocent. **Lizzie Borden's lawyer convinced the jury she was innocent, so Lizzie went free. What did the lawyer say?** Explain that Lizzie's lawyer wrote a Defense Closing Argument which he recited at her trial. (The actual Defense Closing Argument can be found online by searching "Lizzie Borden.")

   Distribute Writing Blackline Master page 7. Have students look at the page and follow along as you explain the assignment. Tell them to make any notes on the page that will help them, but they will turn in the page with the assignment.

2. **The defense lawyers's closing argument gave facts that proved why Lizzie was innocent. The lawyer used emotional words such as "terrible act" and "wrongly punished" and spoke in a persuasive voice to convice the jury that Lizzie was innocent. Imagine you are the prosecuting lawyer who wants to convince the jury that Lizzie is guilty.**

3. Form groups of four students. Each group is a law firm that will work together to write a Prosecution Closing Argument. Have groups name their law firm.

Prewrite

Lizzie's lawyer used facts, reason, and emotions to convince the jury. As a whole group, brainstorm facts and reasons why Lizzie is guilty. Then, brainstorm emotional statements to convince the jury. Write students' responses such as the following on the board:

Why Lizzie Is Guilty
The maid might have helped Lizzie.

Appeal to the Emotions
Lizzie was heartless because she did not love her stepmother.

Have students return to Anthology pages 56–62 to find information.

Draft

Look at the first four lines of the Grading Rubric at the bottom of your page. Direct groups to follow this organization as they write drafts of the Prosecution Closing Argument. Each group member should choose one of the sections and write a paragraph about it. Assign point values, and have students write them in the rubric.

- Introduction to the judge and jury
- Overview of the crime
- Reasons Lizzie is the murderer
- Reasons why the jury must find her guilty

Revise

Have students reread their drafts, using the following revision steps. After each step, have students make the revisions and write their final paragraph.

- **Check the organization.** What paragraphs or sentences should you move so the information flows in the right order?
- **Check your purpose.** Did you address your topic? What facts and emotions can you add to convince the jury that Lizzie is guilty?
- **Check mechanics.** Do fragments or run-on sentences need to be rewritten? What words might be misspelled? Do all sentences begin with capital letters and end with proper punctuation?

Present

Have students in their "legal firms" combine their paragraphs for their Prosecution Closing Argument. Then, each group can rehearse the presentation before reading it to the class, which acts as the jury.

Assess

I will assess your closing arguments based on the rubric on your page. To assess students' closing arguments, use the rubric from the Writing Blackline Master.

Real-World Reading

Jury Summons

1. Direct students to Student Book pages 118 and 119. Tell students that one of a citizen's civic duties is to serve on a jury. **Our Constitution gives us the right to be judged by a jury of our peers. What are peers?** (Regarding a jury, they are people of the same legal status.) **A jury is a group of people picked at random who listens to court cases. What do you know about what jurors do?** (Jurors are citizens who listen to a trial and decide who is guilty or innocent.) **Where have you seen a juror before?** Allow students to describe jurors they have seen on TV or in a real courtroom. **When you receive a jury summons in the mail, it is important to follow the instructions.**

   Review the meanings of the following words with students and clarify their understanding:

   - **exemption** (n) *reason you can be excused*
   - **affidavit** (n) *signed legal statement*
   - **terminate** (v) *end something*
   - **summons** (n) *an order saying you must appear*

2. **Imagine you are an adult with a daytime job. You have received notice you must serve as a juror, which is jury duty. Take a few minutes to read this before I ask some questions.** Allow students to read the Jury Summons. Then, have students locate and highlight (have them circle the last bulleted question) the information that answers the following questions:

   - **How can you file an exemption if you need one?** (Complete the affidavit and mail or fax both sides to the court.)
   - **What will happen if you do not respond to the summons to go to jury duty?** (You will be fined.)
   - **Once you have served on a jury, how long can you be excused from future jury duty?** (24 months)
   - **What should you bring with you to the jury room? Circle this on the form.** (the entire summons)

   Instruct students to complete the Juror Information Form.

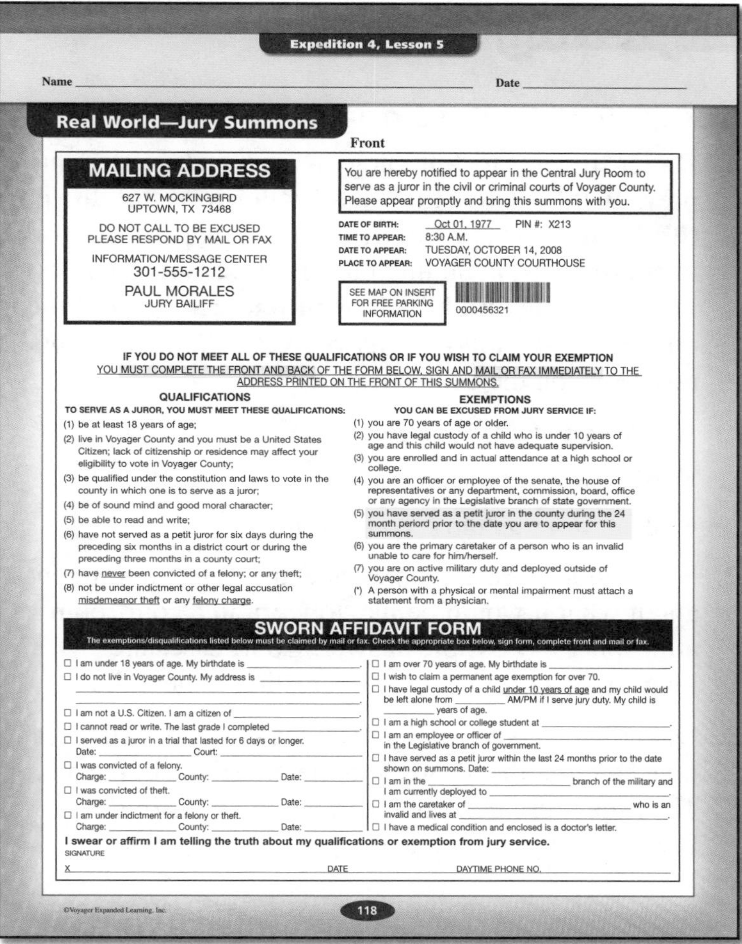

Expedition 4, Lesson 5

Name ______________________ Date ______________

Real World—Jury Summons

Front

MAILING ADDRESS

627 W. MOCKINGBIRD
UPTOWN, TX 73468

DO NOT CALL TO BE EXCUSED
PLEASE RESPOND BY MAIL OR FAX

INFORMATION/MESSAGE CENTER
301-555-1212

PAUL MORALES
JURY BAILIFF

You are hereby notified to appear in the Central Jury Room to serve as a juror in the civil or criminal courts of Voyager County. Please appear promptly and bring this summons with you.

DATE OF BIRTH: Oct 01, 1977 PIN #: X213
TIME TO APPEAR: 8:30 A.M.
DATE TO APPEAR: TUESDAY, OCTOBER 14, 2008
PLACE TO APPEAR: VOYAGER COUNTY COURTHOUSE

SEE MAP ON INSERT FOR FREE PARKING INFORMATION

0000456321

IF YOU DO NOT MEET ALL OF THESE QUALIFICATIONS OR IF YOU WISH TO CLAIM YOUR EXEMPTION
YOU MUST COMPLETE THE FRONT AND BACK OF THE FORM BELOW, SIGN AND MAIL OR FAX IMMEDIATELY TO THE ADDRESS PRINTED ON THE FRONT OF THIS SUMMONS.

QUALIFICATIONS

TO SERVE AS A JUROR, YOU MUST MEET THESE QUALIFICATIONS:

(1) be at least 18 years of age;
(2) live in Voyager County and you must be a United States Citizen; lack of citizenship or residence may affect your eligibility to vote in Voyager County;
(3) be qualified under the constitution and laws to vote in the county in which one is to serve as a juror;
(4) be of sound mind and good moral character;
(5) be able to read and write;
(6) have not served as a petit juror for six days during the preceding six months in a district court or during the preceding three months in a county court;
(7) have never been convicted of a felony; or any theft;
(8) not be under indictment or other legal accusation misdemeanor theft or any felony charge.

EXEMPTIONS

YOU CAN BE EXCUSED FROM JURY SERVICE IF:

(1) you are 70 years of age or older.
(2) you have legal custody of a child who is under 10 years of age and this child would not have adequate supervision.
(3) you are enrolled and in actual attendance at a high school or college.
(4) you are an officer or employee of the senate, the house of representatives or any department, commission, board, office or any agency in the Legislative branch of state government.
(5) you have served as a petit juror in the county during the 24 month periord prior to the date you are to appear for this summons.
(6) you are the primary caretaker of a person who is an invalid unable to care for him/herself.
(7) you are on active military duty and deployed outside of Voyager County.
(*) A person with a physical or mental impairment must attach a statement from a physician.

SWORN AFFIDAVIT FORM

The exemptions/disqualifications listed below must be claimed by mail or fax. Check the appropriate box below, sign form, complete front and mail or fax.

☐ I am under 18 years of age. My birthdate is ____________.
☐ I do not live in Voyager County. My address is ____________
____________.
☐ I am not a U.S. Citizen. I am a citizen of ____________.
☐ I cannot read or write. The last grade I completed ____________.
☐ I served as a juror in a trial that lasted for 6 days or longer.
Date: ________ Court: ________
☐ I was convicted of a felony.
Charge: ________ County: ________ Date: ________
☐ I was convicted of theft.
Charge: ________ County: ________ Date: ________
☐ I am under indictment for a felony or theft.
Charge: ________ County: ________ Date: ________

☐ I am over 70 years of age. My birthdate is ____________.
☐ I wish to claim a permanent age exemption for over 70.
☐ I have legal custody of a child under 10 years of age and my child would be left alone from ________ AM/PM if I serve jury duty. My child is ________ years of age.
☐ I am a high school or college student at ____________.
☐ I am an employee or officer of ____________ in the Legislative branch of government.
☐ I have served as a petit juror within the last 24 months prior to the date shown on summons. Date: ____________
☐ I am in the ____________ branch of the military and I am currently deployed to ____________.
☐ I am the caretaker of ____________ who is an invalid and lives at ____________.
☐ I have a medical condition and enclosed is a doctor's letter.

I swear or affirm I am telling the truth about my qualifications or exemption from jury service.

SIGNATURE

X ____________ DATE ____________ DAYTIME PHONE NO. ____________

118

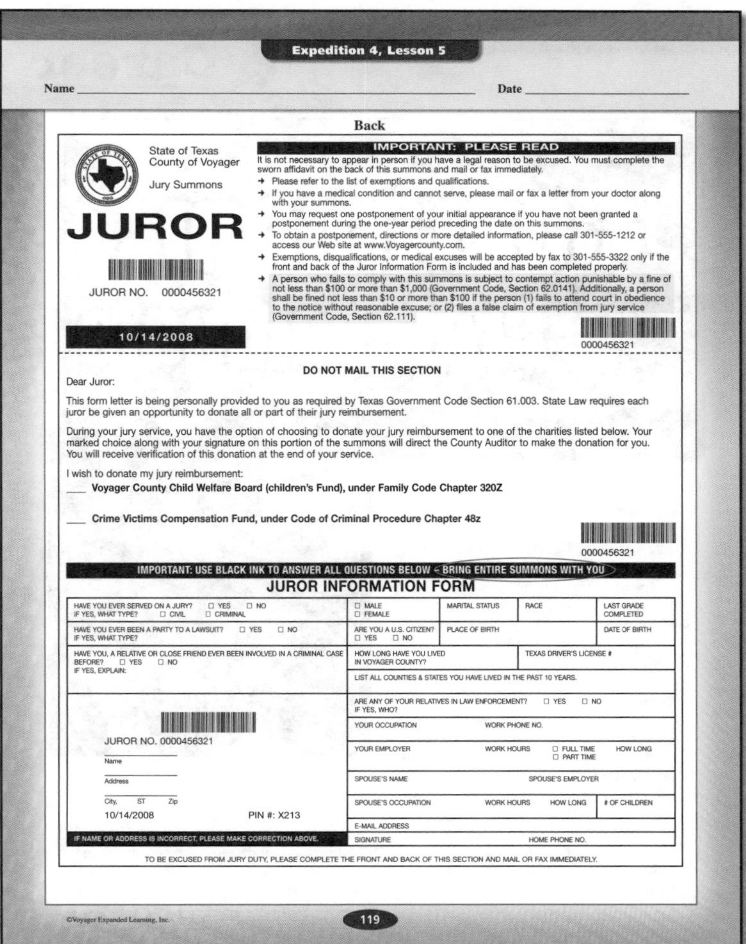

Expedition 4, Lesson 5

Name ______________________ Date ______________

Back

State of Texas
County of Voyager

Jury Summons

JUROR

JUROR NO. 0000456321

10/14/2008

IMPORTANT: PLEASE READ

It is not necessary to appear in person if you have a legal reason to be excused. You must complete the sworn affidavit on the back of this summons and mail or fax immediately.

→ Please refer to the list of exemptions and qualifications.
→ If you have a medical condition and cannot serve, please mail or fax a letter from your doctor along with your summons.
→ You may request one postponement of your initial appearance if you have not been granted a postponement during the one-year period preceding the date on this summons.
→ To obtain a postponement, directions or more detailed information, please call 301-555-1212 or access our Web site at www.Voyagercounty.com.
→ Exemptions, disqualifications, or medical excuses will be accepted by fax to 301-555-3322 only if the front and back of the Juror Information Form is included and has been completed properly.
→ A person who fails to comply with this summons is subject to contempt action punishable by a fine of not less than $100 or more than $1,000 (Government Code, Section 62.0141). Additionally, a person shall be fined not less than $10 or more than $100 if the person (1) fails to attend court in obedience to the notice without reasonable excuse; or (2) files a false claim of exemption from jury service (Government Code, Section 62.111).

0000456321

DO NOT MAIL THIS SECTION

Dear Juror:

This form letter is being personally provided to you as required by Texas Government Code Section 61.003. State Law requires each juror be given an opportunity to donate all or part of their jury reimbursement.

During your jury service, you have the option of choosing to donate your jury reimbursement to one of the charities listed below. Your marked choice along with your signature on this portion of the summons will direct the County Auditor to make the donation for you. You will receive verification of this donation at the end of your service.

I wish to donate my jury reimbursement:

___ **Voyager County Child Welfare Board (children's Fund), under Family Code Chapter 320Z**

___ **Crime Victims Compensation Fund, under Code of Criminal Procedure Chapter 48z**

0000456321

IMPORTANT: USE BLACK INK TO ANSWER ALL QUESTIONS BELOW – BRING ENTIRE SUMMONS WITH YOU

JUROR INFORMATION FORM

HAVE YOU EVER SERVED ON A JURY? ☐ YES ☐ NO
IF YES, WHAT TYPE? ☐ CIVIL ☐ CRIMINAL

☐ MALE ☐ FEMALE | MARITAL STATUS | RACE | LAST GRADE COMPLETED

HAVE YOU EVER BEEN A PARTY TO A LAWSUIT? ☐ YES ☐ NO
IF YES, WHAT TYPE?

ARE YOU A U.S. CITIZEN? ☐ YES ☐ NO | PLACE OF BIRTH | DATE OF BIRTH

HAVE YOU, A RELATIVE OR CLOSE FRIEND EVER BEEN INVOLVED IN A CRIMINAL CASE BEFORE? ☐ YES ☐ NO
IF YES, EXPLAIN:

HOW LONG HAVE YOU LIVED IN VOYAGER COUNTY? | TEXAS DRIVER'S LICENSE #

LIST ALL COUNTIES & STATES YOU HAVE LIVED IN THE PAST 10 YEARS.

ARE ANY OF YOUR RELATIVES IN LAW ENFORCEMENT? ☐ YES ☐ NO
IF YES, WHO?

YOUR OCCUPATION | WORK PHONE NO.

YOUR EMPLOYER | WORK HOURS | ☐ FULL TIME ☐ PART TIME | HOW LONG

SPOUSE'S NAME | SPOUSE'S EMPLOYER

SPOUSE'S OCCUPATION | WORK HOURS | HOW LONG | # OF CHILDREN

E-MAIL ADDRESS

SIGNATURE | HOME PHONE NO.

JUROR NO. 0000456321

Name

Address

City, ST Zip

10/14/2008 PIN #: X213

IF NAME OR ADDRESS IS INCORRECT, PLEASE MAKE CORRECTION ABOVE.

TO BE EXCUSED FROM JURY DUTY, PLEASE COMPLETE THE FRONT AND BACK OF THIS SECTION AND MAIL OR FAX IMMEDIATELY.

119

Exploring Careers

Courtroom Professionals

1. Direct students to Anthology page 63. Have students preview the photos, title, and headings. **What do you think this passage will be about?** (people who work in courtrooms, including bailiffs and court reporters) **Turn the title and headings into questions and focus on finding the answers as you read.** Write students' responses on the board, such as:
   - *Who are courtroom professionals?*
   - *What are the tasks of a bailiff?*
   - *What does a court reporter do?*
2. Have students read the passage and make an inference about what it would be like to work in a courtroom atmosphere. (Possible answer: Court cases are interesting so it would be interesting to hear them.)
3. Direct students to Student Book page 120. Tell them they can find the answers to the questions in the text. They may research other careers in books or online. Have students complete the page.

Expedition 4, Lesson 5

Name ______________________ Date ____________

Exploring Careers: Courtroom Professionals

A. Answer the following questions about careers in the courtroom.

1. Who are some professionals that work in a courtroom?
   bailiff; attorney; judge; court reporter
2. What responsibility does a bailiff have?
   The bailiff protects the people in the courtroom and ensures that the judge's orders are followed and that jurors follow the rules.
3. What is the average yearly salary for a bailiff in the United States?
   around $50,000
4. What is the average length of time that a court reporter is in training?
   2–3 years
5. Contrast the skills needed to be a court reporter with those of a bailiff.
   A court reporter must have a specific skill to type with great speed and accuracy, while the bailiff must know the rules of the courtroom and work with different people to keep order.

B. Use the Internet to research other possible career choices in this field and complete the chart.

Career	
Responsibilities	
Education Required	
Average Salary	
Is this a career you might pursue?	
Why or why not?	
Career	
Responsibilities	
Education Required	
Average Salary	
Is this a career you might pursue?	
Why or why not?	

120

Career

Courtroom Professionals

Many people work in the United States legal system to ensure that all Americans receive a fundamental right when charged with a crime: to be judged by a jury of their peers. Most people expect the professionals in a courtroom trial to be the judge, the defendant's attorney, and the prosecution. Many others are also important to the trial. Two such positions are the bailiff and the court reporter.

Bailiff

The bailiff prepares the courtroom for use, making sure necessary items are in place for the trial. These include everything from paper and pencils to pitchers of water. The bailiff protects the people in the courtroom and in the courthouse. He or she might wear a uniform and carry a gun. He or she makes sure everyone follows the judge's orders and follows the rules. If someone causes a disturbance in the courtroom, the bailiff can make that person leave. The bailiff takes care of the jurors' needs when they are deliberating, or deciding, the verdict. He or she makes sure no one has contact with the jurors. The bailiff also receives the verdict

One of the bailiff's duties is swearing in witnesses.

Criminology 63

Career

from the jury and presents it to the court clerk for reading.

People who apply for the position of bailiff must be U.S. citizens, at least 21 years old with a high school diploma or GED certificate. They must be in good physical condition, and their weight should be proportionate to their height. Several pre-employment tests, aptitude screenings, and psychological examinations, as well as a background investigation, may be required. As a trusted officer of the court, bailiffs are expected to have a good reputation and moral character. Depending on the state or county, new hires will successfully complete a basic corrections officer's program, which may be up to five weeks long. As of 2008, a bailiff's salary ranged from $30,000 to $40,000 a year.

Court Reporter

Every trial has a court reporter who uses a special machine to record every word said during the trial. The machine has 22 special keys that allow the court reporter, also called a stenographer, to capture what everyone says by pressing key combinations. Today's machines then translate the keys into words. Years ago, the stenographer would have to transcribe the typed shorthand by retyping it in words. The court reporter may also use abbreviations. It's similar to text messaging except the stenographer can type up to 240 words per minute. That is much faster than most people type.

Anyone who has graduated from high school and completed an accredited court reporting school program can become a court reporter. It takes some time to develop this skill, and some court reporting college programs can be 2,700 class hours. During that time, a skilled stenographer may record almost 39 million words! It takes the average student two to three years to complete the program. Court reporter salaries range from $30,000 to $40,000 a year according to 2008 statistics. Some stenographers are freelance, charging an hourly rate as companies hire them. Courtrooms are not the only place you will find stenographers. Some companies use them to record meetings.

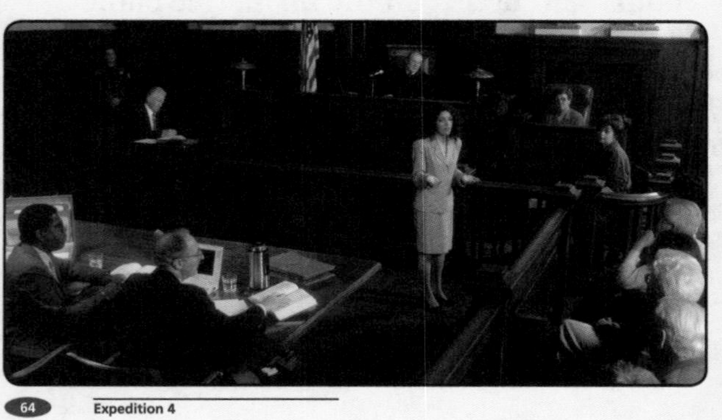

64 Expedition 4

English Language Learner Overview

The ELL signals when extra support is provided to students during the lesson. As needed, use the Blackline Masters for English language learners. For vocabulary, students also may use the online technology component to practice Expedition words or other content-area vocabulary and designated ELL word sets.

Introduce Vocabulary

Lesson 6

Distribute six index cards to each student. Have students write one vocabulary word from Lesson 6 on each card. Read aloud each definition and model how you would remember the meaning. ***Nominal*** **means "very little in amount." It makes me think of "not very much." So I will write that on the card.** Have students write or draw a clue on each card to help them remember the meaning. Provide students with the following sentences. Have them choose words from the cards to complete each sentence.

Before the trial, a jury cannot _______ someone is guilty. (presume)

The driver _______ his car into the small parking space. (wedged)

Some old advertisements _______ people about what products could do. (deceived)

The cost of a bag of chips is _______. (nominal)

Our team arrived an hour late, so we had to _______ the soccer game. (forfeit)

The rumor that the concert would be free turned out to be a _______. (fraud)

Lesson 8

Have students give the part of speech of each vocabulary word. On the board, write *Nouns, Adjectives,* and *Adverbs*. List words under the correct heading. **A noun is a person, place, thing, or idea.** ***Labyrinth*** **is a noun. Is a** ***labyrinth*** **a person, place, thing, or idea?** (thing)

An adjective is a word that describes a noun. The adjective ***grave*** **can describe different nouns. Would you describe a birthday party as** ***grave*****?** (no) **Why not?** (Because a birthday party is a happy occasion.) Repeat this process with the adjectives *shabby* and *stagnant*.

An adverb is a word that describes a verb or an adjective. Would you listen ***keenly*** **if you wanted to understand something that was being said?** (yes) **Why?** (Listening keenly means listening with sharpness and sensitivity.) Repeat this process with *merely*.

Practice Vocabulary

In Lesson 7, provide support for the context words *candidate* and *perceive*. **A** ***candidate*** **is someone who may be elected or chosen for a job. If there are two** ***candidates*** **for a job, will both** ***candidates*** **get the job?** (no) **How can we tell which** ***candidate*** **is best for a job?** Write the following sentence starter on the board: *The best candidate is* _______. (hardworking; qualified)

When you ***perceive*** **something, you use one of your five senses. I** ***perceive*** **that you are upset because I see you crying. How do you** ***perceive*** **that something in the oven is burning?** (You smell it burning or see smoke.) Write the following sentence starter on the board: *I perceive that it is morning because* _______. (I see the sun rising; I hear the alarm clock ringing and birds chirping; I smell breakfast cooking.)

In Lesson 9, provide support for the context words *contemplation* and *animated*. ***Contemplation*** **is the act of thinking about something. It takes me a few days of** ***contemplation*** **to make a big decision. Think about different decisions you have made. Which decisions needed** ***contemplation*****?** (important or difficult decisions) Write the following sentence frame on the board: *A decision to* _______ *requires contemplation.* (move to another town)

Something that is ***animated*** **moves around a lot. If I said that a person was very** ***animated*****, what might that person be doing?** (moving their hands; pacing the room) Write the following sentence starter on the board: *Someone who is animated is <u>not</u>* _______. (sitting still)

Apply the Target Skill: Story Elements

For students who need additional practice identifying story elements, Blackline Master page 24 asks them to match story elements with their definitions. Have students read the story and identify its elements.

Apply the Target Skill: Story Elements and Inference

Provide support and practice for making inferences. Have students work with a partner to create questions about the mystery and use text evidence to make inferences. Have students reflect on how their inferences help them understand the mystery.

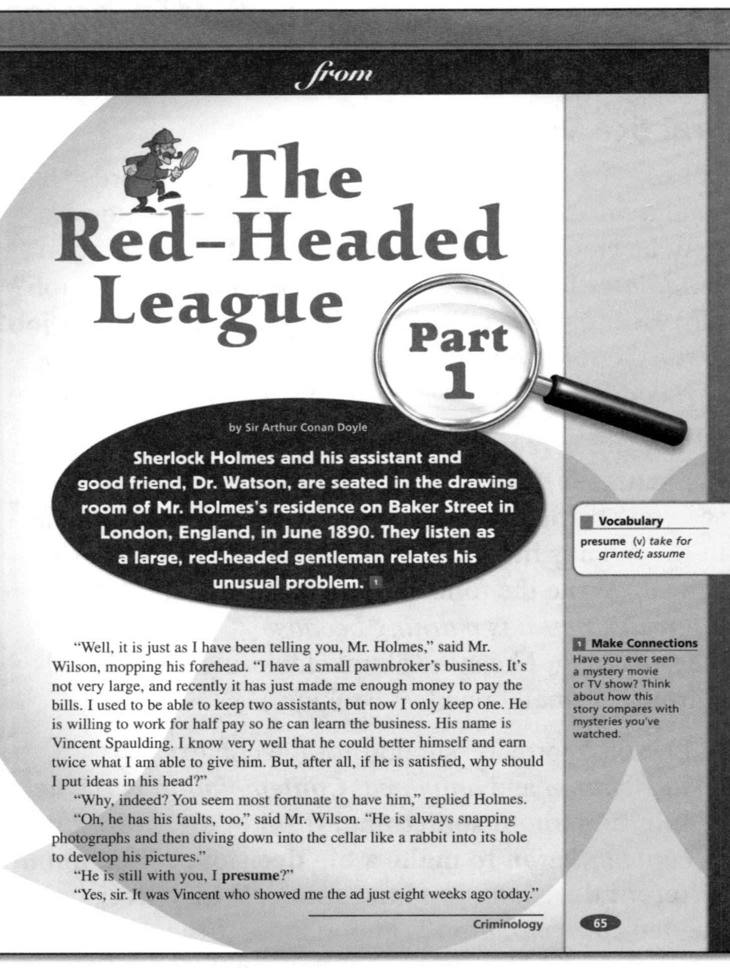

from

The Red-Headed League

Part 1

by Sir Arthur Conan Doyle

Sherlock Holmes and his assistant and good friend, Dr. Watson, are seated in the drawing room of Mr. Holmes's residence on Baker Street in London, England, in June 1890. They listen as a large, red-headed gentleman relates his unusual problem. 1

"Well, it is just as I have been telling you, Mr. Holmes," said Mr. Wilson, mopping his forehead. "I have a small pawnbroker's business. It's not very large, and recently it has just made me enough money to pay the bills. I used to be able to keep two assistants, but now I only keep one. He is willing to work for half pay so he can learn the business. His name is Vincent Spaulding. I know very well that he could better himself and earn twice what I am able to give him. But, after all, if he is satisfied, why should I put ideas in his head?"

"Why, indeed? You seem most fortunate to have him," replied Holmes.

"Oh, he has his faults, too," said Mr. Wilson. "He is always snapping photographs and then diving down into the cellar like a rabbit into its hole to develop his pictures."

"He is still with you, I **presume**?"

"Yes, sir. It was Vincent who showed me the ad just eight weeks ago today."

Vocabulary
presume (v) *take for granted; assume*

1 Make Connections
Have you ever seen a mystery movie or TV show? Think about how this story compares with mysteries you've watched.

Vocabulary
wedged (v) *forced your way into or through*

2 Summarize
This is part of a larger story. Stop every so often to summarize what you have read. What do you know so far?

"Here's another vacancy on the League of the Red-Headed Men, says he. It's worth quite a little fortune to any man who gets it."

"Why, what is it, then, an opening?" I asked.

"You've never heard of the League of the Red-Headed Men?" he asked. "The League was founded by an American millionaire. He was himself red-headed. When he died, he left his fortune to provide easy jobs to men whose hair is of that color. It is splendid pay and very little to do." 2

"Vincent Spaulding seemed to know so much about it. So we shut the business up and started off for the address.

"I hope I never see such a sight again, Mr. Holmes. Every man who had a shade of red in his hair had tramped into the city to answer the advertisement. Fleet Street was choked with red-headed folk, and Pope's Court looked like a sea of oranges. We **wedged** in as well as we could and soon found ourselves in the office.

"A small man with a head that was even redder than mine said a few words to each candidate, then he always managed to find some fault in these men who seemed qualified for the position. Getting a vacancy did not seem to be such a very easy matter, after all. However, when our turn came the little man closed the door as we entered.

"This is Mr. Jabez Wilson," said my assistant, "and he is willing to fill a vacancy in the League."

"And he is admirably suited for it," the other answered. "He has every requirement." He took a step backward and gazed at my hair. Then suddenly he plunged forward, shook my hand, and congratulated me warmly on my success.

"You will, however, I am sure, excuse me for taking an obvious precaution," he said. With that he seized my hair in both his hands, and tugged until I yelled with the pain. "There is water in your eyes," said he as he released me. "I perceive from your tears, that all is as it should be. But we have to be careful, for we have twice been **deceived** by wigs and once by paint." He stepped over to the window and shouted that the vacancy was filled. The folk all trooped away in different directions until there was not a red head to be seen except my own and that of the manager. 3

"My name," said he, "is Mr. Duncan Ross. When shall you be able to start?"

"Well, it is a little awkward, for I have a business already," said I.

"Oh, never mind about that, Mr. Wilson!" said Vincent Spaulding. "I should be able to look after that for you."

"What would be the hours?" I asked.

"Ten to two."

"Now a pawnbroker's business is mostly done on an evening, Mr. Holmes, especially Thursday and Friday evening, which is just before payday; so it would suit me very well to earn a little in the mornings. Besides, I knew that my assistant was a good man, and that he would see to anything that turned up.

"That would suit me very well," said I. "And the pay?"

"Is 4 pounds a week."

"And the work?"

"Is purely **nominal**."

"What do you call purely nominal?"

"Well, you have to be in the office, or at least in the building, the whole time. If you leave, you **forfeit** your whole position forever."

"And the work?"

"Is to copy out the Encyclopedia Britannica. You must find your own ink, pens, and blotting paper, but we provide this table and chair. Will you be ready tomorrow?"

Vocabulary
deceived (v) *fooled or tricked; misled*
nominal (adj) *trifling; insignificant*
forfeit (v) *have to give up or lose something because of a failure to do something*

3 Visualization
Mr. Wilson has begun telling his story of his experience with Vincent Spaulding. Picture in your mind the scene as it is described.

Vocabulary
fraud (n) *an act of deceiving or misrepresenting; a trick*

4 Inference
Why would Mr. Wilson think this? What in the text helps you make your inferences?

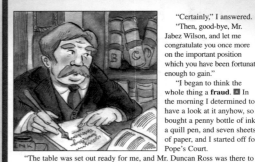

"Certainly," I answered.

"Then, good-bye, Mr. Jabez Wilson, and let me congratulate you once more on the important position which you have been fortunate enough to gain."

"I began to think the whole thing a **fraud**. 4 In the morning I determined to have a look at it anyhow, so I bought a penny bottle of ink, a quill pen, and seven sheets of paper, and I started off for Pope's Court.

"The table was set out ready for me, and Mr. Duncan Ross was there to see that I started my work without any problems. He started me off upon the letter A, and then he left me; but he would drop in from time to time. At two o'clock he told me good-bye and locked the door of the office after me.

"This went on day after day, Mr. Holmes, and on Saturday the manager came in and plunked down four golden coins for my week's work.

"Eight weeks passed like this. I had written about Abbots and Archery and Armour. And then suddenly the whole business came to an end."

"To an end?"

"Yes, sir. And no later than this morning. I went to my work as usual at ten o'clock, but the door was shut and locked, with a sign. Here, you can read for yourself."

The Red-Headed League is Dissolved. October 9, 1890

He held up a piece of white cardboard. Sherlock Holmes and I surveyed this announcement until the comical side of the affair completely overcame us. We both burst out into a roar of laughter.

"I cannot see there is anything very funny," cried our client, his red face flushing up to the roots of his flaming head.

"No, no," cried Holmes. "I really wouldn't miss your case for the world. But, there is something just a little funny about it. What steps did you take when you found the card?"

"I called at the offices round, but none of them seemed to know anything about it. The landlord said the red-headed man I knew as Duncan Ross moved out yesterday. He said he had never heard of the Red-Headed League."

"Your case is an exceedingly remarkable one," said Holmes, "and I shall be happy to look into it." End

"The Red-Headed League," Part 1

Before Reading

Introduce Vocabulary

1. Have students turn to Student Book page 121 and scan the boldfaced vocabulary words. Read aloud the vocabulary words, and have students rate their knowledge of each word.
2. Ask students to share what they know about any words they rated with 3.
3. Read the part of speech, definition, and example sentence for each word. **Do the meanings match what you first thought?**
4. Read aloud the instructions for Part B. Have students complete the activity independently. Ask students to share their responses.

Refer to Blackline Master page 23 to extend vocabulary practice.

Have students use the *Passport Reading Journeys* online technology component to practice and reinforce vocabulary and comprehension skills.

Introduce the Target Skill: Story Elements

1. Write the words *story elements* on the board. Ask students to name a TV show and tell who is in it and when and where it takes place. **Every TV show you named had people or characters and a setting. They took place at a particular place and time. If I ask you what the show was about, you would tell what happened. That is the plot.** Write *characters, setting,* and *plot* below *story elements* on the board. **All stories have these story elements.**
2. **Plots have a beginning, middle, and end as well as a problem that results in a solution.**

Introduce the Passage

1. Have students preview "The Red-Headed League," Part 1 by looking at the title and illustrations. **What clues tell you what the passage is about?**

Expedition 4, Lesson 6

Name ______ Date ______

Vocabulary

"The Red-Headed League," Part 1

A. Rate your knowledge of each boldfaced word.
3 familiar word
2 somewhat familiar word
1 unknown word

☐ **presume** (v) *take for granted; assume*
Detectives should not *presume* to know anything before they hear all the facts.

☐ **wedged** (v) *forced your way into or through*
They *wedged* their way through the crowd to get to the office door.

☐ **deceived** (v) *fooled or tricked; misled*
Unfortunately, some people *deceived* others to get a job.

☐ **nominal** (adj) *trifling; insignificant*
Most people would not think that copying an entire encyclopedia is *nominal* work.

☐ **forfeit** (v) *have to give up or lose something because of a failure to do something*
If leaving the room meant I would *forfeit* my bonus money, I would stay put.

☐ **fraud** (n) *an act of deceiving or misrepresenting; a trick*
If someone wanted to pay me to copy the dictionary by hand, I would think it was a *fraud*.

B. Read each statement. Circle either true or false for each statement.

1. If you pay a **nominal** amount for something, you pay a lot. true (false)
2. If you lose a concert ticket, you **forfeit** the chance to attend. (true) false
3. When witnesses **deceived** the court, they told the truth. true (false)
4. If you **wedged** into the crowded room, you would be outside. true (false)
5. When you **presume** something, you believe it to be true. (true) false
6. If you win a contest through **fraud**, you win fairly. true (false)

 121

Vocabulary

presume (v) *take for granted; assume*
Detectives should not *presume* to know anything before they hear all the facts.

wedged (v) *forced your way into or through*
They *wedged* their way through the crowd to get to the office door.

deceived (v) *fooled or tricked; misled*
Unfortunately, some people *deceived* others to get a job.

nominal (adj) *trifling; insignificant*
Most people would not think that copying an entire encyclopedia is *nominal* work.

forfeit (v) *have to give up or lose something because of a failure to do something.*
If leaving the room meant I would *forfeit* my bonus money, I would stay put.

fraud (n) *an act of deceiving or misrepresenting; a trick*
If someone wanted to pay me to copy the dictionary by hand, I would think it was a *fraud*.

(the illustrations, the title) **Who is the author?** (Sir Arthur Conan Doyle) **What kind of story do you think this passage is? Why?** (fiction, probably a mystery; the illustration shows a magnifying glass.) Explain that Sir Arthur Conan Doyle was the famous author of many mysteries. Sherlock Holmes and Dr. Watson are the primary characters in his mysteries.

2. Remind students that the margin prompts will help focus their attention on the story and guide their understanding.
3. Teach these terms from the passage:
    - *League* means "a group of people with a certain purpose."
    - A *drawing room* is a living room. A *residence* means where someone lives.
    - *Ink* and *blotting* paper refer to the liquid used in quill pens, and the thick paper used to soak up blobs of ink.
    - *Pounds* is the main British unit of money, similar to the U.S. dollar.
    - *Flushing up to the roots of his flaming head* means "blushing so hard his face looked as red as his hair."

During Reading

1. To select reading options that support your students' levels and classroom needs, see Reading Differentiation, page xxxii, if needed.
2. As students read, have them complete Part A of the story map on Student Book page 122 to identify the characters and setting. Part B will be completed in Lesson 7.

After Reading

Check Comprehension

1. Have students check their responses in Part A of Student Book page 122 as you ask the questions.
    - **Who are the main characters in this story?** (Mr. Holmes, Mr. Wilson, Mr. Spaulding, Dr. Watson, and Mr. Ross)
    - **Where and when does the story take place?** (London, England; June 1890; drawing room) **You will complete the story map in another lesson.**

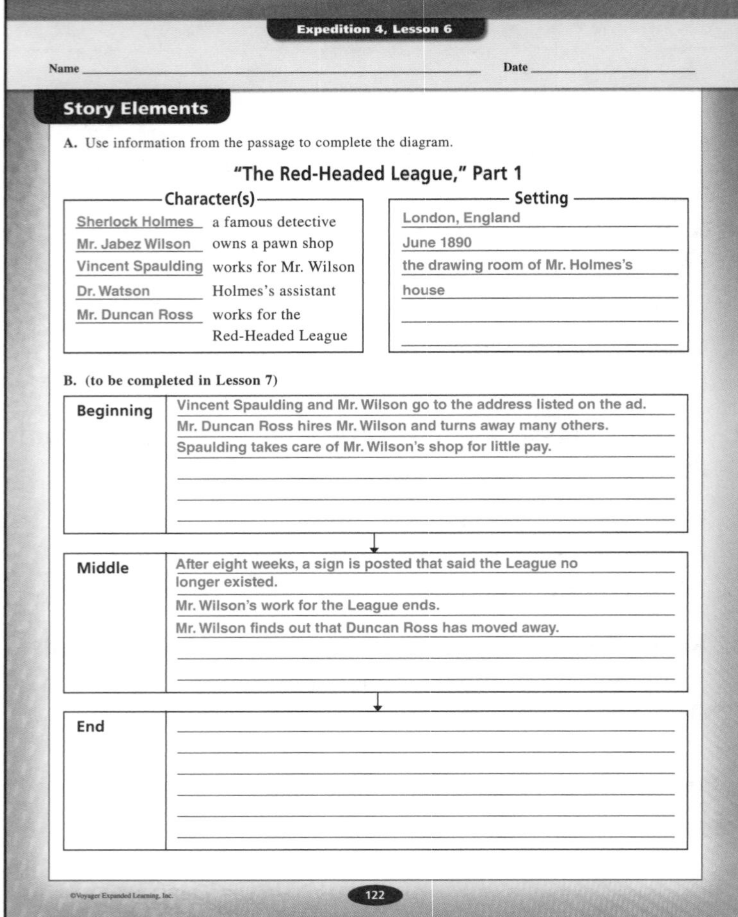

Expedition 4, Lesson 6

Name ______ Date ______

Story Elements

A. Use information from the passage to complete the diagram.

"The Red-Headed League," Part 1

Character(s)	
Sherlock Holmes	a famous detective
Mr. Jabez Wilson	owns a pawn shop
Vincent Spaulding	works for Mr. Wilson
Dr. Watson	Holmes's assistant
Mr. Duncan Ross	works for the Red-Headed League

Setting
London, England
June 1890
the drawing room of Mr. Holmes's house

B. (to be completed in Lesson 7)

Beginning	Vincent Spaulding and Mr. Wilson go to the address listed on the ad. Mr. Duncan Ross hires Mr. Wilson and turns away many others. Spaulding takes care of Mr. Wilson's shop for little pay.
Middle	After eight weeks, a sign is posted that said the League no longer existed. Mr. Wilson's work for the League ends. Mr. Wilson finds out that Duncan Ross has moved away.
End	

©Voyager Expanded Learning, Inc. 122

- **What is the Red-Headed League? Who joins it?** (a club whose purpose is to provide easy jobs to men with red hair; Mr. Jabez Wilson, a business owner)
- **What is the story problem?** (Mr. Wilson worked for the Red-Headed League until it was suddenly dissolved. No one has heard of it.)
- **What do you predict will happen in Part 2? Why?** (Sherlock Holmes will solve the mystery of what happened to the Red-Headed League. He says he will look into it.)

2. Ask students to share their visualizations from Anthology page 67.
3. Have students share their responses to the Inference margin prompt on Anthology page 68.

ACADEMIC SKILL Tell students that they can make inferences about the events that happen during a certain time and place when they read social studies texts.

Remind students to choose books from the *Passport Reading Journeys* Library for independent reading.

"The Red-Headed League," Part 1

Prepare to Reread

Introduce the Lesson

Tell students they will reread Part 1 of "The Red-Headed League" and review story elements.

Practice Vocabulary

1. Have students respond to the following questions.
   - **What does Mr. Holmes *presume*?** (Vincent Spaulding is still working for Mr. Wilson.)
   - **Where were Mr. Wilson and Mr. Spaulding *wedged* when they answered the ad?** (Fleet Street outside of the League office)
   - **The people at the League worried they might be *deceived* by whom?** (people applying who did not really have red hair)
   - **Why would Mr. Wilson want to do *nominal* work?** (because he had another job as a pawnbroker)
   - **What action would cause Mr. Wilson to *forfeit* the position with the League?** (leaving the building during work hours)
   - **Why did Mr. Wilson think the position was a *fraud*?** (The work was unnecessary, and the rules were unusual and strict.)
2. Remind students that they can use context clues to find the meanings of unknown words. Have students turn to Anthology page 66. **What do you think the word *vacancy* means?** (open job) **What clues in the text help you figure out the meaning?** (ad; an opening)
   - **candidate** (n) *person applying for a position*, Anthology page 66
   - **perceive** (v) *understand*, Anthology page 67
   - **comical** (adj) *funny*, Anthology page 68
   - **flushing** (v) *blushing*, Anthology page 68
3. Have students turn to Student Book page 123. Read Part A aloud, then have students complete the page.

Expedition 4, Lesson 7

Name ______ Date ______

Word Building

A. A noun is a person, place, thing, or idea. A verb shows action. An adjective modifies, or describes, a noun. Below are variations of your vocabulary words. Think about the meanings you know for the vocabulary words in blue. Notice the base word in each variation. Prefixes or suffixes have changed the base words to different parts of speech.

Nouns	Verbs	Adjectives
deceit	deceived	deceptive
fraud	defraud	fraudulent
presumption	presume	presumptuous

B. Choose from the list in Part A to complete the sentences. Use each word only once.

1. I __presume__ by your surprised look that you didn't know about this. (verb)
2. Duncan Ross would __defraud__ his own mother to make easy money. (verb)
3. His plan is a common but __deceptive or fraudulent__ practice that has fooled many people. (adjective)
4. His __fraudulent or deceptive__ offer sounds too good to be true, so many people fall for it. (adjective)
5. Personally, I think he was being __presumptuous__ when he thought he could fool you. (adjective)
6. Ross __deceived__ people because they didn't consider the facts. (verb)
7. The man is so sincere and charming that people don't expect to find __deceit__ at the core of his plan. (noun)
8. You could have determined his entire offer was a __fraud__. (noun)
9. Look carefully at the facts next time before making a __presumption__ that the offer is genuine. (noun)

©Voyager Expanded Learning, Inc. 123

Reread

Apply the Target Skill: Story Elements

1. **As you read "The Red-Headed League," Part 1 today, look for the key events in the story.** Have students turn to Student Book page 122 and complete Part B as they reread. **In the last lesson, we listed the characters in the story as we read. Looking carefully at the events and using what you know will help you make inferences to solve the mystery.**
2. When students finish reading, ask them to share the events they listed.
3. Have students use information from the text to make inferences and begin to solve the mystery.
   - **What inference can you make about why Mr. Wilson was chosen for the Red-Headed League?** As students share possible inferences, have them identify the evidence in the text that supports their inferences.

(Possible response: They were specifically looking for Mr. Wilson. Text evidence: No one else was qualified, and they didn't interview him.)

- **What inferences can you make about the job Mr. Wilson is doing for the Red-Headed League?** (They want to keep Mr. Wilson away from his store from 10 to 2. Text evidence: Mr. Ross was emphatic that Mr. Wilson had to stay in the building from 10 to 2.) The job and the Red-Headed League are a fraud. (Text evidence: Both are useless, and no one would pay that much to copy the encyclopedia.)

Refer to Blackline Master page 24 to extend practice with story elements and inference.

Write in Response to Reading

1. Have students turn to Student Book page 124. **Do you think the position with the Red-Headed League was a fraud? Why?** (Yes, the work was too easy and paid too much.) Have students read the instructions and write an advertisement that Duncan Ross may have placed in the newspaper.
2. **You can imagine more about the characters based on what you know from the passage.** Have students read the Part B instructions and write the messages.

EXPEDITION ORGANIZER **Criminology**

Pause to have students turn to Student Book pages 100 and 101. Have students complete the following:

- Write answers or notes below one or more of the probing questions. Encourage them to write a question of their own.
- Think about their own idea from "The Red-Headed League," Part 1. Tell students to write it in the appropriate oval in Part B.

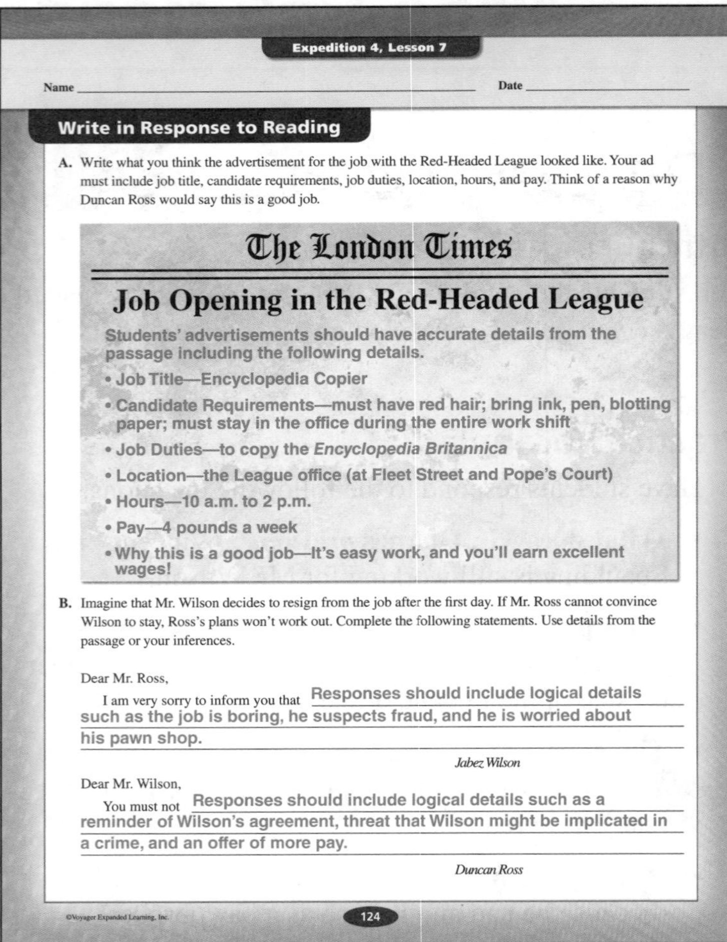

Expedition 4, Lesson 7

Name ______________ Date ______________

Write in Response to Reading

A. Write what you think the advertisement for the job with the Red-Headed League looked like. Your ad must include job title, candidate requirements, job duties, location, hours, and pay. Think of a reason why Duncan Ross would say this is a good job.

The London Times

Job Opening in the Red-Headed League

Students' advertisements should have accurate details from the passage including the following details.
- Job Title—Encyclopedia Copier
- Candidate Requirements—must have red hair; bring ink, pen, blotting paper; must stay in the office during the entire work shift
- Job Duties—to copy the *Encyclopedia Britannica*
- Location—the League office (at Fleet Street and Pope's Court)
- Hours—10 a.m. to 2 p.m.
- Pay—4 pounds a week
- Why this is a good job—It's easy work, and you'll earn excellent wages!

B. Imagine that Mr. Wilson decides to resign from the job after the first day. If Mr. Ross cannot convince Wilson to stay, Ross's plans won't work out. Complete the following statements. Use details from the passage or your inferences.

Dear Mr. Ross,

I am very sorry to inform you that Responses should include logical details such as the job is boring, he suspects fraud, and he is worried about his pawn shop.

Jabez Wilson

Dear Mr. Wilson,

You must not Responses should include logical details such as a reminder of Wilson's agreement, threat that Wilson might be implicated in a crime, and an offer of more pay.

Duncan Ross

©Voyager Expanded Learning, Inc. 124

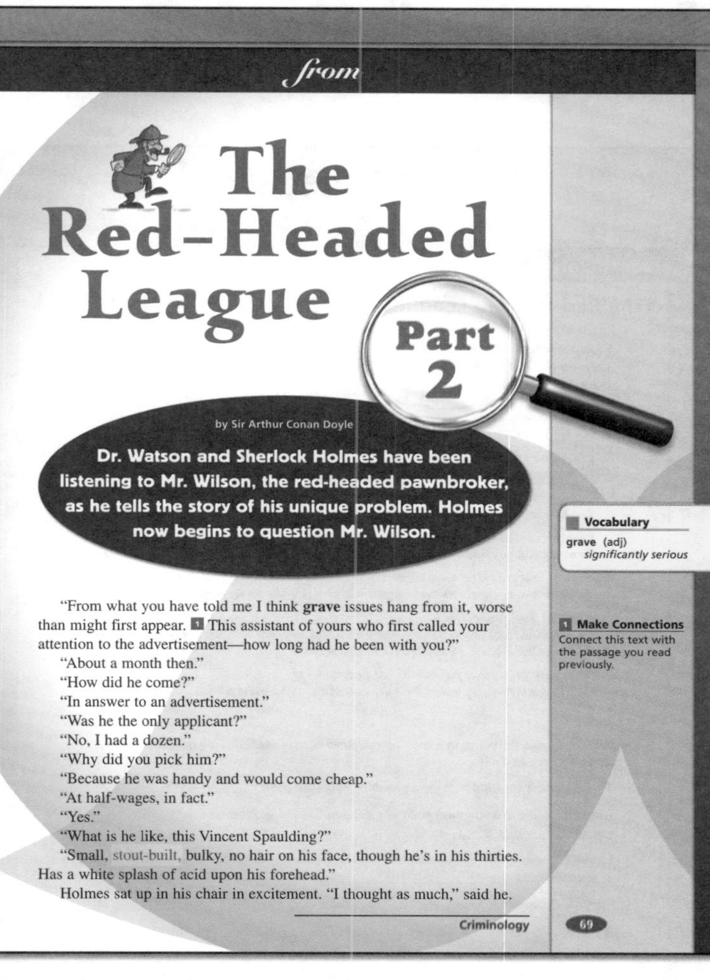

from

The Red-Headed League Part 2

by Sir Arthur Conan Doyle

Dr. Watson and Sherlock Holmes have been listening to Mr. Wilson, the red-headed pawnbroker, as he tells the story of his unique problem. Holmes now begins to question Mr. Wilson.

Vocabulary
grave (adj) *significantly serious*

"From what you have told me I think **grave** issues hang from it, worse than might first appear. [1] This assistant of yours who first called your attention to the advertisement—how long had he been with you?"

1 Make Connections
Connect this text with the passage you read previously.

"About a month then."

"How did he come?"

"In answer to an advertisement."

"Was he the only applicant?"

"No, I had a dozen."

"Why did you pick him?"

"Because he was handy and would come cheap."

"At half-wages, in fact."

"Yes."

"What is he like, this Vincent Spaulding?"

"Small, stout-built, bulky, no hair on his face, though he's in his thirties. Has a white splash of acid upon his forehead."

Holmes sat up in his chair in excitement. "I thought as much," said he.

Vocabulary
shabby (adj) *run-down; falling apart*
keenly (adv) *being sharp and quick*
merely (adv) *only; no more than*
stagnant (adj) *not active*

"Have you ever observed that his ears are pierced for earrings?"

"Yes, sir. He told me a gypsy had done it for him when he was a lad."

"That will do, Mr. Wilson. I shall be happy to give you an opinion upon the subject in a day or two. Today is Saturday, and I hope that by Monday we may come to a conclusion."

We traveled to Saxe-Coburg Square. A brown board with "JABEZ WILSON" upon a corner house announced the place where our red-headed client carried on his business. Sherlock Holmes walked slowly up the **shabby** street and then down again to the corner, still looking **keenly** at the dingy houses. [2] Finally he returned to the pawnbroker's, and, having thumped vigorously upon the pavement with his walking stick two or three times, he went up to the door and knocked. It was instantly opened by a bright-looking, clean-shaven young fellow.

2 Visualize
Make a mental picture of the scene. What do you see?

"I only wished to ask you how you would go from here to the Strand," said Holmes.

"Third right, fourth left," answered the assistant promptly, closing the door.

"Smart fellow, that," observed Holmes as we walked away.

"Evidently," said I, "Mr. Wilson's assistant counts for a good deal in this mystery of the Red-Headed League. I am sure that you inquired your way **merely** so you might see him."

"Not him."

"What then?"

"The knees of his trousers."

"And what did you see on his pants?"

"What I expected to see."

"Why did you beat the pavement?"

"My dear doctor, this is a time for observation, not for talk. We know something of Saxe-Coburg Square. Let us now explore the parts which lie behind it."

We turned round the corner to one of the main streets of the City. The line of fine shops and stately businesses abutted on the other side bordering the faded and **stagnant** square which we had just left.

"Let me see," said Holmes. "There is Mortimer's, the little newspaper shop, the Coburg branch of the City and Suburban Bank, the Vegetarian Restaurant, and McFarlane's carriage building depot. That carries us right on to the other block. [3]

3 Summarize
What do you know about the mystery so far?

"This business at Coburg Square is serious," Holmes said. "A considerable crime is in contemplation and it has been considered for quite some time. I believe we shall be in time to stop it. I shall want your help tonight."

"At what time?"

"Ten will be early enough."

"I shall be at Baker Street at ten."

"Very well. And, I say, Doctor, there may be some little danger, so kindly put your army revolver in your pocket."

It was a quarter past nine when I made my way to Baker Street. I found

Vocabulary
labyrinth (n) *a place full of intricate passageways*

Holmes in animated conversation, his hand moving about as he talked with two men, one of whom I recognized as Peter Jones, the official police agent. The other man was a stranger to me.

"Ha! Our party is complete," said Holmes, buttoning up his peajacket and taking his heavy hunting crop from the rack. "Watson, I think you know Mr. Jones of Scotland Yard? Let me introduce you to Mr. Merryweather, who is to be our companion in tonight's adventure."

"It is the first Saturday night for seven-and-twenty years that I have not had my card game," said Mr. Merryweather.

"I think you will find," said Sherlock Holmes, "that you will play for a higher stake tonight than you have ever done yet, and the play will be more exciting. For you, Mr. Merryweather, the stake will be some 30,000 pounds; and for you, Jones, it will be the man upon whom you wish to lay your hands." [4]

4 Ask Questions
What questions do you still need answers to before you can solve the mystery?

We rattled through an endless **labyrinth** of gaslit streets until we emerged into Farrington Street.

"This fellow Merryweather is a bank director and personally interested in the matter," my friend remarked.

We had reached the same crowded main street in which we had found ourselves in the morning. Mr. Merryweather stopped to light a lantern and conducted us down a dark, earth-smelling passage into a huge vault, or cellar, which was piled all round with crates and massive boxes. [5] End

5 Summarize
Explain to your partner how the new events affect your understanding of the events in the previous passage.

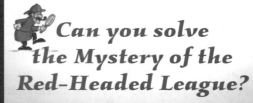

Can you solve the Mystery of the Red-Headed League?

"The Red-Headed League," Part 2

Before Reading

Introduce Vocabulary

1. Have students turn to Part A on Student Book page 125. **Scan the boldfaced vocabulary words to determine if you've seen, heard, or read any of these words that you'll read in the second part of this mystery.** Read aloud the instructions and have students complete Part A.
2. **Which number did you use most? least? There are many ways to learn new words. Everyone is exposed to vocabulary from sources in and out of school: on TV, in music, and in everyday conversations.**
3. Discuss words with 1 ratings. Tell students to pay special attention to those words as you read aloud each definition, part of speech, and example sentence. For each word, ask, **Did the meaning and example match what you already knew about the word? Why or why not?** Have students complete Part B.

Refer to Blackline Master page 25 to extend vocabulary practice.

Students may use the *Passport Reading Journeys* online technology component to practice and reinforce vocabulary and comprehension skills.

Apply the Target Skill: Story Elements and Inference

1. List the following story elements on the board and briefly review the meaning of each.
   - **characters**—who the story is about
   - **setting**—time and place the story takes place
   - **plot**—main events
   - **problem**—struggle or conflict between characters that needs a solution
2. **When you read a story, you can use plot events to make inferences about what the story does not directly tell you. You can find details, add them to what you already know, and make an inference.**

Expedition 4, Lesson 8

Name ______________________ Date ______________

Vocabulary

"The Red-Headed League," Part 2

A. Write one or more numbers next each boldfaced word to show how well you know it.

5 I use it in everyday conversation.
4 I heard it on TV or on the radio.
3 I heard or used it in school.
2 I read it in a book, magazine, or online.
1 I have not read, heard, or used this word.

☐ **grave** (adj) *significantly serious*
Somehow Holmes knew this was a *grave* situation and called the police.

☐ **shabby** (adj) *run-down; falling apart*
The pawnbroker's store looked *shabby* compared with newer stores on the other street.

☐ **keenly** (adv) *being sharp and quick*
Sherlock Holmes is always looking *keenly* at the evidence and seldom misses a clue.

☐ **merely** (adv) *only; no more than*
Dr. Watson was *merely* trying to figure out why Holmes spoke to the man.

☐ **stagnant** (adj) *not active*
The street in front of the pawnbroker's shop was *stagnant* compared with when they went to see about the vacancy in the Red-Headed League.

☐ **labyrinth** (n) *a place full of intricate passageways*
Dr. Watson was easily lost in the *labyrinth* of the cellar passageways.

B. Now, you will read the words in a new context. Read each of the following questions. Then, write the answers on the lines.

1. Would a **grave** situation be a car accident or a football game? a car accident
2. Would the water in a **stagnant** pond be clear and fresh or greenish and dirty? greenish and dirty
3. Lila said, "Aunt Molly **merely** laughed when I accidentally broke her vase." Was Aunt Molly angry or unconcerned? unconcerned
4. Would a **shabby** coat be new and clean or old and worn? old and worn
5. If you tried to get out of a **labyrinth**, would you have to walk in a long, straight path or take many turns? take many turns
6. If you looked **keenly** at a painting, would you be concentrating or not paying attention? concentrating

125

Vocabulary

grave	(adj) *significantly serious* Somehow Holmes knew this was a *grave* situation and called the police.
shabby	(adj) *run-down; falling apart* The pawnbroker's store looked *shabby* compared with newer stores on the other street.
keenly	(adv) *being sharp and quick* Sherlock Holmes is always looking *keenly* at the evidence and seldom misses a clue.
merely	(adv) *only; no more than* Dr. Watson was *merely* trying to figure out why Holmes spoke to the man.
stagnant	(adj) *not active* The street in front of the pawnbroker's shop was *stagnant* compared with when they went to see about the vacancy in the Red-Headed League.
labyrinth	(n) *a place full of intricate passageways* Dr. Watson was easily lost in the *labyrinth* of the cellar passageways.

Read Anthology page 69 aloud. Model making an inference by saying: **I read the detail that Spaulding was willing to work for much less money than other applicants. I already know that people do not offer to work for little money, so I can make the inference that Spaulding was determined to get that job for a secret reason.**

3. **Why does Holmes become excited on page 69?** Guide students to make this inference:

   Details: Holmes guessed correctly that Spaulding had a white mark on his forehead.

   What You Know: Famous detectives know about and meet many criminals.

   Inference: Spaulding is a criminal whom Holmes knows of or has met.

Introduce the Passage

1. Have students preview the passage by reading the introduction on Anthology page 69 and then reading the red script at the bottom of page 72. **What does the author want the reader to do?** (figure out the solution to the mystery) **What do you see in the illustrations on pages 71 and 72?**
2. Direct students' attention to the margin prompts. Remind them to stop for these reading guides and think about the text as they read. Also, tell them to read the vocabulary definitions in the margin if they forget the meaning of a word.
3. Teach these terms from the passage:
   - *Would come cheap* means "I wouldn't have to pay him much."
   - *Scotland Yard* is the London police department headquarters.
   - *Seven-and-twenty* means "27."

ELL Students may not be familiar with TV detective stories. Have students provide examples of crime stories they know. List their responses on the board. Tell students to give their opinions about which stories they think are the most interesting and why.

During Reading

1. To select reading options that support your students' levels and classroom needs, see Reading Differentiation, page xxxii, if needed.
2. Have students read "The Red-Headed League," Part 2, paying close attention to the characters, setting, and plot.

After Reading

Check Comprehension

1. **Reread the Visualize margin prompt on Anthology page 70.** Have students draw the image they have from their reading, then share their work with the class. **How does your mental picture add to what you read?** (Students should describe the shabby houses and shops on a dim city street in the 1800s, including Wilson's pawn shop.)
2. Ask individuals to share their responses to the Summarize margin prompt on Anthology page 71. **What other important ideas would you add to the summary?** (Possible answer: After Holmes investigates the pawnbroker's street, he taps on the sidewalk and asks Spaulding a question so he can look at his knees. They see the bank backs up to the pawnbroker's shop. Holmes arranges to go to the bank's cellar that night with the bank director and Peter Jones from Scotland Yard. Therefore, the Red-Headed League was not the crime. Something else is happening.)

ACADEMIC SKILL Remind students that they can make inferences when they read other texts. **In history you can make inferences to determine the causes of particular events.**

Remind students to choose books from the *Passport Reading Journeys* Library for independent reading.

"The Red-Headed League," Part 2

Prepare to Reread

Introduce the Lesson

Tell students that they will make inferences to solve "The Red-Headed League" mystery.

Practice Vocabulary

1. Write *grave*, *shabby*, and *stagnant* on the board. **An adjective describes something.** Read the following definitions, and ask students to supply other uses.
   - ***Grave* describes a serious issue or problem. What are two other things that *grave* can describe?**
   - ***Shabby* describes a run-down street. What are two other things that *shabby* can describe?**
   - ***Stagnant* describes a quiet, still town square where there's no activity. What are two other things that *stagnant* can describe?**

   Write *keenly* and *merely* on the board. **Some adverbs tell how something is done.**
   - ***Keenly* describes how carefully Sherlock Holmes looked at the dingy houses. What are two other actions that *keenly* can describe?**
   - **Dr. Watson thinks that Holmes *merely* inquired. What is another way to say that?** (Holmes only asked. Holmes just asked.)

   Write *labyrinth* on the board. **Some nouns name places or things.**
   - **In the passage, a *labyrinth* describes streets that twist and turn. What are two other things that are like a *labyrinth*?** (a maze; a long, twisting tunnel)
2. Have students turn to Anthology page 69. Reread the last three paragraphs. **What do you think the phrase *stout-built* means?** (fat; not thin) **Find clues in the text that help you figure out the meaning. How do the clues help you?** (Bulky defines *stout-built*.) Repeat this process for the following words.
   - **trousers** (n) *pants*, Anthology page 70
   - **abutted** (v) *next to; alongside of,* Anthology page 70
   - **in contemplation:** *intended; expected to happen*, Anthology page 71
   - **animated** (adj) *excited; lively*, Anthology page 72

Expedition 4, Lesson 9

Name ______________________ Date ____________

Word Building

A. By adding *-ly* to a word, you change it to an adverb, meaning the way in which something is done. Read the paragraph, then add *-ly* to the following words to complete the paragraph. The first one is done for you.

loud	glad	keen	animated	complete	fortunate

It was Friday evening at Central Bank. After a long week, the workers had gladly gone home. Later that night, the alarm rang loudly. Within minutes, squad cars roared up. People walking by the bank were completely surprised when a burglar ran out. Fortunately, the police arrived just in time to catch the burglar. Some witnesses had keenly observed the burglar. They told the officers important details. On Monday morning, the workers returned to the bank. They all talked animatedly about the attempted burglary.

B. Change each word into an adverb. Use the correct adverb to complete the sentence.

grave	*significantly serious*	gravely
mysterious	*very hard to explain or understand*	mysteriously
cautious	*being careful; using caution*	cautiously
sly	*crafty; secretive*	slyly
serious	*solemn; thoughtful*	seriously

1. Jack slyly crept down the hall to avoid being seen.
2. Jack saw a shadow mysteriously move across the wall.
3. He became gravely aware of footsteps following him.
4. He seriously thought his life was in danger.
5. Being very careful, he cautiously proceeded down the hall.

C. Use a boldfaced word from Part B and write a sentence explaining what Jack saw.
Answers will vary.

©Voyager Expanded Learning, Inc. 126

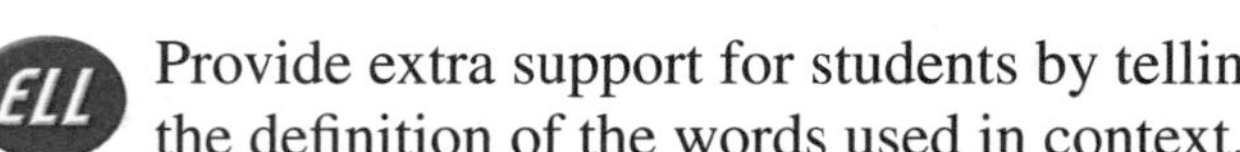

ELL Provide extra support for students by telling them the definition of the words used in context.

3. Have students turn to Student Book page 126. Read aloud the instructions. Have students complete the activity, then share responses with partners.

Reread

Apply the Target Skill: Story Elements and Inference

1. Have students turn to Student Book page 127. **Who are the new characters in Part 2?** (Peter Jones, a policeman and Mr. Merryweather, a bank director)
2. **Reread the passage and fill in the beginning, middle, and end events of Part 2. Be sure to note the change in setting.**
3. When students finish, discuss the main events. **What inference can you make about why Holmes asks Mr. Merryweather to meet him and the police?** (Holmes suspects a bank robbery.)

4. **What is the solution to the mystery?** (Spaulding and Ross have been digging a tunnel from the pawn shop's cellar to the bank vault to steal the money.) **What clues led you to that solution?** (The shop is behind the bank. They trick Wilson to get him out of his pawn shop. Holmes taps on the street and looks at Spaulding's knees because he suspects the man is digging a tunnel.)

Write in Response to Reading

1. Have students turn to Student Book page 128. **When you change one event in the plot, the story may end differently.** Have students read the instructions and complete the new ending.
2. Have partners use details in the text to draw their maps for Part B.

EXPEDITION ORGANIZER **Criminology**

Pause to have students turn to Student Book pages 100 and 101. Have students complete the following:

- Write answers or notes below one or more of the probing questions. Encourage them to write a question of their own.
- Think about their own idea from "The Red-Headed League," Part 2. Tell students to write it in the appropriate oval in Part B and complete the center oval.

Build Background DVD 4.2
Briefly discuss the Expedition passages. Then, watch the DVD together. After watching, review student responses to the probing questions using the Expedition Organizer.

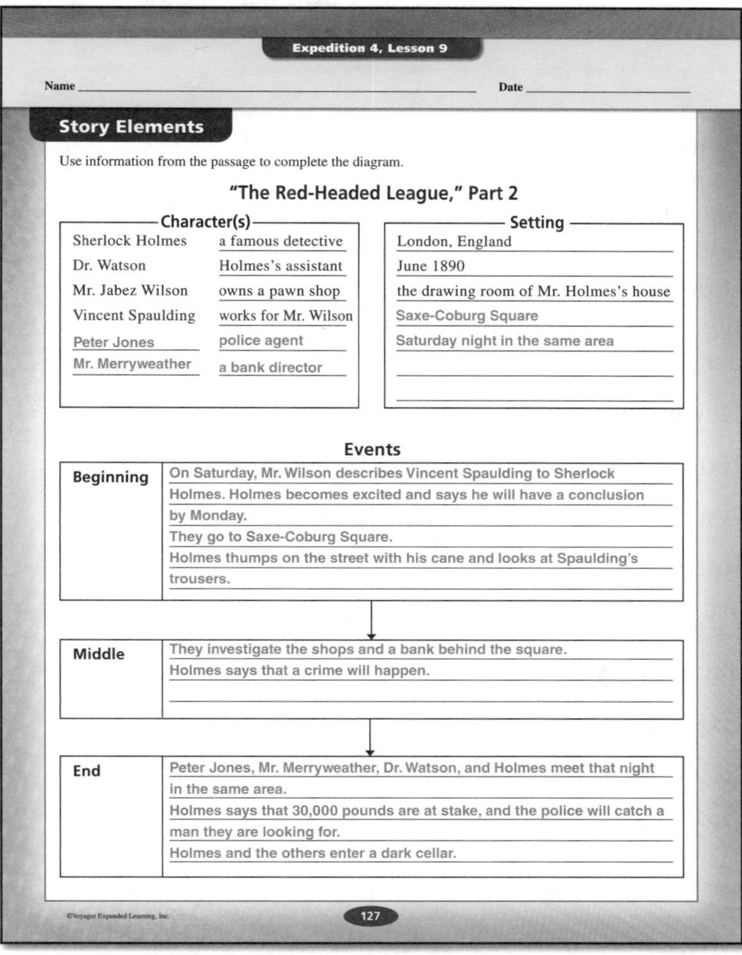

Expedition 4, Lesson 9

Name ______ Date ______

Story Elements

Use information from the passage to complete the diagram.

"The Red-Headed League," Part 2

Character(s)		Setting
Sherlock Holmes	a famous detective	London, England
Dr. Watson	Holmes's assistant	June 1890
Mr. Jabez Wilson	owns a pawn shop	the drawing room of Mr. Holmes's house
Vincent Spaulding	works for Mr. Wilson	Saxe-Coburg Square
Peter Jones	police agent	Saturday night in the same area
Mr. Merryweather	a bank director	

Events

Beginning	On Saturday, Mr. Wilson describes Vincent Spaulding to Sherlock Holmes. Holmes becomes excited and says he will have a conclusion by Monday. They go to Saxe-Coburg Square. Holmes thumps on the street with his cane and looks at Spaulding's trousers.
Middle	They investigate the shops and a bank behind the square. Holmes says that a crime will happen.
End	Peter Jones, Mr. Merryweather, Dr. Watson, and Holmes meet that night in the same area. Holmes says that 30,000 pounds are at stake, and the police will catch a man they are looking for. Holmes and the others enter a dark cellar.

©Voyager Expanded Learning, Inc. 127

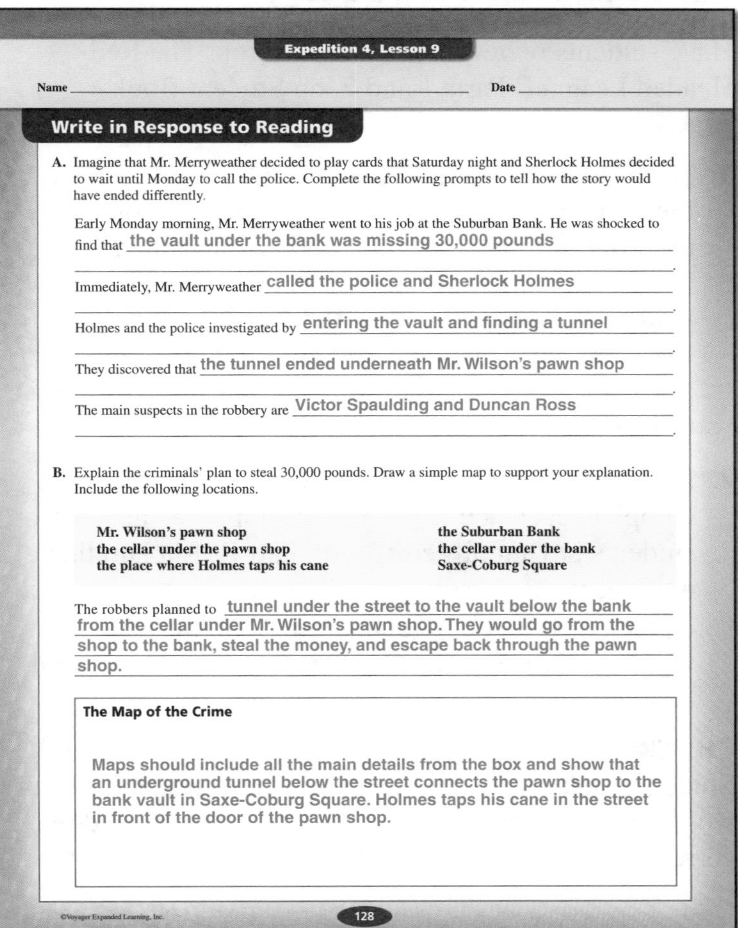

Expedition 4, Lesson 9

Name ______ Date ______

Write in Response to Reading

A. Imagine that Mr. Merryweather decided to play cards that Saturday night and Sherlock Holmes decided to wait until Monday to call the police. Complete the following prompts to tell how the story would have ended differently.

Early Monday morning, Mr. Merryweather went to his job at the Suburban Bank. He was shocked to find that the vault under the bank was missing 30,000 pounds.

Immediately, Mr. Merryweather called the police and Sherlock Holmes.

Holmes and the police investigated by entering the vault and finding a tunnel.

They discovered that the tunnel ended underneath Mr. Wilson's pawn shop.

The main suspects in the robbery are Victor Spaulding and Duncan Ross.

B. Explain the criminals' plan to steal 30,000 pounds. Draw a simple map to support your explanation. Include the following locations.

Mr. Wilson's pawn shop	the Suburban Bank
the cellar under the pawn shop	the cellar under the bank
the place where Holmes taps his cane	Saxe-Coburg Square

The robbers planned to tunnel under the street to the vault below the bank from the cellar under Mr. Wilson's pawn shop. They would go from the shop to the bank, steal the money, and escape back through the pawn shop.

The Map of the Crime

Maps should include all the main details from the box and show that an underground tunnel below the street connects the pawn shop to the bank vault in Saxe-Coburg Square. Holmes taps his cane in the street in front of the door of the pawn shop.

©Voyager Expanded Learning, Inc. 128

Review, Extend, Assess

In today's lesson, as in Lessons 5 and 10 of every Expedition, there are options from which to choose. You may do any or all of the options listed. Activities for each option are given on the following pages. Each option will support or extend previously taught objectives. Choose the option(s) appropriate for your students and prepare accordingly.

Review Vocabulary

Extend Vocabulary

Assess Comprehension and Vocabulary

Reteach

Passport Reading Journeys Library

Technology

Expedition Project

Real-World Reading

Exploring Careers

Review Vocabulary

Have students review the vocabulary for "The Red-Headed League," Parts 1 and 2, on Student Book page 101.

1. Have students turn to Student Book page 129. Tell them that in the passages, the vocabulary words are used in the context of a Sherlock Holmes mystery. **Now you will use the vocabulary in different contexts. Remember that the words will have the same meanings. As you complete the review activity, check the definitions to make sure you use the words correctly.**
2. Read the instructions aloud and have students complete each activity. Provide support as needed for students having difficulty with Part B. Explain that a noun names a person, place, or thing. A thing may be an idea or something intangible. A verb is an action word, and actions include thinking and other mental actions. An adjective describes a noun.

CHECKPOINT Have students share their answers for Student Book page 129. For Part B, have students use the words in sentences to check that they have selected the correct part of speech for each word.

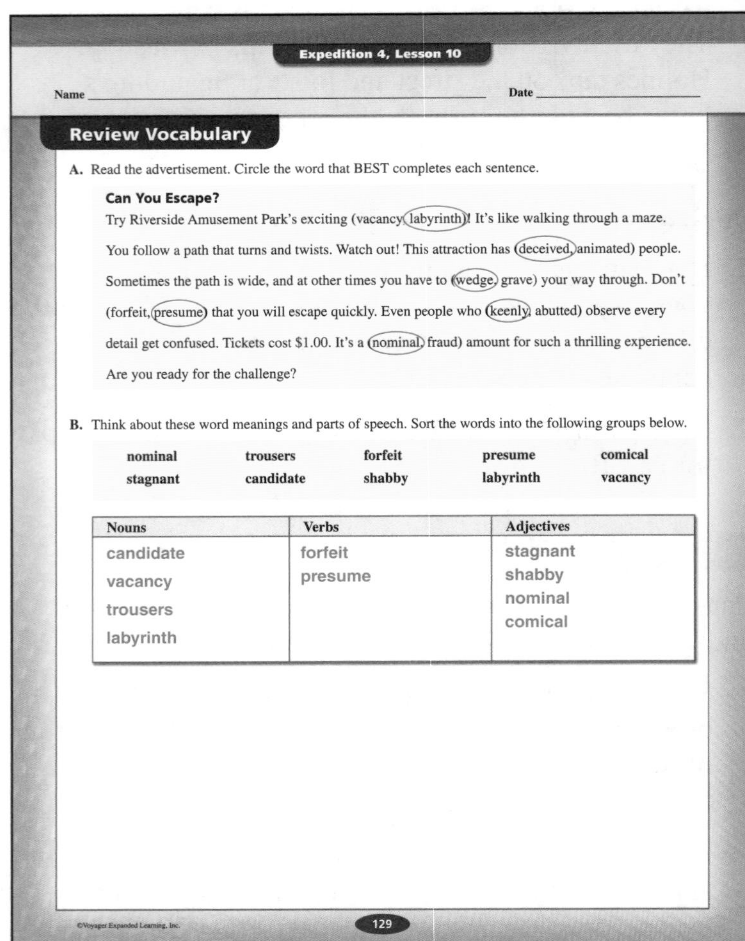
Expedition 4, Lesson 10

Name ______ Date ______

Review Vocabulary

A. Read the advertisement. Circle the word that BEST completes each sentence.

Can You Escape?

Try Riverside Amusement Park's exciting (vacancy, labyrinth)! It's like walking through a maze. You follow a path that turns and twists. Watch out! This attraction has (deceived, animated) people. Sometimes the path is wide, and at other times you have to (wedge, grave) your way through. Don't (forfeit, presume) that you will escape quickly. Even people who (keenly, abutted) observe every detail get confused. Tickets cost $1.00. It's a (nominal, fraud) amount for such a thrilling experience. Are you ready for the challenge?

B. Think about these word meanings and parts of speech. Sort the words into the following groups below.

nominal	trousers	forfeit	presume	comical
stagnant	candidate	shabby	labyrinth	vacancy

Nouns	Verbs	Adjectives
candidate	forfeit	stagnant
vacancy	presume	shabby
trousers		nominal
labyrinth		comical

129

Extend Vocabulary

1. Direct students to Student Book page 130. **Some words have more than one meaning. When a word doesn't make sense in a sentence, it might have a different meaning in addition to the one you know.** Have students tell two definitions of *mean*. (to state or signify; nasty, bad-tempered)
2. Have students read the instructions and complete Part A. For Part B, have students tell where they have heard these words. (in conversation, in school texts, on TV or the radio)

CHECKPOINT When students share their answers, listen for errors that are common to several students. Pause to explain and correct the answers.

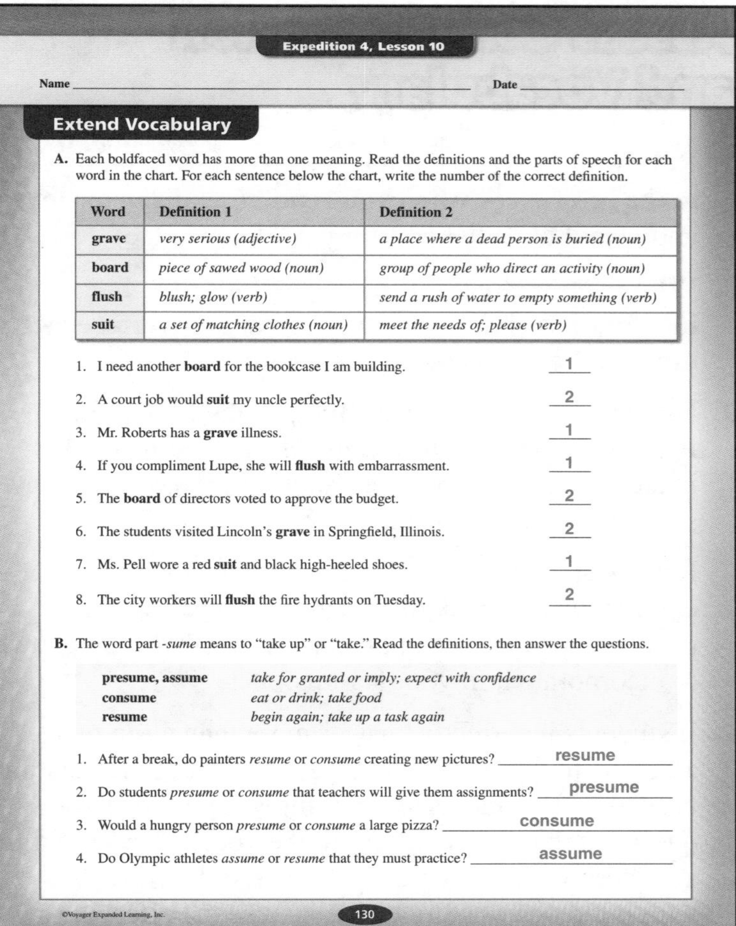

Expedition 4, Lesson 10

Name ________ Date ________

Extend Vocabulary

A. Each boldfaced word has more than one meaning. Read the definitions and the parts of speech for each word in the chart. For each sentence below the chart, write the number of the correct definition.

Word	Definition 1	Definition 2
grave	*very serious (adjective)*	*a place where a dead person is buried (noun)*
board	*piece of sawed wood (noun)*	*group of people who direct an activity (noun)*
flush	*blush; glow (verb)*	*send a rush of water to empty something (verb)*
suit	*a set of matching clothes (noun)*	*meet the needs of; please (verb)*

1. I need another **board** for the bookcase I am building. 1
2. A court job would **suit** my uncle perfectly. 2
3. Mr. Roberts has a **grave** illness. 1
4. If you compliment Lupe, she will **flush** with embarrassment. 1
5. The **board** of directors voted to approve the budget. 2
6. The students visited Lincoln's **grave** in Springfield, Illinois. 2
7. Ms. Pell wore a red **suit** and black high-heeled shoes. 1
8. The city workers will **flush** the fire hydrants on Tuesday. 2

B. The word part *-sume* means to "take up" or "take." Read the definitions, then answer the questions.

presume, assume	*take for granted or imply; expect with confidence*
consume	*eat or drink; take food*
resume	*begin again; take up a task again*

1. After a break, do painters *resume* or *consume* creating new pictures? resume
2. Do students *presume* or *consume* that teachers will give them assignments? presume
3. Would a hungry person *presume* or *consume* a large pizza? consume
4. Do Olympic athletes *assume* or *resume* that they must practice? assume

130

Part A

1. Distribute eight index cards to each student. Read aloud the two definitions for the word *grave*. Have students draw an illustration for each of the two meanings on separate cards. Repeat the process for the other multiple-meaning words.
2. Point out the Spanish cognate *grave*, meaning "very serious." **The Spanish word *grave* /gro veh/ can mean "very serious." However, the Spanish word does not mean "a place where a dead person has been buried."**
3. Read the instructions for Part A. Read the sentences aloud, and have students show the card with the correct response.

Part B

1. Write the words *presume, assume, consume,* and *resume* on the board. Underline the word part *-sume* in each word and emphasize its meaning.
2. Have students read each question aloud. Direct them to reread the definitions of the two word choices. Model your thought process by asking questions such as the following: **After a break, would a painter begin painting pictures again?** (yes) **After a break, would a painter eat or drink new pictures?** (no)

Assess Comprehension and Vocabulary

1. Review how to make inferences. **What do you use to make inferences when you read?** (details in the text and what I already know, or prior knowledge)

2. **When you make inferences, you "fill in" information that is not in the text. Your inferences must make sense, or be reasonable.**

3. Direct students to Student Book pages 131–133. Preview the pages, showing students that they will make reasonable inferences about brief passages. Have students complete the pages.

   Review student answers. Whenever possible, provide elaborative feedback to student responses. Refer to page xl for examples of elaborative feedback and how to incorporate it in your lessons.

   If students incorrectly answer more than 4 out of 15 assessment questions, evaluate what kind of reteaching is needed. If students are missing vocabulary questions, have them return to the vocabulary activities and work with the words they missed. For errors with inference or story elements, use the reteaching suggestions on page 169.

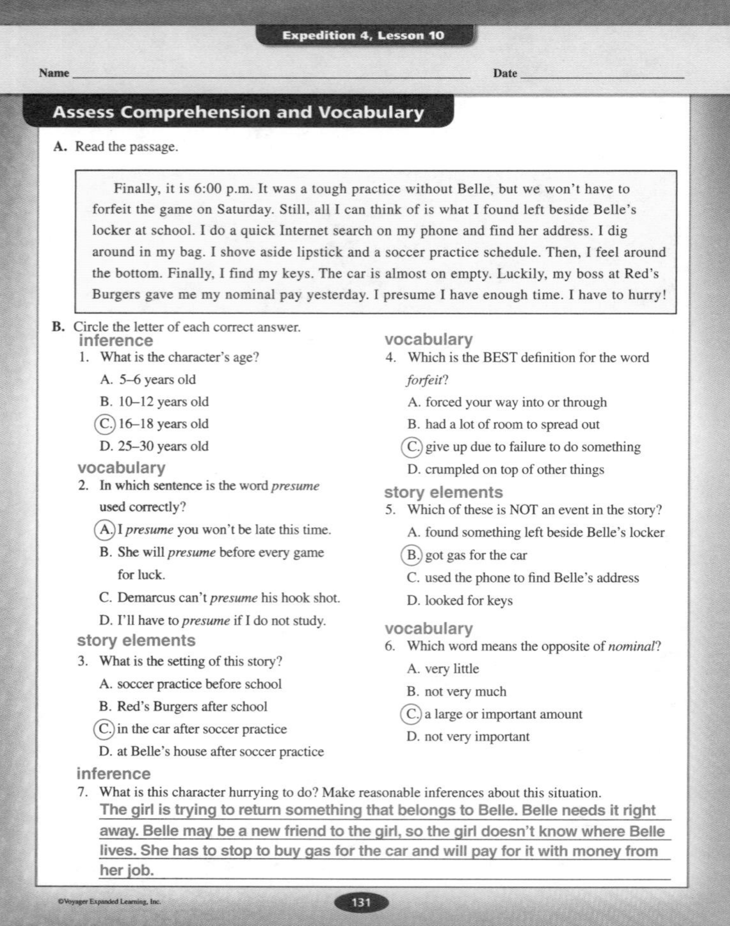

Expedition 4, Lesson 10

Name ______ Date ______

Assess Comprehension and Vocabulary

A. Read the passage.

> Finally, it is 6:00 p.m. It was a tough practice without Belle, but we won't have to forfeit the game on Saturday. Still, all I can think of is what I found left beside Belle's locker at school. I do a quick Internet search on my phone and find her address. I dig around in my bag. I shove aside lipstick and a soccer practice schedule. Then, I feel around the bottom. Finally, I find my keys. The car is almost on empty. Luckily, my boss at Red's Burgers gave me my nominal pay yesterday. I presume I have enough time. I have to hurry!

B. Circle the letter of each correct answer.

inference
1. What is the character's age?
   A. 5–6 years old
   B. 10–12 years old
   (C.) 16–18 years old
   D. 25–30 years old

vocabulary
2. In which sentence is the word *presume* used correctly?
   (A.) I *presume* you won't be late this time.
   B. She will *presume* before every game for luck.
   C. Demarcus can't *presume* his hook shot.
   D. I'll have to *presume* if I do not study.

story elements
3. What is the setting of this story?
   A. soccer practice before school
   B. Red's Burgers after school
   (C.) in the car after soccer practice
   D. at Belle's house after soccer practice

vocabulary
4. Which is the BEST definition for the word *forfeit*?
   A. forced your way into or through
   B. had a lot of room to spread out
   (C.) give up due to failure to do something
   D. crumpled on top of other things

story elements
5. Which of these is NOT an event in the story?
   A. found something left beside Belle's locker
   (B.) got gas for the car
   C. used the phone to find Belle's address
   D. looked for keys

vocabulary
6. Which word means the opposite of *nominal*?
   A. very little
   B. not very much
   (C.) a large or important amount
   D. not very important

inference
7. What is this character hurrying to do? Make reasonable inferences about this situation.
   The girl is trying to return something that belongs to Belle. Belle needs it right away. Belle may be a new friend to the girl, so the girl doesn't know where Belle lives. She has to stop to buy gas for the car and will pay for it with money from her job.

©Voyager Expanded Learning, Inc. 131

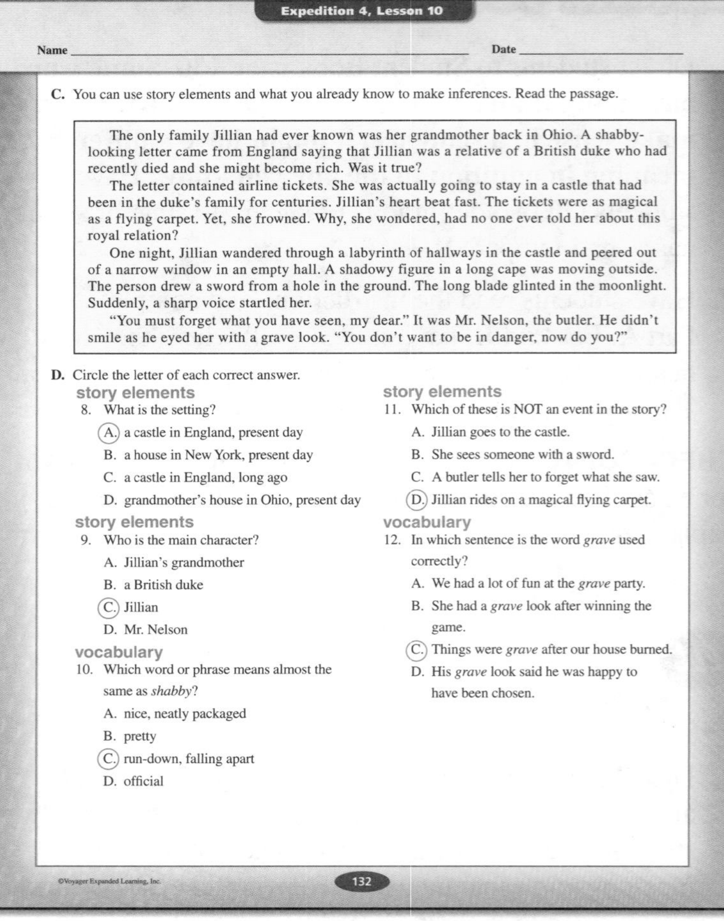

Expedition 4, Lesson 10

Name ______ Date ______

C. You can use story elements and what you already know to make inferences. Read the passage.

> The only family Jillian had ever known was her grandmother back in Ohio. A shabby-looking letter came from England saying that Jillian was a relative of a British duke who had recently died and she might become rich. Was it true?
>
> The letter contained airline tickets. She was actually going to stay in a castle that had been in the duke's family for centuries. Jillian's heart beat fast. The tickets were as magical as a flying carpet. Yet, she frowned. Why, she wondered, had no one ever told her about this royal relation?
>
> One night, Jillian wandered through a labyrinth of hallways in the castle and peered out of a narrow window in an empty hall. A shadowy figure in a long cape was moving outside. The person drew a sword from a hole in the ground. The long blade glinted in the moonlight. Suddenly, a sharp voice startled her.
>
> "You must forget what you have seen, my dear." It was Mr. Nelson, the butler. He didn't smile as he eyed her with a grave look. "You don't want to be in danger, now do you?"

D. Circle the letter of each correct answer.

story elements
8. What is the setting?
   (A.) a castle in England, present day
   B. a house in New York, present day
   C. a castle in England, long ago
   D. grandmother's house in Ohio, present day

story elements
9. Who is the main character?
   A. Jillian's grandmother
   B. a British duke
   (C.) Jillian
   D. Mr. Nelson

vocabulary
10. Which word or phrase means almost the same as *shabby*?
   A. nice, neatly packaged
   B. pretty
   (C.) run-down, falling apart
   D. official

story elements
11. Which of these is NOT an event in the story?
   A. Jillian goes to the castle.
   B. She sees someone with a sword.
   C. A butler tells her to forget what she saw.
   (D.) Jillian rides on a magical flying carpet.

vocabulary
12. In which sentence is the word *grave* used correctly?
   A. We had a lot of fun at the *grave* party.
   B. She had a *grave* look after winning the game.
   (C.) Things were *grave* after our house burned.
   D. His *grave* look said he was happy to have been chosen.

©Voyager Expanded Learning, Inc. 132

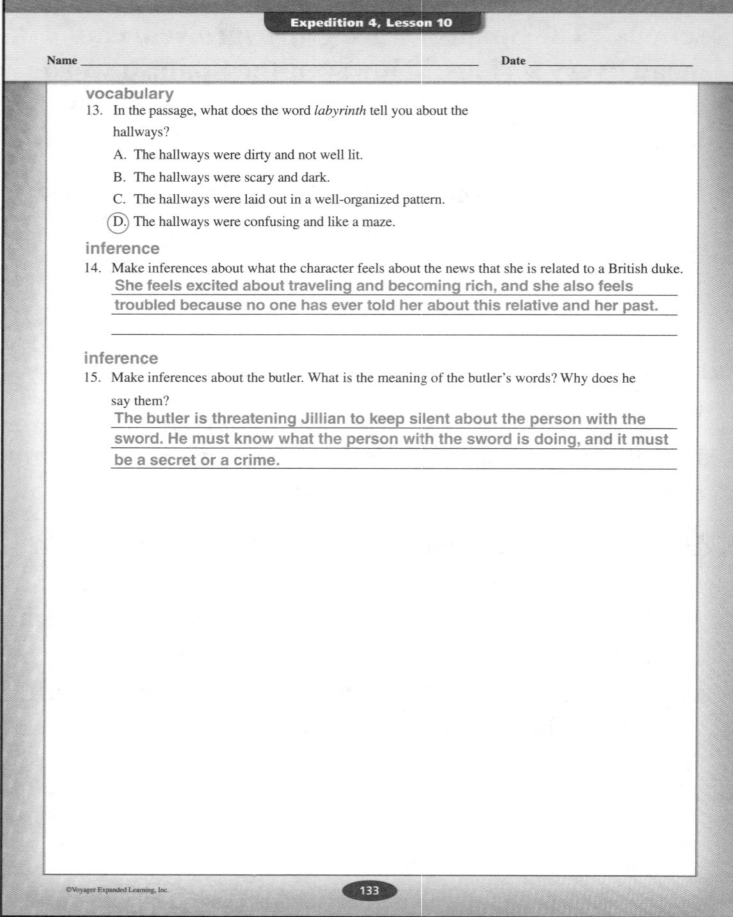

Expedition 4, Lesson 10

Name ______ Date ______

vocabulary
13. In the passage, what does the word *labyrinth* tell you about the hallways?
   A. The hallways were dirty and not well lit.
   B. The hallways were scary and dark.
   C. The hallways were laid out in a well-organized pattern.
   (D.) The hallways were confusing and like a maze.

inference
14. Make inferences about what the character feels about the news that she is related to a British duke.
   She feels excited about traveling and becoming rich, and she also feels troubled because no one has ever told her about this relative and her past.

inference
15. Make inferences about the butler. What is the meaning of the butler's words? Why does he say them?
   The butler is threatening Jillian to keep silent about the person with the sword. He must know what the person with the sword is doing, and it must be a secret or a crime.

©Voyager Expanded Learning, Inc. 133

Reteach

Inference and Story Elements

1. Direct students to Student Book pages 134 and 135. Read the passage in Part A aloud, then review the first graphic organizer. **To make inferences, start with what you read in the text.** Have a student read the first box aloud. **Do you agree with those facts? Check back in the text.** Have another student read the second box aloud. **Do you agree? What else do you know that is not directly stated?** Have students make an inference.
2. **Sometimes you make an inference right away. Then you need to make sure it is a reasonable inference.** Read aloud the inference in the second graphic organizer. **Why do you think the inference is reasonable?** Remind students that they can use what they already know and what they read in any order as they tell why the inference is reasonable. Have students complete Part A.
3. For Part B, explain that knowing story elements will help students make inferences. After students read the passage, have them discuss what Pete and Luke are like. **What clues in the text help you make those inferences about the characters?** Have students complete the dialogue and share their lines with the class. Allow others to decide if the dialogue fits with the characters' traits. Extend the activity by having students use what they know about the characters to imagine how Pete and Luke solve the problem of finding a place for Thalia's party.

ELL Focus on reteaching making inferences and identifying story elements.

1. Focus on details in the assessment to reteach making inferences for students having difficulty with Part A.
   - **Which details in the passage are clues about the character's age and gender?**
   - **What do you already know about high school activities and teens that can help you make an inference about what the girl's interests are?**
   - **What do you know about this character and high school life that help you make an inference about why she is hurrying?**
2. For Part B: **You can examine story elements to make inferences about the events in a story.** Encourage students to review the passage to answer questions about setting, events, and characters.

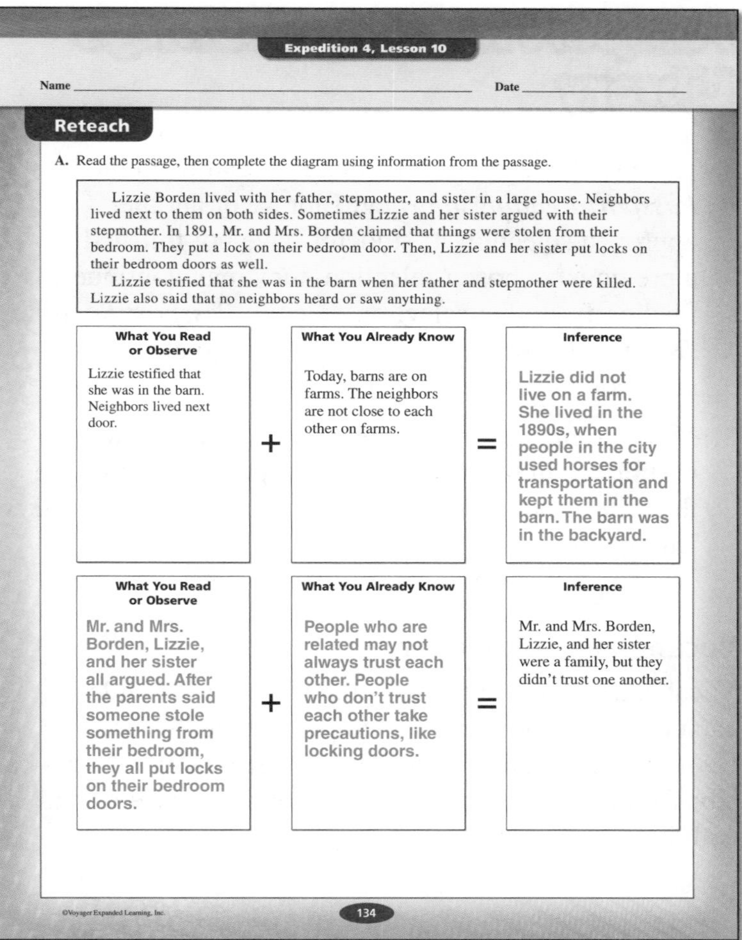

Expedition 4, Lesson 10

Name ______ Date ______

Reteach

A. Read the passage, then complete the diagram using information from the passage.

Lizzie Borden lived with her father, stepmother, and sister in a large house. Neighbors lived next to them on both sides. Sometimes Lizzie and her sister argued with their stepmother. In 1891, Mr. and Mrs. Borden claimed that things were stolen from their bedroom. They put a lock on their bedroom door. Then, Lizzie and her sister put locks on their bedroom doors as well.

Lizzie testified that she was in the barn when her father and stepmother were killed. Lizzie also said that no neighbors heard or saw anything.

What You Read or Observe		What You Already Know		Inference
Lizzie testified that she was in the barn. Neighbors lived next door.	+	Today, barns are on farms. The neighbors are not close to each other on farms.	=	Lizzie did not live on a farm. She lived in the 1890s, when people in the city used horses for transportation and kept them in the barn. The barn was in the backyard.
Mr. and Mrs. Borden, Lizzie, and her sister all argued. After the parents said someone stole something from their bedroom, they all put locks on their bedroom doors.	+	People who are related may not always trust each other. People who don't trust each other take precautions, like locking doors.	=	Mr. and Mrs. Borden, Lizzie, and her sister were a family, but they didn't trust one another.

©Voyager Expanded Learning, Inc. 134

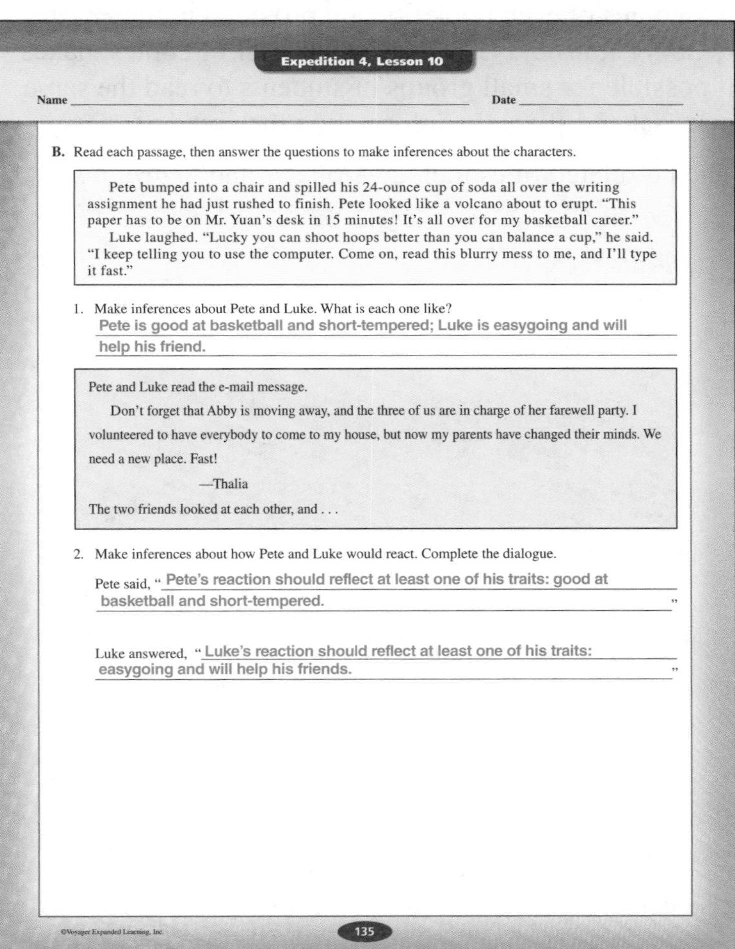

Expedition 4, Lesson 10

Name ______ Date ______

B. Read each passage, then answer the questions to make inferences about the characters.

Pete bumped into a chair and spilled his 24-ounce cup of soda all over the writing assignment he had just rushed to finish. Pete looked like a volcano about to erupt. "This paper has to be on Mr. Yuan's desk in 15 minutes! It's all over for my basketball career."

Luke laughed. "Lucky you can shoot hoops better than you can balance a cup," he said. "I keep telling you to use the computer. Come on, read this blurry mess to me, and I'll type it fast."

1. Make inferences about Pete and Luke. What is each one like?
   Pete is good at basketball and short-tempered; Luke is easygoing and will help his friend.

Pete and Luke read the e-mail message.

Don't forget that Abby is moving away, and the three of us are in charge of her farewell party. I volunteered to have everybody to come to my house, but now my parents have changed their minds. We need a new place. Fast!

—Thalia

The two friends looked at each other, and . . .

2. Make inferences about how Pete and Luke would react. Complete the dialogue.

   Pete said, "Pete's reaction should reflect at least one of his traits: good at basketball and short-tempered."

   Luke answered, "Luke's reaction should reflect at least one of his traits: easygoing and will help his friends."

©Voyager Expanded Learning, Inc. 135

Passport Reading Journeys Library

1. Have students choose reading material from the *Passport Reading Journeys* Library or another approved selection. If students have not finished a previously chosen selection, they may continue reading from that selection. See the *Passport Reading Journeys* Library Teacher's Guide for material on selection guidelines.
2. You also may use this time to allow students to participate in book clubs or book presentations. Use the criteria specified in the *Passport Reading Journeys* Library Teacher's Guide.

Vocabulary Connections

Vocabulary words are listed in the Teacher's Guide for each book. These words are content-related or used frequently in reading material. The selected words can be a basis for independent or small-group discussions and activities.

Student Opportunities

Six copies of each book title are provided in the *Passport Reading Journeys* Library. The number of copies makes it possible for small groups of students to read the same material and share the information they read.

Theme-related titles include *Monster* and *Scorpions*.

Technology

1. Depending on your classroom configuration and computer access, you may have all students work through the technology in a lab setting or have individuals or small groups of students work on desktops or laptops while other students participate in other suggested activities, such as the *Passport Reading Journeys* Library.
2. The online technology component provides additional support for students to work with selected vocabulary words. Students will work through a series of activities to strengthen their word knowledge, then apply that knowledge to passage reading. Refer to the online technology component User Guide for more information.

   Theme-related word sets include U.S. History, Literature, and Chemistry.

Expedition Project

Courtroom Newscast

Ask students to imagine how today's news media would have covered the Lizzie Borden trial or the news of Sherlock Holmes preventing a bank robbery. **You will present TV newscasts of one of the two events as they might have happened.** Have students form groups of four, and distribute copies of Project Blackline Master page 8. Have students look at the page and follow along as you explain the assignment. Assign point values, and have students write them in the rubric. Tell them to make any notes on the page that will help them, but they will turn in the page with the assignment. Instruct students to follow these steps:

1. **Draw a storyboard sequence to design a newscast of the Lizzie Borden trial or the final scene of "The Red-Headed League."** Tell students the sequences should include . . .
   - at least four scenes.
   - the roles of a TV news reporter at the scene, an on-the-scene witness, and a news analyst who gives opinions.
   - information from a variety of sources, such as the Expedition passages, their writing assignment about the closing arguments, the Build Background DVD, Writing in Response to Reading activities during the lessons, and outside research.
2. Instruct students to choose roles.
   - The TV news reporter at the scene presents facts that answer *who*, *what*, *when*, *where*, *why*, and *how* and describes other information.
   - The news analyst presents opinions based on facts or other logical information.
   - The on-the-scene witness presents a personal viewpoint and provides interesting details that fit with the character.
   - The newscast director makes sure that the scenes in the newscast follow quickly in order and that the viewers can understand the information.
3. **Use notebook paper to write the script for each storyboard scene. In the script, use at least three vocabulary words from the Expedition.**
4. Instruct students to rehearse the newscast in their roles and note any needed changes.
5. **Revise the script after you rehearse. Make sure your presentation has each of the features listed in the Grading Rubric.**
6. After students make all their changes, have them write the final script on individual sheets of paper to use as teleprompter cards. They can prepare visuals to support the presentation.
7. Have students present their newscasts during class.
8. **I will assess your newscast based on the rubric on your page.** To assess students' newscasts, use the rubric from the Project Blackline Master.

Real-World Reading

Reading a Newspaper Article

1. Direct students to Student Book page 136. Explain that when you read something in the "real world," you read to find information, such as the news of the day. Have students preview the banner and headings. **What do you know about this text already?** (It is a newspaper article from the *Los Angeles Times*; the topic is how luminol can help solve a crime.) **Do you think a writer is reporting news or a columnist is writing an opinion? Why?** (The dateline Ventura shows it is news from a certain place; the headline indicates the article has facts, not opinions.) Prompt students to tell what they already know about luminol from reading "CSI at the Lizzie Borden Crime Scene." (Luminol reacts with blood stains and glows; using it may destroy a sample.)
2. Write the following questions on the board. Have students keep these questions in mind as they read. They will use these as main ideas to help them give a brief summary. Tell them to highlight and number the text when they find each answer.
   - *Whose bloodstains were found?* (1)
   - *What important evidence did luminol help reveal?* (2)
   - *What other tools did investigators use?* (3)
3. Have students read and underline the sentences with the following words from the article. Then, have them tell the meanings. Clarify their understanding as needed:
   - **compile** (v) *compose or put together from different materials*
   - **urban** (adj) *relating to the city*
   - **lengthy** (adj) *very long; extended*
4. Have students work with partners to use the highlighted information and their own ideas to write one sentence at the top of the Student Book page that briefly summarizes the article. Acknowledge the students who have the most accurate summary with the fewest words.

Expedition 4, Lesson 10

Name ______________________ Date ____________

Real World—Newspaper Article

Los Angeles Times

Luminol Reveals Bloodstains Years Old

Ventura: Katrina (1) Montgomery left a party on November 28, 1992, and the 20-year-old college student seemingly disappeared into thin air. Five years later the cold case was given to a young Ventura County Deputy District Attorney. Working with an experienced investigator, the two men tracked down clues that led to three suspects. One of the suspects was Justin Merriman, a former classmate of Montgomery. All three suspects were friends and refused to "rat" on each other.

But the district attorney and investigator would not give up. Wire taps and hidden cameras recorded the suspects as the investigators asked them about the missing girl. The investigators led two suspects to believe they had plenty of evidence against them. As a result, one of the suspects gave important information about the missing girl and Justin Merriman. Investigators were then able to compile enough evidence to get a search warrant for the home of Merriman's mother. They suspected Merriman had killed the young woman in a room in this home.

(2) Although it was five years later, using the chemical luminol, investigators uncovered bloodstains that showed the room in the house was the crime scene. Even though the stains had been cleaned up and were many years old, they were still visible when sprayed with luminol. However, Merriman maintained he was innocent of any crime. Montgomery's body still had not been found. Without a body, the investigating team could not prove Merriman was guilty.

The other two men finally came forward and confessed they had seen Merriman attack and murder Montgomery in his mother's home. One of the men took investigators to where he had helped Merriman hide the body. What was the edge of a forest in 1992 was now an urban area with highways. They would be unable to find the woman's remains. The only way the District Attorney could get a conviction now would be to get a confession from Merriman. At this point, a former girlfriend of Merriman came forward wanting to help. (3) With more wire taps and hidden cameras, the investigators allowed the girlfriend to meet with the suspected murderer. They recorded Merriman saying things to his former girlfriend that connected him to the crime. They finally gathered enough evidence to arrest Merriman for first-degree murder.

After a lengthy trial, the jury found 28-year-old Justin Merriman guilty. Almost 10 years after the crime, Merriman was given the death penalty. He is now on death row awaiting execution for his crime.

136

Exploring Careers

Detectives

1. Direct students to Anthology page 73. Have students preview the photos, title, and headings. **Turn the title and headings into questions, and focus on finding the answers as you read. Use question words such as *who*, *what*, *how*, and *why*.** Write student responses on the board, such as:
   - *What do detectives do?*
   - *How much education is required?*
   - *What is the training like?*
   - *How much does a detective work?*
   - *What are typical salaries for this career?*
2. Have students read the passage and state three reasons a career as a detective would or would not appeal to them. (Possible answers: training in use of firearms and the law; solving cases; salary)
3. Direct students to Student Book page 137. Have them find answers to the questions in the passage. Have students research related careers in books or online. Have students complete the page.

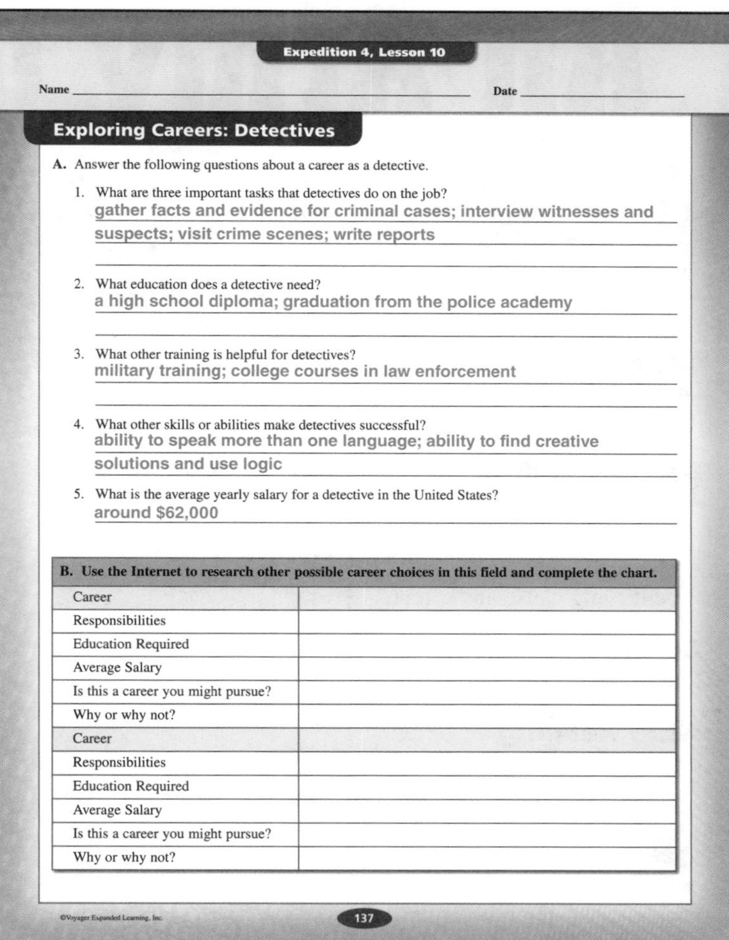

Expedition 4, Lesson 10

Name ______________________ Date ______________

Exploring Careers: Detectives

A. Answer the following questions about a career as a detective.

1. What are three important tasks that detectives do on the job?
gather facts and evidence for criminal cases; interview witnesses and suspects; visit crime scenes; write reports
2. What education does a detective need?
a high school diploma; graduation from the police academy
3. What other training is helpful for detectives?
military training; college courses in law enforcement
4. What other skills or abilities make detectives successful?
ability to speak more than one language; ability to find creative solutions and use logic
5. What is the average yearly salary for a detective in the United States?
around $62,000

B. Use the Internet to research other possible career choices in this field and complete the chart.	
Career	
Responsibilities	
Education Required	
Average Salary	
Is this a career you might pursue?	
Why or why not?	
Career	
Responsibilities	
Education Required	
Average Salary	
Is this a career you might pursue?	
Why or why not?	

©Voyager Expanded Learning, Inc.

137

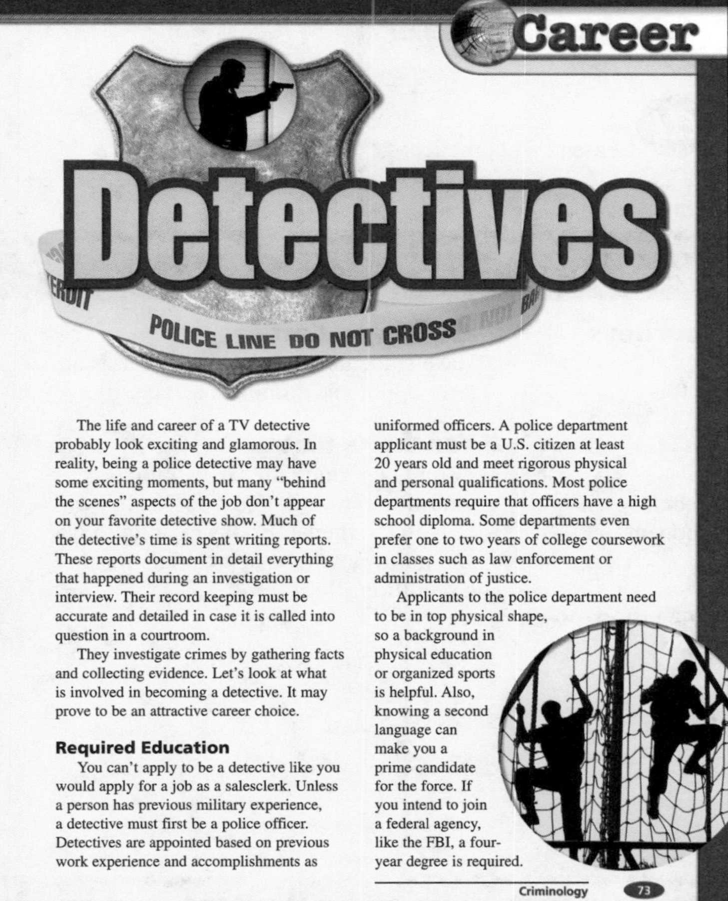

Detectives

The life and career of a TV detective probably look exciting and glamorous. In reality, being a police detective may have some exciting moments, but many "behind the scenes" aspects of the job don't appear on your favorite detective show. Much of the detective's time is spent writing reports. These reports document in detail everything that happened during an investigation or interview. Their record keeping must be accurate and detailed in case it is called into question in a courtroom.

They investigate crimes by gathering facts and collecting evidence. Let's look at what is involved in becoming a detective. It may prove to be an attractive career choice.

Required Education

You can't apply to be a detective like you would apply for a job as a salesclerk. Unless a person has previous military experience, a detective must first be a police officer. Detectives are appointed based on previous work experience and accomplishments as uniformed officers. A police department applicant must be a U.S. citizen at least 20 years old and meet rigorous physical and personal qualifications. Most police departments require that officers have a high school diploma. Some departments even prefer one to two years of college coursework in classes such as law enforcement or administration of justice.

Applicants to the police department need to be in top physical shape, so a background in physical education or organized sports is helpful. Also, knowing a second language can make you a prime candidate for the force. If you intend to join a federal agency, like the FBI, a four-year degree is required.

Criminology 73

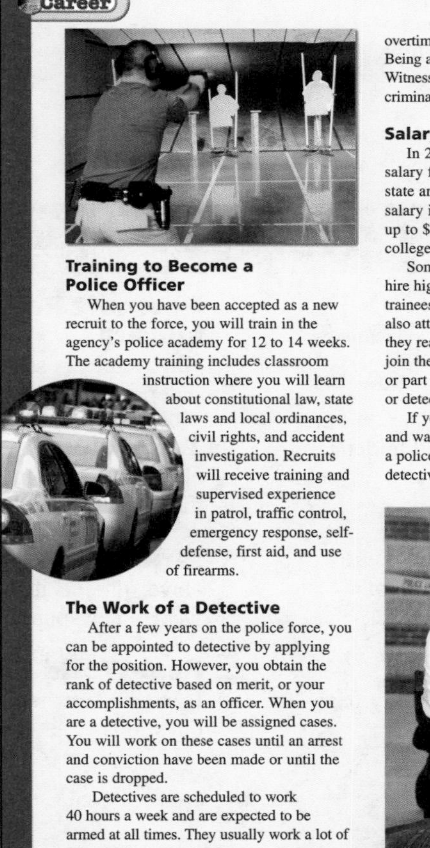

Training to Become a Police Officer

When you have been accepted as a new recruit to the force, you will train in the agency's police academy for 12 to 14 weeks. The academy training includes classroom instruction where you will learn about constitutional law, state laws and local ordinances, civil rights, and accident investigation. Recruits will receive training and supervised experience in patrol, traffic control, emergency response, self-defense, first aid, and use of firearms.

The Work of a Detective

After a few years on the police force, you can be appointed to detective by applying for the position. However, you obtain the rank of detective based on merit, or your accomplishments, as an officer. When you are a detective, you will be assigned cases. You will work on these cases until an arrest and conviction have been made or until the case is dropped.

Detectives are scheduled to work 40 hours a week and are expected to be armed at all times. They usually work a lot of overtime, for which they receive overtime pay. Being a detective is dangerous and stressful. Witnessing death and suffering caused by criminals can affect a detective's personal life.

Salary

In 2008 the national average annual salary for a detective was around $60,000 at state and local levels. The annual detective salary in the federal executive branch was up to $85,000; these positions require a college degree.

Some police departments in large cities hire high school students as police cadets or trainees to do clerical work. These students also attend classes for one to two years until they reach the minimum age requirement to join the force. Many police agencies pay all or part of college tuition if the police officer or detective wants to pursue a higher degree.

If you are interested in criminal justice and want to help your community, becoming a police officer and working your way up to detective may just be the career for you.

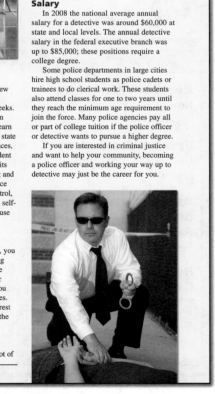

74 Expedition 4

An Army of Progress

"Military Technology"

Lesson 1

Introduce the Expedition
Discuss probing questions about the military.

Before Reading
- Introduce and practice using passage vocabulary.
- Introduce and practice identifying cause and effect.

During Reading
Read "Military Technology."

After Reading
Check comprehension.

Have students practice vocabulary using the online technology component.

Have students select books for independent reading.

ELL Extend and practice.

Lesson 2

Prepare to Reread
- Review and practice using passage vocabulary.
- Practice using context clues.
- Build new words using affixes and multiple meanings.

Reread
- Review and practice identifying cause and effect.
- Write about a new way to use something familiar.

ELL Extend and practice.

"Women in the Military"

Lesson 3

Before Reading
- Introduce and practice using passage vocabulary.
- Practice identifying cause and effect.
- Introduce the passage by previewing the photos and making predictions.

During Reading
Read "Women in the Military."

After Reading
Check comprehension.

Have students practice vocabulary using the online technology component.

Have students select books for independent reading.

ELL Extend and practice.

Lesson 4

Prepare to Reread
- Review and practice using passage vocabulary.
- Practice using context clues.
- Build new words using roots and affixes.

Reread
- Review and practice identifying cause and effect.
- Write about a character and a personal experience.

ELL Extend and practice.

Lesson 5—Review, Extend, Assess

Review Vocabulary
Review and practice using passage vocabulary.

Extend Vocabulary
Use root words to build and understand new words.

Assess Comprehension and Vocabulary
Assess student understanding of vocabulary and cause and effect.

Reteach
Have students complete activity pages for reteaching cause and effect.

Passport Reading Journeys Library
Have students select books for independent reading.

Technology
Have students practice vocabulary using the online technology component.

Writing Process
Have students use the writing process to write a newspaper article.

Real-World Reading
Have students read an e-mail and answer questions.

Exploring Careers
Have students read about a career as an Army pilot and complete an activity.

Teacher's Note
Before beginning the Expedition, ask your librarian to suggest books that will fit with the theme. Books relating to war and military will be appropriate for this Expedition.

"Military Medical Innovations"		"Buffalo Soldiers"	
Lesson 6	**Lesson 7**	**Lesson 8**	**Lesson 9**
Before Reading • Introduce and practice using passage vocabulary. • Practice identifying cause and effect. **During Reading** Read "Military Medical Innovations." **After Reading** Check comprehension. Have students practice vocabulary using the online technology component. Have students select books for independent reading. ELL Extend and practice.	**Prepare to Reread** • Review and practice using passage vocabulary. • Practice using context clues. • Build new words using affixes. **Reread** • Review and practice identifying cause and effect. • Write a letter. ELL Extend and practice.	**Before Reading** • Introduce and practice using passage vocabulary. • Introduce and practice taking notes. • Introduce the passage by previewing and making predictions. **During Reading** Read "Buffalo Soldiers." **After Reading** Check comprehension. Have students practice vocabulary using the online technology component. Have students select books for independent reading. ELL Extend and practice.	**Prepare to Reread** • Review and practice using passage vocabulary. • Practice using context clues. • Build new words using suffixes. **Reread** • Practice taking notes. • Review and practice identifying cause and effect. • Write a speech. ELL Extend and practice.

Lesson 10—Review, Extend, Assess

Review Vocabulary
Review and practice using passage vocabulary.

Extend Vocabulary
Use affixes to build and understand new words.

Assess Comprehension and Vocabulary
Assess student understanding of vocabulary and cause and effect.

Reteach
Have students complete activity pages for reteaching cause and effect.

Passport Reading Journeys Library
Have students select books for independent reading.

Technology
Have students practice vocabulary using the online technology component.

Expedition Project
Have students research and prepare for a military branch presentation.

Real-World Reading
Have students read a monument map and answer questions.

Exploring Careers
Have students read about careers in the Navy and complete an activity.

Expedition 5

Introduce the Expedition

1. Have students study the photograph that opens Expedition 5. **Equipment like this is used by the various branches of the military, or the armed troops that defend nations and people from enemy attacks.** Have students brainstorm words they associate with the word *military*. Write student responses on the board and have them use their ideas to answer: **What do you expect of the U.S. military forces?** Use their examples to explain how their brainstormed words often are tied to their emotions and experiences. For example, one of the words may be *protect*, and their expectations would include having the United States *protected* here and abroad during war or peace.

2. Have partners discuss possible responses to the following probing questions. Ask them to support their thinking from something they've previously learned from reading, experiences, or other sources. **These questions will guide what you are about to learn.**
   - **How does the modern military differ from the military of the past?**
   - **How has the role of soldiers changed over the years?**
   - **What military inventions have become a part of the lives of American people?**

Build Background DVD 5.1
Tell students they will view a brief DVD that provides background information about the military. **As you watch, listen for any unfamiliar words and write them down.** Have students share any words that were unfamiliar, then explain the definitions.

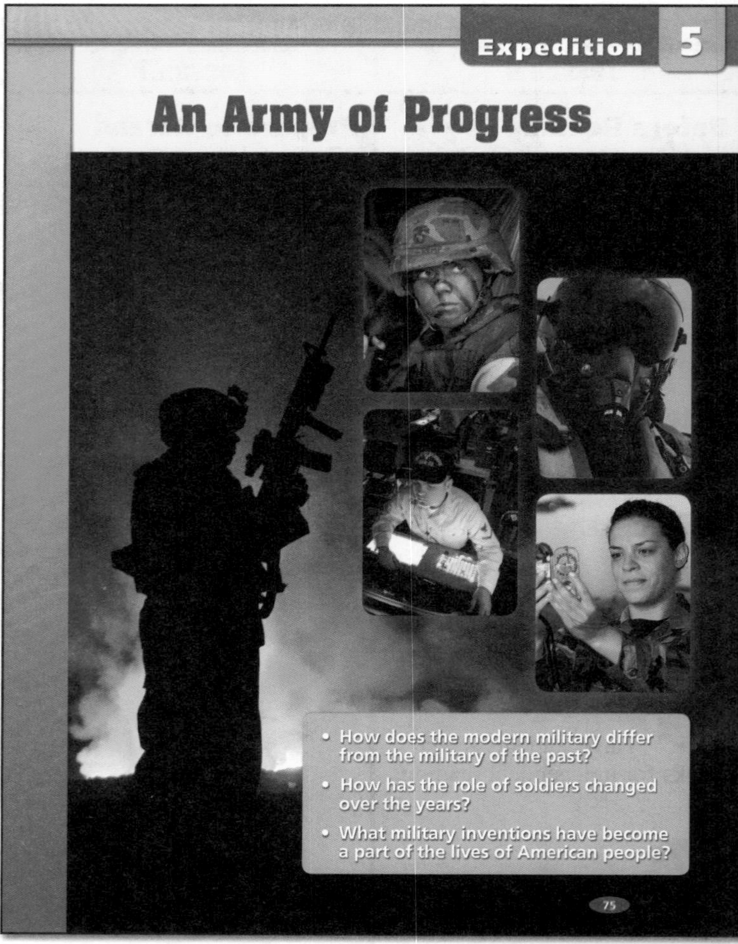
Expedition 5
An Army of Progress
• How does the modern military differ from the military of the past?
• How has the role of soldiers changed over the years?
• What military inventions have become a part of the lives of American people?
75

3. Point out the parts of the Expedition 5 Organizer on Student Book pages 138 and 139. **Use this organizer to write your own ideas and questions about the passages you read in this Expedition.**

   Suggestions for how students can add ideas to the Expedition Organizer appear in this Teacher's Edition at the end of Lessons 2, 4, 7, and 9. If students have responses now, allow them to write them in Part A.

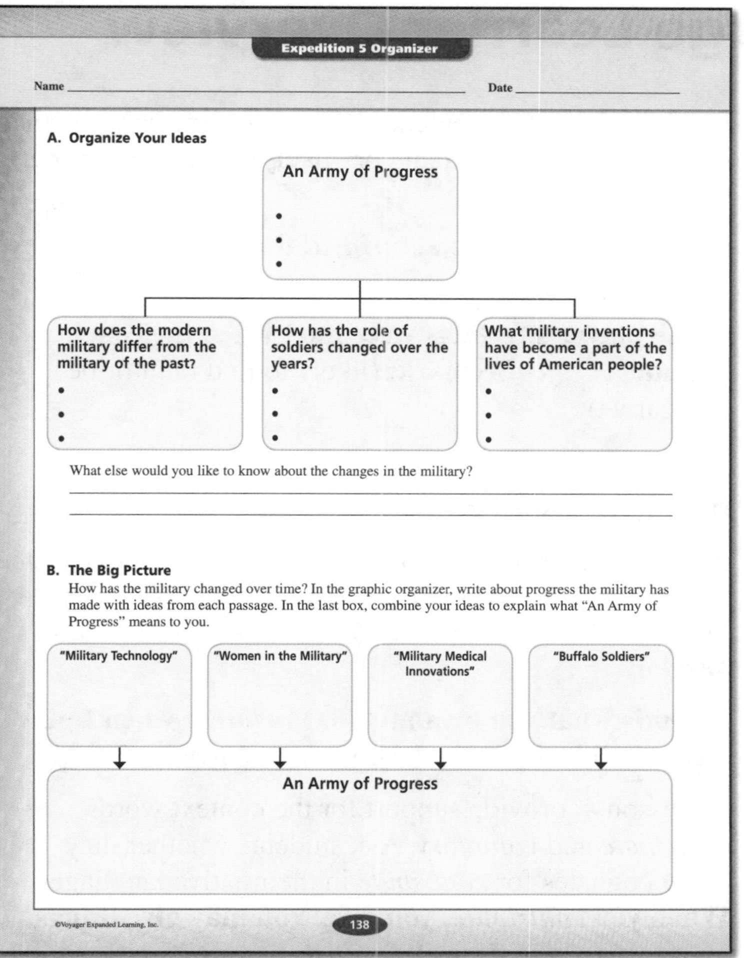

Expedition 5 Organizer

Name ____________________ Date ____________

A. Organize Your Ideas

An Army of Progress
•
•
•

How does the modern military differ from the military of the past?	How has the role of soldiers changed over the years?	What military inventions have become a part of the lives of American people?
• • •	• • •	• • •

What else would you like to know about the changes in the military?

____

B. The Big Picture

How has the military changed over time? In the graphic organizer, write about progress the military has made with ideas from each passage. In the last box, combine your ideas to explain what "An Army of Progress" means to you.

"Military Technology"	"Women in the Military"	"Military Medical Innovations"	"Buffalo Soldiers"

An Army of Progress

©Voyager Expanded Learning, Inc. 138

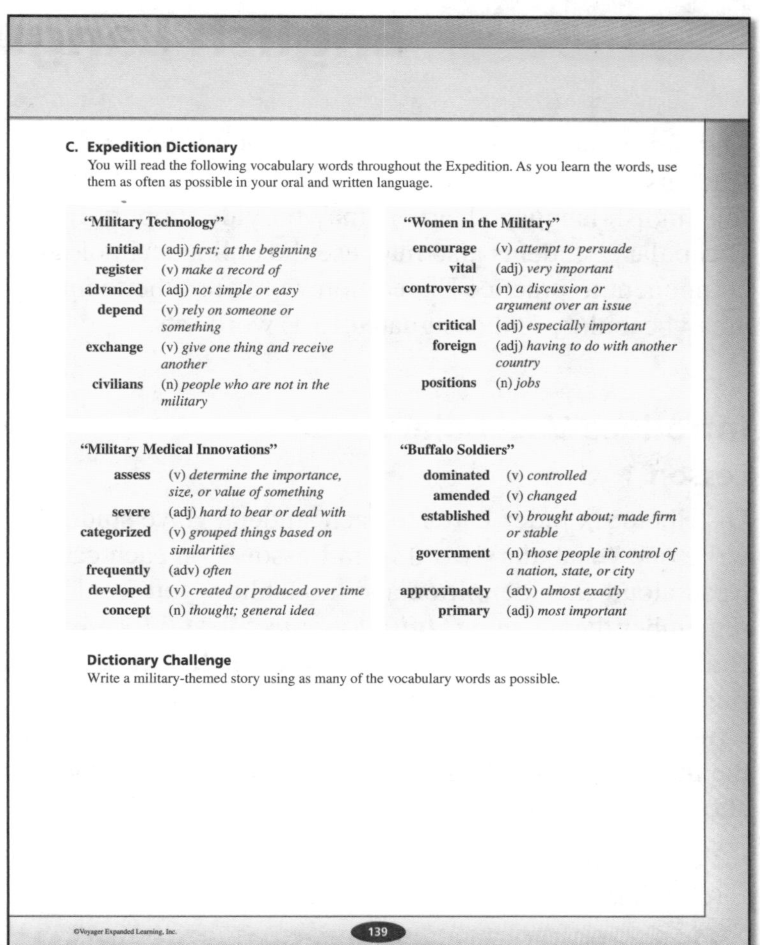

C. Expedition Dictionary

You will read the following vocabulary words throughout the Expedition. As you learn the words, use them as often as possible in your oral and written language.

"Military Technology"

- **initial** (adj) *first; at the beginning*
- **register** (v) *make a record of*
- **advanced** (adj) *not simple or easy*
- **depend** (v) *rely on someone or something*
- **exchange** (v) *give one thing and receive another*
- **civilians** (n) *people who are not in the military*

"Women in the Military"

- **encourage** (v) *attempt to persuade*
- **vital** (adj) *very important*
- **controversy** (n) *a discussion or argument over an issue*
- **critical** (adj) *especially important*
- **foreign** (adj) *having to do with another country*
- **positions** (n) *jobs*

"Military Medical Innovations"

- **assess** (v) *determine the importance, size, or value of something*
- **severe** (adj) *hard to bear or deal with*
- **categorized** (v) *grouped things based on similarities*
- **frequently** (adv) *often*
- **developed** (v) *created or produced over time*
- **concept** (n) *thought; general idea*

"Buffalo Soldiers"

- **dominated** (v) *controlled*
- **amended** (v) *changed*
- **established** (v) *brought about; made firm or stable*
- **government** (n) *those people in control of a nation, state, or city*
- **approximately** (adv) *almost exactly*
- **primary** (adj) *most important*

Dictionary Challenge

Write a military-themed story using as many of the vocabulary words as possible.

©Voyager Expanded Learning, Inc. 139

ELL

Making Connections

Have students share prior knowledge about the military. Begin by asking what the military is and what it does. Write basic terms on the board, such as *soldiers*, *war*, and *defense* as students mention them. **Do you know anyone who has served in the military?**

Preview the vocabulary word *government* as you discuss the military. English language learners may recognize cognates for *government* in their native languages. Allow them to say related words in their native languages and tell what they already know about these words.

A *government* is the group of people who control a city, state, or country. In the United States, the president is commander in chief of the military; the president is more powerful than the generals. The *government* also makes decisions about who serves in its military.

Discuss the U.S. government and its military policies using the following prompts:

- **Currently in the United States, do you have to serve in the military, or is it your choice?** (It is your choice.) **Males do have to sign up for Selective Service when they are 18. If there is ever a draft, their names will be drawn from this list.**
- **Do men and women both serve in the U.S. military?** (yes)
- **Who cannot serve in the U.S. military?** (People younger than 17 years of age cannot serve. People with health problems may not be able to serve in certain roles.)

In some countries, the military has more power than it does in the United States. Encourage students to share their knowledge of the military's role in countries with which they are familiar. If possible, have them share photographs of men and women serving in the U.S. military and other militaries.

English Language Learner Overview

The *ELL* signals when extra support is provided for students during the lesson. As needed, Blackline Masters for English language learners may provide support. For vocabulary, students also may use the online technology component to practice Expedition words or other content-area vocabulary and designated ELL word sets.

Introduce Vocabulary

Lesson 1

Distribute six index cards to each student. Have students write one vocabulary word from Lesson 1 on each card. Read aloud each definition and model how you would remember the meaning. ***Initial*** **means "first." I know that *initials* are the first letters of a word, such as a name. So, I will write that on the card.** Have students write or draw a clue on each card to help them remember the meaning. Read the following sentences. Have students choose words from the cards to complete each sentence.

- **People who are not in the military are called _____.** (civilians)
- **Algebra is an _____ math skill compared with addition.** (advanced)
- **I really need my friend's help; I _____ on it.** (depend)
- **We used our second plan because our _____ plan did not work.** (initial)
- **This week, the university will _____ its new students.** (register)
- **This coat does not fit, so I will _____ it for another size.** (exchange)

Lesson 3

The word *critical* has a second meaning. Write *likely to find fault or be negative* on the board. **Someone who is *critical* always notices things that are wrong. The *critical* dinner guest complained that the soup was too cold. What would you expect a *critical* person to say about a movie?** (that the movie was not good)

Read the following sentences. Have students say whether *critical* means "important" or "likely to find fault or be negative."

- **A good night's sleep is *critical* the night before a test.** (important)
- **The player's feelings were hurt when the coach made a *critical* remark.** (likely to find fault or be negative)

Practice Vocabulary

In Lesson 2, provide support for the context words *target* and *intent*. **A *target* is a mark you aim for. When I play basketball, my *target* is the basket. It is the mark I aim for.**

***Intent* is what you mean to do. My *intent* when I play basketball is to hit the basket, my target.**

In Lesson 4, provide support for the context words *contribute* and *voluntary*. Ask students whether they know cognates for *contribute* in their native languages. **When you *contribute*, you give. You may give things, or you may give time and effort. I *contribute* to an animal shelter by giving money. I *contribute* to a clean neighborhood by helping to clean up litter in the park. How do you *contribute* to your family?** (by helping with chores; baby-sitting; repairing things that are broken)

Ask students whether they know cognates for *voluntary* in their native languages. **Something *voluntary* is something you do because you want to. You are not forced to do something that is *voluntary*. Is coming to school *voluntary*?** (no) **Is an extra credit project *voluntary*?** (yes)

Apply the Target Skill: Cause and Effect

Some students may need additional practice identifying causes and effects. Blackline Master page 27 extends the oral activity in Lesson 2 by having students identify which part of a sentence is the cause and which is the effect. Students then write their own causes and effects and practice using signal words to combine them in complete sentences.

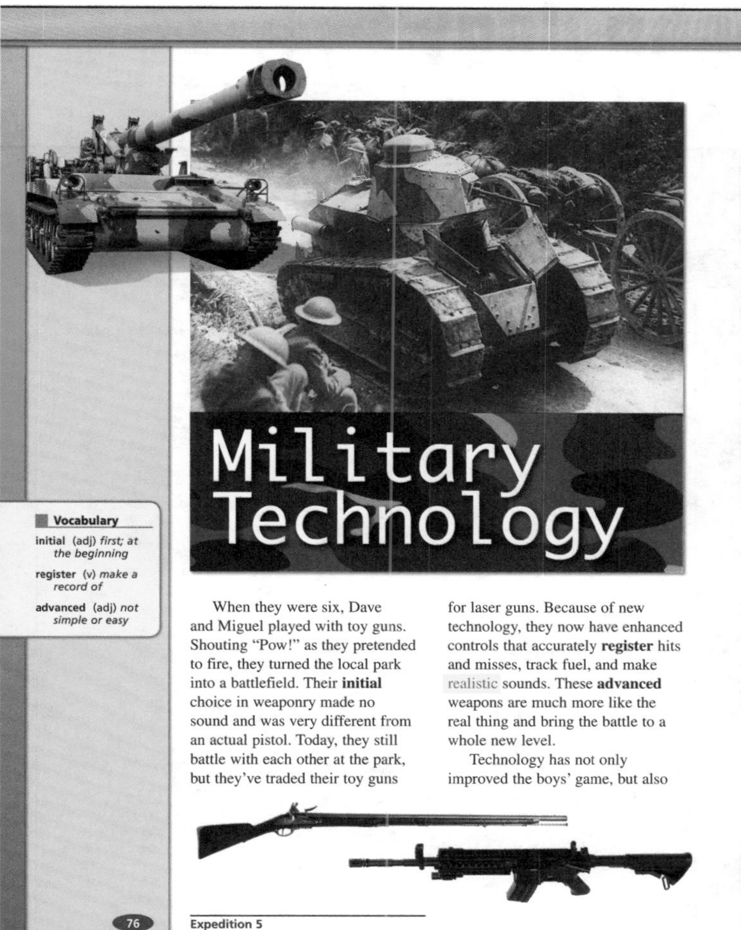

Military Technology

Vocabulary
initial (adj) *first; at the beginning*
register (v) *make a record of*
advanced (adj) *not simple or easy*

When they were six, Dave and Miguel played with toy guns. Shouting "Pow!" as they pretended to fire, they turned the local park into a battlefield. Their **initial** choice in weaponry made no sound and was very different from an actual pistol. Today, they still battle with each other at the park, but they've traded their toy guns for laser guns. Because of new technology, they now have enhanced controls that accurately **register** hits and misses, track fuel, and make realistic sounds. These **advanced** weapons are much more like the real thing and bring the battle to a whole new level.

Technology has not only improved the boys' game, but also has improved military weapons. During the Revolutionary War, American soldiers used weapons such as cannons, which could hit targets from about half a mile away. [1] Even if a cannonball made a direct hit, it wouldn't kill that many people. But, at the time, these were the most up-to-date weapons available. Today, they are considered antiques. They have been replaced by machine guns, chemical hand grenades, and nuclear weapons. A modern smart bomb can be aimed at a mark, fired from miles away, and hit the specific target the size of a postage stamp. Today's nuclear weapons can devastate, or destroy, entire cities.

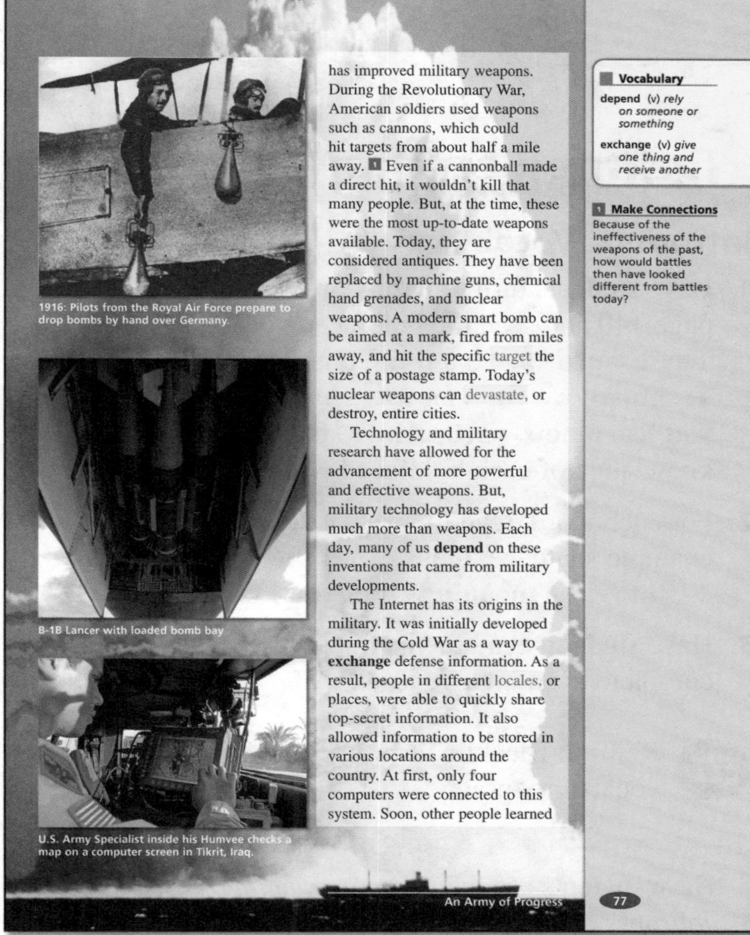

1916: Pilots from the Royal Air Force prepare to drop bombs by hand over Germany.

B-1B Lancer with loaded bomb bay

U.S. Army Specialist inside his Humvee checks a map on a computer screen in Tikrit, Iraq.

Vocabulary
depend (v) *rely on someone or something*
exchange (v) *give one thing and receive another*

1 Make Connections
Because of the ineffectiveness of the weapons of the past, how would battles then have looked different from battles today?

Technology and military research have allowed for the advancement of more powerful and effective weapons. But, military technology has developed much more than weapons. Each day, many of us **depend** on these inventions that came from military developments.

The Internet has its origins in the military. It was initially developed during the Cold War as a way to **exchange** defense information. As a result, people in different locales, or places, were able to quickly share top-secret information. It also allowed information to be stored in various locations around the country. At first, only four computers were connected to this system. Soon, other people learned about it and also wanted to be able to exchange information over the network. Then, the military began sharing the network with others. Today, the Internet is used in homes and businesses around the world. [2]

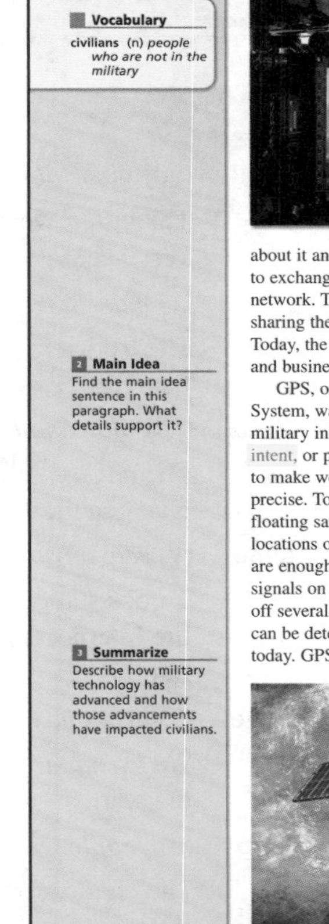

Vocabulary
civilians (n) *people who are not in the military*

2 Main Idea
Find the main idea sentence in this paragraph. What details support it?

3 Summarize
Describe how military technology has advanced and how those advancements have impacted civilians.

GPS, or Global Positioning System, was developed by the military in the late 1970s. The intent, or purpose, of GPS was to make weapon delivery more precise. To do this, the system uses floating satellites to determine locations on Earth. Because there are enough satellites in orbit for signals on the ground to bounce off several at once, exact locations can be determined in most cases today. GPS is still owned and operated by the U.S. Department of Defense but is used widely by American **civilians**. GPS units are commonly installed in cars, boats, and cell phones, so people depend on them to find destinations, map their routes, register past trips, or calculate the distance between two locations.

As technology research continues, our military will develop new tools to help defend our country. Today's smart bombs will probably become the antiques of the future. Civilians will continue to benefit from these advances, and these new applications, or uses, may soon become common for many people. [3] End

"Military Technology"

Before Reading

Introduce Vocabulary

1. Have students turn to Part A on Student Book page 140 and scan the boldfaced vocabulary words. **These words are from the passage "Military Technology." You can use what you know to help you learn new words.** Have students rate their knowledge of each boldfaced word.
2. For each word, read the part of speech, definition, and example sentence. **Check that the words you rated 2–5 have the meanings that you know.**
3. Have students read the instructions for Part B and complete the activity.

ELL Refer to Blackline Master page 26 to extend vocabulary practice.

Have students use the *Passport Reading Journeys* online technology component to practice and reinforce vocabulary and comprehension skills.

Introduce the Target Skill: Cause and Effect

1. **Any event can be a cause, an effect, or both. A cause is why something happened. An effect is what happened. I hear a group sing on the radio, so I buy a CD. The *cause* is that I heard them; the *effect* is that I buy their CD.** Have students think of examples of causes and effects and write them on the board.
2. **When you read, notice signal words like *because of*, *so*, *caused*, *as a result*, and *the reason is*. They tell you what the causes and effects are. Use signal words to create sentences from our causes and effects list.**
3. Direct students to Student Book page 141. Read aloud the instructions. **What is happening in this picture?** If students have trouble identifying what is happening, explain the effects of the atomic bomb and its use during World War II.
4. Have students complete the page and share their answers with a partner. Ask students to explain why the effects do or do not make sense with the photo.

Expedition 5, Lesson 1

Name ______________________ Date ____________

Vocabulary

"Military Technology"

A. Write one or more numbers next to each boldfaced word to show when you have seen, heard, or used this word.

5 I use it in everyday conversation.
4 I heard it on TV or on the radio.
3 I heard or used it in school.
2 I read it in a book, magazine, or online.
1 I have not read, heard, or used this word.

initial (adj) *first; at the beginning*
The *initial* weapons of the U.S. Army weren't very accurate.

register (v) *make a record of*
The troops *register* the names of soldiers lost in battle.

advanced (adj) *not simple or easy*
The *advanced* weapons used by the military have changed the way wars are fought.

depend (v) *rely on someone or something*
Troops stationed away from home *depend* on the Internet for correspondence with friends and family.

exchange (v) *give one thing and receive another*
We *exchange* goods for weapons to help us win the war.

civilians (n) *people who are not in the military*
The *civilians* were accidentally hurt by the bomb intended for the military base.

B. Complete each sentence with the correct vocabulary word from Part A.

1. Soldiers carry communication equipment because they ___depend___ on information to keep them safe.
2. The submarine has a(n) ___advanced___ radar system that finds hidden targets in the water.
3. The ___initial___ step to being an Army soldier is attending boot camp.
4. High-tech firing targets can ___register___ hits when lasers successfully hit them.
5. When two countries are friendly, they ___exchange___ information about their enemies.
6. The ___civilians___ are not allowed on the Army base without a special pass.

 140

Vocabulary

initial (adj) *first; at the beginning*
The *initial* weapons of the U.S. Army weren't very accurate.

register (v) *make a record of*
The troops *register* the names of soldiers lost in battle.

advanced (adj) *not simple or easy*
The *advanced* weapons used by the military have changed the way wars are fought.

depend (v) *rely on someone or something*
Troops stationed away from home *depend* on the Internet for correspondence with friends and family.

exchange (v) *give one thing and receive another*
We *exchange* goods for weapons to help us win the war.

civilians (n) *people who are not in the military*
The *civilians* were accidentally hurt by the bomb intended for the military base.

Introduce the Passage

1. Have students turn to Anthology page 76 to preview "Military Technology." **How do the photos relate to the title "Military Technology"?** Have students make predictions.
2. Remind students to pause and respond to the margin prompts as they read.
3. Teach these terms from the passage:
   - *Machine guns* are rapidly firing, automatic guns that continually fire when the trigger is engaged.
   - *Chemical hand grenades* can be lethal. The grenade has a delay mechanism that allows it to be thrown or fired. The area of effect is small.
   - *Nuclear weapons* are devices, such as bombs, whose great explosive power derives from the release of nuclear energy (splitting and dividing atoms).
   - A *smart bomb* is a bomb that can be guided by radio waves or a laser beam to its target.

During Reading

1. Have students read "Military Technology." To select reading options that support your students' levels and classroom needs, see Reading Differentiation, page xxxii, if needed.
2. Instruct students to look for causes and effects.

After Reading

Check Comprehension

1. **Compare your prediction to the information that you read in the passage. Was your prediction correct?**
2. Help students respond to the Make Connections margin prompt on Anthology page 77. **What TV shows have you seen, or books have you read about historical battles? Think about how advanced technology is used in the military today. How have things changed?** (Today, military strikes are more precise; there is less hand-to-hand fighting.)

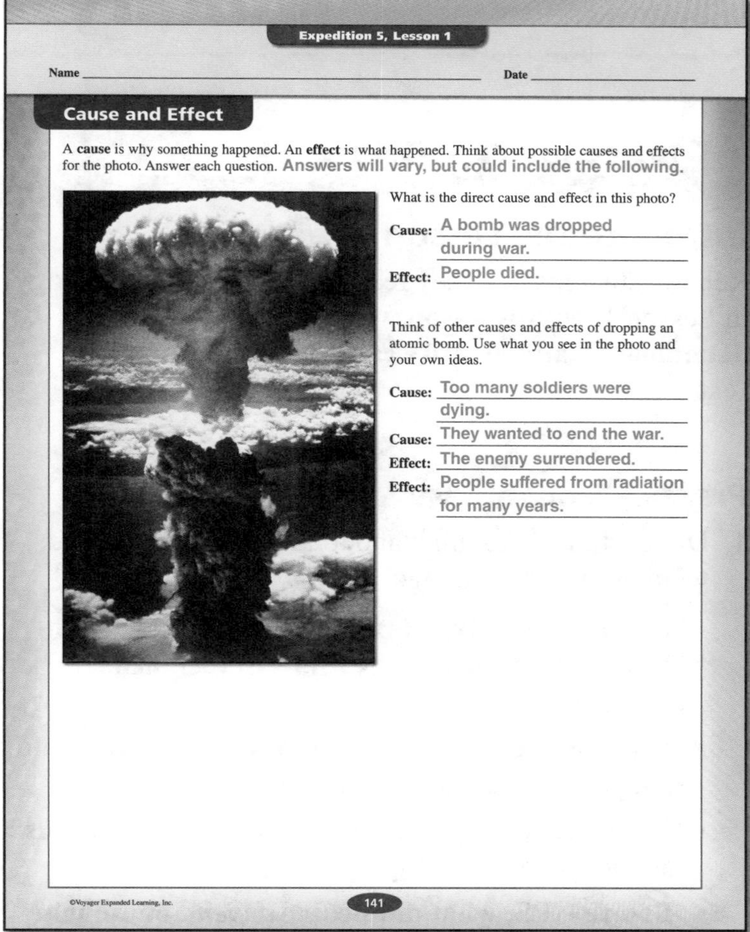

Expedition 5, Lesson 1

Name ______________________ Date ____________

Cause and Effect

A **cause** is why something happened. An **effect** is what happened. Think about possible causes and effects for the photo. Answer each question. Answers will vary, but could include the following.

What is the direct cause and effect in this photo?

Cause: A bomb was dropped during war.

Effect: People died.

Think of other causes and effects of dropping an atomic bomb. Use what you see in the photo and your own ideas.

Cause: Too many soldiers were dying.

Cause: They wanted to end the war.

Effect: The enemy surrendered.

Effect: People suffered from radiation for many years.

©Voyager Expanded Learning, Inc.

141

3. Guide students to find cause-and-effect signal words in the passage.
   - **Because** of new technology, they now have enhanced controls that accurately register hits and misses, track fuel, and make realistic sounds. (p. 76)
   - **As a result**, people in different locales, or places, were able to quickly share top-secret information. (p. 77)
   - **Because** there are enough satellites in orbit to bounce off one another, exact locations can be determined in most cases today. (p. 78)
   - GPS units are commonly installed in cars, boats, and cell phones, **so** people depend on them to find destinations, map their routes, register past trips, or calculate the distance between two locations. (p. 78)
4. Ask students to share other causes and effects they noticed in the passage.

Remind students to choose books from the *Passport Reading Journeys* Library for independent reading.

"Military Technology"

Prepare to Reread

Introduce the Lesson

Remind students that they read about military technology in Lesson 1. **In this lesson, we'll reread "Military Technology" and identify causes and effects in the text.**

Practice Vocabulary

1. Direct students to think about how vocabulary words were used in the passage.
   - **Lila is in the Navy, but her *initial* choice was to be a Marine. What was Lila's first choice?** (to be a Marine)
   - **If you had to *register* hits and misses, how would you do it?** (I'd make a tally for every hit.)
   - **What is a weapon that is not *advanced*?** (Swords are not advanced weapons.)
   - **Before GPS, what did people *depend* on to help with navigation?** (maps and compasses)
   - **How did the Internet help the military *exchange* information?** (The Internet helped them send and receive information to and from faraway places.)
   - **Do you see more *civilians* or military members at a Navy base? Explain.** (more military members because they live and work on the base)
2. Have students turn to Anthology page 76. Reread the last two sentences of the first paragraph. **The first sentence uses the word *realistic* to describe the sounds of laser weapons. What phrase in the second sentence is a clue to the meaning of *realistic*?** (like the real thing)

   Repeat this process for the following words.
   - **target** (n) *a mark you aim for*, Anthology page 77
   - **devastate** (v) *destroy*, Anthology page 77
   - **locales** (n) *places*, Anthology page 77
   - **intent** (n) *purpose*, Anthology page 78
   - **applications** (n) *uses*, Anthology page 78

ELL Directly explain the definitions of the words used in context. Allow students to find clues in the text that support the definition.

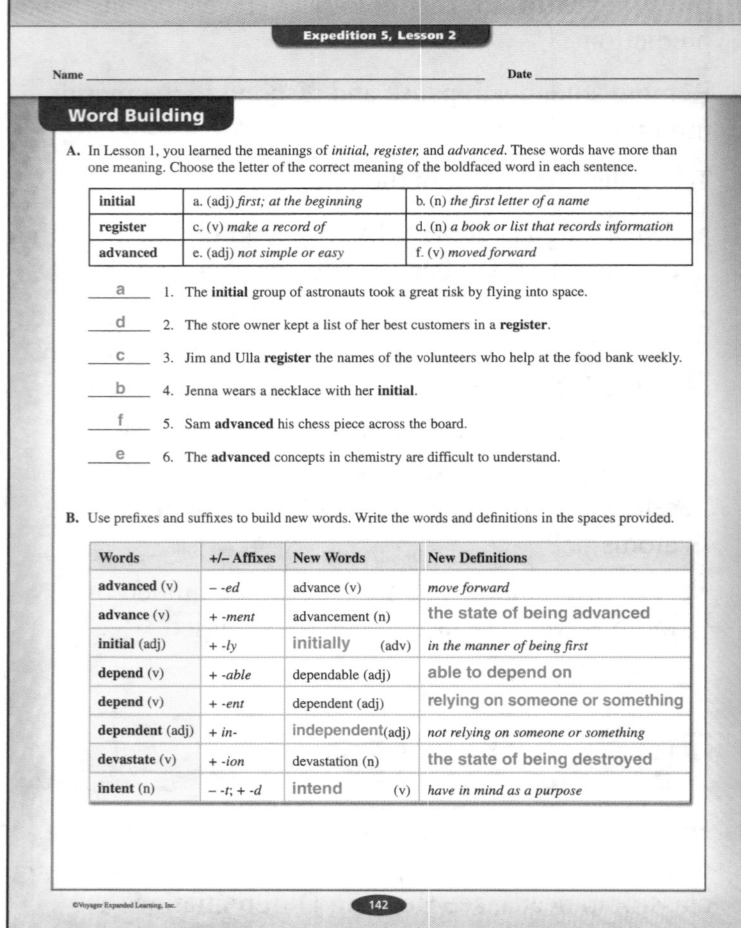

Expedition 5, Lesson 2

Name ______________________ Date ______________

Word Building

A. In Lesson 1, you learned the meanings of *initial, register,* and *advanced*. These words have more than one meaning. Choose the letter of the correct meaning of the boldfaced word in each sentence.

initial	a. (adj) *first; at the beginning*	b. (n) *the first letter of a name*
register	c. (v) *make a record of*	d. (n) *a book or list that records information*
advanced	e. (adj) *not simple or easy*	f. (v) *moved forward*

__a__ 1. The **initial** group of astronauts took a great risk by flying into space.

__d__ 2. The store owner kept a list of her best customers in a **register**.

__c__ 3. Jim and Ulla **register** the names of the volunteers who help at the food bank weekly.

__b__ 4. Jenna wears a necklace with her **initial**.

__f__ 5. Sam **advanced** his chess piece across the board.

__e__ 6. The **advanced** concepts in chemistry are difficult to understand.

B. Use prefixes and suffixes to build new words. Write the words and definitions in the spaces provided.

Words	+/– Affixes	New Words	New Definitions
advanced (v)	– *-ed*	advance (v)	*move forward*
advance (v)	+ *-ment*	advancement (n)	the state of being advanced
initial (adj)	+ *-ly*	initially (adv)	*in the manner of being first*
depend (v)	+ *-able*	dependable (adj)	able to depend on
depend (v)	+ *-ent*	dependent (adj)	relying on someone or something
dependent (adj)	+ *in-*	independent (adj)	*not relying on someone or something*
devastate (v)	+ *-ion*	devastation (n)	the state of being destroyed
intent (n)	– *-t*; + *-d*	intend (v)	*have in mind as a purpose*

142

3. Have students turn to Student Book page 142. Read the instructions for Parts A and B, and have students complete the activities.

CHECKPOINT After students complete Part A, have them identify one item that confused them. Have students substitute each definition for the multiple-meaning word to figure out which makes more sense.

Reread

Apply the Target Skill: Cause and Effect

1. **Sometimes signal words alert you to a cause-and-effect relationship in the text. For example: *As a result* of the availability of the Internet, people in different locations were able to quickly share information. In this example, *as a result* signals the cause-and-effect relationship.**

ELL Support the word *result* in the phrase *as a result of*. Tell students *result* means the same as *effect*. Refer to Blackline Master page 27 to extend practice with cause and effect.

2. **Sometimes you will not see signal words in a passage. Cannons used in the American Revolutionary War are considered antiques today. This is an effect. What caused this to happen?** (The cannons were replaced by more advanced weapons.)
3. Have students turn to Student Book page 143. Read the instructions aloud, and have students complete the activity independently using the passage.

ACADEMIC SKILL Remind students that finding causes and effects can help them in other subjects. Science lessons often focus on the effects of experiments and their causes.

Write in Response to Reading

1. Have students turn to Student Book page 144. Read the instructions for Part A aloud. Encourage students to write about what they believe the military does for the United States.
2. **In "Military Technology," you learned about how military technology was repurposed, or used for a different reason.** Have students read the instructions for Part B and complete the activity.

EXPEDITION ORGANIZER **An Army of Progress**

Pause to have students turn to Student Book pages 138 and 139. Have students complete the following:

- Respond to the probing questions in Part A. Encourage them to add their own questions.
- Think about how "Military Technology" shows the progress of the military. Write their ideas in the graphic organizer in Part B.

Expedition 5, Lesson 2

Name ________________ Date ________

Cause and Effect

Reread "Military Technology." Write the missing causes and effects in the boxes, then write a cause-and-effect statement for each using a signal word.

1.

Cause	Effect
The military needed to make weapon delivery more precise.	It developed GPS.

The military needed to make weapon delivery more precise, so it developed GPS.

2.

Cause	Effect
People in the military needed a way to exchange information easily.	The Internet was invented to communicate over long distances.

Because people in the military needed a way to exchange information easily, the Internet was invented to communicate over long distances.

3.

Cause	Effect
People in the military wanted to create improved weaponry.	People in the military concentrated on developing technology.

People in the military concentrated on developing technology because they wanted to create improved weaponry.

143

Expedition 5, Lesson 2

Name ________________ Date ________

Write in Response to Reading

A. Think about what you know and have read about the U.S. military. Answer the questions.
Answers will vary.

Before reading "Military Technology," my ideas about the military in the United States were . . .

After reading "Military Technology," I can add these ideas.

B. Think of an item in your home or school or something in your community. How would you use it for another purpose?

What it is: ________________

Describe the original purpose for it.

Describe how you would use it in a new way.

144

Women in the Military

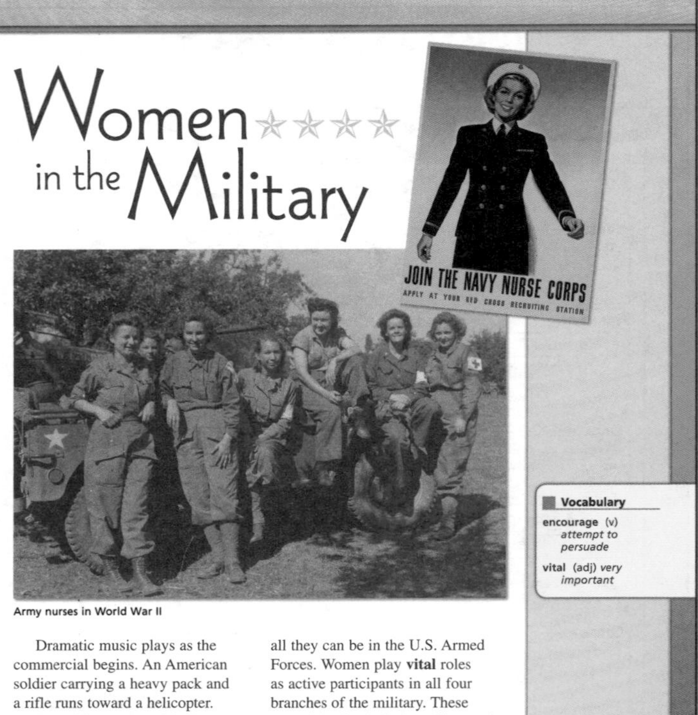

JOIN THE NAVY NURSE CORPS
APPLY AT YOUR RED CROSS RECRUITING STATION

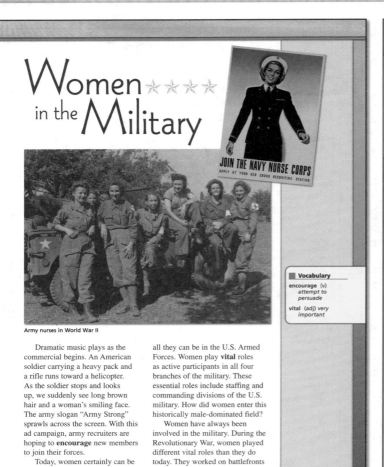

Army nurses in World War II

Vocabulary

encourage (v) *attempt to persuade*

vital (adj) *very important*

Dramatic music plays as the commercial begins. An American soldier carrying a heavy pack and a rifle runs toward a helicopter. As the soldier stops and looks up, we suddenly see long brown hair and a woman's smiling face. The army slogan "Army Strong" sprawls across the screen. With this ad campaign, army recruiters are hoping to **encourage** new members to join their forces.

Today, women certainly can be all they can be in the U.S. Armed Forces. Women play **vital** roles as active participants in all four branches of the military. These essential roles include staffing and commanding divisions of the U.S. military. How did women enter this historically male-dominated field?

Women have always been involved in the military. During the Revolutionary War, women played different vital roles than they do today. They worked on battlefronts

Vocabulary

controversy (n) *a discussion or argument over an issue*

critical (adj) *especially important*

foreign (adj) *having to do with another country*

positions (n) *jobs*

as nurses, cooks, and laundresses. Since then, the role of women in the military has changed dramatically.

During World War II, many new opportunities opened up for women wanting to serve their country. Across America, females were encouraged to help with the war effort. The war was being fought in Europe. Despite the **controversy** over whether women should work outside the home, some American women took up the countless jobs left behind by the fighting men. 1 Many others chose to contribute to, or play a significant part in, the war effort by joining the military. Their voluntary participation in the military was controversial at first. 2 Although they chose to join, many people had trouble accepting the idea of women in uniform. But, America's female military members quickly erased those doubts. They became a **critical** part of the U.S. forces.

More than 150,000 women served in the Women's Army Corps (WAC). They were the first women besides nurses to serve in the U.S. Army. For the first time, women were sent to basic training camps and deployed, or sent into action. They did not see any frontline combat. However, WACs served as medical technicians, radio operators, and secretaries in the United States and in **foreign** countries. They also worked as training instructors, mechanics, photo interpreters, and parachute riggers. Women in the WAC happily took these **positions**. This freed up men to fight the war in foreign countries.

Soon after the WAC was created, other branches of the armed forces encouraged women to enlist, or join. The WAVES (Women Accepted for

1 Inference
What is the controversy about women working outside the home?

2 Context Clues
Using the surrounding sentences, determine what the word *voluntary* means.

Volunteer Emergency Service) was the female unit of the Navy. These women held many of the same positions as their counterparts in the Army. However, some took on even more responsibility. WAVES were the first women in the U.S. military whose duties were exactly the same as male aircrew members. The number of women volunteering to enlist was amazing. By the end of the war, there were more than 8,000 female officers and close to 80,000 enlisted WAVES.

The first women trained to fly American military aircraft were members of WASP, the Women Airforce Service Pilots. These women were a vital part of the Air Force. There were about 1,000 female pilots who were a part of this branch, and they flew almost every type of military plane. Combined, they flew more than 60 million miles, or 2,500 times around the world, in three years. 3

Although they may not have known it, they were paving the way for future generations of American women to become members of the armed forces. By the 1970s, each of these separate divisions was disbanded, or broken up, and women became active parts of the Army, Navy, Air Force, and Marines.

Women in the military are becoming more common. Today, about 20 percent of the military is female. They hold a wide variety of positions and are a critical part of the armed forces. Many of them are

3 Summarize
What were the three military units created for women?

WACs inspecting an airplane

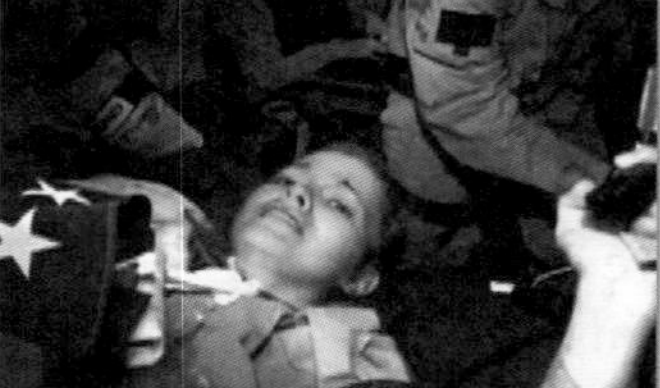

Jessica Lynch was the first female POW to be successfully rescued.

stationed in foreign countries. As more and more females enlist in the military, they continue to break new ground.

In the 1990s, women began to be recognized as military leaders. During this decade, many women were promoted to become commanding officers. The Marine Corps opened pilot positions to women. The Air Force assigned the first woman to command an Intercontinental Ballistic Missile unit.

Female soldier Jessica Lynch made national headlines when she was taken as a prisoner of war (POW) in 2003. She was captured by Iraqi forces when her unit was ambushed. Lynch was rescued about a week later. It was the first time an American female POW had been saved. It was also the first successful rescue of an American POW since World War II.

While some people still see their involvement as controversial, women are in active combat roles on land, at sea, and in the air. Some have graduated in the top of their class at military academies. Others hold high-ranking positions, managing others and making important tactical decisions, critical for each battle's victory. With the many opportunities the military offers its members, women continue to prove that they can be all they can be. 4 End

4 Ask Questions
Think about what you just read. Was there a part that was confusing? Reread the sections that are still unclear.

U.S. Army Capt. Cindy Stockamp counts with children of Afghanistan.

"Women in the Military"

Before Reading

Introduce Vocabulary

1. Have students turn to Part A on Student Book page 145 and scan the boldfaced vocabulary words. **You will see these words when you read the passage "Women in the Military." What do you already know about these words?** Have students rate their knowledge of each boldfaced word.
2. For each word, read the part of speech, definition, and example sentence.
3. For each word that students did not know, have them give an everyday example of the word.
4. Read the instructions for Part B aloud, and have students complete the activity independently. Have partners share answers.

Refer to Blackline Master page 28 to extend vocabulary practice.

Have students use the *Passport Reading Journeys* online technology component to practice and reinforce vocabulary and comprehension skills.

Apply the Target Skill: Cause and Effect

1. **What does *cause* mean? What does *effect* mean?** Write student responses on the board.
2. Write the following effect on the board, and have students provide a cause: *Jesse fell down the steps because ____.* Ask for student responses.

   What is the signal word? (because) **Sometimes you have to infer what a cause or effect is. When you infer the cause or effect, you use what you read and what you already know to figure it out.**
3. **Grant ate a whole pizza and a shake, then he ate two slices of pumpkin pie. Grant felt sick. What is the cause and effect?** (The cause is that Grant ate too much; the effect is that he felt sick.) **The text does not directly state the cause of Grant's sickness. You inferred that eating too much made him sick. What made you infer that cause?** (I know that when people eat too much, they often get sick and have stomachaches.)

Expedition 5, Lesson 3

Name ____________________ Date ____________

Vocabulary

"Women in the Military"

A. Rate your knowledge of each boldfaced word.
3 I know what this word means, and I can use it in a sentence.
2 I have an idea of this word's meaning, but I need to know more.
1 I don't know what this word means.

☐ **encourage** (v) *attempt to persuade*
The ads for the military hope to *encourage* women to join the armed forces.

☐ **vital** (adj) *very important*
Women have played a *vital* role in many wars of the past.

☐ **controversy** (n) *a discussion or argument over an issue*
Whether women should work or stay at home has been a *controversy* for the last 75 years.

☐ **critical** (adj) *especially important*
Each battle is *critical* to the outcome of the war and can't be taken for granted.

☐ **foreign** (adj) *having to do with another country*
Military women often leave the United States to fight wars in *foreign* countries.

☐ **positions** (n) *jobs*
Women hold a variety of *positions* in the military from nurse to commander.

B. Read each question, then write the answer on the line.

1. When salespeople **encourage** a customer to buy a shirt, would they say the shirt is too expensive or the best color and style? the best color and style
2. To win a basketball game, is it **vital** to practice as a team or to befriend the other team's players? to practice as a team
3. Which two people have a **controversy**: two people discussing the nice weather or two people discussing the pros and cons of school uniforms? two people discussing the pros and cons of school uniforms
4. To be safe while riding in a boat, would it be **critical** to wear a life jacket or to know the kinds of fish that live in the lake? to wear a life jacket
5. If you are in a **foreign** city, do you live there or are you visiting? visiting
6. If you listen to people explain the **positions** they hold, do you hear about their hobbies or their work? their work

 145

Vocabulary

encourage	(v) *attempt to persuade* The ads for the military hope to *encourage* women to join the armed forces.
vital	(adj) *very important* Women have played a *vital* role in many wars of the past.
controversy	(n) *a discussion or argument over an issue* Whether women should work or stay at home has been a *controversy* for the last 75 years.
critical	(adj) *especially important* Each battle is *critical* to the outcome of the war and can't be taken for granted.
foreign	(adj) *having to do with another country* Military women often leave the United States to fight wars in *foreign* countries.
positions	(n) *jobs* Women hold a variety of *positions* in the military from nurse to commander.

4. **During the Revolutionary War, American soldiers used weapons such as cannons, which could hit targets from about half a mile away. Why? What is the cause?** (They didn't want to get too close; they wanted to stay safe.)

Introduce the Passage

1. Have students turn to Anthology page 79 and preview "Women in the Military." **Predict what this passage will be about.** Allow students to make predictions.
2. Direct students to pause and think about the margin prompts as they read. **When you see these prompts, pause and read them. Try to respond if you can. If you can't, continue reading, but keep the prompt in mind.**
3. Teach these terms from the passage:
   - *Parachute riggers* are people who inspect, repair, and pack or fold parachutes.
   - *Paving the way* means "making it easier for others to follow."
   - A *prisoner of war* is a person taken by or surrendering to enemy forces in wartime.

ELL Support the academic vocabulary word *infer*. Remind students that they practiced making inferences in Expedition 4. Write the word *inference* and underline the base word *infer*. Review the definition.

During Reading

1. Have students read "Women in the Military." To select reading options that support your students' levels and classroom needs, see Reading Differentiation, page xxxii, if needed.
2. **Look for causes and effects as you read "Women in the Military."**

After Reading

Check Comprehension

1. Have students think about the predictions they made about this passage. **What information did you expect to find in this passage? What information surprised you?** Have students evaluate their predictions.
2. Ask students to share their responses to the Inference margin prompt on Anthology page 80. **What kinds of work do people do at home?** (clean; cook; take care of children) **What does this tell you about what some people expected women to do with their lives?** (Some people expected women only to take care of the home.) Discuss with students why this view could be controversial.

   To make the most of the discussion time, remember to incorporate strategies that encourage and extend student involvement. Refer to page xxxviii for a comprehensive discussion of these strategies.
3. For the Context Clues margin prompt on Anthology page 80, have students reread the paragraph. **Pay special attention to the sentences around the word *voluntary*. How did women in World War II get involved in the military?** (They chose to join and contribute.) **Based on these clues, what does the word *voluntary* mean?** (*Voluntary* refers to something that is chosen freely.)
4. Discuss cause and effect in the following manner. **On the first page of the passage, it says that women were cooks, nurses, and laundresses, but it doesn't say why these were the only jobs available to them. Based on what you already know, can you infer the cause? Why did women hold these jobs?** (Women were expected to be caretakers and to do household chores; men didn't do these jobs.) Have students turn to the second page. **Why did women start working outside of the home?** (Men left jobs to fight in the war; people were needed to fill the jobs.) **There were no signal words to help us, but we were able to infer the cause.**

Remind students to choose books from the *Passport Reading Journeys* Library for independent reading.

"Women in the Military"

Prepare to Reread

Introduce the Lesson

Remind students that they read about women's roles in the military in Lesson 3. **In this lesson, we'll revisit "Women in the Military" to practice inferring causes and effects.**

Practice Vocabulary

1. Direct students to think about how vocabulary words were used in the passage.
   - **How might recruiters *encourage* new members to join the Army?** (They might tell about the positive reasons for joining.)
   - **If the military is missing *vital* people, what might happen? Explain.** (The military would be weaker because important people are missing.)
   - **People were involved in a *controversy* about women joining the military. State that in another way.** (People argued about whether women should be in the military.)
   - **How were women in America *critical* to the war effort during World War II?** (Women worked, making materials for the military and letting men fight.)
   - **If you are a soldier in a *foreign* war, where do you fight?** (in a country that is not my home)
   - **What were some *positions* women had in the WAC?** (Women were medical technicians, radio operators, and secretaries.)

ELL Check student knowledge of additional words, such as *recruiter*. **Does an Army *recruiter* encourage people to join the Army or to leave the Army?** (join the Army)

2. Have students turn to Anthology page 80. Read aloud the third sentence of the second full paragraph. **This sentence uses the word *deployed*. What does this word mean?** (sent into action) **What words help you figure out the meaning?** (sent into action)

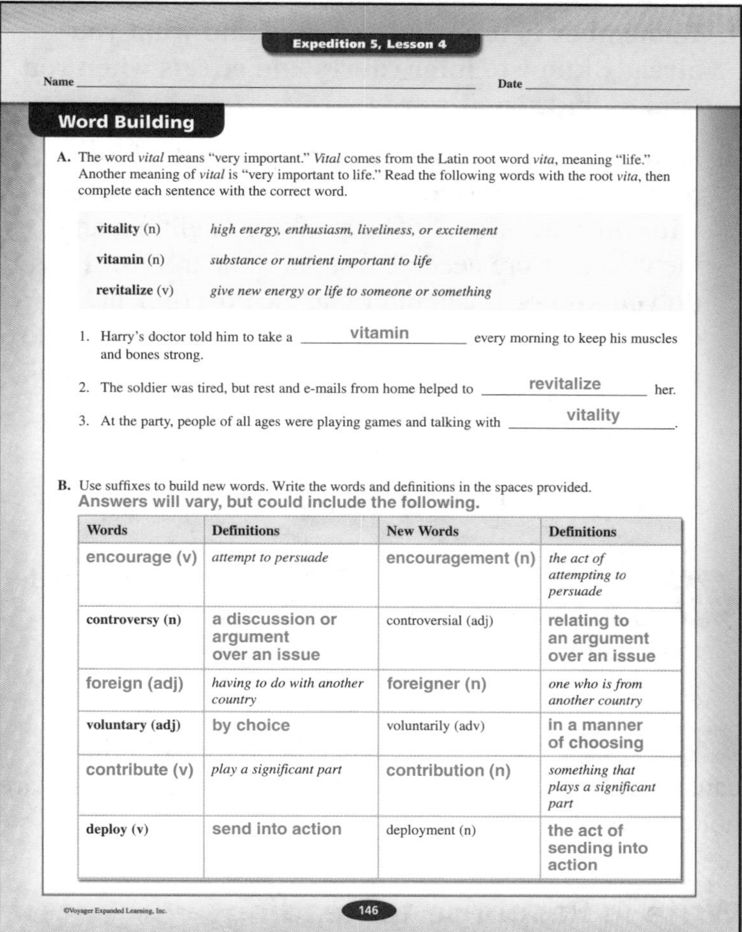

Expedition 5, Lesson 4

Name ______ Date ______

Word Building

A. The word *vital* means "very important." *Vital* comes from the Latin root word *vita*, meaning "life." Another meaning of *vital* is "very important to life." Read the following words with the root *vita*, then complete each sentence with the correct word.

vitality (n) *high energy, enthusiasm, liveliness, or excitement*

vitamin (n) *substance or nutrient important to life*

revitalize (v) *give new energy or life to someone or something*

1. Harry's doctor told him to take a vitamin every morning to keep his muscles and bones strong.
2. The soldier was tired, but rest and e-mails from home helped to revitalize her.
3. At the party, people of all ages were playing games and talking with vitality.

B. Use suffixes to build new words. Write the words and definitions in the spaces provided.
Answers will vary, but could include the following.

Words	Definitions	New Words	Definitions
encourage (v)	*attempt to persuade*	encouragement (n)	*the act of attempting to persuade*
controversy (n)	a discussion or argument over an issue	controversial (adj)	relating to an argument over an issue
foreign (adj)	*having to do with another country*	foreigner (n)	*one who is from another country*
voluntary (adj)	by choice	voluntarily (adv)	in a manner of choosing
contribute (v)	*play a significant part*	contribution (n)	*something that plays a significant part*
deploy (v)	send into action	deployment (n)	the act of sending into action

©Voyager Expanded Learning, Inc. 146

Repeat this process for the following words.

- **contribute** (v) *play a significant part*, Anthology page 80
- **voluntary** (adj) *by choice*, Anthology page 80
- **enlist** (v) *join*, Anthology page 80
- **disbanded** (v) *broken up*, Anthology page 81
- **tactical** (adj) *having to do with a battle*, Anthology page 82

3. Have students turn to Student Book page 146. Read aloud the instructions, and have students complete the activities independently.

CHECKPOINT After students complete Part B, have them identify one item that confused them. Ask students to identify the part of speech of the missing word. Tell students that this is one way to narrow down their choices.

Reread

Apply the Target Skill: Cause and Effect

1. **Remember to use what you read and what you already know to infer causes and effects when you cannot find signal words.**
2. Have students reread the fourth paragraph of the passage. **Why were females encouraged to help with the war effort?** (The men were fighting, and the women were needed to support the troops.) **How do you know?** (I can infer that the government encouraged women to help with the war effort because the men were away fighting.)
3. Have students turn to Student Book page 147. Read the instructions aloud. Explain that students will complete the page using the passage.

ELL Explain that some people believe women should not work outside the home. Encourage students to share their own ideas about women's roles.

ACADEMIC SKILL Remind students that they will infer causes and effects in other classes. Explain that causes are not always obvious.

Write in Response to Reading

1. **Before World War II, the government and men in the military doubted that women could do difficult military work.** Have students share experiences about themselves or others facing doubt when trying to accomplish something. Have students turn to Student Book page 148. Read the instructions for Part A aloud, and have students complete the activity.
2. **How might you feel if you were not allowed to show your talents? How might you respond?** Read the instructions for Part B aloud, and have students complete the activity.

EXPEDITION ORGANIZER **An Army of Progress**

Pause to have students turn to Student Book pages 138 and 139. Have students complete the following:

- Write answers or notes for the probing questions in Part A. Encourage them to add their own questions.
- Think about how "Women in the Military" shows progress. Have students fill in the appropriate space in the graphic organizer in Part B.

Expedition 5, Lesson 4

Name ______ Date ______

Cause and Effect

Reread the passage "Women in the Military" to complete the sentences. Find a cause, effect, and signal word in each sentence or group of sentences. Some signal words are *because*, *since*, and *so*.

1. Complete the sentences in the box. Infer the cause and effect, then write them in the boxes. Add a signal word.

Women were not allowed to officially join the military until World War II. There was controversy over whether women should work outside the home. Many men did not believe women were able to meet the same demands as men.

Cause	Signal Word	Effect
men did not believe that women should work outside the home or could do the things that were necessary to be in the military	therefore	women were not allowed to officially join the military until World War II

2. Complete the sentences in the box. Infer the cause and effect, then write them in the boxes. Add a signal word.

Over the years, women had shown their courage and skill both on and off the battlefield. They had graduated near the top in military academies. In the 1990s, women began to be recognized as military leaders.

Effect	Signal Word	Cause
in the 1990s, women began to be recognized as military leaders	because	women had shown great courage and had graduated near the top in military academies

 147

Expedition 5, Lesson 4

Name ______ Date ______

Write in Response to Reading

A. Think about a character from TV, movies, or books who wanted to do something or achieve something, but others doubted that he or she could do it or opposed him or her. How did that character prove himself or herself? What happened? Describe the character by completing the chart.

Answers will vary.

Name of Character	
Who the Character Was and What He or She Wanted to Do	
What People Thought of the Character	
What the Character Did to Prove Himself or Herself	

B. Have you or someone you know ever been doubted by others? What happened? How did it feel? Write about how you or the person you know thought and acted.

Student answers should reflect an understanding of the inequality experienced by figures like American women who joined the military during and right after World War II. Students should show an understanding of difficult situations and the heroism that may come out of dealing with those situations.

 148

Review, Extend, Assess

In today's lesson, as in Lessons 5 and 10 of every Expedition, there are options from which to choose. You may do any or all of the options listed. Activities for each option are given on the following pages. Each option will support or extend previously taught objectives. Choose the option(s) appropriate for your students and prepare accordingly.

Review Vocabulary

Extend Vocabulary

Assess Comprehension and Vocabulary

Reteach

Passport Reading Journeys Library

Online Technology Component

Writing Process

Real-World Reading

Exploring Careers

Review Vocabulary

Direct students to review the vocabulary for "Military Technology" and "Women in the Military" on Student Book page 139. Have students reread the meanings of the words.

1. Have students turn to Student Book page 149. **You have read these vocabulary words in the passages. Now you will read the vocabulary in different contexts. In other words, the topics will be different, but the words will have the same meanings.** Read the instructions aloud, and have students complete the activity. As students finish, have them check the definitions to ensure they used the words correctly. Have students share their answers.
2. In Part A, if students have difficulty identifying synonyms, remind them that the sentence will mean the same with the underlined word or the synonym. Have them read the sentence twice. The first time, they should read for the general understanding of the sentence. The second time, have students use the phrase *another word for* before the underlined word. For Part B, complete three items with students who have difficulty, then have them complete the remaining items independently.

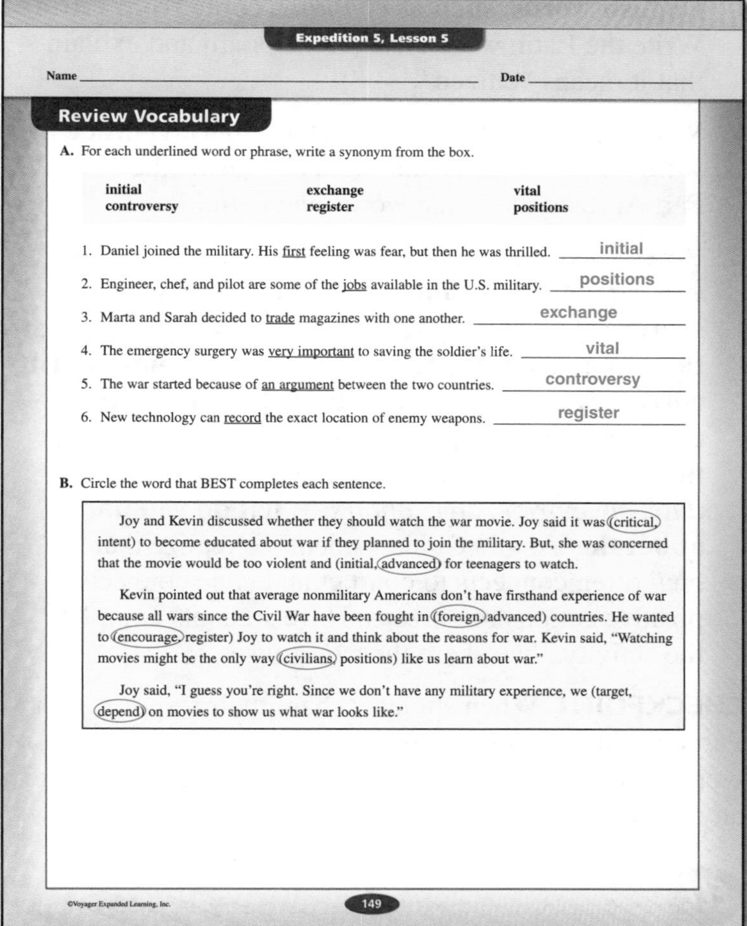

Expedition 5, Lesson 5

Name ______ Date ______

Review Vocabulary

A. For each underlined word or phrase, write a synonym from the box.

initial	exchange	vital
controversy	register	positions

1. Daniel joined the military. His first feeling was fear, but then he was thrilled. initial
2. Engineer, chef, and pilot are some of the jobs available in the U.S. military. positions
3. Marta and Sarah decided to trade magazines with one another. exchange
4. The emergency surgery was very important to saving the soldier's life. vital
5. The war started because of an argument between the two countries. controversy
6. New technology can record the exact location of enemy weapons. register

B. Circle the word that BEST completes each sentence.

Joy and Kevin discussed whether they should watch the war movie. Joy said it was (critical, intent) to become educated about war if they planned to join the military. But, she was concerned that the movie would be too violent and (initial, advanced) for teenagers to watch.

Kevin pointed out that average nonmilitary Americans don't have firsthand experience of war because all wars since the Civil War have been fought in (foreign, advanced) countries. He wanted to (encourage, register) Joy to watch it and think about the reasons for war. Kevin said, "Watching movies might be the only way (civilians, positions) like us learn about war."

Joy said, "I guess you're right. Since we don't have any military experience, we (target, depend) on movies to show us what war looks like."

©Voyager Expanded Learning, Inc. 149

CHECKPOINT Provide additional support for students who had difficulty choosing words in Part B. Have students read the sentences aloud. Tell them to read the sentence twice, inserting one of the words each time. Ask students which word makes the most sense or sounds right.

Extend Vocabulary

1. Direct students to Student Book page 150. **Many English words, such as *civilians*, come from Latin.** Write the Latin word *civis* on the board and explain that it means "citizen."
2. Write *civilians* on the board. Underline *civi* inside the word. Have students underline *civi* inside the words in Part A. Read aloud the words and definitions.
3. Read aloud the instructions for Parts B and C. **You can reread the definitions to help complete the sentences in Part B. Which two words have almost the same meaning?** (civic; civil) **To use these words correctly, pay attention to how they are used in texts and how people use them in speech.** Provide these examples: *civil strife*, *civil disobedience*, *civic duty*, *civic pride*, *civic affairs*. **What do you notice about the usage?** Guide students to realize that *civil* often connects to conflict and *civic* connects to positive actions of citizens. Have students complete the activity, then share their responses.

CHECKPOINT When students share their responses for Parts B and C, listen to ensure that they used the new words in the correct contexts. Pause to explain and correct any errors.

Part A

1. Write the boldfaced words and underline the letters *civi* in each. **Roots may come from other languages. Do you know any words in other languages that come from the root *civis*?**
2. Explore each new word by reading the definition, using the words in a sentence, then asking students to answer a question about the word. ***Civilians* are people who are not in the military. During a war, *civilians* may have to leave the area. How is war dangerous for *civilians*?** Have students answer using the following sentence starter: *War is dangerous for civilians because* _____. (They may be hurt; they don't have weapons.)

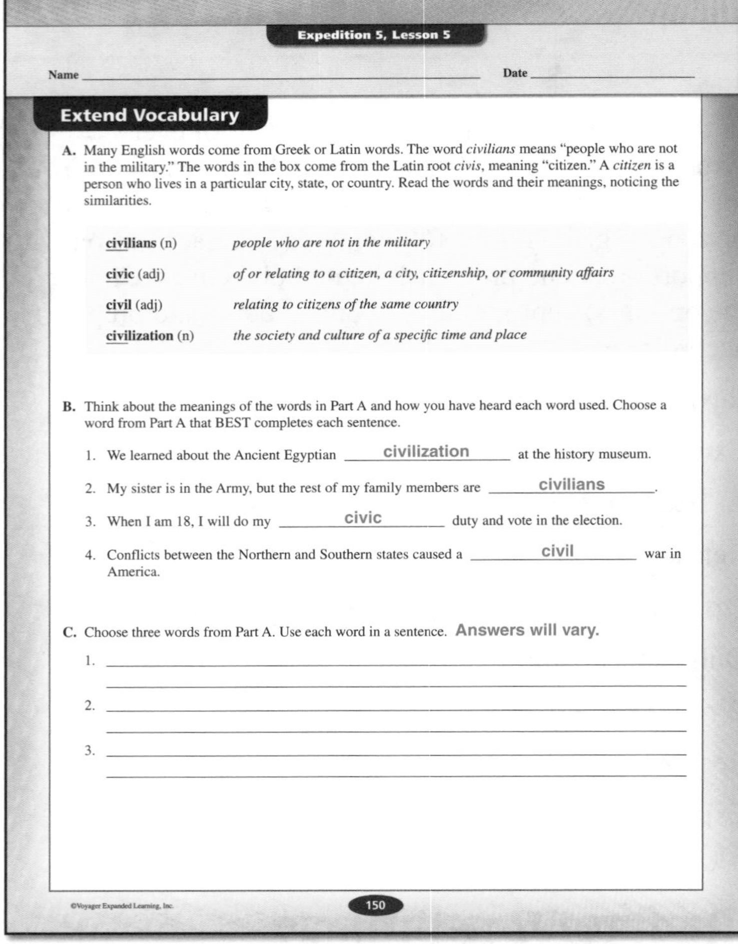

Expedition 5, Lesson 5

Name ______________________ Date ____________

Extend Vocabulary

A. Many English words come from Greek or Latin words. The word *civilians* means "people who are not in the military." The words in the box come from the Latin root *civis*, meaning "citizen." A *citizen* is a person who lives in a particular city, state, or country. Read the words and their meanings, noticing the similarities.

civilians (n)	*people who are not in the military*
civic (adj)	*of or relating to a citizen, a city, citizenship, or community affairs*
civil (adj)	*relating to citizens of the same country*
civilization (n)	*the society and culture of a specific time and place*

B. Think about the meanings of the words in Part A and how you have heard each word used. Choose a word from Part A that BEST completes each sentence.

1. We learned about the Ancient Egyptian ___civilization___ at the history museum.
2. My sister is in the Army, but the rest of my family members are ___civilians___.
3. When I am 18, I will do my ___civic___ duty and vote in the election.
4. Conflicts between the Northern and Southern states caused a ___civil___ war in America.

C. Choose three words from Part A. Use each word in a sentence. Answers will vary.

1. ______________________
2. ______________________
3. ______________________

150

Part B

If students have difficulty completing the sentences, turn the sentence frame into a question with the blank as an answer. **We learned about the ancient Egyptian *civilization* at the history museum. What things did we learn about at the museum?** (ancient Egyptian civilization)

Assess Comprehension and Vocabulary

1. Remind students that they learned about and practiced finding causes and effects as they read the Anthology passages. **How do you look for causes and effects as you read?** Have students explain the strategy in their own words.

2. Direct students to Student Book pages 151–153. Preview the pages, showing students that they will read two passages, find causes and effects, and answer questions. Have students complete the pages independently.

   Review student answers. Whenever possible, provide elaborative feedback to student responses. Refer to page xl for examples of elaborative feedback and how to incorporate it in your lessons.

   If students incorrectly answer more than 4 out of 15 assessment questions, evaluate what kind of reteaching is needed. If students miss vocabulary questions, have them return to the vocabulary activities and work with the words they missed. For cause and effect errors, use the reteaching suggestions on page 192.

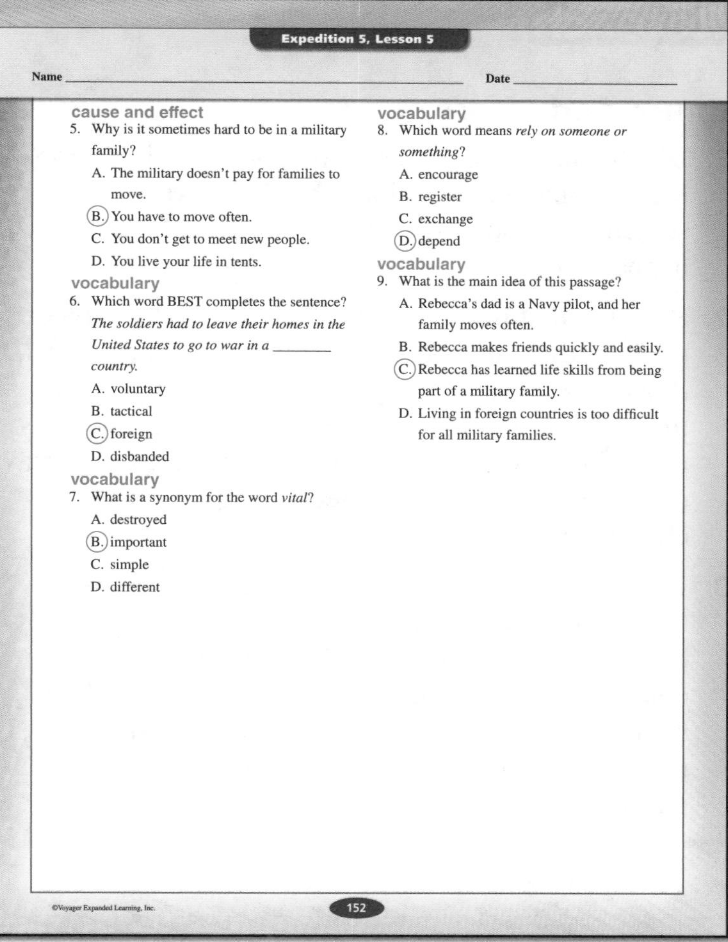

Expedition 5, Lesson 5

Name ____________ Date ____________

cause and effect

5. Why is it sometimes hard to be in a military family?
   A. The military doesn't pay for families to move.
   (B.) You have to move often.
   C. You don't get to meet new people.
   D. You live your life in tents.

vocabulary

6. Which word BEST completes the sentence? *The soldiers had to leave their homes in the United States to go to war in a ________ country.*
   A. voluntary
   B. tactical
   (C.) foreign
   D. disbanded

vocabulary

7. What is a synonym for the word *vital*?
   A. destroyed
   (B.) important
   C. simple
   D. different

vocabulary

8. Which word means *rely on someone or something*?
   A. encourage
   B. register
   C. exchange
   (D.) depend

vocabulary

9. What is the main idea of this passage?
   A. Rebecca's dad is a Navy pilot, and her family moves often.
   B. Rebecca makes friends quickly and easily.
   (C.) Rebecca has learned life skills from being part of a military family.
   D. Living in foreign countries is too difficult for all military families.

©Voyager Expanded Learning, Inc. 152

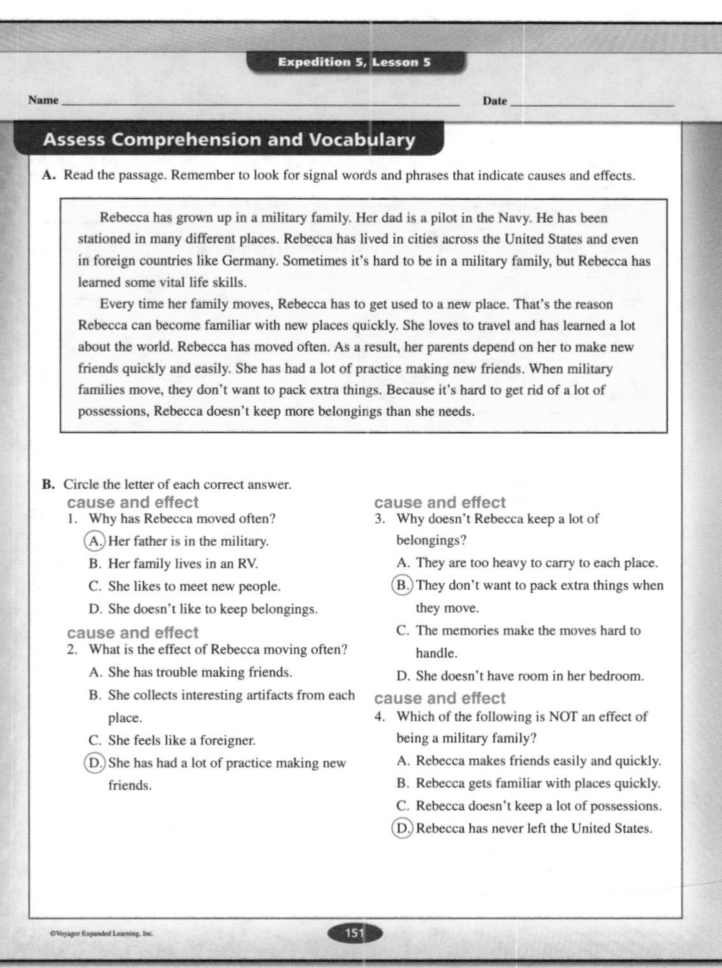

Expedition 5, Lesson 5

Name ____________ Date ____________

Assess Comprehension and Vocabulary

A. Read the passage. Remember to look for signal words and phrases that indicate causes and effects.

Rebecca has grown up in a military family. Her dad is a pilot in the Navy. He has been stationed in many different places. Rebecca has lived in cities across the United States and even in foreign countries like Germany. Sometimes it's hard to be in a military family, but Rebecca has learned some vital life skills.

Every time her family moves, Rebecca has to get used to a new place. That's the reason Rebecca can become familiar with new places quickly. She loves to travel and has learned a lot about the world. Rebecca has moved often. As a result, her parents depend on her to make new friends quickly and easily. She has had a lot of practice making new friends. When military families move, they don't want to pack extra things. Because it's hard to get rid of a lot of possessions, Rebecca doesn't keep more belongings than she needs.

B. Circle the letter of each correct answer.

cause and effect

1. Why has Rebecca moved often?
   (A.) Her father is in the military.
   B. Her family lives in an RV.
   C. She likes to meet new people.
   D. She doesn't like to keep belongings.

cause and effect

2. What is the effect of Rebecca moving often?
   A. She has trouble making friends.
   B. She collects interesting artifacts from each place.
   C. She feels like a foreigner.
   (D.) She has had a lot of practice making new friends.

cause and effect

3. Why doesn't Rebecca keep a lot of belongings?
   A. They are too heavy to carry to each place.
   (B.) They don't want to pack extra things when they move.
   C. The memories make the moves hard to handle.
   D. She doesn't have room in her bedroom.

cause and effect

4. Which of the following is NOT an effect of being a military family?
   A. Rebecca makes friends easily and quickly.
   B. Rebecca gets familiar with places quickly.
   C. Rebecca doesn't keep a lot of possessions.
   (D.) Rebecca has never left the United States.

©Voyager Expanded Learning, Inc. 151

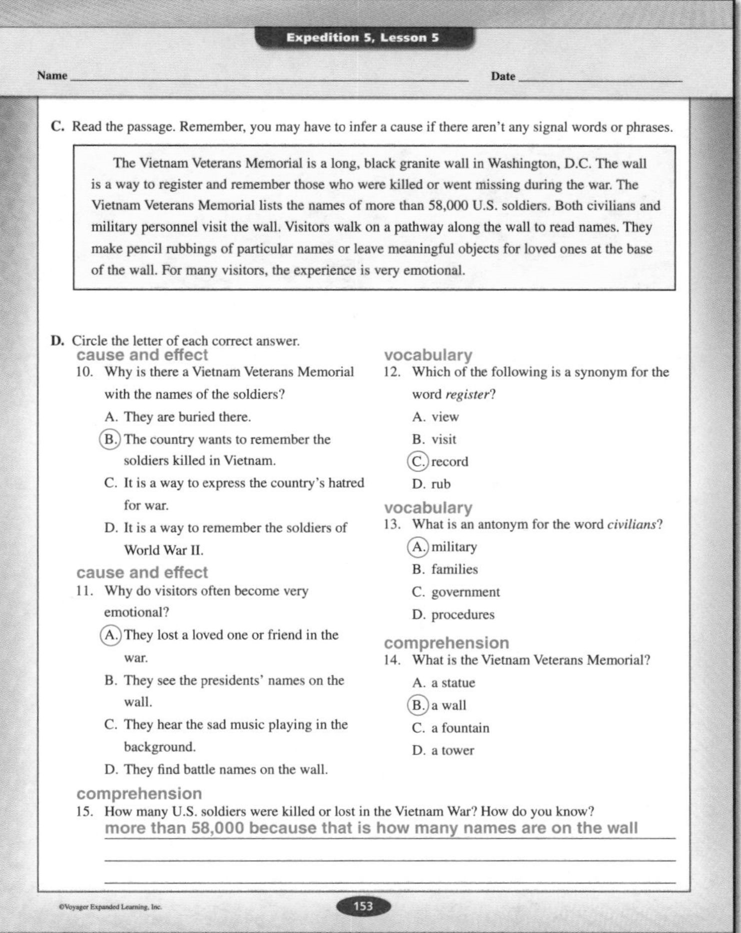

Expedition 5, Lesson 5

Name ____________ Date ____________

C. Read the passage. Remember, you may have to infer a cause if there aren't any signal words or phrases.

The Vietnam Veterans Memorial is a long, black granite wall in Washington, D.C. The wall is a way to register and remember those who were killed or went missing during the war. The Vietnam Veterans Memorial lists the names of more than 58,000 U.S. soldiers. Both civilians and military personnel visit the wall. Visitors walk on a pathway along the wall to read names. They make pencil rubbings of particular names or leave meaningful objects for loved ones at the base of the wall. For many visitors, the experience is very emotional.

D. Circle the letter of each correct answer.

cause and effect

10. Why is there a Vietnam Veterans Memorial with the names of the soldiers?
    A. They are buried there.
    (B.) The country wants to remember the soldiers killed in Vietnam.
    C. It is a way to express the country's hatred for war.
    D. It is a way to remember the soldiers of World War II.

cause and effect

11. Why do visitors often become very emotional?
    (A.) They lost a loved one or friend in the war.
    B. They see the presidents' names on the wall.
    C. They hear the sad music playing in the background.
    D. They find battle names on the wall.

vocabulary

12. Which of the following is a synonym for the word *register*?
    A. view
    B. visit
    (C.) record
    D. rub

vocabulary

13. What is an antonym for the word *civilians*?
    (A.) military
    B. families
    C. government
    D. procedures

comprehension

14. What is the Vietnam Veterans Memorial?
    A. a statue
    (B.) a wall
    C. a fountain
    D. a tower

comprehension

15. How many U.S. soldiers were killed or lost in the Vietnam War? How do you know?
    more than 58,000 because that is how many names are on the wall

©Voyager Expanded Learning, Inc. 153

Reteach

Cause and Effect

1. Direct students to Student Book pages 154 and 155. Read the instructions aloud. **What is a cause?** (why something happened) **What is an effect?** (what happened)
2. Read the first passage aloud. **What signal words or phrases do you see?** (as a result) **What happened?** (Civilians saw photographs of the war for the first time.) **What made that happen?** (Photography was a new invention.) Remind students that the cause may come before or after the effect. Complete the first chart together.
3. **Remember, you may not always see signal words. You may have to use details and what you already know to infer cause and effect.** Have students complete the remaining charts independently. After students complete the pages, have them compare responses. Identify common errors and clarify misconceptions.

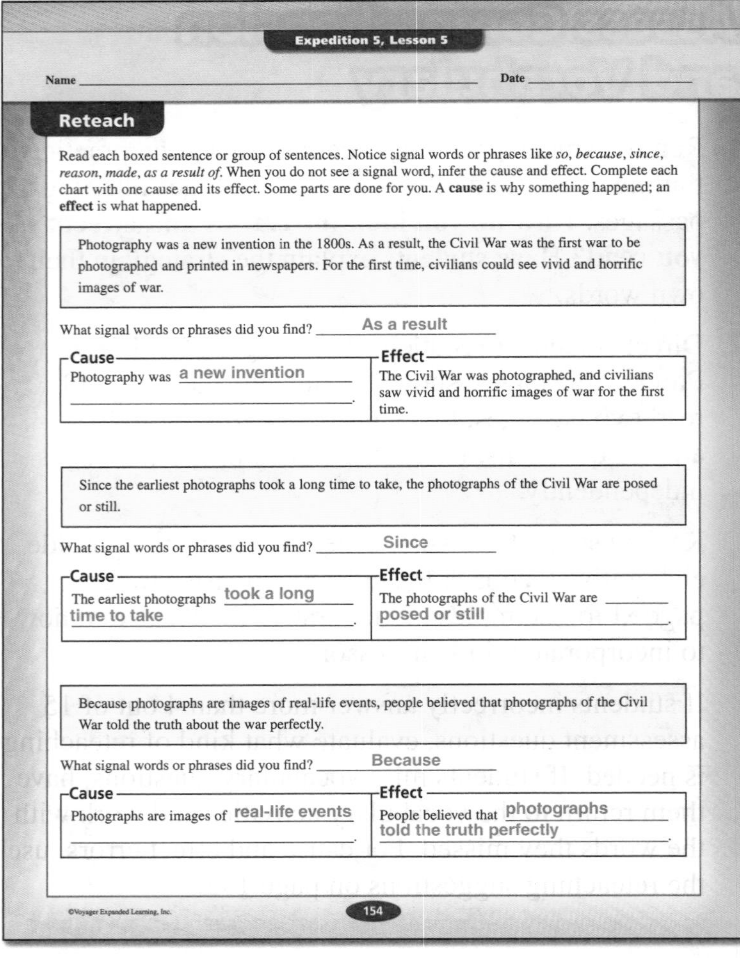

Expedition 5, Lesson 5

Name ______ Date ______

Reteach

Read each boxed sentence or group of sentences. Notice signal words or phrases like *so, because, since, reason, made, as a result of.* When you do not see a signal word, infer the cause and effect. Complete each chart with one cause and its effect. Some parts are done for you. A **cause** is why something happened; an **effect** is what happened.

Photography was a new invention in the 1800s. As a result, the Civil War was the first war to be photographed and printed in newspapers. For the first time, civilians could see vivid and horrific images of war.

What signal words or phrases did you find? As a result

Cause	Effect
Photography was a new invention.	The Civil War was photographed, and civilians saw vivid and horrific images of war for the first time.

Since the earliest photographs took a long time to take, the photographs of the Civil War are posed or still.

What signal words or phrases did you find? Since

Cause	Effect
The earliest photographs took a long time to take.	The photographs of the Civil War are posed or still.

Because photographs are images of real-life events, people believed that photographs of the Civil War told the truth about the war perfectly.

What signal words or phrases did you find? Because

Cause	Effect
Photographs are images of real-life events.	People believed that photographs told the truth perfectly.

©Voyager Expanded Learning, Inc.

154

Expedition 5, Lesson 5

Name ______ Date ______

Photographers during the Civil War used the new technology to excite the public. They would often stage the photos to make it look like their side was winning or to cause anger over the actions of the enemy. People's opinion often changed because of the photographs.

Why would photographers make it look like their side was winning? Infer the cause.
to give people hope

Cause	Effect
Photographers stage photographs.	People's opinions changed.

The invention of photography changed how people "saw" war. Infer the effect this has had on modern warfare.
Answers will vary, but should reflect knowledge of changing war coverage and people's attitudes about war.

©Voyager Expanded Learning, Inc.

155

Passport Reading Journeys Library

1. Have students choose reading material from the *Passport Reading Journeys* Library or another approved selection. If students have not finished a previously chosen selection, they may continue reading from that selection. See the *Passport Reading Journeys* Library Teacher's Guide for material on selection guidelines.
2. You also may use this time to allow students to participate in book clubs or book presentations. Use the criteria specified in the *Passport Reading Journeys* Library Teacher's Guide.

Vocabulary Connections

Vocabulary words for each book are listed in the Teacher's Guide. These words are content-related or used frequently in reading material. The selected words can be a basis for independent or small-group discussions and activities.

Student Opportunities

Six copies of each book title are provided in the *Passport Reading Journeys* Library. The number of copies makes it possible for small groups of students to read the same material and share the information they read.

Theme-related titles include *The Lightning Thief* and *Scorpions.*

Technology

1. Depending on your classroom configuration and computer access, you may have all students work through the technology in a lab setting or have individuals or small groups of students work on desktops or laptops while other students participate in other suggested activities, such as the *Passport Reading Journeys* Library.
2. The online technology component provides additional support for students to work with selected vocabulary words. Students will work through a series of activities to strengthen their word knowledge, then apply that knowledge to passage reading. Refer to the online technology component User Guide for more information.

   Theme-related word sets include World History, U.S. History, Technology, and Government.

Writing Process

Newspaper Article

Distribute Writing Blackline Master page 9. **You will write a newspaper article based on a Civil War photograph.** Provide images from library books with photographs by Matthew Brady and his team of photographers. These can be found online in numerous places.

If you are unable to obtain Civil War photos, have students use the photographs found in "Women in the Military."

Have each student choose a photograph to write a newspaper article. **Imagine you are reporters from the time of the Civil War. What are newspaper articles generally about?** (current events) **You will write about the events as if they have just happened. What sorts of words do you use to tell a story or talk about an event?** (action words; verbs)

Assign point values as you see fit, and have students write them in the rubric. Tell students to make any notes on the page that will help them, but they will turn the page in with the assignment.

Prewrite

You will tell the story as best as you can from what you already know about the Civil War and from looking at the photograph and the caption. Use details in the picture and what you already know about war and history to infer details for a story about the picture even if you do not know much about it. Your newspaper articles should answer *who*, *what*, *when*, *where*, *why*, and *how* questions. Have students prepare a chart with the words *who*, *what*, *when*, *where*, *why*, and *how* down the left side on separate lines. Have students answer the questions about the photo on the right side of the chart. **Use the details in your chart to write your newspaper articles.**

Draft

You will use these standards, or criteria, as you write your newspaper articles. Have students note the special criteria listed on their grading rubric that relates to this assignment.

- The newspaper article answers *who*, *what*, *when*, *where*, *why*, and *how* questions.
- The newspaper article uses details from the photograph to explain it.
- The newspaper article shows evidence of prior knowledge about the Civil War.
- The writing contains strong action verbs.

Revise

Have partners read each other's articles and provide feedback. Then have students reread the drafts, using the following revision steps and questions. After each step, have students make the revisions and write their final drafts.

- **Check the organization.** What paragraphs or sentences should you move so that the information flows in the right order?
- **Check the explanation.** Did you clearly inform the reader of the event and people in the photograph? Did you answer *who*, *what*, *when*, *where*, *why*, and *how* questions? What information might you clarify?
- **Check mechanics.** Do fragments or run-on sentences need to be rewritten? What words might be misspelled? Do all sentences begin with capital letters and end with proper punctuation?

Present

Have students present their newspaper articles. Students may tell each other what details or explanations were unclear.

Assess

I will assess your writing and presentation based on the rubric. To assess student newspaper articles, use the rubric from the Writing Blackline Master.

Real-World Reading

E-Mail

1. Direct students to Student Book page 156. **You will read an e-mail. What ways do you communicate with your friends?** (phone calls; text messages; e-mails) Have students scan the e-mail to find out who and where the e-mail is from. **What can you expect to learn from this e-mail?** (what it is like to be in the military in Iraq)
2. Direct students to read the e-mail, then complete the following:
    - Circle where the writer is writing from.
    - Draw a box around where the writer is from.
    - Underline the information about the writer's job.
    - Double underline the places where the writer spends her time.
3. Have students share their answers. **Have you ever received a letter or e-mail from someone serving in the military? Imagine an e-mail was sent to you. What would it include? How would it make you feel?**

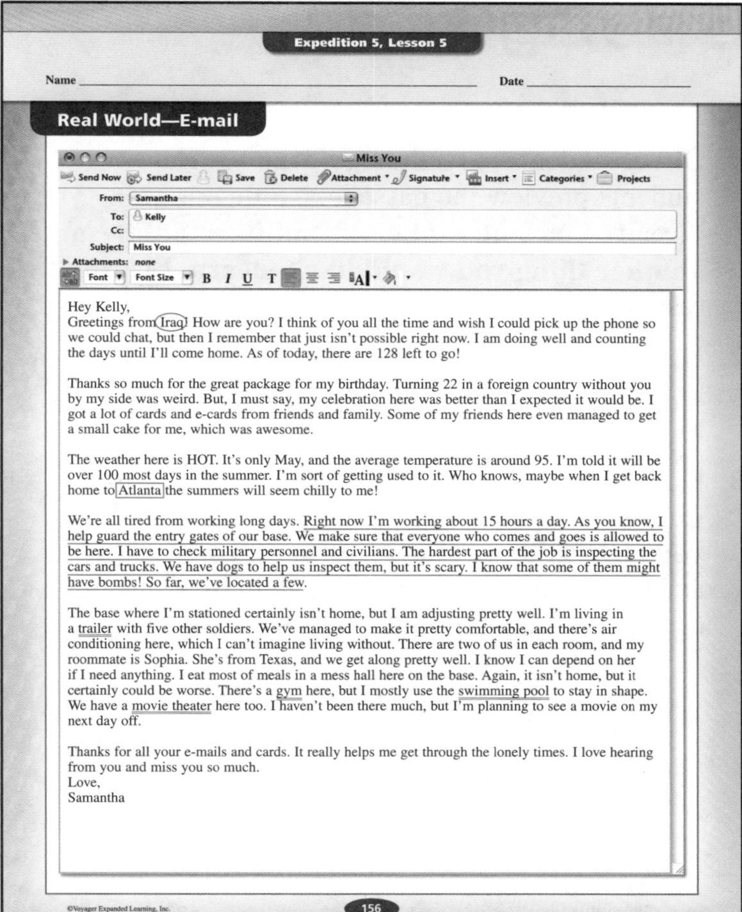
Expedition 5, Lesson 5

Name ______ Date ______

Real World—E-mail

Miss You

From: Samantha
To: Kelly
Cc:
Subject: Miss You
Attachments: none

Hey Kelly,
Greetings from Iraq! How are you? I think of you all the time and wish I could pick up the phone so we could chat, but then I remember that just isn't possible right now. I am doing well and counting the days until I'll come home. As of today, there are 128 left to go!

Thanks so much for the great package for my birthday. Turning 22 in a foreign country without you by my side was weird. But, I must say, my celebration here was better than I expected it would be. I got a lot of cards and e-cards from friends and family. Some of my friends here even managed to get a small cake for me, which was awesome.

The weather here is HOT. It's only May, and the average temperature is around 95. I'm told it will be over 100 most days in the summer. I'm sort of getting used to it. Who knows, maybe when I get back home to Atlanta the summers will seem chilly to me!

We're all tired from working long days. Right now I'm working about 15 hours a day. As you know, I help guard the entry gates of our base. We make sure that everyone who comes and goes is allowed to be here. I have to check military personnel and civilians. The hardest part of the job is inspecting the cars and trucks. We have dogs to help us inspect them, but it's scary. I know that some of them might have bombs! So far, we've located a few.

The base where I'm stationed certainly isn't home, but I am adjusting pretty well. I'm living in a trailer with five other soldiers. We've managed to make it pretty comfortable, and there's air conditioning here, which I can't imagine living without. There are two of us in each room, and my roommate is Sophia. She's from Texas, and we get along pretty well. I know I can depend on her if I need anything. I eat most of meals in a mess hall here on the base. Again, it isn't home, but it certainly could be worse. There's a gym here, but I mostly use the swimming pool to stay in shape. We have a movie theater here too. I haven't been there much, but I'm planning to see a movie on my next day off.

Thanks for all your e-mails and cards. It really helps me get through the lonely times. I love hearing from you and miss you so much.
Love,
Samantha

156

Exploring Careers

Army Pilot

1. Direct students to Anthology page 83. Have students preview the passage. **Name one thing you already know about being a military pilot. Name another thing you would like to learn.** List student responses on the board.
2. Have students read the passage. **What surprised you about this career? Which aspect appeals to you? Which aspect doesn't appeal to you?**
3. Direct students to Student Book page 157. **Answer the questions using the Anthology passage and what you already know.** Have students answer questions and complete the chart at the bottom by researching a career as a military pilot in books or online.

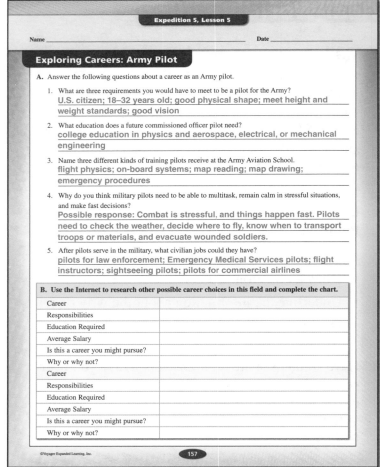

Expedition 5, Lesson 5

Name ______ Date ______

Exploring Careers: Army Pilot

A. Answer the following questions about a career as an Army pilot.

1. What are three requirements you would have to meet to be a pilot for the Army?
U.S. citizen; 18–32 years old; good physical shape; meet height and weight standards; good vision
2. What education does a future commissioned officer pilot need?
college education in physics and aerospace, electrical, or mechanical engineering
3. Name three different kinds of training pilots receive at the Army Aviation School.
flight physics; on-board systems; map reading; map drawing; emergency procedures
4. Why do you think military pilots need to be able to multitask, remain calm in stressful situations, and make fast decisions?
Possible response: Combat is stressful, and things happen fast. Pilots need to check the weather, decide where to fly, know when to transport troops or materials, and evacuate wounded soldiers.
5. After pilots serve in the military, what civilian jobs could they have?
pilots for law enforcement; Emergency Medical Services pilots; flight instructors; sightseeing pilots; pilots for commercial airlines

B. Use the Internet to research other possible career choices in this field and complete the chart.

Career	
Responsibilities	
Education Required	
Average Salary	
Is this a career you might pursue?	
Why or why not?	
Career	
Responsibilities	
Education Required	
Average Salary	
Is this a career you might pursue?	
Why or why not?	

Career

When most people tried to pilot a helicopter in the video game Battlefield 2: Modern Combat, they would either crash into the nearest building or quickly end up shot down by another player. David was the exception. The controls were complex, but he quickly mastered them. He was able to pilot the helicopter all over the map and lead his team to victory, round after round.

He knew it was just a video game, but while he played, he really felt like he was flying. He loved it! Perhaps a military career as a helicopter pilot might be a perfect fit for David. But, becoming a pilot isn't as easy as playing a video game.

The Army has requirements prospective pilots must meet before beginning their training. Candidates must be U.S. citizens between 18 and 32 years of age. They must be in good physical shape. They also have to meet the Army's height and weight standards. Finally, future pilots must have good vision. They cannot be color-blind nor have vision worse than 20/50 in either eye. After meeting these basic requirements, future pilots must take two tests: the Armed Forces Vocational Aptitude Test and the Flight Aptitude Selection Test. Soldiers must meet minimum scores on each of these tests before they can move on to the next step in the process.

Becoming a pilot involves a lot of training. Future pilots must be prepared to complete a demanding program. The Army has two types of helicopter pilots: commissioned officers and warrant officers. You must have a college degree to become a commissioned officer. Many people who choose to take this route study physics and aerospace, electrical, or mechanical engineering in college.

However, many people join the Army right after high school and become warrant officers. To become a warrant officer, candidates must complete nine weeks of Basic Combat Training. Then, they attend Warrant Officer Candidate School in Alabama for nearly seven weeks. At this school, they are tested on self-discipline, attention to detail, and time management. Additionally, the program tests decision-making skills in very stressful environments. Once these qualities have been proven, soldiers move on to specific training for helicopter pilots.

Specific flight training takes place at the Army Aviation School. Here students learn basic flying skills. They spend a lot of time in classrooms learning everything about helicopters. There are also in-depth lessons in flight physics, on-board systems,

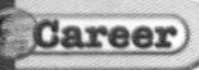

map reading, map drawing, and emergency procedures.

After the classroom portion of the training, soldiers start their in-flight education. To begin, they spend several hours in a flight simulator. Once this requirement is met, they then complete between 70 and 150 hours of in-flight training. In this phase, students further develop their technique and learn basic combat flight skills.

The last phase of this intense training program requires students to specialize in one of four types of the Army's helicopters. Students do not get to choose their specialty. It is assigned to them by the Army. During this phase, they learn all of the details and characteristics of a Kiowa, Black Hawk, Apache, or Chinook helicopter. The whole program takes about one year to complete.

In addition to having a strong desire to fly a helicopter, pilots must have the ability to multitask and remain calm in stressful situations. During training, they are frequently forced to make on-the-spot choices. Then, they must explain their decisions. Also, there is much more to becoming a pilot than just flying the helicopters. Before taking off, they need to prepare flight plans and check weather reports. While in the air, pilots must monitor the cockpit control panels, engines, and other systems on board the helicopter. Additionally, they need to be prepared to perform military operations, transport troops and materials, and evacuate wounded soldiers.

Most experts agree that learning to fly with the military is the absolute best flight training a pilot can get. Upon entering the Army, training is a soldier's job. Soldiers get paid while learning, instead of paying for classes. Generally, a beginning Army salary is about $30,000 a year for an officer. With time and experience, officers have the potential to earn close to $100,000 a year. Army service also makes soldiers eligible for other benefits, such as health care, retirement pay, and free or subsidized food, housing, and education. However, if they pursue this path, pilots must remember that their primary responsibility is to be a soldier first and a helicopter pilot second. The needs of the Army always come first.

Once pilots finish their service with the military, many choose to take their flight skills to a civilian job. Some work as pilots for law enforcement and earn around $90,000 a year. Others become Emergency Medical Services (EMS) pilots. Salaries for this job are about $60,000 annually. Other civilian job opportunities include flight instructors or sightseeing pilots who fly tourists over city attractions. Salaries for these jobs are about $60,000 a year.

David was impressed with all the opportunities available to him. The training will be difficult, but he thinks it will be worth it. Before long, he might be flying in a foreign country, helping serve his country and earning a living doing something he loves.

English Language Learner Overview

The ELL signals when extra support is provided for students during the lesson. As needed, Blackline Masters for English language learners may provide support. For vocabulary, students also may use the online technology component to practice Expedition words or other content-area vocabulary and designated ELL word sets.

Introduce Vocabulary

Lesson 6

Write the words *categorized* and *developed* and tell students that the inflected ending *-ed* changes a verb from present tense to past tense. Draw a line between the verb and the inflected ending. ***Categorize* means "group things based on similarities." I *categorize* my clothing into shirts, pants, and sweaters. When I add *-ed* to the end, that means I put things into groups in the past—perhaps yesterday or earlier today. Yesterday, I *categorized* my CDs by the year they came out.** Repeat this process for *developed*. Point out that some verbs need spelling changes when *-ed* is added.

Lesson 8

Distribute six index cards to each student. Have students write one vocabulary word from Lesson 8 on each card. Read aloud each definition, and model how you would remember the meaning. ***Dominated* means "controlled." It makes me think of *bossed around*, so I will write that on the card.** Have students write or draw a clue on each card to help remember the meaning. Provide students with the following sentences. Have them choose words from the cards to complete each sentence.

- **White men _____ the military until others were allowed to join.** (dominated)
- **When conditions in a country change, laws can be _____.** (amended)
- **The founders of the town _____ this school in 1942.** (established)
- **Citizens pay taxes to the state and federal _____ .** (government)
- **I don't know exactly how much money I have, but I know _____ how much I have.** (approximately)
- **A good diet is the _____ factor in maintaining a healthy weight.** (primary)

Practice Vocabulary

In Lesson 7, provide support for the context words *protocol* and *alleviate*. **A *protocol* is the way you are supposed to do things in a certain situation. Our school has a *protocol* for getting out of the building when there is a fire. What is our *protocol* for when there is a fire?** Write the following sentence starter on the board: *When there is a fire, our protocol is* _____. (to exit the building in an orderly fashion)

When you *alleviate* pain, you decrease or take away the pain. I will *alleviate* your discomfort by giving you a pillow. What are some ways to *alleviate* the symptoms of a cold? Write the following sentence starter on the board: *You can alleviate the symptoms of a cold by* _____. (drinking juice; eating hot soup; sleeping; taking vitamin C)

In Lesson 9, provide support for the context words *sacred* and *deserted*. **If something is *sacred*, it is considered holy. People who practice the Hindu religion consider the cow a *sacred* animal. Name something that is considered *sacred* in another religion.**

If you *deserted* something, you left it behind. The word *desert* is spelled the same as *desert*, but the two words are pronounced differently. Write *desert (noun)* and *desert (verb)* on the board. Pronounce both words, and have students repeat. **It is very dry in the *desert*, so few animals and plants can live there.** Under *desert (noun)*, draw a simple desert with a sun and one cactus. **When you *desert* something, you leave it behind. I felt afraid of the empty parking lot, so I *deserted* it.** Under *desert (verb)*, draw a simple house with a person walking away. **You may have heard the word *dessert*, meaning a sweet treat you eat after a meal. Although it sounds the same as the word *desert*, meaning to leave it behind, it is spelled differently.** Write *dessert* on the board. **When you are talking about the treat you have after a meal, there are two *s*'s.**

Apply the Target Skill: Cause and Effect

Some students may need additional practice identifying multiple causes with one effect. Blackline Master page 31 begins with a brief activity that provides additional practice identifying causes and effects.

After the massive freeway accident, emergency workers immediately sprang into action. They quickly arrived at the accident scene. Then, they began to **assess** the damage. The workers evaluated the injured with the triage system. They rapidly identified who needed the most immediate treatment. A few of the injured were placed in ambulances and medical helicopters to be taken to local hospitals. Others with less **severe** injuries would be treated on-site. Some would need blood transfusions, but they would survive this horrible crash. The people on the scene may not have realized it, but all of these modern medical techniques originated from military medical practices.

Vocabulary

assess (v) *determine the importance, size, or value of something*

severe (adj) *hard to bear or deal with*

categorized (v) *grouped things based on similarities*

frequently (adv) *often*

Triage

Triage is a process for classifying injured people into groups. The word *triage* comes from the French verb *trier*, which means "to sort." The injured are quickly assessed, sorted, and **categorized** based on the severity of their injuries. Today, this system is used **frequently** in emergency rooms and at disaster sites. Triage helps categorize the wounded; allocate, or distribute, scarce resources; and maximize the number of survivors.

Vocabulary

developed (v) *created or produced over time*

concept (n) *thought; general idea*

This standard practice did not originate in hospitals. It was **developed** on battlefields in France during the 1800s. A French doctor in Napoleon's army came up with this method to sort and categorize wounded soldiers. This was a huge change in protocol, or procedure. Prior to this, soldiers were treated in order of rank. The highest ranking officers were always treated first, a **concept** that led to many unnecessary deaths. [1] With the triage system, soldiers who could be quickly treated and returned to combat were now the highest priority. Doctors then turned their attention to wounded soldiers who would probably recover in a few days. Those who were severely injured and probably wouldn't live were left to die on the battlefield.

1 Make Connections
Think about a time when you felt like someone was treated better than you because of who they were. How did that make you feel?

2 Inference
Why did the soldiers become addicted to the drugs? How do you know?

Painkillers

Issuing painkillers to the wounded is another medical technique that was frequently used by military doctors and is standard practice today. Painkillers were often used during the Civil War to keep soldiers comfortable. Many battlefield doctors used morphine to alleviate, or relieve, pain. The morphine was often given in opium pills. Opium is an addictive narcotic that comes from opium poppy seeds. Almost 10 million opium pills, along with 2.8 million ounces of other forms of opium, were given to Union soldiers during the war.

Opium was used to numb the wounded and reduce their pain. The physicians also used it to treat diarrhea, dysentery, and malaria. It provided soldiers with relief from the pain. However, it caused other problems. By 1880, a large number of Union soldiers were addicted to morphine. The newspapers of the day referred to this addiction as "Soldier's Disease." [2]

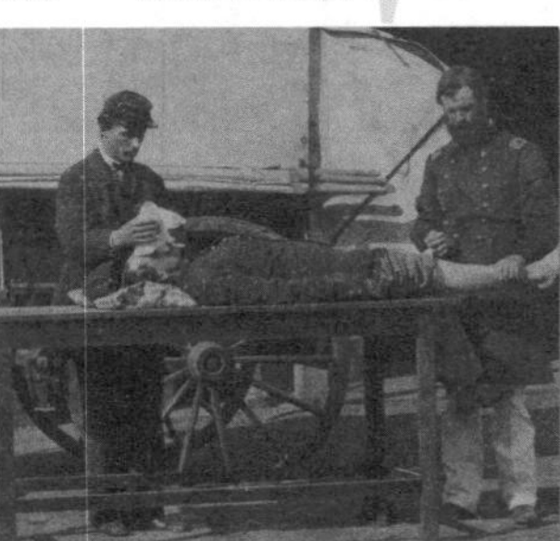
Civil War surgeon at work

A wounded soldier is brought to a mobile hospital by ambulance during battle.

Transporting Blood, Supplies, and Patients

The first known ambulance service was created by the Knights of St. John during the Crusades (decades of wars fought over religion) in the 11th century. They would transport the wounded to medical tents for assessment and treatment. Over time, this concept continued to develop. During French wars in the early 1800s, Napoleon's chief physician improved upon the existing ambulance system. His idea was to remove injured soldiers from the battlefield while fighting was still taking place, instead of waiting for the battle to end. He used horse-drawn wagons to quickly transport the injured. Additionally, he had trained attendants moving the wounded. By doing this, treatment could begin before they arrived at the hospital or medical tent. Previously, the injured soldiers had to wait until the battle ended to receive any medical care. As technology improved, motorized vehicles began to replace horse-drawn ambulances. Soon, this military invention was being used by civilian hospitals. Today, ambulances are used frequently by emergency personnel around the world. Emergency workers arrive on the scene and quickly transport the wounded and ill to the hospital. [3]

3 Context Clues
What clues from this paragraph help you understand the meaning of the word *personnel*?

During the Spanish Civil War in the 1930s, Dr. Norman Bethune created the first mobile medical unit. Severe blood loss was a frequent cause of death on the battlefield. Bethune realized that he could provide blood transfusions on the battlefront. This could save many soldiers' lives. The very first mobile unit he developed had medical supplies for 100 operations and dressings for 500 wounds. This could all be carried on a mule. Blood and medical supplies could now be transported very close to the front lines. Others quickly saw the benefits of this concept. Bethune's units became the models for American Mobile Army Surgical Hospital (MASH) units, which were used frequently in later wars. In 2006, the last MASH unit was closed and converted, or transformed, to a Combat Support Hospital (CSH). The CSH has improved upon Bethune's concept and provides state-of-the-art medical care near the front lines.

A patient is wheeled out from the intensive care unit at the U.S. Mobile Army Surgical Hospital (MASH) in November 2005 in Muzaffarabad, Pakistan, after an earthquake.

4 Main Idea
What is the stated main idea of this paragraph?

The use of helicopters to transport the injured is another practice used at the accident site that developed during a war. Medical helicopters were first used in the 1950s during the Korean War. When helicopters were used to transport the wounded soldiers, the injured could be even more quickly evacuated to hospitals. Trips that would have taken hours on the road were reduced to minutes in the air. [4]

A Baltimore doctor wanted to make this military transportation method available to civilian patients. In 1968, he worked to have patients brought into his shock trauma unit by military helicopters. This work opened the doors for faster transportation to hospitals for civilians. A few years later, the first hospital-based helicopter program was started in Denver, Colorado. Today, medical transport in the air is commonplace. Most trauma units have their own helicopters and landing pads. This allows patients to quickly arrive at hospitals for treatment.

As wars wage around the globe, the battlefields will continue to be laboratories for the medical field. As military surgeons conceptualize and perfect new techniques, civilians will benefit from their hard work. End

"Military Medical Innovations"

Before Reading

Introduce Vocabulary

1. Have students turn to Part A on Student Book page 158 and scan the boldfaced vocabulary words. **You will see these new words in "Military Medical Innovations." Remember that what you already know will help you learn new vocabulary.** Have students rate their knowledge of each boldfaced word.
2. Have students find words that they assigned a 3 rating, share the meanings they know, and use each word in a sentence or phrase.
3. Read the part of speech, definition, and example sentence for each word. **Do any of the words you assigned a 3 rating have the meaning you know? If the meaning is different, then you have to learn the new meaning of the word.**
4. Have students read the instructions for Part B and complete the activity.

Refer to Blackline Master page 29 to extend vocabulary practice.

Have students use the *Passport Reading Journeys* online technology component to practice and reinforce vocabulary and comprehension skills.

Apply the Target Skill: Cause and Effect

1. **You already have learned to recognize cause and effect in texts. Consider this example. A man is driving too fast. It is raining, and the streets are slippery. A squirrel runs across the street, and the man cannot stop in time. He swerves to miss it and hits the curb. What caused the man to hit the curb?** (He was driving too fast. The slippery streets made it hard to stop. He swerved to miss the squirrel.) **There were three causes.**
2. **In some cases, an effect may have multiple causes, or more than one cause.** Write *Cause 1* + *Cause 2* + *Cause 3* = *Effect* on the board.

Expedition 5, Lesson 6

Name ______________________ Date ____________

Vocabulary

"Military Medical Innovations"

A. Rate your knowledge of each boldfaced word.
3 I know what this word means, and I can use it in a sentence.
2 I have an idea of this word's meaning, but I need to know more.
1 I don't know what this word means.

☐ **assess** (v) *determine the importance, size, or value of something*
Doctors must quickly *assess* the severity of the injury in emergency situations.

☐ **severe** (adj) *hard to bear or deal with*
The *severe* injuries left the soldier unable to continue in battle.

☐ **categorized** (v) *grouped things based on similarities*
The nurse *categorized* her patients based on how severe their injuries were.

☐ **frequently** (adv) *often*
Army doctors *frequently* try new things to help save lives.

☐ **developed** (v) *created or produced over time*
New medical treatments are *developed* after years of experience.

☐ **concept** (n) *thought; general idea*
The *concept* of evaluating the level of injuries during emergencies developed on the battlefield.

B. Complete each sentence with the correct vocabulary word from Part A.

1. Doctors may prescribe painkillers for ___severe___ pain.
2. Ambulance service is a ___concept___ that was first used by the military.
3. Because of dangerous conditions, soldiers are ___frequently___ injured.
4. Certain jobs in the military are ___categorized___ according to skill levels.
5. Soldiers in the field quickly ___assess___ their surroundings to decide whether an area is safe.
6. Sasha ___developed___ an interest in journalism when she wrote for an Army newspaper.

 158

Vocabulary

assess	(v) *determine the importance, size, or value of something* Doctors must quickly *assess* the severity of the injury in emergency situations.
severe	(adj) *hard to bear or deal with* The *severe* injuries left the soldier unable to continue in battle.
categorized	(v) *grouped things based on similarities* The nurse *categorized* her patients based on how severe their injuries were.
frequently	(adv) *often* Army doctors *frequently* try new things to help save lives.
developed	(v) *created or produced over time* New medical treatments are *developed* after years of experience.
concept	(n) *thought; general idea* The *concept* of evaluating the level of injuries during emergencies developed on the battlefield.

3. **Jordan was late to school one morning. What might have caused him to be late?** Write one student response under Cause 1 on the board. **What else might have happened that made him even later?** Write another student response under Cause 2 on the board. Continue the process until you have three or more causes. Ask students what effect these multiple causes produced. (Jordan was late.)

Introduce the Passage

1. Have students preview "Military Medical Innovations" on Anthology page 85. **Predict what the passage is about.** Write student predictions on the board.

ELL Write the word *innovations* and tell students it means "changes in the way people do things." **A major *innovation* in communication is that people use e-mail instead of writing letters.**

2. Direct student attention to the margin prompts. **As you read the passage, pause to respond to these prompts.**
3. Teach these terms from the passage:
   - *triage* (trē äzh')
   - A *blood transfusion* is replacing one person's blood with blood from someone else.
   - A *trauma* is an injury or wound.
   - The *Crusades* were hundreds of years of war between Catholics and Muslims over land and religion.

During Reading

1. Have students read "Military Medical Innovations." To select reading options that support your students' levels and classroom needs, see Reading Differentiation, page xxxii, if needed.
2. Instruct students to look for causes and effects as they read "Military Medical Innovations."

Remind students to choose books from the *Passport Reading Journeys* Library for independent reading.

After Reading

Check Comprehension

1. When students finish reading, have them reread the title of the passage. Write *Military Medical Innovations* on the board. **What military medical innovations are mentioned in the passage?** List student responses under the title. (triage; painkillers; ambulance service; mobile medical units; using helicopters)
2. **The photographs show emergency situations both in the military and elsewhere. How are military medical emergencies similar to other medical emergencies? How does the passage show these similarities?** (In both types of emergencies, people need help as quickly as possible. The passage shows how military medical techniques also work in other medical emergencies.)
3. Have students share their responses to the Make Connections margin prompt on Anthology page 86. **Before triage was used, lower-ranking officers had to wait a long time for medical care even when they needed it badly. How do you think those lower-ranking officers felt about waiting? How do you think the officers making them wait felt? What are the factors that cause one group to be privileged over another? Does this still happen today? Explain.**

   To make the most of the discussion time, remember to incorporate strategies that encourage and extend student involvement. Refer to page xxxviii for a comprehensive discussion of these strategies.
4. Ask students what causes and effects they noticed. Read the following and ask students to identify the causes and effects:
   - **The highest ranking officers were always treated first, a concept that led to many unnecessary deaths.** (p. 86 cause: high ranking officers treated first; effect: many unnecessary deaths)
   - **Painkillers often were used during the Civil War to keep soldiers comfortable.** (p. 86 cause: pain killers used; effect: soldiers were comfortable)
   - **However, it caused other problems. By 1880, a large number of Union soldiers were addicted to morphine.** (p. 86 cause: use of morphine as painkiller; effect: addicted to morphine)

"Military Medical Innovations"

Prepare to Reread

Introduce the Lesson

Remind students that they read about military medical innovations in Lesson 6. **In this lesson, we'll revisit "Military Medical Innovations" and practice identifying causes and effects.**

Practice Vocabulary

1. Direct students to think about how vocabulary words were used in the passage.
   - **What do emergency workers do when they quickly *assess* damage after a disaster?** (They figure out what problems to address first and what kind of help to provide.)
   - **What do patients with *severe* injuries need?** (to go to a hospital or get treatment)
   - **How are patients *categorized* by emergency room doctors?** (by the severity of their condition)
   - **What do emergency workers *frequently* do at disaster sites?** (They frequently treat the most serious injuries first.)
   - **Who *developed* the triage system?** (a French doctor in Napoleon's army)
   - **Why did the *concept* of giving morphine to soldiers come about?** (They were in pain.)

ELL Have a student tell you what *assess* means. **Why must emergency workers quickly decide on the amount of damage after a disaster?** (This helps them decide how much assistance, how many supplies, and how many vehicles they need.)

2. Remind students that they can use context clues to find the meanings of unfamiliar words. Have students turn to Anthology page 86. Reread the last sentence of the first partial paragraph. **What do you think the word *allocate* means?** (distribute) **What clue in the text helped you figure out the meaning?** (or distribute)

   Repeat this process for the following words.
   - **protocol** (n) *procedure*, Anthology page 86
   - **alleviate** (v) *relieve*, Anthology page 86

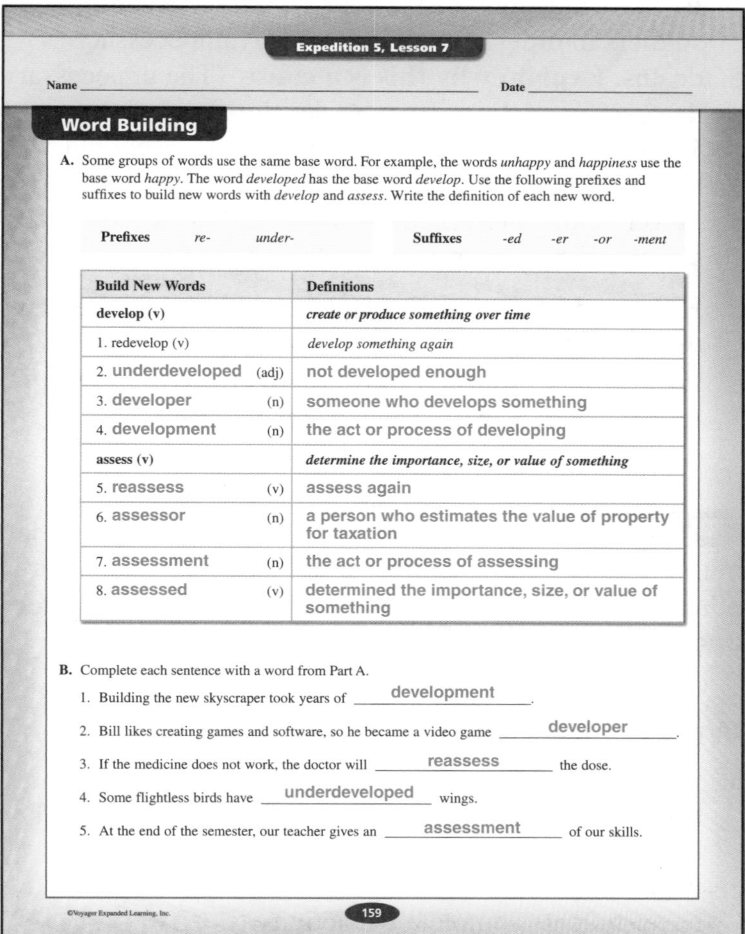

Expedition 5, Lesson 7

Name ______ Date ______

Word Building

A. Some groups of words use the same base word. For example, the words *unhappy* and *happiness* use the base word *happy*. The word *developed* has the base word *develop*. Use the following prefixes and suffixes to build new words with *develop* and *assess*. Write the definition of each new word.

Prefixes *re-* *under-* **Suffixes** *-ed* *-er* *-or* *-ment*

Build New Words	Definitions
develop (v)	***create or produce something over time***
1. redevelop (v)	*develop something again*
2. underdeveloped (adj)	not developed enough
3. developer (n)	someone who develops something
4. development (n)	the act or process of developing
assess (v)	***determine the importance, size, or value of something***
5. reassess (v)	assess again
6. assessor (n)	a person who estimates the value of property for taxation
7. assessment (n)	the act or process of assessing
8. assessed (v)	determined the importance, size, or value of something

B. Complete each sentence with a word from Part A.

1. Building the new skyscraper took years of development.
2. Bill likes creating games and software, so he became a video game developer.
3. If the medicine does not work, the doctor will reassess the dose.
4. Some flightless birds have underdeveloped wings.
5. At the end of the semester, our teacher gives an assessment of our skills.

©Voyager Expanded Learning, Inc. 159

   - **personnel** (n) *workers*, Anthology page 87
   - **converted** (v) *transformed*, Anthology page 88

3. Have students turn to Student Book page 159. Read the instructions for each part of the page, and have students complete the activities.

CHECKPOINT After students complete Part A, have them identify one item they had difficulty with. Have students explain how they determined the definitions of their new words.

Reread

Apply the Target Skill: Cause and Effect

1. Model how to apply the skill to the passage. **I want to know what caused the military to begin using the triage system, so I scan the section on triage. I ask myself, *Why did the military start using triage?***

2. Write the following sentence on the board: *The military started using triage.* Label the sentence *Effect.* **This is what happened, but what caused it?** Have students scan to find the cause: Treating soldiers in order of rank led to many unnecessary deaths. **Explain why this is a cause.** (The unnecessary deaths caused the military to develop a new system.) **What is another cause?** (Medical workers would treat patients who would likely die from their wounds. Fewer soldiers returned to battle, so they needed a new system that would save more lives.)

3. Have students turn to Student Book page 160. Review the cause-and-effect charts. **Reread the text and locate causes that led to each effect. Remember, to find the cause, ask, *Why did this happen?***

ACADEMIC SKILL Remind students that they can determine multiple causes for one effect when they read texts for other classes. **If you understand causes, you will better understand the effect.**

Write in Response to Reading

1. **Think about what it would be like to live during the 1800s when ambulance service was a relatively new idea.** Have students turn to Student Book page 161. Read the instructions for Part A aloud, and have students complete the activity.

2. Have students write their letters, using the ideas they generated in Part A. If students have difficulty beginning, write the following sentence starter on the board: *Today I was wounded in battle. I saw ____.*

EXPEDITION ORGANIZER **An Army of Progress**

Pause to have students turn to Student Book pages 138 and 139. Have students complete the following:

- Respond to one or more of the probing questions in Part A. If they have not yet added a question, encourage them to add one.
- Write their own important idea about "Military Medical Innovations" in the appropriate box in Part B.

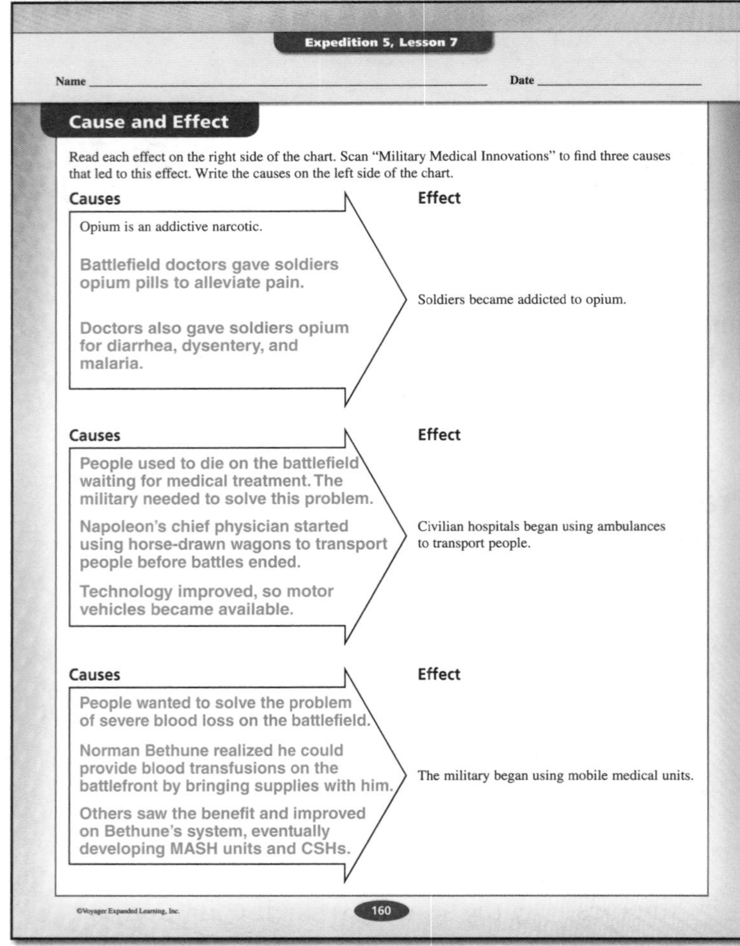
Expedition 5, Lesson 7

Name __________ Date __________

Cause and Effect

Read each effect on the right side of the chart. Scan "Military Medical Innovations" to find three causes that led to this effect. Write the causes on the left side of the chart.

Causes	Effect
Opium is an addictive narcotic. Battlefield doctors gave soldiers opium pills to alleviate pain. Doctors also gave soldiers opium for diarrhea, dysentery, and malaria.	Soldiers became addicted to opium.
People used to die on the battlefield waiting for medical treatment. The military needed to solve this problem. Napoleon's chief physician started using horse-drawn wagons to transport people before battles ended. Technology improved, so motor vehicles became available.	Civilian hospitals began using ambulances to transport people.
People wanted to solve the problem of severe blood loss on the battlefield. Norman Bethune realized he could provide blood transfusions on the battlefront by bringing supplies with him. Others saw the benefit and improved on Bethune's system, eventually developing MASH units and CSHs.	The military began using mobile medical units.

 160

Expedition 5, Lesson 7

Name __________ Date __________

Write in Response to Reading

A. Imagine you are a soldier in Napoleon's army. You are badly wounded on the battlefield, probably by a sword or a sharp bayonet instead of a bullet. A horse-drawn wagon transports you from the battlefield. You write a letter to a friend telling about the new ambulance service that saved you. Complete the chart to write some ideas to use in your letter. Answers will vary.

What I Saw	How I Felt	What Happened Later

B. Compose your letter to your friend. Use specific details from the passage that show how it would feel to fight and be wounded as a soldier in Napoleon's army in the early 1800s.

Dear __________,

Student letters should use details that relate to the military medical innovations described in the passage, such as ambulance service and triage, and describe feelings of a soldier of Napoleon's time.

 161

Buffalo Soldiers

Many people are familiar with Bob Marley's hit "Buffalo Soldier." Few know that it is more than just a popular song with a reggae beat. This song, which provides a brief glimpse at a part of U.S. history, speaks of the role of African Americans in the U.S. Army. Marley sings, "I'm just a Buffalo Soldier in the heart of America. Stolen from Africa. Brought to America. Fighting on arrival, fighting for survival; Said he was a Buffalo Soldier win the war for America."

Historians say Marley's song highlights the work of African American soldiers in an Army **dominated** by whites. Despite racism and discrimination, this group of soldiers did its job bravely and with honor.

African Americans Officially Join the Army

After the Civil War, the Army was reorganized and former "all-white" policies were **amended**. Two cavalry and four infantry units of African American soldiers were **established** by the **government**. 1 For the first time, the government made African Americans a part of the regular Army. Additionally, these men were the first African American soldiers in any peacetime army.

Initially, there were **approximately** 5,000 men in these units. The Civil War brought an end to slavery, and the **primary** reason many freed slaves enlisted was because they feared they wouldn't find other employment. Most of these volunteers were illiterate, and they hoped the Army would teach them to read and write. Others chose to enlist because they felt patriotic. Shortly after the war, the government passed a constitutional amendment to officially abolish, or end, slavery. The government also passed additional amendments that gave African Americans citizenship

Vocabulary

dominated (v) *controlled*

amended (v) *changed*

established (v) *brought about; made firm or stable*

government (n) *those people in control of a nation, state, or city*

approximately (adv) *almost exactly*

primary (adj) *most important*

1 Word Reading
You will come across words you might not know, like *cavalry* and *infantry.* Keep reading. When you finish reading, if you still do not know what the word means, use a dictionary to define the word.

These men pose during a lunch break while on patrol in Montana. The 10th Cavalry was stationed at Fort Custer, Montana, (near present day Billings) from 1892 to 1896.

and African American men the right to vote. These changes encouraged some to serve their country. 2

2 Make Connections
Would you have fought to protect the United States after decades of being a slave with a government that protected the slave owner?

The Nickname "Buffalo Soldier"

The men in these new units soon became known as the buffalo soldiers. The Cheyenne are credited with giving this nickname to the troops. They had never seen African American soldiers before, and the Native Americans were very impressed with their opponents' ability to fight. Some say the Cheyenne gave the nickname to the African American troops out of respect. The buffalo was a sacred, or holy, animal to the Native Americans. They say the Native Americans saw the same fighting spirit in the soldiers as they saw in the buffalo. Others believe the nickname was created because the soldiers' curly hair looked like the buffalo's mane. Even though the

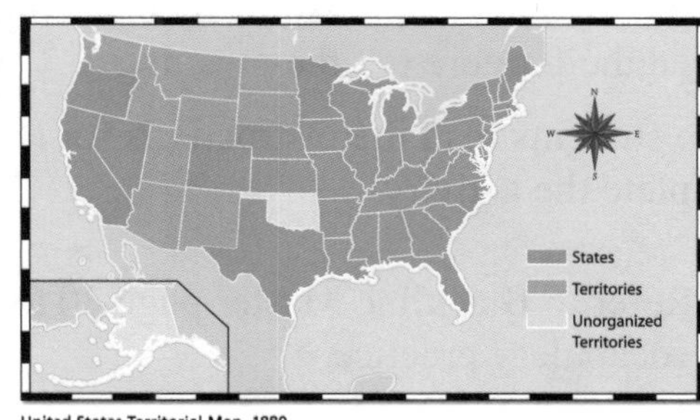

United States Territorial Map, 1880

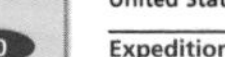

Major Charles Young (left), son of slaves, was the third African American to graduate from West Point Military Academy in 1889. He distinguished himself throughout his military career with the Buffalo Soldiers of the 9th and 10th Cavalries.

soldiers rarely used the name to describe themselves, they did take the nickname as a compliment. 3

3 Summarize
What are the two theories behind the name given to the soldiers?

The Work and Life of Buffalo Soldiers

The buffalo soldiers quickly established that they were dominant warriors. As the United States was rebuilding after the Civil War, many Americans were moving west. As they moved, the government forced Native Americans from their homes to reservations. The Native Americans were not pleased with this and fought back. Initially, the buffalo soldiers' primary task was to fight the Native Americans in the Indian Wars of the late 1800s. During the Indian Wars, approximately 20 percent of the U.S. troops were African Americans. They fought in more than 177 battles.

After the Indian Wars, the buffalo soldiers fought in the Spanish-American War. They made up approximately 40 percent of the cavalrymen in this war. Many of these soldiers charged up San Juan Hill during the now-famous battle. They also served in the Philippines, Hawaii, and Mexico.

The buffalo soldiers were primarily stationed, or positioned, throughout the Midwest and Southwestern United States. In addition to fighting battles with Native Americans, they were responsible for accompanying settlers, cattle herds, and railroad crews on their journeys west. They were there to protect the settlers from possible attacks from Native Americans and dominating outlaws. 4

4 Visualize
Think about what you have read. How do you picture the buffalo soldiers looking? Picture their surroundings.

When they were not fighting, the regiments built forts and roads, dug wells, and installed telegraph lines. They also drew maps indicating water sources in the West. They helped establish the groundwork for westward expansion, a concept that the American people believed was

Cpl. Isaiah Mays, a buffalo soldier, is shown wearing the Medal of Honor he received in 1890. Mays, who was born a slave, joined the 10th Cavalry and was stationed in Arizona, where in 1889 bandits attacked a payroll wagon he was guarding. Shot in both legs, Mays crawled two miles to sound an alarm and was awarded the Medal of Honor for his bravery.

the destiny for the country.

Others were assigned to protect what would become Yosemite, Sequoia, and Kings Canyon National Parks. Although national parks did not yet formally exist, these soldiers worked as our nation's first park rangers. 5 Each day, they patrolled the grounds, made maps, and helped build trails. They also enforced, or carried out, laws. The buffalo soldiers made sure that all the natural resources, such as trees, were not destroyed as settlers made their new homes in the West.

5 Context Clues
Using context clues, what is a *park ranger*?

Life as a buffalo soldier was difficult. For the most part, their uniforms and equipment consisted of what was left over from the Civil War armies. They generally had to do their jobs with limited resources. They were often given older horses, little ammunition, and malfunctioning equipment. Most of their meals consisted primarily of boiled beef, hash, beans, and cornbread. Occasionally, they had sweet potatoes or a piece of fruit. Finally, they frequently faced discrimination from their commanding officers and the civilians they encountered. Despite these poor conditions, very few buffalo soldiers deserted, or left, the Army. Most enlisted for five years and served their entire term. For their efforts, they were paid approximately $13 a month, plus room and board—much less than their white counterparts.

Honoring Those Who Served

Twenty-six buffalo soldiers have been awarded Congressional Medals of Honor. This prestigious, or respected, award celebrates the bravery and courage of military heroes. Today, many states honor the buffalo soldiers. They hold special ceremonies and reenactments. Artwork of the buffalo soldiers is displayed each February at Guadalupe Mountains National Park. The state of Texas established July as "Texas Buffalo Soldiers Heritage Month." Throughout the month, the memory of these soldiers is honored at exhibitions, living history demonstrations, and festivals. In Houston, visitors can tour the Buffalo Soldiers National Museum. End

"Buffalo Soldiers"

Before Reading

Introduce Vocabulary

1. Have students turn to Part A on Student Book page 162 and scan the boldfaced vocabulary words. **When you read "Buffalo Soldiers," you will see these new words. You might know the meanings of some of them.** Have students rate their knowledge of each boldfaced word.
2. Have students share words that they have seen, but are not sure about. Ask students where they saw the word being used and if there were any clues that may have helped them figure out the meaning.
3. Have students read the instructions for Part B and complete the activity.

Refer to Blackline Master page 30 to extend vocabulary practice.

Have students use the *Passport Reading Journeys* online technology component to practice and reinforce vocabulary and comprehension skills.

Introduce the Target Skill: Note Taking

1. **Taking notes about what you read can help you find the most important details for a topic. It also can help you remember those details.** Remind students they have used strategies like noticing text features and scanning text for a purpose. **Now you'll find a new purpose for using the strategies. You'll pay attention to titles and subheadings and scan text to take notes.**
2. Have students turn to Anthology page 59. **In Expedition 4, you previewed and asked questions about this passage.** Focus student attention to the subhead Drawbacks of Luminol on page 62. **What question can you make out of this heading?** Have students write their question on a separate sheet of paper and share it with a partner.

Expedition 5, Lesson 8

Name ______________________ Date ______________

Vocabulary

"Buffalo Soldiers"

A. Put a check mark in each row to indicate how well you know each boldfaced word.

	Know This Word	Have Seen This Word	Don't Know This Word
dominated (v) *controlled* Native Americans *dominated* the West in the 1800s.			
amended (v) *changed* Laws can be *amended* to protect people's rights.			
established (v) *brought about; made firm or stable* Buffalo soldiers *established* a good relationship with many Native American tribes.			
government (n) *those people in control of a nation, state, or city* The *government* makes laws to keep people safe.			
approximately (adv) *almost exactly* There were *approximately* 500 soldiers in the battle.			
primary (adj) *most important* The *primary* reason buffalo soldiers won battles was their bravery.			

B. Read each question, then write the answer on the line.

1. If an army **dominated** its opponent, would it most likely win or lose the battle? win the battle
2. If the government **amended** the Selective Service rules, what would young men have to do? find out how the rules changed
3. If soldiers **established** a fort on the frontier, did they destroy it or plan and build it? plan and build it
4. Does a **government** control a nation or live in a nation? control a nation
5. If a war lasted **approximately** 10 years, did that war last fewer than 10 years, about even with, or much longer than 10 years? about even with 10 years
6. What is a **primary** reason for attending school? learning; getting an education; required by law

©Voyager Expanded Learning, Inc. 162

Vocabulary

dominated (v) *controlled*
Native Americans *dominated* the West in the 1800s.

amended (v) *changed*
Laws can be *amended* to protect people's rights.

established (v) *brought about; made firm or stable*
Buffalo soldiers *established* a good relationship with many Native American tribes.

government (n) *those people in control of a nation, state, or city*
The *government* makes laws to keep people safe.

approximately (adv) *almost exactly*
There were *approximately* 500 soldiers in the battle.

primary (adj) *most important*
The *primary* reason buffalo soldiers won battles was their bravery.

ELL Write *drawbacks* on the board and tell students it means "problems." **The head suggests that luminol has drawbacks, or problems, but we don't know what those problems are.**

3. Have students scan the section for answers to their questions. Encourage students to use sticky notes or a separate sheet of paper to mark parts of the text where they find answers. Tell students that they may not find all the answers to their question in the text.
4. Explain that when students write the answers to the question, they are taking notes. **When you take notes, you do not have to use complete sentences. You should use words and phrases that are easy for you to understand and remember.** Write on the board:

   My Question

   - *What are the drawbacks of luminol?*

   My Notes

   - *Luminol's drawbacks:*

     1. destroys DNA in blood

     2. can give false-positive reaction

     3. not CSI's first choice

   These are my notes about this section of the passage. Notice that I left out details that weren't important to answering my question.

Introduce the Passage

1. Have students turn to Anthology page 89 to preview "Buffalo Soldiers." **What do you predict the passage is about?** Allow students to discuss their predictions.
2. Have students read the title and subheads. **Write the title at the top of a sheet of paper. Then, write a question for each subhead leaving plenty of space underneath.**
   - *Subheading* 1: **Who are buffalo soldiers?**
   - *Subheading* 2: **Why did African Americans officially join the Army?**
   - *Subheading* 3: **Where did they get the nickname?**
   - *Subheading* 4: **What was life like for buffalo soldiers in the Army?**
   - *Subheading* 5: **How are buffalo soldiers honored?**

   You will use this paper tomorrow.
3. Remind students to pay attention to the margin prompts.
4. Teach these terms from the passage:
   - *Cheyenne* (shī an')
   - *Yosemite* (yō se' mə tē)
   - *Sequoia* (si kwo' i ə)
   - *Malfunctioning* means "not working properly."
   - *Reenactments* are plays where actors act out a specific battle in history.

During Reading

1. Have students read "Buffalo Soldiers." To select reading options that support your students' levels and classroom needs, see Reading Differentiation, page xxxii, if needed.
2. Instruct students to look for the most important information and answers to the questions they asked in their notes about buffalo soldiers.

After Reading

Check Comprehension

1. **Now that you've read the passage, was your prediction correct?**
2. Have students share their responses to the Make Connections margin prompt on Anthology page 90. **Imagine that you were often mistreated by a group of people, then that group asked you for help. How would you respond?** Remind students to think about what they know about African American slavery and the Civil War.

   To make the most of the discussion time, remember to incorporate strategies that encourage and extend student involvement. Refer to page xxxviii for a comprehensive discussion of these strategies.

Remind students to choose books from the *Passport Reading Journeys* Library for independent reading.

"Buffalo Soldiers"

Prepare to Reread 

Introduce the Lesson

We will revisit "Buffalo Soldiers" to practice taking notes.

Practice Vocabulary

1. Direct students to think about how vocabulary words were used in the passage.
   - **Who *dominated* the military in the late 1800s?** (white males)
   - **When lawmakers *amended* the Constitution to abolish slavery, what did they do?** (changed it)
   - **Which city *established* a museum that honors the buffalo soldiers?** (Houston)
   - **After the Civil War, how did the *government* help African Americans?** (They passed amendments allowing them to be citizens and vote.)
   - **What is another way of saying *approximately* 5,000 troops?** (nearly 5,000 troops)
   - **Who was the *primary* enemy the United States was fighting in the late 1800s?** (certain Native American tribes)
2. Remind students to use context clues for unfamiliar words. **Turn to Anthology page 91 and read the first sentence of the third paragraph under The Work and Life of Buffalo Soldiers. What could the word *stationed* mean?** (positioned) **What context clues helped you figure out this meaning?** (or positioned)

   Repeat this process for the following words.
   - **illiterate** (adj) *unable to write or read*, Anthology page 89
   - **sacred** (adj) *considered holy*, Anthology page 90
   - **enforced** (v) *carried out*, Anthology page 92
   - **deserted** (v) *left*, Anthology page 92
3. Have students turn to Student Book page 163, read the instructions, then complete the page.

CHECKPOINT If students have difficulty with Part B, suggest they combine the meanings of the words in Part A with the meaning of *-ment*: "the result of or the object of." Then, have students substitute the combined meanings in the sentences.

Expedition 5, Lesson 9

Name ______________________ Date ______________

Word Building

A. Think about the meaning of each boldfaced word and the examples. Add one example to each list.
Answers will vary.

1. Things you can **amend**:	a decision	a rule	________
2. What people **employ** others to do:	drive a truck	teach a class	________
3. How someone can **entertain** others:	singing	acting	________
4. Things you can **establish**:	a club	a fort	________

B. The suffix *-ment* can mean "the result of" or "the object of." Add the suffix *-ment* to the boldfaced words in Part A to complete the sentences.

1. Hector is a good swimmer, so he is looking for employment as a lifeguard this summer.
2. Most teenagers in the state agreed with the amendment to the driving law.
3. When I have free time, I look for entertainment like movies and concerts.
4. The citizens celebrated the establishment of the new library.

C. List other words that end in *-ment* and their definitions. Use a dictionary if you need help.
Answers will vary.

©Voyager Expanded Learning, Inc. 163

Apply the Target Skill: Note Taking

1. **Let's find the answers to your questions. We won't read the whole passage again, but we will look for answers to the specific questions.**
2. Direct students to their questions. Use the following discussion while looking for the answers as a class.
   - **Who are buffalo soldiers?** (Paragraph 1: African American soldiers in the Army)
   - **Why did African Americans officially join the Army?** (Paragraph 3: All-white policies were amended. Paragraph 4: They hoped to learn to read and write and feared they wouldn't find a job; government had passed laws to abolish slavery, give them the right to vote, and make them citizens so they felt patriotic.)
   - **Where did they get the nickname?** (Paragraph 5: Native Americans thought they were brave like the buffalo; their hair reminded Native Americans of buffalo hair.)

- **What was life like for buffalo soldiers in the Army?** (Paragraph 8: They were stationed in the Midwest and Southwest and protected settlers from Native Americans. Paragraph 9: They built forts and roads, dug wells, installed telegraph lines, and drew maps. Paragraph 11: They were given few resources, treated badly, and paid less than Caucasians.)
- **How are buffalo soldiers honored?** (Paragraph 12: medals, ceremonies, reenactments, museums, displays, festivals)

3. Encourage students to reread the notes they wrote, think of cause-and-effect statements about buffalo soldiers, and share them with a partner.
4. Have students turn to Student Book page 164. Read the instructions for Parts A and B, then have students complete the activities independently.

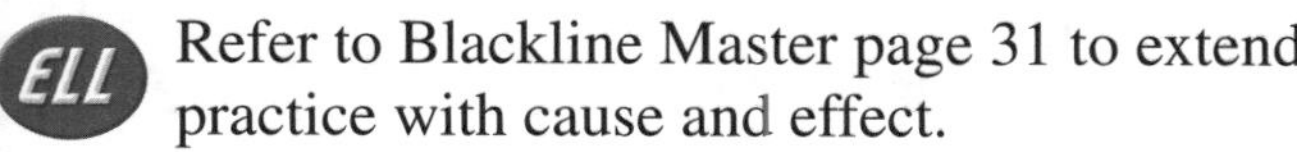

ELL Refer to Blackline Master page 31 to extend practice with cause and effect.

ACADEMIC SKILL Remind students that they can easily identify cause and effect in history texts.

Write in Response to Reading

1. Have students turn to Student Book page 165. Read the instructions for Part A aloud, and have students complete the activity.
2. **Imagine that you have an award to present. Who would deserve this award?** Tell students that they will write a presentation speech to introduce the award winner.

EXPEDITION ORGANIZER **An Army of Progress**

Pause to have students turn to Student Book pages 138 and 139. Have students complete the following:

- Write answers to one or more of the probing questions in Part A. Try to answer their questions.
- Think about how "Buffalo Soldiers" showed military progress and how the passages are connected to complete Part B.
- Complete the Dictionary Challenge in Part C.

Build Background DVD 5.2
Briefly discuss the Expedition passages. Then, watch the DVD together. After watching, review student responses to the probing questions using the Expedition Organizer.

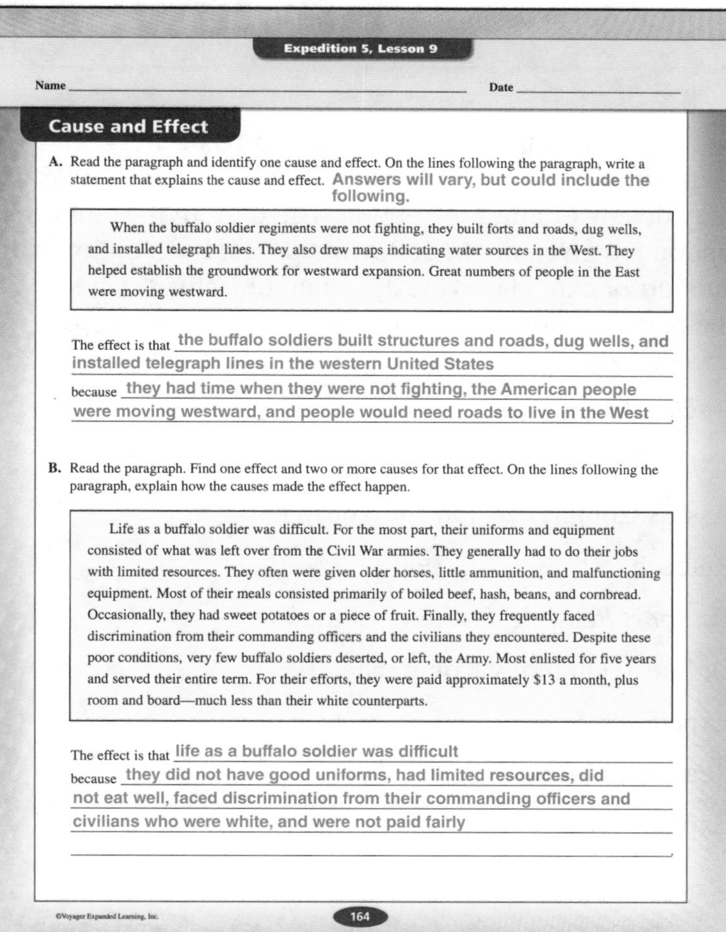

Expedition 5, Lesson 9

Name ______________________ Date ______________

Cause and Effect

A. Read the paragraph and identify one cause and effect. On the lines following the paragraph, write a statement that explains the cause and effect. Answers will vary, but could include the following.

When the buffalo soldier regiments were not fighting, they built forts and roads, dug wells, and installed telegraph lines. They also drew maps indicating water sources in the West. They helped establish the groundwork for westward expansion. Great numbers of people in the East were moving westward.

The effect is that the buffalo soldiers built structures and roads, dug wells, and installed telegraph lines in the western United States

because they had time when they were not fighting, the American people were moving westward, and people would need roads to live in the West.

B. Read the paragraph. Find one effect and two or more causes for that effect. On the lines following the paragraph, explain how the causes made the effect happen.

Life as a buffalo soldier was difficult. For the most part, their uniforms and equipment consisted of what was left over from the Civil War armies. They generally had to do their jobs with limited resources. They often were given older horses, little ammunition, and malfunctioning equipment. Most of their meals consisted primarily of boiled beef, hash, beans, and cornbread. Occasionally, they had sweet potatoes or a piece of fruit. Finally, they frequently faced discrimination from their commanding officers and the civilians they encountered. Despite these poor conditions, very few buffalo soldiers deserted, or left, the Army. Most enlisted for five years and served their entire term. For their efforts, they were paid approximately $13 a month, plus room and board—much less than their white counterparts.

The effect is that life as a buffalo soldier was difficult

because they did not have good uniforms, had limited resources, did not eat well, faced discrimination from their commanding officers and civilians who were white, and were not paid fairly.

 164

Expedition 5, Lesson 9

Name ______________________ Date ______________

Write in Response to Reading

A. Imagine characters and real people showing acts of bravery and honor. Use the chart to describe how a courageous person acts or what the person does. Use each word in a sentence that shows what you imagine. The first one is done for you. Answers will vary.

Words	Sentences
strength	A firefighter is using all her strength to pull a child from a burning house.

B. Imagine that you are giving an award for bravery, courage, and honor. To whom would you give the award? Write a short speech you would use to present an award to a person you think has acted bravely and honorably. Include why you think the person deserves the award. Use two words from Part A.

I would like to present this award to ______________________ because Student responses should reflect an understanding of bravery and honor and should include reasons that support and explain their choices.

 165

Review, Extend, Assess

In today's lesson, as in Lessons 5 and 10 of every Expedition, there are options from which to choose. You may do any or all of the options listed. Activities for each option are given on the following pages. Each option will support or extend previously taught objectives. Choose the option(s) appropriate for your students and prepare accordingly.

Review Vocabulary

Extend Vocabulary

Assess Comprehension and Vocabulary

Reteach

Passport Reading Journeys Library

Online Technology Component

Expedition Project

Real-World Reading

Exploring Careers

Review Vocabulary

Direct students to review the vocabulary for "Military Medical Innovations" and "Buffalo Soldiers" on Student Book page 139. Have students reread the meanings of the words.

1. Have students turn to Student Book page 166. **You have read these vocabulary words in the reading passages. Now you will read the vocabulary in different contexts. In other words, the topics you will read about will be different, but the vocabulary words will have the same meanings.** Read the instructions aloud, and have students complete the activity. As students finish, have them check the definitions to ensure they used the words correctly. Have students share their answers for Parts A and B.
2. In Part A, if students have difficulty identifying antonyms, have them skim the list of boxed words and keep in mind that these words complete the meanings of the sentences. Have students read the sentence twice. The first time, they should read for the general sentence meaning. The second time, have students use the phrase *the opposite of* before the underlined word. For Part B, complete three items with students who have difficulty, then have students complete the remaining items independently.

Expedition 5, Lesson 10

Name ______ Date ______

Review Vocabulary

A. For each underlined word, write an antonym from the box.

severe	**frequently**	**developed**
primary	**dominated**	**approximately**

1. One of Leslie's <u>minor</u> life goals is to graduate. primary
2. The photo was taken in a helicopter <u>exactly</u> 2 miles above ground. approximately
3. We stayed indoors because of the <u>mild</u> storm warning. severe
4. The country <u>destroyed</u> plans to defend its land from invaders. developed
5. Peju <u>rarely</u> makes plans to spend time with her friends. frequently

B. Complete each sentence by writing a context clue that supports the meaning of the boldfaced word. The first one is done for you. Answers will vary, but could include the following.

1. The news reports **assess**, or **rate**, the damage caused by the war.
2. The memorial **categorized**, or grouped, the names of the veterans by military branch.
3. The people in our **government**, such as senators and the president, are elected by the citizens.
4. The United States of America **established** its independence after the Revolutionary War. The war brought about a new independent nation.
5. Photographing battles was a new **concept**, or idea, during the Civil War.
6. The Army **amended**, or changed, its policies to allow both men and women to serve.
7. The British government **dominated**, or controlled, the American colonies in the early 1700s.

 166

CHECKPOINT Provide additional support for students who had difficulty creating context clues in Part B by confirming that students understand the types of context clues: an example, a synonym (a word that means the same), an antonym (a word that means the opposite), or a brief explanation (restatement or appositive). **In sentence 2, the context clue begins with *or*. What type of context clue includes this word?** (synonym) Continue having students identify the type of context clue they need to write to prompt their answers.

Extend Vocabulary

1. **You will work with words that begin with the prefixes *il-* and *mal-*. What words can you think of that begin with these prefixes? What do you think these prefixes mean?** Explain that the prefix *il-* means "not." **For example, the word *illegal* begins with this prefix. It means "not legal."** Explain that the prefix *mal-* means "inadequately, poorly, or improperly." **For example, the word *malnourished* means "not fed enough" or "fed inadequately."**
2. Have students turn to Student Book page 167. Read aloud the words and definitions in the chart at the top of the page. Have students read Part A.
3. **Which of the words in the chart would you use most often? What other words do you know or use that begin with *il-* or *mal-*?** Read aloud the instructions for Parts B and C. Have students complete the activities, then share their responses.

CHECKPOINT When students share their responses for Part B, listen to ensure the new words they included use the correct meaning of the prefixes.

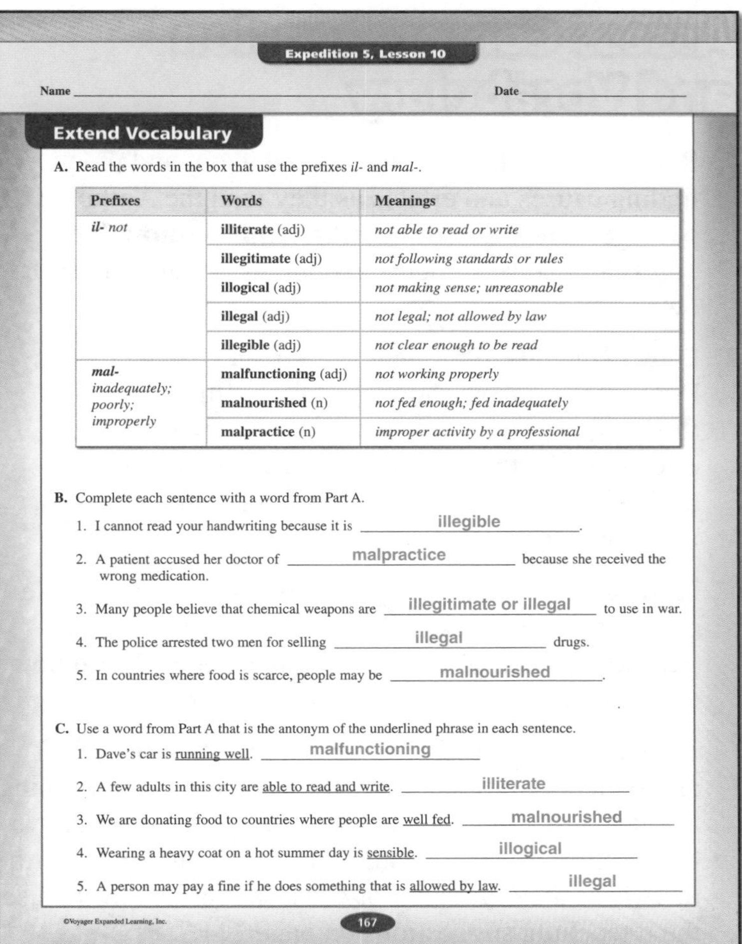

Expedition 5, Lesson 10

Name ______________________ Date ____________

Extend Vocabulary

A. Read the words in the box that use the prefixes *il-* and *mal-*.

Prefixes	Words	Meanings
il- not	**illiterate** (adj)	*not able to read or write*
	illegitimate (adj)	*not following standards or rules*
	illogical (adj)	*not making sense; unreasonable*
	illegal (adj)	*not legal; not allowed by law*
	illegible (adj)	*not clear enough to be read*
mal- inadequately; poorly; improperly	**malfunctioning** (adj)	*not working properly*
	malnourished (n)	*not fed enough; fed inadequately*
	malpractice (n)	*improper activity by a professional*

B. Complete each sentence with a word from Part A.

1. I cannot read your handwriting because it is illegible.
2. A patient accused her doctor of malpractice because she received the wrong medication.
3. Many people believe that chemical weapons are illegitimate or illegal to use in war.
4. The police arrested two men for selling illegal drugs.
5. In countries where food is scarce, people may be malnourished.

C. Use a word from Part A that is the antonym of the underlined phrase in each sentence.

1. Dave's car is running well. malfunctioning
2. A few adults in this city are able to read and write. illiterate
3. We are donating food to countries where people are well fed. malnourished
4. Wearing a heavy coat on a hot summer day is sensible. illogical
5. A person may pay a fine if he does something that is allowed by law. illegal

©Voyager Expanded Learning, Inc.

167

Part A

1. Write the words. Draw a line between the prefix *il-* and the base word. Explore the base words, first asking whether students know the meanings. Then, directly provide the meanings. ***Literate* means "able to read and write." When we add *il-*, the meaning changes to the opposite. *Illiterate* means "not able to read and write." Is a professor of writing *illiterate*?** (no) **Is someone who never learned to read or write *illiterate*?** (yes)

   Continue the process with the rest of the words beginning with *il-*. Use a similar process to show that *mal-* means "inadequately" or "improperly."
2. If students have trouble completing the activity, read aloud the sentence frames. Then, rephrase them as questions. For example: *I cannot read your handwriting because it is* _____. can be rephrased as *What would someone's handwriting look like if that person wrote too quickly?*

Part B

Provide sentence frames to help students use their chosen words. For example: *It would be illogical to join the military if* _____. (you did not want to fight in a war; you did not like to travel to foreign places)

Part C

Have students read the sentences aloud and insert *the opposite of* before the underlined word or phrase.

Assess Comprehension and Vocabulary

1. Remind students that they learned about and practiced finding causes and effects as they read the Anthology passages. **How do you identify causes and effects as you read?** Have students explain the strategy in their own words.
2. Direct students to Student Book pages 168–170. Preview the pages, showing students that they will read two passages and find the causes that lead to effects. Then, they will answer questions about both passages. Have students complete the pages independently.

   Review student answers. Whenever possible, provide elaborative feedback to student responses. Refer to page xl for examples of elaborative feedback and how to incorporate it in your lessons.

   If students incorrectly answer more than 4 out of 15 assessment questions, evaluate what kind of reteaching is needed. If students miss vocabulary questions, have them return to the vocabulary activities and work with the words they missed. For cause and effect errors, use the reteaching suggestions on page 211.

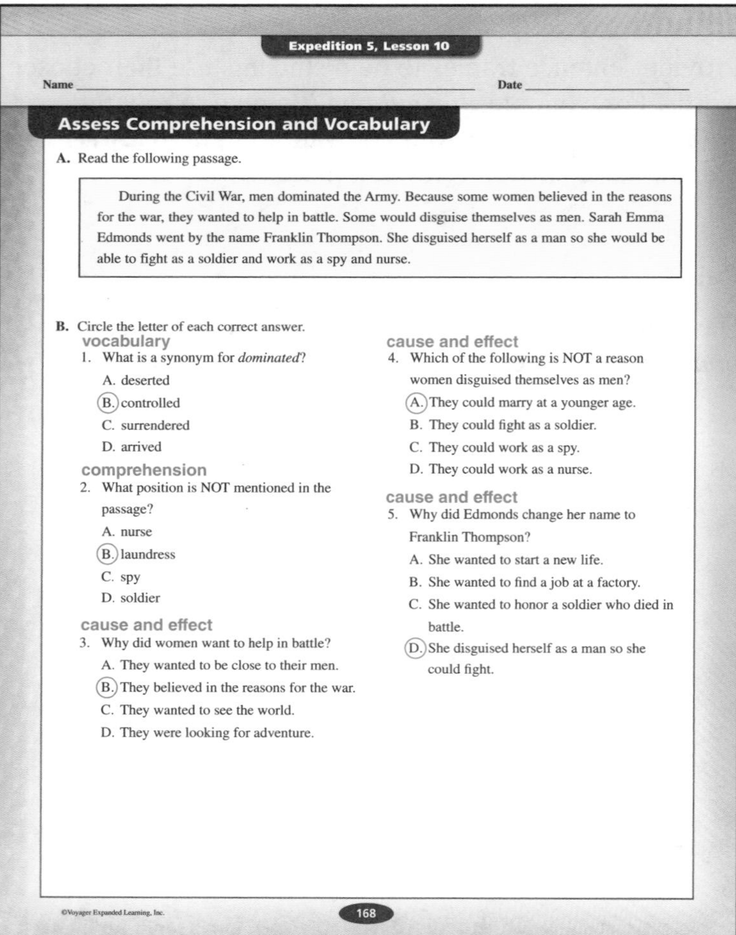

Expedition 5, Lesson 10

Name ____________ Date ____________

Assess Comprehension and Vocabulary

A. Read the following passage.

> During the Civil War, men dominated the Army. Because some women believed in the reasons for the war, they wanted to help in battle. Some would disguise themselves as men. Sarah Emma Edmonds went by the name Franklin Thompson. She disguised herself as a man so she would be able to fight as a soldier and work as a spy and nurse.

B. Circle the letter of each correct answer.

vocabulary
1. What is a synonym for *dominated*?
   A. deserted
   (B.) controlled
   C. surrendered
   D. arrived

comprehension
2. What position is NOT mentioned in the passage?
   A. nurse
   (B.) laundress
   C. spy
   D. soldier

cause and effect
3. Why did women want to help in battle?
   A. They wanted to be close to their men.
   (B.) They believed in the reasons for the war.
   C. They wanted to see the world.
   D. They were looking for adventure.

cause and effect
4. Which of the following is NOT a reason women disguised themselves as men?
   (A.) They could marry at a younger age.
   B. They could fight as a soldier.
   C. They could work as a spy.
   D. They could work as a nurse.

cause and effect
5. Why did Edmonds change her name to Franklin Thompson?
   A. She wanted to start a new life.
   B. She wanted to find a job at a factory.
   C. She wanted to honor a soldier who died in battle.
   (D.) She disguised herself as a man so she could fight.

©Voyager Expanded Learning, Inc. 168

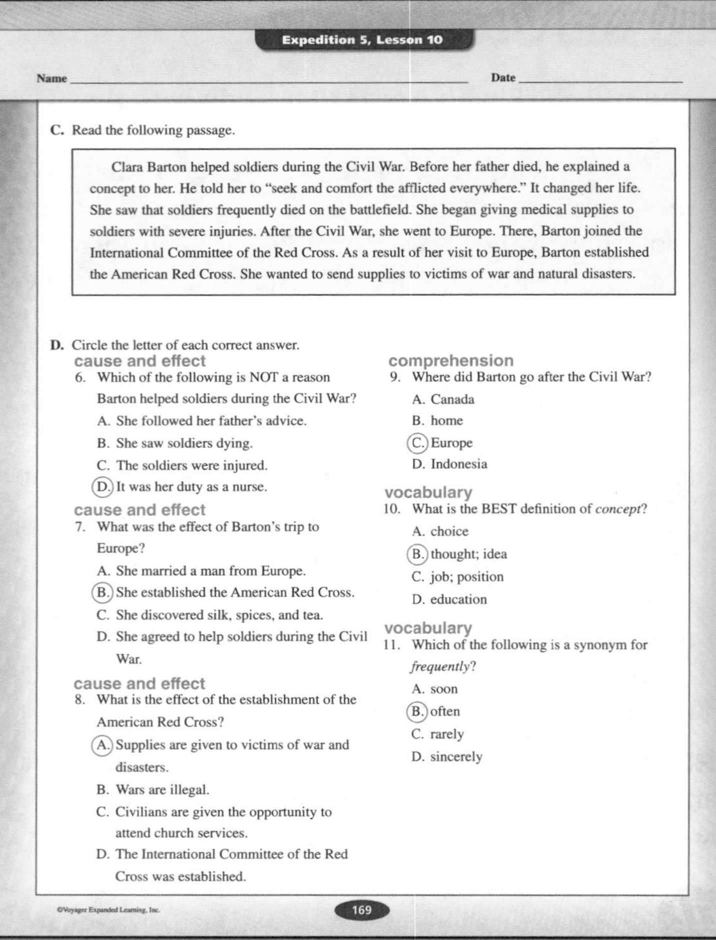

Expedition 5, Lesson 10

Name ____________ Date ____________

C. Read the following passage.

> Clara Barton helped soldiers during the Civil War. Before her father died, he explained a concept to her. He told her to "seek and comfort the afflicted everywhere." It changed her life. She saw that soldiers frequently died on the battlefield. She began giving medical supplies to soldiers with severe injuries. After the Civil War, she went to Europe. There, Barton joined the International Committee of the Red Cross. As a result of her visit to Europe, Barton established the American Red Cross. She wanted to send supplies to victims of war and natural disasters.

D. Circle the letter of each correct answer.

cause and effect
6. Which of the following is NOT a reason Barton helped soldiers during the Civil War?
   A. She followed her father's advice.
   B. She saw soldiers dying.
   C. The soldiers were injured.
   (D.) It was her duty as a nurse.

cause and effect
7. What was the effect of Barton's trip to Europe?
   A. She married a man from Europe.
   (B.) She established the American Red Cross.
   C. She discovered silk, spices, and tea.
   D. She agreed to help soldiers during the Civil War.

cause and effect
8. What is the effect of the establishment of the American Red Cross?
   (A.) Supplies are given to victims of war and disasters.
   B. Wars are illegal.
   C. Civilians are given the opportunity to attend church services.
   D. The International Committee of the Red Cross was established.

comprehension
9. Where did Barton go after the Civil War?
   A. Canada
   B. home
   (C.) Europe
   D. Indonesia

vocabulary
10. What is the BEST definition of *concept*?
   A. choice
   (B.) thought; idea
   C. job; position
   D. education

vocabulary
11. Which of the following is a synonym for *frequently*?
   A. soon
   (B.) often
   C. rarely
   D. sincerely

©Voyager Expanded Learning, Inc. 169

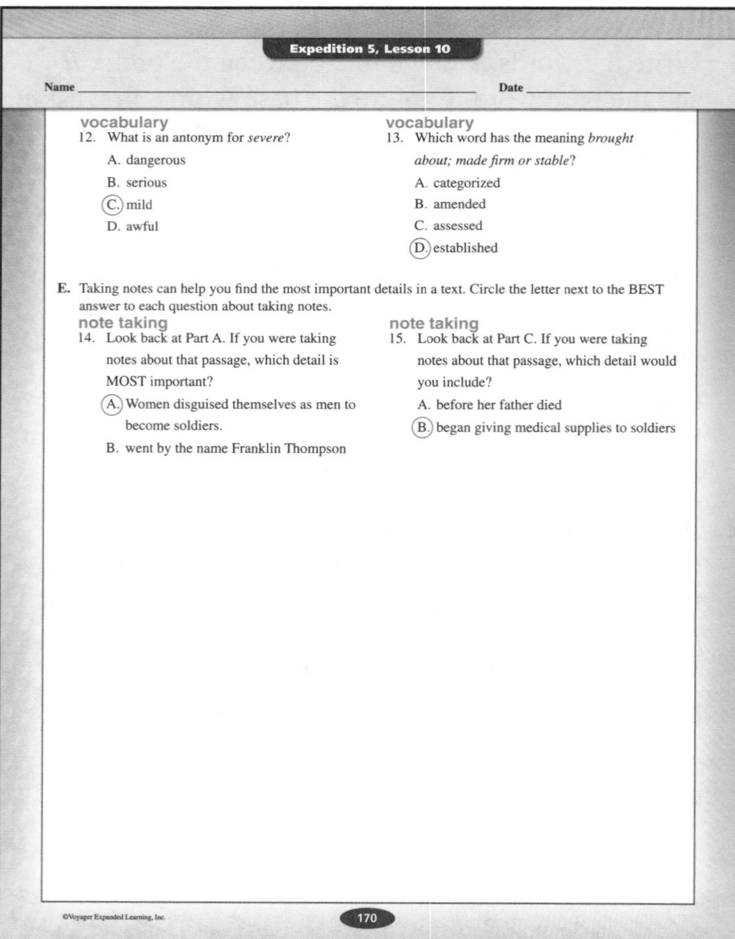

Expedition 5, Lesson 10

Name ____________ Date ____________

vocabulary
12. What is an antonym for *severe*?
   A. dangerous
   B. serious
   (C.) mild
   D. awful

vocabulary
13. Which word has the meaning *brought about; made firm or stable*?
   A. categorized
   B. amended
   C. assessed
   (D.) established

E. Taking notes can help you find the most important details in a text. Circle the letter next to the BEST answer to each question about taking notes.

note taking
14. Look back at Part A. If you were taking notes about that passage, which detail is MOST important?
   (A.) Women disguised themselves as men to become soldiers.
   B. went by the name Franklin Thompson

note taking
15. Look back at Part C. If you were taking notes about that passage, which detail would you include?
   A. before her father died
   (B.) began giving medical supplies to soldiers

©Voyager Expanded Learning, Inc. 170

Reteach

Cause and Effect

1. Direct students to Student Book pages 171 and 172. **When you read a confusing text, stop to figure out what the causes and effects are. Using this strategy may make the text's meaning clear.** Read the instructions aloud. **What is a cause?** (why something happens) **What is an effect?** (what happened)
2. Read the first passage aloud. **What signal words or phrases do you see?** (as a result) **What happened?** (Tammy Duckworth won three medals.) **Why did that happen?** (She was wounded, brave, and heroic.) Remind students that sometimes more than one thing can cause something to happen. Complete the first chart together. Have a student restate the cause and effect using the signal word.
3. Remind students that they may not always see signal words. **You may have to use details and what you already know to infer cause and effect.** Have students complete the last three charts independently. After students complete the pages, have them compare responses.

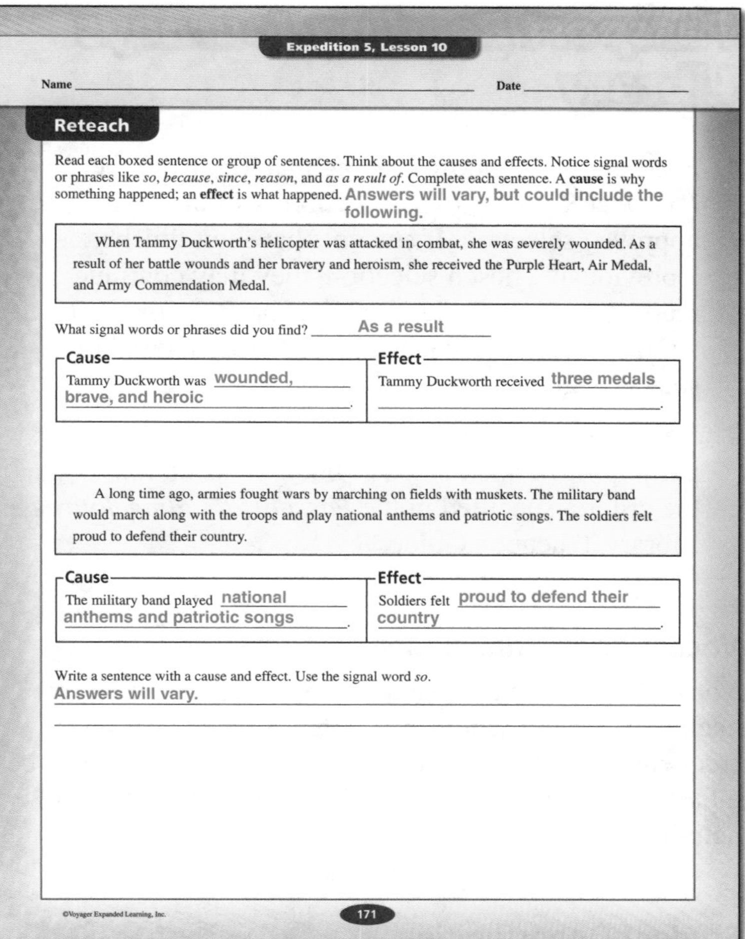

Expedition 5, Lesson 10

Name ______ Date ______

Reteach

Read each boxed sentence or group of sentences. Think about the causes and effects. Notice signal words or phrases like *so*, *because*, *since*, *reason*, and *as a result of*. Complete each sentence. A **cause** is why something happened; an **effect** is what happened. Answers will vary, but could include the following.

When Tammy Duckworth's helicopter was attacked in combat, she was severely wounded. As a result of her battle wounds and her bravery and heroism, she received the Purple Heart, Air Medal, and Army Commendation Medal.

What signal words or phrases did you find? As a result

Cause	Effect
Tammy Duckworth was wounded, brave, and heroic.	Tammy Duckworth received three medals.

A long time ago, armies fought wars by marching on fields with muskets. The military band would march along with the troops and play national anthems and patriotic songs. The soldiers felt proud to defend their country.

Cause	Effect
The military band played national anthems and patriotic songs.	Soldiers felt proud to defend their country.

Write a sentence with a cause and effect. Use the signal word *so*.
Answers will vary.

©Voyager Expanded Learning, Inc. 171

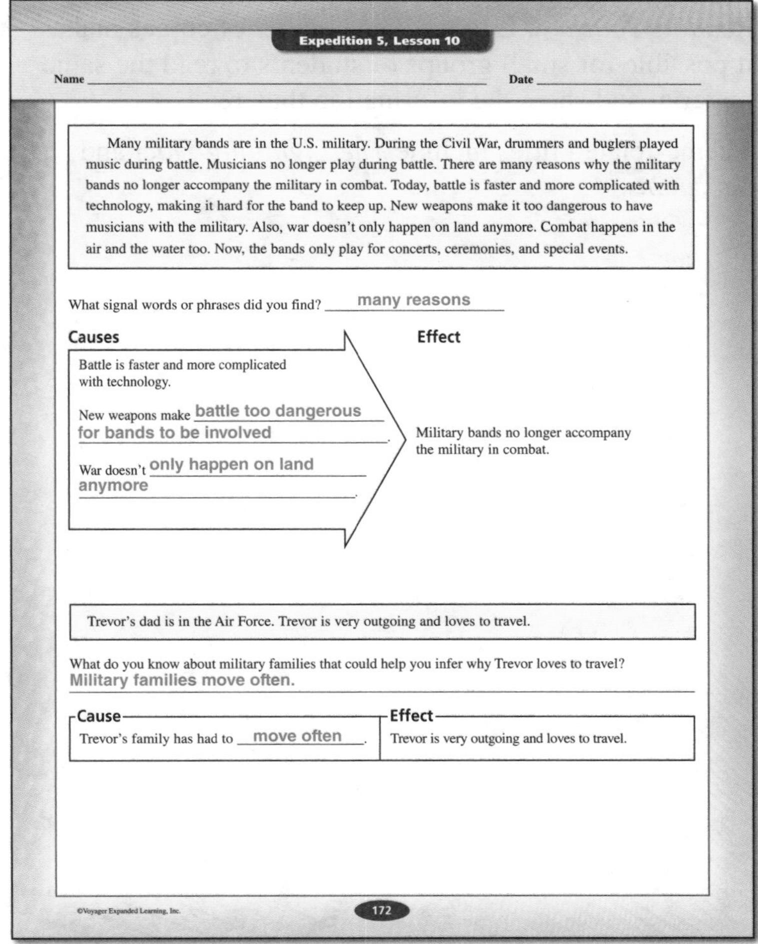

Expedition 5, Lesson 10

Name ______ Date ______

Many military bands are in the U.S. military. During the Civil War, drummers and buglers played music during battle. Musicians no longer play during battle. There are many reasons why the military bands no longer accompany the military in combat. Today, battle is faster and more complicated with technology, making it hard for the band to keep up. New weapons make it too dangerous to have musicians with the military. Also, war doesn't only happen on land anymore. Combat happens in the air and the water too. Now, the bands only play for concerts, ceremonies, and special events.

What signal words or phrases did you find? many reasons

Causes	Effect
Battle is faster and more complicated with technology. New weapons make battle too dangerous for bands to be involved. War doesn't only happen on land anymore.	Military bands no longer accompany the military in combat.

Trevor's dad is in the Air Force. Trevor is very outgoing and loves to travel.

What do you know about military families that could help you infer why Trevor loves to travel?
Military families move often.

Cause	Effect
Trevor's family has had to move often.	Trevor is very outgoing and loves to travel.

©Voyager Expanded Learning, Inc. 172

Passport Reading Journeys Library

1. Have students choose reading material from the *Passport Reading Journeys* Library or another approved selection. If students have not finished a previously chosen selection, they may continue reading from that selection. See the *Passport Reading Journeys* Library Teacher's Guide for material on selection guidelines.
2. You also may use this time to allow students to participate in book clubs or book presentations. Use the criteria specified in the *Passport Reading Journeys* Library Teacher's Guide.

Vocabulary Connections

Vocabulary words are listed in the Teacher's Guide for each book. These words are content-related or used frequently in reading material. The selected words can be a basis for independent or small-group discussions and activities.

Student Opportunities

Six copies of each book title are provided in the *Passport Reading Journeys* Library. The number of copies makes it possible for small groups of students to read the same material and share the information they read.

Theme-related titles include *The Lightning Thief* and *Scorpions.*

Technology

1. Depending on your classroom configuration and computer access, you may have all students work through the technology in a lab setting or have individuals or small groups of students work on desktops or laptops while other students participate in other suggested activities, such as the *Passport Reading Journeys* Library.
2. The online technology component provides additional support for students to work with selected vocabulary words. Students will work through a series of activities to strengthen their word knowledge, then apply that knowledge to passage reading. Refer to the online technology component User Guide for more information.

   Theme-related word sets include World History, U.S. History, Technology, and Government.

Expedition Project

Military Branch Presentation

Distribute copies of Project Blackline Master page 10. **You will do a group presentation on a branch of the U.S. military. You have read about a few military branches in the Anthology. Now you will focus on one branch of the military to learn more about it.** Have students form small groups, and assign each group a military branch to research and present. If possible, cover each branch, including the Army, Navy, Marines, Air Force, Coast Guard, and National Guard.

Assign point values as you see fit, and have students write them in the rubric. Tell students to make any notes on the page that will help them, but they will turn the page in with the assignment.

For students to have a meaningful experience completing tasks as a group, certain strategies need to be employed. Group dynamics and interactions can be improved with strategic planning for group work. Refer to page xxxvi for information on effective grouping strategies.

Have groups follow these steps:

1. **Research your assigned military branch with library books and reliable Internet sites. Find out what the military branch does. Compile a list of job positions, ranks, or the equipment and vehicles used. Interview people you know who are or were members of your chosen military branch.**
2. **Gather or create visuals. Visuals might be posters you create or recruiting brochures from your school's academic counseling office. Images might include pictures of the branch's equipment, vehicles, and uniforms.**
3. **As a group, discuss the benefits and drawbacks to joining the military branch you research.**
4. **Take roles and do assigned tasks for the project that include taking notes, listing needed visuals, creating an outline of the presentation, and leading the discussion.**
5. **Presentations should fit the following criteria:**
    - **Informative and clear explanation of the duties of the military branch**
    - **Detailed visuals that connect to the presentation**
    - **Organized delivery and personal opinions about the benefits and drawbacks of joining the military branch and reasons for the opinions**
6. **Rehearse presentations. Each group member should take one role, such as presenting the duties, job positions, ranks, uniforms, vehicles, and awards of the branch.**
7. **Present informational military branch presentations during class.**
8. **I will assess your writing and presentation based on the rubric on your page.** To assess student presentations, use the rubric from the Project Blackline Master.

Real-World Reading

Map

1. Direct students to Student Book pages 173 and 174. Explain that they will read a map. **What do the markings on the map point out?** (locations of buffalo soldier monuments) **What is a monument?** (a statue or structure built to honor and remember people or events) **What is the text about?** (The text gives information on each monument and the buffalo soldiers at each location.)

2. Have students find the following terms in the text. Define these terms:

   - *To pay tribute* means "show thanks and respect."
   - *Cavalry* means "military troops riding horses."
   - *Preserve* means "protect, or keep safe from harm or aging."

3. Have students look at the map and read the information on each location. **Follow the instructions to mark the text and map.**

4. **Which location would you be most interested in visiting? Explain.**

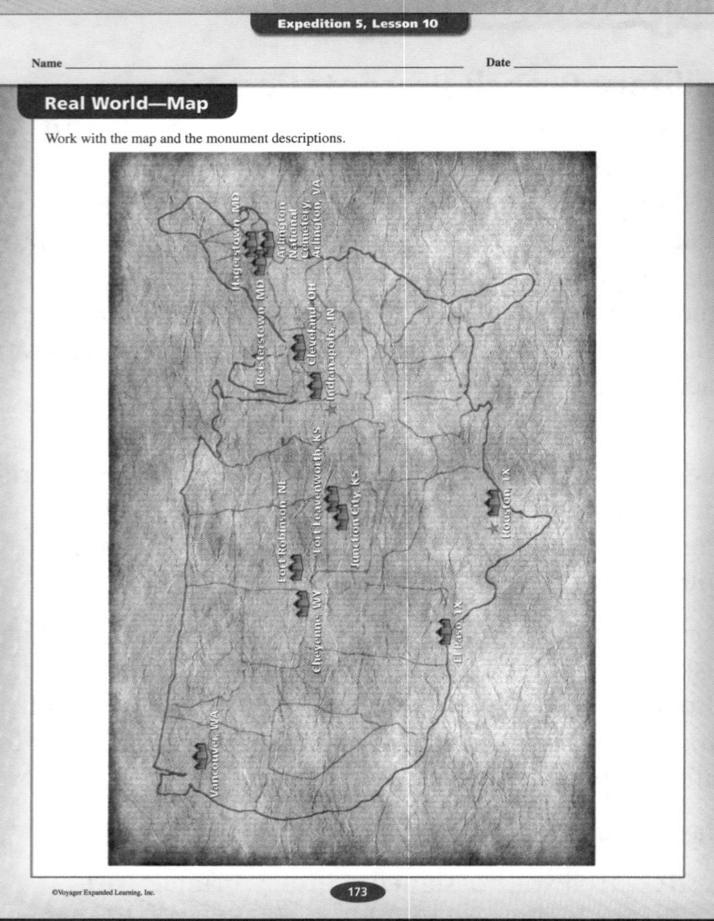

Expedition 5, Lesson 10

Name ____________ Date ____________

Real World—Map

Work with the map and the monument descriptions.

173

Expedition 5, Lesson 10

Name ____________ Date ____________

- Circle the names of buffalo soldiers.
- Place a star on the map where there are buffalo soldier museums.
- Underline the names of wars.
- Draw the route you would take to drive across the country to see all of the buffalo soldier monuments.

Vancouver, WA
The Infantry Barracks
This marker is near the oldest structure in the Vancouver Barracks. A unit of buffalo soldiers stayed here from 1899–1900. It pays tribute to their work and their participation in community events.

Cheyenne, WY
Buffalo Soldier Monument
This statue is at F.E. Warren Air Force Base. It honors the African American Cavalry units that served here in the 1900s.

Fort Robinson, NE
Buffalo Soldiers at Fort Robinson
This marker stands in Fort Robinson State Park near the buffalo soldier barracks. Buffalo soldiers were stationed here for 18 years.

Junction City, KS
Buffalo Soldier Memorial
This memorial is a 9-foot statue of a buffalo soldier from the World War I era. He is standing next to his horse, holding the reins. Dedicated to those who served in the 9th and 10th Cavalry units, it stands near buffalo soldiers' old quarters.

Fort Leavenworth, KS
Buffalo Soldier Memorial
This bronze statue of a buffalo soldier riding his horse honors the soldiers of the 9th and 10th Calvary. The 10th Calvary was formed and activated in Fort Leavenworth in 1867.

El Paso, TX
Buffalo Soldier Memorial
This 3,000-pound bronze statue of an African American soldier on his horse stands at the entrance to Fort Bliss. This pays tribute to the buffalo soldiers who served at Fort Bliss from 1866–1899.

Houston, TX
The Buffalo Soldiers National Museum
This museum gives an overview of African American military history from the Revolutionary War to the Persian Gulf War.

Indianapolis, IN
Buffalo Soldier Research Museum
This museum was founded to research and document the histories of the people who served as buffalo soldiers in the Army. It also has a collection of preserved military artifacts from 1866–1945.

Cleveland, OH
Colonel Charles Young
This monument honors Colonel Charles Young. It has an image of his face and a brief biography of his accomplishment. As a buffalo soldier, he served in the Spanish-American War and in the Philippines. He was the first African American to become a colonel in the Army.

Hagerstown, MD
Corporal William Othello Wilson
This marker pays tribute to Corporal William Othello Wilson, a native of Hagerstown, MD. He earned a Congressional Medal of Honor for his bravery and service in the Indian Wars.

Reisterstown, MD
"Buffalo Soldiers"
This plaque honors First Sgt. Augustus Walley, a Reisterstown native. He was awarded the Medal of Honor for bravery during the Spanish-American War.

Arlington National Cemetery, Arlington, VA
Buffalo Soldiers Centennial Ceremony
This small monument in the cemetery is dedicated to the buffalo soldiers, 9th and 10th Cavalry, and the 24th and 25th Infantry Regiments who served in the Spanish-American War. They charged up San Juan Hill with Teddy Roosevelt and the Rough Riders.

174

Exploring Careers

U.S. Navy

1. Direct students to Anthology page 93. Have students preview the title and subheads. **What Navy careers most interest you? Explain.** Direct students to pay close attention when they read the descriptions.
2. Have students read the passage.
3. Direct students to Student Book page 175. Tell them to answer the questions using the Anthology passage. Then, they can complete the chart at the bottom by researching a career in the U.S. Navy in books or online. If they already know another military career that they are interested in, have them write it in the chart and research it.

Expedition 5, Lesson 10

Name ______________________ Date ____________

Exploring Careers: U.S. Navy

A. Answer the following questions about careers in the U.S. Navy.

1. What are five important job titles in the Navy?
air traffic controller; culinary specialist; diver; musician; photographer
2. Why is it important that a Navy diver be in top physical shape and able to work under pressure?
Diving is physically very difficult. Deconstructing ocean mines would be stressful because it has to be done quickly.
3. What are the Navy's purposes for taking photographs?
to record the news; to record ceremonies; to record troops in combat; to record historical events; to make maps
4. What is the range of annual salaries for careers in the U.S. Navy?
$16,000–$80,000
5. What are three benefits that the Navy provides?
bonuses and paid vacations; health and dental insurance; retirement plans; discounted travel; paid college tuition

B. Use the Internet to research other possible career choices in this field and complete the chart.

Career	
Responsibilities	
Education Required	
Average Salary	
Is this a career you might pursue?	
Why or why not?	
Career	
Responsibilities	
Education Required	
Average Salary	
Is this a career you might pursue?	
Why or why not?	

175

Career

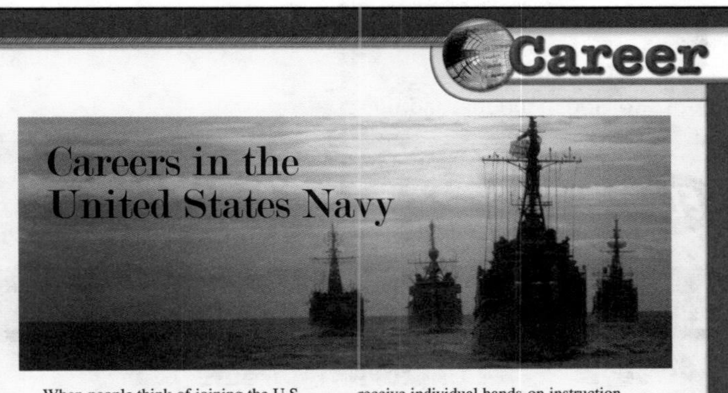

Careers in the United States Navy

When people think of joining the U.S. Navy, they often think of life aboard a large ship or submarine. But, the Navy offers much more than life at sea. For those who choose to join this branch of the military, there are many career options available.

Many people enlist in the Navy right after high school. Most initial terms of enlistment are between two and five years. After enlisting, all sailors must complete eight weeks of Navy Boot Camp. This is an intense introduction to life in the Navy. After this, sailors move on to specific skill training for their chosen career path. Navy personnel can pursue a variety of career paths, ranging from cook to civil engineer to foreign language translator.

Air Traffic Controller

Navy air traffic controllers are responsible for directing aircraft from airports or decks of aircraft carriers. They use radios and radar to communicate with other controllers and pilots. They also update aeronautical charts and maps. After their technical training, air traffic controllers spend up to two years in on-the-job training to further develop their skills. They take additional courses and receive individual hands-on instruction. Many sailors earn college credits during this training. New recruits must enlist for five years to pursue careers as air traffic controllers. After their work in the Navy, many move on to become civilian air traffic controllers.

Culinary Specialists

Those with a passion for cooking will be right at home in the Navy. After a four-week training program, sailors can become culinary specialists. They work on every ship and base in the Navy. After starting out in a mess hall, many work their way up to become head chefs. Some even have the opportunity to cook five-star meals for guests at the White House. After their Navy career, many culinary specialists pursue jobs in the hospitality field. They manage restaurants or become chefs. Others become nutritionists or personal chefs.

Diver

The competition to become a diver for the Navy is intense. Candidates must complete an in-depth mental and physical training program. When they are done, a select few men and women will become Navy divers. Divers may

An Army of Progress  93

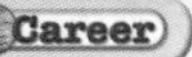

work to deconstruct ocean mines. Some salvage aircraft that were shot down during combat. Others specialize in search-and-rescue missions. Prospective candidates must be in top physical shape and be able to work well under pressure. Divers are given special pay for their hard work. There is an enlistment bonus of up to $30,000. Additionally, these men and women receive dive pay on top of their regular salary each month.

Musician

A musician is another career option available to enlisted sailors. To join this program, enlisted men and women must audition. Then, some sailors have the opportunity to be a part of one of the best music programs in the country. Naval musicians must attend a five-month training program. Upon completion of this course, musicians are then assigned to a Navy Band in the United States, Japan, or Italy. They perform all types of music, from classical to contemporary rock. During this time, training continues. Naval musicians get paid for training while earning college credits and performing around the world. After their service in the Navy, many move on to join professional bands and orchestras as vocalists, musicians, conductors, and composers.

Photographer

Naval photographers use state-of-the-art still and video cameras. They cover news events, ceremonies, and troops in combat. They also take photos for historical purposes. Some of their work includes aerial photography for mapmaking. Other assignments include editing and producing public relations videos. Photographers may also cover press conferences. Some may work as underwater photographers. Navy-provided training for this job often counts as college credit. As civilians, many Navy photographers pursue careers as journalists, portrait photographers, or film editors.

Salaries

Enlisted salaries start at about $16,000 a year. The earning potential quickly increases with training and years of service. Officers can earn close to $80,000 a year. There are many other benefits involved in joining the Navy. Some of these include bonuses and paid vacations. Sailors also receive health and dental insurance. Retirement savings plans and discounted travel are two other military benefits. Military veterans are also eligible for continuing education benefits, such as the GI Bill. After 90 days of active duty, sailors are eligible to receive full college tuition. Additionally, they get $1,000 a year for books, and a monthly housing allowance.

The Navy offers a wide variety of careers that reach far beyond sailing a ship. The specialized classes and on-the-job training can prepare enlisted sailors for a lifelong Navy career. They also can help people make a smooth transition to the civilian workforce. While developing personally and professionally, many complete college degrees, build retirement savings, and achieve their lifelong career goals.

 94 Expedition 5

Now You See It

"Fly Guy"		"Graffiti: Vandalism or Art?"	
Lesson 1	**Lesson 2**	**Lesson 3**	**Lesson 4**
Introduce the Expedition Discuss probing questions about graphic arts. **Before Reading** • Introduce and practice using passage vocabulary. • Introduce and practice identifying problems and solutions. **During Reading** Read "Fly Guy." **After Reading** Check comprehension. Have students practice vocabulary using the online technology component. Have students select books for independent reading. ELL Extend and practice.	**Prepare to Reread** • Review and practice using passage vocabulary. • Practice using context clues. • Build new words using the prefix *anti-*. **Reread** • Review and practice identifying problems and solutions. • Write a comic strip and a dialogue. ELL Extend and practice.	**Before Reading** • Introduce and practice using passage vocabulary. • Introduce and practice identifying point of view and bias. • Introduce the passage by previewing and making predictions. **During Reading** Read "Graffiti: Vandalism or Art?" **After Reading** Check comprehension. Have students practice vocabulary using the online technology component. Have students select books for independent reading. ELL Extend and practice.	**Prepare to Reread** • Review and practice using passage vocabulary. • Practice using context clues. • Build new words using the suffixes *-able* and *-ible.* **Reread** • Review and practice identifying point of view and bias. • Write a persuasive letter. ELL Extend and practice.

Lesson 5—Review, Extend, Assess

Review Vocabulary
Review and practice using passage vocabulary.

Extend Vocabulary
Use base words to build and understand new words.

Assess Comprehension and Vocabulary
Assess student understanding of point of view and bias.

Reteach
Reteach identifying problem/solution and point of view/bias using student activity pages.

Passport Reading Journeys Library
Have students select books for independent reading.

Technology
Have students practice vocabulary using the online technology component.

Writing Process
Have students use the writing process to write a persuasive argument.

Real-World Reading
Have students read online messages and complete student activity page.

Exploring Careers
Have students read about a career as a comic book writer and complete an activity page.

Teacher's Note
Before beginning the Expedition, ask your librarian to suggest books that will fit with the theme. Graphic novels or books relating to films or plays will be appropriate for this Expedition.

"When Videos Turn Bad"		"Animation and Gaming Graphics"	
Lesson 6	**Lesson 7**	**Lesson 8**	**Lesson 9**
Before Reading • Introduce and practice using passage vocabulary. • Practice identifying point of view and bias. • Introduce the passage by previewing and making predictions. **During Reading** Read "When Videos Turn Bad." **After Reading** Check comprehension. Have students practice vocabulary using the online technology component. Have students select books for independent reading. ELL Extend and practice.	**Prepare to Reread** • Review and practice using passage vocabulary. • Practice using context clues. • Build new words using the Latin roots *volvere* and *tenere*. **Reread** • Review and practice identifying point of view and bias. • Write an interview. ELL Extend and practice.	**Before Reading** • Introduce and practice using passage vocabulary. • Introduce and practice Big Picture note-taking. • Introduce the passage by previewing and making predictions. **During Reading** Read "Animation and Gaming Graphics." **After Reading** Check comprehension. Have students practice vocabulary using the online technology component. Have students select books for independent reading. ELL Extend and practice.	**Prepare to Reread** • Review and practice using passage vocabulary. • Practice using context clues. • Practice using multiple-meaning words *project* and *produce*. **Reread** • Review and practice Big Picture note-taking. • Write a description of movie or video game graphics. ELL Extend and practice.

Lesson 10—Review, Extend, Assess

Review Vocabulary
Review and practice using passage vocabulary.

Extend Vocabulary
Use Latin root words to build and understand new words.

Assess Comprehension and Vocabulary
Assess student understanding of point of view and bias.

Reteach
Reteach identifying point of view/bias and Big Picture note-taking using student activity pages.

Passport Reading Journeys Library
Have students select books for independent reading.

Technology
Have students practice vocabulary using the online technology component.

Writing Process
Have students research and prepare for a debate dialogue.

Real-World Reading
Have students read movie reviews and complete student activity page.

Exploring Careers
Have students read about a career as a graphic artist and complete an activity page.

Expedition 6

Introduce the Expedition

1. Have students turn to Anthology page 95 and view the opening photograph. **What do you see in the photograph?** (video; computer graphics) **What kinds of arts or artists are you interested in?** (Allow students to discuss their interests.)
2. **Historically, graphic arts referred to the artistic process of drawing or printmaking. Today, however, it refers to the trade of a graphic designer who uses a computer to create drawings and designs.** Have students explain what graphic arts they encounter daily. Encourage students to talk about art they create.
3. Have partners discuss initial responses to the following probing questions. Explain that they will consider these questions throughout the Expedition.
   - **How has technology changed visual expression?**
   - **How are graphic arts the same as or different from fine art?**
   - **What graffiti, if any, should be outlawed?**

Build Background DVD 6.1
Tell students that they will view a brief DVD that provides background information about graphic arts. **As you watch, listen for ideas that connect to the responses you discussed.**

Expedition 6
Now You See It
How has technology changed visual expression?
How are graphic arts the same as or different from fine art?
What graffiti, if any, should be outlawed?
95

4. To make the most of the discussion time, remember to incorporate strategies that encourage and extend student involvement. Refer to page xxxviii for a comprehensive discussion of these strategies.
5. Point out the parts of the Expedition 6 Organizer on Student Book pages 176 and 177. **You will use this organizer to write your own ideas and questions about the passages you read in this Expedition.**

   Suggestions for how students can add ideas to these pages appear in this Teacher's Edition at the end of Lessons 2, 4, 7, and 9. Allow students to write initial responses in the probing questions graphic organizer in Part A.

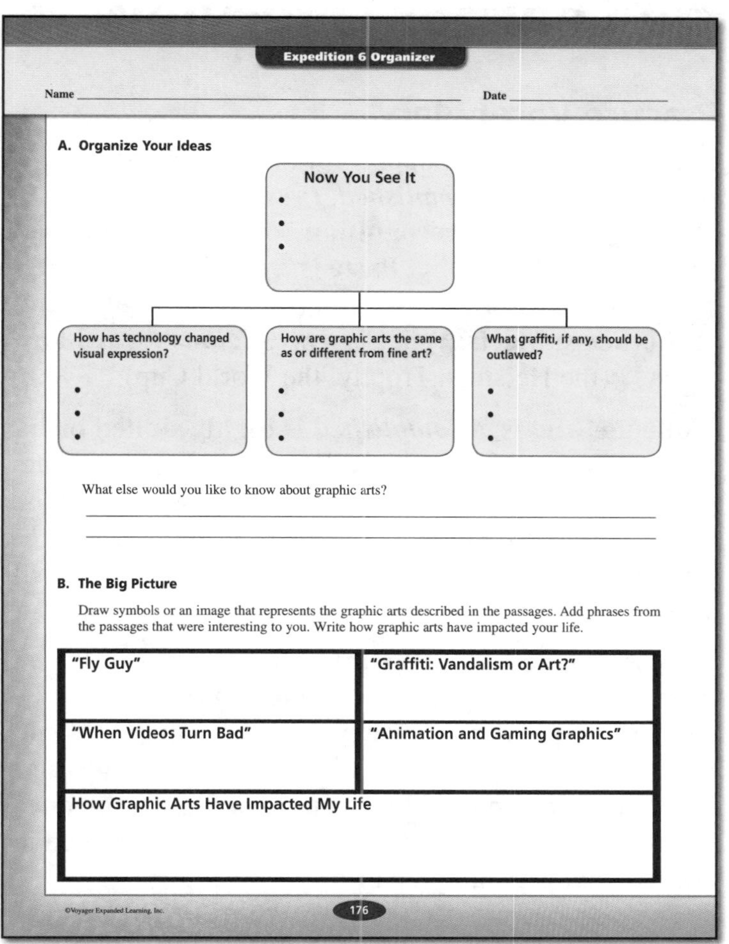

Expedition 6 Organizer

Name ______________________ Date ____________

A. Organize Your Ideas

Now You See It
-
-
-

How has technology changed visual expression?	How are graphic arts the same as or different from fine art?	What graffiti, if any, should be outlawed?
• • •	• • •	• • •

What else would you like to know about graphic arts?

____

____

B. The Big Picture

Draw symbols or an image that represents the graphic arts described in the passages. Add phrases from the passages that were interesting to you. Write how graphic arts have impacted your life.

"Fly Guy"	"Graffiti: Vandalism or Art?"
"When Videos Turn Bad"	"Animation and Gaming Graphics"
How Graphic Arts Have Impacted My Life	

©Voyager Expanded Learning, Inc. 176

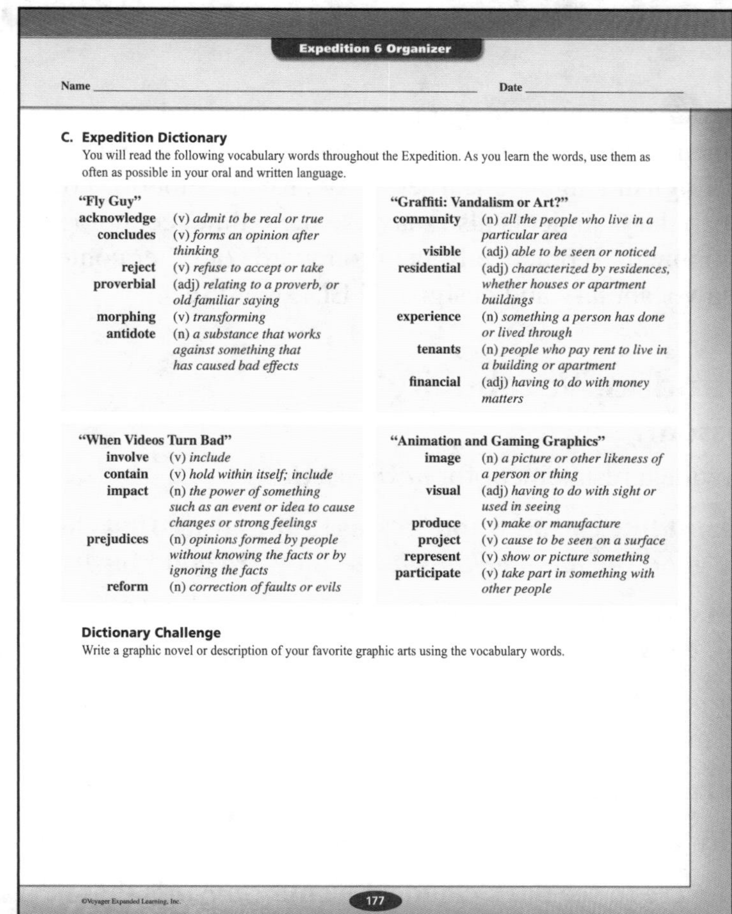

Expedition 6 Organizer

Name ______________________ Date ____________

C. Expedition Dictionary

You will read the following vocabulary words throughout the Expedition. As you learn the words, use them as often as possible in your oral and written language.

"Fly Guy"
acknowledge (v) *admit to be real or true*
concludes (v) *forms an opinion after thinking*
reject (v) *refuse to accept or take*
proverbial (adj) *relating to a proverb, or old familiar saying*
morphing (v) *transforming*
antidote (n) *a substance that works against something that has caused bad effects*

"Graffiti: Vandalism or Art?"
community (n) *all the people who live in a particular area*
visible (adj) *able to be seen or noticed*
residential (adj) *characterized by residences, whether houses or apartment buildings*
experience (n) *something a person has done or lived through*
tenants (n) *people who pay rent to live in a building or apartment*
financial (adj) *having to do with money matters*

"When Videos Turn Bad"
involve (v) *include*
contain (v) *hold within itself; include*
impact (n) *the power of something such as an event or idea to cause changes or strong feelings*
prejudices (n) *opinions formed by people without knowing the facts or by ignoring the facts*
reform (n) *correction of faults or evils*

"Animation and Gaming Graphics"
image (n) *a picture or other likeness of a person or thing*
visual (adj) *having to do with sight or used in seeing*
produce (v) *make or manufacture*
project (v) *cause to be seen on a surface*
represent (v) *show or picture something*
participate (v) *take part in something with other people*

Dictionary Challenge

Write a graphic novel or description of your favorite graphic arts using the vocabulary words.

©Voyager Expanded Learning, Inc. 177

ELL

Making Connections

Have students share prior knowledge about graphic arts. Begin by writing the art genres—*graphic novel, comic book, graffiti, film,* and *computer animation*—on the board. Encourage students to name examples of the different genres representing different cultures and language backgrounds such as anime from Japan.

Preview the vocabulary word *visual* as you introduce the Expedition. English language learners may know cognates for *visual, graphic, video, film,* and *movie* in their home languages. Allow them to say related words and phrases in their home languages and to share what they already know about these words. Tell students that the arts being discussed are all visual because they involve things you can see.

English language learners will recognize many other cognates in the Expedition 6 vocabulary relating to art and film, such as *artist, paint,* and *camera*. During your discussions, offer opportunities for students to point out cognates by asking questions such as: **What's the word for *artist* in Spanish?**

English Language Learner Overview

The (ELL) signals when extra support is provided for students during the lesson. As needed, Blackline Masters for English language learners may provide support. For vocabulary, students also may use the online technology component to practice Expedition words or other content-area vocabulary and designated ELL word sets.

Introduce Vocabulary

Lesson 1

Provide a restatement for *acknowledge*.

I don't like eating whole grains, but I admit that they are good for me. I *acknowledge* they are good for me.

You didn't think you would like the movie, but you did. Now will you *acknowledge* that you liked it?

For *antidote* and *conclude*, use familiar examples to teach the meanings.

You can go to a doctor to get an *antidote* for a poison.

Why would an *antidote* help you if you were poisoned?

If I were to see dark clouds, I would *conclude* that it will rain.

If you see someone bringing a pizza, what do you *conclude*?

Use *reject* with the antonym *accept* to teach the meaning.

Here is a book. Will you *accept* or *reject* it?

I will give you an invitation to a party. Will you *accept* or *reject* it?

Lesson 3

Have students tell the part of speech of each vocabulary word. Write the headings *Nouns* and *Adjectives* on the board. List words under the correct heading. **A *noun* is a person, place, thing, or idea.** Show items around the classroom as you give examples of nouns, such as *table*. ***Community* is a noun. Is a *community* a person, place, thing, or idea?** (thing) Repeat the process with the nouns *experience* (idea) and *tenants* (person/people).

An *adjective* is a word that describes a noun. Make your facial expressions show the meaning of examples of adjectives, such as *happy*. **The adjective *visible* can describe different nouns. Would you describe the air as *visible*?** (no) **Why not?** (*Visible* means "able to be seen," and air can't be seen.) Repeat the process with the adjectives *residential* and *financial*.

Practice Vocabulary

In Lesson 2, provide support for the context words *prestigious* and *accomplished*. ***Prestigious* means "having respect or recognition" or "famous for being important." The Nobel Prize is a *prestigious* award for people who achieve great things in science, literature, and other subjects. What is a *prestigious* award for sports?** (the Heisman Trophy; the World Cup)

Someone who is *accomplished* is highly skilled or has proven that he or she is excellent at something. The person may or may not be famous. Jennifer Hudson is an *accomplished* singer. My cousin is an *accomplished* dancer. Who is an *accomplished* actor? (Answers will vary.)

In Lesson 4, provide support for the context word *defaced*. **If a person *defaced* something, he or she spoiled the appearance or ruined the way it looked. I accidentally *defaced* the door to my building when I spilled paint on it. What would you do if someone *defaced* your property?** (repair it; find who defaced it and ask that person to repair it)

Apply the Target Skill: Problem/Solution

Have students review the definitions of the academic vocabulary words *problem* and *solution*. Practice identifying Brian's problem in "Fly Guy" by asking yes/no questions, including **Is Brian's problem that he wins the science competition?** (no) **Is his problem that the other students don't like him?** (yes) Have students identify the solution to Brian's problem, answering with yes/no or with phrases or sentences.

Apply the Target Skill: Point of View and Bias

Students may need additional practice with point of view and bias. Practice identifying the author's point of view in "Graffiti: Vandalism or Art?" by providing the following sentence starters: *At the beginning of the interview, Muriel thinks or believes ________. At the beginning of the interview, Josh thinks or believes ________.*

FLY GUY
SOME THINGS NEVER CHANGE. BRIAN "BRAIN" RAYNES WINS THE PRESTIGIOUS SCI-TECH COMPETITION—FOR THE SECOND YEAR IN A ROW.
HERE IS YOUR $5,000 CHECK, YOUNG MAN. CONGRATULATIONS.
UM... THANKS... AGAIN.
YEAH, BRAIN. GO! GO AWAY.
DON'T EVEN, CHAD. YOU COULD AT LEAST ***ACKNOWLEDGE*** THAT HE WON.
I INVENTED A FRUIT HYBRIDIZER RAY THAT COMBINES A CANTALOUPE AND A HONEYDEW MELON. VOILÀ! A CANTADEW!
LAST YEAR, BRIAN INVENTED A MICROFYING GLASS.
I DIRECT A LASER BEAM THROUGH THE GLASS ONTO THESE SPOTS ON THE CARPET. VOILÀ! THEY... SHRINK!
TOO BAD HE CAN'T GET HIS MACHINE TO WORK ON HIS ZITS.
WHATEVER!
YOU MUST BE VERY PROUD, SON.
SURE.
DON'T SPEND IT ALL IN ONE PLACE. HA!
I WON'T...
MY HOUSE AT EIGHT. DON'T BE LATE.
I'VE WON, BUT I'M STILL A GLORK.*
THE OTHER KIDS ARE GOING TO A PARTY. I'M GOING... NOWHERE. WHY?
*GLORK = GEEK + LOSER + DORK.
MAYBE I SHOULD GO TO THE PARTY, ANYWAY, AND FIND OUT WHY I WASN'T INVITED.
NAH. THEY'LL JUST ***REJECT*** ME.
96 Expedition 6

THE TEEN SCIENCE WHIZ ***CONCLUDES*** THAT HE NEEDS TO STUDY THE "COOL" KIDS IN THEIR NATIVE HABITAT.
IF I KNOW WHAT THEY LIKE, I CAN BE THE KIND OF PERSON THEY WILL LIKE.
BUT, HOW CAN I GET INTO THE PARTY WITHOUT AN INVITATION?
OF COURSE!
I'LL USE THE MICROFYING GLASS ON MYSELF!
I'LL SHRINK MYSELF DOWN TO THE SIZE OF A BUG.
GO TO THE PARTY... AND BE LIKE THE ***PROVERBIAL*** FLY ON THE WALL... IF I SURVIVE.
CLICK!
MEANWHILE... A FAMILY OF FAMISHED FRUIT FLIES FEAST ON THE SPOILS OF BRIAN'S HYBRIDIZER EXPERIMENTS.
GO AWAY. SHOO, FLIES.
WHAT IS HAPPENING TO ME? THIS IS ***MORPHING*** ME INTO A FLY. OH, NO!
COOL! I CAN SEE IN MULTIPLE DIRECTIONS. I CAN LOOK UP, DOWN, ALL AROUND.
THIS ISN'T WHAT I PLANNED, BUT SCIENCE... MARCHES ON! MAKE THAT FLIES ON... OFF TO THE PARTY. FIRST, ONE MORE GRAPE.
ZZZZZZZ
CHAD'S HOUSE LATER THAT NIGHT...
I'M BORED.
PLAYING VIDEO GAMES. TALKING ON THE PHONE. NAPPING?
Now You See It 97

WHAT DO YOU WANT TO DO?
I DON'T KNOW. WHATEVER YOU WANT TO DO.
I DON'T KNOW. WHAT DO YOU WANT TO DO?
SOME PARTY.
YOU KNOW WHO WOULD HAVE SOME IDEAS?
WHO?
BRIAN.
BRIAN BRAIN?
BRIAN DOESN'T SIT AROUND DOING... NOTHING. HE IS ACCOMPLISHED. HE MAKES THINGS HAPPEN.
YOU MAY BE RIGHT.
HE'S CUTE TOO.
BRIAN BRAIN?
BRIAN BRAIN. I'D TELL HIM, BUT... I'M AFRAID HE WILL REJECT ME.
WOO HOO!
BRIAN BUZZES HAPPILY AROUND THE PARTY.
GREAT! SHE FINALLY ACKNOWLEDGES ME AND I'M A FLY! I WANTED TO BE LIKE THESE KIDS WHEN THEY WANTED TO BE LIKE ME. THIS EXPERIMENT IS OVER. TIME FOR THE ANTIDOTE.
WHAT'S WITH THIS CRAZY FLY?
NOW I KNOW WHAT WE CAN DO!
GET THAT FLY!
SWAT!
NO! DON'T HURT THE POOR LITTLE FLY.
GET THAT FLY OFF YOUR NOSE.
WHEW!
HE'S COMING WITH ME. GOODBYE.
YES!
THE ***ANTIDOTE*** WILL COUNTERACT THE EFFECTS OF THE HYBRIDIZER AND MICROFYING RAYS IN ABOUT TWO MINUTES. I'LL BE MY HUMAN SELF AGAIN AND IN A PERFECT POSITION TO GIVE LUCY A KISS—
OH! TOMATOES. I LOVE TOMATOES.
TOM'S PRODUCE
THE END (FOR NOW)
98 Expedition 6

"Fly Guy"

Before Reading

Introduce Vocabulary

1. Have students turn to Part A on Student Book page 178. Read aloud the ratings for vocabulary words and have students rate their knowledge of these words.
2. Read aloud the part of speech, definition, and example sentence for each word.
3. Explain that an *antidote* can be a substance like a medicine. Write on the board: *Jim took an antidote to stop the effects of a poison.* **An *antidote* also can be something you can't see or touch.** Write on the board: *A good antidote for Brian's loneliness would be to make more friends.* **How is *antidote* used in the sentence?** (as something you can't see or touch)
4. Have students read the instructions for Part B and complete the activity.

Refer to Blackline Master page 32 to extend vocabulary practice.

Have students use the *Passport Reading Journeys* online technology component to practice and reinforce vocabulary and comprehension skills.

Introduce the Target Skill: Problem/Solution

1. **People face problems and look for solutions daily. For example, you want your friend to help you spread awareness about mistreated animals, but she thinks it's useless. What is the problem?** (Your friend doesn't agree with you.) **How might you solve it?** Allow students to discuss their solutions.
2. Tell students that in stories, characters might have problems. **Events in stories often follow the characters through the process of solving a problem. The solution is how the problem is solved.**
3. Direct students to Student Book page 179. Read aloud the instructions. **What is happening in this picture?** Have students name possible problems and solutions or outcomes. Have students complete the page.
4. Have students share identified problems and solutions.

Expedition 6, Lesson 1

Name ____________ Date ____________

Vocabulary

"Fly Guy"

A. Rate your knowledge of each boldfaced word.
3 I know what this word means, and I can use it in a sentence.
2 I have an idea of this word's meaning, but I need to know more.
1 I don't know what this word means.

☐ **acknowledge** (v) *admit to be real or true*
Brian's competitors had to *acknowledge* that he won first place at the science fair.

☐ **concludes** (v) *forms an opinion after thinking*
Chad *concludes* that Brian really enjoys science.

☐ **reject** (v) *refuse to accept or take*
Brian did not want Lucy to *reject* his friendship.

☐ **proverbial** (adj) *relating to a proverb, or old familiar saying*
Brian picked up the *proverbial* lucky penny when he saw it on the ground.

☐ **morphing** (v) *transforming*
Most teenagers wish they would discover they were *morphing* into someone with a photographic memory just before a test.

☐ **antidote** (n) *a substance that works against something that has caused bad effects*
Sometimes the best *antidote* for the flu is a shot.

B. Complete each sentence with the correct vocabulary word from Part A.

1. The nurse said that antibiotics often are the best ___antidote___ against infection.
2. When Isaac was the third player to be beaten by Demarcus, we yelled the ___proverbial___ saying, "Another one bites the dust!"
3. Erin loves playing video games with her friends and would never ___reject___ an invitation.
4. After examining different posters in the art show, the judge ___concludes___ that mine is the best.
5. I was surprised to hear the famous artists ___acknowledge___ they like to read graphic novels.
6. When Tim pushes a button on his toy robot, it starts ___morphing___ into a bat.

 178

Vocabulary

acknowledge (v) *admit to be real or true*
Brian's competitors had to *acknowledge* that he won first place at the science fair.

concludes (v) *forms an opinion after thinking*
Chad *concludes* that Brian really enjoys science.

reject (v) *refuse to accept or take*
Brian did not want Lucy to *reject* his friendship.

proverbial (adj) *relating to a proverb, or old familiar saying*
Brian picked up the *proverbial* lucky penny when he saw it on the ground.

morphing (v) *transforming*
Most teenagers wish they would discover they were *morphing* into someone with a photographic memory just before a test.

antidote (n) *a substance that works against something that has caused bad effects*
Sometimes the best *antidote* for the flu is a shot.

Introduce the Passage

1. Have students preview the passage. **How is this passage different from the others you've read?** (It looks like a comic strip.) **What do you notice that will help you preview the story?** Students should identify text boxes, dialogue balloons, thought balloons, and art as clues to what kind of story it is.
2. **Based on the title and the pictures, what do you predict the passage is about?** (a boy who turns into a fly)
3. Due to the design of this passage, there are no margin prompts. Discuss with students how they can monitor their comprehension using the strategies often found in margin prompts.

During Reading

1. Have students read "Fly Guy." To select reading options that support your students' levels and classroom needs, see Reading Differentiation, page xxxii, if needed.
2. Remind students that when they read the comic panels, they read the narration and thought and speech balloons from left to right, moving from top to bottom.
3. **Look for the problems that the character solves in the story as you read.**

After Reading

Check Comprehension

1. When students finish reading, ask them the following questions:
   - **Who is the main character in this story?** (Brian)
   - **What is the setting of this story?** (school, during the school day; Chad's house, later that night)
   - **How did Brian turn into a fly?** (He uses the microfying glass on himself, shrinks, and morphs into a fly.)
   - **What did Brian learn by watching the other teens at the party?** (They are bored. One girl respects and likes him.)
2. **Compare your prediction to the information that you read in the passage. What was different about your prediction?** Have students share their responses.

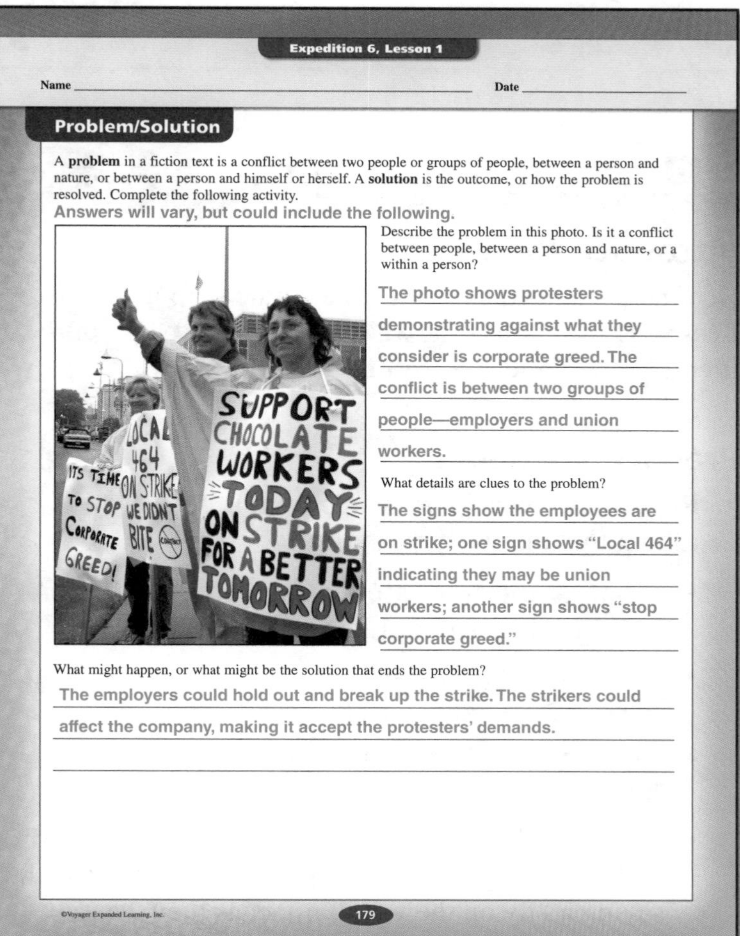

Expedition 6, Lesson 1

Name ____________________ Date ____________

Problem/Solution

A **problem** in a fiction text is a conflict between two people or groups of people, between a person and nature, or between a person and himself or herself. A **solution** is the outcome, or how the problem is resolved. Complete the following activity.

Answers will vary, but could include the following.

Describe the problem in this photo. Is it a conflict between people, between a person and nature, or a within a person?

The photo shows protesters demonstrating against what they consider is corporate greed. The conflict is between two groups of people—employers and union workers.

What details are clues to the problem?

The signs show the employees are on strike; one sign shows "Local 464" indicating they may be union workers; another sign shows "stop corporate greed."

What might happen, or what might be the solution that ends the problem?

The employers could hold out and break up the strike. The strikers could affect the company, making it accept the protesters' demands.

©Voyager Expanded Learning, Inc. 179

3. **The character in this story had several problems that were solved. What was the main problem?** (Brian wanted to be liked by others.) **How did he solve the problem?** (He morphed into a fly and went to the party. He found out that Lucy liked him.)

ACADEMIC SKILL Remind students that identifying problems and their solutions can help them understand information in other subjects. They can examine how effective solutions are.

Remind students to choose books from the *Passport Reading Journeys* Library for independent reading.

"Fly Guy"

Prepare to Reread

Introduce the Lesson

Remind students that they read a comic strip in Lesson 1. **In this lesson, we'll revisit "Fly Guy" and identify problems and solutions in the story.**

Practice Vocabulary

1. Review the vocabulary words from Lesson 1 by asking the following questions.
   - **What do the other students *acknowledge* about Brian?** (He is smart; Lucy says he is cute.)
   - **Brian *concludes* something about the friends at the party. What is it?** (They are bored.)
   - **How do the other students show they *reject* Brian?** (They don't invite him to the party.)
   - **Brian decides to become the *proverbial* fly on the wall. Why is this *proverbial*?** (People often use the saying a "fly on the wall"; it means they want to listen or watch in a way that no one will notice.)
   - **What happens when Brian begins the *morphing* process?** (He changes into a fly.)
   - **Why does Brian need an *antidote*?** (to counteract the effects of the hybridizer and microfying rays)

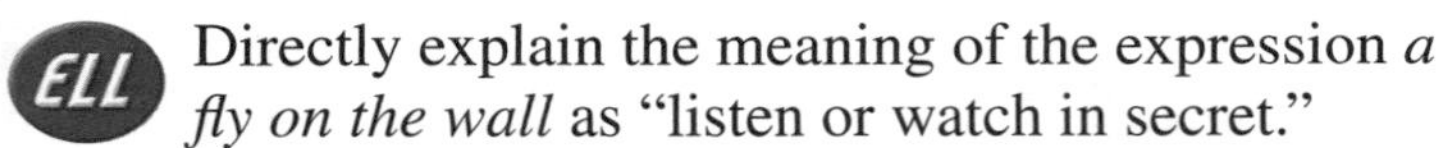

ELL Directly explain the meaning of the expression *a fly on the wall* as "listen or watch in secret."

2. Have students turn to Anthology page 96. **What do you think the word *prestigious* means?** (having respect or recognition) **What clues in the text help you determine this?** (The whole school recognizes Brian's science achievement.)

   Repeat this process for the following words.
   - **voilá** (interj) *see there; French expression to express success*, Anthology page 96
   - **multiple** (adj) *many*, Anthology page 97
   - **accomplished** (adj) *highly skilled*, Anthology page 98

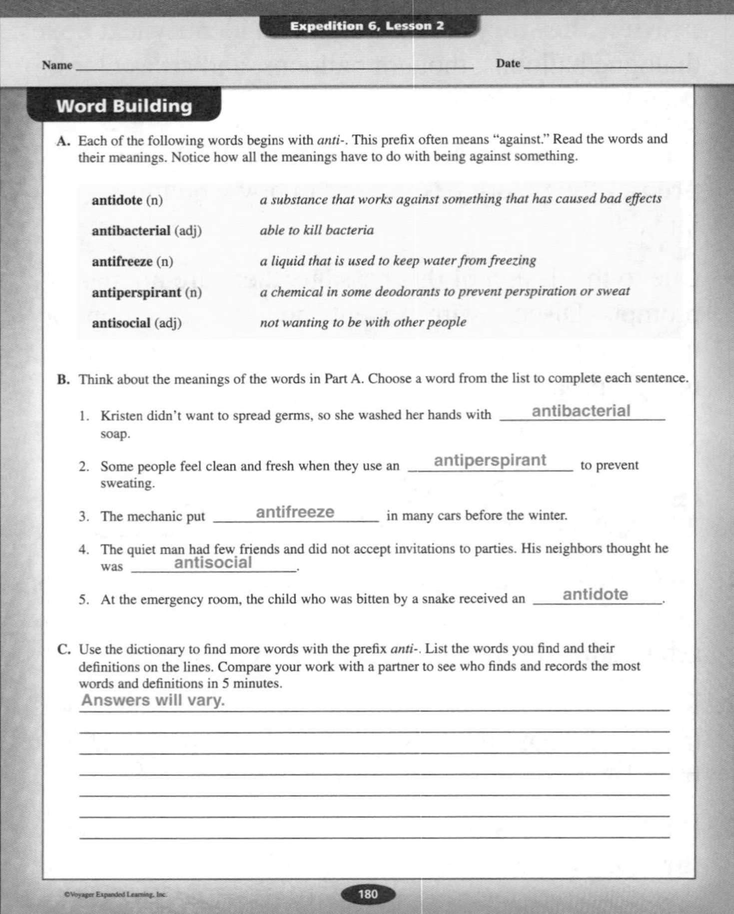

Expedition 6, Lesson 2

Name ______________________ Date __________

Word Building

A. Each of the following words begins with *anti-*. This prefix often means "against." Read the words and their meanings. Notice how all the meanings have to do with being against something.

antidote (n)	*a substance that works against something that has caused bad effects*
antibacterial (adj)	*able to kill bacteria*
antifreeze (n)	*a liquid that is used to keep water from freezing*
antiperspirant (n)	*a chemical in some deodorants to prevent perspiration or sweat*
antisocial (adj)	*not wanting to be with other people*

B. Think about the meanings of the words in Part A. Choose a word from the list to complete each sentence.

1. Kristen didn't want to spread germs, so she washed her hands with __antibacterial__ soap.
2. Some people feel clean and fresh when they use an __antiperspirant__ to prevent sweating.
3. The mechanic put __antifreeze__ in many cars before the winter.
4. The quiet man had few friends and did not accept invitations to parties. His neighbors thought he was __antisocial__.
5. At the emergency room, the child who was bitten by a snake received an __antidote__.

C. Use the dictionary to find more words with the prefix *anti-*. List the words you find and their definitions on the lines. Compare your work with a partner to see who finds and records the most words and definitions in 5 minutes.

Answers will vary.

©Voyager Expanded Learning, Inc. 180

3. Have students turn to Student Book page 180. **You learned the word *antidote*, which begins with the prefix *anti-*. You can build on what you know about *antidote* to learn other words that begin with *anti-*.** Read the instructions for each part of the page, and have students complete the page.

CHECKPOINT After students complete Part B, have them identify one item they had difficulty with. Have students explain how they used the meanings of *anti-* in the sentence to determine the correct answer.

Reread

Apply the Target Skill: Problem/Solution

1. **When you read fiction, you should think about the main problem as you follow the events to reach the solution.**
2. **A character usually faces one main problem, and the solution happens near the end of the story. The character faces minor problems as well, and these move the plot forward to the final solution.**
3. Have students turn to Student Book page 181. **The problem is what goes wrong for the character. What do the character's actions lead to?** (a solution) Read the instructions aloud, then have students complete Part A independently. After completing Part A, have students share their responses.
4. Have partners complete Part B. After completing Part B, have partners share their story extensions with the class.

Write in Response to Reading

1. Have students turn to Student Book page 182. **What do you know about Brian that the other characters do not know?** (Brian morphed into a fly.) **Sometimes the reader knows something that the characters of a story do not.** Read the instructions aloud, then have students complete the activity.
2. When students finish, have them share their responses in small groups.

EXPEDITION ORGANIZER **Now You See It**

Pause to have students turn to Student Book pages 176 and 177. Have students complete the following:

- Write answers or notes below one or more of the probing questions. Encourage them to write a question of their own.
- Think about "Fly Guy." Have students write their thoughts in the appropriate box in Part B.

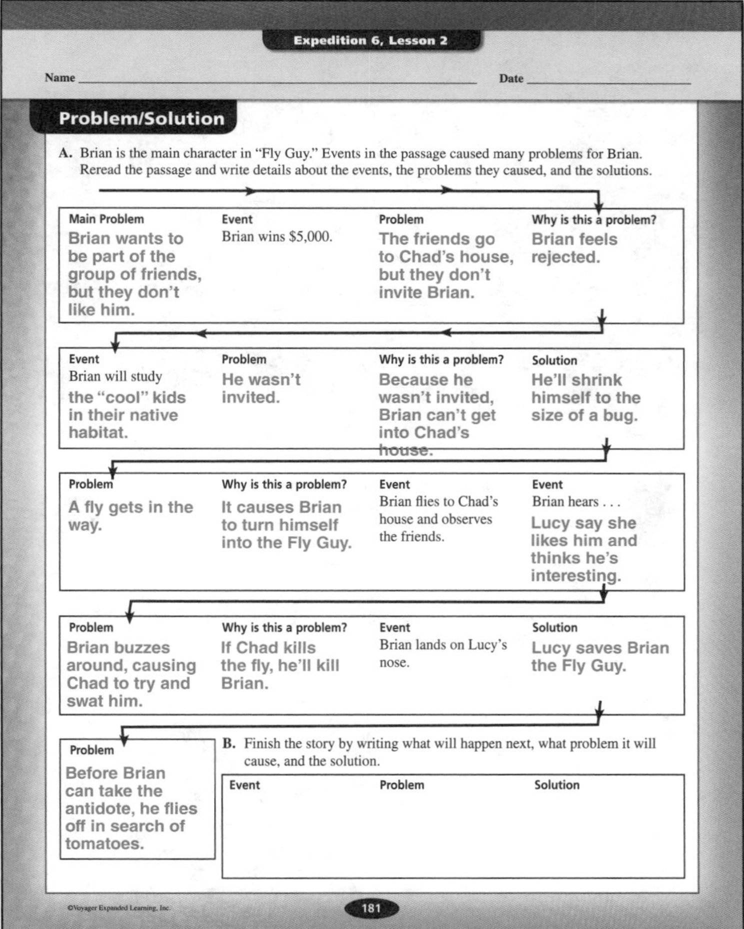

Expedition 6, Lesson 2

Name ______________________ Date ____________

Problem/Solution

A. Brian is the main character in "Fly Guy." Events in the passage caused many problems for Brian. Reread the passage and write details about the events, the problems they caused, and the solutions.

Main Problem	Event	Problem	Why is this a problem?
Brian wants to be part of the group of friends, but they don't like him.	Brian wins $5,000.	The friends go to Chad's house, but they don't invite Brian.	Brian feels rejected.

Event	Problem	Why is this a problem?	Solution
Brian will study the "cool" kids in their native habitat.	He wasn't invited.	Because he wasn't invited, Brian can't get into Chad's house.	He'll shrink himself to the size of a bug.

Problem	Why is this a problem?	Event	Event
A fly gets in the way.	It causes Brian to turn himself into the Fly Guy.	Brian flies to Chad's house and observes the friends.	Brian hears . . . Lucy say she likes him and thinks he's interesting.

Problem	Why is this a problem?	Event	Solution
Brian buzzes around, causing Chad to try and swat him.	If Chad kills the fly, he'll kill Brian.	Brian lands on Lucy's nose.	Lucy saves Brian the Fly Guy.

Problem
Before Brian can take the antidote, he flies off in search of tomatoes.

B. Finish the story by writing what will happen next, what problem it will cause, and the solution.

Event	Problem	Solution

©Voyager Expanded Learning, Inc.

181

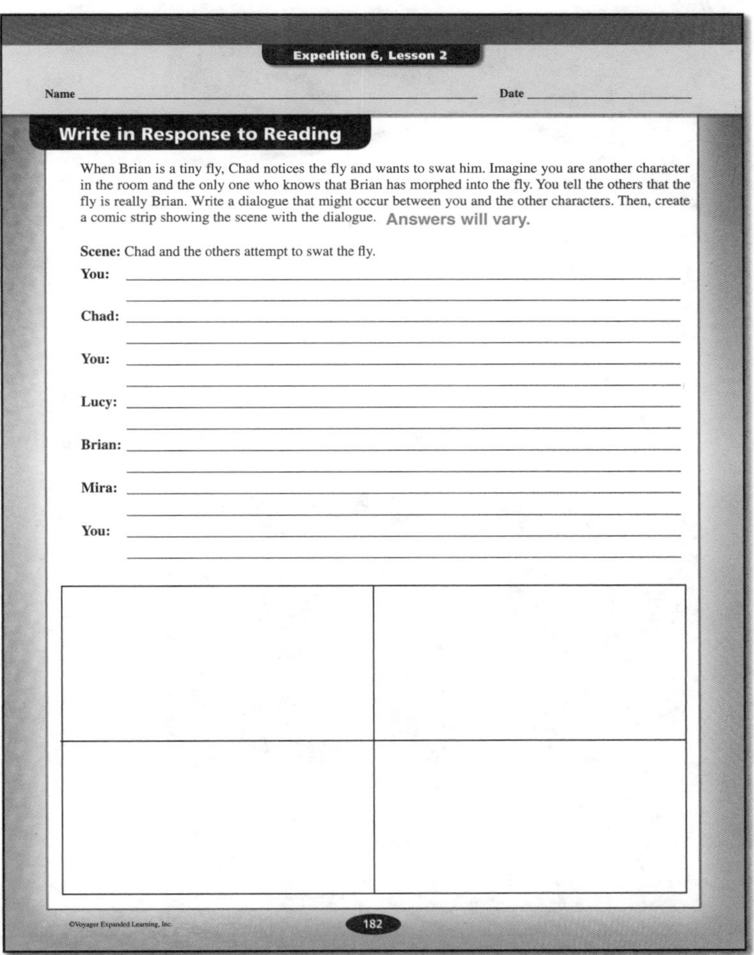

Expedition 6, Lesson 2

Name ______________________ Date ____________

Write in Response to Reading

When Brian is a tiny fly, Chad notices the fly and wants to swat him. Imagine you are another character in the room and the only one who knows that Brian has morphed into the fly. You tell the others that the fly is really Brian. Write a dialogue that might occur between you and the other characters. Then, create a comic strip showing the scene with the dialogue. Answers will vary.

Scene: Chad and the others attempt to swat the fly.

You: ______________________

Chad: ______________________

You: ______________________

Lucy: ______________________

Brian: ______________________

Mira: ______________________

You: ______________________

©Voyager Expanded Learning, Inc.

182

Narrator: Welcome to *Sign of the Times*, the talk show devoted to what's going on in our **community** of Westridge. Today, we're focusing on the subject of graffiti. These pictures and words drawn or painted on streets, walls, and buildings are **visible** to us all when we walk or drive through town.

Our two local guests in the studio today feel really strongly about this topic. Muriel Johnson is a longtime resident of our community. She has always been active in community service. Our second guest is a young man, Josh Harding. Josh calls himself an artist. First, let's hear from Muriel, whose apartment building was recently vandalized.

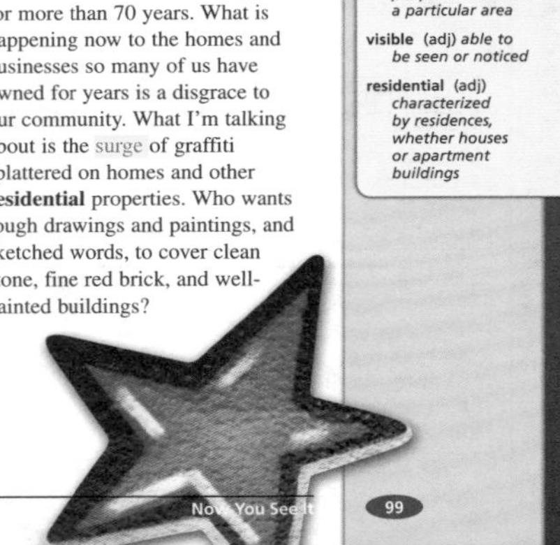

Muriel: Thank you, Ms. Gonzales, for having me on your show. I have lived in Westridge for more than 70 years. What is happening now to the homes and businesses so many of us have owned for years is a disgrace to our community. What I'm talking about is the surge of graffiti splattered on homes and other **residential** properties. Who wants rough drawings and paintings, and sketched words, to cover clean stone, fine red brick, and well-painted buildings?

Vocabulary

community (n) *all the people who live in a particular area*

visible (adj) *able to be seen or noticed*

residential (adj) *characterized by residences, whether houses or apartment buildings*

Vocabulary

experience (n) *something a person has done or lived through*

tenants (n) *people who pay rent to live in a building or apartment*

financial (adj) *having to do with money matters*

Narrator: Muriel, tell us about your **experience** with this recent outburst of graffiti.

Muriel: Well, one of my residential buildings, an apartment complex I bought nearly 40 years ago, was recently defaced. One morning last week, I received call after call from the **tenants** who rent my apartments. Each one complained about the disturbing pictures and messages that appeared overnight on the walls of the apartment building. Moreover, the wall across the street also was covered with graffiti. They all have to look at the graffiti because it can be seen from their front windows. The calmness of their homes has been replaced with an uproar over the vandalism. Besides that, my tenants feel personally attacked in what was a safe residential area.

I have a **financial** responsibility to clean up the apartment building. It will take a lot of money. To make my tenants happy, I may even have to pay to have the wall cleaned. I don't make a large profit renting my apartments, and I'm retired. The apartment building is my sole source of income, so this will be a financial burden. These young people who vandalize homes should consider how they affect other community members. They should stop defacing property. The police should find them and make them clean up their damage. They should pay for restoration. 1

1 Visualize
Picture how Muriel's apartment building looks with the graffiti.

Narrator: Muriel, thank you for sharing your experience. It's easy to see why you find graffiti so

upsetting. I'm sure you aren't alone in your concerns about graffiti. But, our next guest, Josh Harding, has a different perspective on the issue. Josh, I understand you call yourself a "graffiti artist." Do those words really go together?

Josh: You bet. I am working with a group of guys to add art to otherwise drab gray streets in business and residential areas of our community. If Muriel's building and street had been tagged with *our* graffiti, Muriel and her tenants would have been proud of the work of art visible on her building. The art would have enhanced the property. 2

You see, just because people call my art graffiti doesn't mean it defaces buildings and walls—it improves them, adds living colors and pleasing designs. Even more important, what my group incorporates in our graffiti is a social message. We want to wake people up to the need for tolerance. We want to show people we care about the beauty of the environment. We want to shake people out of

2 Ask Questions
A question to ask yourself is: How does Josh's viewpoint compare to Muriel's view?

their gray worlds and bring them light and color. If you've never looked at places we've tagged, you wouldn't know how sad they seemed before. We bring life to them, art to them, and meaning. 3

3 Visualize
Picture the graffiti described by Josh.

Narrator: That is a different way of looking at graffiti—as an art form and social commentary. What do you think, Muriel? Does this change your feelings about your experience?

Muriel: It still won't pay for the cleanup of my apartment building on Summit Avenue. But, I can begin to understand there is more to graffiti than just vandalizing property. I didn't realize these young people feel they are adding art and expressing important messages. I thought they just wanted to destroy other people's property.

Josh: Ah, is your apartment building at 228 Summit Avenue? Is it that gray building across from a concrete wall?

Muriel: Yes, do you know who painted my building?

Josh: Sorry, Muriel, but that's one of the pieces of art and social commentary I was just describing. My group tagged your building and the wall across the street. I'm sorry we've caused trouble and cost you money. We really don't mean to hurt individuals. We just want to express what we feel so others can feel it. Our medium is the gray walls of the community.

Muriel: Josh, thank you for being honest and admitting what you did to my building. What you've said gives me something to think about. Perhaps what you did is art, but you should ask permission from the owner first. Maybe you boys could meet me tomorrow to discuss a cleanup project—at your cost. 4

4 Summarize
How have the opinions of Muriel and Josh changed?

Josh: Yes, ma'am.

Narrator: A surprising turn of events here, but our time is up. See you next week on *Sign of the Times*. End

"Graffiti: Vandalism or Art?"

Before Reading

Introduce Vocabulary

1. Have students turn to Student Book page 183. Scan the boldfaced vocabulary words in Part A. **These words appear in "Graffiti: Vandalism or Art?"** Have students rate their knowledge of these words by marking where they encountered them.
2. Have students share words they know, along with where they saw or heard the words. Ask students to use words they know in sentences.
3. Read aloud the part of speech, definition, and example sentence for each word. **Do the meanings match the meanings you know? If not, adjust your rating on the chart.**
4. Have students read the instructions for Part B and complete the activity.

Refer to Blackline Master page 33 to extend vocabulary practice.

Have students use the *Passport Reading Journeys* online technology component to practice and reinforce vocabulary and comprehension skills.

Introduce the Target Skill: Point of View and Bias

1. **Authors have points of view, or opinions, on the topics they write about. When an author's writing shows a very strong preference for a particular point of view, the author shows more than a mere opinion. The author shows a bias.** Tell students that the best way to find an author's point of view is to ask questions about the text, then find answers. Write the following prompts on the board:
   - *Does the author have a personal connection to the topic? What is that connection?*
   - *Does the text contain negative words like never, not, bad, and poor, or positive words like best, great, wonderful, and rich?*

   Ask and answer these kinds of questions to determine the author's point of view and bias. Also, notice words that affect you emotionally.

Expedition 6, Lesson 3

Name ______________________ Date ______________

Vocabulary

"Graffiti: Vandalism or Art?"

A. Write one or more numbers next to each boldfaced word to show when you have seen, heard, or used this word.

5 I use it in everyday conversation.
4 I heard it on TV or on the radio.
3 I heard or used it in school.
2 I read it in a book, magazine, or online.
1 I have not read, heard, or used this word.

☐ **community** (n) *all the people who live in a particular area*
The people in this *community* work hard to keep the streets clean by picking up the trash.

☐ **visible** (adj) *able to be seen or noticed*
The wall across the street is *visible* from my bedroom window.

☐ **residential** (adj) *characterized by residences, whether houses or apartment buildings*
The *residential* section of Westridge is pretty with beautiful houses and well-kept apartment buildings.

☐ **experience** (n) *something a person has done or lived through*
My *experience* with graffiti artists has been quite pleasant, so I asked them to paint my building.

☐ **tenants** (n) *people who pay rent to live in a building or apartment*
The *tenants* in the apartment building wanted the owner to pay for damages to the property.

☐ **financial** (adj) *having to do with money matters*
Cleaning graffiti is a large *financial* burden for business owners.

B. Answer each question with a vocabulary word from Part A.

1. Which word describes people who pay rent to live in apartments?
tenants
2. Which word would you use to describe the kind of business banks do?
financial
3. Which word describes an area that has houses, but not stores or businesses?
residential
4. Which word goes with neighbors, business owners, and friends in your area?
community
5. Which word goes with your sense of sight? visible
6. Which word goes with "skill and understanding that you have learned"?
experience

 183

Vocabulary

community (n) *all the people who live in a particular area*
The people in this *community* work hard to keep the streets clean by picking up trash.

visible (adj) *able to be seen or noticed*
The wall across the street is *visible* from my bedroom window.

residential (adj) *characterized by residences, whether houses or apartment buildings*
The *residential* section of Westridge is pretty with beautiful houses and well-kept apartment buildings.

experience (n) *something a person has done or lived through*
My *experience* with graffiti artists has been quite pleasant, so I asked them to paint my building.

tenants (n) *people who pay rent to live in a building or apartment*
The *tenants* in the apartment building wanted the owner to pay for damages to the property.

financial (adj) *having to do with money matters*
Cleaning graffiti is a large *financial* burden for business owners.

2. Write the following sentences on the board: *The best music was made in the 1970s. Groups like Led Zeppelin and my favorite band, Queen, showed amazing creativity. Even today, bands cannot match the high musical quality of the 1970s.* **I can ask questions about these statements to find the author's point of view.**
   - **What personal connection does the author have to the topic?** (Queen is the author's favorite band.)
   - **What positive or negative words does the author use?** (positive words: *best; favorite; amazing creativity; high musical quality*)
   - **What is the author's purpose for using these words?** (to convince the reader to agree with his or her point of view)
3. **What point of view, or opinion, did the author express in the text?** (The best music was made in the 1970s.) **How does the author support this point of view?** (The author uses positive words. The author's favorite band is from the 1970s.)
4. Explain that bias is not the same as point of view. ***Bias* is a strong preference for one point of view and not others. After determining the author's point of view, scan for clues that point to an author's bias. How do you know the author of this text feels strongly?** (The author uses many positive words and confidently states that 1970s music is the best of all.) **Does this author show bias? How do you know?** (Yes, the author praises 1970s music, but only writes about rock music in the 1970s and ignores other kinds of music or other opinions about 1970s music.) Explain that different opinions exist about most topics and that people have reasons for their opinions. **An author shows bias by presenting only one side of an argument and leaving out important facts that contradict that bias.**

ELL Support academic language by defining the word *narrator* in the passage as "someone who tells a story."

Introduce the Passage

1. Have students turn to Anthology page 99 to preview "Graffiti: Vandalism or Art?" Have students read the title and speaker tags (Narrator and Muriel) in the text.
   - **What do these tell you about what you will read?** (They indicate that the passage is about graffiti and will be some sort of play or interview.)
   - **Do the photos support this? Explain.** (Yes, the photos show graffiti and reporters, so this is probably an interview.)
2. Direct student attention to the margin prompts. **As you read, pause to consider these prompts. You may have to reread parts of the passage to answer the prompts.**

During Reading

1. To select reading options that support your students' levels and classroom needs, see Reading Differentiation, page xxxii, if needed.
2. Have students read "Graffiti: Vandalism or Art?" and look for Muriel and Josh's points of view.

After Reading

Check Comprehension

1. Have students look at the Ask Questions margin prompt on Anthology page 101. **How does Josh's viewpoint compare to Muriel's?** Have students discuss the two viewpoints.
2. Have students respond to the Visualize margin prompt on Anthology page 102. **How did the picture in your mind change when you realized that Josh created the graffiti?**
3. Have students discuss their responses to the Summarize margin prompt on Anthology page 102.

ACADEMIC SKILL Remind students to use a variety of sources when doing research and to be careful not to use biased source material.

Remind students to choose books from the *Passport Reading Journeys* Library for independent reading.

"Graffiti: Vandalism or Art?"

Prepare to Reread

Introduce the Lesson

Remind students they read an interview that contained two points of view. **Now we'll reread "Graffiti: Vandalism or Art?" to study point of view and bias.**

Practice Vocabulary

1. Have students think about how vocabulary words were used in the passage with these questions.
   - **What people are part of your *community*?** (parents; shopkeepers; neighbors)
   - **How is graffiti more *visible* than paintings in a museum?** (Graffiti is visible to anyone who may walk or drive by it.)
   - **What makes a *residential* area different from other areas in a city?** (It has only homes and apartments; other areas have businesses and shops.)
   - **What is one important part of Muriel's life *experience*?** (She has lived in Westridge for 70 years; she owns a building.)
   - **Is it surprising that Muriel's *tenants* would complain about the graffiti? Why?** (Answers will vary.)
   - **What *financial* problem did the graffiti cause?** (Muriel must pay to clean up the graffiti.)
2. Have students turn to Anthology page 100. Point out the word *defaced*. **What does *defaced* mean?** (spoiled appearances) **What clue helps you know this meaning?** (disturbing pictures)

   Repeat this process for the following words.
   - **surge** (n) *rush or sweep*, Anthology page 99
   - **restoration** (n) *a return of something to a former, original, normal, or unimpaired condition*, Anthology page 100
   - **tolerance** (n) *the condition of being willing to accept differences in others*, Anthology page 101

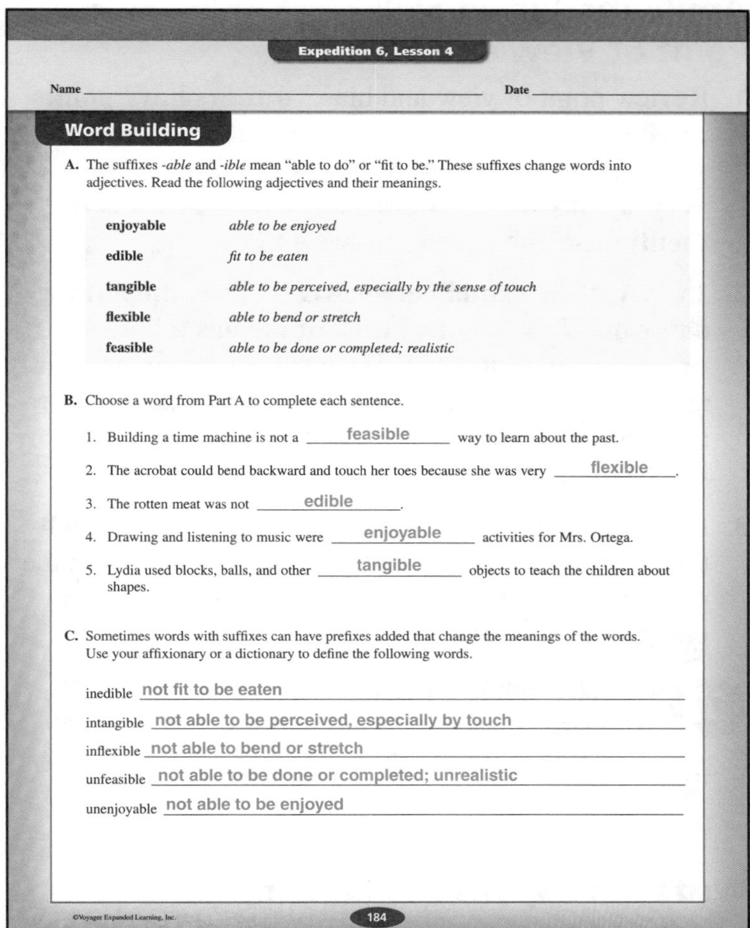

Expedition 6, Lesson 4

Name ______ Date ______

Word Building

A. The suffixes *-able* and *-ible* mean "able to do" or "fit to be." These suffixes change words into adjectives. Read the following adjectives and their meanings.

enjoyable	*able to be enjoyed*
edible	*fit to be eaten*
tangible	*able to be perceived, especially by the sense of touch*
flexible	*able to bend or stretch*
feasible	*able to be done or completed; realistic*

B. Choose a word from Part A to complete each sentence.

1. Building a time machine is not a feasible way to learn about the past.
2. The acrobat could bend backward and touch her toes because she was very flexible.
3. The rotten meat was not edible.
4. Drawing and listening to music were enjoyable activities for Mrs. Ortega.
5. Lydia used blocks, balls, and other tangible objects to teach the children about shapes.

C. Sometimes words with suffixes can have prefixes added that change the meanings of the words. Use your affixionary or a dictionary to define the following words.

inedible not fit to be eaten

intangible not able to be perceived, especially by touch

inflexible not able to bend or stretch

unfeasible not able to be done or completed; unrealistic

unenjoyable not able to be enjoyed

©Voyager Expanded Learning, Inc. 184

3. Have students turn to Student Book page 184. **The word *visible* contains the suffix *-ible*.** Read aloud the instructions, words, and definitions, and have students complete the activities.

CHECKPOINT After students complete Part B, have them identify one item that confused them. Have students substitute each definition for each missing word to figure out the correct answer.

ELL Explain that *restoration* has *restore* in it, which means "to fix." **If you *restore* a house so that it looks new, you have completed a *restoration*.**

Reread

Apply the Target Skill: Point of View and Bias

1. Review point of view and bias. **Authors have points of view, or opinions, on the topics they choose to write about. When an author's point of view is very strong and the opposing point of view is not mentioned, the author shows a bias.**
2. **In "Graffiti: Vandalism or Art?", does the author show bias? Do you feel the author has a bias for or against graffiti?** (no) Have students support their answers. Students might respond that the author allowed fair representations of the characters. **Who in the passage did show bias?** (Muriel and Josh)
3. Have students turn to Student Book page 185. Read the instructions aloud, and have partners complete the page. **Reread "Graffiti: Vandalism or Art?" and complete the chart.**

ELL Directly define *fair* and *unfair*. Have students compare fair and unfair situations: *It is fair when* ________. *It is unfair when* ________.

Expedition 6, Lesson 4

Name ________ Date ________

Point of View

List information about Muriel and Josh and how they feel about graffiti. Include their points of view and the reasons behind their views. Reread "Graffiti: Vandalism or Art?" to complete the following chart.

Points of View	
Muriel	Josh
• older, retired woman; fixed income • building owner for 40 years • feels responsible for a clean building and happy tenants	• younger boy who creates graffiti art • socially conscious of issues in the world • feels graffiti adds beauty and life to boring buildings

How can they resolve their conflict about their differences?

They can understand better if Muriel explains the costs of running a building and Josh shows the artistry of graffiti. Josh could resolve to respect other people's property and ask permission to put his graffiti on it.

 185

Write in Response to Reading

1. **If Josh were an author of an article about graffiti, what would his point of view be?** (Graffiti improves drab residential areas and sends an important message to the community.) **What is Josh's personal connection to graffiti?** (He is a graffiti artist.) **Do you think Josh has a bias? Explain.** (Answers may vary.)
2. Have partners use similar questions to identify Muriel's point of view. **Does Muriel have a bias? How do you know?** (Yes, she owns a building that has to be cleaned; she uses *spoiled*, *damaged*, and *vandalism* to describe graffiti.)
3. Have students turn to Student Book page 186. Read aloud the instructions. Have students share letters.

Expedition 6, Lesson 4

Name ________ Date ________

Write in Response to Reading

Write a letter to the editor on the following lines to support either Josh or Muriel. Remember to include details from "Graffiti: Vandalism or Art?" in your letter.

Answers will vary, but should include details that support each point of view. For Josh, graffiti brings life, art, and meaning to drab areas. For Muriel, graffiti defaces property, costing money for cleanup and making residents feel unsafe.

 186

EXPEDITION ORGANIZER **Now You See It**

Pause to have students turn to Student Book pages 176 and 177. Have students complete the following:

- Write answers or notes below one or more of the probing questions. Encourage students to write their own questions.
- Think about their own ideas about the passage. Have students write them in the appropriate box in Part B.

Review, Extend, Assess

In today's lesson, as in Lessons 5 and 10 of every Expedition, there are options from which to choose. You may do any or all of the options listed. Activities for each option are given on the following pages. Each option will support or extend previously taught objectives. Choose the option(s) appropriate for your students and prepare accordingly.

Review Vocabulary

Extend Vocabulary

Assess Comprehension and Vocabulary

Reteach

Passport Reading Journeys Library

Online Technology Component

Writing Process

Real-World Reading

Exploring Careers

Review Vocabulary

Direct students to review the vocabulary for "Fly Guy" and "Graffiti: Vandalism or Art?" on Student Book page 177.

1. **We have read these vocabulary words in these passages. You will read the vocabulary in different contexts, but the meanings will not change.** Have students turn to Student Book page 187. Read the instructions aloud, and have students complete the activity. As students finish, have them check the definitions to ensure they used the words correctly. Have students share their answers for Part A.
2. For Part B, have students read through the entire interview once to gain an understanding of the interview. Then they can go back and write answers. If students have difficulty choosing correct words, remind them that the clues in parentheses might be part of the words' definitions. Have them review the definitions on Student Book page 177.
3. When all students finish, have them share their responses.

Expedition 6, Lesson 5

Name ______________________ Date ______________

Review Vocabulary

A. Complete each sentence with a vocabulary word that supports the meaning of the underlined word or phrase. The first one is done for you.

community **antidote** **morphing** **acknowledge** **multiple**

1. Ryan was afraid his friends would not accept, or **reject**, his idea for a video.
2. The graffiti artists tagged multiple buildings, not just one.
3. The whole community, including neighbors and kids, cleaned up graffiti in the park.
4. Leah had a stressful day. She needed an antidote, such as a cup of tea.
5. The robots were transforming into something powerful, morphing into villains.
6. Kelsey hoped her friends would acknowledge, not ignore, her graphic design.

B. Read the following interview. Write a word from the box that BEST completes each sentence. Use the words in parentheses as clues.

tenants **experience** **concludes** **financial** **surge**
visible **prestigious** **accomplished** **residential**

Beth: Everyone is talking. Your recent graphic novel is visible (seen or noticed) everywhere! How does the surge (rush or sweep) in popularity feel?

Adrian: Everyone? I know my girlfriend concludes (forms an opinion after thinking) that it is a great book, but she's biased! Actually, I did spend many months writing and drawing.

Beth: This book won a prestigious (giving fame or respect) award. You've also gained some financial (having to do with money) success. You must feel proud and accomplished (highly skilled) as a writer and artist. What's your secret?

Adrian: I enjoy practicing my skill. My success has a lot to do with hard work, practice, and my past experience (what a person has done).

Beth: People identify with your characters who live in a residential (characterized by apartments and houses) area of St. Louis. Is that what you mean by "past experience"?

Adrian: Yes, my family was like the characters in the book who are tenants (people who rent an apartment) in the building. I know those situations so I can write about them.

 187

CHECKPOINT Provide additional support for students who had difficulty in Part A by having students match the underlined words or phrases to the definitions in their Expedition Dictionary.

Extend Vocabulary

1. Direct students to Student Book page 188 and read the instructions for Part A aloud. ***Conclude* is a base word. You can create new words by adding prefixes, suffixes, and inflectional endings to base words. Words that share the same base word are in the same word family.** Have students read the words and definitions related to *conclude*.
2. **What is the base word for the vocabulary word *residential*?** (reside) Have students read the words and definitions.
3. Have students complete the activity, then share their responses.

CHECKPOINT When students share their responses for Parts A and B, listen to ensure they used the new words in the correct contexts. Pause to explain and correct any errors.

Part A

1. Read aloud the definitions and have students tell which are least familiar. Provide additional examples for those words, and observe whether students need help as they answer items with those words.
2. For the word family with *conclude*, use a familiar or exaggerated prompt. **What would you *conclude* if a freshman was chosen for the varsity team?** (He is a very good player.) **Would your friends agree with your *conclusion*? Would this be a *conclusive* decision for the coach? Could you say *conclusively* that the coach made the right decision?**

Part B

Have students substitute each definition for each missing word to figure out the correct answer.

Part C

1. Have students say their sentences first, then write them.
2. Partners can work together to write new sentences with the words.

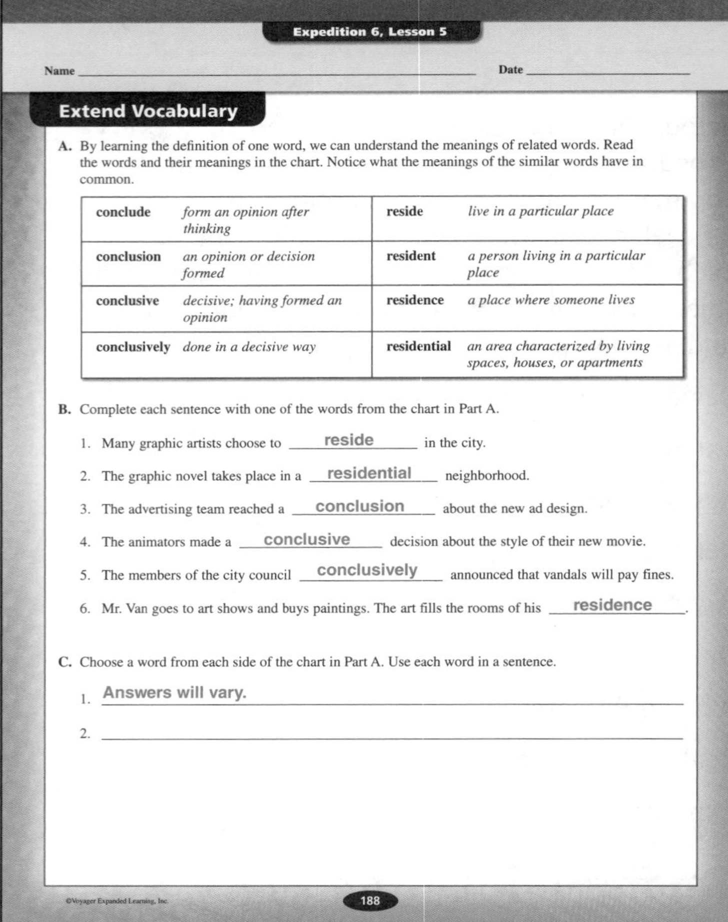

Expedition 6, Lesson 5

Name ______ Date ______

Extend Vocabulary

A. By learning the definition of one word, we can understand the meanings of related words. Read the words and their meanings in the chart. Notice what the meanings of the similar words have in common.

conclude	*form an opinion after thinking*	**reside**	*live in a particular place*
conclusion	*an opinion or decision formed*	**resident**	*a person living in a particular place*
conclusive	*decisive; having formed an opinion*	**residence**	*a place where someone lives*
conclusively	*done in a decisive way*	**residential**	*an area characterized by living spaces, houses, or apartments*

B. Complete each sentence with one of the words from the chart in Part A.

1. Many graphic artists choose to __reside__ in the city.
2. The graphic novel takes place in a __residential__ neighborhood.
3. The advertising team reached a __conclusion__ about the new ad design.
4. The animators made a __conclusive__ decision about the style of their new movie.
5. The members of the city council __conclusively__ announced that vandals will pay fines.
6. Mr. Van goes to art shows and buys paintings. The art fills the rooms of his __residence__.

C. Choose a word from each side of the chart in Part A. Use each word in a sentence.

1. Answers will vary.
2. ______

 188

Assess Comprehension and Vocabulary

1. **What is an author's point of view?** (the author's opinion about a topic) **How can an author have an unbiased point of view?** (by telling both sides) **If an author only told one point of view, would that be fair or biased?** (biased)
2. **If a police officer writes about tagging and graffiti artists, what bias might the article have?** (a negative view because most graffiti is illegal)
3. Direct students to Student Book pages 189–191. Have students complete the pages independently.

   Review student answers. Whenever possible, provide elaborative feedback to student responses. Refer to page xl for examples of elaborative feedback and how to incorporate it in your lessons.

   If students incorrectly answer more than 4 out of 15 assessment questions, evaluate what kind of reteaching is needed. If students miss vocabulary questions, have them return to the activities and work with the words they missed. For errors recognizing point of view and bias, use the reteaching suggestions on page 234.

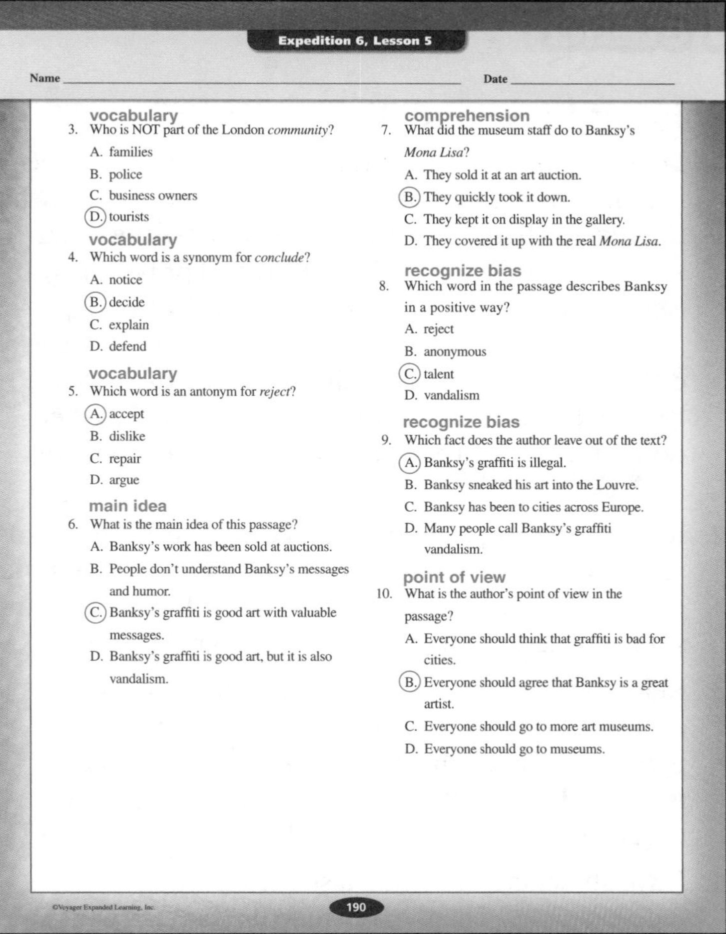

Expedition 6, Lesson 5

Name ______________________ Date __________

vocabulary
3. Who is NOT part of the London *community*?
   A. families
   B. police
   C. business owners
   (D.) tourists

vocabulary
4. Which word is a synonym for *conclude*?
   A. notice
   (B.) decide
   C. explain
   D. defend

vocabulary
5. Which word is an antonym for *reject*?
   (A.) accept
   B. dislike
   C. repair
   D. argue

main idea
6. What is the main idea of this passage?
   A. Banksy's work has been sold at auctions.
   B. People don't understand Banksy's messages and humor.
   (C.) Banksy's graffiti is good art with valuable messages.
   D. Banksy's graffiti is good art, but it is also vandalism.

comprehension
7. What did the museum staff do to Banksy's *Mona Lisa*?
   A. They sold it at an art auction.
   (B.) They quickly took it down.
   C. They kept it on display in the gallery.
   D. They covered it up with the real *Mona Lisa*.

recognize bias
8. Which word in the passage describes Banksy in a positive way?
   A. reject
   B. anonymous
   (C.) talent
   D. vandalism

recognize bias
9. Which fact does the author leave out of the text?
   (A.) Banksy's graffiti is illegal.
   B. Banksy sneaked his art into the Louvre.
   C. Banksy has been to cities across Europe.
   D. Many people call Banksy's graffiti vandalism.

point of view
10. What is the author's point of view in the passage?
   A. Everyone should think that graffiti is bad for cities.
   (B.) Everyone should agree that Banksy is a great artist.
   C. Everyone should go to more art museums.
   D. Everyone should go to museums.

©Voyager Expanded Learning, Inc. 190

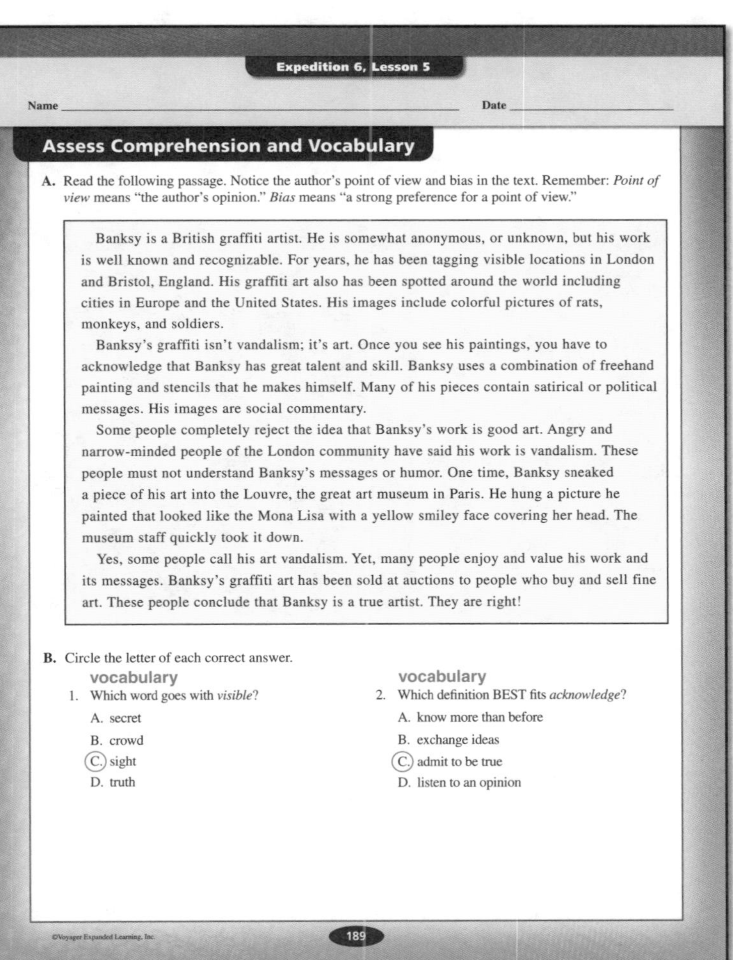

Expedition 6, Lesson 5

Name ______________________ Date __________

Assess Comprehension and Vocabulary

A. Read the following passage. Notice the author's point of view and bias in the text. Remember: *Point of view* means "the author's opinion." *Bias* means "a strong preference for a point of view."

Banksy is a British graffiti artist. He is somewhat anonymous, or unknown, but his work is well known and recognizable. For years, he has been tagging visible locations in London and Bristol, England. His graffiti art also has been spotted around the world including cities in Europe and the United States. His images include colorful pictures of rats, monkeys, and soldiers.

Banksy's graffiti isn't vandalism; it's art. Once you see his paintings, you have to acknowledge that Banksy has great talent and skill. Banksy uses a combination of freehand painting and stencils that he makes himself. Many of his pieces contain satirical or political messages. His images are social commentary.

Some people completely reject the idea that Banksy's work is good art. Angry and narrow-minded people of the London community have said his work is vandalism. These people must not understand Banksy's messages or humor. One time, Banksy sneaked a piece of his art into the Louvre, the great art museum in Paris. He hung a picture he painted that looked like the Mona Lisa with a yellow smiley face covering her head. The museum staff quickly took it down.

Yes, some people call his art vandalism. Yet, many people enjoy and value his work and its messages. Banksy's graffiti art has been sold at auctions to people who buy and sell fine art. These people conclude that Banksy is a true artist. They are right!

B. Circle the letter of each correct answer.

vocabulary
1. Which word goes with *visible*?
   A. secret
   B. crowd
   (C.) sight
   D. truth

vocabulary
2. Which definition BEST fits *acknowledge*?
   A. know more than before
   B. exchange ideas
   (C.) admit to be true
   D. listen to an opinion

©Voyager Expanded Learning, Inc. 189

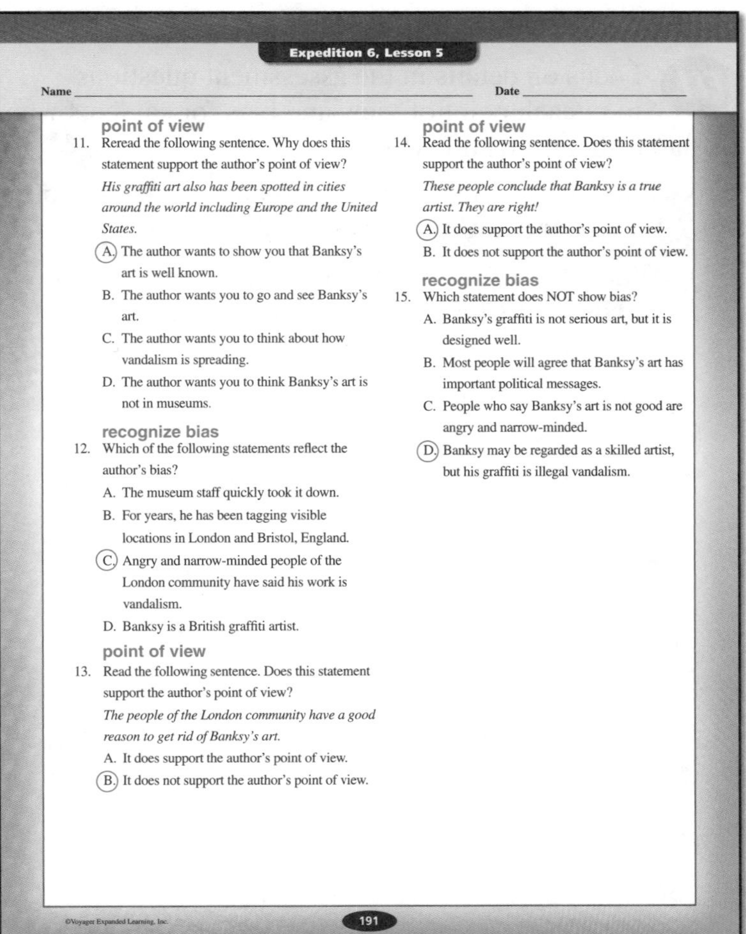

Expedition 6, Lesson 5

Name ______________________ Date __________

point of view
11. Reread the following sentence. Why does this statement support the author's point of view?
   His graffiti art also has been spotted in cities around the world including Europe and the United States.
   (A.) The author wants to show you that Banksy's art is well known.
   B. The author wants you to go and see Banksy's art.
   C. The author wants you to think about how vandalism is spreading.
   D. The author wants you to think Banksy's art is not in museums.

recognize bias
12. Which of the following statements reflect the author's bias?
   A. The museum staff quickly took it down.
   B. For years, he has been tagging visible locations in London and Bristol, England.
   (C.) Angry and narrow-minded people of the London community have said his work is vandalism.
   D. Banksy is a British graffiti artist.

point of view
13. Read the following sentence. Does this statement support the author's point of view?
   The people of the London community have a good reason to get rid of Banksy's art.
   A. It does support the author's point of view.
   (B.) It does not support the author's point of view.

point of view
14. Read the following sentence. Does this statement support the author's point of view?
   These people conclude that Banksy is a true artist. They are right!
   (A.) It does support the author's point of view.
   B. It does not support the author's point of view.

recognize bias
15. Which statement does NOT show bias?
   A. Banksy's graffiti is not serious art, but it is designed well.
   B. Most people will agree that Banksy's art has important political messages.
   C. People who say Banksy's art is not good are angry and narrow-minded.
   (D.) Banksy may be regarded as a skilled artist, but his graffiti is illegal vandalism.

©Voyager Expanded Learning, Inc. 191

Reteach

Point of View and Bias

1. Direct students to Student Book page 192. Read the instructions aloud. **Is the author's point of view what the author believes, or is the author telling what someone else believes?** (what the author believes) **Should you agree with every author? Explain.** (No, the author may not be correct or may just have a different belief.) **Some authors' points of view are biased. Should you rely on just one author when doing research?** (No, you should have a variety of sources.)
2. Read the passage aloud. **Positive and negative words are clues to the author's point of view and possible bias.** Have volunteers read sentences aloud while other students identify the positive and negative words.
3. Read each question aloud and have students find answers. Have students identify bias in the third paragraph. Guide them to realize that the author is biased because the author does not present any negative points about the mural.
4. Have students answer the last question box independently. Then, have students share responses and take the opportunity to clarify misconceptions.

ELL Focus on details in the assessment questions to reteach point of view and bias for students who had difficulty with Part B.

- **What words or details in the passage lead you to believe the author likes or dislikes Banksy?**
- **What details are near the negative or positive words in the text?**

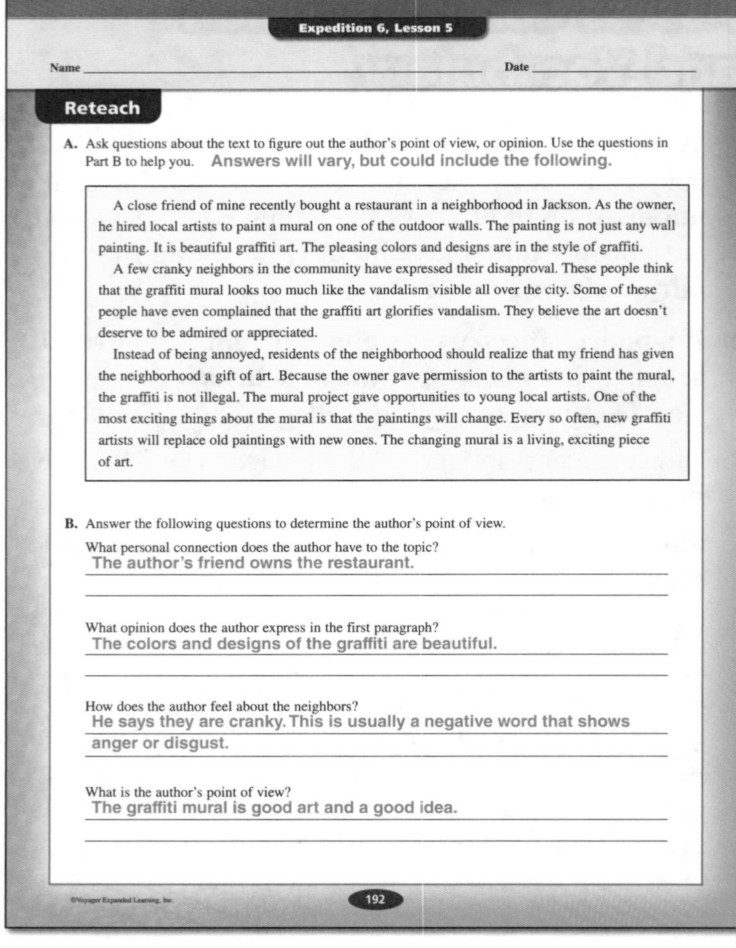

Expedition 6, Lesson 5

Name ______________________ Date ______________

Reteach

A. Ask questions about the text to figure out the author's point of view, or opinion. Use the questions in Part B to help you. Answers will vary, but could include the following.

A close friend of mine recently bought a restaurant in a neighborhood in Jackson. As the owner, he hired local artists to paint a mural on one of the outdoor walls. The painting is not just any wall painting. It is beautiful graffiti art. The pleasing colors and designs are in the style of graffiti.

A few cranky neighbors in the community have expressed their disapproval. These people think that the graffiti mural looks too much like the vandalism visible all over the city. Some of these people have even complained that the graffiti art glorifies vandalism. They believe the art doesn't deserve to be admired or appreciated.

Instead of being annoyed, residents of the neighborhood should realize that my friend has given the neighborhood a gift of art. Because the owner gave permission to the artists to paint the mural, the graffiti is not illegal. The mural project gave opportunities to young local artists. One of the most exciting things about the mural is that the paintings will change. Every so often, new graffiti artists will replace old paintings with new ones. The changing mural is a living, exciting piece of art.

B. Answer the following questions to determine the author's point of view.

What personal connection does the author have to the topic?
The author's friend owns the restaurant.

What opinion does the author express in the first paragraph?
The colors and designs of the graffiti are beautiful.

How does the author feel about the neighbors?
He says they are cranky. This is usually a negative word that shows anger or disgust.

What is the author's point of view?
The graffiti mural is good art and a good idea.

192

Passport Reading Journeys Library

1. Have students choose reading material from the *Passport Reading Journeys* Library or another approved selection. If students have not finished a previously chosen selection, they may continue reading from that selection. See the *Passport Reading Journeys* Library Teacher's Guide for material on selection guidelines.
2. You also may use this time to allow students to participate in book clubs or book presentations. Use the criteria specified in the *Passport Reading Journeys* Library Teacher's Guide.

Vocabulary Connections

Vocabulary words are listed in the Teacher's Guide for each book. These words are content-related or used frequently in reading material. The selected words can be a basis for independent or small-group discussions and activities.

Student Opportunities

Six copies of each book title are provided in the *Passport Reading Journeys* Library. The number of copies makes it possible for small groups of students to read the same material and share the information they read.

Theme-related titles include *Monster* and *Walk Two Moons*.

Technology

1. Depending on your classroom configuration and computer access, have students work through the technology in a lab setting or have individuals or small groups of students work on desktops or laptops while other students participate in other suggested activities, such as the *Passport Reading Journeys* Library.
2. The online technology component provides additional support for students to work with selected vocabulary words. Students will work through a series of activities to strengthen their word knowledge, then apply that knowledge to passage reading. Refer to the online technology component User Guide for more information.

   Theme-related word sets include Math and Technology.

Writing Process

Write a Persuasive Argument

Is graffiti vandalism or art? Explain that students will choose a position to defend and write a persuasive paragraph to support their position. Remind students that they read two opposing positions in "Graffiti: Vandalism or Art?" Have students review the passage.

Distribute copies of Writing Blackline Master page 11. Have students look at the page and follow along as you explain the assignment. Assign point values, and have students write them in the rubric. Tell them to make any notes on the page that will help them, but they will turn in the page with the assignment.

Prewrite

Have partners discuss Muriel's and Josh's positions about graffiti and the arguments they used to defend their positions. Instruct students to write these arguments in their chart and use them as a base to build their own arguments. Students should fill in both sides of the chart on their Blackline Master, then choose which position they agree with. Make a two-column chart on the board for the opposing arguments with the headings *Vandalism* and *Art*. After students work with their partner, have them share what they wrote in their charts. Write their responses on the board, and, as needed, help them to elaborate to add validity to their points. Have students add information to their charts based on the group discussion.

Have students choose three arguments from their chart that support their opinion and one counterargument from the other column that they want to refute in their writing.

Draft

Direct student attention to the rubric at the bottom of Writing Blackline Master page 11. **You will use these steps as you write your persuasive arguments.**

- **Begin with a clear opinion statement that tells your point of view.**
- **Provide three reasons that support your opinion.**
- **Then, make a counterargument. This is the information you chose from the column that argues against your opinion.**
- **Next, you will argue against the opposing argument, or counterargument, telling why you disagree.**
- **Finally, write a concluding statement that refers back to your opinion.**

Have students work independently to draft their persuasive arguments. Remind them that they will be able to revise their work.

Revise

Have students trade papers, read their partner's draft, and give each other feedback. Direct students to use the rubric to frame their discussion as they tell their partner which arguments are the most persuasive and which arguments may need elaboration. Have students trade again and reread their own drafts, using the following revision steps and questions. After each step, have students make the revisions and write their final draft.

- **Check the organization.** What sentences should you move so the information will flow in the right order?
- **Check your purpose.** Did you address the arguments that oppose your opinion? What facts and emotions can you add to persuade the reader?
- **Check mechanics.** Do fragments or run-on sentences need to be rewritten? What words might be misspelled? Do all sentences begin with capital letters and end with proper punctuation?

Present

Have students present their persuasive arguments to the class, alternating between the vandalism position and the art position.

Assess

I will assess your persuasive arguments based on the rubric on your page. To assess student persuasive arguments, use the rubric from the Writing Blackline Master.

Real-World Reading

FaceStart Wall-to-Wall

1. **Do you communicate with your friends on an online social networking site?** Allow students to discuss their experiences. Direct students to Student Book pages 193 and 194. Explain that they will read messages that are like the kind they may read on an online social networking site.
2. Direct students to read the messages. **Mark the text to answer the questions.**
   - **Circle the names of the friends. How many people are having this conversation?** (two)
   - **Underline negative and positive words. Put a plus sign above positive words and a minus sign above negative words.**
   - **Highlight what Aditya thinks is prejudiced.**
3. Have students read and place a star by the following words. Have them write the meanings in the margins. Clarify their understanding as needed.
   - ***Participated* means "took part in something with other people."**
   - ***Representation* means "something that shows or pictures something."**
   - ***Prejudiced* means "having opinions without knowing the facts or while ignoring the facts."**
   - ***Reform* means "correct faults or evils."**
4. **Pretend Aditya and Jen are your friends. Write a short message to them in response.**

Expedition 6, Lesson 5

Name ______________________ Date ____________

Real World—FaceStart Wall-to-Wall

FaceStart Home Profile Friends Inbox Aditya Settings Logout Search

My Wall-to-Wall with Jen

Jen's Profile | Back to My Profile

Share

Aditya Have you seen any videos lately? The one that Ms. Monet showed my French class today had some really weird dancers. Two kids started off with a crowd watching. The lighting flashed brightly, the scene got fuzzy, and then, suddenly, everyone participated in the dance, flailing their arms about and shaking their bodies. You know, the dance looked as if they were all chasing away bees, and the costumes were ridiculous. But, the music was really awesome, really electric, and I'd listen to it as long as I didn't have to see the dance.

May 4 at 10:52 am - Comment - Like

Jen Don't be so negative; I think the costumes were slick. You may be a good judge of music—that's electro house music, by the way—but you just don't understand dance. I saw that same video last year in Ms. Monet's class. The combinations of moves are powerful, almost poetic, in Tecktonik dance—that's what it's called, you know, but I think it's a mix of hip-hop and techno.

May 4 at 11:13 am - Comment - Like

Aditya Poetic? A poet in a frenzy, maybe. Anyway, I do have some appreciation for dance. How about that video of the dancing cows? Did you see that one? The split screen images that cut the cows in pieces created such a hysterical visual representation, I nearly split myself with laughter.

May 4 at 11:19 am - Comment - Like

Jen Right! You would think dancing cows are great. Zoe told me about that one, and I thought it was in bad taste, especially when the cow collapsed from exhaustion in the middle of the mucky field.

May 4 at 11:22 am - Comment - Like

Aditya That was faked. Don't think of it as a real cow really falling dead. Think of it as the image of a cow that happily danced itself to death.

May 4 at 11:26 am - Comment - Like

Jen So, that's not much better. My idea of hilarity is Mark Johnson's videos of his dog doing tricks—Mark goes to our school, you know. He's posted a lot of these humorous dog-doing-tricks videos, and I watch them over and over. The dog always does something so stupid, but it's really funny the way everything happens.

May 4 at 11:28 am - Comment - Like

©Voyager Expanded Learning, Inc. 193

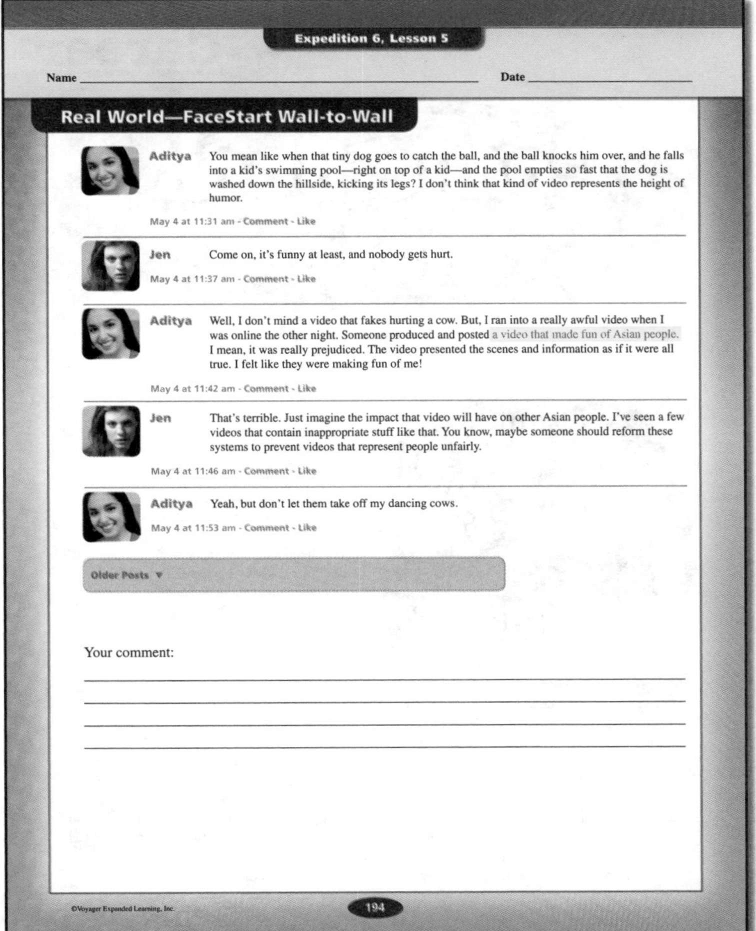

Expedition 6, Lesson 5

Name ______________________ Date ____________

Real World—FaceStart Wall-to-Wall

Aditya You mean like when that tiny dog goes to catch the ball, and the ball knocks him over, and he falls into a kid's swimming pool—right on top of a kid—and the pool empties so fast that the dog is washed down the hillside, kicking its legs? I don't think that kind of video represents the height of humor.

May 4 at 11:31 am - Comment - Like

Jen Come on, it's funny at least, and nobody gets hurt.

May 4 at 11:37 am - Comment - Like

Aditya Well, I don't mind a video that fakes hurting a cow. But, I ran into a really awful video when I was online the other night. Someone produced and posted a video that made fun of Asian people. I mean, it was really prejudiced. The video presented the scenes and information as if it were all true. I felt like they were making fun of me!

May 4 at 11:42 am - Comment - Like

Jen That's terrible. Just imagine the impact that video will have on other Asian people. I've seen a few videos that contain inappropriate stuff like that. You know, maybe someone should reform these systems to prevent videos that represent people unfairly.

May 4 at 11:46 am - Comment - Like

Aditya Yeah, but don't let them take off my dancing cows.

May 4 at 11:53 am - Comment - Like

Older Posts ▼

Your comment:

____

____

____

____

©Voyager Expanded Learning, Inc. 194

Exploring Careers

Comic Book Writer

1. Direct students to Anthology page 103. Have students preview the title and photograph. **What do you think this article will be about?** (a career as a comic book writer) **What is one thing you already know about writing comic books? What is one thing you would like to learn about this career?** List student responses on the board.
2. Have students read the article. **What surprised you about this career? Which aspects appeal to you? Which aspects do not appeal to you?**
3. Direct students to Student Book page 195. **Use information from the passage to answer the questions, then complete the chart by researching careers in books or online.**

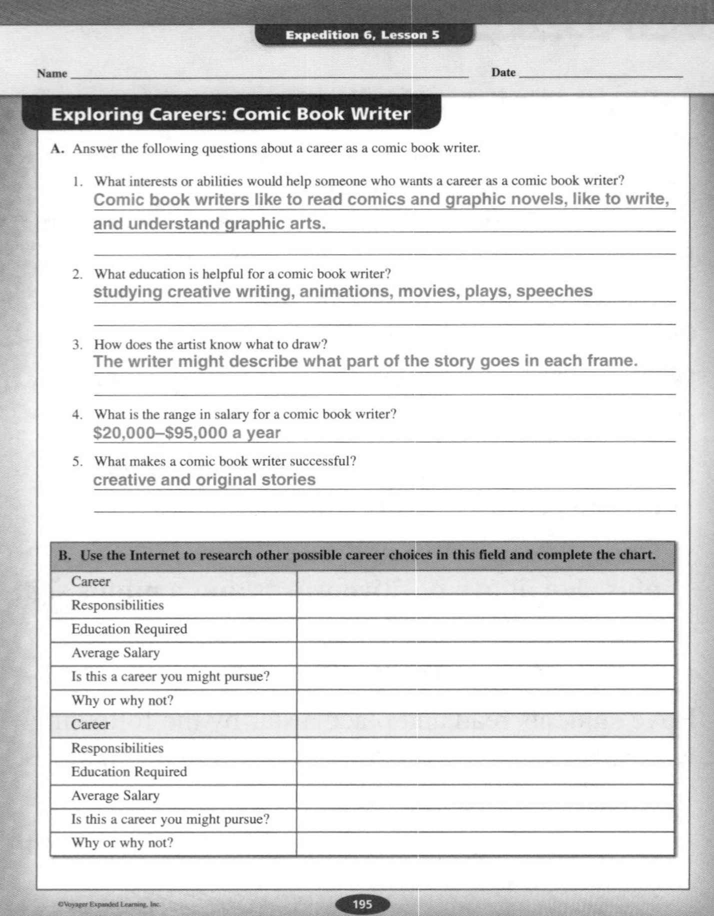

Expedition 6, Lesson 5

Name ______________________ Date ______________

Exploring Careers: Comic Book Writer

A. Answer the following questions about a career as a comic book writer.

1. What interests or abilities would help someone who wants a career as a comic book writer?
Comic book writers like to read comics and graphic novels, like to write, and understand graphic arts.
2. What education is helpful for a comic book writer?
studying creative writing, animations, movies, plays, speeches
3. How does the artist know what to draw?
The writer might describe what part of the story goes in each frame.
4. What is the range in salary for a comic book writer?
$20,000–$95,000 a year
5. What makes a comic book writer successful?
creative and original stories

B. Use the Internet to research other possible career choices in this field and complete the chart.

Career	
Responsibilities	
Education Required	
Average Salary	
Is this a career you might pursue?	
Why or why not?	
Career	
Responsibilities	
Education Required	
Average Salary	
Is this a career you might pursue?	
Why or why not?	

©Voyager Expanded Learning, Inc. 195

Comic Book Writer

Words with Punch, Images with Pizzazz

If you are a reader of comic books or graphic novels, and you like to write, you might be interested in a career as a comic book writer. Don't let the limited number of words you see in those conversation balloons fool you. Writing comic books involves a clear understanding of language. It requires an ability to use language well to tell a story. Writing also requires knowledge of graphic arts. You will need to imagine, and explain, how the story will be told visually.

Think about what you see in each frame of a comic. The images that are visible on the page are supported by the words, and the words are supported by the images. An accomplished writer knows how to show just enough and say just enough to tell the story powerfully. Each frame of the comic needs to move logically to the next frame. In this way, a comic book or a graphic novel is more like an animated cartoon you'd see on television than a cartoon in the newspaper, called a still cartoon.

Of course the story itself must be something you, as a comic book writer, want to develop in your own special way. The characters and events will need to seem fresh and exciting, even though most plots—or at least parts of plots—and all the basic themes have been used countless times before:

Now You See It 103

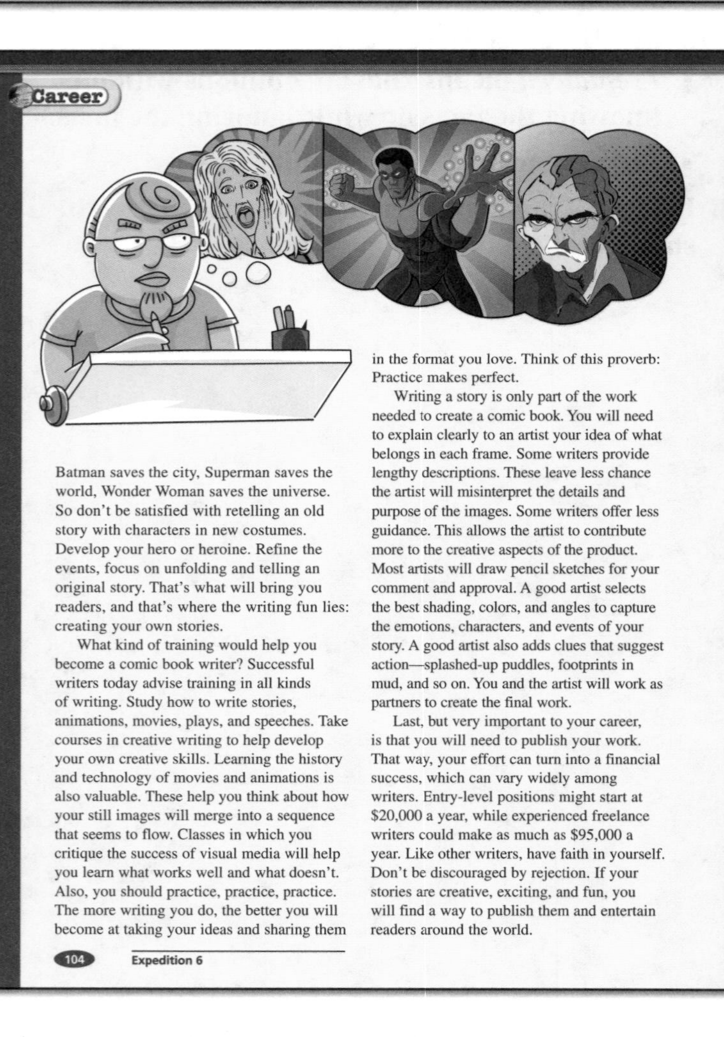

Batman saves the city, Superman saves the world, Wonder Woman saves the universe. So don't be satisfied with retelling an old story with characters in new costumes. Develop your hero or heroine. Refine the events, focus on unfolding and telling an original story. That's what will bring you readers, and that's where the writing fun lies: creating your own stories.

What kind of training would help you become a comic book writer? Successful writers today advise training in all kinds of writing. Study how to write stories, animations, movies, plays, and speeches. Take courses in creative writing to help develop your own creative skills. Learning the history and technology of movies and animations is also valuable. These help you think about how your still images will merge into a sequence that seems to flow. Classes in which you critique the success of visual media will help you learn what works well and what doesn't. Also, you should practice, practice, practice. The more writing you do, the better you will become at taking your ideas and sharing them in the format you love. Think of this proverb: Practice makes perfect.

Writing a story is only part of the work needed to create a comic book. You will need to explain clearly to an artist your idea of what belongs in each frame. Some writers provide lengthy descriptions. These leave less chance the artist will misinterpret the details and purpose of the images. Some writers offer less guidance. This allows the artist to contribute more to the creative aspects of the product. Most artists will draw pencil sketches for your comment and approval. A good artist selects the best shading, colors, and angles to capture the emotions, characters, and events of your story. A good artist also adds clues that suggest action—splashed-up puddles, footprints in mud, and so on. You and the artist will work as partners to create the final work.

Last, but very important to your career, is that you will need to publish your work. That way, your effort can turn into a financial success, which can vary widely among writers. Entry-level positions might start at $20,000 a year, while experienced freelance writers could make as much as $95,000 a year. Like other writers, have faith in yourself. Don't be discouraged by rejection. If your stories are creative, exciting, and fun, you will find a way to publish them and entertain readers around the world.

104 Expedition 6

English Language Learner Overview

The ELL signals when extra support is provided for students during the lesson. As needed, Blackline Masters for English language learners may provide support. For vocabulary, students also may use the online technology component to practice Expedition words or other content-area vocabulary and designated ELL word sets.

Introduce Vocabulary

Lesson 6

Point out the word *prejudices*. Pronounce the English word slowly, and have students repeat after you. If applicable, have a Spanish-speaking student model the pronunciation of the Spanish cognate *prejuicio*. Then, read aloud the definition and have students respond to the following questions.

- **If I already dislike a movie before I have seen it, do I have *prejudices* about the movie?** (yes)
- **If I see a movie, think about it carefully, and then decide I don't like it, do I have *prejudices* about the movie? Why?** (no, because I carefully evaluated it)
- **Why might I have *prejudices* about a movie before I have seen it?** (A friend might have influenced your opinion. You might have read an article that said the movie was bad.)

Lesson 8

Have students read aloud the definition of each vocabulary word. Ask the following questions.

- **Does a photograph show an *image*?** (yes)
- **Do you experience sound in a *visual* way?** (no)
- **When you *produce* something, do you make it?** (yes)
- **Would you *project* a picture if you did not want anyone to see it?** (no)
- **Do movies always *represent* people truthfully?** (no)
- **Can anyone *participate* in a professional soccer game?** (no)

Practice Vocabulary

In Lesson 7, provide support for the context words *traditionally* and *commercial*. **If something is done *traditionally*, it is done in keeping with traditions or customs. *Traditions* are the ways people have always done things. *Traditionally*, people eat dessert after dinner. When do people *traditionally* brush their teeth?** (in the morning; before bed)

Have students discuss their favorite commercial. **What is the purpose of a *commercial*?** (to advertise something) **Why do companies want to have a *commercial* on TV or the radio?** (to make people aware of their product or service so they will become customers)

In Lesson 9, provide support for the context words *succession* and *transparent*. **When things happen in *succession*, they happen one after the other. I hit the drum three times in rapid *succession*.**

When something is *transparent*, you can see through it. Computer animation made the person's skin appear *transparent*. If someone's skin were *transparent*, what would you be able to see? (muscles; veins)

Apply the Target Skill: Point of View and Bias

Students may need additional practice with point of view and bias. On Blackline Master page 35, students identify positive and negative words in sentences. Then, students read short passages and analyze the point of view through multiple-choice questions. Remind students that point of view is the author's opinion or feelings about a subject.

WHEN VIDEOS TURN BAD
How would you define a "film"?
Is it something you have to see in a theater or own on a DVD?
Or, could any video clip, no matter how trivial, be considered a "film"?

What Is a Film?

These questions all **involve** some truth. The word *film* describes the material traditionally, or usually, used to capture images. In that way, anything using the material of film to record the world could be considered a film. But, there are also cultural and historical ideas involved. Film is often seen as necessarily artistic. A great movie may be called a film, but a commercial for a product would not be, even though they are both created with the same media. Whether a film is considered one we can sell depends on what content it will **contain**, not what it's made of.

Vocabulary
involve (v) *include*
contain (v) *hold within itself; include*

How Films Began

The motion picture has been around since the 1860s. The earliest films were a series of still frames, or pictures, attached to a spinning drum and viewed through a small window. This is like making a flip book of still images. When you fan the pages quickly, the drawings appear to move. By the 1880s, the earliest motion-picture cameras had been made. These cameras allowed for the creation of movies much like those of today, but they could not record sound. The first films were silent, consisting purely of a sequence of images, nothing else. Dialogue was written on cards and filmed for the audience to read. These popular films had a great **impact** on society because they changed the way people viewed their lives.

Vocabulary
impact (n) *the power of something such as an event or idea to cause changes or strong feelings*

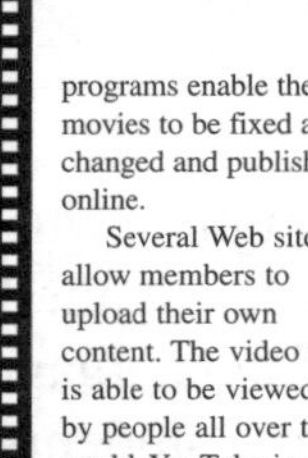

Later, inventors figured out how to play sound with the movie. Then the moviegoer could actually hear the dialogue and the sounds of things happening. Eventually, people devised a way to edit film to create special effects, which are illusions that could not be filmed with the rest of the movie. The growth of the film industry has impacted many areas of life, driving the expansion of television and online video services. 1

1 Make Connections
Think about what you know about movies. How were early movies different from what you see now?

Everyone's a Filmmaker

Modern digital technology takes filmmaking from the studio and allows it to be done by individuals. Cell phones, digital cameras, and camcorders all can record video with both images and sound. Affordable computer editing programs enable these movies to be fixed and changed and published online.

Several Web sites allow members to upload their own content. The video then is able to be viewed by people all over the world. YouTube is one of the best known, with a huge database of user-created content. Some of these videos share interesting news, expose different viewpoints, and create humor. These videos often contain important political or social comments.

However, with these beneficial uses come other uses that are perhaps inappropriate. Some videos criticize

and attack, just to destroy someone's image or reputation. Individuals or groups may be attacked in ways most people, and sometimes the law, consider unacceptable. Such videos often contain racist, sexist, or otherwise bigoted material. Different people have different **prejudices**. YouTube and similar Web sites are places that can be used to share interesting or helpful information. Unfortunately, people also can post biased and sometimes offensive films.

Where Does It End?

Many of these films can be—and are intended to be—personally damaging. Others may impact people's lives in ways the film creator did not intend. Some filmmakers just wanted to laugh at someone else's mistakes. Some hoped to make a film that gained fame. However, because these films are visible to millions, the films can be incredibly embarrassing for the subjects of the videos. Moreover, the person being portrayed often cannot block or limit the spread of the video.

Even if the "attacked" person can get the site to take down the video, the film could still be circulated. Popular videos are often passed along by individual users. Then the videos can be published on other sites. This practice can make the spread of the material nearly impossible to stop. The prejudiced, incorrect, and harmful messages these videos contain can be hurtful. How would you like it if your whole school started talking about a video someone had made about you that contained false information? 2

Vocabulary
prejudices (n) *opinions formed by people without knowing the facts or by ignoring the facts*
reform (n) *correction of faults or evils*

2 Recognize Bias
Describe the bias reflected by the author in these paragraphs.

Free Speech or Slander?

The issue of personal videos becomes a problem of individual rights. The Constitution guarantees citizens freedom of speech, but this freedom does not extend to spreading lies. The force of YouTube and other sites can be positive and powerful. It can spread constructive information about politics or events that make the public wiser, and help people make good decisions. But, some **reform** is needed, because untrue and damaging content is inappropriate.

The sites hosting the content should be held accountable to remove prejudiced films that spread lies or personally damage people. However, a citizen's right to criticize must be maintained. This makes reform of the system a difficult and touchy area. Just as we asked, "What is a film?" we also have to ask, "What is appropriate?" Uploading a video of someone slipping and falling on ice, for the purpose of making fun of them personally, is not appropriate. However, a video of several people slipping and falling in front of a business that refuses to clean its walkway might be worthwhile commentary. The second video may actually affect people's lives positively by forcing the business to act.

3 Summarize
Explain what is the question of great importance mentioned in this paragraph.

So if you were to reform the system and remove content, would you remove one, both, or neither? Why? The decision is difficult because it involves both people's right to privacy and their right to freedom. Now that individuals can create films on their cell phones, digital cameras, or other video equipment, this has become a question of great importance. 3 End

"When Videos Turn Bad"

Before Reading

Introduce Vocabulary

1. Have students turn to Part A on Student Book page 196 and scan the boldfaced vocabulary words. **You will see these words when you read "When Videos Turn Bad."** Have students rate their knowledge of each boldfaced word.
2. Have students share words they know and provide example sentences using the words. Read the part of speech, definition, and example sentence aloud. **Do the words you marked with a 3 have the same meaning you know?** Have students adjust their ratings if necessary.
3. Read the instructions for Part B aloud, then have students complete the activity.

ELL Refer to Blackline Master page 34 to extend vocabulary practice.

Have students use the *Passport Reading Journeys* online technology component to practice and reinforce vocabulary and comprehension skills.

Apply the Target Skill: Point of View and Bias

1. Remind students that an author's point of view is the author's opinion on a topic. **A *bias* is a strong preference for a point of view. Texts with biases may not be entirely truthful. Why might you be suspicious of a text written by a biased author?** (might not reveal important facts that don't agree with the author's bias)
2. Write the following sentences on the board: *Graffiti is on its way out as an art form. City workers are covering up graffiti faster than taggers can create it. It's about time. Now, maybe the true artists like myself won't be compared with those criminals.*

   Imagine that Anna, an artist, wrote this text. Have students determine the author's point of view by asking the following questions. **Does she have a bias? How do you know?** (The author hopes all graffiti art will end. She uses emotional words telling her own side. She seems biased because she does not tell other sides.)

Expedition 6, Lesson 6

Name ______ Date ______

Vocabulary

"When Videos Turn Bad"

A. Rate your knowledge of each boldfaced word.
3 I know what this word means, and I can use it in a sentence.
2 I have an idea of this word's meaning, but I need to know more.
1 I don't know what this word means.

☐ **involve** (v) *include*
Making a film used to *involve* a lot of equipment and people, but now I can use my cell phone.

☐ **contain** (v) *hold within itself; include*
Does that movie *contain* violence or bad language?

☐ **impact** (n) *the power of something such as an event or idea to cause changes or strong feelings*
Jared did not realize the *impact* his video clip of Marcus falling down would have on his friend.

☐ **prejudices** (n) *opinions formed by people without knowing the facts or by ignoring the facts*
The Internet video incited *prejudices* against the politician because people didn't know the truth.

☐ **reform** (n) *correction of faults or evils*
Many people feel a *reform* is needed on a Web site that promotes violence.

B. Complete each sentence with a vocabulary word from Part A.

1. Creating films and commercials __involves__ actors and directors working together.
2. The movie had a negative __impact__ on me because it showed how people mistreat one another.
3. Films can help eliminate __prejudices__ by showing the reasons cultures are different.
4. Films that __contain__ violence are rated inappropriate for children.
5. Some consumers want cable companies to agree to a __reform__ and lower their rates.

 196

Vocabulary

involve (v) *include*
Making a film used to *involve* a lot of equipment and people, but now I can use my cell phone.

contain (v) *hold within itself; include*
Does that movie *contain* violence or bad language?

impact (n) *the power of something such as an event or idea to cause changes or strong feelings*
Jared did not realize the *impact* his video clip of Marcus falling down would have on his friend.

prejudices (n) *opinions formed by people without knowing the facts or by ignoring the facts*
The Internet video incited *prejudices* against the politician because people didn't know the truth.

reform (n) *correction of faults or evils*
Many people feel *reform* is needed on a Web site that promotes violence.

ELL Provide support for students by telling them that negative words relate to *no*, *not*, and what is wrong with something; positive words relate to what someone thinks is good and right.

Introduce the Passage

1. Have students preview "When Videos Turn Bad" on Anthology page 105. **What features of this passage should you use to preview?** (photos; title; questions below the title; headings) **Using these clues, what do you predict the passage will be about?** Have students share their predictions and explain how clues in the text helped them make their predictions. Write predictions on the board.
2. Remind students to pay attention to the margin prompts as they read. **When you see a margin prompt, pause and think about the prompt. You may have to keep reading to find information.**

During Reading

1. To select reading options that support your students' levels and classroom needs, see Reading Differentiation, page xxxii, if needed.
2. Have students read "When Videos Turn Bad." **The passage presents two points of view about the regulation, or control, of online video content. Each point of view is supported by details in the text. As you read, look for the points of view and determine if you think the author shows a bias, or a strong preference, for one point of view.**

After Reading

Check Comprehension

1. Have students compare their predictions to what they read in the passage.
2. Help students respond to the Make Connections margin prompt on Anthology page 106. Have students name the oldest movies they can remember. **How are today's movies better or more advanced than those older movies?** (Possible response: Today's movies have better special effects.) Some students may be interested in older movies as well as modern movies. Have them describe which aspects of older movies appeal to them.
3. Focus on the Recognize Bias margin prompt on Anthology page 107. Have students reread the Where Does It End? section. **What point of view does the author express in this section?** (Videos online are dangerous, damaging, and uncontrollable.) **Is the author biased? Explain your answer.** (Yes, the author does not present positive reasons for having online content and only gives the negative.)
4. Discuss with students whether or not they think other sections of the passage show bias. If students detect bias, have them support their answer with evidence from the text.

ACADEMIC SKILL Tell students to keep point of view and bias in mind as they read texts in other classes. Point of view and bias can help students understand the authors of historical texts.

Remind students to choose books from the *Passport Reading Journeys* Library for independent reading.

"When Videos Turn Bad"

Prepare to Reread

Introduce the Lesson

Remind students they read about the pros and cons of online videos. **We'll reread "When Videos Turn Bad" to discover the author's point of view and whether the author has a bias.**

Practice Vocabulary

1. Encourage students to use the vocabulary words where possible in their responses to these questions.
    - **Does it *involve* a lot of work to circulate a video? Explain.** (No, you just post it on the Internet.)
    - **For a movie to be appropriate for young children, what kind of characters might it *contain*?** (cartoon characters; animals)
    - **What *impact* would an embarrassing video of you have?** (a negative impact)
    - **Some people watch videos and form opinions. Why might the opinions be *prejudices*?** (They might not consider other facts.)
    - **Some people want to *reform* YouTube and other Internet sites. How could you say that another way?** (Some people think YouTube and other Internet sites need to reform to correct problems.)
2. Have students turn to Anthology page 105. Point out the term *still frames* at the beginning of the How Films Began section. **The term *still frames* is used to describe early films. What clue helps you know the meaning of this term?** (or pictures)

    Repeat this process for the following words.
    - **traditionally** (adv) *usually*, Anthology page 105
    - **commercial** (n) *advertisement*, Anthology page 105
    - **special effects** (n) *illusions that would not be possible*, Anthology page 106
    - **bigoted** (adj) *intolerant of any belief or opinion that differs from one's own*, Anthology page 107
3. Have students turn to Student Book page 197. **The words *involve* and *contain* come from Latin roots.** Read aloud the instructions, words, and definitions in Part A. Provide support as needed to help students see the connection of "to turn" in today's meaning of *involve* and *evolve.* Have students read the instructions for Parts B and C and complete the activities.

Expedition 6, Lesson 7

Name ______________________ Date ______________

Word Building

A. The word *involve* uses the Latin root *volvere*, which means "to turn." The word *contain* uses the Latin root *tenere*, which means "to hold." Read the following words and their meanings. With a partner, discuss how the meanings we use today come from the Latin root meanings.

Words	Definitions	Words	Definitions
involve	*roll up; wrap; include*	**contain**	*hold within itself*
revolve	*move around a central point*	**retain**	*keep; have a hold of*
evolve	*slowly develop (unfold) or become more complex*	**obtain**	*hold onto; possess; gain*

B. Think about the word meanings in Part A and how you have heard each word used. Choose a word from the list to complete each sentence.

1. The coach did not want to lose her players. She wanted to ___retain___ them for the coming season.
2. How many writers and people with cameras will you ___involve___ in the video project?
3. The small computer store owner decided to ___obtain___ a larger space in a mall.
4. The chef's plans for a simple dinner often ___evolve___ into a huge banquet.
5. Astronauts repair satellites that ___revolve___ around Earth.
6. How many discs does this DVD case ___contain___?

C. Draw two panels of a cartoon. Use at least two words from Part A in speech or thought bubbles, a caption, or story boxes.

©Voyager Expanded Learning, Inc. 197

CHECKPOINT After students complete Part B, have them identify one item that confused them. Have students substitute each definition for the missing word to determine the correct answer.

ELL Have students share their experience with movies and special effects. Be aware that some students may be unfamiliar with movies if their culture does not allow students to watch movies or television.

Reread

Apply the Target Skill: Point of View and Bias

1. Have students turn to Anthology page 105. **What question would you ask to find the author's point of view?** (What does the author think about the subject or topic? Which words does the author choose?) Write student responses on the board.

2. Have students turn to Student Book page 198. **Reread the passage to find supporting details for each point of view on the chart.** Have partners complete the chart. Ask students to share their answers.

3. **How is bias different from point of view?** (Point of view is the author's opinion about a topic. Bias is a strong, one-sided preference for a point of view.) **How do you recognize bias?** (The author has a personal or emotional reaction to the topic; the author tells only one side of the topic.) **Does the author show bias in this passage?** (No, the author does not show a personal reaction; the author fairly presents good and bad points about YouTube.)

Refer to Blackline Master page 35 to extend practice with finding point of view and bias.

Write in Response to Reading

1. Have students turn to Student Book page 199. Read the instructions for Part A aloud. **A closed-ended question has only a *yes* or *no* response, such as *Have you watched videos on YouTube?* Good interview questions are open-ended and encourage discussion, such as *What videos have you watched on YouTube?*** Guide partners to write open-ended questions covering protecting or eliminating online video sites like YouTube, possible dangers of free online uploads, or potential solutions to problems raised in "When Videos Turn Bad." Have them change partners and interview each other.

2. **Now, you can explain what you think about the same topic.** Have students read the instructions for Part B and complete the activity. Ask students to share their responses.

EXPEDITION ORGANIZER **Now You See It**

Pause to have students turn to Student Book pages 176 and 177. Have students complete the following:

- Write answers or notes below one or more of the probing questions. Encourage them to write their own questions.
- Think about the story "When Videos Turn Bad" and write your thoughts in the appropriate box in Part B.

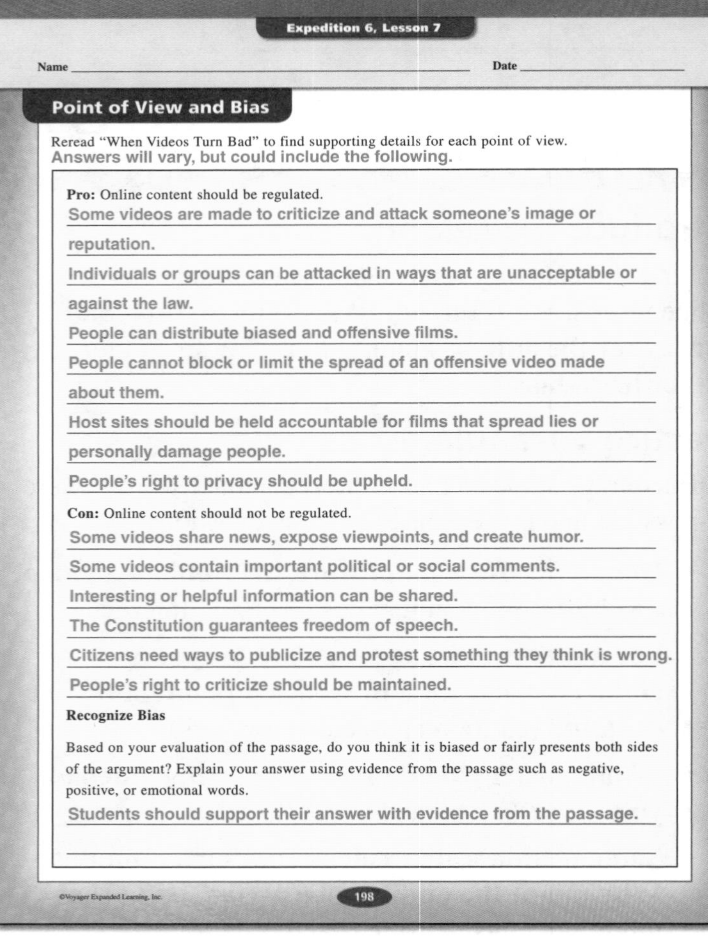

Expedition 6, Lesson 7

Name ______ Date ______

Point of View and Bias

Reread "When Videos Turn Bad" to find supporting details for each point of view.
Answers will vary, but could include the following.

Pro: Online content should be regulated.
Some videos are made to criticize and attack someone's image or reputation.
Individuals or groups can be attacked in ways that are unacceptable or against the law.
People can distribute biased and offensive films.
People cannot block or limit the spread of an offensive video made about them.
Host sites should be held accountable for films that spread lies or personally damage people.
People's right to privacy should be upheld.

Con: Online content should not be regulated.
Some videos share news, expose viewpoints, and create humor.
Some videos contain important political or social comments.
Interesting or helpful information can be shared.
The Constitution guarantees freedom of speech.
Citizens need ways to publicize and protest something they think is wrong.
People's right to criticize should be maintained.

Recognize Bias

Based on your evaluation of the passage, do you think it is biased or fairly presents both sides of the argument? Explain your answer using evidence from the passage such as negative, positive, or emotional words.
Students should support their answer with evidence from the passage.

Expedition 6, Lesson 7

Name ______ Date ______

Write in Response to Reading

A. Someone is making a video of you while you interview another person to find out how often he or she watches videos on YouTube, whether he or she has posted a video, and what he or she thinks about videos made by other people. Write the interview using questions with *who, what, where, when, why,* and *how*. Include a question about how the person reacts to offensive videos.

Interview topic: What do you think about watching videos people post on Web sites?

You: Hi! What do you know about free speech and Web sites like YouTube? Watch as I interview ______.

Question: Interviews should include a variety of questions and answers
Response: about what someone feels and thinks about videos posted
Question: to the Internet by users. Questions can be about protecting
Response: or eliminating online video sites like YouTube, the possible
Question: dangers of free online uploads, potential solutions to the
Response: problems raised in "When Videos Turn Bad," and related points.
Question: ______
Response: ______
Question: ______
Response: ______

B. After the interview, state how your own point of view is similar to or different from the person you interviewed. Is your point of view biased or unbiased? Explain.

I believe that sites like YouTube ______.

The person I interviewed believes that ______.

My point of view is (biased/unbiased) because ______.

The person I interviewed has a/an (biased/unbiased) point of view because ______
Student responses should compare their point of view and the one of the person in the interview and should reflect an understanding of bias.

On the Scene

Suddenly, you feel transported to a mountain. Huge bats—shiny with glaring eyes and sharply pointed teeth—swoop down at you as you cringe in your seat. For a second, the movie made you feel as if you were there. 1

If you've read graphic novels or comic books, you may have discovered they can be difficult to follow. Sometimes one frame doesn't seem to continue in the next one. People and objects unexpectedly change position from one **image** to the next. The still pictures allow little sense of movement.

Animation is an important **visual** tool for telling a story. It allows viewers to see a story unfold in front of them. It also makes everything realistic and natural.

Early Animation

People began to **produce** animation a long time ago. Beginning in the 16th century, people created objects called "magic lanterns" that would **project** a series of still images onto a screen, much like a modern projector. Images had to be switched by hand. These were very

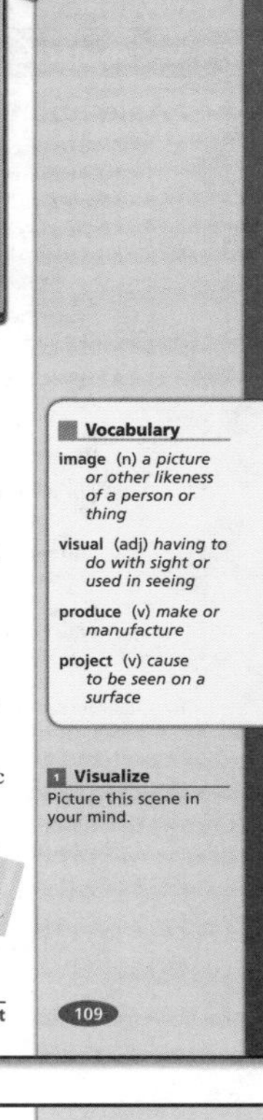

Vocabulary

image (n) *a picture or other likeness of a person or thing*

visual (adj) *having to do with sight or used in seeing*

produce (v) *make or manufacture*

project (v) *cause to be seen on a surface*

1 Visualize
Picture this scene in your mind.

Vocabulary

represent (v) *show or picture something*

primitive animating devices. Flip books, created in the 1800s, showed "moving" drawings—simple animated cartoons. The artist would draw a scene on a page, then redraw the scene with subtle changes to an object on subsequent, or following, pages. When the pages were bound in a book and quickly flipped through, the object in the scene appeared to move.

In the 1860s, people developed mechanical devices to project a series of images in quick succession. This also produced the effect of movement. With the invention of the film camera, animators developed stop-motion animation in which a picture is taken of each image that is redrawn with slight changes. When the images are played back quickly, the objects appear to move seamlessly. This new and different way to **represent** objects showed the world in motion, not at rest. 2

2 Summarize
What is the sequence of how animation developed?

Animation Leaps Ahead

The computer has helped people create new types of visual art. Yet, modern computer animation is done in the same way as stop-motion animation. Design programs allow three-dimensional shapes to be created with the computer by adding shadows and highlights. These can be rotated, stretched, and moved across the screen. The designer can put these shapes together and turn them into representations of objects, such as cars, trees, and people. Images can be applied to the surface of objects to make them look as if

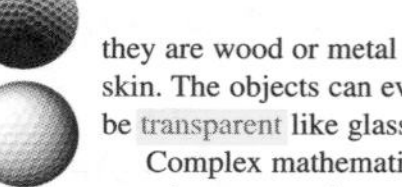

they are wood or metal or skin. The objects can even be transparent like glass.

Complex mathematical equations are used to determine how light reflects from these surfaces. These math equations compute how much shading or highlighting is needed on an object. This allows the production of realistic visual effects. As the objects change and move, a still image is recorded every fraction of a second. When these images are strung together into video, the objects appear to move. These techniques are used in movies to create amazing things, such as alien worlds, spaceships, futuristic cities, and gigantic bats. Also, computer animation is used to film scenes that would be too difficult or dangerous to do in reality, such as jumping off a building or going over a waterfall.

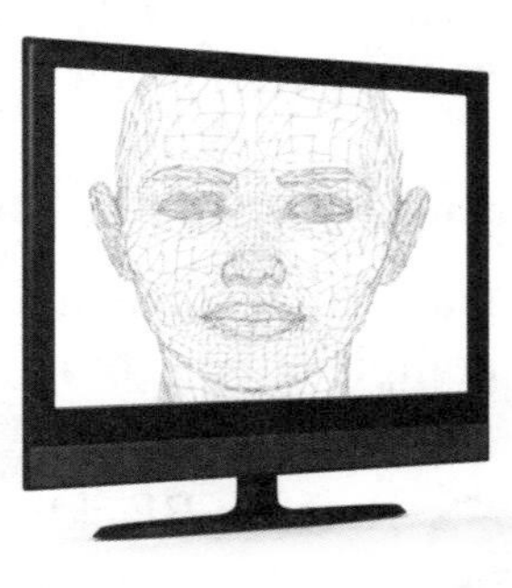

Graphics Take to Gaming

As computers became more powerful, these techniques of movement, shading, and highlighting were adapted to computer gaming. Colorful lines and circles made up early computer games such as Pac-Man. The user, as if looking down on the action from above, manipulated a yellow dot to chomp up blue dots through a labyrinth of paths. Computer game users now get to **participate** in the action as if they were immersed, or put into, the game. They are no longer remote from the world represented on screen, but feel as if they are walking through it. Users interact with this animated world and affect it.

Computer games work similarly to the earlier computer animation software. As the player's character moves, objects appear to move past, getting bigger as they come close, just as objects do in real life. Making the object grow bigger creates the illusion that the object is coming closer. Each fraction of a second, a still image is displayed on the screen. These images show the objects around the player with their correct locations and sizes, making the world appear realistic. These frames are shown one after the other. The eye cannot tell they are still.

Years ago, the most advanced games had only simple geometric shapes like cubes and triangles. Many old games used wire-frame graphics, showing the edges of objects but not filling in their faces. However, modern games have become incredibly realistic. Using lines, shadows, and highlights to create visual illusions, graphic artists trick the eye into seeing movement. Reflections on water look real, characters have flowing hair and rippling clothes, and the textures of brick walls and tree bark are lifelike because of creative uses of lines, shadows, and highlights. 3

Vocabulary

participate (v) *take part in something with other people*

3 Summarize
Explain the techniques used by graphic artists to make animation look 3-D and move.

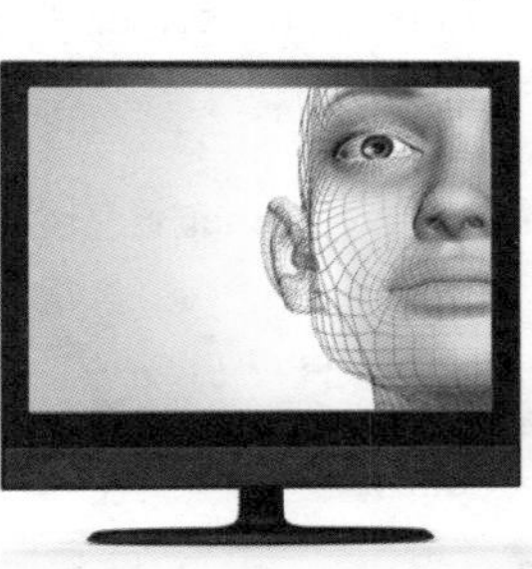

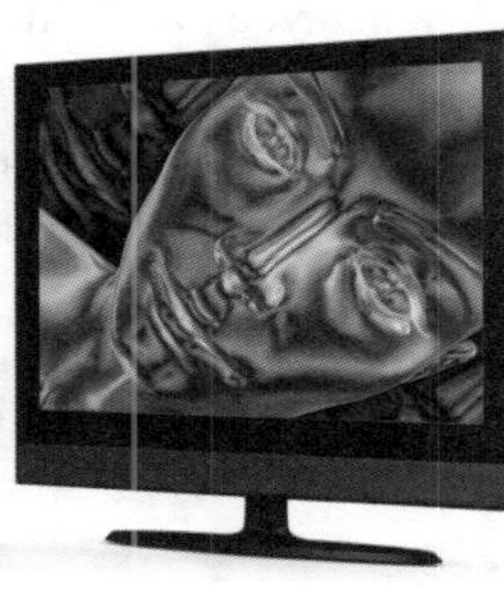

Today, game development doesn't stop when the game leaves the game studio. Participants in the game can add their own content. This addition of user-generated content is called *modding*, from the word *modify*, meaning "change." Players, using the same design software as the developers, can create new objects, new characters, or even new worlds. For example, a player can create a building that looks like his or her school and insert it into the game. This used to be impossible. But, computers have advanced so much that even complicated visual design software runs on many home computers. This trend, in which a game's participants create added objects, has become part of video game culture. A person can use the software to design a map for a popular Internet game and put it on his or her personal Web site for others to download and use. Some people have become so good at this kind of designing that game companies have hired these "modders" based on their work on the Internet, not on any technical education.

Engaging Other Senses

The visual aspect of games, creating three-dimensional objects, is a vital part of the development process. However, anyone who has played a game with the sound turned off knows that makes the experience less exciting. The creation of music to heighten the sense of game excitement is an important step. Also, each action in the game must have an associated sound. No matter how realistic the game looks, walking and jumping will never seem real if there is no sound. Recently, game developers have designed controllers that vibrate. These give tactile feedback the player can feel, enhancing the realism. 4

4 Context Clues
Reread the last two sentences. What clues help you understand the meaning of *tactile*?

Animation is the most fundamental aspect of computer gaming. However, only by combining visual input with audible and tactile input does a game seem real. What started as a simple attempt to show movement on a page has evolved into a complex virtual world. We can see, hear, and seemingly feel as if we are walking through this world by the creative use of lines and shadows. End

"Animation and Gaming Graphics"

Before Reading

Introduce Vocabulary

1. Have students turn to Part A on Student Book page 200 and scan the boldfaced vocabulary words. **These words are from "Animation and Gaming Graphics."** Have students rank their knowledge of the words.
2. Have partners compare their word rankings. Direct students to discuss the words they rated as 1 and 2.
3. Read the part of speech, definition, and example sentences for each word aloud. **Do the meanings you know match the meanings of the definition?** Direct students to adjust their ratings if necessary.
4. Have students read the instructions for Part B and complete the activity.

ELL Refer to Blackline Master page 36 to extend vocabulary practice.

Introduce the Target Skill: Big Picture Notes

1. Remind students that they learned how to take notes in Expedition 5. **You asked questions, then took notes. Now you will read and take notes, then ask questions about your notes. You'll follow steps that will help you take organized notes. It is an easy way to figure out the "big picture," or main ideas.**
2. Have students turn to Anthology page 29. **Let's see how you can use Big Picture notes for this passage.** On the board, draw a large rectangle to represent a sheet of notebook paper. Draw a vertical line down the middle of the right-hand side as in Student Book page 202. Write the heading *Benefits of Online Shopping* on the left side. (See page 249 for an example of how to draw this notes page.)

Expedition 6, Lesson 8

Name ____________________ Date ____________

Vocabulary

"Animation and Gaming Graphics"

A. Read the boldfaced words. Rate the words in order of how well you know them.

5 I use it in everyday conversation.
4 I heard it on TV or on the radio.
3 I heard or used it in school.
2 I read it in a book, magazine, or online.
1 I have not read, heard, or used this word.

☐ **image** (n) *a picture or other likeness of a person or thing*
Our art teacher used the animated *image* of a stick figure to show movement.

☐ **visual** (adj) *having to do with sight or used in seeing*
A picture is a *visual* tool that will help me understand a story.

☐ **produce** (v) *make or manufacture*
When did they *produce* the first animated cartoon?

☐ **project** (v) *cause to be seen on a surface*
When you *project* the pictures on the screen, everyone can see them.

☐ **represent** (v) *show or picture something*
The way they *represent* the hero in that video game is exciting.

☐ **participate** (v) *take part in something with other people*
I like to *participate* in that online game and play against people in other countries.

B. Complete each sentence with the correct vocabulary word from Part A.

1. The cartoon artist drew one frame, then showed the ___image___ to another artist.
2. Computer animation is a ___visual___ art.
3. The director and the animation studio will ___produce___ a full-length cartoon.
4. Each week, I have time to ___participate___ in playing video games with other gamers.
5. The neighbors decided to ___project___ the movie on the side of a building.
6. How can an artist draw a character who appears to ___represent___ good but does evil things?

 200

Vocabulary

image (n) *a picture or other likeness of a person or thing*
Our art teacher used the animated *image* of a stick figure to show movement.

visual (adj) *having to do with sight or used in seeing*
A picture is a *visual* tool that will help me understand a story.

produce (v) *make or manufacture*
When did they *produce* the first animated cartoon?

project (v) *cause to be seen on a surface*
When you *project* the pictures on the screen, everyone can see them.

represent (v) *show or picture something*
The way they *represent* the hero in that video game is exciting.

participate (v) *take part in something with other people*
I like to *participate* in that online game and play against people in other countries.

- **Write notes on the left side of your paper beginning with the heading. You've already learned how to turn the headings into questions. What questions can I write in my question column?** (What are the benefits of online shopping?)
- Have students read the section and give three important notes; write these on the board. (Possible responses: convenience; price comparison; merchants avoid costs of traditional stores.)
- **When you finish reading, think about the notes and write questions on the right side. These questions will help you study.** Call on a student to ask questions about the notes, and write them on the right side. Guide students to ask helpful study questions such as, "Why can Internet merchants offer better prices?"
- **Last, review what you wrote in the columns and write a summary.** Have a volunteer dictate a summary. Have students notice how the questions on the right side become guides for writing the summary.

3. Point out that students can use Big Picture notes in all classes. **Keep the notes you take. Study by folding back the paper on the vertical line so only the questions show.**
4. **You will take Big Picture notes in Lesson 9.** Ask students what questions they have and what might be the most difficult step for them—taking notes while reading, thinking of questions, or writing the summary. Discuss their questions and note expected difficulties to address in Lesson 9.

ACADEMIC SKILL Tell students that they can use Big Picture notes in all subjects. Explain that they can write a set of notes for different sections or chapters of their textbooks. Remind students that the foldable notes are an easy study guide.

Introduce the Passage

1. Have students turn to Anthology page 109 to preview "Animation and Gaming Graphics." **What will you use to preview the passage?** (the title; subheadings; photos) **What clues do they give you about the passage?** (The photos and title show that computers are used to make animation; the headings are about the history of animation.) **Predict what the passage is about.** Write student predictions on the board.
2. Remind students to pay attention to the margin prompts. **When you see a prompt, pause and try to answer it. You may have to reread a part of the passage.**

During Reading

1. Have students read "Animation and Gaming Graphics." To select reading options that support your students' levels and classroom needs, see Reading Differentiation, page xxxii, if needed.
2. **As you read, pay attention to the information you think is important to remember.**

After Reading

Check Comprehension

1. **How are your predictions different from what you just read?** Ask students to share the differences between their predictions and the passage. Have students identify text features that influenced their predictions.
2. Focus student attention to the Visualize margin prompt on Anthology page 109. **Which words in the first two sentences appeal to your five senses?** (mountain; huge bats; shiny; glaring eyes; sharply pointed teeth; swoop; cringe) **Use these words to create a mental picture of what you read.**
3. Point out the Summarize margin prompt on Anthology page 110. **Pay attention to dates and signal words like *first*, *beginning*, *next*, and *finally* that show the order of events. What was the earliest kind of animation?** (magic lanterns)
4. Have students share what they thought were important ideas.

Remind students to choose books from the *Passport Reading Journeys* Library for independent reading.

"Animation and Gaming Graphics"

Prepare to Reread

Introduce the Lesson

Remind students that they read about computer animation in the previous lesson. **We'll revisit "Animation and Gaming Graphics" and take Big Picture notes.**

Practice Vocabulary

1. Have students think about how vocabulary words were used in the previous lesson by asking the following questions.
   - **What fantastic *image* from a film or game looks real to you?** (Answers will vary.)
   - **What are the *visual* differences between a cartoon and a comic book?** (Comic books have still images, and cartoons move.)
   - **What do you need to *produce* an image?** (paint; computer; other art devices)
   - **How do images look when you *project* them on theater screens?** (very large; exciting)
   - **If you were an animator, how would you *represent* a superhero?** (Answers will vary.)
   - **Who must *participate* in creating a cartoon?** (animators; sound engineers; writers)

ELL Have students give cognates and the meanings for vocabulary words. Confirm that the meaning in English is the same, or clarify the difference in the English meaning. Slowly pronounce vocabulary words and have students repeat.

2. Have students turn to Anthology pages 109 and 110 and read the first paragraph under Early Animation. **What does *subsequent* mean?** (following) **What context clues help you figure out this meaning?** (or following)

   Repeat this process for the following words.
   - **succession** (n) *the act or process of following in order; sequence*, Anthology page 110
   - **transparent** (adj) *like glass; see-through*, Anthology page 110
   - **immersed** (v) *put into; completely occupied by something*, Anthology page 111

Expedition 6, Lesson 9

Name ______ Date ______

Word Building

A. Some words have more than one meaning. In this lesson, you learned the meanings and pronunciations of the words *project* and *produce* as verbs.

Project (/pro' jekt/) also can be a noun that means "a task that requires time, effort, and planning."
Sally and I decided to do a science *project* that shows and explains how fish gills work.

Produce (/prō' düs/) also can be a noun that means "fruits and vegetables that are products of farms."
I bought *produce* like lettuce, carrots, tomatoes, and cucumbers to make salad for dinner.

B. Choose *A, B, C,* or *D* as the correct meaning of the boldfaced word in each sentence.

project
A. (v) *cause to be seen on a surface*
B. (n) *a task that requires time, effort, and planning to complete*

produce
C. (v) *make or manufacture*
D. (n) *fruits and vegetables that are products of farms*

D 1. The store ran out of fresh **produce** because deliveries were slow.
A 2. In the summer, the city parks **project** movies outdoors so people can watch them for free.
C 3. My boss at the candle shop taught me to **produce** beautiful candles.
B 4. Fixing the old house was a **project** for our whole family.
D 5. The only kind of **produce** I dislike is radishes.
A 6. The teacher chose to **project** her presentation on the board so all students could see.

C. Use either *project* or *produce* in two different sentences, one for each meaning.
1. Answers will vary.
2. ______

©Voyager Expanded Learning, Inc. 201

3. Have students turn to Student Book page 201. Read the instructions aloud. Model the pronunciation of the words as they are used for the different meanings. Have students complete the page.

CHECKPOINT After students complete Part B, have them identify one item that confused them. Direct students to try both definitions in place of the word.

Reread

Apply the Target Skill: Big Picture Notes

1. Have students turn to Student Book page 202 and prepare to take Big Picture notes about "Animation and Gaming Graphics." **The first step in taking Big Picture notes is to write the headings, then write important ideas while you read or listen. For this activity, the headings have been completed. Notice how they match the passage.** Have students reread the *Early Animation* section, take notes, and share their notes.

2. **For the second step, write questions.** Have students use the notes they wrote to write questions.
3. **What is the last step?** (Write the summary.) Remind students they should use words in the questions as hints when writing the summary. Instruct students to read the remaining sections, take notes, and write questions.
4. Have partners compare notes. **Everyone's notes will be different.**
5. Have students give examples of each part of Big Picture notes. **Would you take notes differently next time? How?** Have students tell how they might improve their own note-taking process.

ELL Remind students that a summary contains only the most important facts and ideas and clearly states the main idea.

Write in Response to Reading

1. **Have you seen films or played games with animation? How did it engage your senses?** Have students turn to Student Book page 203. Read the instructions for Part A aloud, and have students complete the activity.
2. **What would the characters and settings be in your own animation? Would you make the animation funny, scary, or serious?** Have students read the instructions for Part B and complete the activity.

EXPEDITION ORGANIZER **Now You See It**

Pause to have students turn to Student Book pages 176 and 177. Have students complete the following:

- Write answers or notes below the probing questions. Encourage students to add their questions.
- Use their ideas about the passages to complete the last box in Part B, "How Graphic Arts Have Impacted My Life."

Build Background DVD 6.2

Briefly discuss the Expedition passages. Then, watch the DVD together. After watching, review student responses to the probing questions using the Expedition Organizer.

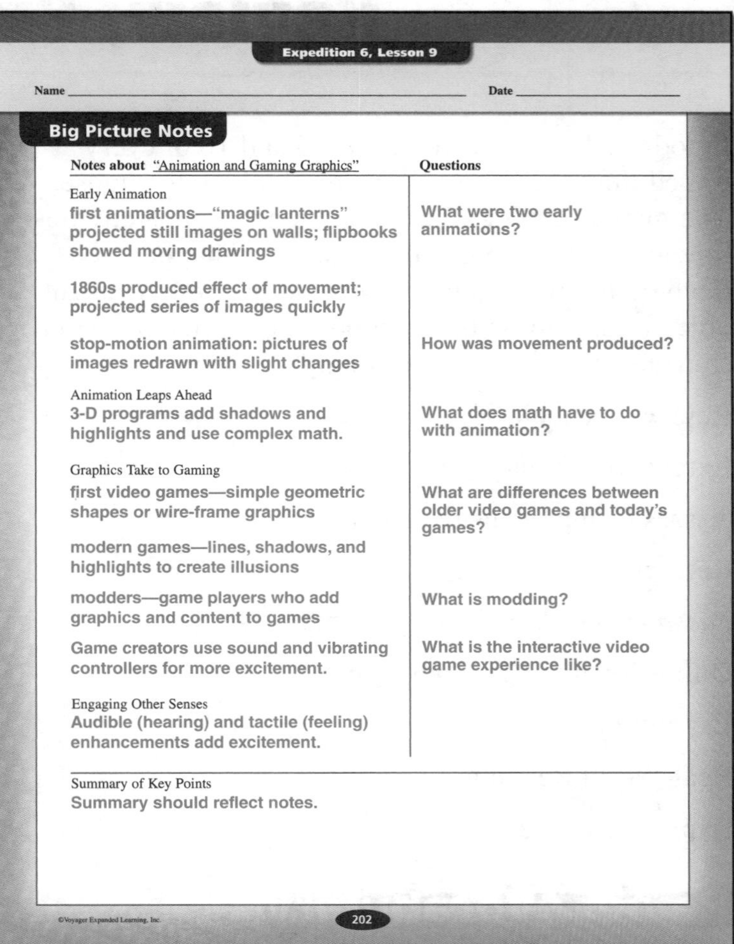

Expedition 6, Lesson 9

Name ______________________ Date ____________

Big Picture Notes

Notes about "Animation and Gaming Graphics"	Questions
Early Animation first animations—"magic lanterns" projected still images on walls; flipbooks showed moving drawings	What were two early animations?
1860s produced effect of movement; projected series of images quickly	
stop-motion animation: pictures of images redrawn with slight changes	How was movement produced?
Animation Leaps Ahead 3-D programs add shadows and highlights and use complex math.	What does math have to do with animation?
Graphics Take to Gaming first video games—simple geometric shapes or wire-frame graphics	What are differences between older video games and today's games?
modern games—lines, shadows, and highlights to create illusions	
modders—game players who add graphics and content to games	What is modding?
Game creators use sound and vibrating controllers for more excitement.	What is the interactive video game experience like?
Engaging Other Senses Audible (hearing) and tactile (feeling) enhancements add excitement.	

Summary of Key Points
Summary should reflect notes.

©Voyager Expanded Learning, Inc. 202

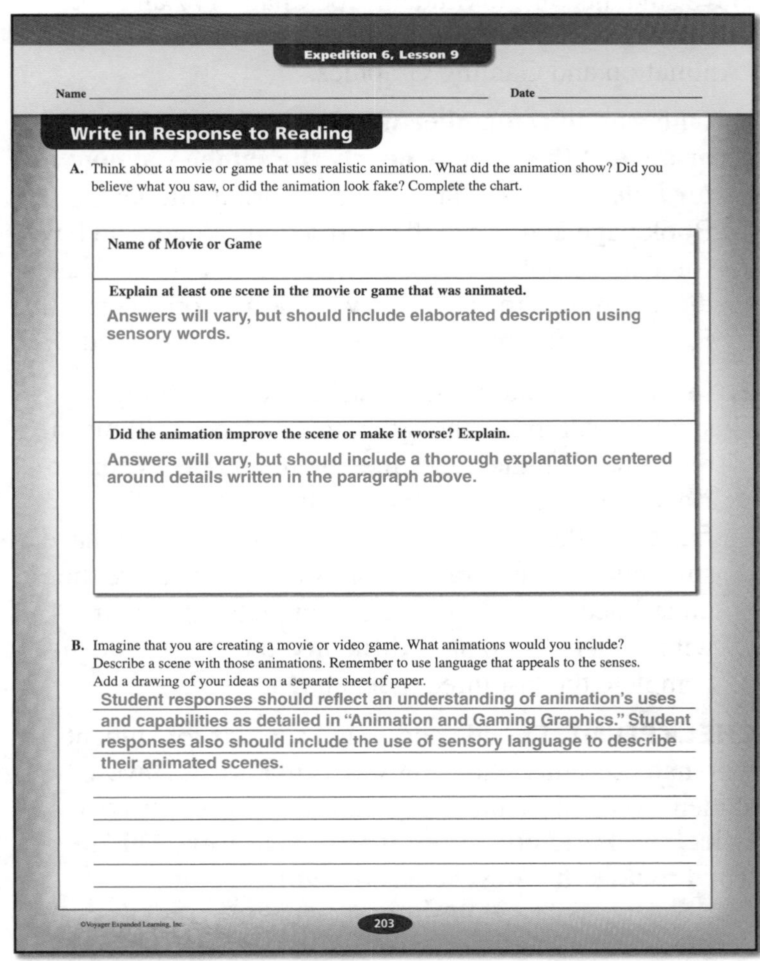

Expedition 6, Lesson 9

Name ______________________ Date ____________

Write in Response to Reading

A. Think about a movie or game that uses realistic animation. What did the animation show? Did you believe what you saw, or did the animation look fake? Complete the chart.

Name of Movie or Game
Explain at least one scene in the movie or game that was animated. Answers will vary, but should include elaborated description using sensory words.
Did the animation improve the scene or make it worse? Explain. Answers will vary, but should include a thorough explanation centered around details written in the paragraph above.

B. Imagine that you are creating a movie or video game. What animations would you include? Describe a scene with those animations. Remember to use language that appeals to the senses. Add a drawing of your ideas on a separate sheet of paper.
Student responses should reflect an understanding of animation's uses and capabilities as detailed in "Animation and Gaming Graphics." Student responses also should include the use of sensory language to describe their animated scenes.

©Voyager Expanded Learning, Inc. 203

Review, Extend, Assess

In today's lesson, as in Lessons 5 and 10 of every Expedition, there are options from which to choose. You may do any or all of the options listed. Activities for each option are given on the following pages. Each option will support or extend previously taught objectives. Choose the option(s) appropriate for your students and prepare accordingly.

Review Vocabulary

Extend Vocabulary

Assess Comprehension and Vocabulary

Reteach

Passport Reading Journeys Library

Online Technology Component

Expedition Project

Real-World Reading

Exploring Careers

Review Vocabulary

Have students turn to Student Book page 177 and review the vocabulary for "When Videos Turn Bad" and "Animation and Gaming Graphics."

1. **One way to remember words is to learn a synonym, or a word that means nearly the same. A synonym for *happy* is *glad*.** Have students turn to Student Book page 204. Read the instructions aloud, and have students complete the activity. Tell students to check the definitions to ensure they used the words correctly. Have students share their answers for Parts A and B.
2. In Part A, if students have difficulty identifying synonyms, remind them that the sentence will mean the same with the underlined word and the synonym. Have them read through the sentence twice. The first time, they read for sense. The second time, have students use the phrase *another word for* before the underlined word. For Part B, complete three items with students who have difficulty, then have students complete the last three independently.

CHECKPOINT Provide additional support for students who had difficulty choosing words in Part B. Have students read the sentences aloud. **Read the sentence twice, inserting one of the words each time. Which word makes the most sense or sounds right?**

Expedition 6, Lesson 10

Name ______________________ Date ______________

Review Vocabulary

A. For each underlined word or phrase, write a synonym, or a word that has the same or a similar meaning. Choose your answers from the words in the box.

reform **transparent** **image** **participate** **impact** **contain**

1. The picture on Kurt's T-shirt is a design by his favorite artist. image
2. The invention of the computer had a huge effect on artists and animators. impact
3. The candidate planned to bring change if she became mayor of the town. reform
4. Chris Ware's book cover designs include interesting shapes and colors. contain
5. Jeremy decided to join in the video game with his friends. participate
6. The visual effects made the animated ghosts look see-through. transparent

B. Circle the word that BEST completes each sentence.

James and Megan went to see the latest superhero movie. They couldn't wait for the theater to (participate, project) their favorite superhero on the big screen. Megan already had read all the comic books, so she had formed some (prejudices, immersed) about the movie. Before seeing the movie, Megan was sure no movie could (reform, represent) the story and hero as well as the comics. After the movie, Megan acknowledged how well the computer animators could (commercial, produce) the action scenes. James said that making those scenes had to (involve, impact) a lot of new computer technology. They both thought that the movie was great (visual, subsequent) entertainment.

C. Choose three words from Part A. Write a sentence about graphic arts using each vocabulary word.

1. Answers will vary.
2. ______________________
3. ______________________

204

Extend Vocabulary

1. Direct students to Part A on Student Book page 205. **Many words in English, such as *visual*, come from Latin.**
2. Write the word *visual* on the board. Underline *vis* inside the word. Read aloud Part A. Have students underline *vis* inside the words in Part A. Read aloud the words and definitions. **How do these words relate to the meaning of *sight*?** Tell students that knowing roots will help them understand other words with the same root when they read.
3. Read aloud the instructions for Parts B and C. **You can reread the definitions to help you complete the sentences in Part B.** Have students complete the activity, then share their responses.

CHECKPOINT When students share their responses for Parts B and C, listen to ensure that they used the new words in the correct contexts. Pause to explain and correct any errors.

Part A

1. Write the boldfaced words and underline the root *vis* in each of them. **Root words may come from other languages. What words in your home language contain the root *vis*? Explain the meanings.** If the meaning is related to *sight*, tell students the meaning can help them remember English words with *vis*. If the meanings are different, emphasize the English meaning.
2. Explore each new word by reading the definition, using the words in a sentence, then asking students to answer a question about the word. **To *visit* is to go to see and spend time with. I would like to *visit* my grandmother. Who would you like to *visit*?** Have students answer using the following sentence starter: *A person I would like to visit is ______.*

Expedition 6, Lesson 10

Name ______________________ Date ______________

Extend Vocabulary

A. Each of the following words comes from the Latin root word *visus*, which means "sight." Read the words and their meanings. Notice how all the meanings connect to the word *sight*.

visual	(adj) *having to do with sight or used in seeing*	**supervisor**	(n) *person who keeps watch over*
vision	(n) *the ability to see*	**visit**	(v) *go to see and spend time*
visible	(adj) *able to be seen or noticed*		

B. Think about the meanings of the words in Part A and how you have heard each word used. Choose a word from the list to complete each sentence.

1. Jacqui plans to ___visit___ the museum of graphic design Tuesday.
2. The large lettering on the poster is ___visible___ from across the room.
3. Daniel works as the ___supervisor___ of a team of illustrators and designers for graphic novels.
4. The film critic said the new movie was a great work of ___visual___ art.
5. Graphic artists who work long hours at the computer can strain their ___vision___.

C. Choose four words from Part A to use in a sentence about comics or movies.

1. Answers will vary.
2. ______________________
3. ______________________
4. ______________________

 205

Part B

If students have difficulty completing a sentence, turn the sentence into a question with the blank as an answer: *The tall building is ______ from far away.* **What is something that is able to be seen or noticed?** (visible)

Part C

1. Before students choose their words, have them rate each word: 1—do not know it; 2—have heard it but am not sure of the meaning; 3—use it in conversation or in school.
2. Have students choose words they rated as 2 or 3 for the activity. If students do not have enough words rated 2 or 3, have them look at the definitions.

Assess Comprehension and Vocabulary

1. Remind students they learned to recognize an author's point of view and bias. **How can you recognize the author's point of view?** (identify positive and negative words; decide if the author has a personal reason for thinking a certain way; identify the author's opinions)
2. Direct students to Student Book pages 206–208. Remind students to notice the author's point of view and any bias. Have them complete the pages.

   Review student answers. Whenever possible, provide elaborative feedback to student responses. Refer to page xl for examples of elaborative feedback and how to incorporate it in your lessons.

   If students incorrectly answer more than 4 out of 15 assessment questions, evaluate what kind of reteaching is needed. If students miss vocabulary questions, have them return to the vocabulary activities and work with the words they missed. For errors recognizing point of view and bias, use the reteaching suggestions on page 253.

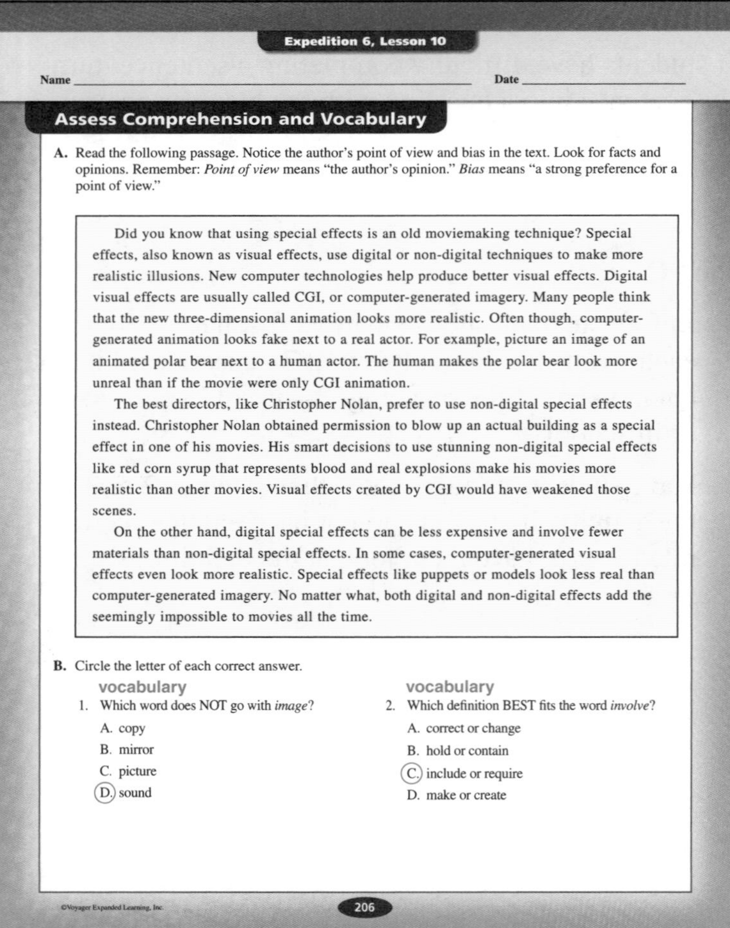

Expedition 6, Lesson 10

Name ____________________ Date ____________

Assess Comprehension and Vocabulary

A. Read the following passage. Notice the author's point of view and bias in the text. Look for facts and opinions. Remember: *Point of view* means "the author's opinion." *Bias* means "a strong preference for a point of view."

Did you know that using special effects is an old moviemaking technique? Special effects, also known as visual effects, use digital or non-digital techniques to make more realistic illusions. New computer technologies help produce better visual effects. Digital visual effects are usually called CGI, or computer-generated imagery. Many people think that the new three-dimensional animation looks more realistic. Often though, computer-generated animation looks fake next to a real actor. For example, picture an image of an animated polar bear next to a human actor. The human makes the polar bear look more unreal than if the movie were only CGI animation.

The best directors, like Christopher Nolan, prefer to use non-digital special effects instead. Christopher Nolan obtained permission to blow up an actual building as a special effect in one of his movies. His smart decisions to use stunning non-digital special effects like red corn syrup that represents blood and real explosions make his movies more realistic than other movies. Visual effects created by CGI would have weakened those scenes.

On the other hand, digital special effects can be less expensive and involve fewer materials than non-digital special effects. In some cases, computer-generated visual effects even look more realistic. Special effects like puppets or models look less real than computer-generated imagery. No matter what, both digital and non-digital effects add the seemingly impossible to movies all the time.

B. Circle the letter of each correct answer.

vocabulary
1. Which word does NOT go with *image*?
   A. copy
   B. mirror
   C. picture
   D. sound

vocabulary
2. Which definition BEST fits the word *involve*?
   A. correct or change
   B. hold or contain
   C. include or require
   D. make or create

©Voyager Expanded Learning, Inc. 206

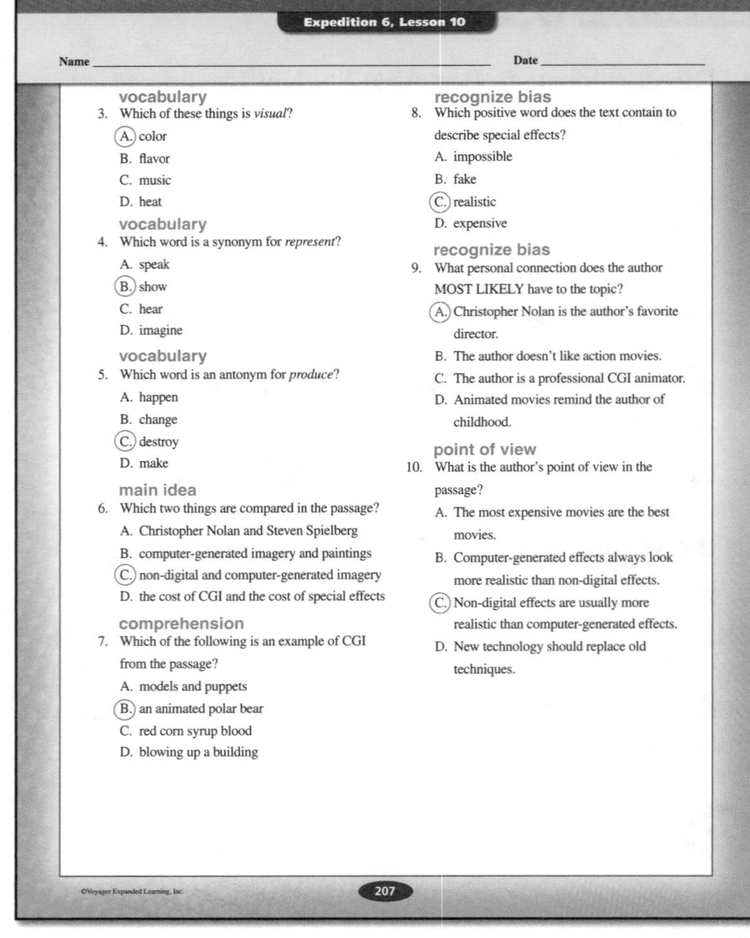

Expedition 6, Lesson 10

Name ____________________ Date ____________

vocabulary
3. Which of these things is *visual*?
   A. color
   B. flavor
   C. music
   D. heat

vocabulary
4. Which word is a synonym for *represent*?
   A. speak
   B. show
   C. hear
   D. imagine

vocabulary
5. Which word is an antonym for *produce*?
   A. happen
   B. change
   C. destroy
   D. make

main idea
6. Which two things are compared in the passage?
   A. Christopher Nolan and Steven Spielberg
   B. computer-generated imagery and paintings
   C. non-digital and computer-generated imagery
   D. the cost of CGI and the cost of special effects

comprehension
7. Which of the following is an example of CGI from the passage?
   A. models and puppets
   B. an animated polar bear
   C. red corn syrup blood
   D. blowing up a building

recognize bias
8. Which positive word does the text contain to describe special effects?
   A. impossible
   B. fake
   C. realistic
   D. expensive

recognize bias
9. What personal connection does the author MOST LIKELY have to the topic?
   A. Christopher Nolan is the author's favorite director.
   B. The author doesn't like action movies.
   C. The author is a professional CGI animator.
   D. Animated movies remind the author of childhood.

point of view
10. What is the author's point of view in the passage?
   A. The most expensive movies are the best movies.
   B. Computer-generated effects always look more realistic than non-digital effects.
   C. Non-digital effects are usually more realistic than computer-generated effects.
   D. New technology should replace old techniques.

©Voyager Expanded Learning, Inc. 207

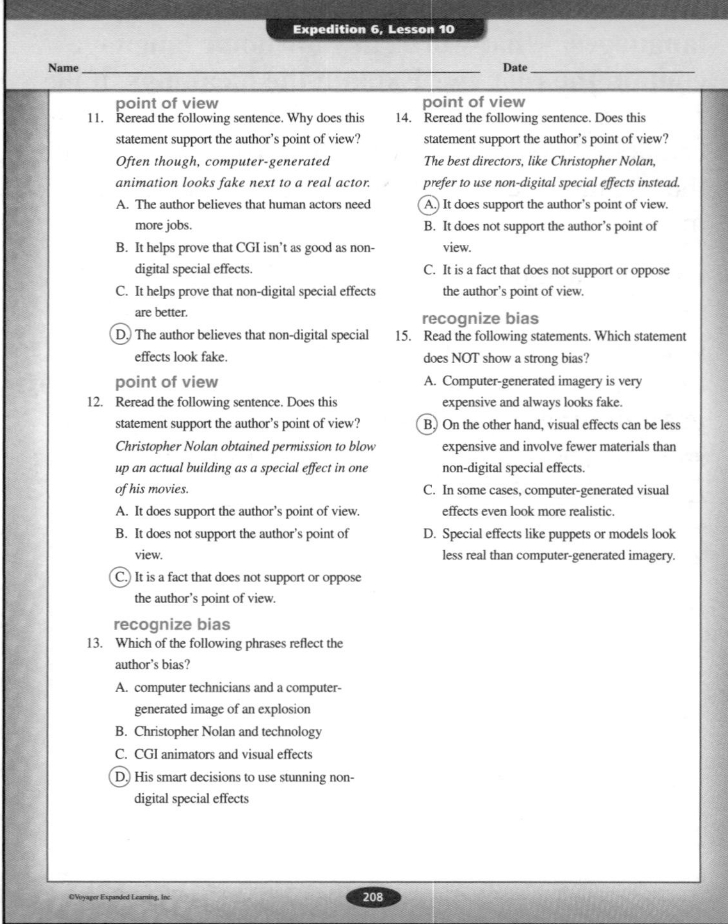

Expedition 6, Lesson 10

Name ____________________ Date ____________

point of view
11. Reread the following sentence. Why does this statement support the author's point of view?
   Often though, computer-generated animation looks fake next to a real actor.
   A. The author believes that human actors need more jobs.
   B. It helps prove that CGI isn't as good as non-digital special effects.
   C. It helps prove that non-digital special effects are better.
   D. The author believes that non-digital special effects look fake.

point of view
12. Reread the following sentence. Does this statement support the author's point of view?
   Christopher Nolan obtained permission to blow up an actual building as a special effect in one of his movies.
   A. It does support the author's point of view.
   B. It does not support the author's point of view.
   C. It is a fact that does not support or oppose the author's point of view.

recognize bias
13. Which of the following phrases reflect the author's bias?
   A. computer technicians and a computer-generated image of an explosion
   B. Christopher Nolan and technology
   C. CGI animators and visual effects
   D. His smart decisions to use stunning non-digital special effects

point of view
14. Reread the following sentence. Does this statement support the author's point of view?
   The best directors, like Christopher Nolan, prefer to use non-digital special effects instead.
   A. It does support the author's point of view.
   B. It does not support the author's point of view.
   C. It is a fact that does not support or oppose the author's point of view.

recognize bias
15. Read the following statements. Which statement does NOT show a strong bias?
   A. Computer-generated imagery is very expensive and always looks fake.
   B. On the other hand, visual effects can be less expensive and involve fewer materials than non-digital special effects.
   C. In some cases, computer-generated visual effects even look more realistic.
   D. Special effects like puppets or models look less real than computer-generated imagery.

©Voyager Expanded Learning, Inc. 208

Reteach

Point of View and Bias

1. Direct students to Student Book pages 209 and 210. Read the instructions aloud. **If you read different articles about the same topic, do the authors have the same opinion?** (Possible response: No, the authors probably have different opinions.) **How can you tell which opinions to agree with?** (Look for the point of view; find different sides of the topic; look for bias; read books on the topic so that you become knowledgeable about the facts.)
2. **As the passage is read aloud, underline positive and negative words in the text. Those words are clues about the author's opinion.** Have volunteers read sentences aloud and other students identify positive and negative words to underline.
3. Have students share their first idea of what the author's point of view is. Then, read aloud the first three questions and have students discuss possible answers. Have students answer the last question independently, compare this answer with one they wrote earlier, then tell how their statements changed after they answered the questions.

ELL Focus on details in the assessment questions to reteach point of view and bias for students who had difficulty with Part B.

- **What words or details in the passage reveal what the author likes or dislikes?**
- **What emotion does the author feel?**
- **What details are near the negative or positive words in the text?**

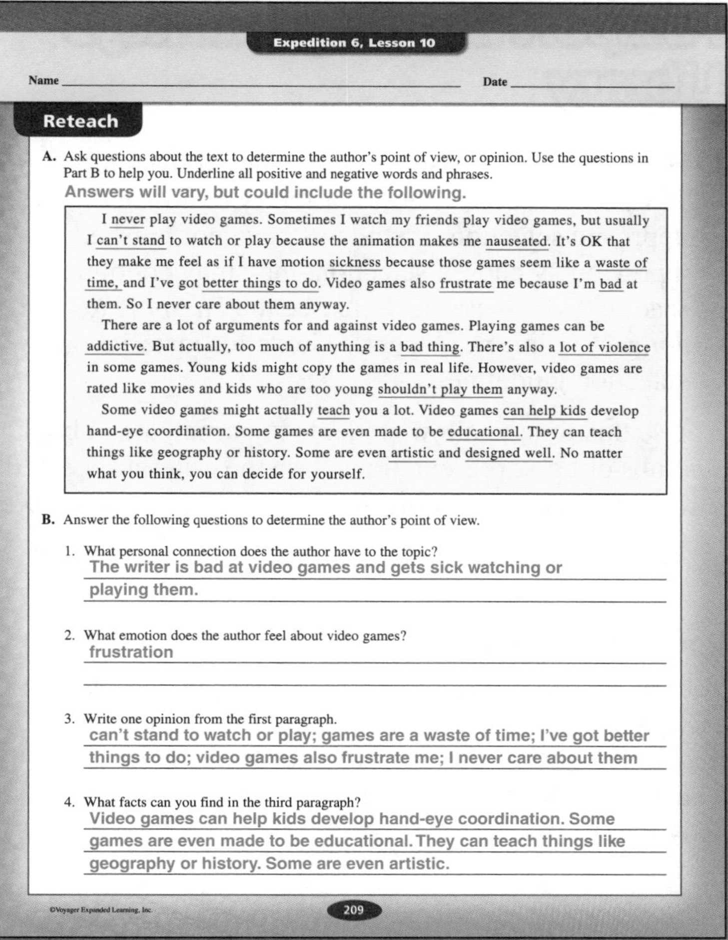

Expedition 6, Lesson 10

Name ______ Date ______

Reteach

A. Ask questions about the text to determine the author's point of view, or opinion. Use the questions in Part B to help you. Underline all positive and negative words and phrases.

Answers will vary, but could include the following.

I never play video games. Sometimes I watch my friends play video games, but usually I can't stand to watch or play because the animation makes me nauseated. It's OK that they make me feel as if I have motion sickness because those games seem like a waste of time, and I've got better things to do. Video games also frustrate me because I'm bad at them. So I never care about them anyway.

There are a lot of arguments for and against video games. Playing games can be addictive. But actually, too much of anything is a bad thing. There's also a lot of violence in some games. Young kids might copy the games in real life. However, video games are rated like movies and kids who are too young shouldn't play them anyway.

Some video games might actually teach you a lot. Video games can help kids develop hand-eye coordination. Some games are even made to be educational. They can teach things like geography or history. Some are even artistic and designed well. No matter what you think, you can decide for yourself.

B. Answer the following questions to determine the author's point of view.

1. What personal connection does the author have to the topic?
The writer is bad at video games and gets sick watching or playing them.
2. What emotion does the author feel about video games?
frustration
3. Write one opinion from the first paragraph.
can't stand to watch or play; games are a waste of time; I've got better things to do; video games also frustrate me; I never care about them
4. What facts can you find in the third paragraph?
Video games can help kids develop hand-eye coordination. Some games are even made to be educational. They can teach things like geography or history. Some are even artistic.

©Voyager Expanded Learning, Inc. 209

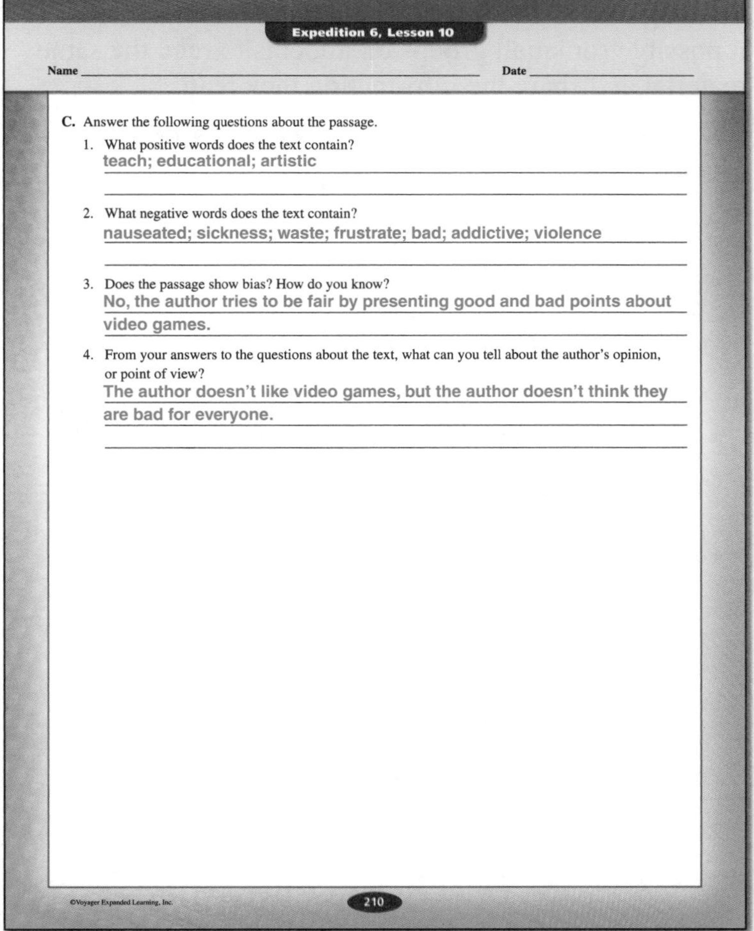

Expedition 6, Lesson 10

Name ______ Date ______

C. Answer the following questions about the passage.

1. What positive words does the text contain?
teach; educational; artistic
2. What negative words does the text contain?
nauseated; sickness; waste; frustrate; bad; addictive; violence
3. Does the passage show bias? How do you know?
No, the author tries to be fair by presenting good and bad points about video games.
4. From your answers to the questions about the text, what can you tell about the author's opinion, or point of view?
The author doesn't like video games, but the author doesn't think they are bad for everyone.

©Voyager Expanded Learning, Inc. 210

Passport Reading Journeys Library

1. Have students choose reading material from the *Passport Reading Journeys* Library or another approved selection. If students have not finished a previously chosen selection, they may continue reading from that selection. See the *Passport Reading Journeys* Library Teacher's Guide for material on selection guidelines.
2. Use this time to allow students to participate in book clubs or book presentations. Use the criteria specified in the *Passport Reading Journeys* Library Teacher's Guide.

Vocabulary Connections

Vocabulary words are listed in the Teacher's Guide for each book. These words are content-related or used frequently in reading material. The selected words can be a basis for independent or small-group discussions and activities.

Student Opportunities

Six copies of each book title are provided in the *Passport Reading Journeys* Library. The number of copies makes it possible for small groups of students to read the same material and share the information they read.

Theme-related titles include *Monster* and *Walk Two Moons*.

Technology

1. Depending on your classroom configuration and computer access, have students work through the technology in a lab setting or have individuals or small groups of students work on desktops or laptops while other students participate in other suggested activities, such as the *Passport Reading Journeys* Library.
2. The online technology component provides additional support for students to work with selected vocabulary words. Students will work through a series of activities to strengthen their word knowledge, then apply that knowledge to passage reading. Refer to the online technology component User Guide for more information.

   Theme-related word sets include Math and Technology.

Expedition Project

Graffiti Debate

You have learned to recognize point of view and bias. In your written persuasive arguments, you explained your opinion or point of view. Now, you will use those ideas in an oral debate. Distribute Project Blackline Master page 12. Have students look at the page and follow along as you explain the assignment. Assign point values, and have students write them in the rubric. Tell them to make any notes on the page that will help them, but they will turn in the page with the assignment. Have students form groups of four and follow these steps:

1. Have each group split into two sides: Team A and Team B with two students in each team. Team A will present the argument that graffiti is art. Team B will present graffiti is vandalism. Students may review their prewriting charts from their persuasive arguments.

   For students to have a meaningful experience completing tasks as a group, certain strategies should be employed. Group dynamics and interactions can be improved with strategic planning for group work. Refer to page xxxvi for information on effective grouping strategies.

2. Have students preplan a dialogue for a debate that includes each group member. Teams will take turns replying to opposing arguments and giving further arguments for their claims.

3. Debate dialogues should resemble the following format.

   Team A, Student 1: Make argument that graffiti is art.

   Team B, Student 1: Make argument for opposing the claim that graffiti is art; make a new argument why graffiti is vandalism.

   Team A, Student 2: Refute opposing opinion; make new argument.

   Team B, Student 2: Refute that opposing opinion; make new argument.

   The number of dialogue lines may vary.

4. Student presentations should fit these criteria:
   - Well-developed arguments for the main opinions
   - Direct responses to opposing opinions
   - Organized delivery; includes facts and opinions and logical arguments

5. Rehearse presentations. Each group member should have a copy of the debate dialogue.

6. Present debates. Two members of the group should follow up the debate with an evaluation as to which side presented the strongest case.

7. **I will assess your debates based on the rubric on your page.** To assess student debates, use the rubric from the Project Blackline Master.

Real-World Reading

Movie Reviews

1. Direct students to Student Book pages 211 and 212. **You will read movie reviews. Do you ever read movie reviews in the newspaper or online to decide which movies you would like to see?** Have students preview the movie reviews by identifying the names of the movies and the film critic.

2. Direct students to read the film reviews.
   - **Underline negative and positive words. Put a plus sign above positive words and a minus sign above negative words.**
   - **Put a star next to the titles of the movies the critic recommends. Put an *X* next to the titles of the movies the critic does not recommend.**
   - **Circle movies you would be interested in watching. Your opinion does not have to match the film critic's opinion.**

3. Have students read and place a check mark by the following words. Then, have them write the meanings in the margins. Clarify their understanding as needed:
   - ***Residential* means "characterized by residences, whether houses or apartment buildings."**
   - ***Antidote* means "a substance that works against something that caused bad effects."**
   - ***Accomplished* means "highly skilled."**
   - ***Proverbial* means "relating to a proverb, or old familiar saying."**

4. **If you read these movie reviews online, which movie would you choose to see on Friday night? Do you believe all the opinions of the film critic? Explain.**

Expedition 6, Lesson 10

Name ____________________ Date __________

Real World—Movie Reviews

R.D. Jameison, Film Critic

At the Movies

The Cellar X

This is the third—and worst—in the series of movies written by P.F. Hill. Charlie Dock suffers from a dual personality about as original as Dr. Jekyll and Mr. Hyde. The plot is an unbelievable series of events that fails to develop the slightest bit of suspense. Moreover, unexpected and unnecessary violence abounds. Reg Flint falls into the cellar, ripping his arm off on the metal trap door. On a safe, residential street, Clara Gregory gets knifed in the stomach. With the unrealistic (I mean inexistent) plot, the only antidote to dullness is the fine actress Jessica Lawn. She portrays Tessie Finkel rather nicely. Otherwise, *The Cellar* remains totally in the cellar.

Taking Chances ★

This romantic comedy is worth the money. The plot turns on a series of miscommunications and mistaken identities. Young Erik Lee and Alexis Trueben find each other. They break up and find each other again. Though the plot is classical romantic comedy, the twists are cleverly done. The dialogue is human yet humorous, and every conversation is surprising. Clark Statton plays an exceptional Lee, delivering his witty lines with visible ease. Laura Back bubbles as the lovely but sometimes perplexed Trueben. I recommend that you take a chance on this superb film.

Super Vacuum X

The title of this new science-fiction movie says it all—empty, empty, empty. Space explorers Van and Dora Jones, along with their bumbling team, encounter a super vacuum in space. This weird and totally unbelievable phenomenon is controlled by an alien life-form. The aliens' plan is to rip apart the galaxy by planting super vacuums throughout space. Actors Brad Yolan and Melissa Marks have damaged their careers by playing Van and Dora. A disastrously boring plot, coupled with no character development and plenty of useless action, made me wish the super vacuum would just suck up everyone in the movie. Then we could leave the theatre as soon as possible.

The Hidden Door ★

What happens when a door that you can't find is guarded by dragons you can't see, yet the door holds a secret vital to your survival? You get the entertaining fantasy movie, *The Hidden Door*. Maya Truth is played excellently by accomplished actress Melody Sanchez. She is the mysterious and beautiful woman who can help Adi Ino, the hero. Ino will find the hidden door, but only if he is clever enough to gain Truth's respect by trusting the incredible things she says. Luke Tonto portrays Ino as an innocent young warrior coming of age. Ino is the warrior who must give up fighting to win the real prize. When you step behind the hidden door with Truth and Ino, you will be amazed at what you find.

211

Expedition 6, Lesson 10

Name ____________________ Date __________

Real World—Movie Reviews

Goss Manor ★

This Victorian romance has a stellar cast. Gary Wu portrays the dark, mysterious Roderick Marshall. Petra Boland plays the beautiful, independent Jane Harding. Harding's possessive relatives make her life a proverbial misery. While Harding loves Marshall, she is forced by her father into a loveless marriage with Willard Cookson. In the dark Victorian manor house, people disappear for months at a time. Throughout the movie, finances and fortunes change, and Harding finds herself rejected and alone. Will she ever learn what became of Marshall? The answer lies hidden in *Goss Manor*.

1. If you read these movie reviews online, which movie would you choose to see on Friday night?
   Answers will vary.

2. Do you believe all the opinions of the film critic? Explain.

212

Exploring Careers

Graphic Artist

1. Direct students to Anthology page 113. Have students preview the title and type of passage. **What do you think this article will be about?** (a career as a graphic artist) **What kinds of things do you think a graphic artist might design or illustrate?** List responses on the board. If needed, name printed things students might see every day, such as ads, newspapers, packaging, and labels.
2. Have students read the article. **As you read, note any skills or characteristics that might describe you. Also, notice tools you would like to learn to use.**
3. Direct students to Student Book page 213. **Use the passage to answer the questions, then complete the chart by researching careers in books or online.**

Expedition 6, Lesson 10

Name ____________________ Date ____________

Exploring Careers: Graphic Artist

A. Answer the following questions about a career as a graphic artist.

1. What are three different businesses or groups that need graphic artists?
   advertising agency; magazine publisher; nonprofit organization; many large businesses
2. Where do a graphic artist's designs appear? Name three items or products.
   posters; book illustrations; magazine layouts; covers of books
3. Why does a graphic artist need to be interested in new ideas?
   Concepts and styles can be different for each project; technology changes.
4. What education do most graphic artists have?
   degree from a four-year college or a two- to three-year design school
5. What other training is helpful for a graphic artist?
   training in design technology; training in computer graphics; training in design software

B. Use the Internet to research other possible career choices in this field and complete the chart.

Career	
Responsibilities	
Education Required	
Average Salary	
Is this a career you might pursue?	
Why or why not?	
Career	
Responsibilities	
Education Required	
Average Salary	
Is this a career you might pursue?	
Why or why not?	

 213

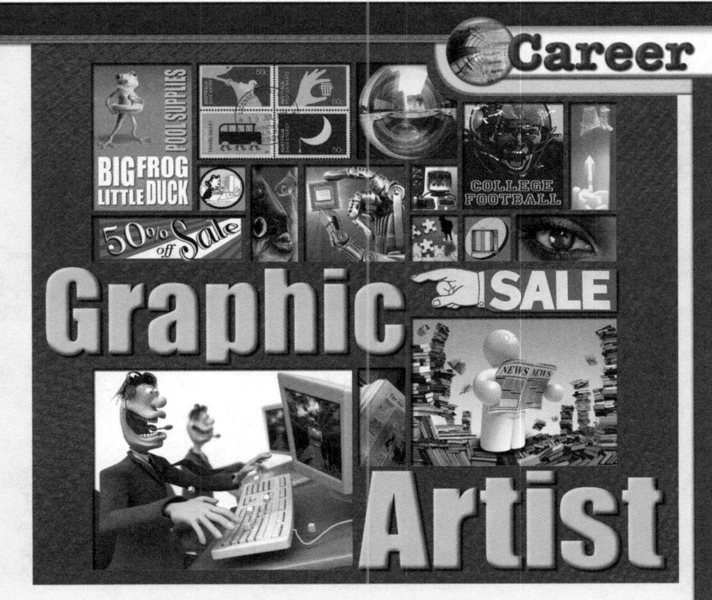

Design Your Own Career

When your brother asks you for directions to the mall, you draw a map. Your random sketches and doodles really impress your friends. As you whiz around buildings in a video game, trying to find and destroy the enemy, you wish the graphics were more varied and realistic. These are examples of skills and interests in art and design that could be applied to the job of a graphic artist. You would find the career competitive, challenging, and personally rewarding.

Graphic artists, or graphic designers, work for many groups, either alone or with a team. They may design for businesses, Internet companies, nonprofit organizations, or the government. They may work for printers as well as publishers of newspapers, magazines, and books. Some artists are hired to work full-time in-house, or at an office. They may participate in a team that creates designs. Others are freelance designers, meaning they are self-employed and often work from home. Representing themselves, they seek out contracts for work. This freedom enables them to select the types of projects they are skilled at and find enjoyable. A few graphic artists work entirely for themselves. They may, for example, create graphic novels, animate cartoons, or design multimedia shows.

Now You See It  113

Career

Graphic artists at work "in-house." They work for a company at its office.

Graphic artists are the people who create visual images to communicate ideas. As a designer, you would use varying forms of media for your work. You might produce print materials such as posters, logos, and pamphlets for an advertising campaign, or sketch the illustrations for a children's book. For a textbook publisher, you might draw tables, maps, and graphs. You might lay out the photos and information for magazine pages, or create computer-generated art or edit photos for a calendar. Think of the art you see on Web sites, on a video or DVD, on television, and so on. A graphic artist designed that art.

If you were a graphic artist, you would create images that inspire the trust of your client and spark the interest of the target audience. Your ideas would have to be presented with a keen sense of design. Your knowledge of color theory and typography—the type of lettering—would help. Moreover, you would need to communicate verbally to understand what clients want and to explain what you can do. Your willingness to incorporate others' ideas would show in your sketches and finished art. You would use problem solving to get your ideas to mesh with the job's requirements. And, you would apply technical skills related to the media you work in.

A graphic artist also needs to be open to change. The artist reforms concepts and styles as jobs or consumers change. You may have been creating advertising for a huge automobile manufacturer. Suddenly, you are called on to design a Web site for a company that sells an automobile with a low impact on the environment. You might have been designing brochures for a fishing company. Next, you are planning a multimedia show for a nonprofit group. If you work in technological design, you could be asked to create an entirely modern cellular phone. If you work in industrial design, you may be hired to draw a plan for a better chair.

Education and Salary

A graphic designer is educated in the terms and technology necessary for the job. The designer studies common design practices and many graphic styles and forms. Most companies require a degree from a four-year college or a two- to three-year design school. Computer graphics and design software knowledge are essential. And, the designer must stay on top of technological advances. Most beginning designers receive on-the-job training. Some achieve higher levels in companies, becoming team leaders or managers. Some teach design at schools and colleges. Average annual salaries for graphic artists in 2008 ranged from $35,000 to $45,000.

Or, maybe this really is your dream job: You are sitting at a computer, and instead of hunting for the enemy, you are creating the background in which an exciting new video game takes place. If you train to be a graphic artist, this dream could become reality.

114 Expedition 6

Across Cultures

"Rats Rule!"

Lesson 1

Introduce the Expedition
Discuss probing questions.

Before Reading
- Introduce vocabulary.
- Introduce and practice comparing and contrasting.

During Reading
Read "Rats Rule!"

After Reading
Check comprehension.

Have students practice vocabulary using the online technology component.

Have students select books for independent reading.

ELL Extend and practice.

Lesson 2

Prepare to Reread
- Review and practice using passage vocabulary.
- Practice using context clues.
- Build new words using roots.

Reread
- Review and practice comparing and contrasting.
- Write a travel brochure and journal entries.

ELL Extend and practice.

"Adventures in Eating"

Lesson 3

Before Reading
- Introduce and practice using passage vocabulary.
- Review and practice comparing and contrasting.
- Introduce the passage by previewing and making predictions.

During Reading
Read "Adventures in Eating."

After Reading
Check comprehension.

Have students practice vocabulary using the online technology component.

Have students select books for independent reading.

ELL Extend and practice.

Lesson 4

Prepare to Reread
- Review and practice using passage vocabulary.
- Practice using context clues.
- Build new words using synonyms and antonyms.

Reread
- Review and practice comparing and contrasting.
- Write a description of peculiar foods.

ELL Extend and practice.

Lesson 5—Review, Extend, Assess

Review Vocabulary
Review and practice using passage vocabulary.

Extend Vocabulary
Use root words to build and understand new words.

Assess Comprehension and Vocabulary
Assess student understanding of vocabulary and comparing and contrasting.

Reteach
Have students complete activity pages for reteaching comparing and contrasting.

Passport Reading Journeys Library
Have students select books for independent reading.

Technology
Have students practice vocabulary using the online technology component.

Writing Process
Have students use the writing process to write about a cultural experience.

Real-World Reading
Have students read and complete a job application.

Exploring Careers
Have students read about being a chef and complete an activity page.

Teacher's Note
Before beginning the Expedition, ask your librarian to suggest books that will fit with the theme. Books relating to cultural traditions, travel, feeling strange because of your family, and learning a language will be appropriate for this Expedition.

"The Multicultural Search for Beauty"

Lesson 6

Before Reading
- Introduce and practice using passage vocabulary.
- Practice comparing and contrasting.
- Introduce the passage by previewing and making predictions.

During Reading
Read "The Multicultural Search for Beauty."

After Reading
Check comprehension.

Have students practice vocabulary using the online technology component.

Have students select books for independent reading.

ELL Extend and practice.

Lesson 7

Prepare to Reread
- Review and practice using passage vocabulary.
- Practice using context clues.
- Build new words using roots.

Reread
- Review and practice comparing and contrasting.
- Write a persuasive argument.

ELL Extend and practice.

"A Big Mac for Everyone?"

Lesson 8

Before Reading
- Introduce and practice using passage vocabulary.
- Review taking Big Picture notes.
- Introduce the passage by previewing and making predictions.

During Reading
Read "A Big Mac for Everyone?"

After Reading
Check comprehension.

Have students practice vocabulary using the online technology component.

Have students select books for independent reading.

ELL Extend and practice.

Lesson 9

Prepare to Reread
- Review and practice using passage vocabulary.
- Practice using context clues.
- Build new words using multiple meanings and roots.

Reread
- Practice taking Big Picture notes.
- Write journal entries.

ELL Extend and practice.

Lesson 10—Review, Extend, Assess

Review Vocabulary
Review and practice using passage vocabulary.

Extend Vocabulary
Use root words to build and understand new words.

Assess Comprehension and Vocabulary
Assess student understanding of vocabulary and comparing and contrasting.

Reteach
Have students complete activity pages for reteaching comparing and contrasting.

Passport Reading Journeys Library
Have students select books for independent reading.

Technology
Have students practice vocabulary using the online technology component.

Expedition Project
Have students research and prepare for a folktale presentation.

Real-World Reading
Have students read an airplane travel sign and complete instructions.

Exploring Careers
Have students read about a career in film and complete an activity page.

Expedition 7

Introduce the Expedition

1. Have students preview the photographs throughout the Expedition. Write the following on the board: *culture—a way of life, ideas, customs, and traditions specific to a group of people*. **What activities, or interests, are universal?** (Many people wear makeup and jewelry, cook food, practice religions, play games, and listen to music.) Record student responses on the board.
2. Discuss the following probing questions. Explain that the questions will guide what students will learn in this Expedition.
   - **What cultural practices seem strange to you?**
   - **What does your culture eat or do that other people might see as strange?**
   - **What ideas of nutrition, beauty, and worship do you have that are shared by people in other places?**

   To make the most of the discussion time, remember to incorporate strategies that encourage and extend student involvement. Refer to page xxxviii for a comprehensive discussion of these strategies.

Build Background DVD 7.1
Tell students they will view a brief DVD that provides background information about cultures across the world. **As you watch, listen for ideas that connect to the questions we discussed.**

3. Point out the parts of the Expedition 7 Organizer for Across Cultures on Student Book pages 214 and 215. **You will use this organizer to write your own ideas and questions about the passages you read in this Expedition.**

   Suggestions for how students can add ideas to these pages appear in this Teacher's Edition at the end of Lessons 2, 4, 7, and 9. Allow students to write initial responses in the probing questions graphic organizer in Part A.

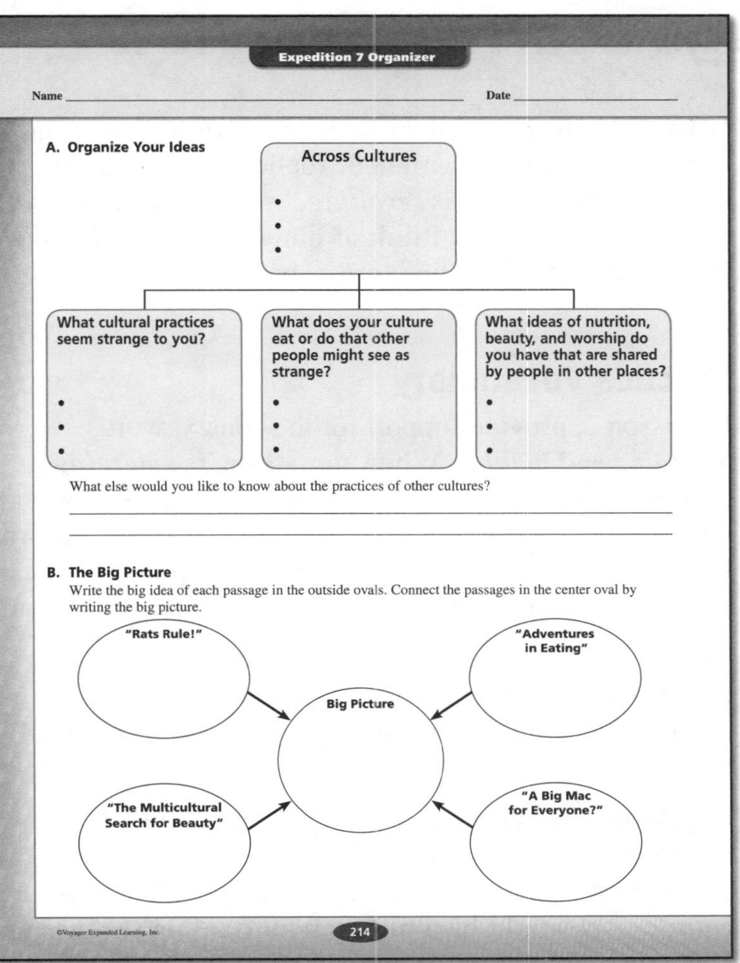

Expedition 7 Organizer

Name ______________________ Date ____________

A. Organize Your Ideas

Across Cultures
-
-
-

What cultural practices seem strange to you?
-
-
-

What does your culture eat or do that other people might see as strange?
-
-
-

What ideas of nutrition, beauty, and worship do you have that are shared by people in other places?
-
-
-

What else would you like to know about the practices of other cultures?

____

____

B. The Big Picture

Write the big idea of each passage in the outside ovals. Connect the passages in the center oval by writing the big picture.

©Voyager Expanded Learning, Inc. 214

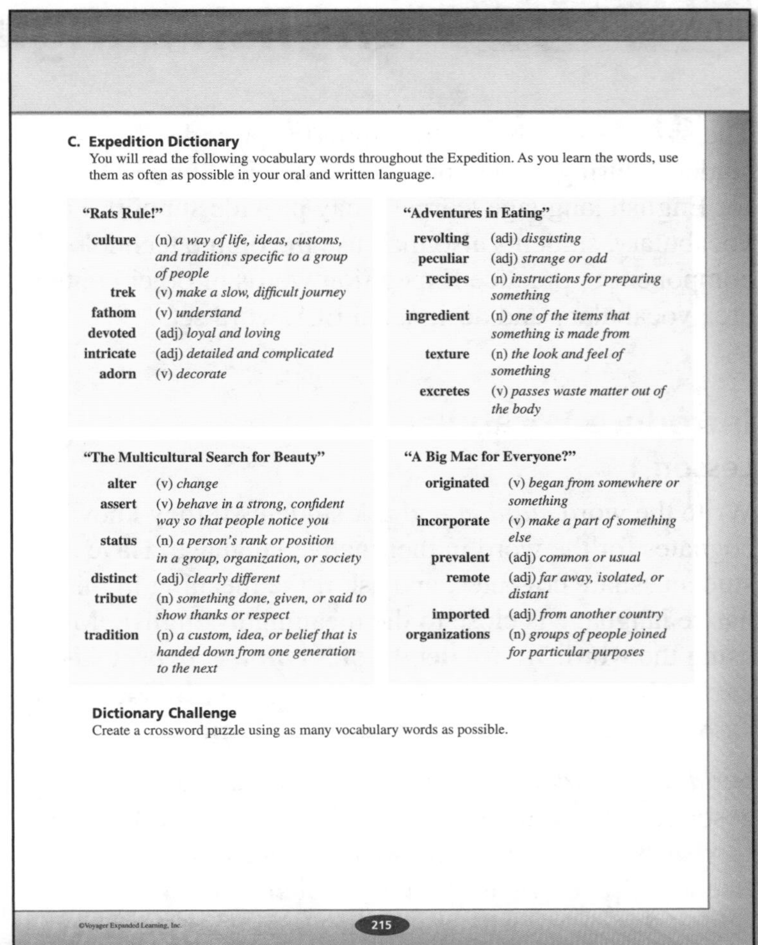

C. Expedition Dictionary

You will read the following vocabulary words throughout the Expedition. As you learn the words, use them as often as possible in your oral and written language.

"Rats Rule!"

culture	(n) *a way of life, ideas, customs, and traditions specific to a group of people*
trek	(v) *make a slow, difficult journey*
fathom	(v) *understand*
devoted	(adj) *loyal and loving*
intricate	(adj) *detailed and complicated*
adorn	(v) *decorate*

"Adventures in Eating"

revolting	(adj) *disgusting*
peculiar	(adj) *strange or odd*
recipes	(n) *instructions for preparing something*
ingredient	(n) *one of the items that something is made from*
texture	(n) *the look and feel of something*
excretes	(v) *passes waste matter out of the body*

"The Multicultural Search for Beauty"

alter	(v) *change*
assert	(v) *behave in a strong, confident way so that people notice you*
status	(n) *a person's rank or position in a group, organization, or society*
distinct	(adj) *clearly different*
tribute	(n) *something done, given, or said to show thanks or respect*
tradition	(n) *a custom, idea, or belief that is handed down from one generation to the next*

"A Big Mac for Everyone?"

originated	(v) *began from somewhere or something*
incorporate	(v) *make a part of something else*
prevalent	(adj) *common or usual*
remote	(adj) *far away, isolated, or distant*
imported	(adj) *from another country*
organizations	(n) *groups of people joined for particular purposes*

Dictionary Challenge

Create a crossword puzzle using as many vocabulary words as possible.

©Voyager Expanded Learning, Inc. 215

ELL

Making Connections

Expedition 7 invites students to compare and contrast their culture with other cultures. The passages, probing questions, and discussion prompts offer rich opportunities for English language learners to share information about their native culture. However, students may feel uncomfortable discussing their background in ways that set them apart from other students.

Phrase questions in a way that allows students to talk about their own experiences or the experiences of someone they know or have heard of.

- Encourage students to discuss similarities between cultures as well as differences.
- Avoid generalizations about nations and cultures, pointing out that the passages describe the way *some* members eat, dress, or think, but not *all*, and that customs among regions within countries may vary widely.

Students may need more background information to understand Karni Mata's temple in the first passage. Explain that a temple is a religious building. Preview the vocabulary word *trek*. Write the definition on the board, and tell students that some people *trek* to temples or other religious sites as part of their worship. If possible, draw a building and a road leading to it with arrows indicating the direction of a trek. Tell students that in English the word *pilgrimage* has the sense of "religious trek" or "religious journey." Encourage students to share prior knowledge about religious treks or other types of journeys.

When you discuss the Karni Mata temple, model your own reaction to the idea of rats in a religious building: **I have heard of temples, but I have never heard of a temple with rats in it. What do we usually think of being in a temple?** Without judging the Karni Mata temple, let students know it is natural to be surprised by it.

Continue this process as you read the other passages. Return frequently to the first and second probing questions, allowing students to share their ideas and feelings but also to consider the ideas and feelings of others.

English Language Learner Overview

The signals when extra support is provided for students during the lesson. As needed, Blackline Masters for English language learners may provide support. For vocabulary, students also may use the online technology component to practice Expedition words or other content-area vocabulary and designated ELL word sets.

Introduce Vocabulary

Lesson 1

Write the word *culture*, and ask students if they know cognates for the word in their native language. Have students share cognates, and ask if the meaning in their native language is close to the meaning in English. Model using the word: **In my neighbor's *culture*, people kiss each other on both cheeks when they say hello. In my *culture*, it is more common to shake hands.**

For *devoted*, *adorn*, and *trek*, use familiar examples and gestures to teach the meaning. **My *devoted* brother came to visit me every day when I was sick. Would a *devoted* friend help you if you had a problem? Before the school dance, we will *adorn* the room with streamers and balloons. How will you *adorn* yourself before the school dance? The store near my house was closed, so I had to *trek* all the way across town to another store. If you were going somewhere in a car and it broke down, where might you have to *trek*?**

Use *intricate* with the antonym *simple*, and use or draw examples to teach the meaning. **The first pattern is very simple, but the second pattern is *intricate*. I could play the simple piece of music, but I had trouble playing the *intricate* piece.**

Lesson 3

Have students name the two vocabulary words that are adjectives. Write the words *revolting* and *peculiar* as students say them. If students have difficulty identifying the adjectives, remind them to look at the part of speech listed in the definition.

Remind students that an adjective is a word that describes a noun. **If I say, "Katie has a big dog," what's the adjective in my sentence?** (big) **If I say, "Katie has a *peculiar* dog," what's the adjective?** (peculiar) **What is Katie's dog like if it is a *peculiar* dog?** (strange or odd) **If I say, "I think blood sausage is delicious," what's the adjective in my sentence?** (delicious) **If I say, "I think blood sausage is *revolting*," what's the adjective?** (revolting) **What do I think of blood sausage if I think it's *revolting*?** (disgusting; gross; bad-tasting)

Practice Vocabulary

In Lesson 2, provide support for the context words *emerging* and *inhabit*. **When something is *emerging*, it is coming forth or out from inside a place. I saw a man *emerging* from the school library this morning. He was leaving the library. When you are *emerging* from a car, are you getting into the car or getting out?** (getting out)

When you *inhabit* a place, you live there. I *inhabit* a neighborhood a few miles away from this school. Birds *inhabit* the trees near my house. What kinds of animals *inhabit* the ocean? (fish; whales)

In Lesson 4, provide support for the context word *counterpart*. **If something has a *counterpart*, it has something similar to it in another place. My German *counterpart* would be a high school reading teacher in Germany. What kind of person in Germany could be your *counterpart*?** (a German high school student)

Apply the Target Skill: Compare and Contrast

Students may be unfamiliar with the graphic organizers used to compare and contrast in Lessons 1–5. Blackline Master page 39 offers additional practice making a T-chart. To model creating a Venn diagram, compare and contrast soccer and U.S. football. Have students supply information as you write. In the overlapping section, write that both games use a ball, are played on a grass field, and involve scoring points. In the nonoverlapping sections, list the distinct qualities of each sport.

Rats! In the sewers, in the Dumpsters, and in the streets, rats feed on the leftover food and scraps of humans. They dwell in the filthiest places imaginable. Few creatures in the animal kingdom have a more negative image than the rat. Around the world, rats are seen as revolting, vicious, unclean animals that damage food supplies and spread deadly diseases. However, some people actually keep rats as pets. What's more, the view of rats varies from **culture** to culture more than you might think.

Span the globe and you'll find cultures in Southeast Asia, Australia, and Africa that eat rats as part of their daily diet. In China, the rat is the first of 12 animals in the zodiac. People born in the Year of the Rat are thought to possess such admirable qualities as creativity, honesty, and generosity. 1

Of all the different ideas about rats, however, one of the most unusual is found in northwest India at the Karni Mata temple. Throughout the year, worshippers **trek** to this 600-year-old temple to show their devotion and pay their respects to its holy residents—20,000 brown rats!

Vocabulary
culture (n) *a way of life, ideas, customs, and traditions specific to a group of people*

1 Make Connections
Have you ever seen a menu in a Chinese restaurant with the signs of the zodiac? What other animals are represented?

Rats scrounging the sewers for food

Durga, the Hindu goddess of power and victory

The Legend of Karni Mata

Why on earth would anyone want to worship rats? To **fathom** the answer, you must first know the story of Karni Mata, the Hindu mystic. Born in the 14th century, Karni was believed to be the reincarnation of Durga, the goddess of power and victory. From a young age, this reborn goddess performed many miraculous, or unexplainable, healings, which earned her a **devoted** flock of followers.

As the legend goes, one day a child of one of her tribesmen drowned. When Karni attempted to revive the child, Yama, the god of death, informed her that the child had already been reincarnated. She was too late, so she made a deal with Yama and rats began emerging, or coming forth, from her small sanctuary. Word of the event spread near and far—Karni had made a deal with Yama. From that day forward, Karni's tribespeople would be reborn as rats until they could be born back into the tribe as humans. "Karni's rats" have been treated like royalty ever since.

A Temple for Rats

In the early 1900s, a local ruler named Maharaja Ganga Singh constructed the temple as a tribute to Karni Mata. He generously donated huge silver gates and **intricate** marble panels. Silver and gold ornaments **adorn** the interior walls of the structure. In the inner temple is a small shrine that many believe Karni Mata made herself, some 600 years ago. Today, the temple is one of India's most famous religious sites. 2

Rats are treated like royalty at the Karni Mata temple in India.

Royal Rodents

The temple's rats are known as *kabas*, and they rule like kings and queens! Priests set bowls of milk and water around the temple, and

Vocabulary
trek (v) *make a slow, difficult journey*
fathom (v) *understand*
devoted (adj) *loyal and loving*
intricate (adj) *detailed and complicated*
adorn (v) *decorate*

2 Main Idea
What is the main idea of this paragraph?

A baby splashes in the milk set out to feed Karni's rats.

pilgrims who have made the trek to the temple feed the rats sweet treats called *prasad*. Worshippers drink milk and eat food that's been sampled by a rat; it's considered a great blessing.

However, there is one blessing that's very rare: the sighting of a white rat. 3 Of the thousands of rats that inhabit, or live in, the temple there are said to be only about five white ones. They are thought to be especially holy. Seeing one of these rats is considered very lucky because they are believed to be the manifestation of Karni Mata and her family.

The creation of a rat temple may be hard to fathom, especially given the animal's link with disease. But, during the last century, there has never been an outbreak of illness among the devoted pilgrims who have visited, which may be a miracle in itself! The Karni Mata temple is not for the squeamish. But, if you could transform into any animal, you might consider becoming one of the temple's royal residents. After all, few animals live such charmed lives as the followers of the rat goddess. End

3 Ask Questions
Think about what you have read. Could you tell a friend about the rat temple?

Some people believe a sacred white rat could be Karni Mata herself.

"Rats Rule!"

Before Reading

Introduce Vocabulary

1. Have students turn to Part A on Student Book page 216 and scan the boldfaced vocabulary words. Read aloud the six vocabulary words, and have students rate their knowledge of the words in the chart.
2. For each word, read the part of speech, definition, and example sentence. **Check to make sure you know the correct meaning of the words.**
3. For words students were unfamiliar with, have them use the word in a sentence.
4. Read aloud the instructions for Part B. Have students complete the activities independently. Have partners compare answers.

ELL Refer to Blackline Master page 37 to extend vocabulary practice.

Have students use the *Passport Reading Journeys* online technology component to practice and reinforce vocabulary and comprehension skills.

Introduce the Target Skill: Compare and Contrast

1. **As you read, pay attention to similarities and differences between elements of a text. You might compare and contrast people, places, actions, and plots in text. You also can compare and contrast descriptions and ideas.** Write the following on the board:
   - *compare—recognize what is similar, or alike, between two or more things*
   - *contrast—recognize what is different between two or more things*
2. **Signal words such as *like* and *in addition* show comparisons, and *but* and *unlike* show differences.**

Expedition 7, Lesson 1

Name ______ Date ______

Vocabulary

"Rats Rule!"

A. Put a check mark in each row to indicate how well you know each boldfaced word.

	Know This Word	Have Seen This Word	Don't Know This Word
culture (n) *a way of life, ideas, customs, and traditions specific to a group of people* The food they ate and the holidays they celebrated were a part of their *culture*.			
trek (v) *make a slow, difficult journey* People *trek* long distances to spend time with the rats.			
fathom (v) *understand* I can't *fathom* why people would want to travel many miles to eat with rats.			
devoted (adj) *loyal and loving* My *devoted* grandmother has been to the temple to show her loyalty to the goddess.			
intricate (adj) *detailed and complicated* The *intricate* details on the walls are difficult to copy.			
adorn (v) *decorate* He used beautiful artwork to *adorn* the temple walls.			

B. For each underlined word or phrase, choose a word from Part A that is a synonym.

1. I can't understand why anyone would live in the Arctic. fathom
2. I will make a slow and difficult journey through the rain forest. trek
3. The detailed and complicated pattern on the scarf was beautiful. intricate
4. I am fascinated by the way of life, ideas, and customs of the Australian Aborigines. culture
5. Many people decorate their homes with cultural artifacts. adorn
6. My loyal and loving father doesn't miss any of our cultural heritage festivals. devoted

 216

Vocabulary

culture (n) *a way of life, ideas, customs, and traditions specific to a group of people*
The food they ate and the holidays they celebrated were a part of their *culture*.

trek (v) *make a slow, difficult journey*
People *trek* long distances to spend time with the rats.

fathom (v) *understand*
I can't *fathom* why people would want to travel many miles to eat with rats.

devoted (adj) *loyal and loving*
My *devoted* grandmother has been to the temple to show her loyalty to the goddess.

intricate (adj) *detailed and complicated*
The *intricate* details on the walls are difficult to copy.

adorn (v) *decorate*
He used beautiful artwork to *adorn* the temple walls.

3. Have students think of two music groups and describe how they are the same. **When you describe similarities, you compare.** List the groups and student responses on the board. **When you describe differences, you contrast things.** Have students describe the differences. As students respond, write signal words they use on the board. **We often compare and contrast many aspects of things like we did with these groups. Which items relate to the bands' appearance? What relates to their style of music? How long have the bands been playing?**
4. Direct students to Student Book page 217. Have students read the instructions and complete the activity. Discuss their responses as a class.

Introduce the Passage

1. **What do you think of rats?** Generate a class discussion about students' image of rats and what they do when they see one.
2. Have students preview "Rats Rule!" and predict what the passage will be about.
3. Remind students to pause and respond to the margin prompts as they read.
4. Teach these terms from the passage:
   - A *mystic* is one who has a personal relationship with the spirit world.
   - *Charmed lives* are lives that seem to be perfect.
   - *Karni Mata* (kär' nē ma' ta)
   - *Maharaja Ganga Singh* (mä hə rä jo gahn jə sing)
   - *kabas* (ka' bas)
   - *prasad* (prə sod')

1. Have students read "Rats Rule!" To select reading options that support your students' levels and classroom needs, see Reading Differentiation, page xxxii, if needed.
2. Instruct students to pay attention to similarities and differences as they read "Rats Rule!"

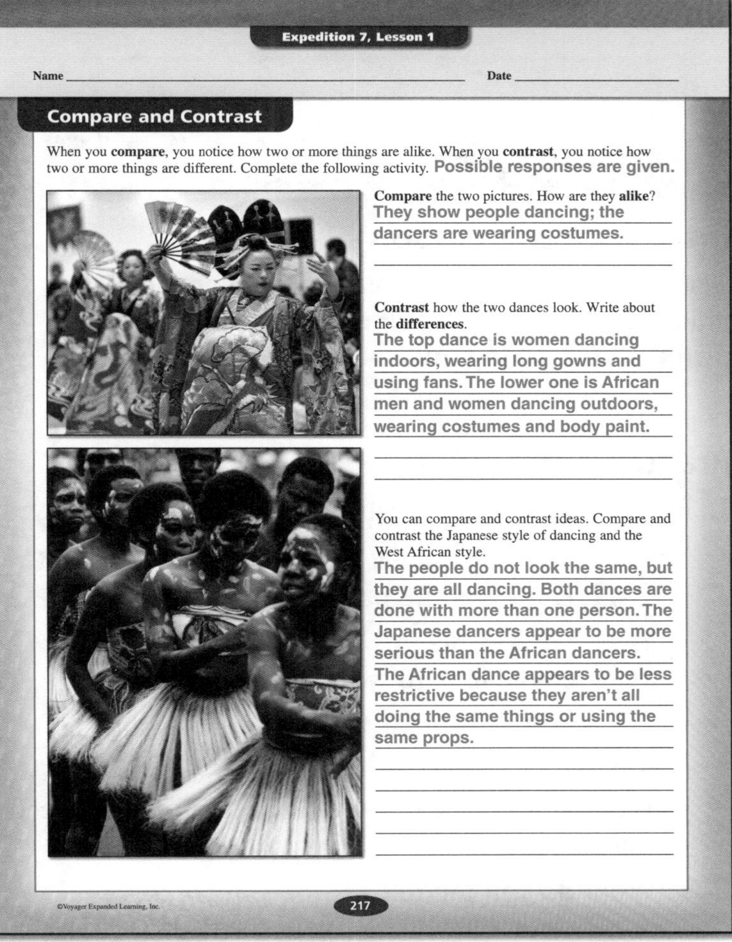

Expedition 7, Lesson 1

Name ______ Date ______

Compare and Contrast

When you **compare**, you notice how two or more things are alike. When you **contrast**, you notice how two or more things are different. Complete the following activity. Possible responses are given.

Compare the two pictures. How are they **alike**?
They show people dancing; the dancers are wearing costumes.

Contrast how the two dances look. Write about the **differences**.
The top dance is women dancing indoors, wearing long gowns and using fans. The lower one is African men and women dancing outdoors, wearing costumes and body paint.

You can compare and contrast ideas. Compare and contrast the Japanese style of dancing and the West African style.
The people do not look the same, but they are all dancing. Both dances are done with more than one person. The Japanese dancers appear to be more serious than the African dancers. The African dance appears to be less restrictive because they aren't all doing the same things or using the same props.

©Voyager Expanded Learning, Inc.

217

Check Comprehension

1. Ask students the following questions:
   - **Who is the rat goddess, and why do people worship her?** (Karni Mata was a Hindu mystic who performed miracles.)
   - **What do people do at her temple?** (feed the rats; share milk and food with the rats)
2. Have students evaluate the predictions they made about this passage.
3. **What do many Americans think of rats?** (gross; dirty) **What do the people who visit the Karni Mata temple think of rats?** (holy; sacred) **Is this is a similar view or a contrasting view?** (contrasting) **Express this with one sentence.** (Many Americans think rats are gross and dirty, but trekkers to the Indian temple worship rats as sacred animals.)

Remind students to choose books from the *Passport Reading Journeys* Library for independent reading.

"Rats Rule!"

Prepare to Reread

Introduce the Lesson

Remind students that they read about a temple for rats in India. **In Lesson 2, we'll revisit the passage and practice comparing and contrasting.**

Practice Vocabulary

1. Remind students of vocabulary words and how they were used in the passage.
   - **What *culture* is the passage about?** (Indian)
   - **Where do people *trek* to visit rats?** (the Karni Mata temple in northwest India)
   - **What seems difficult to *fathom*?** (why anyone would honor rats)
   - **What do *devoted* visitors do at the temple?** (feed and eat with the rats)
   - **What do you picture the *intricate* marble panels look like?** (They have detailed carvings or decorations.)
   - **What things *adorn* the temple?** (silver and gold ornaments)
2. Remind students that they can use context clues to find the meanings of unknown words. Have students turn to Anthology page 117. **What do you think the word *reincarnation* means?** (reborn) **What clues in the text helped you determine the meaning?** (The word *reincarnation* is restated as "reborn.")

   Repeat this process for the following words.
   - **miraculous** (adj) *unexplainable*, Anthology page 117
   - **emerging** (v) *coming forth*, Anthology page 117
   - **donated** (v) *gave generously*, Anthology page 117
   - **pilgrims** (n) *those who travel to visit a holy place*, Anthology page 118
   - **inhabit** (v) *live in*, Anthology page 118

ELL Support students as they use context clues. Use the word *emerging* as you demonstrate how a hand can emerge from a coat sleeve or how a person can emerge from another room.

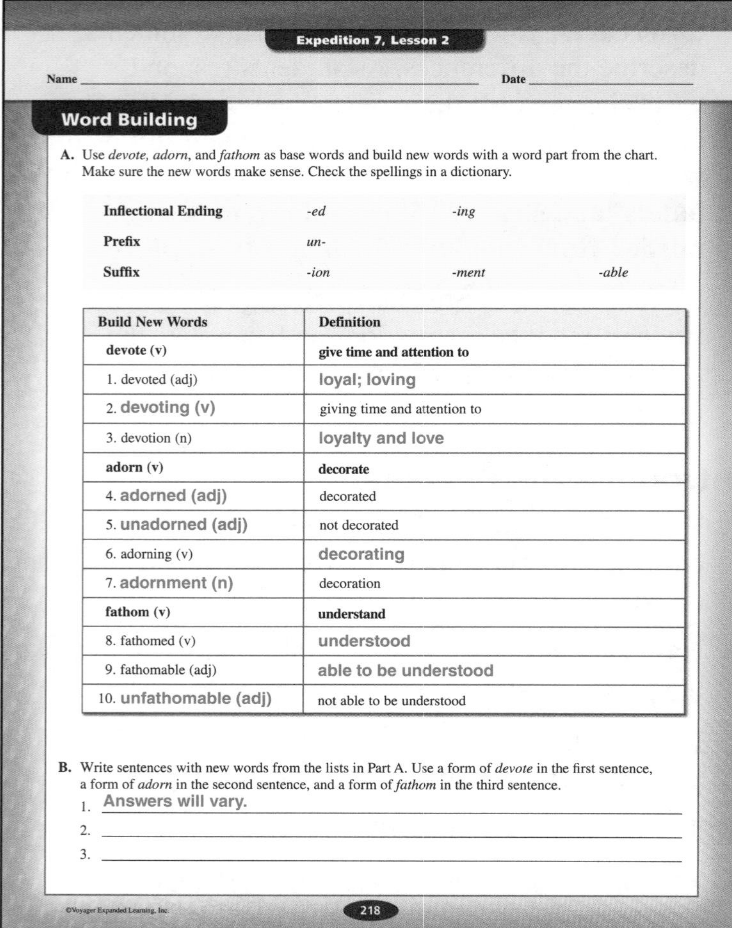

Expedition 7, Lesson 2

Name ______ Date ______

Word Building

A. Use *devote, adorn,* and *fathom* as base words and build new words with a word part from the chart. Make sure the new words make sense. Check the spellings in a dictionary.

Inflectional Ending	*-ed*	*-ing*	
Prefix	*un-*		
Suffix	*-ion*	*-ment*	*-able*

Build New Words	Definition
devote (v)	**give time and attention to**
1. devoted (adj)	loyal; loving
2. devoting (v)	giving time and attention to
3. devotion (n)	loyalty and love
adorn (v)	**decorate**
4. adorned (adj)	decorated
5. unadorned (adj)	not decorated
6. adorning (v)	decorating
7. adornment (n)	decoration
fathom (v)	**understand**
8. fathomed (v)	understood
9. fathomable (adj)	able to be understood
10. unfathomable (adj)	not able to be understood

B. Write sentences with new words from the lists in Part A. Use a form of *devote* in the first sentence, a form of *adorn* in the second sentence, and a form of *fathom* in the third sentence.

1. Answers will vary.
2. ______
3. ______

218

3. Have students turn to Student Book page 218. Read the word parts at the top of the page. Explain that the vocabulary word *devoted* contains the word *devote*. ***Devote*, *adorn*, and *fathom* are base words. You can create new words by adding prefixes, suffixes, and inflectional endings to base words. Words that share the same base word are in the same word family.** Read aloud the instructions, and have students complete the activities.

CHECKPOINT If students have difficulty with Part B, suggest that they check the meanings and spellings of the words in a dictionary.

Reread

Apply the Target Skill: Compare and Contrast

1. **When reading a text, you can compare and contrast descriptions, events, people, places, things, or plots. You can compare and contrast ideas too.**
2. Have students scan the passage and identify things, ideas, or customs and tell why they are the same or different from what they have experienced. Tell students to use signal words as they answer.
3. Have students turn to Student Book page 219. Preview the Venn diagram. **A Venn diagram is a graphic organizer to help you compare and contrast things. Read the labels on each circle, and write facts from the passage. In the center, write how the two items are the same.** Have students complete the activity.

ACADEMIC SKILL Remind students that contrasting can help them in other subjects. Knowing the differences between two things can help them understand each one better.

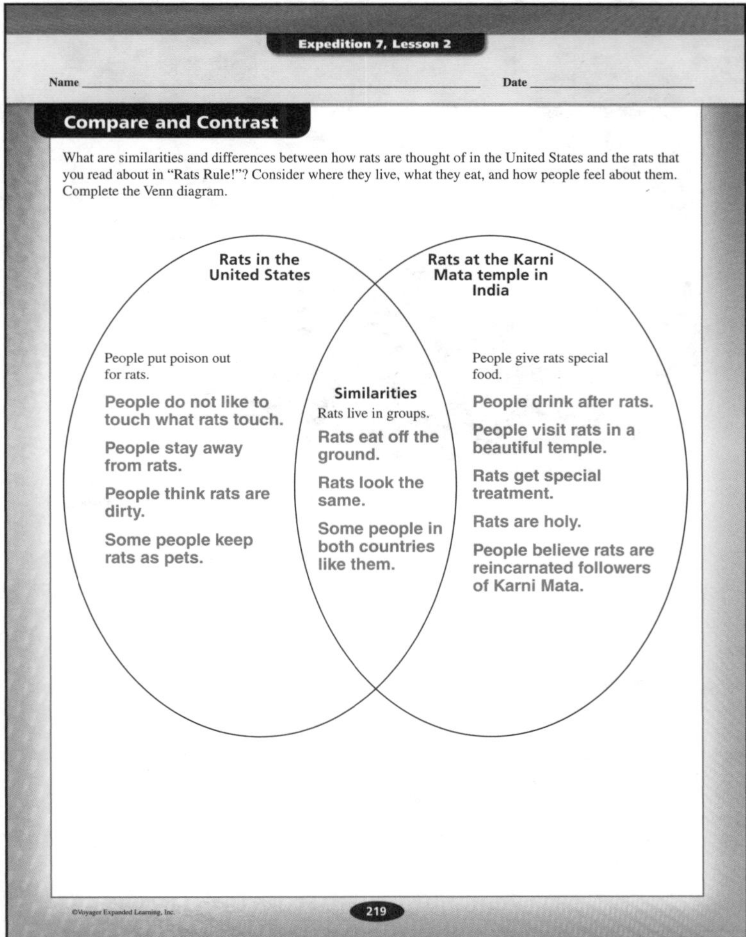

Expedition 7, Lesson 2

Name ______________________ Date ____________

Compare and Contrast

What are similarities and differences between how rats are thought of in the United States and the rats that you read about in "Rats Rule!"? Consider where they live, what they eat, and how people feel about them. Complete the Venn diagram.

©Voyager Expanded Learning, Inc. 219

Write in Response to Reading

1. Prepare students to complete the writing activities on Student Book page 220. Display examples of brochures. **What is the purpose and tone of a tourism brochure?** (Tourism brochures have the purpose of advertising and promoting a place to travel to; the tone is usually excited.) Read aloud the instructions for Part A, and have students complete the activity.
2. **Think of a place that is so important to you that you would travel a long distance to get there.** Read aloud the instructions for Part B. Have students complete the activity independently.

EXPEDITION ORGANIZER **Across Cultures**

Pause to have students turn to Student Book pages 214 and 215. Have students complete the following:

- Write answers to one or more of the probing questions in Part A. Encourage them to write a question of their own.
- Think about the big idea from "Rats Rule!" Tell students to write it in the graphic organizer in Part B.

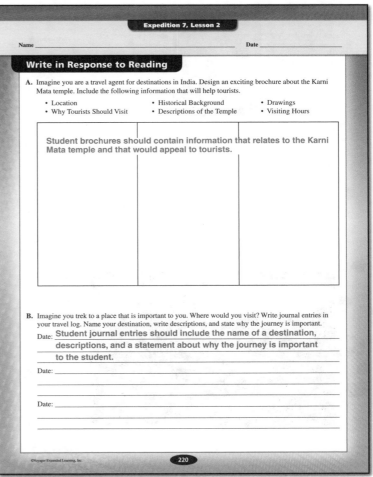

Expedition 7, Lesson 2

Name ______________________ Date ____________

Write in Response to Reading

A. Imagine you are a travel agent for destinations in India. Design an exciting brochure about the Karni Mata temple. Include the following information that will help tourists.

- Location
- Why Tourists Should Visit
- Historical Background
- Descriptions of the Temple
- Drawings
- Visiting Hours

Student brochures should contain information that relates to the Karni Mata temple and that would appeal to tourists.

B. Imagine you trek to a place that is important to you. Where would you visit? Write journal entries in your travel log. Name your destination, write descriptions, and state why the journey is important.

Date: Student journal entries should include the name of a destination, descriptions, and a statement about why the journey is important to the student.

Date: ______________________

Date: ______________________

©Voyager Expanded Learning, Inc. 220

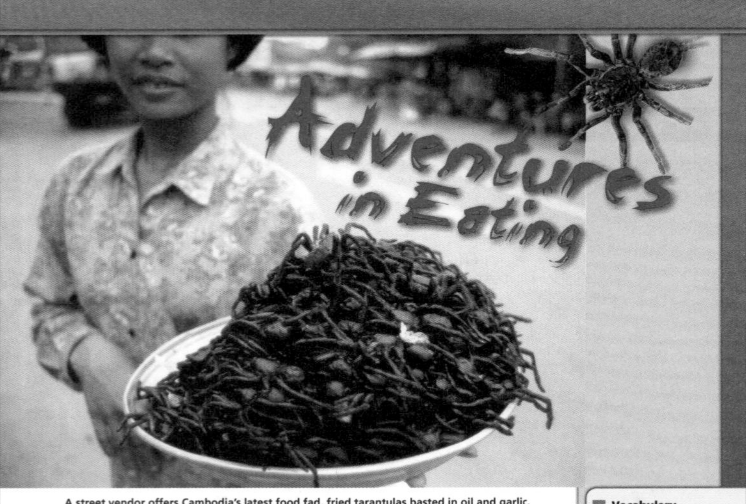

A street vendor offers Cambodia's latest food fad, fried tarantulas basted in oil and garlic.

Vocabulary
revolting (adj) *disgusting*
peculiar (adj) *strange or odd*

Everyone has a favorite food. Whatever yours is, chances are that food would seem pretty strange to some people. Every culture around the world has delicious food, but most cultures also have a few recipes that sound odd or even **revolting** to other people. Fried spiders are favorite snacks in the Cambodian town of Skuon. These spiders are specially bred, or raised, in holes in the ground, and each is about as large as a human hand. Eating iguanas is an ancient tradition for the people of Costa Rica. Fried grasshoppers are popular in Africa, and many cultures enjoy chocolate-covered ants.

You're Eating What?

These foods might sound a little **peculiar** to you. But, some of the strangest foods Americans eat have been around for so long that nobody gives them a second thought. Take cheese, for instance. Many Chinese people do not include milk in their diets. They might find the idea of milk ripened by bacteria, an organism that can sometimes cause disease, rather gross. It may not seem peculiar for you to imagine eating crab legs or lobster tails, but in other parts of the world these foods are disturbing.

Vocabulary
recipes (n) *instructions for preparing something*
ingredient (n) *one of the items that something is made from*

In fact, plenty of dishes in the United States, such as scrapple or head cheese, created out of a pig's head and organs, are positively revolting to people of other cultures.

Fans of Fat

It's not surprising that the food of a culture reflects what is close at hand and what makes the most nutritional sense. For the Inuit, who live in parts of Alaska, Greenland, and Canada, seal and whale blubber have long been an important part of their diet. Plain fat from other animals is also popular in other cultures with cold climates. 1 In the Ukraine, *salo*, or salted pig fat, is eaten raw, smoked, fried, or boiled. 2

1 Context Clues
Using context clues, define *blubber*.

2 Ask Questions
Think about what you read. How are the foods described different from what you eat?

It's in the Blood

Then there's blood. Many cultures around the world include blood in some of their favorite **recipes**. Blood sausage is exactly what it sounds like and is eaten for breakfast in various European countries. It's a sausage made of pigs' blood, fat, and organs and is usually fried. Some places call it blood pudding or black pudding, but it's pretty much the same dish. In Sweden, cooks make blood dumplings out of flour, blood, and salt and serve them with butter and jam. Many Chinese cook with jelled, or firmed, duck or pigs' blood. In the Philippines, a favorite dish is blood stew, which is made with pork and blood. 3

3 Main Idea
Which sentence in this paragraph states the main idea?

The Maasai of Tanzania drink a mixture of cow's blood and milk. Different cultures in Asia and Eastern Europe also include blood soup among their favorite dishes. In Mexico, a special type of soup uses goat's blood as the main **ingredient**. Why blood? It has plenty of iron, and it helps thicken sauces and soups. It is truly a multipurpose food. But, some cultures do not allow blood in their meals. In Jewish and Muslim cultures, religious law forbids people to eat blood. Instead, the preparation of meat must be supervised to make sure that as much blood as possible is removed before cooking.

Making blood sausages after slaughtering a pig at the Wushi Village, China

Heads to Toes

Eating the ribs of a cow or pig is normal in the United States. What other animal body parts are enjoyed around the world? Jellied cow's foot

is a Polish dish that is just what it sounds like: a cow's foot cooked for many hours in water with garlic and spices until it takes on a jellied **texture**. Norwegians have a traditional dish of sheep's head that is often served around Christmas. 4 The head is boiled and all of it is eaten, including the eyes, tongue, and ears. The French counterpart to this dish is called *tête de veau* or "calf's head." The brain is served on a plate with the head. Mexicans also serve brains in a similar dish called *tacos sesos*, or tacos made with cow's brains. A traditional Scottish dish called *haggis* is basically a sausage, except the sausage casing is made from a sheep's stomach. Seal flipper pie is traditionally eaten at Easter in Newfoundland, Canada. What is the secret ingredient? You guessed it: seal flippers!

Raw haggis

Vocabulary
texture (n) *the look and feel of something*

4 Make Connections
What traditional dish does your family serve for special holidays?

An Unusual Nest

Some delicacies around the world are not only unusual, they're extraordinarily expensive. For hundreds of years, Chinese cooks have made a dish called "bird's nest soup." The main ingredient in this recipe is the nest of tiny birds called cave swifts. If you're thinking of a textured structure made of twigs and straw, think again. Cave swifts make nests entirely out of their own spit, which hardens in the air. When combined with water, the hard nests

A man collects nests for bird's nest soup.

Vocabulary
excretes (v) *passes waste matter out of the body*

The Asian Palm Civet plays an important role in making the world's most expensive coffee.

become squishy in texture and a lot like gelatin. Millions of cave swifts' nests are pulled off cave walls each year. Then they are cleaned and sold to restaurants, where they are served as bird's nest soup. The work of pulling the nests off cave walls is extremely dangerous. Because of this, cave swifts' nests are one of the most expensive animal products people can buy. Eating bird spit may seem revolting to you, but people in Hong Kong will pay between 30 and 100 U.S. dollars for a bowl.

Beastly Beverage

People all over the world drink coffee, but Kopi Luwak is the most expensive coffee in the world. Most coffee comes from berries picked from coffee trees. The seeds inside the berries are roasted to make coffee beans. But, Kopi Luwak goes a step further. In Indonesia, the Asian Palm Civet, an animal that looks like a cat, eats coffee berries as part of its diet. Then, it **excretes** the partially digested beans. The excreted beans are washed and lightly roasted. These beans are used to make this incredibly expensive coffee. It is said that the process of going through the Asian Palm Civet's digestive system gives the coffee beans a very peculiar flavor. It's got to be special because people are willing to pay astonishing prices for it. 5

5 Ask Questions
Think about what you read. Ask yourself questions about things you don't understand or things that leave you wondering. For example, how did people discover these foods to be tasty?

The next time you eat a cheese sandwich or a burger and fries, just think—someone across the world who is snacking on fried spiders might think your dinner is really disgusting. End

"Adventures in Eating"

Before Reading

Introduce Vocabulary

1. Have students turn to Part A on Student Book page 221 and scan the boldfaced vocabulary words. **You will find these words in the passage "Adventures in Eating." Words you have seen, heard, or used can help you understand these meanings. Complete Part A.**
2. Read each word, the part of speech, definition, and example sentence. **Be sure you understand the meaning for words you assigned a 1 that you have not read, heard, or used before.**
3. Have students read the instructions for Part B and choose the correct usage for each word.

ELL Refer to Blackline Master page 38 to extend vocabulary practice.

Have students use the *Passport Reading Journeys* online technology component to practice and reinforce vocabulary and comprehension skills.

Apply the Target Skill: Compare and Contrast

1. **A comparison shows how things are alike. A contrast shows how things are different. You can compare and contrast almost anything.** Draw a T-chart on the board with the headings *Taco* and *Hamburger*. **Let's compare a taco and a hamburger. Both can be made with beef.** Write *beef* under both headings. **Now contrast a taco and a hamburger.** Write *served in a shell* below Taco and *served on a bun* below Hamburger. **A hamburger is served on a bun, but a taco is served in a shell.** Have students think of additional comparisons and contrasts, and list them on the chart.

Expedition 7, Lesson 3

Name ______ Date ______

Vocabulary

"Adventures in Eating"

A. Write one or more numbers next to each boldfaced word to show when you have seen, heard, or used this word.

5 I use it in everyday conversation.
4 I heard it on TV or on the radio.
3 I heard or used it in school.
2 I read it in a book, magazine, or online.
1 I have not read, heard, or used this word.

☐ **revolting** (adj) *disgusting*
The *revolting* smell of cooked blood made me sick.

☐ **peculiar** (adj) *strange or odd*
Although they seem normal to me, some American foods are *peculiar* to other people.

☐ **recipes** (n) *instructions for preparing something*
There are several *recipes* for blood pudding, but they all taste similar.

☐ **ingredient** (n) *one of the items that something is made from*
The main *ingredient* in beef stew is beef.

☐ **texture** (n) *the look and feel of something*
The gritty *texture* of the food made it difficult to eat.

☐ **excretes** (v) *passes waste matter out of the body*
Your body uses the vitamins and minerals in food and *excretes* what's left.

B. Read each question, then write the answer on the line.

1. Would a **revolting** smell in a restaurant make you want to stay or leave? leave
2. Would a food seem **peculiar** to you if you eat it every day or have never tasted it before? if you have never tasted it before
3. Would you use **recipes** to find your way to the mall or make blood sausage? make blood sausage
4. Are tomatoes or chocolate the main **ingredient** in salsa? tomatoes
5. Does the **texture** of ice cream make it difficult or easy to eat? easy
6. When an animal **excretes**, is it getting rid of something it doesn't need or hunting for its next meal? getting rid of something it doesn't need

 221

Vocabulary

revolting (adj) *disgusting*
The *revolting* smell of cooked blood made me sick.

peculiar (adj) *strange or odd*
Although they seem normal to me, some American foods are *peculiar* to other people.

recipes (n) *instructions for preparing something*
There are several *recipes* for blood pudding, but they all taste similar.

ingredient (n) *one of the items that something is made from*
The main *ingredient* in beef stew is beef.

texture (n) *the look and feel of something*
The gritty *texture* of the food made it difficult to eat.

excretes (v) *passes waste matter out of the body*
Your body uses the vitamins and minerals in food and *excretes* what's left.

2. Write the following sentences on the board: *Both can be made with beef. A hamburger is served on a bun, but a taco is served in a shell.* Read the sentences aloud. **Notice the words that signal a comparison or a contrast.** Circle the signal words *both* and *but*. ***Both* signals a comparison, or likeness. *But* signals a contrast, or difference.** List additional signal words such as *like*, *as well as*, *similarly*, *unlike*, *on the other hand*, and *although*.

ELL Support academic vocabulary words *compare* and *contrast*. Write *same* next to *compare* and *different* next to *contrast*. Have students tell words for *same* and *different* in their native languages.

Introduce the Passage

1. Have students turn to Anthology page 119 and preview "Adventures in Eating." Have them predict what the passage is about.
2. Point out the margin prompts. **Use the information in the passage and what you already know to address the prompts as you read.**
3. Teach these terms from the passage:
   - *Inuit* (in' yū it)
   - *Ukraine* (yū krān')
   - *Maasai* (mo sī')
   - *Tanzania* (tan' z ə nē ə)
   - *tête de veau*: (tet də vō)
   - *civet* (siv' it)
   - *Give it a second thought* means "to think about it."
   - *Close at hand* means "easy to get or available."

ELL Point out the Context Clues margin prompt on Anthology page 120. Ask for translations of *blubber* in students' native languages.

During Reading

1. Have students read "Adventures in Eating." To select reading options that support your students' levels and classroom needs, see Reading Differentiation, page xxxii, if needed.
2. As students read, have them make a note when they see similarities and differences.

After Reading

Check Comprehension

1. When students finish reading, have them look back at the text to review information. Have students answer the following questions.
   - **What American foods are described as unappealing or strange to other cultures?** (cheese; crab; lobster; head cheese; cow and pig ribs)
   - **How does the climate where people live affect what they eat?** (Cultures eat what is available. For example, people in cold climates eat whales, seals, and pig fat.)
   - **What types of dishes are made with blood? Why do people use blood as an ingredient?** (blood sausage, blood dumplings, blood stew, blood soup; it has iron and helps thicken sauces.)
   - **How is Kopi Luwak coffee made?** (The Asian Palm Civet eats coffee berries and excretes them; the waste is collected, and the beans are washed and roasted.)
2. Direct students' attention to the predictions they wrote about the passage. **Was your prediction correct? Why or why not?**
3. Review the Ask Questions margin prompt on Anthology page 120. ***Contrasts* show how things are different.** Have students share contrasts between U.S. food and food eaten in other countries.
4. Have students share their responses to the Main Idea margin prompt on Anthology page 120. (Many cultures around the world include blood in some of their favorite recipes.)

Remind students to choose books from the *Passport Reading Journeys* Library for independent reading.

"Adventures in Eating"

Prepare to Reread

Introduce the Lesson

Ask students what they think of U.S. foods compared with foods eaten by other cultures. **We will reread "Adventures in Eating" to practice using vocabulary and comparing and contrasting foods from many cultures.**

Practice Vocabulary

1. Recall vocabulary words from the passage and how they were used.
   - **What U.S. food do people from other cultures find *revolting*?** (scrapple or head cheese)
   - **What foods did you find *peculiar*?** (Answers will vary but could include fried spiders, blood sausage, bird's nest soup, or Kopi Luwak.)
   - **Where do you find *recipes* for meals or certain dishes?** (in a cookbook or online)
   - **What *ingredient* is used in a favorite food that you like?** (Answers will vary.)
   - **What do you think a jelled *texture* is like?** (smooth, soft, and wiggly like jelly)
   - **What happens when an animal *excretes* coffee beans?** (Coffee beans come out in its waste.)
2. Remind students that context clues can help them find meanings for unknown words. Have students turn to Anthology page 119. **What does the word *bred* mean?** (raised) **How does the clue in the sentence help you understand the meaning of the word *bred*?** (*Raised* is a synonym for bred.)

   Repeat this process for the following words.
   - **bacteria** (n) *microscopic organism that can cause disease*, Anthology page 119
   - **jelled** (adj) *firm*, Anthology page 120
   - **counterpart** (n) *similar*, Anthology page 121
   - **delicacies** (n) *unusual, expensive food*, Anthology page 121
3. Have students turn to Student Book page 222. **You can understand unknown words by thinking about synonyms or antonyms.** Guide students to complete the synonym and antonym chart. Have students complete Parts B and C independently. Review the answers as a class.

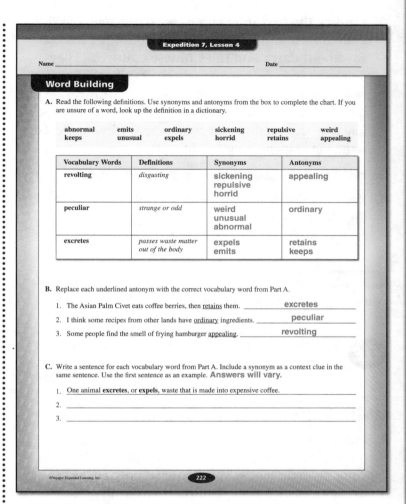

Expedition 7, Lesson 4

Name ____________ Date ____________

Word Building

A. Read the following definitions. Use synonyms and antonyms from the box to complete the chart. If you are unsure of a word, look up the definition in a dictionary.

abnormal	**emits**	**ordinary**	**sickening**	**repulsive**	**weird**
keeps	**unusual**	**expels**	**horrid**	**retains**	**appealing**

Vocabulary Words	Definitions	Synonyms	Antonyms
revolting	*disgusting*	sickening repulsive horrid	appealing
peculiar	*strange or odd*	weird unusual abnormal	ordinary
excretes	*passes waste matter out of the body*	expels emits	retains keeps

B. Replace each underlined antonym with the correct vocabulary word from Part A.

1. The Asian Palm Civet eats coffee berries, then retains them. excretes
2. I think some recipes from other lands have ordinary ingredients. peculiar
3. Some people find the smell of frying hamburger appealing. revolting

C. Write a sentence for each vocabulary word from Part A. Include a synonym as a context clue in the same sentence. Use the first sentence as an example. **Answers will vary.**

1. One animal **excretes**, or **expels**, waste that is made into expensive coffee.
2. ____________
3. ____________

©Voyager Expanded Learning, Inc. 222

CHECKPOINT If students have difficulty creating sentences, provide a sentence frame such as _____ *is considered revolting, or disgusting,* _____. (Eating crab legs or lobster is considered revolting, or disgusting, by some cultures.)

Reread

Apply the Target Skill: Compare and Contrast

1. Have students review the notes they wrote while reading "Adventures in Eating." **When I read, I ask myself: How are these ideas alike? How are they different? Do I see signal words that help me determine similarities and differences?**

2. Have students turn to Student Book page 223. Read the instructions for Part A aloud. Model scanning the passage "Adventures in Eating" to complete the chart. **I notice the first item compares dairy foods in the United States and China. What does the passage say about dairy and the Chinese culture?** (They do not include milk in their diets.) **Write this on the chart under Typical Foods in Other Cultures. What dairy products do people eat in the United States?** (cheese; ice cream; milk; sour cream) Have students write the responses in the chart.
3. Have students scan the passage to complete the chart.
4. Read the instructions for Part B. Have partners work together for support as necessary and share their comparisons and contrasts as well as their sentences.

ACADEMIC SKILL Remind students that they can look for comparisons and contrasts when reading textbooks.

Refer to Blackline Master page 39 to extend practice with compare and contrast.

Write in Response to Reading

1. Prepare students to complete the writing activities on Student Book page 224. **Think about three of your favorite foods. What ingredients are used to make them? Why would other cultures find some ingredients unappealing or odd?** Read the instructions for Part A aloud. Have students complete the chart.
2. **Think about the foods described in the passage. Which were the most peculiar to you? Why?** Have students read the instructions for Part B and complete the chart. Read the instructions for Part C. Have students prepare to write by visualizing the scene of the dinner. Then, have students complete the activity.

EXPEDITION ORGANIZER **Across Cultures**

Pause to have students turn to Student Book pages 214 and 215. Have students complete the following:

- Reread and answer one or more of the probing questions in Part A. Encourage students to add a question of their own if they have not already.
- Determine the big idea from "Adventures in Eating." Have students write it in the graphic organizer in Part B.

Expedition 7, Lesson 4

Name ______ Date ______

Compare and Contrast

A. Write facts about foods from U.S. culture and other cultures in the chart. Some parts of the chart are completed for you.

Food Type	Typical Foods in the United States	Typical Foods in Other Cultures
Dairy	cheese; milk; sour cream; ice cream	Parts of China: no milk or dairy
Insects	Eating insects is uncommon.	Africa: fried grasshoppers
Fat	bacon from pigs	Ukraine: salted pig fat eaten raw, smoked, fried, or boiled Inuit of Alaska, Greenland, Canada: seal and whale blubber
Blood	Eating blood is uncommon.	European countries: blood sausage Sweden: blood dumplings China: jellied duck or pig blood Philippines: blood stew Tanzania: milk and blood drink Mexico: goat's blood soup Jewish and Muslim cultures: forbid blood
Body Parts	cow and pig ribs; lobster tails	Poland: jellied cow's foot Norway: boiled sheep's head France: calf's head Mexico: *tacos sesos* (cows' brain tacos) Scotland: haggis (sheep's stomach) Newfoundland, Canada: seal flipper pie
Delicacies	caviar (fish eggs); pâté (goose or chicken liver spread)	China: bird's nest soup Indonesia: Kopi Luwak coffee

B. Read the completed chart in Part A. Use signal words to make a comparison and a contrast between foods. Answers will vary.

1. Compare ______
2. Contrast ______

 223

Expedition 7, Lesson 4

Name ______ Date ______

Write in Response to Reading

A. List three of your favorite foods. Complete the following chart with information about the ingredients in the foods. Include reasons why some cultures may find your favorite foods unappealing.

Favorite Food	Main Ingredients	Why It May Be Unappealing
Answers will vary.		

B. In the passage, you read about foods from other cultures. List three foods you found most peculiar.

Most Peculiar Food	Why It Is Peculiar
Answers will vary.	

C. Imagine you are eating a meal with the most peculiar foods you have ever heard of. Write a description of where the meal takes place, what you are eating, who is with you, and how you and others react. Use vivid words in the description.

Student descriptions should include vivid details about where the meal takes place, food sources and ingredients, who is eating, and the diners' reactions.

 224

Review, Extend, Assess

In today's lesson, as in Lessons 5 and 10 of every Expedition, there are options from which to choose. You may do any or all of the options listed. Activities for each option are given on the following pages. Each option will support or extend previously taught objectives. Choose the option(s) appropriate for your students and prepare accordingly.

Review Vocabulary

Extend Vocabulary

Assess Comprehension and Vocabulary

Reteach

Passport Reading Journeys Library

Online Technology Component

Writing Process

Real-World Reading

Exploring Careers

Review Vocabulary

Direct students to review the vocabulary for "Rats Rule!" and "Adventures in Eating" on Student Book page 215.

1. Have students read each word and definition.
2. Direct students to Student Book page 225. **One way to learn a new word is to learn an antonym. An antonym for *dry* is *wet* or *damp*. When you think of antonyms, you make a word association, which helps you remember the new word.** Read the instructions aloud, and have students complete the activity. Tell students to go back and check the definitions to make sure they are using the words correctly.
3. In Part B, if students have difficulty filling in words, remind them that the clues in parentheses might be part of the word's definition. Have them review the definitions on the Expedition Organizer, page 215.

CHECKPOINT Have students share their answers for both activities on Student Book page 225. If students have difficulty with a word, reteach the definition by using it in a familiar context, such as one related to school.

Expedition 7, Lesson 5

Name ______________________ Date ______________

Review Vocabulary

A. Replace each underlined word or phrase with a vocabulary word that is its antonym, or opposite.

Amira spent two years as a teacher in Cambodia. At first, she thought the Khmer language sounded 1. ordinary. But, after living in Cambodia for a while, she learned to speak and understand the language. Amira was a very 2. unloving teacher. She spent hours helping each student understand the lessons. On her days off, she loved to 3. sit around the market town of Skuon. Amira could 4. misunderstand how everybody traveled for miles on bicycles. She liked riding bikes and cycled all the way to market. The first time she saw fried spiders, she thought they were 5. appealing, but she tried them out of curiosity. Amira also bought clothing with beautiful and 6. simple designs.

1. peculiar
2. devoted
3. trek
4. fathom
5. revolting
6. intricate

B. Choose a word from the box that BEST completes each sentence. Use the words in parentheses as clues.

culture	excretes	texture
ingredient	recipes	adorn

1. Erica has a book of Indian ___recipes___ (instructions to make food) that instruct her on how to make curry dishes.
2. People all over the world ___adorn___ (decorate) their bodies with piercings.
3. In Tibet, the Buddhist religion is an important part of the ___culture___ (way of life).
4. Rice is a common ___ingredient___ (item inside a meal) in Asian cooking.
5. The wool sweater from Scotland has a scratchy ___texture___ (how something feels).
6. The Asian Palm Civet eats coffee berries, then ___excretes___ (passes waste matter out of the body) the beans.

 225

Extend Vocabulary

1. Tell students they will work with words that begin with the prefixes *e-* and *ex-*. **What words can you think of that begin with these prefixes? What do you think these prefixes mean?** Explain that the prefixes *e-* and *ex-* mean "out; away; from." **These prefixes have the same meaning.**
2. Have students turn to Student Book page 226. Read aloud the words and definitions in the chart at the top of the page. Have students read the instructions for Part B and complete the activity.
3. **What words on the chart are new to you? What other words do you know or use that begin with these prefixes?** Read aloud the instructions for Part C. Have students complete the activity, then share their responses.

CHECKPOINT When students share their responses for Part C, listen to ensure the new words they included use the correct meaning of the prefixes.

Part A

Explore and practice the words in the second column. Ask students whether they know the meanings. If not, read the definitions in the third column and model using each word in a sentence. **We saw the word *emerge* in the first passage. It means "come out from." I could say, "I saw the worm *emerge* from the ground." I also could say, "I saw the worm come out from the ground."**

Part B

If students have difficulty completing Part B, read aloud the sentence frames. Support the items with a think-aloud. For item 1: **The sentence describes how candles light a dark room. I know that candle flames make and send out light. What word can mean giving out something that has been made?** (emit) **Let's see if that word makes sense in the sentence.** Read the sentence with *emit* in the blank. Ask students whether that answer makes sense.

Continue the process for items 2–8.

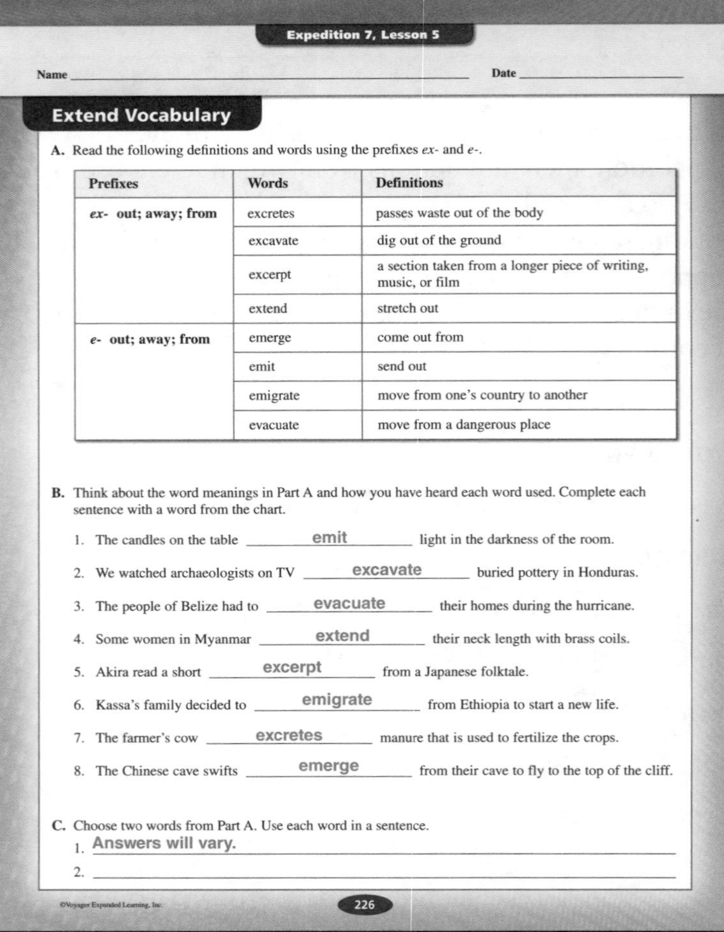

Expedition 7, Lesson 5

Name ______________________ Date ____________

Extend Vocabulary

A. Read the following definitions and words using the prefixes *ex-* and *e-*.

Prefixes	Words	Definitions
ex- out; away; from	excretes	passes waste out of the body
	excavate	dig out of the ground
	excerpt	a section taken from a longer piece of writing, music, or film
	extend	stretch out
e- out; away; from	emerge	come out from
	emit	send out
	emigrate	move from one's country to another
	evacuate	move from a dangerous place

B. Think about the word meanings in Part A and how you have heard each word used. Complete each sentence with a word from the chart.

1. The candles on the table ___emit___ light in the darkness of the room.
2. We watched archaeologists on TV ___excavate___ buried pottery in Honduras.
3. The people of Belize had to ___evacuate___ their homes during the hurricane.
4. Some women in Myanmar ___extend___ their neck length with brass coils.
5. Akira read a short ___excerpt___ from a Japanese folktale.
6. Kassa's family decided to ___emigrate___ from Ethiopia to start a new life.
7. The farmer's cow ___excretes___ manure that is used to fertilize the crops.
8. The Chinese cave swifts ___emerge___ from their cave to fly to the top of the cliff.

C. Choose two words from Part A. Use each word in a sentence.

1. Answers will vary.
2. ______________________

226

Part C

For Part C, have students substitute the definition for the new word to make sure their sentence makes sense.

Assess Comprehension and Vocabulary

1. Remind students that they learned to make comparisons and contrasts. **How do you compare something?** (You show how it is similar.) **How do you contrast?** (You show how something is different.)
2. Direct students to Student Book pages 227–229. Preview the pages, showing students that they will read a passage and answer questions. Remind them to notice similarities and differences. Have students complete the pages independently.

   Review student answers. Whenever possible, provide elaborative feedback to student responses. Refer to page xl for examples of elaborative feedback and how to incorporate it in your lessons.

   If students incorrectly answer more than 4 out of 15 assessment questions, evaluate what kind of reteaching is needed. If students miss vocabulary questions, have them return to the vocabulary activities and work with the words they missed. For errors with compare and contrast, use the reteaching suggestions on page 276.

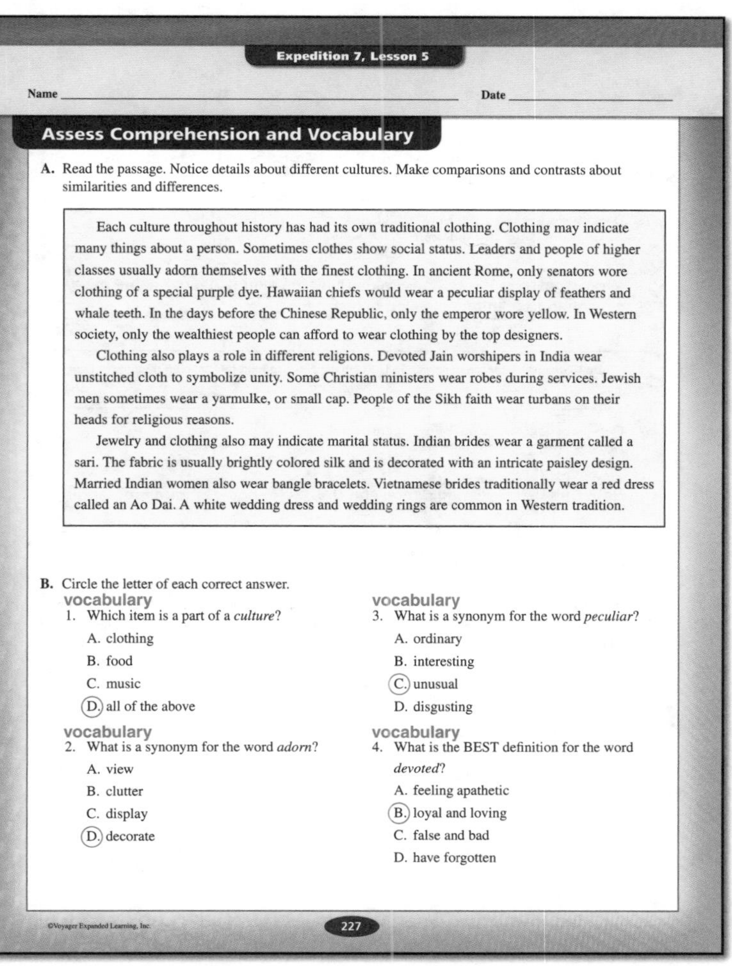
Expedition 7, Lesson 5

Name ______ Date ______

Assess Comprehension and Vocabulary

A. Read the passage. Notice details about different cultures. Make comparisons and contrasts about similarities and differences.

Each culture throughout history has had its own traditional clothing. Clothing may indicate many things about a person. Sometimes clothes show social status. Leaders and people of higher classes usually adorn themselves with the finest clothing. In ancient Rome, only senators wore clothing of a special purple dye. Hawaiian chiefs would wear a peculiar display of feathers and whale teeth. In the days before the Chinese Republic, only the emperor wore yellow. In Western society, only the wealthiest people can afford to wear clothing by the top designers.

Clothing also plays a role in different religions. Devoted Jain worshipers in India wear unstitched cloth to symbolize unity. Some Christian ministers wear robes during services. Jewish men sometimes wear a yarmulke, or small cap. People of the Sikh faith wear turbans on their heads for religious reasons.

Jewelry and clothing also may indicate marital status. Indian brides wear a garment called a sari. The fabric is usually brightly colored silk and is decorated with an intricate paisley design. Married Indian women also wear bangle bracelets. Vietnamese brides traditionally wear a red dress called an Ao Dai. A white wedding dress and wedding rings are common in Western tradition.

B. Circle the letter of each correct answer.

vocabulary
1. Which item is a part of a *culture*?
   A. clothing
   B. food
   C. music
   (D.) all of the above

vocabulary
2. What is a synonym for the word *adorn*?
   A. view
   B. clutter
   C. display
   (D.) decorate

vocabulary
3. What is a synonym for the word *peculiar*?
   A. ordinary
   B. interesting
   (C.) unusual
   D. disgusting

vocabulary
4. What is the BEST definition for the word *devoted*?
   A. feeling apathetic
   (B.) loyal and loving
   C. false and bad
   D. have forgotten

©Voyager Expanded Learning, Inc. 227

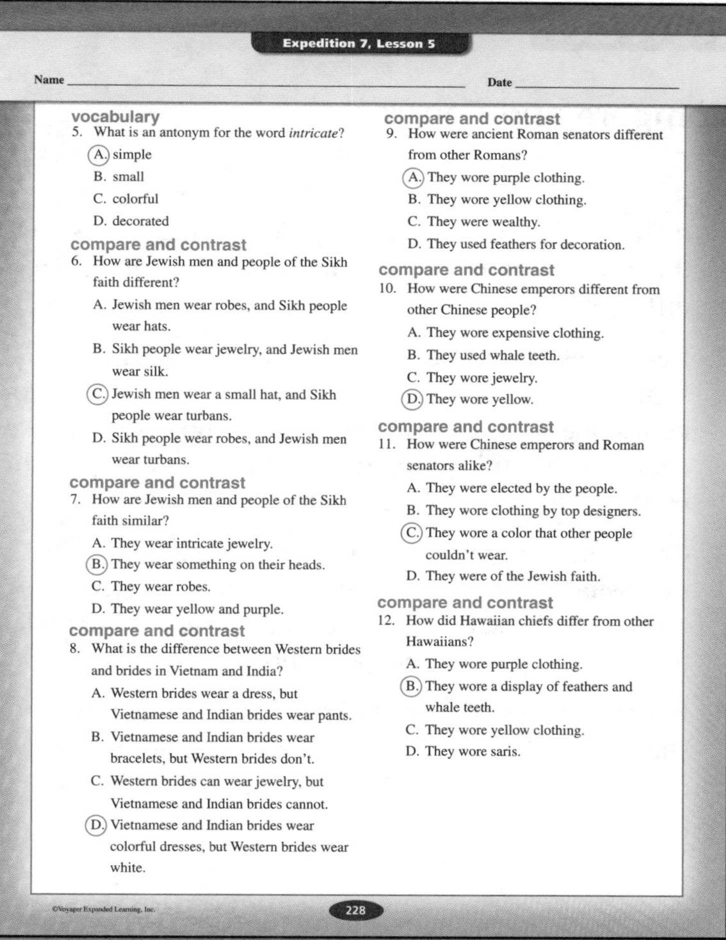
Expedition 7, Lesson 5

Name ______ Date ______

vocabulary
5. What is an antonym for the word *intricate*?
   (A.) simple
   B. small
   C. colorful
   D. decorated

compare and contrast
6. How are Jewish men and people of the Sikh faith different?
   A. Jewish men wear robes, and Sikh people wear hats.
   B. Sikh people wear jewelry, and Jewish men wear silk.
   (C.) Jewish men wear a small hat, and Sikh people wear turbans.
   D. Sikh people wear robes, and Jewish men wear turbans.

compare and contrast
7. How are Jewish men and people of the Sikh faith similar?
   A. They wear intricate jewelry.
   (B.) They wear something on their heads.
   C. They wear robes.
   D. They wear yellow and purple.

compare and contrast
8. What is the difference between Western brides and brides in Vietnam and India?
   A. Western brides wear a dress, but Vietnamese and Indian brides wear pants.
   B. Vietnamese and Indian brides wear bracelets, but Western brides don't.
   C. Western brides can wear jewelry, but Vietnamese and Indian brides cannot.
   (D.) Vietnamese and Indian brides wear colorful dresses, but Western brides wear white.

compare and contrast
9. How were ancient Roman senators different from other Romans?
   (A.) They wore purple clothing.
   B. They wore yellow clothing.
   C. They were wealthy.
   D. They used feathers for decoration.

compare and contrast
10. How were Chinese emperors different from other Chinese people?
   A. They wore expensive clothing.
   B. They used whale teeth.
   C. They wore jewelry.
   (D.) They wore yellow.

compare and contrast
11. How were Chinese emperors and Roman senators alike?
   A. They were elected by the people.
   B. They wore clothing by top designers.
   (C.) They wore a color that other people couldn't wear.
   D. They were of the Jewish faith.

compare and contrast
12. How did Hawaiian chiefs differ from other Hawaiians?
   A. They wore purple clothing.
   (B.) They wore a display of feathers and whale teeth.
   C. They wore yellow clothing.
   D. They wore saris.

©Voyager Expanded Learning, Inc. 228

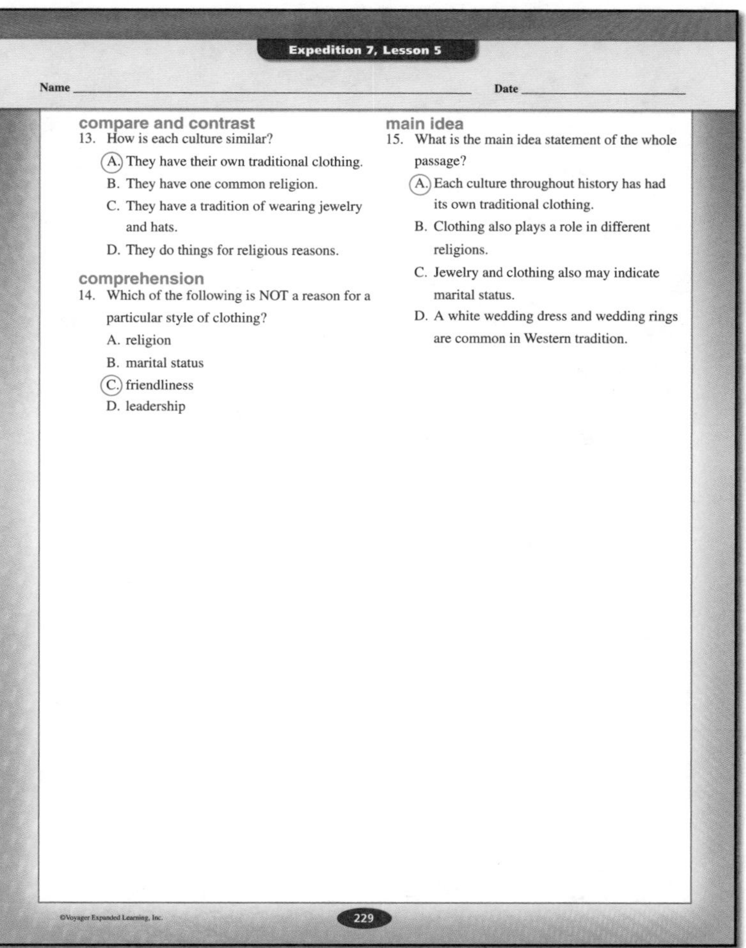
Expedition 7, Lesson 5

Name ______ Date ______

compare and contrast
13. How is each culture similar?
   (A.) They have their own traditional clothing.
   B. They have one common religion.
   C. They have a tradition of wearing jewelry and hats.
   D. They do things for religious reasons.

comprehension
14. Which of the following is NOT a reason for a particular style of clothing?
   A. religion
   B. marital status
   (C.) friendliness
   D. leadership

main idea
15. What is the main idea statement of the whole passage?
   (A.) Each culture throughout history has had its own traditional clothing.
   B. Clothing also plays a role in different religions.
   C. Jewelry and clothing also may indicate marital status.
   D. A white wedding dress and wedding rings are common in Western tradition.

©Voyager Expanded Learning, Inc. 229

Reteach

Compare and Contrast

1. Direct students to Student Book pages 230 and 231. Read the instructions aloud. **How is comparing different from contrasting?** (Comparing shows how things are similar. Contrasting shows how things are different.)
2. Read the brief passages aloud. **Circle words that signal a comparison or contrast.** When you need to help students distinguish between comparisons and contrasts, use this prompt: **Does this text compare or contrast something? How do you know?**
3. Complete the first item with students, having them share their thinking process aloud. Correct misconceptions, and observe students as they complete the remaining items independently.
4. For extra support, give students sentence starters such as: *In both cultures* ____. and *The cultures are different because* ____. After students complete the pages, have them compare responses.

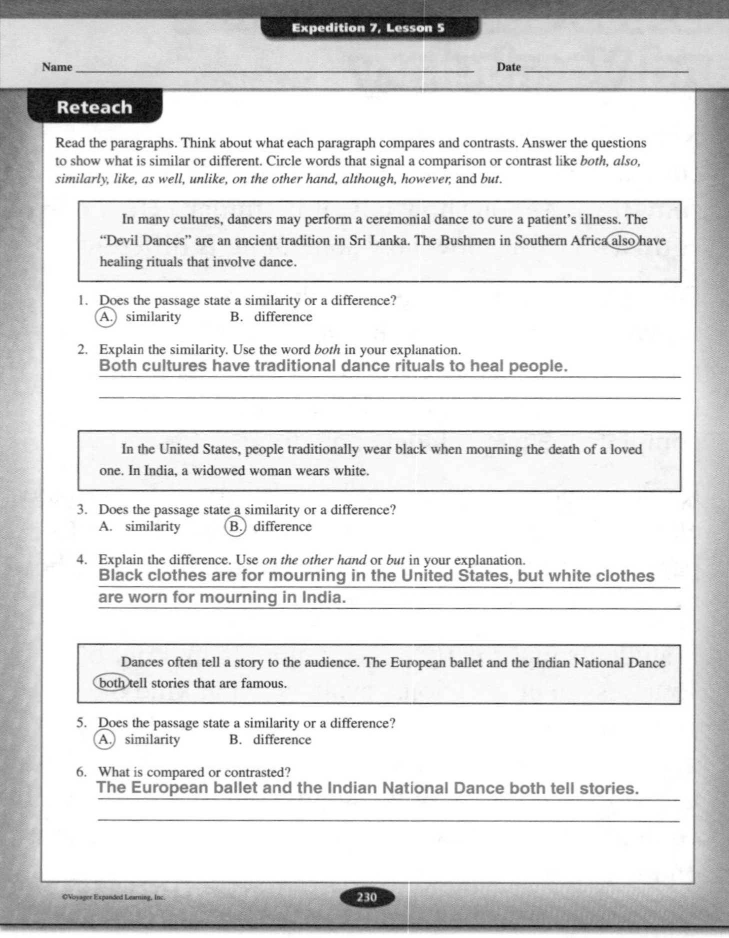

Expedition 7, Lesson 5

Name ____________ Date ____________

Reteach

Read the paragraphs. Think about what each paragraph compares and contrasts. Answer the questions to show what is similar or different. Circle words that signal a comparison or contrast like *both, also, similarly, like, as well, unlike, on the other hand, although, however,* and *but.*

In many cultures, dancers may perform a ceremonial dance to cure a patient's illness. The "Devil Dances" are an ancient tradition in Sri Lanka. The Bushmen in Southern Africa (also) have healing rituals that involve dance.

1. Does the passage state a similarity or a difference?
   (A.) similarity B. difference
2. Explain the similarity. Use the word *both* in your explanation.
   Both cultures have traditional dance rituals to heal people.

In the United States, people traditionally wear black when mourning the death of a loved one. In India, a widowed woman wears white.

3. Does the passage state a similarity or a difference?
   A. similarity (B.) difference
4. Explain the difference. Use *on the other hand* or *but* in your explanation.
   Black clothes are for mourning in the United States, but white clothes are worn for mourning in India.

Dances often tell a story to the audience. The European ballet and the Indian National Dance (both) tell stories that are famous.

5. Does the passage state a similarity or a difference?
   (A.) similarity B. difference
6. What is compared or contrasted?
   The European ballet and the Indian National Dance both tell stories.

©Voyager Expanded Learning, Inc. 230

Expedition 7, Lesson 5

Name ____________ Date ____________

In the United States, many women think that tan skin makes them look more beautiful. (However,) in Asia, many women want clear, milky, pale skin.

7. Does the passage state a similarity or a difference?
   A. similarity (B.) difference
8. What is compared or contrasted?
   Many women in the United States think tan skin is beautiful, but many women in Asia think pale skin is beautiful.

(Both) Spanish flamenco dancers and U.S. tap dancers use loud foot tapping rhythms in their dance.

9. Does the passage state a similarity or a difference?
   (A.) similarity B. difference
10. What is compared or contrasted?
    Both Spanish flamenco dance and U.S. tap dance use loud foot tapping.

Different cultures in history have passed down myths and folktales. Storytellers recited the tales from memory. In the western African country of Gambia, a storyteller would play music on a stringed instrument called the kora. In Cambodia, a storyteller would play a stringed instrument called the chapey.

11. Does the passage state a similarity or a difference?
    (A.) similarity B. difference
12. What is compared or contrasted?
    Both cultures have folktales that storytellers performed with music with stringed instruments.

©Voyager Expanded Learning, Inc. 231

Passport Reading Journeys Library

1. Have students choose reading material from the *Passport Reading Journeys* Library or another approved selection. If students have not finished a previously chosen selection, they may continue reading from that selection. See the *Passport Reading Journeys* Library Teacher's Guide for material on selection guidelines.
2. You may use this time to allow students to participate in book clubs or book presentations. Use the criteria specified in the *Passport Reading Journeys* Library Teacher's Guide.

Vocabulary Connections

Vocabulary words are listed in the Teacher's Guide for each book. These words are content-related or used frequently in reading material. The selected words can be a basis for independent or small-group discussions and activities.

Student Opportunities

Six copies of each book title are provided in the *Passport Reading Journeys* Library. The number of copies makes it possible for small groups of students to read the same material and share the information they read.

Theme-related titles include *The Liberation of Gabriel King, The Green Glass Sea,* and *Loser.*

Technology

1. Depending on your classroom configuration and computer access, you may have students work through the technology in a lab setting or have individuals or small groups of students work on desktops or laptops while other students participate in other suggested activities, such as the *Passport Reading Journeys* Library.
2. The online technology component provides additional support for students to work with selected vocabulary words. Students will work through a series of activities to strengthen their word knowledge, then apply that knowledge to passage reading. Refer to the online technology component User Guide for more information.

   Theme-related word sets include Geography, World History, Sociology, and Economics.

Writing Process

A Personal Narrative

Distribute Writing Blackline Master page 13. **You will write about an event where you experience a different culture.** Ask students to look at the page and follow along as you explain the assignment. Assign point values as you see fit, and ask students to write them in the rubric. Tell them to make any notes on the page that will help them, but they will turn the page in with the assignment. Encourage them to think about cultures other than their own. Explain that the writing style will be a narrative. **You will tell the story of your personal cultural experience.** Tell students that good narratives include descriptions of setting, people, and actions. **Unique cultural experiences need vivid explanations. What kinds of words or phrases will you include in your descriptions?** (adjectives; sensory details) **Adjectives and sensory details create a vivid picture in the reader's mind.** Write the following on the board and tell students they may include descriptions of these things:

- *clothing*
- *food*
- *dance*
- *music*
- *holidays*
- *literature*
- *art*

Prewrite

Your narratives should include sensory descriptions that appeal to the five senses—sight, smell, hearing, taste, and touch. Descriptive words help the reader visualize the story.

Have students think about a personal cultural experience. **You can brainstorm situations and descriptions with a story web.** Model a story web as a class. A few possible cross-cultural experiences are attending a wedding or religious event, purchasing things in another country, working with people from other cultures, and traveling in other countries. Begin a story web on the board with nouns and verbs. Add adjectives and adverbs that describe those nouns and verbs. Have students work on their own webs.

Draft

You will use these standards, or criteria, as you write your narratives. Your narratives must have . . .

- **a specific cultural experience.**
- **a specifically described setting.**
- **sensory details that vividly appeal to the senses.**
- **an explanation of what you learned about the culture.**

Have students work independently to draft their narratives. Remind them that they will be able to revise their work.

Revise

Have students reread the drafts, using the following revision steps and questions. After each step, have students make the revisions and write their final draft.

- **Check the organization.** What paragraphs or sentences should you move so that the information flows in the right order?
- **Check your description.** Did you use vivid sensory details and adjectives? Where do you need to add more details or description?
- **Check mechanics.** Do fragments or run-on sentences need to be rewritten? What words might be misspelled? Do all sentences begin with capital letters and end with proper punctuation?

Present

Have students present their narratives to the class.

Assess

I will assess your writing and presentation based on the rubric on your page. To assess students' personal narratives, use the rubric from the Writing Blackline Master.

Real-World Reading

Job Application

1. Direct students to Student Book pages 232 and 233. Explain that they will complete a job application. **Have you ever applied for a job? What kind of information does an employer need to know to hire someone?** Have students preview the section headings.

   Have students tell the meanings of the following words and clarify their understanding:

   - **anticipate**—*expect*
   - **essential**—*necessary*
   - **accommodation**—*adjustment*
   - **qualifications**—*qualities and experiences that make one right for a job*

2. **Imagine you are looking for a job at a restaurant. Complete this job application.**

3. Tell students that employers will ask them to explain why they are qualified for the job. **Qualifications can be descriptive words like *responsible* or *trustworthy*.** Have partners share their qualifications.

Expedition 7, Lesson 5

Name ______________________ Date ____________

Real World—Job Application

Complete the following job application. Use a dictionary to look up any words you do not know.

Restaurant Job Application

Last name ____________ First name ____________ Middle name ____________
Position desired ____________
Date available to begin employment ____________
Number of hours per week available for employment ____________
What salary do you anticipate for this position? ____________
Are you 18 years of age or older? ☐ Yes ☐ No
If you answered "No"—you are not older than 18—what is your age? ____________
If you are under age 18, do you have an employment/age certificate? ☐ Yes ☐ No
Can you perform the essential functions required of this job, either with or without reasonable accommodation? ____________
Are you legally eligible for employment in the United States? ☐ Yes ☐ No

Have you ever been convicted of a felony? ☐ Yes ☐ No
If so, provide date of conviction and details. ____________

Contact Information
Street address ____________
City ____________ State ____________ Zip ____________
E-mail address ____________
Home phone ____________ Cell phone ____________

Education
Circle the highest grade level completed. 5 6 7 8 9 10 11 12
Circle the number of years of post-high school education. 1 2 3 4 post-college

Educational Institutions

Name and Location of Educational Institution	Degree Received	Major Course of Study

©Voyager Expanded Learning, Inc. 232

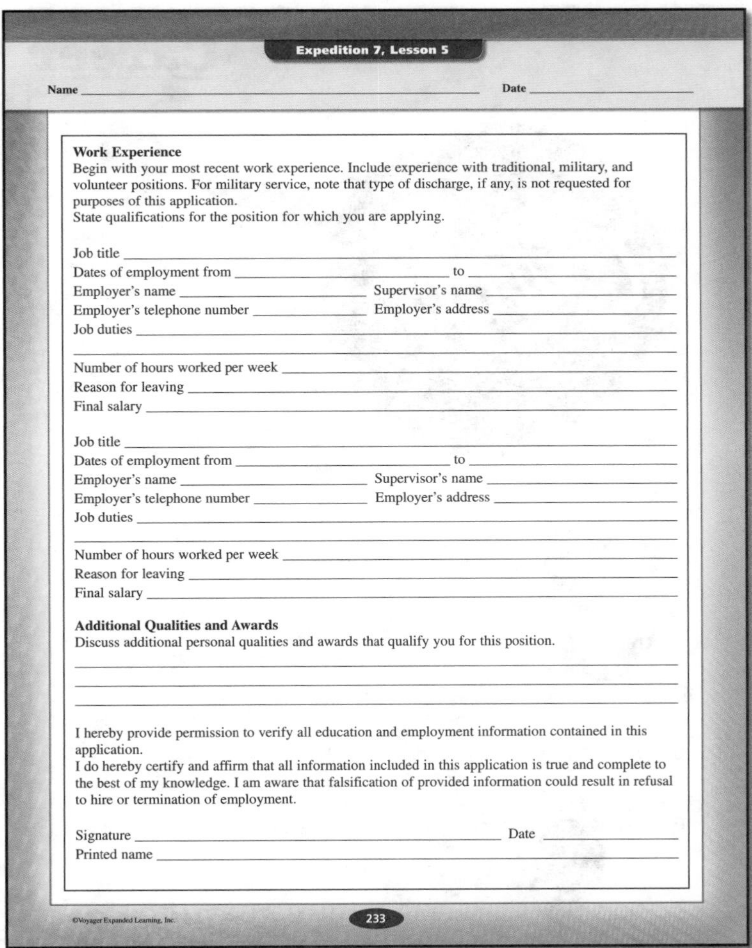

Expedition 7, Lesson 5

Name ______________________ Date ____________

Work Experience
Begin with your most recent work experience. Include experience with traditional, military, and volunteer positions. For military service, note that type of discharge, if any, is not requested for purposes of this application.
State qualifications for the position for which you are applying.

Job title ____________
Dates of employment from ____________ to ____________
Employer's name ____________ Supervisor's name ____________
Employer's telephone number ____________ Employer's address ____________
Job duties ____________

Number of hours worked per week ____________
Reason for leaving ____________
Final salary ____________

Job title ____________
Dates of employment from ____________ to ____________
Employer's name ____________ Supervisor's name ____________
Employer's telephone number ____________ Employer's address ____________
Job duties ____________

Number of hours worked per week ____________
Reason for leaving ____________
Final salary ____________

Additional Qualities and Awards
Discuss additional personal qualities and awards that qualify you for this position.

I hereby provide permission to verify all education and employment information contained in this application.
I do hereby certify and affirm that all information included in this application is true and complete to the best of my knowledge. I am aware that falsification of provided information could result in refusal to hire or termination of employment.

Signature ____________ Date ____________
Printed name ____________

©Voyager Expanded Learning, Inc. 233

Exploring Careers

Chef

1. Direct students to Anthology page 123. Have students preview the title and photograph. **Name one thing you might already know about a chef's job. Name something you would like to learn.** List student responses on the board.
2. Direct students to read the passage. **Do you already know how to bake and cook? If not, are you interested in learning? Which aspect of this career appeals to you; which doesn't?**
3. Have students turn to Student Book page 234. **Answer the questions and complete the chart by researching a career as a chef in books or online.** Have students complete the page.

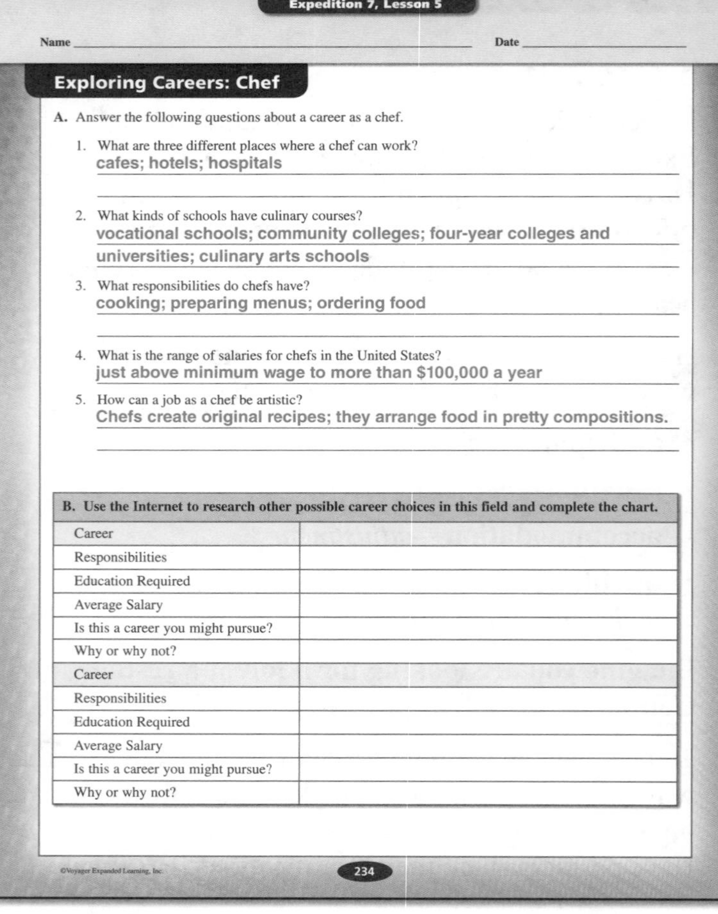

Expedition 7, Lesson 5

Name ______________________ Date ____________

Exploring Careers: Chef

A. Answer the following questions about a career as a chef.

1. What are three different places where a chef can work?
   cafes; hotels; hospitals
2. What kinds of schools have culinary courses?
   vocational schools; community colleges; four-year colleges and universities; culinary arts schools
3. What responsibilities do chefs have?
   cooking; preparing menus; ordering food
4. What is the range of salaries for chefs in the United States?
   just above minimum wage to more than $100,000 a year
5. How can a job as a chef be artistic?
   Chefs create original recipes; they arrange food in pretty compositions.

B. Use the Internet to research other possible career choices in this field and complete the chart.

Career	
Responsibilities	
Education Required	
Average Salary	
Is this a career you might pursue?	
Why or why not?	
Career	
Responsibilities	
Education Required	
Average Salary	
Is this a career you might pursue?	
Why or why not?	

©Voyager Expanded Learning, Inc.

234

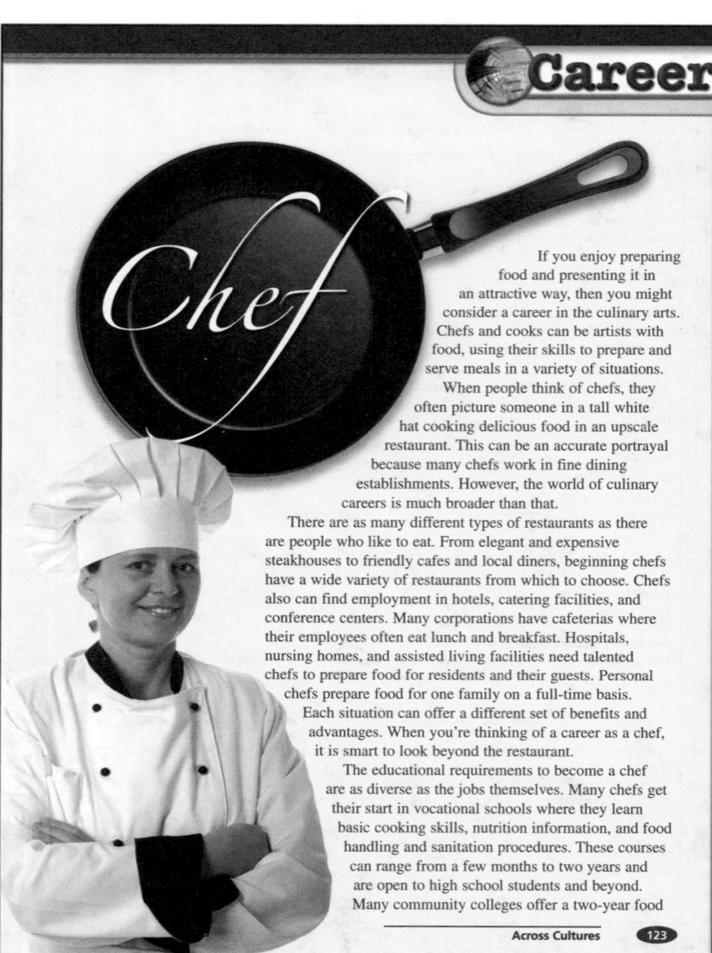

Career

Chef

If you enjoy preparing food and presenting it in an attractive way, then you might consider a career in the culinary arts. Chefs and cooks can be artists with food, using their skills to prepare and serve meals in a variety of situations.

When people think of chefs, they often picture someone in a tall white hat cooking delicious food in an upscale restaurant. This can be an accurate portrayal because many chefs work in fine dining establishments. However, the world of culinary careers is much broader than that.

There are as many different types of restaurants as there are people who like to eat. From elegant and expensive steakhouses to friendly cafes and local diners, beginning chefs have a wide variety of restaurants from which to choose. Chefs also can find employment in hotels, catering facilities, and conference centers. Many corporations have cafeterias where their employees often eat lunch and breakfast. Hospitals, nursing homes, and assisted living facilities need talented chefs to prepare food for residents and their guests. Personal chefs prepare food for one family on a full-time basis.

Each situation can offer a different set of benefits and advantages. When you're thinking of a career as a chef, it is smart to look beyond the restaurant.

The educational requirements to become a chef are as diverse as the jobs themselves. Many chefs get their start in vocational schools where they learn basic cooking skills, nutrition information, and food handling and sanitation procedures. These courses can range from a few months to two years and are open to high school students and beyond. Many community colleges offer a two-year food

Across Cultures 123

Career

services or culinary arts program resulting in an associate's degree.

Some colleges and universities also offer a culinary arts curriculum. These schools usually pair cooking classes with a course in business and hospitality. They may have a four-year program for those who plan to own or manage a restaurant or other food-service business.

Culinary arts schools offer a highly specialized education in various cuisines and cooking styles. If you aspire to be a top chef in a fine restaurant, a culinary arts school might be your best choice. Students usually need from nine to 24 months to complete a culinary arts program at one of these schools.

Chefs do a lot more than just cook. A chef's responsibilities may include preparing menus and ordering food. Many chefs visit local farmers' markets or other suppliers to get the best selection of ingredients for that day's menu.

Most chefs work long hours, especially those who work in restaurants, where the last customer might not leave until midnight. Cooking is also a physically demanding job. Chefs must spend a lot of time on their feet in very hot kitchens. The job also involves a lot of heavy lifting—think of all those huge sacks of flour or sugar. It can be dangerous, too, because chefs handle extremely hot food and sharp knives.

Sometimes the monetary rewards for the hard work are not great. An entry-level chef might make only a few dollars more than minimum wage. However, a top chef or restaurant owner can earn a much larger income. Some chefs can earn more than $100,000 a year. Your skills, where you work, and the type of chef you are will determine where your pay will fall in the salary range from just above minimum wage to more than $100,000.

If you can stand the heat and love to cook, a career in the culinary arts can be a fulfilling path in life.

124 Expedition 7

English Language Learner Overview

The ELL signals when extra support is provided for students during the lesson. As needed, Blackline Masters for English language learners may provide support. For vocabulary, students also may use the online technology component to practice Expedition words or other content-area vocabulary and designated ELL word sets.

Introduce Vocabulary

Lesson 6

Ask students if there is a cognate for *tradition* in their native language. Pronounce the English word slowly, and have students repeat. If applicable, have a student model the pronunciation of the cognate. Read aloud the definition, and have students respond to the following questions.

- **Carmen is the first person in her family to wear a blue wedding dress. Is it a *tradition* in her family to wear a blue wedding dress?** (no)
- **Alex has the same name as his father, his grandfather, and his great-grandfather. Do you think it is a *tradition* to name people Alex in his family?** (yes)
- **What *traditions* have you heard of?** (Answers will vary.)

Lesson 8

Use *remote* with the antonym *close*, and give examples to teach the meaning. **Some parts of Alaska are so *remote*, you can't get to them by car. Other parts are *close* enough to drive to.**

Use *prevalent* with the antonym *uncommon*, and give examples to teach the meaning. **Cell phones are a *prevalent* form of communication, but telegrams are *uncommon*.**

Use *originated* with the synonym *started*, and give examples to teach the meaning. **Computer games that *originated* in Asia have become popular in other parts of the world. Other games that *started* in North America are now popular in Asia.**

Give examples to teach *organizations*. **The American Red Cross is an *organization* that provides medical treatment. The U.S. Soccer Federation is an *organization* in charge of professional soccer. What *organizations* do we have at our school?** (sports teams; clubs; honors society)

Practice Vocabulary

In Lesson 7, provide support for the context words *modified* and *rival*. **If you *modified* something, you changed it. I *modified* my coat by sewing different buttons on it. What *modified* clothes have you seen?** (patches sewn onto a jacket; hems taken up)

If someone is my *rival*, I compete with that person. The two *rivals* arm wrestled to see who was stronger. Are people who play on the same sports team *rivals*? (no) **Why not?** (They compete together, not against each other.)

In Lesson 9, provide support for the context words *adopt* and *drawbacks*. **If you *adopt* a custom or practice, you make it your own. I have decided to *adopt* an Asian style of cooking because I think it is healthy for me. When have you seen someone *adopt* a style of clothing?** (Answers will vary but could include Rastafarian hats, Native American jewelry, and South American hoodies.)

***Drawbacks* are the bad things about a situation or thing. I like my new car, but it has some *drawbacks*—the trunk is too small, and the speakers aren't very loud. What are some *drawbacks* to working after school?** (can't do homework; miss time with friends; interferes with clubs and sports)

Apply the Target Skill: Compare and Contrast

Some students may need additional practice with comparing and contrasting using graphic organizers. Blackline Master page 41 has a Venn diagram using the simple example of three different musical instruments. If possible, provide photographs or other illustrations of the three instruments—an electric guitar, a piano, and a drum—to help students complete the graphic organizer. Guide them in asking questions to determine which statements apply to each instrument.

Vocabulary
alter (v) *change*
assert (v) *behave in a strong, confident way so that people notice you*
status (n) *a person's rank or position in a group, organization, or society*

The 15-year-old was getting ready for a party. First, she painted her nails with a dark red polish and let it dry. Then, looking in a mirror, she applied light powder to her face, ruby red lipstick to her lips, and brown pencil to her shaved eyebrows. Next, she combed her hair, using gloss to make it shine. That done, the girl dressed, and as a finishing touch, fastened a heavy gold necklace around her neck. She checked her reflection once again in the mirror. It was perfect!

This scenario could happen here today. But, you may be surprised to learn that the 15-year-old who used cosmetics, hair product, and jewelry to **alter** her appearance lived in China about 2,000 years ago.

For thousands of years and in different parts of the world, men and women have found ways to enhance their looks for different reasons. Sometimes they altered their body to appear more attractive to the opposite sex. For example, women all over the world wore corsets around their waists for many centuries. The corset was designed to give women a small waist that was considered beautiful. Women wore this unbelievably tight garment under their clothes. Many stories have been told of organ damage and broken ribs in the name of beauty. Other times, people modified their bodies to **assert** their **status** in

Across Cultures 125

Vocabulary
distinct (adj) *clearly different*

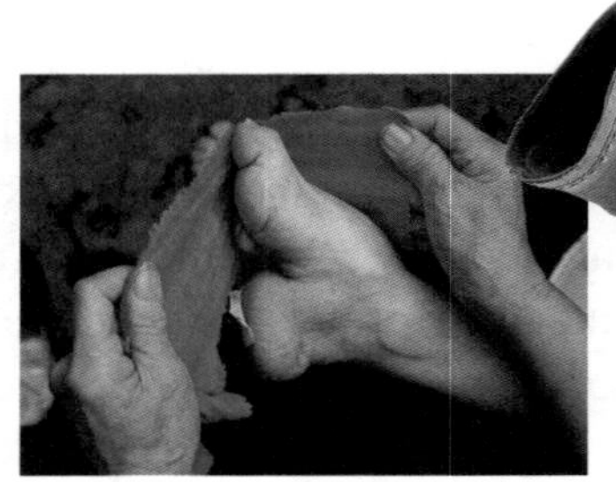

Chinese foot binding shoes (above) and a woman binding deformed feet in Sichuan Province, China

society. Decades ago, wealthy women in China practiced foot binding. Small feet were not only a sign of wealth, they were a sign of beauty. Between the ages of 3 and 11, girls would have someone tightly wrap, or bind, their four small toes on each foot. Done correctly, this would keep the foot from growing, and the toes would actually be wrapped under the foot. Women would end up with tiny feet, one-third the size of normal feet. Many times women would be crippled and left to depend on others for many things. In both cases, extreme measures were taken to be beautiful in the eyes of society. 1

1 Main Idea
Find the main idea sentence in this paragraph. What details support it?

Different cultures emphasize different parts of the body. One culture appreciates full lips. Another culture values long, slender necks. And, what is attractive to one culture may seem odd to another. What stays the same is that some people in all cultures go to great lengths to have others in their society say, "Wow!"

A Necklace of Another Kind

Welcome to Myanmar, a large country in Southeast Asia. This country is known for its majestic mountain ranges, historic temples, and secluded beaches. But, it is also known for a **distinct** tribe of people, the Kayan. The women in this tribe in the northeast of Myanmar have necks that resemble that of a giraffe.

Achieving that look isn't easy, for the women are born with necks that are normal sizes. To attain it, a Kayan woman wraps her neck in a series of high brass coils. The result is that the woman's head stretches very high up and her chin juts out in front, giving the impression that she has an elongated neck. With the coils in place, the distance between her chin and her shoulders can be as great as 12 inches. Made of brass, the coils are smooth and can weigh as much as 12 pounds.

There are theories as to how and why the neck coils originated.

126 Expedition 7

Kayan women show the various stages of neck rings.

Vocabulary
tribute (n) *something done, given, or said to show thanks or respect*
tradition (n) *a custom, idea, or belief that is handed down from one generation to the next*

Some say it was to protect women from being bitten on the neck by tigers or from attacks by rival tribes competing for land and status. Others say it had religious significance, a **tribute** to an ancient deity, or god. No one knows for sure.

The neck coils require maintenance. The women scrub them clean with a solution of lime, straw, and tree bark. Then, the women go about their work, never letting the coils interfere with their chores and everyday living.

You may wonder when Kayan females start wearing neck rings. At age 6, an older woman places a short coil around the girl's neck. Then, at about age 10, the coil is replaced with a longer and heavier spiral. By the time the girl has grown into adulthood, she is wearing a full set.

Admittedly, the rings are uncomfortable, yet women wear them anyway. "It's **tradition**," explained one. Neck rings can be hot, especially in very warm weather.

"We get used to them," said another. Clearly, the practices of one's ancestors have a powerful hold on a culture and its people today. 2

2 Visualize
As you read the descriptions, picture in your mind what you or someone you know would look like with neck rings.

Piercings Abound

While some people adorn their bodies, other people pierce them. People all over the world pierce ears, noses, lips, tongues, and various other body parts. Where did these practices come from? Nose piercing has been traced back 4,000 years. But, its popularity arose in the 16th century when women in India often wore nose rings. Back then, rich women used nose rings to assert their wealth and status. As the family became richer,

Across Cultures 127

the woman wore an increasingly larger ring.

Traditionally, the nose ring was placed in the left nostril, rather than the right. According to Indian medicine, the left side is associated with the female reproduction process and a nose ring is said to lessen the pain of childbirth. Today, however, the nose ring—whether worn in India or in the United States—is often used as decoration. Earlobe piercings are one of the world's most popular piercings and have been around for centuries. The tradition probably started as a way to keep demons and evil spirits out of the body because metal repelled demons, which entered the body through the ears—or so people believed. The oldest mummified body in the world was found frozen in an Austrian Glacier in 1991. Tests showed the body to be more than 5,000 years old. The body had pierced ears, and the holes had been enlarged to roughly the size of a pea.

3 Ask Questions
After reading the last three paragraphs ask yourself, "How are these cultures' views of beauty similar and how are they different?"

Though it, too, began with ancient civilizations, the piercing of the lips is common throughout the world. Many people insert objects into the piercings, such as rings, pins, or disks. The Dogon tribe of Mali and the Nuba of Ethiopia wear rings in their lips for religious purposes. Among tribes of Central Africa and South America, piercings are stretched to extremely large proportions, and large wooden or clay plates are inserted. Women in the Makololo tribe of Malawi wear lip plates in the upper lips to make them beautiful.

Tongue piercing also began with ancient civilizations like the Mayas and Aztecs. The tongue was pierced to draw blood to appease angry gods and to create an altered state of consciousness, allowing communication with the gods. 3

This African tribal woman is a model of beauty in her culture with her enlarged ear piercing and lip disk.

128 Expedition 7

The Greatest of Tattoos

You have probably seen people who sport a tattoo, perhaps a bird in flight or a small heart. The tattoos are a way to distinguish themselves. But, some men in Japan take tattooing to an extreme, covering nearly the whole body—chest, shoulders, upper arms, back, buttocks, and legs—with a full body tattoo. While tattoos in the United States often have personal significance, or importance, such as a tribute to a friend or family member, full body armor, as it is known in Japan, is based on traditional folktales from Japanese theater. As a result, a typical full body tattoo shows one large image from a story of long ago—perhaps a fire-breathing dragon, a savage tiger, or a supernatural being, with abilities beyond that of natural man. The effect can be scary and threatening.

Getting a tattoo is painful, yet men put up with the discomfort. Some do it to test themselves, trying to prove they are "real men," able to endure months of weekly visits to the tattoo artist. Others simply appreciate the beauty of an image from literature.

Whatever their motivation, today, full body tattoos are discouraged in Japan. As a result, few men show their tattoos in public. In fact, to conceal a large tattoo for their customers, tattoo artists cover most of the body with the body art, but leave a blank space down the middle of the customer's chest for occasions when the man wears an open-collar shirt.

American Beauty

Many Americans also go to extremes to become "beautiful." They starve themselves to become thin, lose sleep to keep from messing up their hairdos, undergo risky cosmetic surgery, risk skin cancer to become tan, suffer through piercings and tattoos—all in the name of beauty.

The next time you see a TV ad in America for some sort of body enhancement—like chandelier earrings or musk-scented cologne—think back to body alterations done around the world to achieve a desired effect. Keep in mind that through the years and across many cultures, people have found different ways to assert their status and say, "Check me out!" 4 Practices differ because of each culture's distinctive values, lifestyle, and history. End

4 Make Connections
What do you do to enhance your beauty? Why do you think it makes you more beautiful?

Across Cultures 129

"The Multicultural Search for Beauty"

Before Reading

Introduce Vocabulary

1. Have students turn to Part A on Student Book page 235 and scan the boldfaced vocabulary words. **These words will appear in "The Multicultural Search for Beauty."** Read the instructions as students follow along.
2. **Which words are the most familiar to you? Where have you seen these words used?** For familiar words, tell students to write where they have seen them, such as in school or online. Ask students to pay extra attention to unknown or unfamiliar words and to underline key words in those definitions.
3. Read aloud the part of speech, definition, and example sentence for each word.
4. Read aloud the instructions for Part B. Have students complete the section independently. Have partners compare answers.

ELL Refer to Blackline Master page 40 to extend vocabulary practice.

Have students use the *Passport Reading Journeys* online technology component to practice and reinforce vocabulary and comprehension skills.

Apply the Target Skill: Compare and Contrast

1. Remind students that comparing and contrasting means to determine similarities and differences among two or more ideas. **How are your favorite television shows different? How are they the same?** Create a chart listing titles of television shows, and list differences including topic, audience, and format. Then, list similarities. Have students share additional comparisons and contrasts.
2. Direct students to Anthology page 125. Remind students that they can compare and contrast two or more ideas by reading text or by observing photos.

Expedition 7, Lesson 6

Name ______ Date ______

Vocabulary

"The Multicultural Search for Beauty"

A. Put a check mark in each row to indicate how well you know each boldfaced word.

	Know This Word	Have Seen This Word	Don't Know This Word
alter (v) *change* I did not want to *alter* my appearance to fit in with the group.			
assert (v) *behave in a strong, confident way so that people notice you* The man wore a headdress to *assert* his authority.			
status (n) *a person's rank or position in a group, organization, or society* Her beautiful jewelry indicated her *status* in the tribe.			
distinct (adj) *clearly different* Each culture has a *distinct* idea of beauty that is unlike the ideas of other cultures.			
tribute (n) *something done, given, or said to show thanks or respect* I wear my grandmother's favorite pin every day as a *tribute* to her.			
tradition (n) *a custom, idea, or belief that is handed down from one generation to the next* Long ago, people started the *tradition* of wearing a ring to show they were married.			

B. Read each statement. Circle true or false.

1. Your appearance stays the same when you **alter** it. true (false)
2. You might **assert** your personal style by piercing your ears. (true) false
3. Expensive cars indicate a high **status** in many cultures. (true) false
4. People in various cultures have **distinct** languages. (true) false
5. The **tradition** of wearing white for a wedding is a new idea. true (false)
6. When you give a **tribute** to someone, you dislike the person. true (false)

 235

Vocabulary

alter (v) *change*
I did not want to *alter* my appearance to fit in with the group.

assert (v) *behave in a strong, confident way so that people notice you*
The man wore a headdress to *assert* his authority.

status (n) *a person's rank or position in a group, organization, or society*
Her beautiful jewelry indicated her *status* in the tribe.

distinct (adj) *clearly different*
Each culture has a *distinct* idea of beauty that is unlike the ideas of other cultures.

tribute (n) *something done, given, or said to show thanks or respect*
I wear my grandmother's favorite pin every day as a *tribute* to her.

tradition (n) *a custom, idea, or belief that is handed down from one generation to the next*
Long ago, people started the *tradition* of wearing a ring to show they were married.

ACADEMIC SKILL Remind students that they can compare and contrast as they read texts in other classes.

Introduce the Passage

1. Generate a class discussion about beauty with the following questions. **What is beauty? What influences our image of beauty? Does everyone have the same ideas about beauty?**

   To make the most of the discussion time, remember to incorporate strategies that encourage and extend student involvement. Refer to page xxxviii for a comprehensive discussion of these strategies.

2. Have students preview the photos in the passage "The Multicultural Search for Beauty." ***Conventional ideas* are what most people in your society think. Do you think the passage will be about conventional ideas about beauty in the United States? Why?** (No, the photos show practices uncommon in the United States.) Ask students to preview the passage. **What beauty practices described in the headings are also common here?** (piercings; tattoos) Tell students to form their prediction of what the passage is about. Write examples of predictions on the board. **How do you think this passage will relate to your own personal experience?**
3. Remind students to pause and respond to the margin prompts as they read.
4. Tell students they will find foreign words and some unfamiliar idioms in the passage. Teach these terms from the passage:
   - *Myanmar* (myon' mor)
   - *Kayan* (kī ən)
   - A *Finishing touch* is the last thing done to make something "perfect."
   - *Go to great lengths* means "to do things out of the ordinary or to the extreme."

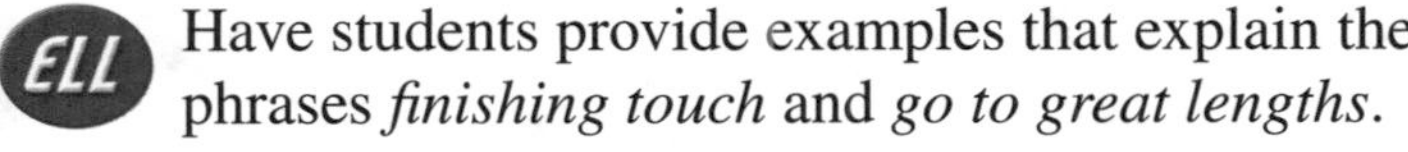

ELL Have students provide examples that explain the phrases *finishing touch* and *go to great lengths*.

During Reading

1. Have students read "The Multicultural Search for Beauty." To select reading options that support your students' levels and classroom needs, see Reading Differentiation, page xxxii, if needed.
2. **Remember to pay attention to the comparisons and contrasts. What will you do if there are no signal words?** (Pause and ask: How are these things alike or different?)

After Reading

Check Comprehension

1. Direct students to think about the predictions they made before reading the passage. **What parts of the passage fit with what you expected? What unexpected information did you learn? What experiences in your life relate to the information in the passage?**
2. Direct students to the Main Idea margin prompt on Anthology page 126. Have students share responses. (Responses should reflect the understanding that some women long ago and today will endure extreme pain and deformity to conform to their cultural ideas of beauty.)
3. Have individuals share their responses to the Ask Questions margin prompt on Anthology page 128.
4. Have students answer the following questions.
   - **What comparisons are made between teenage girls in America today and teenage girls in China 2,000 years ago?** (Both use cosmetics, hair products, and jewelry to alter their appearance.)
   - **Think about the reasons people pierce their noses. Compare the purpose of nose piercings and nose rings in India today and long ago.** (Today, nose rings are decoration; long ago, the size of the nose ring signified a family's wealth and status.)
   - **What beauty ideals from the passage did you find most peculiar? Which were most interesting? Why?** (Answers will vary.)

Remind students to choose books from the *Passport Reading Journeys* Library for independent reading.

"The Multicultural Search for Beauty"

Prepare to Reread

Introduce the Lesson

Remind students that they read about beauty ideals from other cultures. Tell students they will revisit the passage to practice comparing and contrasting.

Practice Vocabulary

1. Direct students to think about the passage vocabulary and how the words were used.
   - **How did the 15-year-old girl in the passage *alter* her appearance?** (She used cosmetics, hair products, and jewelry to change how she looked.)
   - **How did some wealthy women in 16th century India *assert* their importance in the community?** (They wore large nose rings and jewelry.)
   - **If you visited China long ago, how could you recognize a woman of high *status*?** (Her feet would be bound to make them stay very small.)
   - **What is an example of a *distinct* way to make yourself beautiful or attractive?** (Design your own tattoo; use neck rings.)
   - **How do some people use their tattoos as a *tribute* to someone?** (They have a name of someone they love tattooed on their body.)
   - **What is a beauty *tradition* in a culture you know or have read about?** (wearing lipstick and nail polish in the United States; piercings in many)
2. Remind students to use context clues to understand unfamiliar words. Have students turn to Anthology page 125. **What do you think the word *reflection* means? What clues help you determine the meaning?** (She looked in the mirror, so a reflection must be an image seen in the mirror.)

   Repeat this process for the following words.
   - **modified** (v) *altered*, Anthology page 125
   - **rival** (adj) *competing against each other*, Anthology page 127
   - **significance** (n) *importance*, Anthology page 127
   - **supernatural** (n) *beyond natural*, Anthology page 129

Expedition 7, Lesson 7

Name ______________________ Date ____________

Word Building

A. The word *tribute* means "something done, given, or said to show thanks or respect." The English word comes from the Latin word *tributum*, which means "to pay." Read other words that use this root.

tribute *something done, given, or said to show thanks or respect*
distribute *scatter or spread something throughout a particular area or place*
attribute *think of something as caused by a particular circumstance*
contribute *be one of the factors that causes something; give for the benefit of something*

B. Complete each sentence with one of the boldfaced words in Part A.

1. People may ___attribute___ their views about beauty to their values, lifestyle, and culture.
2. Japanese tattoo artists are always careful to ___distribute___ the color on the tattoo evenly.
3. Women wore corsets to make them look more attractive. This practice often would ___contribute___ to making them feel sick. Corsets occasionally caused broken ribs and organ damage.
4. The fashion of wearing neck coils was not always for beauty. At one time, it was a way to pay ___tribute___ to a god or deity.

C. Create new words by adding suffixes to words from Part A. Use your affixionary to write definitions.

Word	Suffix	New Word	New Definition
contribute	+ *-ory*	contributory	relating to giving or causing something
distribute	+ *-tion*	distribution	the act of spreading out
contribute	+ *-tion*	contribution	the act of giving
distribute	+ *-or*	distributor	one who spreads something
contribute	+ *-or*	contributor	one who gives something

©Voyager Expanded Learning, Inc. 236

3. Have students turn to Student Book page 236 and follow along as you read instructions. **You have learned the meaning of the word *tribute*. Other words contain the same root, such as *distribute*, *attribute*, and *contribute*.** Have students complete the page independently. Have partners discuss their responses.

CHECKPOINT If students have difficulty choosing the correct word for sentences in Part B, review the word meanings and use each word orally in a sample sentence.

Reread

Apply the Target Skill: Compare and Contrast

1. Remind students to look for comparisons and contrasts as they reread "The Multicultural Search for Beauty." **When I read, I actively look for similarities and differences among ideas. I can use a Venn diagram to keep track of my ideas.**
2. Have students turn to Student Book page 237. Read the instructions aloud.
3. Point out the overlapping sections and what kind of information to write in each. **What is one thing we know is true for all three?** (Answers will vary.) **Write that in the center section where all three circles overlap.** Have students complete the activity.
4. **Reread or scan the passage to complete the page.** Have partners share their completed diagrams.

ACADEMIC SKILL Remind students to use a Venn diagram when they compare and contrast two or more topics in other texts, such as different characters in literature.

ELL Refer to Blackline Master page 41 to extend practice with comparing and contrasting.

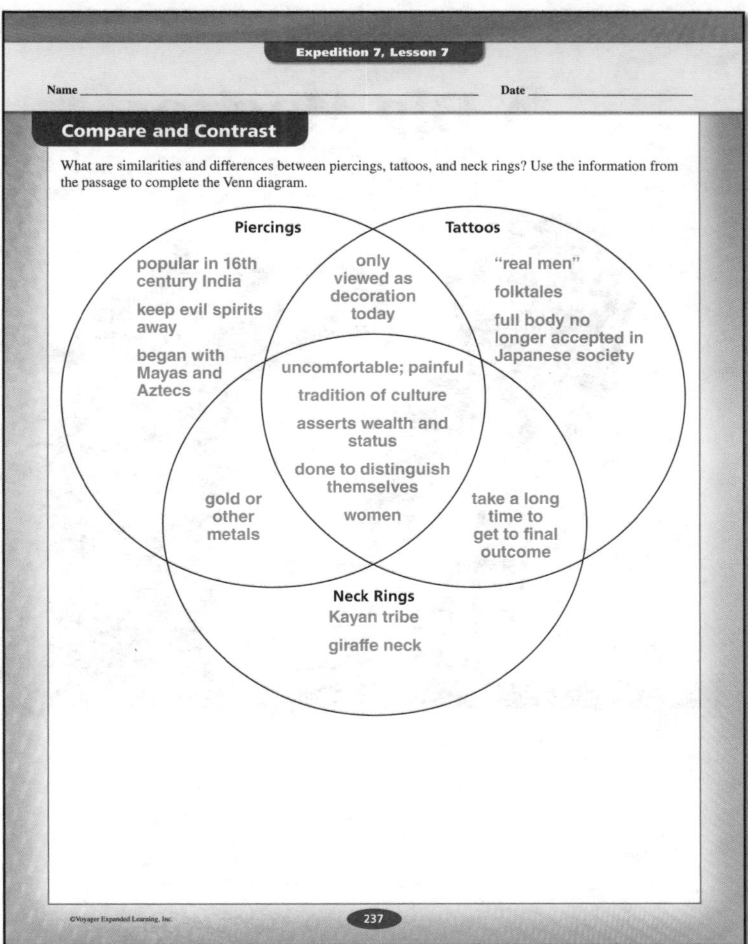

Expedition 7, Lesson 7

Name ____________________ Date ____________

Compare and Contrast

What are similarities and differences between piercings, tattoos, and neck rings? Use the information from the passage to complete the Venn diagram.

©Voyager Expanded Learning, Inc. 237

Expedition 7, Lesson 7

Name ____________________ Date ____________

Write in Response to Reading

A. In the left column, list beauty enhancements from "The Multicultural Search for Beauty." In the middle column, list positive effects of the enhancements. In the right column, list negative effects of the enhancements. The first one is done for you. Possible responses are given.

Enhancements	Positive Effects	Negative Effects
cosmetics and hair products	can make people feel confident and good about themselves	can make people feel inadequate and ugly if they do not use them every day
neck rings	are part of the Kayan tradition; passed on from generation to generation	are heavy and cause a deformed neck
foot binding	once made women feel special and exclusive	painful; causes deformity; makes women unable to walk
nose rings	used as decoration only; may help give people identity and exhibit their personality	can be painful and unsanitary

B. Imagine some people in your community want to pass The Just Plain You Law. If passed, it will be illegal to alter your appearance with beauty enhancements. Each person must appear in public as "natural." Take a position for or against the law by checking a box. Write your argument, and give reasons for your position.

The Just Plain You Law

☐ For ☐ Against

Students should use persuasive techniques to argue for or against the case for beauty. Students taking the "for" position may cite reasons of health and safety concerns (surgery, eating disorders, deformity) as well as how an ideal standard of beauty may be unobtainable and may cause damage to identity and self-esteem. Students taking the "against" position may cite reasons of tradition and culture, as well as personal preference and expression in choosing how they look.

©Voyager Expanded Learning, Inc. 238

Write in Response to Reading

1. Prepare students to complete the writing activity on Student Book page 238. Read the instructions for Part A. **What are the positive and negative effects of beauty enhancements?** Have students complete the chart and share with a partner.
2. Read the instructions for Part B aloud. Remind students to use the chart from Part A, support from "The Multicultural Search for Beauty," and their own prior knowledge as they write their argument.

EXPEDITION ORGANIZER **Across Cultures**

Pause to have students turn to Student Book pages 214 and 215. Have students complete the following:

- Write answers to the probing questions in Part A. If they have not yet added a question, encourage them to add their own.
- Think about the big idea from "The Multicultural Search for Beauty." Tell students to write it in the appropriate section of Part B.

A Big Mac for Everyone?

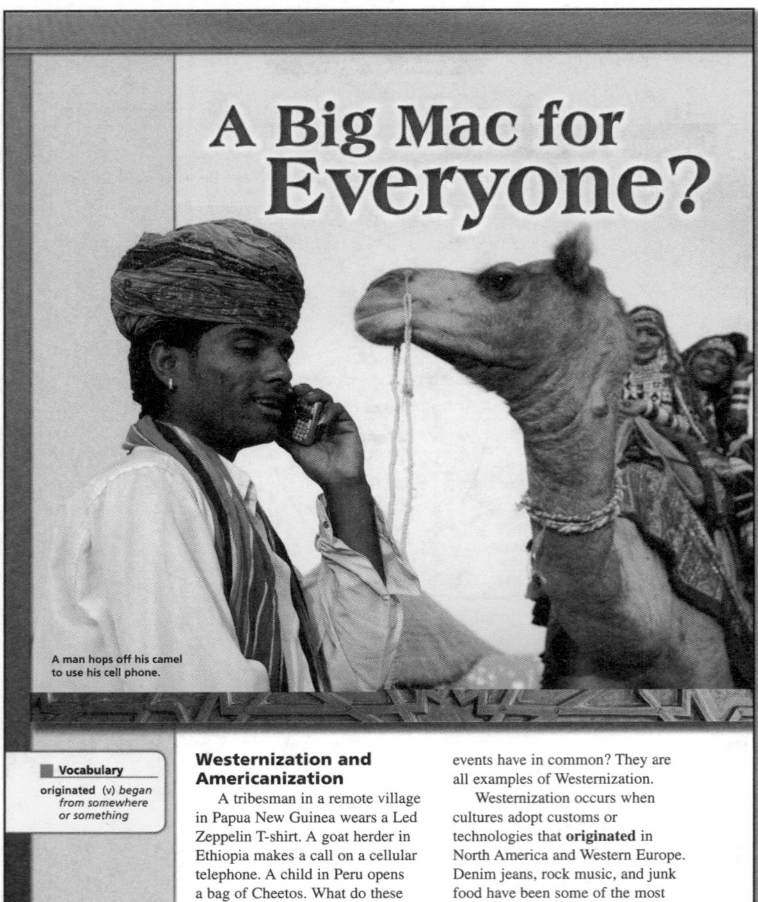

A man hops off his camel to use his cell phone.

Vocabulary

originated (v) *began from somewhere or something*

Westernization and Americanization

A tribesman in a remote village in Papua New Guinea wears a Led Zeppelin T-shirt. A goat herder in Ethiopia makes a call on a cellular telephone. A child in Peru opens a bag of Cheetos. What do these events have in common? They are all examples of Westernization.

Westernization occurs when cultures adopt customs or technologies that **originated** in North America and Western Europe. Denim jeans, rock music, and junk food have been some of the most

American-made washing machines are imported around the world. Why do you think this modern convenience is so popular?

Vocabulary

incorporate (v) *make a part of something else*

prevalent (adj) *common or usual*

remote (adj) *far away, isolated, or distant*

imported (adj) *from another country*

popular fashions and trends that Western culture has brought to the rest of the world. Technologies, like washing machines, refrigerators, cell phones, and computers, have also made their way into other cultures.

Often a culture will adopt some elements of another culture and **incorporate** those elements into their own traditions. Heavy metal music, for example, originated in the United States, but there are countless bands in the Middle East that have made that form of music their own. Many countries have incorporated some elements of Western dress along with their classic clothing. As a result, you might see a Fijian woman wearing Nikes with her traditional grass skirt.

Americanization is Westernization that comes specifically from the culture of the United States. All over the world, American movies, music, clothing, and even foods are **prevalent**. If you visit places as far away as Jerusalem, Cape Town, and Beijing, you will recognize the same chains of restaurants and shops, the same styles of clothing, and the same kinds of technology. However, Americanization is not limited to big cities. In fact, aspects of American culture have made their way to some of the most **remote** places on the planet. **Imported** VCRs or DVD players bring American movies to any town or village with electricity. The products and technology that viewers observe in those movies are often considered modern and desirable, particularly by young people.

However, American culture is often at odds with traditional cultures. Short skirts and tight shirts, for example, are prohibited in many cultures. Graphic song lyrics are offensive; food items may be forbidden. On the other hand, cell phones make communication easier,

A Chinese man delivers Coca-Cola. How is soda transported in the United States?

1 Context Clues

Using context clues, what do you think conveniences means?

and conveniences like washing machines and refrigerators make daily tasks less time-consuming. 1

Some people say that the importation of Western or American technology, foods, medicines, and clothing make people's lives in non-Western countries easier and better. Other people say that Westernization is bad—stripping cultures of what makes them unique and self-sufficient. Many elders believe that the incorporation of any Western way of life is destructive and forces them to rely on other countries, which is perceived as bad. Most likely, the truth is somewhere between those two extremes.

Let's take a look at an example of Americanization that may be familiar to you.

Case Study in Americanization: McDonald's

With more than 13,000 restaurants in the United States, it is likely that there is a McDonald's in your neighborhood. But, did you know that there are McDonald's restaurants in 119 countries and territories across the globe? What started in 1940 as a hamburger stand in San Bernardino, California, became a symbol of American culture throughout the world. When McDonald's opens its first restaurant in a new country or

A McDonald's in Jordan. Do you think they serve any specialty items here?

community, it is generally welcomed as a sign of modernization. People line up to be among the first to eat at the new restaurant. At the grand opening of McDonald's in Kuwait City, the drive-thru line was 7 miles long. [2]

There may be benefits to a community when McDonald's opens a restaurant. Among these benefits is that McDonald's brings money into a community by providing jobs for local employees. In addition, the McDonald's Corporation donates money to local charitable **organizations**. Finally, McDonald's holds to high standards of cleanliness and food quality. A study in Hong Kong showed that the clean public bathrooms available in McDonald's restaurants put pressure on other restaurants to provide the same level of service and hygiene.

There also may be drawbacks, or disadvantages, for a community when McDonald's arrives. Often, elders in a community mourn the loss of traditional foods and ways of life. Rather than eating a home-cooked meal made with local ingredients and taken with extended family, young people can grab a hamburger imported from far away. Although McDonald's makes an effort to include local dishes on its menus, such as rice and beans in Costa Rica and a vegetarian burger in India, those choices are not as prevalent as burgers, fries, and shakes. In addition, the food that McDonald's sells is often higher in fat, salt, and sugar than traditional foods. This unhealthy food can

Vocabulary

organizations (n) *groups of people joined for particular purposes*

[2] Make Connections

What would you be willing to wait in a 7-mile long line for?

[3] Summarize

Summarize the drawbacks of an American restaurant moving into a new country.

[4] Text Features

Using the map can help you understand the text. Why do you think these areas have no McDonald's? What do they have in common?

lead to increases in fatal health conditions, such as heart disease, obesity, and diabetes. [3]

Clearly, Westernization is a complicated issue. While there are benefits, like simplifying household tasks with imported technology, there are also drawbacks, like changing ways of life that have worked for thousands of years.

Un-Westernized Cultures

Whether by choice or because of forces beyond their control, some cultures have not had much contact with the Western world. A map of McDonald's locations shows a number of countries in Africa and Central Asia without McDonald's restaurants. [4] There are probably multiple reasons for this. Perhaps the local people or governments are resistant to Westernization. Equally likely, those places do not have the infrastructure, or basic facilities, to support a McDonald's. Perhaps there are no paved roads, or the roads are damaged or dangerous. Perhaps people do not have enough money to eat at a restaurant because their economy is not money-based. The most remote cultures tend to resist the advances of Westernization most successfully just because they are difficult to access. Imagine trying to set up and stock a McDonald's in a Pakistani village that's an 8-hour hike from the nearest paved road!

As it becomes easier to access technology, even the most remote cultures are likely to be affected by Westernization. This can be good and bad. People would like to have the freedom to choose the things that will make their lives easier and better, regardless of where they originated. At the same time, it would be a very boring world if everyone wore the same clothes, listened to the same music, and ate the same foods. Perhaps a Big Mac should be a choice, but it should not be the only choice. End

McDonald's Spans the Globe

"A Big Mac for Everyone?"

Before Reading

Introduce Vocabulary

1. Have students turn to Part A on Student Book page 239 and scan the boldfaced vocabulary words. **These words will appear in "A Big Mac for Everyone?"** Read the instructions as students follow along. Have students complete Part A.
2. Have partners talk about words they rated as the most familiar.
3. Read the words, parts of speech, definitions, and example sentences aloud. Give an additional example sentence or scenario for the words students rated 1 or 2. **Remember that *prevalent* means something common. For example, ice is *prevalent* in the Arctic.**
4. Read the instructions for Part B. Have students complete the sentences and discuss them with a partner.

ELL Refer to Blackline Master page 42 to extend vocabulary practice.

Have students use the *Passport Reading Journeys* online technology component to practice and reinforce vocabulary and comprehension skills.

Expedition 7, Lesson 8

Name ______ Date ______

Vocabulary

"A Big Mac for Everyone?"

A. Number the vocabulary words in order of how well you know them with 1 as the least familiar and 6 as the most familiar. Compare with a partner. Talk about the words you ranked as most familiar.

6 most familiar → 5 → 4 → 3 → 2 → 1 least familiar

☐ **originated** (v) *began from somewhere or something*
Heavy metal music *originated* in the United States, then spread across the world.

☐ **incorporate** (v) *make a part of something else*
Many cultures try to *incorporate* some Western conveniences into their societies.

☐ **prevalent** (adj) *common or usual*
Many teens still wear blue jeans, which have been a *prevalent* part of teenage clothing for decades.

☐ **remote** (adj) *far away, isolated, or distant*
The man was stranded on a *remote* island with no human contact for one year.

☐ **imported** (adj) *from another country*
U.S. washing machines are an *imported* convenience in many countries.

☐ **organizations** (n) *groups of people joined for particular purposes*
She works for charitable *organizations* that provide food for the hungry.

B. Choose the boldfaced word from Part A that BEST completes each sentence.

1. Discount stores sell many __imported__ products like toys, electronics, and clothes from India.
2. Trekking to a __remote__ village in the mountains is a difficult journey.
3. My family donates to __organizations__ that provide money for cancer research.
4. Rock music has become __prevalent__ throughout the world.
5. Some fast-food restaurants __incorporate__ yogurt, fruit, and salads in their menus.
6. Some say the hamburger sandwich __originated__ in 1885 near Hamburg, New York.

 239

Vocabulary

originated (v) *began from somewhere or something*
Heavy metal music *originated* in the United States, then spread across the world.

incorporate (v) *make a part of something else*
Many cultures try to *incorporate* some Western conveniences into their societies.

prevalent (adj) *common or usual*
Many teens still wear blue jeans, which have been a *prevalent* part of teenage clothing for decades.

remote (adj) *far away, isolated, or distant*
The man was stranded on a *remote* island with no human contact for one year.

imported (adj) *from another country*
U.S. washing machines are an *imported* convenience in many countries.

organizations (n) *groups of people joined for particular purposes*
She works for charitable *organizations* that provide food for the hungry.

Apply the Target Skill: Big Picture Notes

1. Remind students that they already learned about taking Big Picture notes. **When you take Big Picture notes, you divide your paper, write the headings and subheadings with plenty of space beneath them, take notes as you read, write questions on the right, and summarize your notes.**
2. Have students return to their Big Picture notes from Expedition 6 on Student Book page 201. **How do you use each section of the notes?** Remind students that they write notes on the left side of the page as they listen to or read a text; they write questions on the right side when they are done reading or listening; and they review what they wrote in the columns and write a summary.
3. Tell students they will take Big Picture notes in Lesson 9.

ACADEMIC SKILL Remind students that they can use Big Picture notes in other classes to help understand how ideas work together. They can fold their paper to easily study the notes or have someone quiz them.

Introduce the Passage

1. Have students preview "A Big Mac for Everyone?" on Anthology page 130. **Before you read, preview the passage. Predict what the passage is about.** Have students share their predictions.
2. Remind students to pause and respond to the margin prompts as they read. **If you do not know the name of a country or place when reading, what should you do?** (Look back to see if you missed a clue; ask a question about it; keep the question in mind as you continue reading.) **What should you focus on when reading?** (the important ideas)
3. Demonstrate the pronunciation of these terms from the passage:
   - *Papua New Guinea* (pa pu' ə nū gi' nē)
   - *Fijian* (fē jē' ən)
   - *Jerusalem* (jə rü sə ləm)
   - *Beijing* (bā jing)
   - *Pakistani* (pa ki sta' nē)

During Reading

1. **Look for main ideas and important details as you read "A Big Mac for Everyone?"** To select reading options that support your students' levels and classroom needs, see Reading Differentiation, page xxxii, if needed.
2. Remind students to look at the headings within the passage before reading each section.

After Reading

Check Comprehension

1. When students finish reading, have them tell the most important information in the passage. **What did you think was important to remember?** Write the information on the board and leave it for the next lesson.
2. Have students think about their predictions about the passage. **How accurate were your predictions?**
3. Have students share answers to the Make Connections margin prompt on Anthology page 133. **Now put yourself in the place of people described in the passage who waited hours for fast food. Explain how you think the people felt.**

   To make the most of the discussion time, remember to incorporate strategies that encourage and extend student involvement. Refer to page xxxviii for a comprehensive discussion of these strategies.
4. Read aloud the Summarize margin prompt on Anthology page 134, and have partners prepare a brief summary. Have partners state the summary aloud. (The drawbacks to the global expansion of McDonald's are that families do not eat at home together, the food is not as healthful, and people get used to a limited variety of food.)

Remind students to choose books from the *Passport Reading Journeys* Library for independent reading.

"A Big Mac for Everyone?"

Prepare to Reread

Introduce the Lesson

Ask students if they think Westernization has had more of a positive or negative impact in other cultures. **In Lesson 9, we'll revisit "A Big Mac for Everyone?" and practice taking Big Picture notes.**

Practice Vocabulary

1. Remind students how the vocabulary words were used in the passage.
   - **What types of music *originated* in the United States?** (rock music; blues; jazz)
   - **What do you *incorporate* into your life from another culture?** (food; music; fashions)
   - **What types of entertainment are *prevalent* in cultures all over the world?** (movies; music; dance)
   - **How do people in *remote* areas of the world learn about the United States?** (watch movies)
   - **If you live in the United States and you bought an *imported* TV, where was it made?** (in another country)
   - **How is one person working for a purpose different from *organizations* working for the same purpose?** (Organizations are groups of people working together for a cause or purpose.)
2. Direct students to Anthology page 134. **Remember that you can use context clues to determine the meanings of unfamiliar words or phrases. What do you think the word *infrastructure* means?** (basic facilities) **How did you determine the meaning?** (It is written in the text.)

   Repeat this process for the following words.
   - **adopt** (v) *make your own*, Anthology page 131
   - **self-sufficient** (adj) *rely on yourself only*, Anthology page 132
   - **drawbacks** (n) *disadvantages*, Anthology page 133

ELL Directly explain the definition of the words used in context. Allow students to find clues in the text to support the definition. Refer to English Language Learner Overview, page 281, for more activities supporting these words.

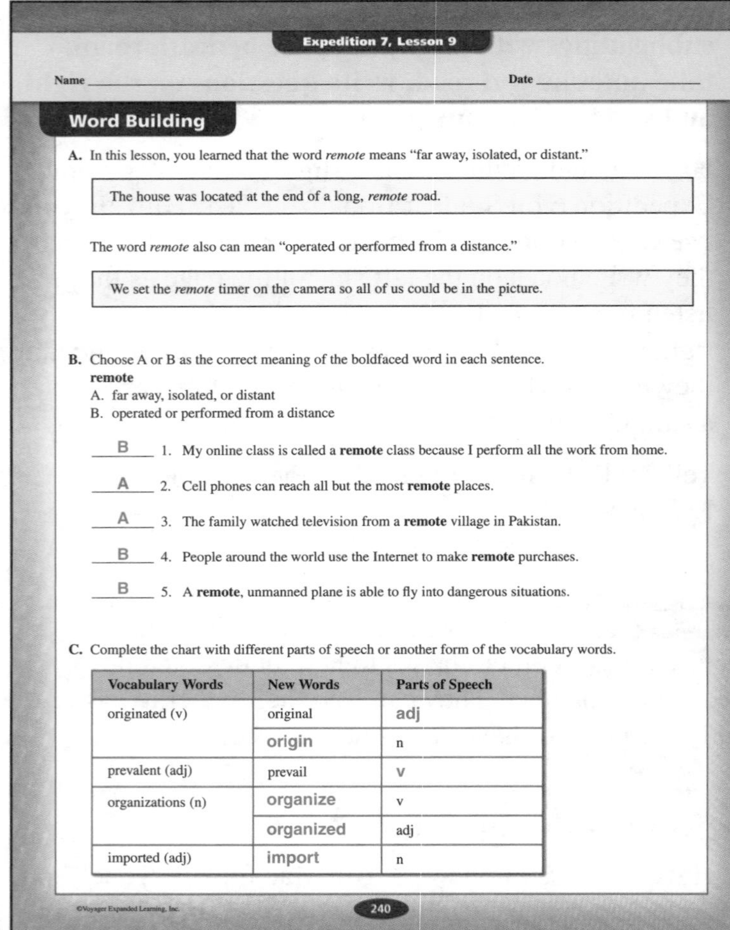

Expedition 7, Lesson 9

Name ______ Date ______

Word Building

A. In this lesson, you learned that the word *remote* means "far away, isolated, or distant."

The house was located at the end of a long, *remote* road.

The word *remote* also can mean "operated or performed from a distance."

We set the *remote* timer on the camera so all of us could be in the picture.

B. Choose A or B as the correct meaning of the boldfaced word in each sentence.
remote
A. far away, isolated, or distant
B. operated or performed from a distance

B 1. My online class is called a **remote** class because I perform all the work from home.
A 2. Cell phones can reach all but the most **remote** places.
A 3. The family watched television from a **remote** village in Pakistan.
B 4. People around the world use the Internet to make **remote** purchases.
B 5. A **remote**, unmanned plane is able to fly into dangerous situations.

C. Complete the chart with different parts of speech or another form of the vocabulary words.

Vocabulary Words	New Words	Parts of Speech
originated (v)	original	adj
	origin	n
prevalent (adj)	prevail	v
organizations (n)	organize	v
	organized	adj
imported (adj)	import	n

©Voyager Expanded Learning, Inc. 240

3. Have students turn to Student Book page 240. **Some words have more than one meaning.** Read the instructions aloud. Have students complete the page.

CHECKPOINT If students have difficulty creating new words for Part C, create a list of possible answers for them to choose from.

Reread

Apply the Target Skill: Big Picture Notes

1. **You will use Student Book page 241 to take Big Picture notes about "A Big Mac for Everyone?" The first step (writing headings) has been done for you.** Have students turn to Anthology page 130 and scan or reread the passage and take notes under each heading.
2. **Next, write questions on the right side.**
3. Finally, remind students that they should use the questions and notes when writing the summary.

4. Point out the information on the board. Discuss which items are important and which items are not. Use the following as a guide to what should be in their notes.
    - **What is the difference between Americanization and Westernization?** (Westernization means using products or ideas that originated in North America or Western Europe; Americanization means using products or ideas that are American.)
    - **When a McDonald's opens in a foreign country, what are the benefits for that country?** (more jobs for local people; cleanliness for the customers; money donated to local organizations)
    - **Why would some cultures not want to become Westernized?** (Local residents and governments do not want to lose their traditions and their unique identities.)

Write in Response to Reading

Have students turn to Student Book page 242. Read the instructions and the start of each journal entry. Remind students that the point of view of the characters may be similar, different, or a combination. **As you learn more facts about an issue or topic, you have more reasons for your ideas.** Encourage students to use facts to support the characters' opinions.

EXPEDITION ORGANIZER **Across Cultures**

Pause to have students turn to Student Book pages 214 and 215. Have students complete the following:

- Write answers to one or more of the probing questions in Part A. Ask students if they can answer their question now that the Expedition is complete. If not, encourage them to research to find the answer.
- Think about the big idea from "A Big Mac for Everyone?" Tell students to write it in the organizer, then read the prompt in the center box and write their response.
- Complete the Dictionary Challenge in Part C.

Build Background DVD 7.2

Briefly discuss the Expedition passages, then watch the DVD together. After watching, review student responses to the probing questions using the Expedition Organizer.

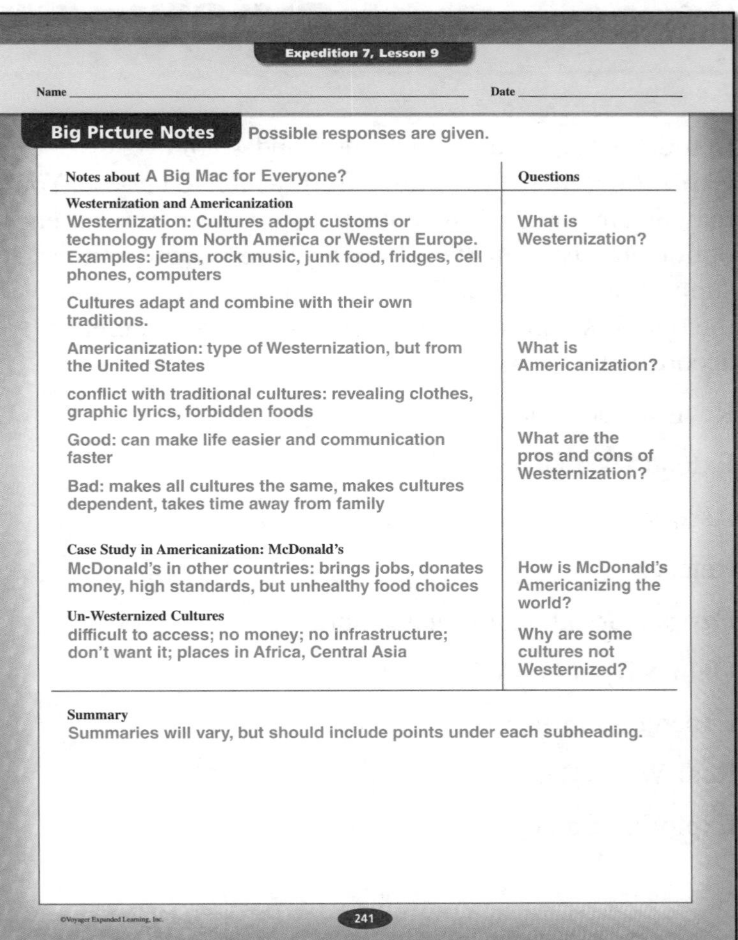

Expedition 7, Lesson 9

Name ______ Date ______

Big Picture Notes Possible responses are given.

Notes about A Big Mac for Everyone?	Questions
Westernization and Americanization Westernization: Cultures adopt customs or technology from North America or Western Europe. Examples: jeans, rock music, junk food, fridges, cell phones, computers	What is Westernization?
Cultures adapt and combine with their own traditions.	
Americanization: type of Westernization, but from the United States	What is Americanization?
conflict with traditional cultures: revealing clothes, graphic lyrics, forbidden foods	
Good: can make life easier and communication faster Bad: makes all cultures the same, makes cultures dependent, takes time away from family	What are the pros and cons of Westernization?
Case Study in Americanization: McDonald's McDonald's in other countries: brings jobs, donates money, high standards, but unhealthy food choices	How is McDonald's Americanizing the world?
Un-Westernized Cultures difficult to access; no money; no infrastructure; don't want it; places in Africa, Central Asia	Why are some cultures not Westernized?

Summary
Summaries will vary, but should include points under each subheading.

©Voyager Expanded Learning, Inc. 241

Expedition 7, Lesson 9

Name ______ Date ______

Write in Response to Reading

Imagine that the first McDonald's restaurant in Bolivia is being built. Read the following journal entries. What opinions and feelings do you think Melissa and Rudolfo have? Will their points of view be similar or different? Complete their journal entries. Use details from the article "A Big Mac for Everyone?" and your own imagination to support the opinions and ideas. Answers will vary.

Journal Entry of Melissa Granger **October 20**

In two weeks, I will leave Greenville. I will travel to South America to work as the manager of the first McDonald's in La Paz, Bolivia. ______

Journal Entry of Rudolfo Mesa **October 20**

Every day, my wife, my three children, and I walk past the construction site of the McDonald's. It will open soon in my town. ______

 242

Review, Extend, Assess

In today's lesson, as in Lessons 5 and 10 of every Expedition, there are options from which to choose. You may do any or all of the options listed. Activities for each option are given on the following pages. Each option will support or extend previously taught objectives. Choose the option(s) appropriate for your students and prepare accordingly.

Review Vocabulary

Extend Vocabulary

Assess Comprehension and Vocabulary

Reteach

Passport Reading Journeys Library

Online Technology Component

Expedition Project

Real-World Reading

Exploring Careers

Review Vocabulary

Direct students to review the vocabulary for "The Multicultural Search for Beauty" and "A Big Mac for Everyone?" on Student Book page 215.

1. Have students read the words and definitions.
2. Have students turn to Student Book page 243. **You previously read these vocabulary words in the reading passages. Now you will read the vocabulary in different contexts, but the words will have the same meanings.** Read the instructions aloud, and have students complete the activities. As students complete the review activity, have them go back and check the definitions to ensure they used the words correctly. Have students share their answers.
3. In Part A, if students have difficulty identifying synonyms, remind them that the sentence will mean the same with the underlined word and the synonym. Have them read through the sentence twice—first for understanding, then using the phrase *another word for* before the underlined word. For Part B, complete three items with students who have difficulty, then have them complete the last three independently.

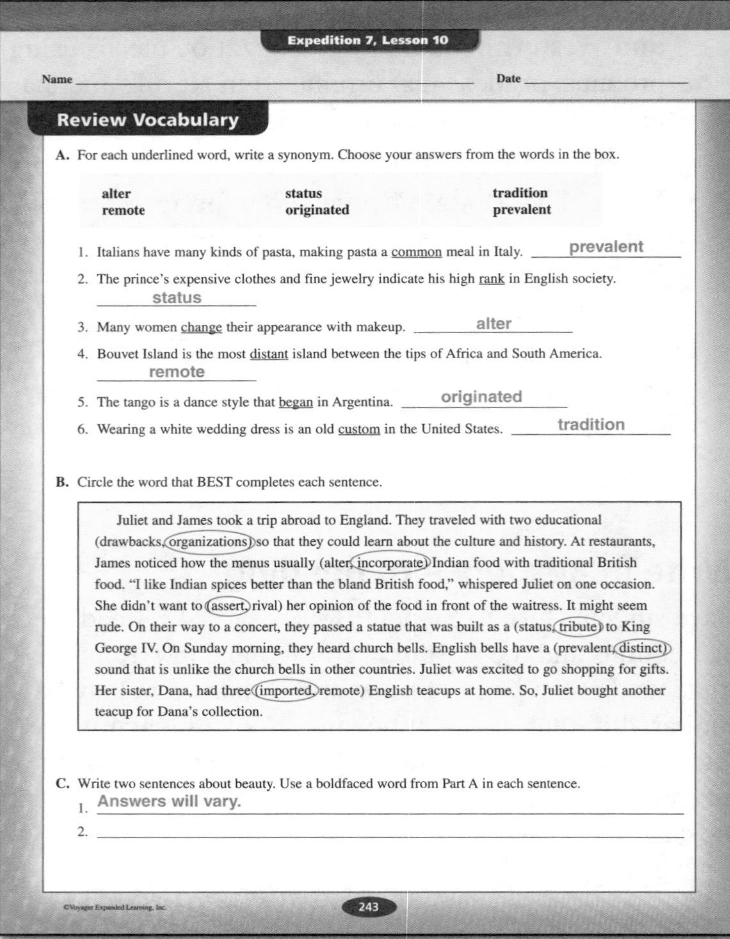
Expedition 7, Lesson 10

Name ________ Date ________

Review Vocabulary

A. For each underlined word, write a synonym. Choose your answers from the words in the box.

alter	**status**	**tradition**
remote	**originated**	**prevalent**

1. Italians have many kinds of pasta, making pasta a common meal in Italy. prevalent
2. The prince's expensive clothes and fine jewelry indicate his high rank in English society. status
3. Many women change their appearance with makeup. alter
4. Bouvet Island is the most distant island between the tips of Africa and South America. remote
5. The tango is a dance style that began in Argentina. originated
6. Wearing a white wedding dress is an old custom in the United States. tradition

B. Circle the word that BEST completes each sentence.

Juliet and James took a trip abroad to England. They traveled with two educational (drawbacks, organizations) so that they could learn about the culture and history. At restaurants, James noticed how the menus usually (alter, incorporate) Indian food with traditional British food. "I like Indian spices better than the bland British food," whispered Juliet on one occasion. She didn't want to (assert, rival) her opinion of the food in front of the waitress. It might seem rude. On their way to a concert, they passed a statue that was built as a (status, tribute) to King George IV. On Sunday morning, they heard church bells. English bells have a (prevalent, distinct) sound that is unlike the church bells in other countries. Juliet was excited to go shopping for gifts. Her sister, Dana, had three (imported, remote) English teacups at home. So, Juliet bought another teacup for Dana's collection.

C. Write two sentences about beauty. Use a boldfaced word from Part A in each sentence.
1. Answers will vary.
2. ________

©Voyager Expanded Learning, Inc. 243

CHECKPOINT Provide additional support for students who had difficulty choosing words in Part B. Have students read the sentences aloud. Tell them to read the sentence twice, inserting one of the words each time. Ask students which word makes the most sense or sounds right.

Extend Vocabulary

1. Direct students to Student Book page 244. **Many words in English, such as *imported*, come from Latin.** Write the Latin word *portare*, meaning "carry" on the board.

   portare: carry

2. Write the word *imported* on the board. Underline *port* inside the word. Have students underline the root *port* in each word in Part A. Read aloud the words and definitions. **What is similar about all of these words?** (They have to do with carrying or moving things or people from one place to another.) **Which are opposites?** (export and import) **Which is a place?** (port) Have students circle the most unfamiliar word in the list. Provide examples for that word.

3. Read aloud the instructions for Parts B and C. **You can reread the definitions to help you.** Have students complete the activities, then share their responses.

CHECKPOINT When students share their responses for Parts B and C, listen to ensure they used the new words in the correct contexts. Pause to explain and correct any errors.

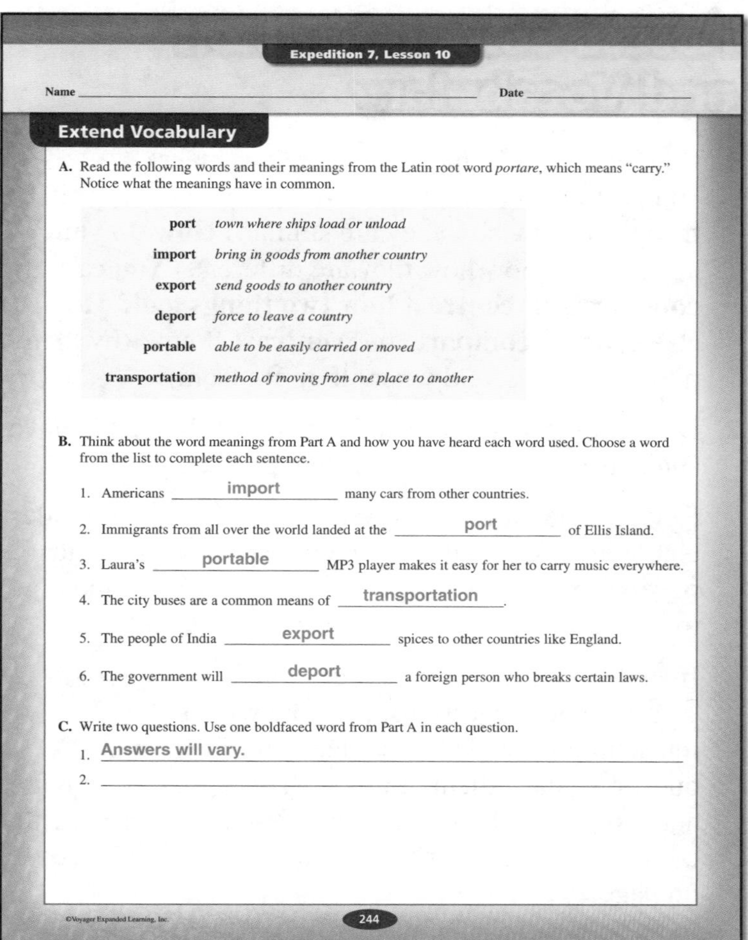

Expedition 7, Lesson 10

Name ______ Date ______

Extend Vocabulary

A. Read the following words and their meanings from the Latin root word *portare*, which means "carry." Notice what the meanings have in common.

port	*town where ships load or unload*
import	*bring in goods from another country*
export	*send goods to another country*
deport	*force to leave a country*
portable	*able to be easily carried or moved*
transportation	*method of moving from one place to another*

B. Think about the word meanings from Part A and how you have heard each word used. Choose a word from the list to complete each sentence.

1. Americans import many cars from other countries.
2. Immigrants from all over the world landed at the port of Ellis Island.
3. Laura's portable MP3 player makes it easy for her to carry music everywhere.
4. The city buses are a common means of transportation.
5. The people of India export spices to other countries like England.
6. The government will deport a foreign person who breaks certain laws.

C. Write two questions. Use one boldfaced word from Part A in each question.

1. Answers will vary.
2. ______

©Voyager Expanded Learning, Inc.

244

Part A

1. Write the boldfaced words, and underline the root *port* in each of them. **Root words may come from other languages. Do you know any words in other languages that contain the root *port*?**

2. Explore each new word by reading the definition, using the words in a sentence, and asking students to answer a question about the word. ***Transportation* is a method of going from one place to another. What *transportation* do you use?** Have students answer using the following sentence frame: *To get from place to place, I use _____ as transportation.*

Part B

If students have difficulty completing the sentences, turn the sentence into a question with the blank as an answer. **Americans _____ many cars from other countries. How do Americans get cars from other countries?** (import them)

Part C

Before students create questions, write *who*, *what*, *where*, *when*, *how*, and *why* on the board. **Think of questions that begin with these words. Picture scenes with words like *port* and *transportation* and use those ideas to form your questions.**

Assess Comprehension and Vocabulary

1. Remind students that they learned to make comparisons and contrasts. **How do you compare things?** (Show how they are similar.) **How do you contrast?** (Show how they are different.) **You can compare and contrast how two things look. How else can you compare and contrast them?** (by their purposes, ideas, and where they are from)

2. Direct students to Student Book pages 245–247. Have students complete the pages independently.

   Review student answers. Whenever possible, provide elaborative feedback to student responses. Refer to page xl for examples of elaborative feedback and how to incorporate it in your lessons.

   If students incorrectly answer more than 4 out of 15 assessment questions, evaluate what kind of reteaching is needed. If students miss vocabulary questions, have them return to the vocabulary activities and work with the words they missed. For errors with compare and contrast, use the reteaching suggestions on page 297.

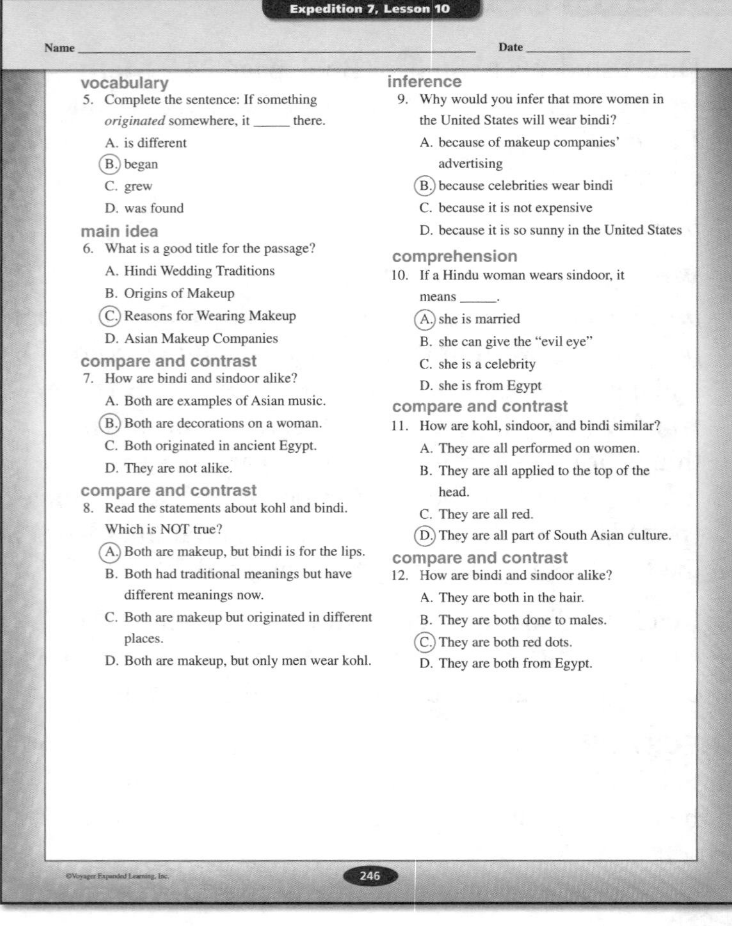

Expedition 7, Lesson 10

Name ____________________ Date ____________

vocabulary
5. Complete the sentence: If something *originated* somewhere, it _____ there.
   A. is different
   (B.) began
   C. grew
   D. was found

main idea
6. What is a good title for the passage?
   A. Hindi Wedding Traditions
   B. Origins of Makeup
   (C.) Reasons for Wearing Makeup
   D. Asian Makeup Companies

compare and contrast
7. How are bindi and sindoor alike?
   A. Both are examples of Asian music.
   (B.) Both are decorations on a woman.
   C. Both originated in ancient Egypt.
   D. They are not alike.

compare and contrast
8. Read the statements about kohl and bindi. Which is NOT true?
   (A.) Both are makeup, but bindi is for the lips.
   B. Both had traditional meanings but have different meanings now.
   C. Both are makeup but originated in different places.
   D. Both are makeup, but only men wear kohl.

inference
9. Why would you infer that more women in the United States will wear bindi?
   A. because of makeup companies' advertising
   (B.) because celebrities wear bindi
   C. because it is not expensive
   D. because it is so sunny in the United States

comprehension
10. If a Hindu woman wears sindoor, it means _____.
   (A.) she is married
   B. she can give the "evil eye"
   C. she is a celebrity
   D. she is from Egypt

compare and contrast
11. How are kohl, sindoor, and bindi similar?
   A. They are all performed on women.
   B. They are all applied to the top of the head.
   C. They are all red.
   (D.) They are all part of South Asian culture.

compare and contrast
12. How are bindi and sindoor alike?
   A. They are both in the hair.
   B. They are both done to males.
   (C.) They are both red dots.
   D. They are both from Egypt.

©Voyager Expanded Learning, Inc. 246

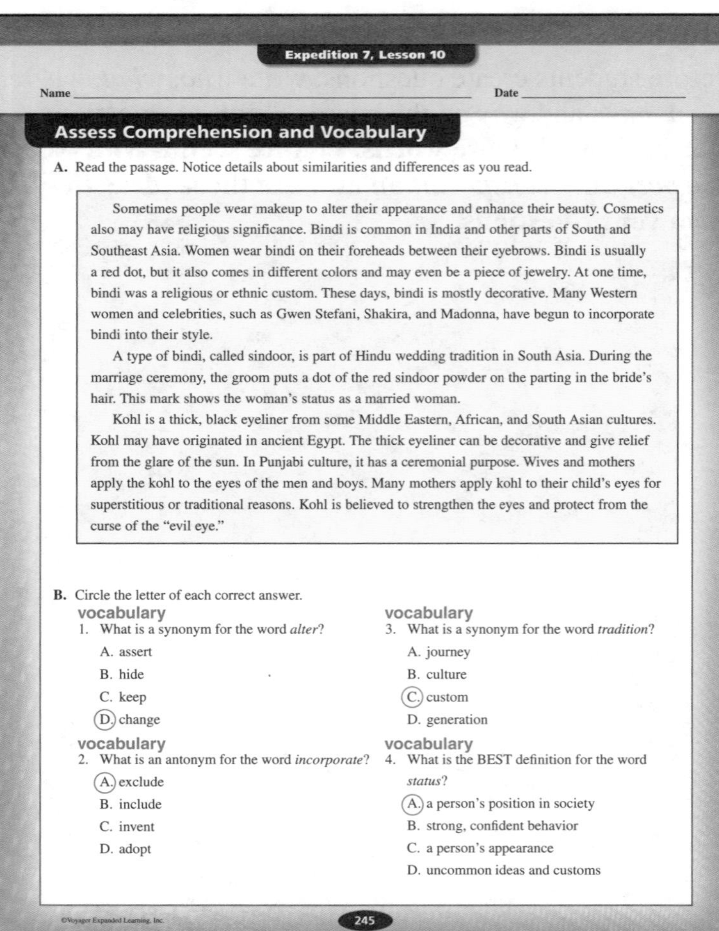

Expedition 7, Lesson 10

Name ____________________ Date ____________

Assess Comprehension and Vocabulary

A. Read the passage. Notice details about similarities and differences as you read.

Sometimes people wear makeup to alter their appearance and enhance their beauty. Cosmetics also may have religious significance. Bindi is common in India and other parts of South and Southeast Asia. Women wear bindi on their foreheads between their eyebrows. Bindi is usually a red dot, but it also comes in different colors and may even be a piece of jewelry. At one time, bindi was a religious or ethnic custom. These days, bindi is mostly decorative. Many Western women and celebrities, such as Gwen Stefani, Shakira, and Madonna, have begun to incorporate bindi into their style.

A type of bindi, called sindoor, is part of Hindu wedding tradition in South Asia. During the marriage ceremony, the groom puts a dot of the red sindoor powder on the parting in the bride's hair. This mark shows the woman's status as a married woman.

Kohl is a thick, black eyeliner from some Middle Eastern, African, and South Asian cultures. Kohl may have originated in ancient Egypt. The thick eyeliner can be decorative and give relief from the glare of the sun. In Punjabi culture, it has a ceremonial purpose. Wives and mothers apply the kohl to the eyes of the men and boys. Many mothers apply kohl to their child's eyes for superstitious or traditional reasons. Kohl is believed to strengthen the eyes and protect from the curse of the "evil eye."

B. Circle the letter of each correct answer.

vocabulary
1. What is a synonym for the word *alter*?
   A. assert
   B. hide
   C. keep
   (D.) change

vocabulary
2. What is an antonym for the word *incorporate*?
   (A.) exclude
   B. include
   C. invent
   D. adopt

vocabulary
3. What is a synonym for the word *tradition*?
   A. journey
   B. culture
   (C.) custom
   D. generation

vocabulary
4. What is the BEST definition for the word *status*?
   (A.) a person's position in society
   B. strong, confident behavior
   C. a person's appearance
   D. uncommon ideas and customs

©Voyager Expanded Learning, Inc. 245

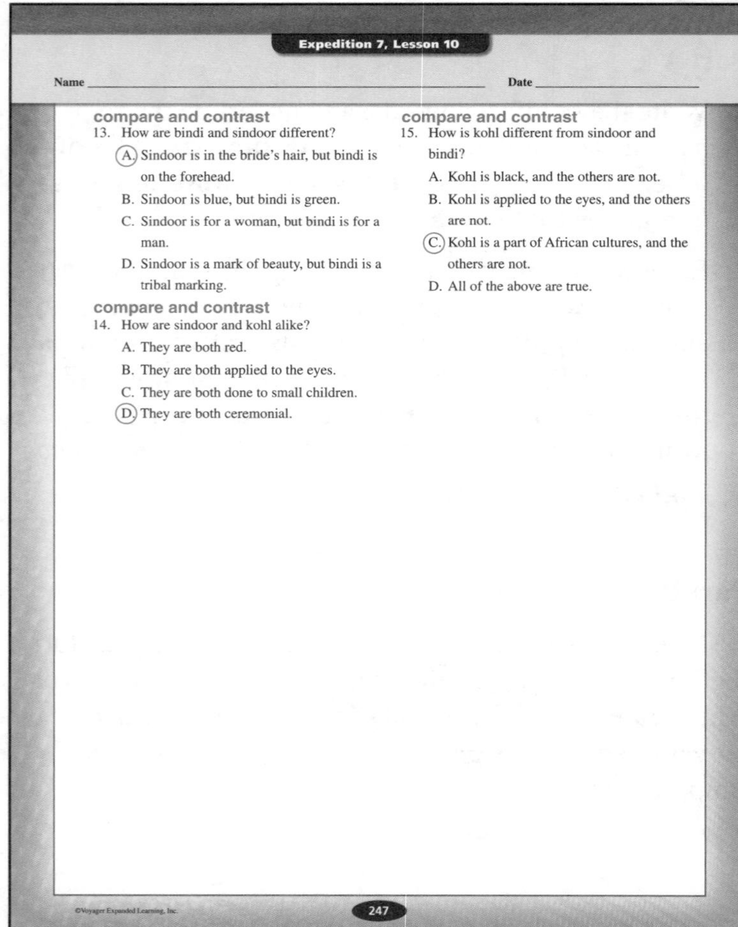

Expedition 7, Lesson 10

Name ____________________ Date ____________

compare and contrast
13. How are bindi and sindoor different?
   (A.) Sindoor is in the bride's hair, but bindi is on the forehead.
   B. Sindoor is blue, but bindi is green.
   C. Sindoor is for a woman, but bindi is for a man.
   D. Sindoor is a mark of beauty, but bindi is a tribal marking.

compare and contrast
14. How are sindoor and kohl alike?
   A. They are both red.
   B. They are both applied to the eyes.
   C. They are both done to small children.
   (D.) They are both ceremonial.

compare and contrast
15. How is kohl different from sindoor and bindi?
   A. Kohl is black, and the others are not.
   B. Kohl is applied to the eyes, and the others are not.
   (C.) Kohl is a part of African cultures, and the others are not.
   D. All of the above are true.

©Voyager Expanded Learning, Inc. 247

Reteach

Compare and Contrast

1. Direct students to Student Book pages 248 and 249. Read the instructions aloud. **How is comparing different from contrasting?** (Comparing shows how things are similar. Contrasting shows how things are different.)

2. Read the passage in Part A aloud. Have students make the drawings for Part B, checking for details in the passage. Have students compare their drawings. Before students complete Part C, have them locate and underline the signal words *But*, *Both*, *But*, and *Unlike*. **Which words signal comparisons, and which words signal contrasts?** Have students complete Part C. Observe students' errors and provide individual instruction before they continue.

3. Have students read aloud the passage in Part D. Have students relate whether they have tasted these foods before. Read the instructions for Parts E and F aloud. Complete the first item with students, and have them complete the remaining items independently.

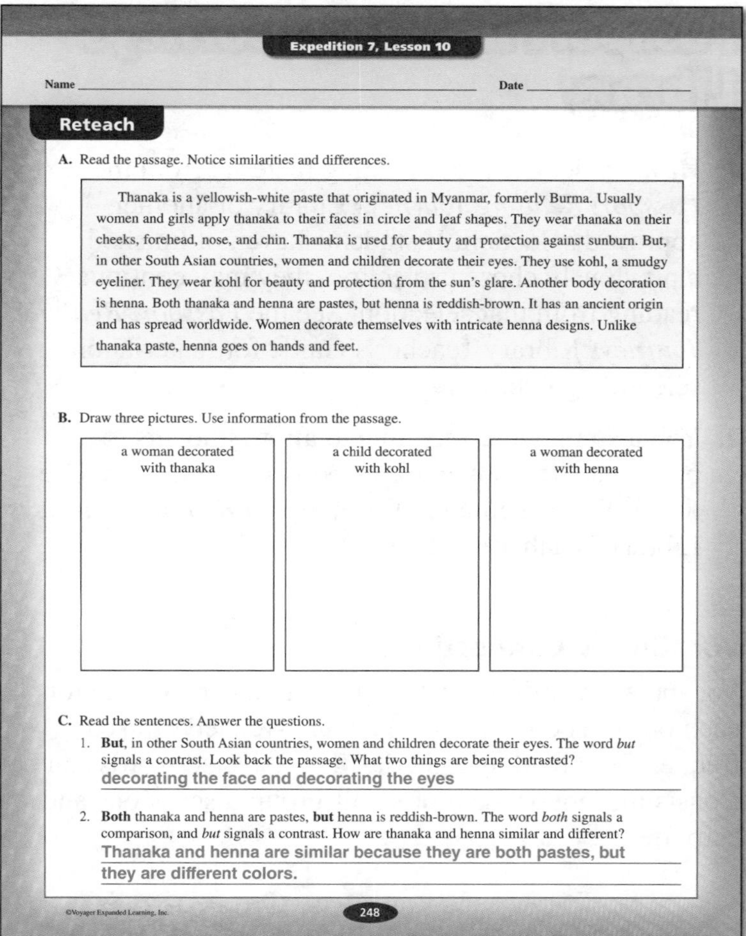

Expedition 7, Lesson 10

Name ______________________ Date ____________

Reteach

A. Read the passage. Notice similarities and differences.

Thanaka is a yellowish-white paste that originated in Myanmar, formerly Burma. Usually women and girls apply thanaka to their faces in circle and leaf shapes. They wear thanaka on their cheeks, forehead, nose, and chin. Thanaka is used for beauty and protection against sunburn. But, in other South Asian countries, women and children decorate their eyes. They use kohl, a smudgy eyeliner. They wear kohl for beauty and protection from the sun's glare. Another body decoration is henna. Both thanaka and henna are pastes, but henna is reddish-brown. It has an ancient origin and has spread worldwide. Women decorate themselves with intricate henna designs. Unlike thanaka paste, henna goes on hands and feet.

B. Draw three pictures. Use information from the passage.

a woman decorated with thanaka	a child decorated with kohl	a woman decorated with henna

C. Read the sentences. Answer the questions.

1. **But**, in other South Asian countries, women and children decorate their eyes. The word *but* signals a contrast. Look back the passage. What two things are being contrasted?
decorating the face and decorating the eyes

2. **Both** thanaka and henna are pastes, **but** henna is reddish-brown. The word *both* signals a comparison, and *but* signals a contrast. How are thanaka and henna similar and different?
Thanaka and henna are similar because they are both pastes, but they are different colors.

©Voyager Expanded Learning, Inc. 248

Expedition 7, Lesson 10

Name ______________________ Date ____________

3. **Unlike** thanaka paste, henna goes on hands and feet. The word *unlike* signals a contrast. Look back in the passage. What two things are being contrasted?
Thanaka decorates the face, but henna decorates hands and feet.

D. Read the passage. Notice similarities and differences.

A delicacy is a rare and expensive food. Some delicacies are from a certain culture. Caviar is a Russian delicacy. It is made of salted fish eggs. Caviar is usually eaten as a spread. The most expensive caviar is usually eaten on special occasions such as weddings. Century egg is a Chinese delicacy. It takes several weeks or months to prepare the duck or chicken egg. The egg sits in a mixture of clay, ash, salt, lime, and rice straw until it is ready to eat. The yolk becomes dark green, and the egg white becomes dark brown. The surface of the eggs have beautiful patterns that look like pine branches.

E. Read the sentences. Notice the signal words and what is compared or contrasted. Write the missing words on the lines to complete each sentence.

1. Caviar and ___century eggs___ are similar because they are both types of ___eggs___.
2. ___Caviar___ is fish eggs. Century eggs are not from fish but from ___ducks or chickens___.
3. Both caviar and century eggs have ___salt___ as an ingredient.
4. Caviar and century eggs are delicacies in different cultures. Caviar is a ___Russian___ delicacy, but century eggs are a ___Chinese___ delicacy.

F. Compare and contrast century eggs or caviar to scrambled eggs. How are they the same and different?
Answers should state similarities and differences and support them with accurate descriptions of both types of eggs.

 249

Passport Reading Journeys Library

1. Have students choose reading material from the *Passport Reading Journeys* Library or another approved selection. If students have not finished a previously chosen selection, they may continue reading from that selection. See the *Passport Reading Journeys* Library Teacher's Guide for material on selection guidelines.
2. You also may use this time to allow students to participate in book clubs or book presentations. Use the criteria specified in the *Passport Reading Journeys* Library Teacher's Guide.

Vocabulary Connections

Vocabulary words are listed in the Teacher's Guide for each book. These words are content-related or used frequently in reading material. The selected words can be a basis for independent or small-group discussions and activities.

Student Opportunities

Six copies of each book title are provided in the *Passport Reading Journeys* Library. The number of copies makes it possible for small groups of students to read the same material and share the information they read.

Theme-related titles include *The Liberation of Gabriel King, The Green Glass Sea,* and *Loser.*

Technology

1. Depending on your classroom configuration and computer access, you may have all students work through the technology in a lab setting or have individuals or small groups of students work on desktops or laptops while other students participate in other suggested activities, such as the *Passport Reading Journeys* Library.
2. The online technology component provides additional support for students to work with selected vocabulary words. Students will work through a series of activities to strengthen their word knowledge, then apply that knowledge to passage reading. Refer to the online technology component User Guide for more information.

   Theme-related word sets include Geography, World History, Sociology, and Economics.

Expedition Project

Folktale Presentation

Distribute Project Blackline Master page 14. Remind students that they have read about different cultures in their Anthology reading passages. **Each culture has its own collection of folktales. Folktales are popular, traditional stories that each generation passes down to the next generation.** Have students name some familiar folktales like *The Frog King, Town Mouse and Country Mouse,* and *Hansel and Gretel*. List student responses on the board. Have students form small groups and direct them in the process.

For students to have a meaningful experience completing tasks as a group, certain strategies need to be employed. Group dynamics and interactions can be improved with strategic planning for group work. Refer to page xxxvi for information on effective grouping strategies.

Have students look at the page and follow along as you explain the assignment. Assign point values, and ask students to write them in the rubric. **Make any notes on the page that will help you, but you will turn the page in with the assignment.**

1. Assign each group a popular tale from a culture outside of the United States. Tales may be stories such as Russia's tales about *Baba Yaga*, West Africa's tales about *Anansi the Spider*, or Japan's tale of *Urashima Taro*.
2. Direct groups to library anthologies and Web sites to research their tales. Students should read the tale several times to become familiar with it so they can retell it to the whole class. Students also should research background about the tale and create an introduction that helps listeners understand cultural differences, such as certain characters being known as tricksters and customs like greetings or titles.
3. **You will use these standards, or criteria, as you create your presentations. Your presentations must have . . .**
   - **an introduction that relates to the tale and the culture.**
   - **a clear, engaging, dramatic retelling of the folktale.**
   - **appropriate costumes or visuals that enhance the dramatic presentation.**
   - **articulate delivery that demonstrates understanding of the tale.**
4. **Gather or create visuals for a dramatic presentation of the story.** Students may choose to act out the story themselves or use hand or stick puppets, felt boards, or posters of story scenes.
5. **Rehearse the folktale presentation. Each group member should take one role as a narrator or character. Make sure the presentation has the previously discussed criteria.**
6. **Present folktales during class.**
7. **I will assess your presentation based on the rubric on your page.** To assess students' presentations, use the rubric from the Project Blackline Master.

Real-World Reading

Airport Travel Instructions

1. Direct students to Student Book page 250. Explain that they will read tips for efficient airport travel. **Have you ever traveled by airplane? What did you do to prepare for your flight?**
2. Point out the following words in the text. Have students draw a star next to the words. Ask students to tell the word meanings. Clarify their understanding. Have them write the meanings in the margins.
   - *Domestic* means "within the same country."
   - *Breaches* means "acts of breaking the law."
   - *Interrogation* means "a process of being questioned by authorities."
3. **Imagine that you are preparing for a flight. What would you want to know?** Direct students to read the instructions on the sign. Instruct them to complete the activity.
4. **To read detailed instructions such as this, you can go back and scan, or search quickly through the text, to find certain information you are looking for.** Have students share their answers. Encourage them to discuss details that they already knew or that surprised them.

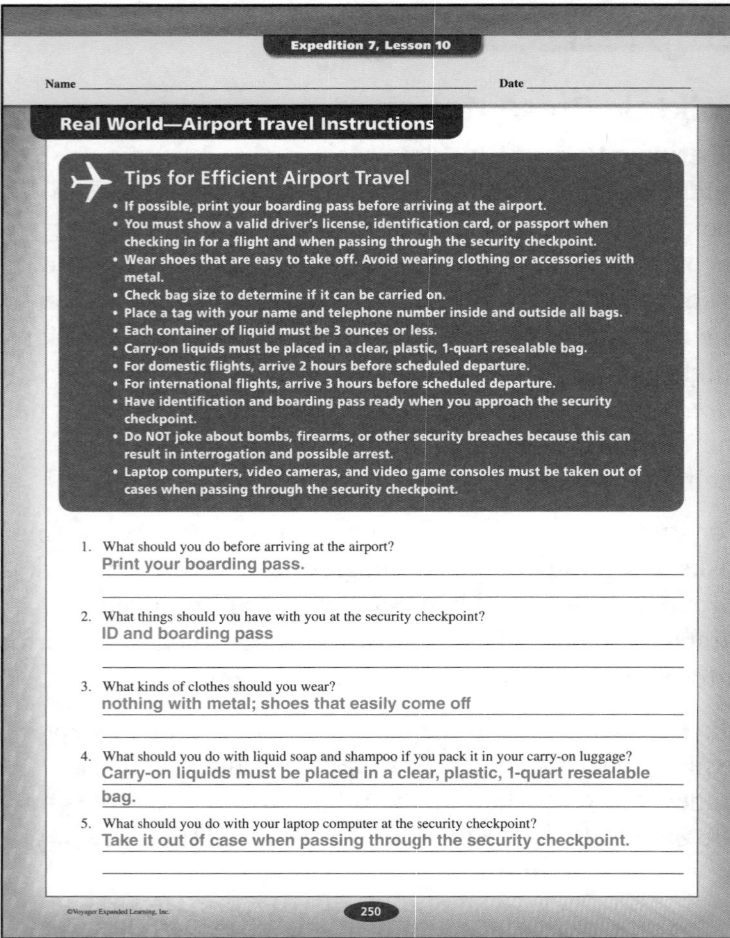
Expedition 7, Lesson 10

Name ______ Date ______

Real World—Airport Travel Instructions

Tips for Efficient Airport Travel

- If possible, print your boarding pass before arriving at the airport.
- You must show a valid driver's license, identification card, or passport when checking in for a flight and when passing through the security checkpoint.
- Wear shoes that are easy to take off. Avoid wearing clothing or accessories with metal.
- Check bag size to determine if it can be carried on.
- Place a tag with your name and telephone number inside and outside all bags.
- Each container of liquid must be 3 ounces or less.
- Carry-on liquids must be placed in a clear, plastic, 1-quart resealable bag.
- For domestic flights, arrive 2 hours before scheduled departure.
- For international flights, arrive 3 hours before scheduled departure.
- Have identification and boarding pass ready when you approach the security checkpoint.
- Do NOT joke about bombs, firearms, or other security breaches because this can result in interrogation and possible arrest.
- Laptop computers, video cameras, and video game consoles must be taken out of cases when passing through the security checkpoint.

1. What should you do before arriving at the airport?
   Print your boarding pass.
2. What things should you have with you at the security checkpoint?
   ID and boarding pass
3. What kinds of clothes should you wear?
   nothing with metal; shoes that easily come off
4. What should you do with liquid soap and shampoo if you pack it in your carry-on luggage?
   Carry-on liquids must be placed in a clear, plastic, 1-quart resealable bag.
5. What should you do with your laptop computer at the security checkpoint?
   Take it out of case when passing through the security checkpoint.

 250

Exploring Careers

A Career in Film

1. Direct students to Anthology page 135. Have students preview the title and photographs. **What kinds of things do you think a person does as a member of a camera crew?** List student responses on the board.

2. Direct students to read the passage. **Do you already know how to use filming equipment? If not, are you interested in learning? Which aspect of this career appeals to you; which doesn't?**

3. Have students turn to Student Book page 251. **Answer the questions and complete the chart by researching the career of camera crew person in books or online.** Have students complete the page.

Expedition 7, Lesson 10

Name ______________________ Date ______________

Exploring Careers: A Career in Film

A. Answer the following questions about a career in film.

1. What positions are on a camera crew?
   camera operator; film loader; assistants; director of photography
2. What are three important tasks that assistants do on the job?
   tell actors where to stand; set up the shot; make sure that actors are in focus during filming
3. What kinds of schools offer courses in this field?
   vocational schools; community colleges; four-year universities
4. What are some ways to gain experience to become a camera crew person?
   school productions; make your own films or music videos; volunteer to get a job at a film or video production house; attend workshops, seminars, and classes
5. What might make an income for a camera crew person unstable?
   They get paid for working on one project at a time, sometimes with gaps in between.

B. Use the Internet to research other possible career choices in this field and complete the chart.	
Career	
Responsibilities	
Education Required	
Average Salary	
Is this a career you might pursue?	
Why or why not?	
Career	
Responsibilities	
Education Required	
Average Salary	
Is this a career you might pursue?	
Why or why not?	

251

Visual images are all around us. Many people enjoy capturing moments and events on camera or video. These experiences can range from taking photos at a family gathering to videotaping a sporting event. But, what if you think bigger? What about shooting video or taking pictures in unusual places at unusual events? Millions of people make their living doing just that. They work on camera crews to shoot documentaries, TV shows, commercials, movies, or music videos.

A camera crew has opportunities for many different kinds of work. The camera operator—the person who takes the photos or shoots the video—is just one part of a large team.

A film loader is one of the most important people on a camera crew. You've probably already figured out that this person's job is to load the film into the cameras, but the job entails much more than that. The film loader needs to make sure the right film is used. He or she has to load the film in a light-free environment, following specific technical instructions so that the film is not damaged. Then, when the film shoot is done, it's up to the film loader to download the film without exposing it to light and dust and send it into production. Film loaders also order all the equipment and film required for a day's photo shoot, coordinate film and equipment deliveries, and inventory all the film at the end of the day before it is handed over to the production crew.

The assistants on a camera crew get the set ready for the cameras to start rolling. Assistants set up the shots, tell actors where to stand, mark the studio floor to indicate actors' positions, and monitor rehearsals to ensure that every actor is in focus while filming a scene.

Across Cultures  135

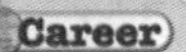

There are different levels of assistants. The first assistant camera person is the top of the ladder, making sure that everything runs properly and managing the set or photo shoot. He or she reports to the project's director of photography, while other assistants and crew people report to the first assistant.

The camera operators are the people who actually film the scenes. The director of photography and the first assistant tell the camera operator what kind of shot they want. They discuss which angles are best, what features to highlight, and what they want the finished product to look like. Then it's up to the operator to film the scene to those specifications. Most movies, music videos, and TV shows have multiple cameras to film scenes, and each camera has its own operator.

A typical workday for a person on a camera crew might go like this. He or she comes to the set and reviews which scenes are being shot that day. The crew person needs to know what type of film and which cameras are being used that day. He or she is responsible for being sure that all the equipment is set up, loaded, and ready. Some test shots are taken to ensure everything is working properly. Then, when the actors arrive and are in place, filming starts. A scene may be filmed more than once to ensure no one makes a mistake, the lighting is just right, and everything looks as the director wants it.

The best way to learn how to be a camera crew person is to train your eye. Begin capturing still images with a camera, then improve your skills from there. Many high schools have video production on campus, and students are involved in all facets of the production. After high school, some vocational schools and community colleges offer courses in this field, as do four-year universities. Get as much experience as you can by working on school productions or making your own films or music videos.

You can volunteer or take a job at a film or video production house and attend workshops, seminars, and classes. Introduce yourself to people you meet who are already in the industry and ask for their advice and assistance—networking is key in any industry, but especially in film.

Working on a camera crew is not the steadiest job because crew people usually work on a project-to-project basis. Every time a project ends, you can be out of work until you find a new assignment. Having a supplemental part-time job can help financially. Salaries vary widely based on job type, region, and experience.

With hard work and the right connections, you might find yourself behind the camera in the career of your dreams. Take your best shot!

136 Expedition 7

Blackline Masters

Blackline

Masters

Name ______________________________ Date ______________

Memoir

You will write a memoir. A memoir is a story about a memory or experience from the writer's own life. It is autobiographical. An autobiography is a story about oneself. Your memoir will be a descriptive narrative that will connect to the Expedition theme "Who Am I?" by retelling a personal experience.

Plan

Choose a personal experience to write about. If you can't think of an actual experience, create an experience that you would like to have.

Prewrite

A narrative tells a story. Descriptive writing includes adjectives, or descriptive words, that help the reader visualize the story.

Brainstorm situations and descriptions with a story web. Put your personal experience or event in the center of your web.

Draft

Write your memoir.

Revise

- **Check the organization.** What paragraphs or sentences should you move so that the story flows in the right order?
- **Check your description.** Did you use vivid sensory details and adjectives? Did you use dialogue that sounds like the characters? Where do you need to add more details or description?
- **Check mechanics.** Do fragments or run-on sentences need to be rewritten? What words might be misspelled? Do all sentences begin with capital letters and end with proper punctuation?

Present

Present your memoir to the class.

Grading Rubric

Criteria	Points Possible	Points Received
Contains a specific personal memory		
Contains a specific setting		
Contains a character with traits, actions, feelings, and dialogue		
Has a clear beginning, middle, and end		
Contains vivid sensory details and adjectives		
Well-organized writing		
Correct mechanics used in writing: punctuation, spelling, and sentence structure		
Spoke clearly during presentation		
Eye contact made during presentation		

Name ______________________________ Date ______________

Biographical Presentation

Partner's Name ______________________________

You will present biographical information about a partner. Think about your own hobbies, interests, family, cultural background, and personality. What things make you who you are? What do you find out about new friends when you are getting to know them?

Introduce yourself to your partner. Share a few brief things with each other, such as hobbies, interests, family, and cultural background.

Use what your partner shared to generate a list of questions to ask him or her. The questions should reflect what you have learned and what you want to know. Write the answers to the questions as you interview your partner.

Gather or create visuals. Visuals might be posters, photographs, favorite possessions, cultural objects, or items used for his or her hobbies. If your partner doesn't provide you with any, draw a visual.

Rehearse presentations. Give your partner positive feedback. Make sure the presentation has each of the features listed.

Present the biography of your partner to the class.

Grading Rubric

Criteria	Points Possible	Points Received
Clear explanation of personal attributes		
Included details about family, culture, hobbies, and interests		
Had detailed visuals that connect to the presentation		
Well-organized presentation that connected to Expedition theme		
On task during class time		
Spoke clearly during presentation		
Eye contact made during presentation		

Name ______________________ Date ____________

Web Site Review

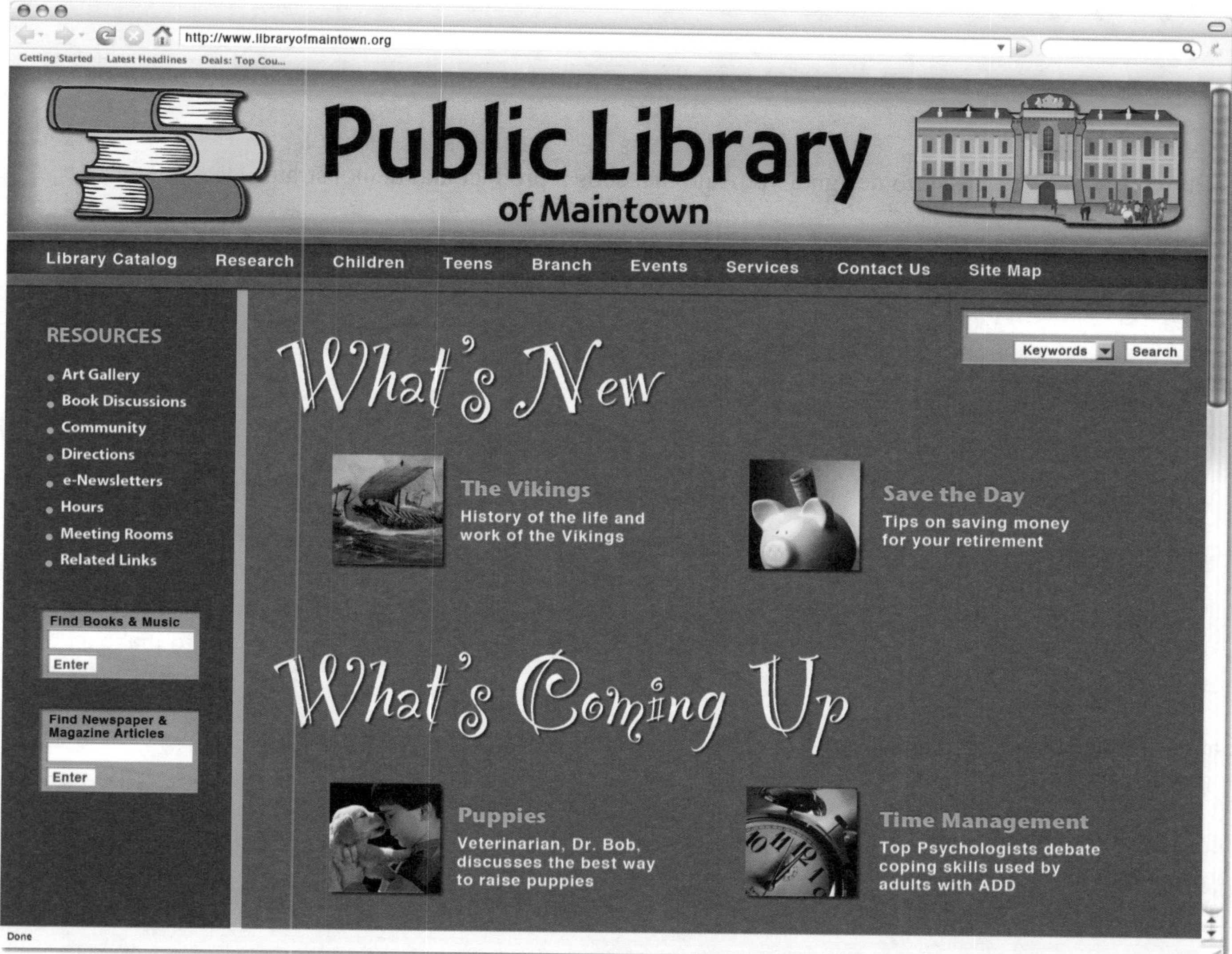

Grading Rubric

Criteria	Points Possible	Points Received
Includes clear description of the Web site features		
Contains four to five criteria of a good Web site		
Explains specific ways the Web site meets the criteria		
Correct mechanics used in writing: punctuation, spelling, and sentence structure		
Well-organized writing		

Name ______________________________ Date ______________

Web Site

Group Members: ______________________ ______________________

______________________ ______________________

You will work with your group to design a Web site that sells a product and demonstrates elements of good design.

Follow these steps to create your Web site:

- Decide what your Web site will sell.
- Design three screens to be accessed on your site.
  - A home page with a link to a catalog
  - A catalog screen that shows the product with a link to the checkout
  - A checkout screen that shows how to order the product
- Assign one screen to one (or two) group members to design. Sketch your ideas on paper.

When everything is mapped out, create posters showing the three screens for your Web site. Use labels to show the different features. Use colored pencils or markers and magazine cutouts or drawings to make a creative poster.

Use at least three vocabulary words from the Expedition in the Web site posters and three more words in your oral presentations.

Present your Web site plan to the class. Rehearse your presentation. Each group member should talk about his or her particular screen, explaining all the features.

Grading Rubric

Criteria	Points Possible	Points Received
Includes clear description of the Web site features		
Contains criteria of a good Web site		
Presentation of three distinct screens		
Uses vocabulary words correctly		
Correct mechanics used in writing: punctuation, spelling, and sentence structure		
Spoke clearly during presentation		
Eye contact made during presentation		
On task during class time		

Name ______________________ Date ____________

Descriptive Essay

You will write a three-paragraph essay describing your favorite band or musician.

Plan

Choose your band or musician.

Prewrite

Your essays should use sensory descriptions that appeal to the five senses: sight, smell, hearing, taste, and touch. In a group, create a list of descriptive words and phrases for each sense. Use this list of words and phrases as you write your essays.

Draft

Write a descriptive essay using the following criteria:

- Musical genre, sound, instruments, and message of lyrics
- Musician's appearance, background, and style
- Reasons why you like the musician or band
- What the music tells you about the time period in which it was written

Revise

- **Check the explanation.** Did you clearly inform the reader about the band/musician? What parts should you clarify or add more information to?
- **Check your description.** Did you use vivid sensory details and adjectives? Where do you need to add more details or description?
- **Check mechanics.** Do fragments or run-on sentences need to be rewritten? What words might be misspelled? Do all sentences begin with capital letters and end with proper punctuation?

Present

Present your essay to the class.

Grading Rubric

Criteria	Points Possible	Points Received
Contains information about musical genre, messages, and time period		
Contains information about artist's appearance, style, and background		
Contains reasons for liking the band/musician		
Has a clear beginning, middle, and end		
Contains vivid sensory details and adjectives		
Well-organized writing		
Correct mechanics used in writing: punctuation, spelling, and sentence structure		
Spoke clearly during presentation		
Eye contact made during presentation		

Name ______________________ Date ______________

Interview

Interviewee's Name ______________________

Group Members: ______________ ______________

______________ ______________

You will interview someone about his or her favorite band or musician. You will present the interview to the class.

Write seven specific questions to ask your subject. Be sure to ask *who*, *what*, *where*, *when*, *why*, and *how* questions.

Interview the person about his or her favorite band.

Research background information about the musical group.

Gather or create visuals such as posters, band memorabilia, album covers, and T-shirts. Discuss how to use samples of actual recordings of the music discussed in the interview during the presentation.

Prepare a presentation that includes the interview and background related to the subject's favorite band or musician, visual aids, and audio samples.

Rehearse the presentation. Each group member should present one particular aspect of the interview. Revise the information.

Present the interview to the class.

Grading Rubric

Criteria	Points Possible	Points Received
Vivid, accurate descriptions and background of the musical genre or musicians		
Quotations and other detailed information from the interview based on specific questions		
Connection to musical origins, culture, history, politics, or topical connections to the Anthology passages		
Detailed visuals and audio samples that connect to the presentation		
Well-organized presentation		
On task during class time		
Spoke clearly during presentation		
Eye contact made during presentation		

Name ____________________ Date ____________

Closing Argument

Police, detectives, and CSI teams find evidence, but lawyers, a judge, and often a jury evaluate the evidence and decide who is guilty or innocent. Lizzie Borden's lawyer convinced the jury she was innocent, so Lizzie went free.

Plan

Imagine you are the prosecuting lawyer who wants to convince the jury Lizzie is guilty. Your group is a law firm that will write a Prosecution Closing Argument. Give a name to your law firm.

Law Firm ____________________

Lawyers: ____________________ ____________________

____________________ ____________________

Prewrite

Lizzie's lawyer used facts, reason, and emotions to convince the jury. As a group, brainstorm facts and reasons why Lizzie is guilty. Then, brainstorm emotional statements that will convince the jury.

Draft

Each group member should choose one of the sections described in the first four lines of the Grading Rubric and write a paragraph about it.

Revise

Reread and revise your draft, using the following steps.

- **Check the organization.** What paragraphs or sentences should you move so the information flows in the right order?
- **Check your purpose.** Did you address your topic? What facts and emotions can you add to convince the jury Lizzie is guilty?
- **Check mechanics.** Do fragments or run-on sentences need to be rewritten? What words might be misspelled? Do all sentences begin with capital letters and end with proper punctuation?

Present

Working with the members of your "legal firms," combine your group Prosecution Closing Argument. Then, rehearse the presentation before reading it to the class, which acts as the jury.

Grading Rubric

Criteria	Points Possible	Points Received
Includes introduction to the judge and jury		
Includes overview of the crime		
Includes reasons why Lizzie is the murderer		
Includes reasons why the jury must find her guilty		
On task during class time		
Spoke clearly during presentation		
Eye contact made during presentation		
Correct mechanics used in writing: punctuation, spelling, and sentence structure		

Name ______________________________ Date ______________

Courtroom Newscast

Design a newscast of the Lizzie Borden trial or the final scene of "The Red-Headed League." The newscast should include . . .

- at least four scenes for your chosen newscast.
- the roles of a newscast director, TV reporter at the scene, an on-the-scene witness, and a news analyst who gives opinions.
- information from a variety of sources, such as the Expedition passages, the writing assignment about the closing arguments, the Build Background DVD, Writing in Response to Reading activities during the lessons, and outside research.

Choose roles. Write your name next to your role.

- The TV news reporter at the scene presents facts that answer *who*, *what*, *when*, *where*, *why*, and *how* and describes other information. ______________________________
- The news analyst presents opinions based on facts or other logical information. ______________________________
- The on-the-scene witness presents a personal viewpoint and provides interesting details that fit with the character. ______________________________
- The newscast director makes sure that the scenes in the newscast follow quickly in order and that the viewers can understand the information. ______________________________

Use notebook paper to write the script for each scene of the newscast. In the script, use at least three vocabulary words from the Expedition. Rehearse the newscast in your roles and note any needed changes. Make sure your presentation has each of the features listed in the Grading Rubric. After making all the changes, write the final script on individual sheets of paper to use as teleprompter cards. You can prepare visuals to support the presentation. Present your newscasts during class.

Grading Rubric

Criteria	Points Possible	Points Received
Has four scenes with information from a variety of sources		
TV news reporter at the scene presents facts that answer *who*, *what*, *when*, *where*, *why*, and *how* and describes other information.		
News analyst presents opinions based on facts or other logical information.		
On-the-scene witness presents a personal viewpoint and provides interesting details that fit with the character.		
Newscast director makes sure that the scenes in the newscast follow quickly in order, and that the viewers can understand the information.		
Contains three vocabulary words		
Spoke clearly during presentation		
Eye contact made during presentation		
On task during class time		

Name ______________________________ Date ______________

Newspaper Article

You will become a reporter and write a newspaper article describing a war photo.

Plan

Tell the story of the photograph. Use information you already know about the Civil War to write your article. Use details in the picture and what you already know about war and history to infer details for a story about the picture.

Prewrite

Prepare a chart with the words *who*, *what*, *when*, *where*, *why*, and *how* down the left side on separate lines. Answer the questions about the photo on the right side of the chart. Use the details in your chart to write your newspaper article.

Draft

Write a newspaper article.

Revise

- **Check the organization.** What paragraphs or sentences should you move so that the information flows in the right order?
- **Check the explanation.** Did you clearly inform the reader of the event and people in the photograph? Did you answer *who*, *what*, *when*, *where*, *why*, and *how* questions? What information might you clarify?
- **Check mechanics.** Do fragments or run-on sentences need to be rewritten? What words might be misspelled? Do all sentences begin with capital letters and end with proper punctuation?

Present

Report the newspaper article.

Grading Rubric

Criteria	Points Possible	Points Received
Who, *what*, *when*, *where*, *why*, and *how* questions answered		
Photograph thoroughly explained		
Prior knowledge about the Civil War in article		
Strong action verbs in writing		
Well-organized writing		
Correct mechanics used in writing: punctuation, spelling, and sentence structure		
Spoke clearly during presentation		
Eye contact made during presentation		

Name ______________________ Date ______________

Military Branch Presentation

You will do a group presentation of a branch of the military.

Group Roles:
Note Taker: ______________________

Art Director: ______________________

Outline Creator: ______________________

Discussion Leader: ______________________

Our Branch of the Military: ______________________

Research your assigned military branch with library books and reliable Internet sites.

Find out what the military branch does. You might put together a list of job positions, ranks, vehicles, or awards. Interview people you know who are or were members of your chosen Armed Forces branch.

Gather or create visuals. Visuals might be posters you create or recruiting brochures from your school's academic counseling office. Images might include pictures of the branch's vehicles, uniforms, and awards.

As a group, discuss the benefits and drawbacks to joining the military branch you are researching.

Rehearse presentations. Each group member should take one role, such as presenting the duties, job positions, ranks, uniforms, vehicles, and awards of the branch.

Present informational presentations on the military during class.

Grading Rubric

Criteria	Points Possible	Points Received
Has informative and clear explanation of the duties of the military branch		
Has detailed visuals that connect to the presentation		
Contains personal opinions about the benefits and drawbacks of joining the military branch and reasons for the opinions		
Well-organized presentation		
On task during class time		
Spoke clearly during presentation		
Eye contact made during presentation		

Name ______________________________ Date ______________

Persuasive Argument

Write a persuasive argument to convince your reader that graffiti is either vandalism or art.

Plan

Think about the two opposing positions in the passage "Graffiti: Vandalism or Art?" from the Anthology.

Prewrite

Review both sides of the positions and the supporting arguments for each. Record your findings on the back of this paper in a chart like the following.

Vandalism	Art

Draft

Choose which side you want to defend: vandalism or art. Write a persuasive argument.

Revise

Reread your draft. Use the following steps to make revisions and write your final draft.

- **Check the organization.** Which paragraphs or sentences should you move so the information will flow in the right order?
- **Check your purpose.** Did you address the arguments that oppose your opinion? What facts and emotions can you add to persuade the reader?
- **Check mechanics.** Do fragments or run-on sentences need to be rewritten? What words might be misspelled? Do all sentences begin with capital letters and end with proper punctuation?

Present

Present your persuasive argument as instructed by your teacher.

Grading Rubric

Criteria	Points Possible	Points Received
Has a clear opinion statement that tells your position		
Has three reasons that support your opinion		
Has a counterargument that opposes your opinion		
Has information that argues against the counterargument		
Has a conclusion		
Correct mechanics used in writing: punctuation, spelling, and sentence structure		
Well-organized writing		
Eye contact made during presentation		
Spoke clearly during presentation		

Name ______________________________ Date ______________

Graffiti Debate

Group Members: ______________________ ______________________

______________________ ______________________

You will prepare for a debate that includes each of your four team members. Teams will take turns replying to opposing arguments and giving further arguments for their opinion. Your team of four will split into Team A and Team B with two students each.

Preplan a dialogue for a debate that includes each group member. The people in your teams will take turns replying to opposing arguments and giving further arguments for their claims. Debate dialogues should use the following format:

Team A, Student 1: Make argument that graffiti is art.
Team B, Student 1: Make argument for opposing claim that graffiti is art; make a new argument why graffiti is vandalism.
Team A, Student 2: Refute opposing opinion; make new argument.
Team B, Student 2: Refute that opposing opinion; make new argument.

As a team, discuss graffiti. Is it vandalism or art? Research your position. Find information on graffiti artists and laws regarding graffiti.

Gather or create visuals, such as posters you create. Presentations should fit the criteria listed in the Grading Rubric.

Rehearse presentations. Each group member should present one argument.

Present debates during class.

Grading Rubric

Criteria	Points Possible	Points Received
Well-developed arguments for the main opinions		
Direct responses to opposing opinions		
Organized delivery		
Includes facts and opinions and logical arguments		
On task during class time		
Spoke clearly during presentation		
Eye contact made during presentation		

Name ______________________________ Date ______________

Personal Narrative

You will tell the story of your personal cultural experience by writing a narrative.

Plan

Tell the story of a personal cultural experience. Base your narrative on an actual experience you have had, or make it up. Use the information you already know about different cultures to write your narrative. Good narratives include descriptions of the setting, people, and actions. Describe clothing, food, dance, music, holidays, literature, and art in your narrative.

Prewrite

Brainstorm situations and descriptions with a story web. Use the details in your story web to write your narratives.

Draft

Write a narrative. Use adjectives and sensory details to create a vivid picture.

Revise

- **Check the organization.** What paragraphs or sentences should you move so that the information flows in the right order?
- **Check your description.** Did you use vivid sensory details and adjectives? Where do you need to add more details or description?
- **Check mechanics.** Do fragments or run-on sentences need to be rewritten? What words might be misspelled? Do all sentences begin with capital letters and end with proper punctuation?

Present

Present your personal narrative to the class.

Grading Rubric

Criteria	Points Possible	Points Received
Addresses a specific cultural experience		
Describes a specific setting and people		
Contains an explanation of what you learned about the culture including clothing, food, dance, music, holidays, literature, and art		
Contains sensory details		
Well-organized writing		
Correct mechanics used in writing: punctuation, spelling, and sentence structure		
Spoke clearly during presentation		
Eye contact made during presentation		

Name ____________________ Date ____________

Folktale Presentation

You will do a group presentation of a folktale. Folktales are popular, traditional stories that some generations pass down to the next generation. You will be given a popular tale from a culture outside of the United States to present to the class.

Group Members: ____________________ ____________________

____________________ ____________________

Our Folktale: ____

Research the background of the tale, and create an introduction that helps listeners understand cultural differences.

Create appropriate costumes or visuals that enhance the dramatic presentation.

Assign parts of the folktale to each member of the group. Memorize your parts of the folktale.

Rehearse presentations. Each group member should provide constructive feedback to the other performers.

Present the background of the folktale and a clear and engaging dramatic retelling of the folktale.

Grading Rubric

Criteria	Points Possible	Points Received
Introduction answers where the tale was from and why that particular culture has this tale.		
Articulate delivery that demonstrates understanding of the tale		
Appropriate costumes or visuals that enhance the dramatic presentation		
Dramatic and engaging retelling of folktale		
Well-organized presentation		
On task during class time		
Spoke clearly during presentation		
Eye contact made during presentation		

Additional

Resources

Pronunciation Guide

Short Vowels

a	/a/	map, cat
e	/e/	ten, test
i	/i/	zip, sip
o	/o/	job, spot
u	/u/	cup, jump

Long Vowels

o	/ō/	vote, woke
i	/ī/	white, bite
a	/ā/	tape, cake
e	/ē/	debate, gene
u	/ū/	tube, chute

Letter Combinations

th	/th/	thin (unvoiced), this (voiced)
oi; oy	/ȯi/	coin; toy
ar	/är/	car, harsh, start
wh	/hw/	whale, whiff
oa	/ō/	coat, boast
qu	/kw/	quit, quest
ea; ee	/ē/	dream; need
oo	/u̇/	book, good
oo	/ü/	food, soon
or	/ȯr/	fork, short
ea	/e/	feather, head

ir; er; ur	/ər/	thirst; perk; burn
ch	/ch/	chip, chop
ai; ay	/ā/	main, brain; stay, play
ou; ow	/au̇/	cloud, pouch; cow, brown
igh	/ī/	might, flight
kn	/n/	knack, knight
al	/ȯl/	salt, hall
ph	/f/	photo, dolphin
wr	/r/	write, wrong
au; aw	/ȯ/	launch, vault; dawn, crawl

Vocabulary

A

abyss
academic
accumulation
accurate
achieve
acknowledge
activities
acute
adhere
adorn
advanced
affect
alter
alternative
amended
amplifies
analysis
anguish
antidote
appropriate
approximately
assembled
assert
assess
associate
attributes
authority
avoid

B

background
bear
behavior
benefit
bias
blunders

C

captured
catalyst
categorized
cautious
characterized
chemicals
civilians
coincidence
collapsed
commerce
commotion
community
compelled
compete
competent
complex
concept
concludes
conditioned
conform
confrontation
conservative
consumers
contain
contemporary
contributes
contrived
control
controversy
convenience
convert
convey
coordinate
correspond
crisis
critical
crucial
culture
current
customs

D

debate
deceived
defend
deliberate
depend
depicted
depleted
design
desperate
determine
develop
developed
devices
devoted
differentiate
diluted
disabilities
disapproval
disastrous
discern
discriminate
distinct
diverged
diverse
domestic
dominated

E

ecology
effects
efficient
elaborate
eliminated
emphasize
employment
encourage
endeavors
energy
enforced
enhance
enrich
environment
established
ethnic
evaluate
exact
except
exchange
excretes
exhibited
expanding
experience
expert
explore
express

F

factors
fashion
fathom
ferocious
fiends
financial
focus
foreign
forfeit
founders
frail
fraud
frequently
fundamental

G

generated
genuine
globe
goods
government
gratitude
grave
gruesome

H

habitat
heroic
hybrid

I

ideal
identity
image
impact
impair
imported
impose
incorporate
incorrigible
indeed
individual
infinitely
influence
ingredient
initial
innocent
inquiry
inspiring
instances
instinct
instruct
instruments
intense
interacted
intricate
involve

J

judgment

K

keenly

L

labyrinth
loyal

M

majority
manage
maneuvers
manifest
manufacture
media
merchant
merely
modern
morphing
motion
motive
mutual

N

nature
negligent
nominal
nominated
nuzzled

O

officials
opinionated
opposed
order
organic
organizations
originated

P

participate
particles
patterns
peculiar
perceptibly
perhaps
persecuted
personal
phase
physical
politics
population
portray
positions
poverty
practical
predict
prejudices
prescribe
preserve
presume
prevalent
primary
probable
produce
profiles
prohibit
project
prominent
protest
proverbial
purpose

Q

qualified

R

range
rational
react
reaction
recipes
reform
register
regulates
reject
remote
renders
replicate
represent
residential
resources
response
reveal
revolting

risk
roots

S

seldom
selection
severe
severed
shabby
significant
situation
social
society
solitude
soluble
spectacle
spectrum
speculate
stagnant
standards
status
stimulus
submit
substance
survive
suspicion
symbol
synthesized
synthetic
system

T

techniques
tenacity
tenants
terminate
texture
theory
tolerance
tolerate
tradition
transaction
transition
transport
treatment
trek
tribute
typically

U

unique
united
universal
urban

V

vainly
valor
various
vary
vast
venture
vicious
viewpoint
vile
visible
visual
vital
volume

W

wedged

Index

F

G

I

K

L